YACHT VOYAGES

Eric Wiberg

Island Books

for Captain Stephen Connett, R/V of *Geronimo*.
He taught me to sail a big boat at night off Cat Island, Bahamas.
&
Captain Aaron Dickson of Halifax.
He saved my life overboard in a snowstorm, off Block Island.

by the same author:

Bahamas in World War II
Mailboats of the Bahamas
U-Boats in the Bahamas
U-Boats off Bermuda
U-Boats in New England
Swan Sinks / Boston Harbor
Round the World in the Wrong Season
Tanker Disasters / Tankers East of Suez
Surviving St. George's / Scars
Published Writing / Juvenilia
Travel Diaries / Sea Stories
Drifting to the Duchess (script with Paolo Pilladi & book)
Napoleon's Battles (with Felix Wiberg)
Åke Wiberg (with Mats Larsson)

Copyright © Eric Troels Wiberg, 2021, ericwiberg.com

All rights reserved. No part of this publication may be reproduced in any manner without the prior written permission of the publisher, except in the case of brief quotations embodied in articles or reviews. Photographs and text are the creation of the author, who asserts his rights to them under copyright and intellectual property laws.

Paper ISBNs: 978-0-9998479-1-6, 0-9998479-1-0
E-Book ISBNs: 978-0-9843998-3-3, 0-9843998-3-6
Library of Congress Control Number: 2019908981

for information, or to contact the author please email eric@ericwiberg.com
design and layout by Abdul Rehman Qureshi, writingpanacea@gmail.com

Printed in the United States of America.

Bermuda Chart, Voyages 1989 - 2005

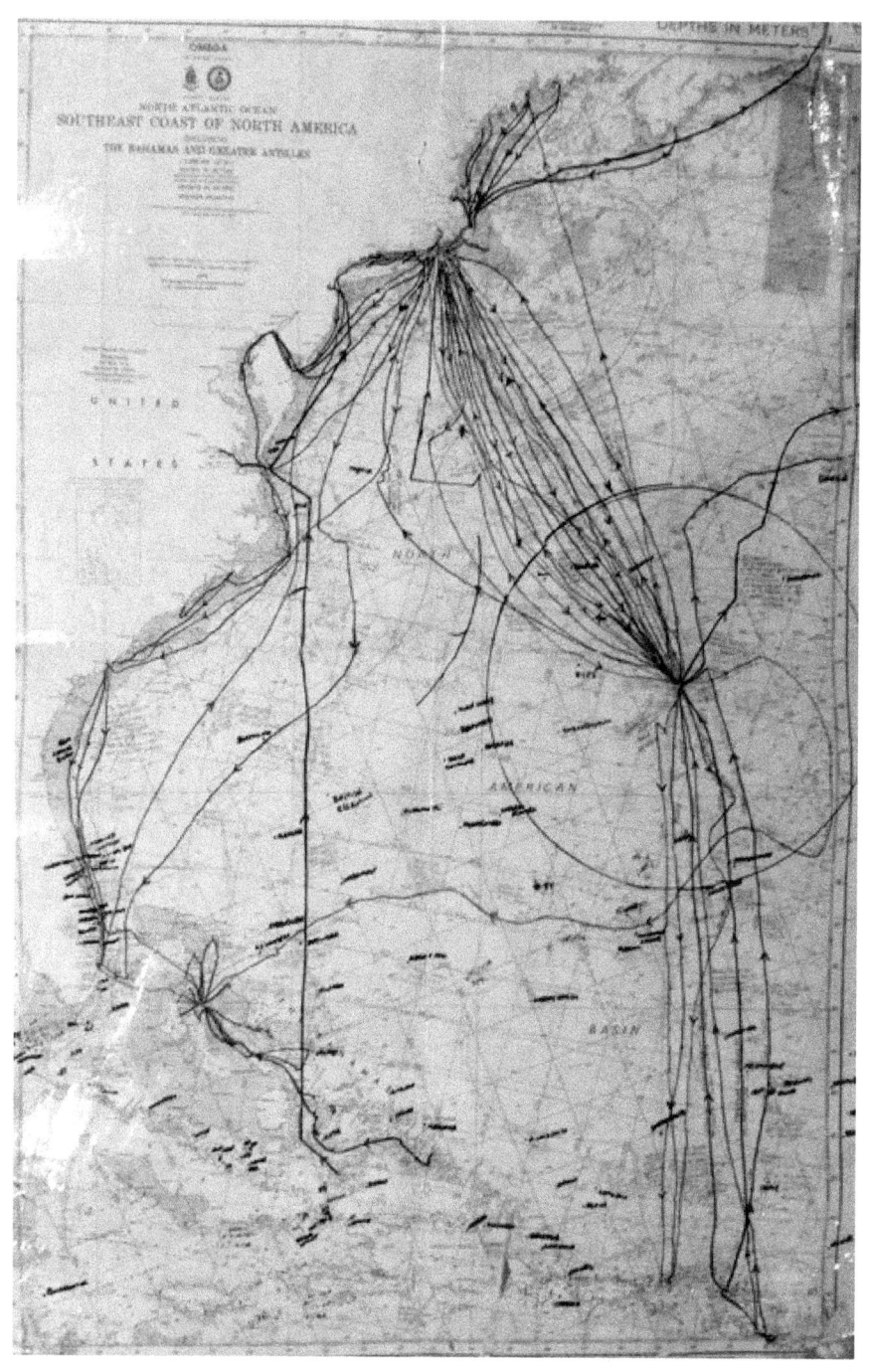

Overview & Origins

Our older sister Ann and mother Jane in our father Sten Anders' first runabout boat in Old Fort Bay, Bahamas, in March 1966, shortly after they married, bought a business and he moved there from Sweden via Brazil and she from the *New Yorker* in NYC.

All four children; James, Eric, John, and Ann at right, in our pool at Cable Beach, Nassau, c.1976. This is one of several inflatable rafts which we bought with rewards for returning people's ID's, wallets, purses periodically dumped (by robbers after only cash) in the woods behind hotels like the one which our parents owned and ran.

James, John and me launching our first handmade raft on Lake Cunningham, behind our home in Nassau, c.1979. It is made of dunnage and a crate, with a nest of palm fronds in the cockpit. Probably Pauli Joseph, the family groundskeeper from Cap-Haïtien, helped. The rig, made of our local branches for mast and boom and our mother's sheet, and clothes line for rigging, is simple lateen or felucca, like on the Nile and, in modern terms, the popular Sunfish model. Not sure how we steered it, but we made it to an islet and had a lunch and fished a-la Huckleberry Finn. I'm quite sure the raft never made it home. It was launched between the caves, the old well (in which we found a dog skull) and the launch ramp and hangar for a seaplane owned by WWII RAF hero Lester Brown, and the Goodwyn brothers. Later we were watching a speedboat race on that same spot with our nanny, Nurse Ulla, and many visitors, when a boat caught its engines in the thick mangrove and flipped, killing its occupant. We soon realized that the dead racer's family were right next to us, some of them our age…

Being shown the ropes by our cousin Eva on a lake in Sweden, in 1980.

With Eva's family boat on the Swedish lake, John looking very captain-like, about age 11. Note the varnished wooden mast and that we still have sail set (and got wet)! We did it! Sister Ann & me on foredeck. Our uncle Göran looking rather patrician...

Returning to St. George's Bermuda as skipper of *Flambé* in 1999. With a crew of lifelong friends, four bachelors all happy with life, this was the halcyon standard of joy for voyages which I didn't come close to achieving that fall, with a succession of seven hurricanes. The Tall Ship over my shoulder was crewed by a young lady who I was walking home one evening when we accidentally took a wrong turn by the white sailboat onto a patch of soft grass on the water..... In front of the pink building I pulled a scientist from the Bio Station and her moped out seven years earlier... I always like to "dress up" into a loose Oxford cotton shirt for arrival; the red line is tied between the back of my hat and the button hole in my shirt to prevent losing the hat... The white tape around the metal backstay is put on after tightening it to prevent the sharp edges of the cotter pins from ripping fabric – or skin (one client lost his finger when it went in that gap close behind a pin that went out).

The small brown wooden rack with stainless screws through it to the right of the Swiss ensign is to mount the outboard motor on the Lifesling on the left is to deploy a floating safety harness to a person, or MOB in the water. You can see both how narrow the cockpit is and how close to the water the helmsman is. Companies like *Swans* and Hinckleys tend to build boats that leave sailors more exposed to the great outdoors, and are made in the Baltic and Maine, with short summers. Little Harbor, Bristol and other boats, while also made in New England and not tropical areas, tend to have center cockpits, more elevated, automated, and protected against falling out, the idea being that owners can buy more privacy and less crew by operating the boat almost entirely from the safety and warmth of a cockpit, which even has radar screens, automatic winches, and motor-furled main and head sails.

Summary of all Yacht Voyages

Over 50 years I've had the privilege of stepping aboard roughly 500 vessels, some of them passenger ships, 90 of which were international and took me to some 75 countries and 250 islands. On average, I travelled some 160 nautical miles (nm) on each boat. I worked on roughly a third of them; including commercial vessels like lobster boats, tankers, and a bulker. This book is about the roughly 100 sailboats which I operated over 50,000 nm, mostly internationally, and 50 power boats for another 4,000 miles, none of them international. Though I raced on 10 boats, I never commanded a boat on an offshore race. And, for the record, I've never won a single boat race in sail, power, or commercial. My crew and I let others chase silver; I was after adventure and gold; payment, in whatever form, often just room, board and a flight home. As a consequence of this career choice I've spent a winter operating a backpacker hut in the Roaring Forties of New Zealand's Stewart Island, a summer at the Seafarer's International House in Manhattan, and eight months at the infamous Mitre Hotel in Singapore; South African divers and maritime detritus upstairs, working women downstairs.

My paid career lasted from age 18 in 1989 to age 50 in 2020, during which I served roughly a third each in crew, mate, and captain capacity, having my first command at age 23. I commanded roughly the same amount of sailing as power boats; about 30 each. We focus here on the roughly 40 yacht deliveries, both sail and power, as well as a dozen or so sailing charters. Though these voyages girth the globe, only leaving a gap between Madras and Mombasa untraveled on the surface (four times I girded the globe; nothing goes upwind like a 747!), the main focus is on the Bahamas, where my siblings and I grew up, Scandinavia, where we have citizenship, New England, where we all went to school for at least a decade, and finally Bermuda and the Caribbean. Bermuda was my yacht delivery hub, with over 30 voyages to or from, and 11 trips in 15 months in 1999-2000.

There are two jokes about delivery skippers; crew who catch them passing the same navigational aids multiple times to rack up more time at sea and more money, and the one I made up about pulling into Bermuda for a few days not just to get fuel and rest but by convincing owners "there's gotta be an occluded front out there somewhere!" (if you haven't heard of this double-barrel warm and cold front, few others have – it sounds and looks scary and has a bit of terror in it for everyone, making an excuse to spend just one more night in port....). Delivery skippers like to moan that they lose more jobs to "the neighbor's son" syndrome than to other skippers; in other words, an owner is fretting about hiring some expensive professional and instead grabs the kid mowing the lawn to do it instead.

Since I have fewer than 100,000 nm experience (just 77,000 or so), and a fairly modest license (100 tons near coastal), and fewer than 100 vessels under command, I have far less experience than many mariners I know. I am much more interested in detailing how those hard-won miles of experience were gained, the anguish and hunger of early years, and some of the triumphant, yet also humbling and scary, experiences of later years. If anyone were to ask me if I would send my son to sea, I would say *No*, yet I know that no-one is going to stop anyone from going to sea. No one stopped me. They say about the shipping industry that it may not be the oldest profession, but someone had to have carried members of the first profession across the water!

Types of Vessel	Number of Vessels	Mileage Per Type	Miles per Vessel
Work boats, some served on	72	6,575	91
Race boats I crewed	10	4,752	475
Leisure boats	96	6,352	66
Delivery, Sail & Power	64	41,141	674
Charter boats	32	3,990	125
Passenger boats, as guest	215	14,669	68
Types	**489**	**77,479**	**159**

Total Mileage by Vessel Type in Nautical Miles

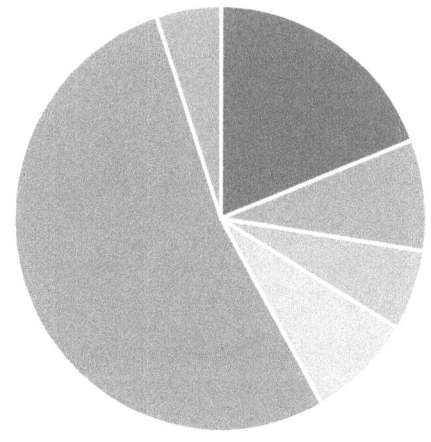

- 215 Pax boats, 215 boats, miles
- 72 Work boats 72, miles are
- 10 Race 10 boats, 4752
- 96 Leisure boats 96, 6,352 miles
- 64 Delivery sail & Power 64, 41,141
- 32 Charter 3,990 32 boats

    Day work included work on docks in many countries, islands, and places. After all global cruising is defined as "repairing your yacht in interesting places." Boats I did day work on must number in the dozens, but some names are *Troika,* and *Night Train,* a 50' Hinckley, 1990 Bermuda-Race prep in Newport, the latter in Barrington as well, *Quintessence,* in Portsmouth, RI, *Flyfly, Geronimo* (Newport mostly), *Maja,* 32' sloop owned by Dick Murphie, in Bermuda during the *Xebec* crossing, and *Pam* and *Mariner* in Wickford and Newport, sanding in winter. I've done work in yards in Nassau for Nigel Bower and

Alan Wardle at Nassau Powerboat Adventures (Brown's Boat Basin), my friend Peder in Singapore's boat at Tanjong Pagar and Changi, and in many ports, from *War Baby* at Brewer's Marine at Pilot's Point to Jamestown RI, and so on. *Flying Magic*, a 98' Dutch-built Jongert under Captain Hans, and *Wave of Peace*, 78' Jongert, Australian Andrew, also in Camden, and the latter in Newport also, in summer 1993.

Day work (casual labor) is a rite of passage, though I remember my shock and muted sadness at seeing a skipper on his hands and knees sanding and varnishing floorboards on Goat Island. Day work is the dirty secret of the industry; everybody does it, even owners. On boats I often took less desired roles like hand-cleaning bilges, toilets, doing dishes, lubricating hand-hanks for the emergency sails, because they are less critical and overseers are less critical too. Besides, you find some neat things in bilges, and in the ocean under immigration docks. I asked an esteemed older yacht captain in Tahiti what makes a good yacht captain. He thought for a moment and replied: a good captain is the first one to do the dishes.

A woman I dated during university who was both European and older, crossed from the Med to Barbados on a large sailing yacht, and brought with them a pig named Aloysius. They anchored off Bridgetown and were most keen after nearly a month at sea, to go ashore. They were, however told by Bajan Customs that under no circumstances was the pig to go ashore, or to pose a porcine risk of going shore. That night a forlorn crew tucked without mirth into fresh pork for supper, washed down with a few glasses of the guilts.

Arriving at Horta, Faial, Azores, aboard the 40' *Swan Dancer* in 2000. The Aussie skipper met me for 15 minutes at RBYC in Bermuda before hiring me, and I had never met the other crew, a Kiwi and an American divinity student, before I stepped aboard. We sailed moments later. We remain in touch. Convinced we were getting lazy in the Azores High (*Anticiclone dos Açores*) with no wind, the skipper unplugged the autopilot, saying it was broken.

Table of Contents

Bermuda Chart, Voyages 1989 - 2005 III
Overview & Origins IV
Summary of all Yacht Voyages VIII
Table of Contents XI
In Memoriam XVI
Forewords XX

Introduction 1
World Map, Islands, Continents & Countries Hailed 30
Islands Visited, 1970 – 2020 31

Chapter 1 34
Voyage 1: *Qu'elle Aime*, the Baltic, Sweden, July, 1988 34
Voyage 2: Family power boats *Viking* and *Ma'Wessel* 1 & 2, Nassau, 1978 – 1994 ... 44
Voyage 3: *Geronimo*, Cat Island, Bahamas, Spring, 1987 49
Voyage 4: *Black Sheep*, Narragansett Bay, 1987-1989 55

Chapter 2 57
Voyage 5: *Rumor*, Marion-Bermuda Race, Bermuda-Newport, June-July, 1989 57
Voyage 6: *Rising Star*, Bermuda to Newport, June, 1991 69

Chapter 3 75
Voyage 7: *Circuit* Bermuda to Nassau and Fort Lauderdale, July, 1991 75
Voyage 8: *Xebec*, Antigua, St. Maarten, Anguilla, Bermuda, Belgium, May-July, 1991 ... 89

Chapter 4 106
Voyage 9: *War Baby*, Lymington, England - Ireland - Brittany, France, 1991 106
Voyage 30: *War Baby*, Marion - Bermuda Race, Newport, then Pilot's Point, CT, 1999 ... 106
Voyage 44: *War Baby*, Newport - Bermuda Race, 2000 106
Voyage 10: *Young Endeavour* Port Canaveral, Florida - Nassau, August, 1992 123

Chapter 5 126
Voyage 11: *Whisper of Maine*, Newport, Vineyard, Nantucket training, 1992-1993 ... 126

Voyage 12: *Whisper of Maine*, Marion - Bermuda Race, June, 1993 126
Voyage 13: *Whisper of Maine*, Bermuda-Camden-Newport, July-September, 1993 126
Voyage 14: *Dovetail* Camden-Penobscot Bay, July-September, 1993 137
Voyage 15: *Wave of Peace*, Daywork, Camden, Newport, August, September 1993 138

Chapter 6 139

Voyage 16: *Breathless*, Newport-Lauderdale via Bahamas, Sept.-October, 1993 139
Voyage 17: *Power Play* Palm Beach, November, 1993 148

Chapter 7 155

Voyage 18: *Stornoway*, Panama-Galapagos, November 1993 to May, 1994 155

Chapter 8 179

Voyage 19: *Goldenhome* Turks & Caicos-Hogsty-Exumas-Nassau, Spring, 1995 179
Voyage 20: *Simpatico*, Crooked, Acklins Islands, Bahamas, Island Expedition, 1995 179
Voyage 21: *The Dollar*, Newport-Block Island, August, 1995 182
Voyage 22: *Luna*, Newport-Bra d'Or, Canada, June-July, 1995 182

Chapter 9 183

Voyage 23: *Endless Summer*, Bermuda-Newport, July, 1996 183
Voyage 27: *Endless Summer* Newport-Bermuda Race, June, 1998 183
Voyage 24: Power boats; Singapore-Sentosa Island, numerous day trips, 1995-1998 187
Voyage 25: *Cheoy Lee sloop*, Jurong-Changi ship yards, Singapore, 1997-1998 189
Voyage 26: *Artemis*, Jurong to Changi Sailing Club, Singapore, 1995-1998 190

Chapter 10 191

Voyage 28: *Youth*, Stratford CT-Portsmouth RI, Spring, 1999 191
Voyage 33: *Youth*, Jamestown-Block-Cuttyhunk, MV-Nantucket, Padanaram, 1999 191
Voyage 59: *Youth*, Newport-Portsmouth RI, Summer 2000 191
Voyage 29: *Flambé*, Antigua - Newport via Bermuda, May-June, 1999 194
Voyage 31: *Diviner*, Southwest Harbor Maine - Jamestown RI, July, 1999 198
Voyage 32: *Pericles*, Lockeport, Nova Scotia-Newport, RI August, 1999 201
Voyage 35: *Marblic*, SW Harbor ME-Newport, September, 1999 202

Chapter 11 203

Voyage 36: *Sarafina* Newport-Port Canaveral via Annapolis & Charleston 207
Voyage 37: *Crested* Newport-Lauderdale via Beaufort, Charleston 210
Voyage 38: *Triton*, Newport-Lauderdale via Norfolk, Charleston 215
Voyage 39: *Femme*, Newport-Tortola, BVI, via Bermuda, November-December, 1999 216

Chapter 12 227

    Voyage 40: *Valentine* Newport, Jamestown, Hundreds of Short Trips, 1999-2001 227

    Voyage 41: *Stiarna*, Chaguaramas, Trinidad-Grenada, February, 2000 229

    Voyage 34: *Sabbatical,* Newport cross-harbor, Mooring to Marina, Winter, 2000 235

    Voyage 42 *Sabbatical*, Newport-Tortola, BVI, via Bermuda, Winter-Spring, 2000 235

    Voyage 43: *Seeadler*, Bermuda-Newport, May, 2000 238

    Voyage 45: *Dancer*, Bermuda-Azores-Channel Islands, UK 240

    Voyage 46: *La Souris Qui Rugit*, Christmas Cove, Maine - Newport, May, 2001 242

Chapter 13 243

    Voyage 47: *Lapwing*, Southwest Harbor, Maine-Bristol RI 243

    Voyage 48: *Ascent*, Rock Hall, MD-Block-Newport-Cuttyhunk-Vineyard-Newport 244

    Voyage 49: *McKinna 57*, Newport-South Norwalk, CT, September, 2000 245

    Voyage 50: *Ivory*, Newport-Bermuda-St. Thomas, April, 2000 245

Chapter 14 248

    Voyage 51: *Sinai*, Antigua-Bermuda-Block Island-Black Rock CT.................................. 248

    Voyage 52: *Samburu*, Marion Bermuda Race, June, 2001 255

    Voyage 53: *Tetiaroa*, Padanaram, Martha's Vineyard, Cuttyhunk, 'Tucket, Padanaram ... 257

    Voyage 54: *Quick Step*, Newport, Portsmouth, Mooring Maintenance, Towing 258

    Voyage 55: Sailboat Tow, Fairhaven MA-Newport 259

    Voyage 56: Launch *Rounder*, Newport–Edgartown Martha's Vineyard 259

    Voyage 57: Launch *Hope* Newport–Block Island, for Oldport 260

    Voyage 64: *Quick Step, Patriot*, Newport-Bristol-Newport; July 4, US Navy Charters 260

    Voyage 58: *Elba*, Barrington-Jamestown 261

    Voyage 60: *Erebus*, Portsmouth-Newport 261

    Voyage 61: *Katahdin*, Newport-Port Jefferson, NY 261

Chapter 15 263

    Voyage 62: *Katabatic*, Hull MA-Jamestown RI 263

    Voyage 63: *Violin,* South Freeport ME-Nahant MA 263

    Voyage 65: *Papaya*, Jamestown RI-Rye NY 264

    Voyage 66: *Maiden 2* (ex-*PlayStation*) Newport-Westport MA 264

    Voyage 67: *Alcyone*, Newport-Bristol 266

    Voyage 68: *Föhn Wind*, Padanaram-Vineyard-Tucket-Hadley-Menemsha, ... 267

    Voyage 69: *Föhn Wind* RI-Block I, Cuttyhunk, Vineyard, Tucket..................................... 267

Chapter 16 269

    Voyage 70: *Turk*, Nantucket-Sag Harbor NY 269

    Voyage 71: *Farr Away*, Bermuda-Port Jefferson, NY 270

    Voyage 72: *Oniwa*, Newport Harbor Christmas Lights, December 274

    Voyage 73: *Congo* Wilmington NC to Beaufort, NC 274

    Voyage 74: *Andromeda*, St. Martin-Bermuda-Sag Harbor, NY 275

Chapter 17 278

    Voyage 75: *Pollux*, Marion-Bermuda Race, 3rd Place 278

    Voyage 76: *Aviatrix*, Newport, Narragansett Bay 279

    Voyage 77: *Impulse*, Newport-Hyannis-Nantucket MA 279

    Voyage 78: *Eclipse*, Bristol-Newport-Bristol RI 279

    Voyage 79: *Regimen*, Islip, Long Island, NY-Portsmouth, RI 281

    Voyage 80: *La Mer*, Padanaram MA-Newport 281

Chapter 18 282

    Voyage 81: *Ranger*, Eliot Maine-Portsmouth, RI 282

    Voyage 82: *Tangerine,* Bermuda–Marion MA, June 284

    Voyage 83: *Endearment*, Newport-Portsmouth 289

    Voyage 84: *Kikynos*, Portsmouth RI-Portland, ME 289

    Voyage 85: *Bellatrix*, Newport-Wilson's Creek, Norwalk CT 289

    Voyage 86: *Williwaw*, Newport RI-Larchmont NY 290

Chapter 19 291

    Voyage 87: *Alpine*, Shelter Island, NY-Block Island-Wickford, RI 291

    Voyage 88: *J-40*, Day-racing, Riverside YC, Connecticut 293

    Voyage 89: *Kamchatka*, Bermuda-Newport 293

    Voyage 90: *Allure*, Old Saybrook-Norwalk CT 295

    Voyage 91: *Water Taxis*, Boston Harbor Cruises, August, 2019-March, 2000 295

    Voyage 92: *Blue Moon*, sea trials Narragansett Bay, Portsmouth RI, July, 2020 298

Chapter 20 300

    Joseph Conrad's *Initiation*, in *The Mirror of the Sea* 300

Conclusion 311

Appendices 317

    Appendix 1 - Echo Yacht Deliveries - Ranks & Roles 317

    Appendix 2 - Sample Echo Yacht Delivery voyages 320

Appendix 3 - Life Ring Story: *Breathless* & ITB *Philadelphia* 322
Appendix 4 - Float Plan for *Ivory* 323
Appendix 5 - Timings of the Loss of *Stiarna* 324
Appendix 6 - Echo Three-Season Summary, to End 1999 325
Appendix 7 - Echo Sample Yacht Delivery Contract 326
Appendix 8 - 2005 Echo Yacht Delivery's Second-Quarterly Summary 330
Appendix 9 - Echo Yacht Delivery Wall of Fame 332
Appendix 10 - Working Voyages: 56 vessels, 1,510 miles 333
Appendix 11 - Passenger Voyages: 178 vessels, 12,240 miles 334
Appendix 12 – "A Summer Under Sail for Eric Aboard *Rumor*" 337
Appendix 13 – "23 Year Old Nassuvian Skippers 70 Foot Sailing Yacht Across Pacific" 339
Appendix 14 - Employer Letterheads 346
Appendix 15 - Law Student Sinks Yacht 349
Appendix 16 - Poem "*War Baby,* Irish cave" 358

Photo Credits, Contributions 359
Acknowledgements 361
About the Author 369

In Memoriam

I would especially like to recognize the many mentioned herein who are no longer with us, including Warren Brown, Charlie Berry, and Teddy Gosling of *War Baby*, Richard Goennel, Dr. Sheldon Brotman of *Whisper of Maine*, Bill and Mrs. Wright, and Lars Lenfeldt of *Qu'elle Aime*. Chris Treahy truly did provide me with the voyage of a lifetime across the Pacific, and taught me a lot to boot. I would like to remember Bob Tiedemann, who hired me on *Pam* and *Mariner*, Jamie Boeckel of *Blue Yankee*, lost in 2002, Trey Topping of *Flying Colours*, and Ron Barr and Tim Davitt of the Armchair Sailor Bookstore where I worked. Ally Zapp, who I knew too briefly at the IYAC, has the Flip-Flop Regatta in her honor, and Nigel Henderson was someone I wanted to be.

For my captain Patty's sake, I salute Mike Plant, lost on *Coyote*. I would like us to remember Dr. Donald E. Hill, killed on *Bellatrix* as it began the 1989 Marion-Bermuda Race, though I did not meet him. We miss Steve Wolmsley and Don Glassie, of *The Arabella*, which hired friends of mine. Commodore Frank Snyder and I had a short gam, he from *Chasseur*, in Nassau Harbour, me on the modest *Ma'Wessel*. I am indebted to Dayton Carr of *Gunga Din* and *Oliver Hazard Perry*, who was always generous and thoughtful. The owner of *Rogue* about whom her captain Dermot Bremner told me, had the misfortune to have grounded her on Cape Hatteras when the boat was named *Ornery*. Through sheer force of will, and by never leaving his boat, he managed to salvage her. On tying the boat up at a Virginia marina, he checked into a local hotel, then suffered a massive stroke and passed.

In the early 1990s a very memorable personality made his presence known in the sailing scene, or at least the Lower Thames sailor's haunts like the International Yacht and Athletic Club (IYAC). As a young man he had his arm caught between two large yachts and severed below the elbow. Despite this, I saw him challenge and beat another larger-than-life character, then-Mayor of Providence, Buddy Cianci, in a game of pool at the IYAC. A few years later I heard that John Horn was killed in Florida after mistaking the wrong house for his crew house, and was shot, or that he died from injuries from a beating outside a Lauderdale bar. Originally from Connecticut, he worked with organizations in support of disabled sailors. Another friend, Malcolm McKay, skipper of the *T'Hell*, recently took one too many wave over the toe rail – fare thee well.

I would like also to remember the sailor and yacht owner who offered me my critical first command, across the Pacific: Christopher Patrick Orient of *Stornoway*. My long-term employer, who I respect greatly, Severin, lost son Rip some years after we all sailed to Canada together on *Luna*, and later his devoted wife, who grew up where I did, in Nassau. My condolences on their absence. I wish they were here to read these accounts. Though I acknowledge her throughout, Barbara Babs Connett and her family have been encouraging role models for me since my teens; she is missed by me and many.

In the shipping side where I worked during much of the preparation of this book, I note the sad loss of Bob Flynn some years ago and more recently the passing of Antonio Litman, an extraordinarily warm person who dropped everything to drive from Manhattan to Connecticut to personally collect my entire maritime law library for Virginia's House of

Hope. I my deepest respect and sympathies for crew-mate Felix Colatanavanua, whose father, David Hamilton-Jones was a beloved artist at our family business Cable Beach Manor for many years painting, and passed after a full life. It is with sorrow that I learned that Felix's lovely younger sister, who their mother would walk to Bay Street every school day for the bus, also passed. Please accept my family's deepest condolences, Felix, in Fiji.

While this book was being prepared, we lost our relative and friend Orjan Lindroth, whose mother, born Gunnel Helgosdotter Wiberg, moved to Nassau in 1952 with her husband Arne Lindroth, to work for the owner of Electrolux at what is now Paradise Island, which Mr. Wenner Gren owned. Orjan and my brother John worked closely together, and I was invited on board *Schooner Queen* for memorable day trips in Abaco, where Orjan developed Schooner Bay, and off Old Fort Bay.

A special show of deference and friendship to Ron Ackman, who for some 20 years was my employer, mentor, neighbor, and friend. We had many long conversations on Young Street, on his boat *Aurora* at Sayer's Wharf. The topics ranging from his friend Lars the captain of the Swedish tall ship *Svanen* on which I wanted to run away age 17, the effects of his time with the US Navy in Vietnam, and much more. He died too early, and is sorely missed by far more than me, and especially by Alexis and Teak.

I gratefully remember revered sailors from my home town, and others taken from us too young: Peter Christie, Esq., Bobby Symonette, Durward Knowles, Troy D'Arville, Shorty Trimmingham, Patrick A. McAleer, BC sailor, lawyer, friend. I fondly recall seeing Louie the Lobsterman in Newport, on my walks to work in the book store, and at Gary's Handy Lunch. I feel those who have passed would also remind us of the great times they had on boats. Many happy friendships and relationships have been furthered or initated on boats. Warren Brown of *War Baby* says that eleven couples he knew of met on his boats over the years. One of my best mates met his spouse indirectly through a voyage via Bermuda. I believe that those no longer with us would be pleased to be assured of that.

Sailboats: Explanatory Diagrams

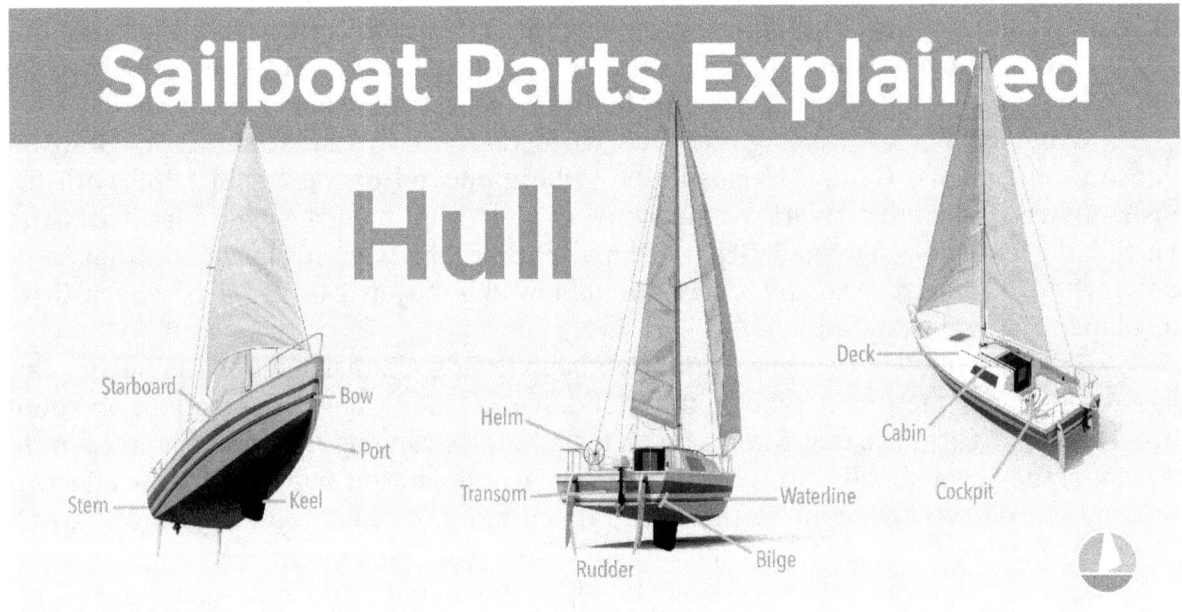

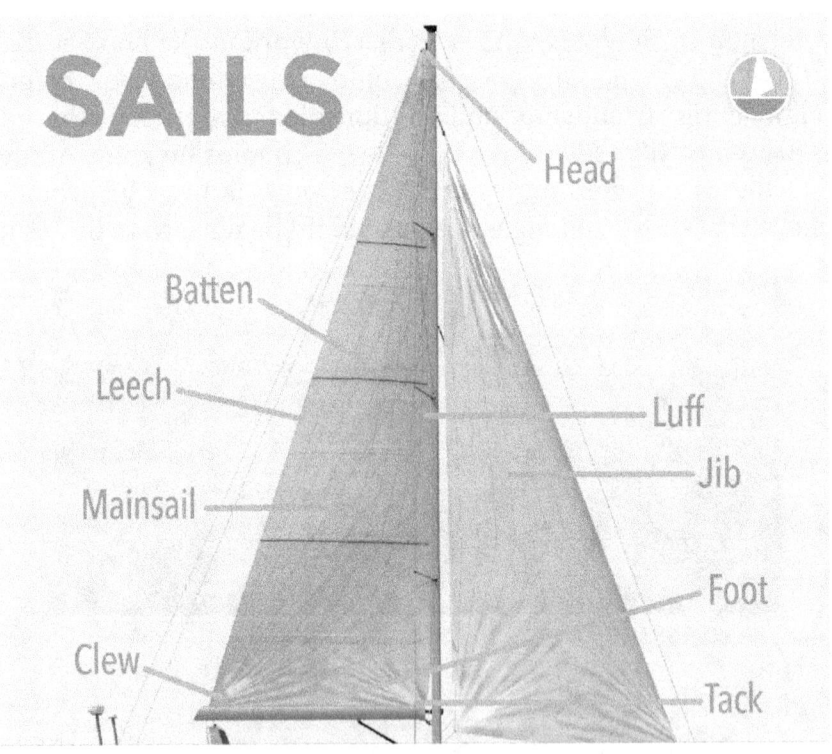

Images created by and courtesy of the editors of improvesailing.com, compliments of Shawn Buckles, Improve Sailing, UK.

Powerboat: Explanatory Diagrams

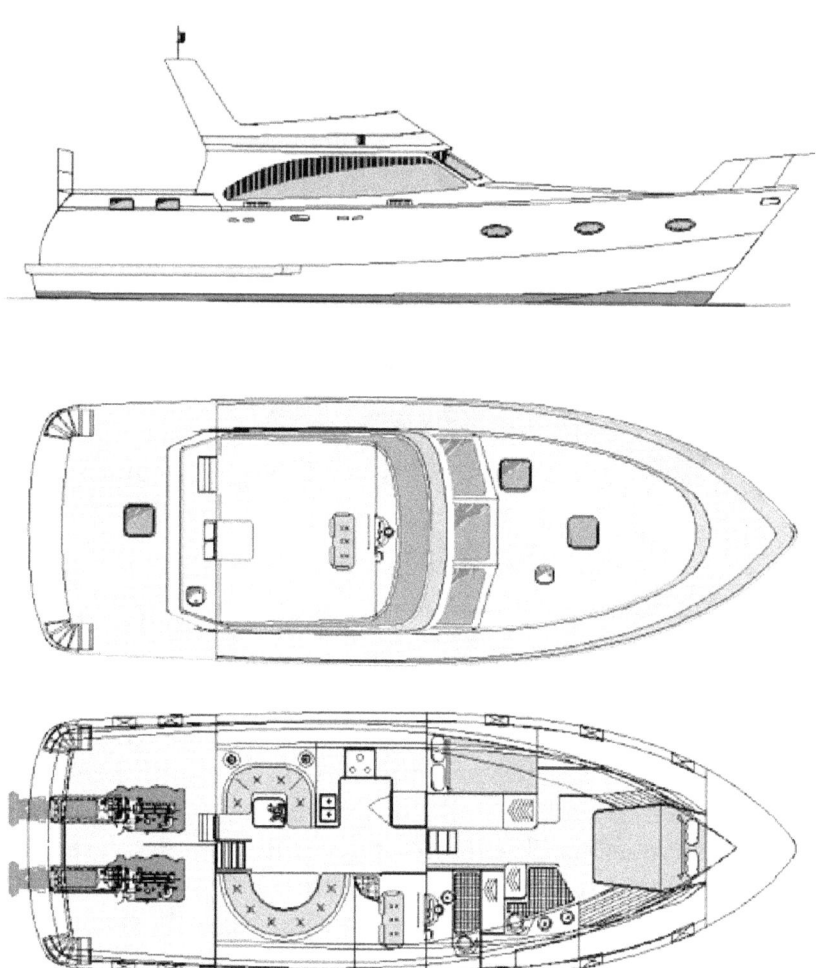

Banjo Roberts-Goodsons' yacht design site in Australia. This particular model is the Euro 1,400, the aft cabin version. This version may be fitted with jet drives or conventional twin engines, situated under the pilot house. From: Banjoroberts.com. I chose this model because it clearly shows the two engines at bottom left, a bit of the interior (which delivery crew almost never use on a power yacht), and the basic deck layout. Unlike sailboats, which have large wide decks, larger motor yachts often have just narrow, thin, tricky to navigate spaces between hull and house. One young man slipped from such a spot – there is little to grab onto, and sank to the bottom of Bannister's Wharf in Newport. I was skipper of a launch right there at the time and am a strong swimmer, and would gladly have hopped in to help find the young man, but no one told us what was going on, just told us to stop, and they waited for a fire department diver, and when they pulled him out he had brain damage but was thankfully alive. You can drown in a bathtub. All boating is dangerous, particularly when you throw alcohol or other stimulants into an environment already dominated by weather, light, wind and rain conditions.

Forewords

I was delighted to be asked to write the foreward for this book containing such outstanding stories about yacht voyages. Countless other books have been written about yachting over the years, but remarkably, very few have described the trials, tribulations and accounts of being a yacht delivery Captain. This book is just that.

I met Eric in a pub in Newport, Rhode Island, one evening in late August of 1999, after having just completed a yacht delivery from Chester, Nova Scotia, Canada to Hyannis Port, Cape Cod, Massachusetts. At that stage of my life, I was young sailor in search of adventure and warmer climes. So, when Eric talked about his new delivery company and described some of his own yachting adventures, and I told him about some my own recent exploits on tall ships, we hit it off pretty good. He subsequently invited me to sail with him as his Chief Mate on a yacht being delivered to Florida. What I thought would be one delivery, ultimately turned into four, and an unforgettable chapter of my life that included tales of survival, extreme weather conditions and even rescue on the high seas. Overall, I believe ours was a good partnership many years ago; he was looking for a dedicated Chief Mate, and I wanted to log some serious ocean time. What we didn't anticipate was that our partnership would turn into a lifelong bond and friendship.

The following pages offer a wonderful collection of first-hand accounts of what it truly means to be a yacht delivery Captain. *Yacht Voyages* makes mention to many of the folks who have played supporting roles as crew, including yours truly. In all the years I have been a seafarer, I can truly say that I've never met a sailor who has logged as many nautical miles on yachts, or has had such an adventurous life on the sea, as Eric. His love of the sea goes deep and his passion for maritime life is truly evident in his writing. So, when I learnt he had finally put this book together of all his yacht voyages, I was excited to read it and truly honored to contribute to it.

Enjoy the read.

Sailor Aaron Dickson

Yacht deliveries and employment as a yacht Captain can range from joy to misery, from a sense of fulfilling accomplishment to terror of violent storms and skirting the law. Eric's experiences show this range through the eyes of a mature man looking back at the challenges of his youth.

Blessed with a keen intellect, emotional sensitivity, and boundless energy, Eric presents the reader with lively tales told from a very personal point of view. Eric begins his voyages as a callow youth and as a promising writer on a mission to collect personal experiences that he wants to tell as part of his wide-ranging maritime life.

It is fascinating to watch Eric develop an adult understanding of human nature, and a system of personal ethics.

I highly recommend this collection of sea stories, which, like all good tales, manage to both delight and instruct.

Stephen Connett

Bahamas Sea Turtle Research
Bahamas Sea Turtle Network

Introduction

"It was then that I knew I'd had enough,
burned my credit card for fuel.
Headed out to where the pavement turns to sand...."

Neil Young & Crazy Horse Band, *Thrasher*
Album *Rust Never Sleeps*, 1979

Overview: *I went to sea, as a writer, having studied the maritime world for years. I concluded that it offered affordable global travel, risk of death (indeed, risk and death), fear and euphoria. Then, like most, I stayed in the maritime industry, and it kept giving me stories. Here are some of them. Knowing this will explain my failings as both a sailor and a writer; I set out not to master being a mariner, but being a writer, which is now my full-time work.*

Our first captain! A nationally ranked, Bahamas hall-of-fame tennis champion who simply never gives up.... Our mother, Jane McDermid Wiberg, originally of Scarsdale, New York, then Nassau since 1965. She in turn entrusted us to German Nurse Ulla in our early years. We were expected to suck it up and tough it out from an early age. Being one of three brothers constantly outdoors further underpinned this. By age 8, we had built and sailed our own scrappy boat on Lake Cunningham, Nassau and admired the sea from the family business, consisting of waterfront apartments for European visitors.

My father was congratulated when we rescued a drowning man at Balmoral Island (once North Cay, Cable Beach) but he was also chastised by fellow Rotarians when we were spotted in badly polluted golf-course ponds. Indeed we all caught Chicken Pox on those fetid messes, as well as hundreds of golf balls and dozens of turtles, which we rehabilitated and released (or sold).

This book set off to be a nautical memoir about a young sailor rising through the ranks aboard over 100 privately owned sailing yachts 35-to-55 feet long. By the end of it, you will have followed me round the world four times, and voyaged to some 250 islands in about 75 countries. The stories start with my being tossed around in a tiny boat in the Baltic Sea off Sweden, then gaining a foothold as a boat-boy for a prominent New England Brahmin family, and racing to Bermuda. This led to my assuming command over a 68-foot wooden yacht across the Pacific.

Firstly, some background on who motivated me to undertake these adventures. I can cover the first 17 years quickly. My brothers and I made a sailboat out of crates, sheets, and sticks and sank in Lake Cunningham, in a diplomatic enclave (our father represented Sweden, my brother now does) outside Nassau, Bahamas; we did make it to an islet. Due to crime in Nassau, we found wallets in the woods between the hotels at Cable Beach and our home, and would return the ID cards and so forth. The recipients would send us rewards, and we always bought inflatable boats (looking back I guess it was blood money of sorts, indirectly benefiting from the crimes enacted on the visitors we depended on...).

Most of our dozen or so inflatable boats were very modest craft limited to pools and ponds. The largest, however was a full Avon grey inflatable dinghy, propelled by a very basic military-grade classic British Seagull Outboard, two-stroke, one-cylinder engine which my father went to great pains to keep working. Though it always seemed to keep the operator breathless due to its sputtering, the little motor took us to the island a mile offshore form our business. Balmoral Island gave us much to explore, including a hollow islet and beaches and bird rookeries, reefs, and a B-26 Marauder bomber plane from the RAF base No. 111 Coastal Operational Training Unit (O.T.U.(C)) during World War II in shallow water, with all killed, and two diesels from a sunken motor vessel which I wrote to the head of *National Geographic* saying were ancient cannons; I still have the wonderful encouraging reply from their president and chairman, Gilbert M. Grosvenor.

My parents then bought a 28-foot Silverton gasoline inboard boat which we ran aground during its maiden voyage, between Silver Cay and Balmoral Island, then our Dad bravely endured shattered window glass to make it to the Exumas in a gale. It was called *Viking* and was a lot of work. We had two kid's boats, all named *Ma'Wessel*, for *My Vessel*, with the name always painted in Rastafarian colors of red, green, and yellow. The first was a non-descript lake-boat, with high side and a single-outboard; visually unappealing but safe. We had *Viking* from my ages 7 to 12 or so, the first *Ma'Wessel*, about age 14 to 16, the second *Ma'Wessel* from ages 17 to 23, and the present grande dame, *Shoal Shaker*, from age 24 to past 50 and still going strong at Old Fort Bay; it was bought at a Florida police auction, so we can imagine the boat must have some stories to tell!

The second and final *Ma'Wessel* was about 15-foot Boston Whaler, very used. These were open rectangles with a couple benches, and the helmsman steering from the back bench, one side, a cable throttle, forward and reverse, with two anchors, one either end, an engine that sometimes trimmed. It was powered by a single Evinrude outboard engine of no more than about 70 horsepower. Any more power and the engine could force the bow to pop into the air, overpowering the boat and endangering persons. I rescued a young fellow from a Whaler which flipped that way, the engine was on the seafloor, dangling from cables, he was lucky to be alive. It was an awkward tow. Boston Whalers are famous as great safe, agile, powerful unsinkable boats for young persons to learn the ropes aboard. They are also popular as yacht business and sailing program support boats, and short-distance recreational trips, in both fresh and salt water.

Ready for anything! Camp Rockmont, Asheville, North Carolina, age 9, 1979.

With a family of six, some unfortunate soul gets to be the one to destroy the boat. We never had overlapping boats, and didn't buy a new one till the former hulk was toted to a garage sale on a trailer and sold "as is;" without the trailer! At age 11 I lost the family windsurf board after paddling it to an island, leaving it, and finding the tide or a mean person had stolen it, and one of several old Sunfish hulls – all of them leaking either in the deck, cockpit or below – sank and was abandoned by me west of Balmoral, though I managed to swim the rig to shore and salvage it and the mast and sails.

Then there was this: I was home from having graduated college and a summer of moving large boats, and returned to Nassau with a rather large reddish goatee; so noticeable that in Miami airport I was asked whether I was a missionary! When I came home from a boating trip on the second *Ma'Wessel* to place the gas cannisters in the tool shed I was surprised that two blonde teenage Dutch girls were playing tennis on my parent's court (Mom is a tennis coach). They were the daughters of our new neighbors, bankers from the Netherlands.

In my effort to make a favorable impression on them, the next day we piled the fuel tanks and family dog into a Brazilian made off-road truck, and went down to *Ma'Wessel*.

The vessel's latest inadequacies having not been made clear to me, or perhaps I having simply minimized them, things went well for the three of us and our dog Chelsea, who had one eye blind but she had four great sea legs. We arrived at the wreck of a crashed drug plane half a mile west of Lyford Cay Marina, which had made great cocktail story fodder, as guests at sunset drinks literally watched as the US Drug Enforcement Agency (DEA) and Bahamian police helicopter forced the small drug plane into the water and the pilot swam ashore with his drugs and a dog, only to be captured.

After a fun snorkel, I started the boat while anchored (which one is supposed to do, before you become adrift), and began heading in calm sunny conditions towards Old Fort Bay, a mile to the east. First we heard a lot of cackling sounds and smelled melting rubber. Then there was smoke and some flames, but no explosion. I quickly disconnected the fuel line, anchored, and had the young ladies sit on the lip of the bow of the boat; the tippy front. They were instructed to jump into the sea if and when the snarling engine exploded. It didn't, which is good, because by the time they registered the engine had exploded, it would have been too late.

I didn't have a cell or a radio, so as the engine still sputtered and simmered and cackled, and there was nothing I could do to stop it after disconnecting the batteries too, except perhaps douse it with water. Since it seemed like some kind of electrical fire, water would not really help. I removed the lid and let it burn down. I decided not to swim the boat to the nearest shore, which was private property above the high-water mark near Lady Todd's casuarina-enshrouded estate a mere 300 or so yards away. Rather, in my youthful exuberance, I opted to swim burning boat, passengers, and dog all the way to the marina entrance about half a miles away, and, if I could, to the family's boat slip. Well, I managed by laughing and keeping spirits high, and swimming my guts out, to get them all into the channel at the entrance of the Lyford Cay Marina. Our family friend Juan was coming out on is large powerboat just then. Naturally, he kindly came alongside and offered to tow us back to our slip.

However, I was so close that even though Juan was in touch with the harbor master, the affable and professional Gino, with whom we are all friendly, I was determined to get the boat back to the slip myself, by swimming in the calm waters the final quarter mile. To them I was beginning a short swim; to me I was in fact *ending* a long swim! Also, I think secretly I was worried that having a strapping lad in a bigger boat that actually functioned as designed – Juan - might tempt the young ladies to jump ship! Befuddled a bit, Juan and others were then treated to the spectacle of their friend swimming through a marina filled with fancy mega-yachts owned by the Aga Khan, the Laura Ashley clan, and others, towing a burning boat, dog and two Dutch girls aboard virtually with his teeth and fumes for energy….

An early date; bring boat paint and let's make a centerboard from scratch! Age 18. She and I were both journalists on the local paper.

The ride home was pretty silent, I never did "get the girl," and was never able to take her for a spin in a working boat. *Ma'Wessel* was sold by placing ads I the local papers emphatically stating "As is, where is" – we could not be bothered to scrap or toss the engine, so we sold it where it fell in the line of duty, cables holding the boat together and all. The boat flexed visibly with water ingress in any kind of sea; when it was rough, it could really only manage downwind. I imagine her as inverted on the sea floor nowadays: perhaps a lobster trap off the Berry Islands, or shelter for a family post-Hurricane.

We all learned from these boats; lessons like remember to top up fuel, to tie off the anchor before setting it (yup, I made that mistake in front of a family of professional mariners who owned *Keewadin* and others). Eventually we became passably good at anchoring, backing down on the beach, finding keys on the sea floor, fishing, spearfishing, lighting fires on the beach using only local materials, navigating at night with no radar or depth sounder, and, sadly the importance of differentiating dangerously inebriated persons according to what hallucinogenic they had ingested, swallowed, snorted, or drank. We also helped others, including Peter Frampton's 'girlfriend' and her other boyfriend, to whom she gave the key to Frampton's power yacht while he was recording at Compass Point nearby, get Frampton's beached boat off Old Ford Beach in winter gale. I learned from a documentary that he was so upset by all the betrayal that he smashed a car into a tree, causing career-impairing injuries; which is why most reader's haven't heard of him. Although the highest order of rescue is to volunteer your boat for BASRA – Bahamas Air Sea Rescue Association – I was never on the island long enough to participate. The small boating community knew much about the accidents that happened in Bahamas, often the victims were visitors, and alcohol was almost always involved, though at times the blinding sun in the operator's eyes contributed.

Then the family purchased *Shoal Shaker* at auction in Fort Lauderdale. It sank on delivery in 1994 (hence the name), and yet was enthusiastically and generously salvaged by Bimini residents and is lovingly restored to this day by our older brother John. As far as sailing goes, we always had a Sunfish or windsurfer lying around our family hotel, Cable Beach Manor, as well as other stuff to play around on, from canoes to boards to inflatables. There were all kinds of other excitements less than a mile offshore on Balmoral Island. In an all-boys Christian camp in the Black Mountains near Asheville, North Carolina, I was taught the fundamentals of sailing by a very kindly counsellor from the Bahamas, named Bruce Stewart. Through his instruction, I finally understood the principals at about age 9, and have always been very fond of the basic, self-operating lateen or felucca rig simplicity. The Sunfish also featured a small cuddy and cockpit on some models. In boarding school I often sketched out details of a one-way voyage to the Exumas from Nassau, with a homemade anchor and food supplies; dreaming about a down-wind voyage taking a day.

Camp Rockmont. We thought we were clever anglers, until I learned later the lake was dammed and then stocked with bass. I took part in the first-ever, mile-long swim race, for which the councilors hand-painted a first-place certificate. On behalf of a dozen Bahamians there, I was proud to be the recipient. Unrelatedly: in camp one rule was "don't mess with a kid who has an older brother in camp." We each had two brothers there, and a handful of fellow Bahamians, some of whom were instructors... so lucky me!

I have spent many joyous hours alone and with others on Sunfish, even though several took on water and became heavy and sluggish, or actually sank. Then I had a failed stint on the St. George's School sailing team, lasting barely a season, in which I failed to efficiently operate 420's and Dragonflies at Ida Lewis Yacht Club in Newport. This was followed by more sub-par stints on small boats like Larks, Techs, Rhodes 19's, and Lasers on the Charles River in Boston, for Boston College, and finally had a breakthrough onto larger boats, which for BC included the coaches' yacht *Face Off*, and Luder 44's, designed for the US Navy, at Annapolis and in New London, Connecticut. Since I was back-up on the big-boat team, I could be found aboard *Colt International* chatting with Capt. Neil and Francis Batt, of Australia about offshore passages (I stayed on *Colt International* right out of college and saw Neil and Francis in Newport and Lymington, UK).

I was not only not a good racer, but a bad one. I T-boned another boat, from Harvard, in a regatta where we shared the same buoy, or mark, but I was not even in the same race!

They made it to shore. I lost the rig near the salt and pepper bridge in Boston while dead downwind trying to light a cigarette, and was banned from using MIT's equipment (I kept the base of the mast). I helped set and monitor the mark for the International 505's world championship in San Francisco in 1989, but would not be able to pick out a 505 from pair of Levi's 505 jeans in a marina lineup. In short, I was the Ferdinand the Bull of competitive sailing; I didn't want to share the boat with anyone, and I didn't give a shit about starting a race, much less winning one.

Lacking any great skill, I found that over time I was assumed, by basis of existing experience, to have an idea about what I was doing. If I was totally honest, my simply having gone to a sailing prep school probably helped. I guess now is the time to re-examine whether privilege played a part, and I am sure that sometimes it did. But no one in my family was in a yacht club, or, in the Americas at least, owned a sailboat, and most of my sailboat voyages were international, with men and women of many nationalities. To get on *War Baby* I hand-wrote and faxed letters and sailing CV's to the harbor masters of all the major sailing ports globally, Auckland, *Kamchatka*, Panama, Cabo San Lucas, London, Gibraltar, and so on. I personally wrote to Earl Heinz in Honolulu, Jimmy Cornell, Bill Buckley, and many, many others over a period or months. Several kindly wrote back.

As the saying goes, fortune tends to favor the prepared. Then, from Bermuda, Warren Brown offered me a berth aboard *War Baby* on a Corinthian (volunteer) basis, which I immediately accepted. I went on to actively sail in *War Baby* for a decade, spending time on her in the UK, Ireland, France, Bermuda, US, and New Zealand. I had some advantages, chose what I wanted to do, and used the hell out of them to get me there. To me, I fit all my dreams, desires and fantasies of danger and adventure *into* sailing, and either the sailing world fit me and accommodated me, or if my skillset lagged, I forced myself to adapt and to step up to the next level.

There is an irony which the reader is trusted to figure out; I was conscientiously running away from two years of horror in boarding school which were not self or student-inflicted. The irony is that I chose a sport which is considered a rich man's game to run away from the world ruled by rich man's rules: prep school. I understand the irony, and accept it. Ocean sailing is not a way of life given to pausing to consider; captains are expected to decide and decide quickly; the wrong decision can be better than no decision, and crew then will know what is expected of them. We call listening to the rigging slapped by the wind into the mast the onset of *marina-itis*; a fear of leaving port. I told a captain with whom I am friendly that I didn't feel well about our up-coming departure from Bermuda that day. His reply was classic:

"You don't feel right because you got shitfaced until 4 am, that's why. And we're not leaving because the weather sucks, not because of your hangover." I don't think I was alone in that I had a pretty persistent drinking problem, and sometimes an attitude problem as well, particularly having been a captain but often doing non-captain work despite being licensed to command. I am not alone in believing that ships and their crews will rot if left in port too long, and that a big part of a skipper's job is psychological. In Tahiti I was party of a small band of young English-speaking sailors, and one week the owner of our boat (I was 23) said he would pay me. I told "the guys" this (Canadians, Brits, French), and everyone got "dressed" and combed their hair. The owner then handed me about $20, in Pape'ete, where a can of Coca-Cola costs about $5. Unperturbed, I told the guys we needed to hit the town, and we did. At the first club we all trampled up the wooden stairs and the doorman somehow let us in. Once in I bought a couple colas and the fellows sat down. As the wealthy locals and visitors would go dancing, they left jars of cola and bottles of rum, to which I would help myself and circulate to my team at irregular intervals. I never got caught, and we all had a good time; for about $3 a person!

As you will read, I still found the adventure I sought, and when letters didn't work, I simply swam out to boats in the harbors of Bermuda, Antigua, even Newport. For every race to Bermuda there is a phalanx of B-teamers like me who show up to move the boats back home. So, as there is a bright and shiny side to yachting, there is a shadier, poorer, more nuanced one as well. Though I haven't done that much cruising (the other end of the racing spectrum), I understand, having seen it first-hand ,the aphorism that the French will build a steel sailboat in their back yard which is half the length of an American yacht, but sail it twice the distance. At the end of a world cruise these steel craft return looking rusty and worse for wear, but they did their job, and the builder had gotten what they wanted from it, and can give it to a neighbor. Many of them manage a world only Francophones know exists: the French-speaking one. A veritable *ancien régime*; Indochine, French Guiana, French Guinea, Cot D'Ivoire, Reunion, Pondichéry, Mauritius, Burkina Faso, Guadeloupe and other French West Indies, Seychelles, Djibouti, French Polynesia, Comoros, Tahiti, Algeria, Senegal, Dahomey, Morocco, Algeria, Tunisia, and many more.

There are many other sayings; buy a boat equivalent in feet to your age in years, what does a sailboat flying a so-and-so ensign mean? "We are broke, and will steal your vegetables!" The hoist (or height) of a yacht ensign, or nautical flag, is meant to be as many inches long as the number of feet the yacht is long. A gin palace is there primarily to look good, nor for performance; it people can't see it (like that pesky bit beneath the water which has the machinery and counterbalances all the bars up top), why bother with it? Me met one stuck in Tahiti; it was delivered there from Panama at a discount to test the market. The market failed, and the delivery ship company refused to come back for it, and it wasn't able to cross oceans on its own. Gin palace. Cruising is also known as the art of repairing your yacht in interesting places…. Or sailing towards the same direction as the little arrow on the top of the mast known as a Windex; or into the wind. Double the power of your engine, I was reminded, does not double the speed. And owners are said to fill the fuel tank of a sailboat in May and don't expect to refill it again that whole summer, they are so cheap.

Although tall ship sailors have a mysticism about them (and I watched them daily signal by semaphore flags in Camden Maine), and sailboat sailors have to master both sail as well as machinery, still some of their brethren in the powerboat community look down on them as "rag-boaters." One theory is that a lot of powerboat officers had their start in sail, and miss it. Of course there is plenty of name-calling. One of the sad cases was the season in the Caribbean where many dozens of expensive and essential and hard-to-replace boat dinghies were stolen, and invariably locals on dozens of islands were blamed. Towards summer, as many boats prepared to cross oceans and return home, a sleuth uncovered a foreign (European) boat jammed with the stolen dinghies and their motors.

We were leaving Bermuda in 1991 on a 50-foot racing machine and I had to ask where the gooseneck was. In case you, also, don't know, it is an important place where the boom meets the mast. It was like starting the Cannonball Run car race across USA, and asking where the axel is. Even as a young captain I made such egregious mistakes as adding oil to engines that showed low on the dip stick simply because they were running. I naively thought that if I simply soaked fan belts in pots with boiling water, I could stretch them onto the alternator without having to stop everything, unbolt, and re-bolt. The owner of a family-run boatyard said he could not understand why I would start sanding or painting in the bow and just move to other areas of the boat with no seeming pattern. I thought of my reply – but did not articulate it; he was a scientist and engineer, I was a poet!

I desperately needed sailing to become the vessel for my wanderlust, which I quickly found cycling and walking could not provide. I realized there was too much land, it was too dangerous (over 30 wars on any given year), and there was much more water. I was desperate for a chance for me to work my way around the planet in all directions, my two passports and love of languages enabling me to gain access to cosmopolitan thrills as well as time-worn spills and scrape. A highlight of my early sailing was when we arrived from Antigua under a Belgian skipper, with a crew from Antigua, US, and New Zealand, and a cat, just as the lovely schooner *Dolphin* emerged from Town Cut, St. George's. We had our yellow flag on the spreader aflutter meaning we were inbound from another country, and they were heading to another country, and we waved joyfully to each other.

Over time, I learned enough so that folks don't get hurt, and heard, and did not utter, the memorable phrase "Don't bleed on my deck!" I strove to remain sober at sea, be punctual for watch, respectful of my mates, and commit no mutiny or sabotage. Between Bahamas where I grew up and New England where I moved, lay Bermuda. I found this pin-prick in a chart of the North Atlantic as a child and wanted to know more about it. I still dream of spending a year writing on the cliffs behind lovely St. George's. As you will see in the diary entries for *Rumor*, I learned to eat what I was offered, and not steal or eat out of line.

On boats under my command I encourage crew to eat as much as they can as often as they can, though we still keep a strict provisioning and cooking and cleaning routine; anyone who has lived with me will know the mantra; *the cook don't clean*. It was fun to have several of your closets friends, armed with a food budget for two weeks plus a margin of safety of 30%, and go hog-wild in one of the mega food stores in the US. My sailing brethren and employers have given me much of the material for the book you are reading, and so much more. And I have also satiated the roaming impulses, the tendency to run towards danger. I prefer the comfort of a writer's perch nowadays, though a recent book took me onto Boston Harbor alone in a motor launch all through winter, serving 26 docks from either 5.45 am to 2 pm or 1.30 pm to 10.30 pm. Though I finished the photo book, I don't miss the job, or the cold. When I learned the hourly rate, I was ecstatic. Later I learned that the housekeepers in the hotel we would seek shelter under made $5 more per hour, plus more in tips, than the licensed mariners responsible for 26 persons' lives.

These are mostly narrative accounts, from logbooks and diaries. Thus they are in real time; with the object and intent to give readers first-hand insight into events as they unfolded, often with the emotional component overlaid. They include being knocked overboard in a snowstorm, the burning and sinking of a classic 1937-built yacht off Trinidad (which led to the seminal maritime law case *Reliance v. Hanover*, 2002) and a trans-Atlantic voyage with a heavy drinker which failed. Yet on another trans-At, which began just hours after I stepped ashore from a Newport-Bermuda Race, was recruited and set off for the Azores, we met the *Empire State*, New York State Maritime College's training ship. We had no email on our small yacht and I called the ship to ask if they could send an email to a girl in the UK – I had had no time on shore to do so. The radio operator said he would, if I kept it short. The message

"Sailing your way, ETA London 10 July, Love Eric" went a long way towards improving my love life on arrival! Another trans-Atlantic was with a playboy whose mother bought him the boat. On arrival in Europe I took her to be the genteel boss, until she plied me with sherry to gather dirt on her son and his girlfriends and debts. Her son hired (but didn't pay) a convicted drug smuggler and addict who assaulted me with a knife mid-ocean - twice. He promised to "look after me," but all payments for seven weeks' work stopped after $9. Then I was told to "stop asking for money." After crossing the Pacific as captain of a 78-footer I applied to me mate or crew on a large charter sailing yacht *Evoee*, in Invercargill The Bluff New Zealand. I wanted to see New Zealand's fjords, Sub-Antarctic Islands, and an albatross. I received a reply from the owners, after learning the existing mate, a Kiwi, had been injured, rather badly. They were asking crew to work with no pay. The same old shit. It used to be "do it for the experience," but once I actually *had* the experience, the pay was still nothing.

I tried, unsuccessfully to cross the North Atlantic at age 19 with two Midwestern friends, both named Roger, a former CIA agent, partially blind and nudist, and a captain whose was upset when I dared to refill his water jug in the cockpit with water, rather than vodka. On top of these were shark attacks in three island nations, mutinous behavior not just by the crew, but when the author became, by financial necessity, crew for other captains again.

I once flew from a job helping operate tankers in Singapore to Bermuda. There I joined a crew sailing to Newport who knew very little about me. On the first night out I was resting yet kept hearing the name *CSL Atlantic Eerie*. The increasingly frantic tones on the VHF radios of dozens of sailboats nearby neared panic. By extraordinary coincidence, given that there are nearly 54,000 merchant ships in the world, 10,000 of them this type of dry-bulk ship, I had spent nearly a month aboard that particular ship as a trainee. Finally, I picked up the Mic and asked to speak to Captain Ben, the Canadian master with whom I had dined from Bahamas to Virginia and New York the summer before.

"Eric? Is that you? Thought you were in Singapore, young man!"

He asked, and I then explained, that some 100 boats were all leaving Bermuda following the awards ceremony, and given the good weather. Few of them had experience with large ships in close proximity, and since there were so many of them, the merchant mariners were unable know adjust course and speed for each caller without knowing which was which or upsetting an entire new group on the new course! Capt. Ben figured this out right away, and as ship captains are wont to do, he acted quickly and decisively:

"OK, Eric, tell you what, we will stop *Atlantic Erie*, throw on our deck lights, and let you and your friends pass. *Bon voyage* and stay in touch!"

Folks in the fleet heading home were then a bit more curious about "that Eric guy!"

Humorous episodes include developing a knack for having huge ships alter course for tiny yachts by sounding larger than we were, grabbing crew out of sundry bars to avoid hurricanes, or leaving undesirables ashore. In college I found myself missing the sea and had the blues, so I conspired to steal a barely-enclosed 19-foot Rhodes-designed inshore boat which we trained on, and take it to France. I doubt I could have survived as far as Cape Cod, had I figured out how to get it out of the Charles River with rig in place to Boston Harbor, which I never did. I started to stockpile cans of food and blankets, though, a-la Christopher McCandless (aka Alexander Supertramp), of *Into the Wild* notoriety. Warren on *War Baby* said often: "If you want to kill yourself in sailing, that's your business, but don't call in other people from their families and lives to come save you if you can help it."

The nomadic life led to fast-paced romances in foreign ports. After a voyage from the US to the UK, the burly Australian skipper forced the young yacht owner to drive in a red Ferrari to London banks until the crew were paid. When over £13,000 were paid out in cash in the pub, the adjacent table of men took a sudden keen interest in us, until I showed them photos of the trip with half a dozen lads in nothing but boxers. This is all the saga of global yacht delivery crew who are the unsung glue who fill in the gap by manning and moving those boats smaller than the mega-yachts and bigger than those which the owners sail themselves. The delivery sweet spot for sailboats is between 35 and 55 feet, or about 11 to 17 meters. Under 35 and I would not take it offshore, and over 55 and the boat probably needs a full-time captain to maintain such a large investment. The few times that owners paid the full agreed amount caused me the most shock, rather than the other way round.

On re-reading this material, I am forced to ask: how will readers relate to or feel empathy, even sympathy, for a young person on the bosom of the sea far from home, unable to contact anyone he knows, and at the mercy of the skills, or at times lack of skills, of persons he met hours or days before? That will be up to you. Over the years, I asked many senior shipping industry executives, navy sailors, tug boat, salvage, and yacht sailors

"What was it like when you first went to sea?" Across the board, man of the men and women from Pakistan, West Africa, the Caribbean, Europe and the US; said they experienced isolation, loneliness, fear, seasickness, anxiety for their safety and other privations like hunger. A friend from Nassau crossed the North Atlantic from Bahamas to the UK in a rare, massive 129-foot, 1933-built J-boat named *Velsheda* in the early 1990s, only to have the deck seams above his bunk open up, soaking him much of the way.

Shortly before this photo was taken on Balmoral Island, some Spanish visitors helped themselves to our snorkeling equipment (see we hid it here, under the towel). Another time the boat completely sank and kayakers helped me swim the sail to shore. One trick to keeping cigarettes dry was to tie them in bags to the mast.

An officer on a super-fast sailing yacht confided his opinion that sailors are still treated as they always have been; *under fed, under slept, and under paid* (that was Jerry on *Stealth* in about 2001). As hard at is to believe when you see these beautiful boats, it's much more hardscrabble than it looks, like the duck pedaling furiously below the surface. It was six years as a professional sailor from my first employer to my first full-time employer until I was fully paid. Some of this is my own fault; the real money is in running a large yacht full time, saving rent, being paid through a tax-free corporation of the flag of the yacht, and making tips. But from the outset I swore I would never stand on the gangway waiting to receive full-time owners, never have to ask or remember how they take their coffee; never have to serve someone like Robert Maxwell, on *Lady Ghislaine*, who, I was told through the yachtie gristmill, wiped himself with the yacht's towels. He fell off her and drowned. The yacht's namesake, his daughter, is still creating an infamy of her own.

One summer my very friendly landlord hired me for a short power yacht trip from Fairhaven to Goat Island on a large power yacht with the word *Toy* in it. Since that experience in Palm Beach with *The Other Woman*, I've largely avoided this genus, except when I friend had a stroke miles off Savannah, and I offered to deliver them a crew to help them get to port. I was paid only for time aboard, and not all the other time to and from ports. Then I knew that short-changing crew was the norm rather than the exception. Of course I spent the trip listening to how the captain hadn't been paid for work on a big sailing boat, as the lead-up to my getting stiffed!

I spent last winter running a water taxi, with tips averaging $1 an hour, whereas I am OK with tipping much more just for picking up or delivering some food; a job not requiring sea-time, safety of life at sea, and years of licensing and drug-testing. Truth is that I went into the line of work above all to gain some adventure, to be able to tell some sea stories from them, and to write the very book you are reading. I only starved on a couple trips, losing about 30 pounds in seven weeks, but we never ate the canned cat food! I asked the skipper, Martin, about his most memorable charter: he said some French men and women flew from Marseilles to Guadeloupe, and when asked:

"Where to?" they unzipped a large bag of cash. They said to Martin:

"Go south to Venezuela, Brazil, wherever – when this money runs out, we fly home."

They were bank robbers, and when the money ran out, after innumerable crazy nights, they flew back to France. A couple years later I was at Mr. Nesbitt's local bar at Delaport Village, Nassau, Bahamas with a childhood friend from New York who wintered at Lyford Cay Club. I asked Theo what his most memorable sailing voyage, he told me, without knowing my back story, that his father called the Coast Guard in the Caribbean to get the family off some totally shitty sailing yacht after telling the French skipper Martin that he would get his entire refund back, and he would regret tangling with a New York City businessman. That boat was *Xebec*, the family evacuated her, and Theo was gob-smacked to learn that I had actually chosen to work with him on that boat across the entire North Atlantic!

I realized over time that I got a lot more than money out of these experiences, and certainly a lot more than if I paid for it. Self-confidence, a better understanding of what leadership styles do and do not work. I also have learned about geography, weather, escapism, how folks from owners to crew have changed the world and made or lost fortunes. Plus a bit of engineering, physics, politics, government, economics, military, fisheries, love, both accretive and the more transactional kind, and the physical planet. I learned to cook a basic onion, potato, and boiled-fish stew with pepper grounds, to smother eggs in Vaseline and turn them every week or two to keep them longer, how to bleed air out of fuel filters and squeeze full into them in rough seas. I learned a bit about courtesy, when to swear and not, though I rarely seem to practice all the boundaries all the time.

    Sailors, accustomed to being surrounded by mates who have their back in thick and thin, have been regarding as over-trusting on land. I learned the hard way that trusting every person I meet does not always work. For example, my Panamanian cab driver, a former cop, told me in Spanish on the way back to the airport that he was upset that after five days he had failed to blackmail me. When I asked him why he would possibly want to do that, he shrugged, and said they would only extort me every month or so! In contrast, Gerasimos, my man on the ground, friend and driver in Piraeus and Athens, once came close to pummeling the commodore of a yacht club over a dispute about his parking spot! A Canadian professor asked me to look after his small sailboat when he was away. When I went back to school I slipped the marina security some cash and asked him to look out for the boat – instead he and his mates stripped it the next night; the even stole the laundry detergent!

    I learned one of the great secrets of sailboat voyages is that, provided you don't have paying passengers, you don't need licenses, some get permission ahead or skip islands for the lack of it, but you are basically allowed a 72-hour emergency layover, or 24-hours anchorage, anywhere if you need it. On ocean passages, you are bringing your home with you, and that is nice. Also, pithy sayings about crew like "if you have to think of kicking them off, the decision is already made," don't always hold up. Just because two women on one boat didn't get along, doesn't mean that two or more on another boat would not. An owner once hired the best light-weather sailor in the Great Lakes to help him win the Bermuda High portion of the Newport to Bermuda Race, which is known as the parking lot. They never saw the fellow after the start gun, poor thing was sick as a dog in the Gulf Stream.

    I learned too that even if the owners or captains don't treat you well, they still are legally obliged to fly you to your home port of origin, or at least the country of your passport. On ships powered by wind, you can travel far for free; often boats don't have the fuel need to get to the next port; you sail or you drift waiting for wind; the fluid most important is not fuel but water, as proved when a steel sailboat was found off the Azores with the skeleton of a man and a dog on it. He got their calculus wrong. And cooperation; they say the mind breaks long before the body. Sure, I spilled a share of teenage tears on these voyages, but me and the other guy who starved kept tallies (he won the goatee competition, I the weight-loss) and three years later he tapped my shoulder in Auckland, New Zealand to ask me for the time.

    I have zero regrets from these trips. I started a bank of my own in Bermuda, using coins hidden in limestone cliffs so that I would never run of cash there again, and replenished it over 30 times. I was fogged in on Block Island with a freshly arrived crew from Ireland and Antigua and asked the federal authorities in Nashville if we might go ashore before formally entering the US in New York. Figuring I blew it by asking, I was taken aback by the bureaucrat's reply

"I didn't see you go ashore," he said. That's the kind of complicit understatement I revel in! In the throes of winter the three of us accounted for about a fifth of the night-life. And it was nicer than the time we had to witness a small plane crash into Block Island's only gas station from the deck of our boat, and later learn that the Fire Chief was half way through putting out the fire when he recognized his mother's car and had to recuse himself.

One odd side effect is my aversion to go pleasure-boating or to buy any pleasure-boat beyond a kayak or two-person dinghy. It's not that I don't find it fun, but being responsible for every last bit of it has worn on me; like sanding a hull till you get to the gel-coat. I'd rather go as a passenger on a ferry. It's just too much of a busman's holiday. I tell people not to buy a boat – many boatyards give away a surplus hull (or two) in the spring, rather than lose revenue on space. I've seen a share of boats chopped up by chainsaw, their metal hardware removed, and the fiberglass carcasses dumped. In some cases a boatyard keeps the best delinquent boat to refurbish themselves. The delinquent boats and parts they have been known to sell. I bought an old engines for $50; I sold the same Volvo Penta two-stroke for scrap for $80, after I had taken apart every bit of it, still failing to comprehend exactly how it propels a boat forward and backward – even sideways nowadays!

I tell people if they charter for four weekends a year they will save money, get more usage and joy out of boats, and be free of ownership. But brokers tell me owners have a compulsion to own a boat, even in colder climates where that might mean a few months or even a few weekends out on the water. Who am I to judge? Yacht owners have put food on my tables, and launched me on whole new adventures, like arriving in Europe by boat from the Caribbean to enroll at Oxford, and landing in Singapore for three years to operate tanker ships.

The original idea of providing every diary and log of every voyage, including on tanker ships and passenger vessels was not achievable for several reasons; many voyages were short and professional. In other words, the only log was left on board the boat, where it belongs, as it's official record. After all, my navigation kit was simply a paper chart, pencil, dividers and protractors, with a hand-held GPS; not much electronic at all. The commercial shipping material was lopped out, and in order to keep the short sailing voyages without the official logs or diary entries, I simply summarized the high or low points for readers. One entry is less than a line long. Mostly I tried to do that with humor, so this isn't a series of woe-is-me teenage rants!

In over 60 cases I altered the names of boats, simply because, if my colleagues and I were paid to perform our voyage, it is not our write to then name names. This is true of most owners and some crew; I feel it only fair that if things are shown in a negative light, the object is to learn from the experience, not naming persons. The biggest culprit and mistake-maker in the book is the author. I also ran the manuscript past dozens of participants, and received some very helpful critical input from many persons. Where I have published articles about an experience – *Young Endeavour* being an exception, I put them in the Appendices. I use owners and captains' names as a sign of my respect for them, as in the cases of the skippers of *Geronimo, War Baby, Whisper of Maine,* and *Rising Star*. Fellow alumni or family of boats I sailed with may think I've been unfairly critical.

But I am sure every sailor agrees that when you are on the working end of offshore passages, with crew you haven't worked with before, for weeks or months, your reportage is not always 100% rosy; in fact, I've been a published journalist on and off since age 17, and 100% is also not creditable; more often its taken as bullshit and inaccurate. Which makes it remarkable that owners bring aboard so many outsiders into their personal space; this is both for social impulses and because large racing boats need lots of crew. And not just greybeards who buy rounds of drinks, but young, physical, risk-taking and broke ones too, because someone's got to change the headsail in Force 7 in the North Atlantic at 3 am.

Nowadays both sail and power yachts are so full of automation that skeleton crews of owners can sail, dock, maneuver, anchor, and make long passages on them. That wasn't always the case, and in racing that is certainly not the case. And, while I spent years looking over the passenger fleets of New York Harbor from an office at 17 Battery Place and Boston Harbor from Eagle Hill in East Boston, where shipbuilder Donald McKay build his clipper ship empire, and now those fleets are at a virtual standstill, the private charter market seems to be booming, particularly for the maneuverable picnic boat variety.

If the stories seem author-centric, it's because they took me some four decades to accrue, and my primary motivation was to share them with you. And since they need to be authentic, I am sharing what I personal experience, witnessed and heard. Writing has always been my main motivator, since my brother John and I put together and sold an illustrated *Turtle Report* in the Bahamas at age 10. I learned how to sail by necessity. And as most who have sailed with me would agree, I possess no natural talent at sailing, nor technical expertise: after sailing for St. George's School and on the Big Boat Team at Boston College, I was quietly dismissed from both, and never achieved even top-three. I was heading solo to Jamestown from Newport when our high school coach caught up to me an turned me around. While lighting a cigarette on the Charles River my mast fell down, and I was never given another.

If I wasn't good at sailing or winning races, or fixing engines, food preparation, sail repair, or the innumerable other skills required to keep you and your mates self-sufficient for months, then what could I do? Although just as important as having technical skill, my ability to communicate instructions succinctly, while conveying the consequences for not doing something, was often lacking. My crew tell me I was either too nice, or said too much. I ordered a crew to hold onto a bow line once while were pulled alongside another yacht off Bermuda to replenish their fuel. I only gave the incoming yacht half my jerry can, since I needed it to get to the US and they were only two miles from port, yet they were peeved with us, and we all knew a boat like that could get more than an hour per gallon. When I felt out boat lurch the wrong way, I looked forward and realized the bow line had been let go, I had to take the young man aside and explain that even though were friendly ashore, at sea what I said had a greater significance. Often a captain has to erase assumptions about crew knowledge.

After a gale in Nuku'Alofa Tonga forced us to abandon our anchor inside an enclosed harbor, the crew and I went out next day to find it in deepish very murky water. I finally grasped the head of the chain and surfaced to have him pull it into the inflatable dinghy. Only some yahoo shell collectors on shore had called him over to get a free ride to a nearby island. He was nattering way with them while I tread water holding a rather heavy anchor chain for a 68-foot yacht, which I didn't want to let go of and have to go back for. I yelled like hell, and when he came back and we were pulling the chain, filthy, muddy, into the white dinghy, I emphasized that faced with choosing between a captain treading water in a busy harbor alone or some strangers asking for freebies, it should not be a difficult choice, and crew-mates always – always – come first. He got it.

The view from my room in Blue Dorm at St. George's School, Middletown, Rhode Island. I could see out to the wide Atlantic, and see the strong lights at Aquinnah Head, Martha's Vineyard and smaller ones at Sakonnet Light and Cuttyhunk Island, where much of this book has been written.

I think most folks I sailed with or moved boats for would agree that I was decent at organizing; I priced out a delivery from Bermuda and the final amount was less than $4 off, including toll and laundry. I would be pragmatic, was honest to a fault about failings, new how to swim pretty well. My first task on any boat was to hop in the water and study the rudder and keel; that knowledge could come in very handy if we faced running aground; that way I taught myself what would hit first; keel or rudder? Before travel-lifts the boat might be designed to sit on a graded railway in a yard and the rudder might, by design, hit first. Also what if a lobster trap tangled in the propeller, or rudder? Where were the through-hull fittings? A lobster trap brought us to a complete halt far from Nantucket, but before jumping in to free it, I had to tie myself to the boat, since when I separated the boat from trap I didn't want to be the only holding the trap, with novice charter guests holding the wheel!

Not only was I able to survive and know when to let go of a trip and return to dock, but as far as I know, none of the over 100 persons I brought aboard and hired were injured (notwithstanding a two-liter soda bottle to eyebrow of a friend's son), and despite a fire and sinking and MOB, no one was killed. The lack of accidents was no accident. At Eaglebrook School for Boys a small stone in the grass was engraved with the words "Brave men shall not die because I faltered," and I haven't. What I really enjoyed was finding the right people to be at sea with, booking them all tickets to and from home, all the many details that go with feeding them and keeping them in good cheer, and benefiting from their skills and experience.

Unless I missed something, it was generally me getting hurt or attacked; by sharks, but knife-wielding crew low on coke and food, getting arrested by Panamanian police in the brothel district for our own safety, and taken back to the boat escorted by cops. Then there were less obvious wounds, like stomach worms and being so malnourished that for decades I had half a dozen surgeries to ameliorate critical anemia. After the last surgery in 2016 I asked the transit cop in New York's Grand Central Station what happened if I fainted in the station and hit my head; he replied "you would die," explained there were no EMTs stationed there, then went back to conducting. I was overboard to the point of hypothermia, lost a bit of the tip of my left index finger that I am writing this with, and was hit in the head by Thai long boat speeding along without a worry in the work off Rai Lay Bay, western Thailand while swimming. And I consider myself fortunate, since I'm able to write this and have you read it!

I also enjoyed the quirky interactions; meeting on the high seas with Captain Gordon of the fishing vessel *Kismet*, out of Point Judith; we were in-bound from Bermuda and had run out of cigarettes, but had plenty of dark rum. He was amenable to a trade; we came up his port quarter under full sail, and we attached a bottle of Goslings Black Seal rum to a string, which they caught and pulled in. Then Gordon's crew threw us three packets of cigarettes. When the black garbage bag was eagerly torn apart, my crew exclaimed

"Menthol?" There were fishermen off Sakonnet marveling at a water taxi far off shore, as I took the launch to the Vineyard, alone. A madman in a workboat 75 miles from Georgia repeatedly try to ram our sailboat, so I had the crew put on different shirts and keep popping out of different hatches while we slowly got ahead of him. I was moving a boat as the US Navy was searching for the plane in which JFK Jr., his wife and sister-in-law were lost off Martha's Vineyard, and the lobstermen with traps in the area were none too pleased about being deprived of their livelihood. In over 30 voyages to and from Bermuda, the only Bermuda-Triangle-esque experience was watching the US Navy retrieve what the military calls "space assets" at night with lots of helicopters. Another time we lost all electronics for days and groped our way from Bermuda to the Virgin Islands feeling very unplugged, we didn't even have speed instruments.

No one is as surprised and pleased as I that I made it this far to share these experiences. On *War Baby* 11 couples – 22 persons – met on the deck and went on to marry. Probably because I had PTSD from crossing the North Atlantic during the weeks before, and was prone to jumping naked out of my bunk stark naked and screaming, I was not one of those who were a lady-crew chose to marry! And there were amazing happy occasions; Captain Jim Leonard being pulled out of the Gulf Stream at night after nearly 42 minutes alone in the sea, not being able to swim, from *War Baby* in a race, and in the Gulf Stream.

Geronimo pulling first a woman in a lifeboat whose captain had killed himself after their small yacht sank, then a Russian merchant mariner who treaded water in Bahamas nearly 24 hours.

Some voyages, where I was close to ended tragically; my first Marion-Bermuda Race in 1989 a man on *Bellatrix* was killed by the boom in an accidental gybe. In the Baltic we found an empty life raft, the entire crew of a boat I rode a hurricane with, *Flying Colors*, was swallowed by the Gulf Stream, Bahamas to Charleston. Two Newport sailors' boats were found empty, one (*Coyote*) mid-Atlantic, another off Bahamas. Several world-class racers lost, but buddies from the sailing pub killed racing. Then stories of a young South African man died on a long passage from fish-borne food poisoning, his cadaver towed behind the boat in a dinghy until the crew could not take it anymore and cut the line.

Even for the survivors there is trauma; seeing my high school teacher break down sobbing on the phone after their yacht was dismasted. I spent writing a 25 page account of sailing to the UK; my classmates at Oxford requested it of me, but it was too soon; too raw. Sunrise found me curled up fetal position, wrapped around the base of my dorm room's only wash basin, sobbing and crying uncontrollably for hours. I hadn't confronted what had happened; the two knife attacks to the throat, the terrifying weather, concomitant noise, the threat to be poisoned, the utter indifference of the skipper to the crew tensions and danger; he was the only person on board over 30 and yet we were lucky to see him for a few minutes every second or third day, and he was the only one who knew what he was doing! We were making 14 knots down waves with all sails destroyed, day after day.

There was much joy and laughter, even love, as well. Except for a few European-style boats when a drink or two might be permitted over dinner, being drunk or drugged on board was not tolerated, and I very rarely saw it. One consequence for this sailor, who was single most of the relevant timeframe, was to over-drink on shore. I was what could be called a happy drunk, a binge drinker, and my drinking more often led to making new friends. One result is that every time I return to Bermuda I walk to the Bermuda Biological Station, and at the reception desk in an airy sunny atrium, I ask:

"Is Rachel on campus?"

Of course she never is, since we met decades ago, but I like to ask. I visit the heart of Sir George Somers in St. George's, which he poetically had buried in Bermuda. In my 20s I missed the last bus from Hamilton back to the boat in St. George's, had no money, was tipsy, and set off on a walk of many hours. Two thirds of the way, I was walking on the main road near the north coast when four youths came my way, saying

"Good evening" as they passed. Soon after, one turned on his heel and innocently asked if had any money.

"Have any money? If I had any money, do you think I would be walking from Hamilton alone at 3 am, drunk, all the way to my boat, in St. George's?" I don't think they factored that I knew the terrain as well as I did. As quickly as they could, the boys had called an uncle, a taxi driver, who showed up and with a couple of the lads ensured I not only got back to the town I was staying, but they gave me some spending money to buy some drinks at the Starlight bar, and ensured the owner treated me well!

Waiting for my boat to sail in from a race at St. David's Light, Bermuda, I was able to see the yacht *Fazizi*, breaking the Cold War barriers under Skip Novak, sail into Bermuda in the early 1990s. A Polish tall ship in France in 1991, as the wall was falling, refused payment for sail repairs, citing brotherhood of the sea. I watched the World War II Liberty Ship SS *Jeremiah O'Brien* arrive in Nassau. And the *Queen Mary II* and the *Normandie* anchor off. On *War Baby* we loved to 'dip colors' by simply lowering our ensign, or yacht flag, for a theatric pause, when near warships of any nation. Immediately some poor crew would dash out of the wheelhouse and run aft to lower their ensign and reciprocate the salute!

And the time my crew and I were ambling down the waterfront at Pomare Boulevard in Pape'ete when we came upon a small frigate or patrol ship of the French Navy. The girls – they were, shall we say, bar girls – waved and giggled at the crew; that was normal. But when they recognized officers on the bridge in gold braid, and called them by name, there were cheeks to make a Burgundy vintner proud, they were so flushed red!

On the same voyage, flushed with my first command, I went to find a fellow Swede, Bengt Danielsson, an anthropologist who married a Tahitian woman. He is an amazing man whose illustrated book charmed me; after crossing the South Pacific with legend Thor Heyerdahl on the balsa raft *Kon Tiki* in 1947, he settled behind Pape'ete, and I hitched a ride with locals and they dropped me near his home. I stood there looking up a winding country lane for a good while, then slowly and deliberately set off by foot to Tahiti'Iti or the Presque'Isle to look at the Paul Gauguin Museum there. I decided that I was in Tahiti forging my own adventures, that I didn't to bother Moitessier or Danielsson to validate my own path.

In the pages ahead, the formats of each entry can vary vastly; from the microscopic detail of notes detailing a weather briefing delivered to a fleet of boats crossing a boisterous Gulf Stream, sent on scratchy voices via SSB or Single Side-Band radio from Herb Hilgenberg on *Southbound II* in Canada, to a short, pithy humorous summation, and much in between. The original title of this book was *Voyage Logs*; it was not meant to be a narrative so much as a recitation of all the vessels and voyages, not just the happy or traumatic ones. I penned a different book named *Sea Stories* to cover the more anecdotal aspects.

This book is meant to inform as much as entertain, and to enable readers to trace the arc from how thrilling a few hours' pleasure outing from Newport is for high school students having a beer with their uncle and girls, to the hum-drum matter-of-factness of two experienced captains driving to some New England port, boarding an unknown boat, and getting underway within an hour for a port equally unknown to them.

The missed voyages the 365 opportunities a year which I drummed up while leading Echo Yacht Delivery Worldwide in Newport from 1999 to 2005 for 100 paying mariners, do not get included, though a sample of them is provided in the Appendix at end. They are not featured in detail here either because the trips went to other captains and crew, went to sailors outside my network, or never happened. One example was a call from a frantic young sailor in Bermuda.

"I need your help," he said.

"Who are you?" I asked

"I'm Johny X.; I just rammed a sailing catamaran into a large sea buoy leaving Hamilton Bermuda for St. George's and the owner is pissed, since the crossbar is broken."

"Johny," I said. "You took that voyage from my colleagues and me without ever telling me, and thus stiffed me out of the finder's fee, and kept all of us it the dark. Then you destroyed the client's boat. Good luck down there. And don't use my or Echo's name."

I ended up selling the company primarily because I was spending more time chasing down finder's fees and commissions than time spent originating and sending the voyages, and I could not afford the admin to manage the bidding "blind." To succeed, I needed to use the Reliance Yacht Charters model of having a staff manage the bidding, which I could not justify on the revenue I made. It wasn't unusual in winter for me stay up till 3 am to find voyages for the sailors, but we so wiped out at graduate school that the lady janitor at URI gave me access to a loft to nap in. One trick I used was to go on gay dating sites for owners seeking a "Man Friday," mostly in Key West in winter, yet no one ever complained. Probably my most shameful non-voyage was one I was due at 4.30 am in Jamestown for, to make the tides for a trip up Long Island Sound. I must have returned from the local sailor's pub (IYAC or Zelda's) after closing at 1 am, because I never made it. I must have blacked out (I finally stopped all drinking in 2006). I am very disappointed to have let the captain down, particularly as he lost the voyage entirely.

Right after my Freshman year in Boston I set off by bike to Newport. That summer I worked a month or so at the Clarke Cooke House on Bannister's Wharf, a job I was proud to occupy, and they invested valuable training in me. However as summer started to peak and the 100 or more yachts prepared to race to Bermuda, I became nervous, excited, distracted. As you will read, I ultimately hopped on a boat voyaging back to Newport from the race that summer, and had the difficult task of quitting.

No one was sure if I made the right decision, however several times that summer I sailed into port and was dropped off at Bannister's Wharf, and marched up the wharf with my white sea bag and green Eaglebrook laundry bag, sunburned and happy as a clam, and when I would catch the manager Michael's eye and wave to my erstwhile colleagues, I know I had made the right decision, for me at least. Sailing can be fun. I hope you enjoy. For me the experience is just the first part; recording it then sharing it as the lasting bit. Seven hundred and thirty-three typed pages from 53 hand-written logs, journals and diaries over 35 years later, I hope that the results meets your expectations.

Living in Newport year-round, near the waterfront, a couple times I was told that single males were scanter – scarcer - than some would like. As it was explained to me, many men – and of course women – headed down to the Caribbean to work in the winter, leaving women dubious as to the reliability of their mates. One outcome was the winter warmer model, in which single locals before dating apps would match in the fall and usually break up during the dawn-to-dusk St. Patrick's Day parade and inebriant, due to egregious behavior of their winter mate in the bathroom of O'Brien's, IYAC, Zelda's, the Red Parrot or many other places. Once the breakup had taken place, the bar-keeps at respective bars where the couple had hung out would usually decree in whose favor the bar ruled; the winner got to drink there and hunt for a new mate, the loser would be banished to bars closer to Queen Anne's Square, Broadway – or even further up town!

Other odd rituals included who to send to pick the purse after an after-hours party, if you bring a half-drunk buttle of wine to a party are you banished forever or just for the season? (forever), and the folks we were really bored and envious would call in sightings of walks of shame while leaving Newport for Boston at 7 am, as in "black leather coat and high heels, rounding Young Street, northbound on Spring past the library." I remember on my return from Singapore refusing to go to Senor Frogs, where Salve Regina students were known to pursue cheap drinks like moth to light (or just like students), because they were way too young; meanwhile they were as old as 21, and I 28. I learned to simplify this complex mating scenario thus; men that went to sea ended up Dead, Drunk, and Divorced. I prefer Cicero's simplification, that there are three types of people; the living the dead, and those at sea.

Since this book covers 50 years, here are five primary epochs:

- 1970-1983: Nassau Bahamas and summer camps in the US; experimenting, motor
- 1983-1993: Boarding schools and colleges in the US and UK; mostly unpaid voyages
- 1989-1999: Freelance paid sailor for any owner, anywhere, mostly on long voyages
- 1999-2005: Echo Yacht Delivery Worldwide; I founded, owned, operated full time
- 2006-2021: Echo was bought, run by Dale, Kevin and Richard, then I bought it back.

The vast majority of voyages took place during summers from age 17 to 24. Then I took a full-time job in Singapore, ages 25-27, still racing to and from Bermuda and in Asia. Then I resumed full-time sailing from ages 28 to 34, by which time I was enrolled in two graduate programs, running a small international real estate company, and then I married. By the time our son was born in 2007, I had swallowed the anchor, with very view exceptions. Then my focus shifted to writing and publishing maritime non-fiction, and as a nautical outlet my brothers and I have been taking our children on long voyages via mailboat in the Bahamas, where my family has been for three generations.

Out of professional and personal courtesy, I have changed the names of the yachts themselves, yet that is not always possible when it comes to photographs of boats and people. The fact is that not only are the events depicted real, as I experienced them, but also usually occurred decades ago, the boats' names have changed, and the relationships were pretty short-lived. If I have caused offense, it was not meant. There is a balance sought between respecting privacy, telling my story as I experienced it, and also giving credit to those who have influenced me.

Motive: Before we cast off, I have to leave off with these thoughts to help you navigate the shoals ahead. Sitting in a dinghy crossing Nuku'Alofa Tonga at age 23, the woman whose family were cruising on a power yacht owned by some Hollywood star in the 1930s, told me that everything comes down to motives. If, as a newly-minted captain or the owners, or anyone, made the effort to truly understand the motives of those around them, their fears and dreams, then they could not only understand their colleagues, lovers, leaders, but also manipulate them. I gave this some thought. So, while they were not quite *apotheoses*, or miraculous visions, here are two of the defining moments motivating me:

In my teens I had an extremely vivid dream wherein I was an adult, walking alone through our empty pre-school. At the water fountain I found my crush (Brandi or Amanda), and of course we fell in love despite the intervening decades. It being the 1970s, in the dream I had sideburns, a moustache and long hair. The point is, that the dream was set in about 2010, when she and I would have been 40 years old. Critically, I considered the age of 40 to be the apogee of life, beyond which you just slide down towards death, holding Brandi's (or Amanda's!) hand. I resolved there and then to live my life as though it would end at 40; and shy away from no risk, because I was going to die at 40 anyway. There was a bit of Colonel Kilgore (Robert Duvall) in *Apocalypse Now;* a sense of invincibility as he walked from the surf line talking about the smell of napalm in the morning and how the enemy doesn't surf and some day the war would end. *He knew he wasn't going to get hit*, the narrator tells us.

Then I had a second lightning-bolt moment. Within a week of joining *Rumor* on my first international blue water passage, at 18 and a week shy of graduating from St. George's. That spring I enjoyed not having a sport, and replaced my failure at sailing with a writing project that was largely self-administered. While watching a sports match, a teacher I barely knew made a passing remark about my physicality; a vague complement. This really triggered something in me, because I had survived two years of sexual, sometimes subtle, abuse, beginning with being groomed the first hour on campus. I really never stood a chance against the guy, Frank, but I did manage to get him fired. I think it is not uncommon for victims in those situations – I prefer the term *survivor* – to blame themselves, and even to self-harm.

In my case I had adolescent fantasies of falling face-first into a campfire so that people "would like me for who I really was, not what I looked like," and blaming my body and physique for having attracted a lecher to me. This created combustible emotions. During and after the abuse, I was already burning and cutting my body, while at school, and in college the nadir was putting out a cigarette in my cheek, slowly, in a room full of people. Clearly I felt very deeply about this. But here's my point: it was *intentional*. I didn't do it for your pity, and I'm not asking for it now; I have plenty of self-pity of my own! In my adolescent mind I was "putting my body in its place" and making it unattractive to others. Shaved head, ear-piercing, cast-off clothing, and so on.

But the real issue is this: at age 18 I made a very deliberate and conscious decision to live a hard physical life, and focus on a cerebral one. I looked carefully at the abuse, and recognized that being an athlete, and my predator being an overweight middle-aged man in poor health, I could have physically overpowered him, yet I did not. This was due to my inexperience, lack of self-confidence at age 16, and adherence to recognized social structures and boundaries. We all know them: respect your elder/teacher/dorm master /choirmaster/faculty advisor/tutor/piano instructor; all that toolbox of control which enable adults to abuse children and institutions get away with it.

I realized that Frank had achieved control over me not physically, but rather mentally; over an intense campaign of letters, invitations, events, conversations, private movie viewings, trips out of town and so forth. I resolved then and there that if I was to fend of advances like his, I would have to become the smartest son-of-a-bitch in the room, and make my brain, not my brawn, the strongest muscle in my body. After some 53 diaries, 6 colleges and universities and nearly 40 books, I'm still trying, and until my divorce I thought I'd been doing pretty well. The exercise is more interesting when the person you've outsmarted isn't aware of it.

But what did all this enlightenment mean for my poor body? Let's just say the near-term prognosis was not good. I decided consciously to trash it, to punish it, to burn it, abuse it, starve it, drown it in alcohol and nicotine, and deprive it of sleep or steady relationships. This lasted nearly two decades, before I stopped drinking in 2006. I quit smoking a decade later, I was at least a pack of cigarettes a day and binge drinking whenever I could afford it. Since I don't know how it would have been possible to have traveled four times round the planet almost constantly, I forewent long-term relationships in favor of the long-distance, letter-writing kind, and, frankly, promiscuity. Since being a licensed mariner at age 25, I have been subject to random drug tests, as well as mandatory ones for renewal and when accidents occur. This means that, while I'm far from a saint, I never grappled with addiction to an array of other substances, even if I experimented with them. I think seeing them abused growing up in the Bahamas put me off them anyway; that and I couldn't afford coke, and in my experience young men are not often offered it for free! So I dodged that bullet.

I sought out and embraced some of the self-punishing and abusive aspects of this profession. Sailing offers young people many things at once: allure and abuse, glamor, grit and misbehavior, along with a dose of discretion. It's nothing like a cruise ship or even a large power yacht – you are literally up front and personal with each other, every body hair, smell, sound and sweat. The living space on a 40-foot yacht with eight persons using one toilet is actually tiny. For a kid with wanderlust, unlike, say, walking or trucking (a prep-school friend is a Teamster; his family renounced him), there is a social cache to sailing which makes otherwise abnormal behavior; taking off unannounced to foreign countries with no money, seems somehow respectable if your son is on a yacht. Because my first stint on a boat outside our family or friends was paid, and my low standing was made clear, and because my family are not in yachting, and have not procured me work in that sector, my view of my self was not always in accord with how others saw me, even if I did join a club.

As I set off from Bahamas to this elite school, my mandate was clear. My free-spirited siblings had run up against prep-school rigidity, so my family gave me a simple mandate: do what ever it takes to graduate; just *do what your told*. So I did; I founded the Poetry Club, led sports teams, set records, ran at least 4-5 clubs, and was on two varsity teams a year all three years (my first year I played JV & some varsity football). My mistake was being coaxed into the choir and letting my faculty advisor pass the trash, sending me to the vice-like grip of a known pedophile. This led by my second year to full nude body rubs from Frank, dawn and midnight. I realized that the broken moral compass wasn't mine, but the school's. With that value system shattered, I got Frank expelled and still, stubbornly, I graduated. On Prize Day I was ignored. But rumors of my compromised masculinity compromised me when looking for a girlfriend. As my classmate KBM put it bluntly years later:

"Weebs, sleeping with a male faculty didn't exactly help your game with the girls!" She was right. Even at home in Nassau, girls I would start dating complained that other women nagged them that I was in fact gay. It was untenable, and I never went back there to live. I needed a new home, a new shell to curl up into. Somewhere that I could prove my masculinity again, since clearly having been a linebacker for three years hadn't been enough. Fortunately, being an islander living on an island, the choice of where to go next was quite clear: to sea.

Looking from campus and in Newport Harbor at the yachts heading away from land, I latched onto the sailing community as my new safe haven; it offered a combination of grit, skill, escapism, untouchability, rebellion, danger, and camaraderie. I ran to it as somewhere to find salvation, damnation, or both. I would let it kill me or save me. By comparison, the administrators at the school made some of the spoilt party animals I knew growing up look like saints. Since my leaders had surrendered the right be trusted, I needed new ones. I needed a new community, with protocols and leadership that I could respect; that wasn't trying to fuck me. The Pied Piper I'd been told to follow turned out to be rotten to the core; a pig with lipstick, which collapsed under the weight of an estimated 100 victims.

Sitting on the sails of a racing boat at a yacht club in Bermuda, my companion was waxing on about all the other prep-school boys involved in the race that year who we knew. To him it was a kind of natural selection. However, I became uncomfortable. All the other kids had parents who owned boats or were members of the big yacht clubs. They didn't get thrown off at the last minute for no fault, burn holes in their hands, and quit their land jobs over it. It reminded me of how tenuous my situation was: my job was always to work. In order to get forward I always had to act like the hired hand, with no fallback. I didn't pay to spend a night in Bermuda for more than 30 trips, until I was married.

It wasn't just money, but the principal. I'd chosen my means of escape and I was going to ride it to the end, whether it killed me or not. Nearly 35 years in, and it hasn't. Despite some internal issues and skin cancers fixed by numerous surgeries, top and bottom, and plenty of near-misses. Overall I'd have to say that sailing has provided me with what I asked of it, without taking my body or mind; at least not both at the same time. And I still get edgy about going on other people's boats for pleasure; I much prefer to be working for pay or paying to get somewhere, and I've never bought my own boat.

Having hitch hiked alone in East Africa, Europe, Scandinavia and the US, I saw sailing as a means towards an end, not a trophy for a case. It wasn't a way for me to hit the road, it *was* the road. On it, I could go anywhere; a yacht going to Scotland went France instead, a boat under way for Portugal ended up in the Bahamas. You might leave for another country in the morning and be back in port that day. I stepped ashore in Bermuda planning to stay for a week, but 20 minutes later I'd been recruited to sail to the Channel Islands via the Azores. When I was done, I walked away, with no physical or monetary stake in the game. And not one trophy. As Neil Young, wrote in *Thrasher*, when he "had enough" he "burned his credit card for fuel, [and] headed out to where the pavement turns to sand." The sea leaves no footprints.

My goal, as it has always been, is to tell a story that is accurate, informs, and entertains. For me to white-wash and glorify events would defeat the purpose of my, and the reader, learning from and being entertained by them. If I scrubbed all the things I should not have done, and all my screw-ups, personal and professional, as well as those of boats, proprietors, officers and crew, this would be a very short – and boring – book. The goal is to given an unvarnished progression of a boy through to a middle-aged man, using voyages as a yardstick. Since the negative experiences are essential in that trajectory, they are retained, however I've watered down some personal attacks or sarcasm and one-on-one dialogues, while retaining the narrator's essential mindset and mood. I should not have to excoriate another person for the reader to understand that I felt I was in an uncomfortable place. It should read more like the arc of a story than the narrator arching his back again. Re-reading it, I'm struck by how drastically domestic situations change on different boats just days apart, and along with it the narrator's sense of place and security. At time it seems like we are vicariously couch-surfing on magic carpets which cross oceans.

If you were looking at this book from 30,000 feet and looking for a glint or hint as to what lies within, you would sensibly assume it might focus on races won or lost, the fastest and best boats, the stormiest or voyages, or their duration and destination. You might even assume it is about mistakes and money made, and boats lost. But really, it's about people. And then it's about the people with the greatest skills and the ones most likely to remain calm and come to your aid and, most importantly keep you out of trouble. And it's not about blaming the folks that didn't do much - the author has tried to take as much blame as possible, which is easy when you are captain.

This book is about explaining why the other crew's actions or in actions caused me fear, which was pretty easy when I was a teenager with very little technical or offshore knowledge. Tear-soaked diaries were not due to harmful people, just a scared kid. I promised that I modified settings, disguised and changed the names of boats and persons in most cases, but the book will simply not be an honest portrayal of coming of age unless it shows the real heartache which arose from my ending up, often through recklessness on my part, with very incompatible captains and crew. After much consultation, and on advice of other sailors, I therefore include them here, with apologies to anyone whose feelings may be hurt. As a parent of a teenager, most of us learn to see situations from more than one angle as we age, and I hope that the reader will do so as well.

Since almost every voyage was shared with other sailors and mariners, they are, or should be, the central characters. Since I do a fair bit of criticizing herein, let me start by describing what I value and cherish in a shipmate. Though this vignette was not on "yachts," like all voyages herein, it is true:

Boston Harbor in January a few months ago. It was blowing a right gale as I tied up port-side-to at the exposed passenger jetty at the end of Sumner Street, East Boston. Located at the base of Main Channel Light #14 sits on a rigid concrete tripod nearby, on what is known to old timers as Whidden's Point; to others this is Lo Presti Park, The Eddy and Reel House, near Jeffries Point. It being a quiet night for water taxi captains, I hunkered down for a couple hours of waiting for a call to pick up passengers at any of 25 stops, but no call came. Then, as expected, at 10 pm our lead captain, Andrew, released all four boats to untie and head back to base in Charlestown. I hopped out of my boat and simply untied the stern line.

That's when things very quickly went wrong. The boats have large plexiglass sides affixed to the aft two thirds of the 26 feet, and this is like a wall, or sail, to wind. I had not realized, sitting inside the boat, just how much the wind had increased, but it was steady at 30 knots and gusting to 40 knots (nearly 47 mph). No sooner had I slacked off the stern line than the boat ran away from me downwind. Very quickly – in seconds – I had to decide to either let go of the line and the stern of the boat, or be pulled into the extremely cold water. I let the line go.

Now, fortunately, the bow line was still attached to the dock, but it wasn't a thick line, and the cleats would only hold the boat for so long – less than an hour. Since the only radio was on board the boat, I had to risk pulling in the bow line, hopping in the bow, and shimmying aft to the only entryway, where I was able to regain the cockpit and the throttles. Naturally, I engaged the gear on the single diesel engine, and just as naturally, the port after docking line which I had only let go a few minutes before was caught by the propeller and seized the engine, rendering it useless to me.

It was then that I made a despondent call to my colleagues, explaining the mess I had made for myself – I'd only started with the company a few months before, after steering nothing more than a desk for over decade. Andrew said he was passing me anyway and would be there in five minutes. I explained exactly what happened, and I watched as the other two boats headed to base. I didn't know Andrew well except that he was always early, very well prepared, coached the newbies on what was the best warm clothing to wear, was cheerful and a woodworker on time off. He had also been a professional commercial diver for some years in New England – in all weather.

I climbed back out of the useless controls area, grabbed some spare lines, and jumped off the bow back onto the dock. Andrew had taught me that the U-shaped bowl in which my boat lay had shallow rocks about 30 yards or less towards Logan Airport. The wind was blowing right down the U-shaped bowl, with my boat hanging by a thread almost in the middle of it. To the starboard, or right side of my boat was the concrete bulkhead about 20 years in, and behind the boat those rocks. The wind and waves meant that the entire mess was what mariners call a "lee shore" – where all the bad bits, or dangerous rocks and docks, are downwind of you, ensuring you will hit them if you do nothing. The only good, or safe bits, are at the entrance, or the mouth, which you must reach either by reversing out to it, since the area was not wide enough to turn around in, or just stay there to begin with.

Since it was ill-advised for an unsupported boat to enter that cauldron on such a night, I really wasn't sure what Andrew planned to do, but he knew. He just didn't tell me.

Andrew arrived in solo command of a 26-foot passengers boat with a Yanmar diesel and single screw, like mine except his was an Oldport Marine Launch, with better bow access and two entries. Very importantly, the captain of these boats has just one place to stand, to steer from, operate the single shift gear, and also to reach out from port forward and tie and untie the primary spring line. Without talking, Andrew hung his boat back the *Andrea*, which lead captains preferred, thinking.

Then, he committed. With 30 knots behind him, he dove in towards the back left end of my boat, making a damn good clip. I had no idea what he intended to do. Just as his window or hatch was about align with my transom, his left hand reached out of the hatch. His right hand was on the throttle, the wheel was unattended. Deftly and as quickly as a street fighter, he flashed out what must have been an extremely sharp knife, and just as he passed the aft cleat, he swung his forearm in its direction and severed the line between cleat and propeller, meaning that tension was now off the prop. Then, just as deftly, Andrew retracted both knife and arm, resumed steering his boat, and jammed his boat in reverse until the propeller dug in and gradually pulled him out of danger. Neither mariner nor vessel had been damaged or hurt.

I hopped onto my boat – it was not possible for me to get to that cleat and I would not have tried until I had help. With great difficulty considering the wind and windage of my boat, I was able to free the prop (Andrew had already freed it), and I worked my boat in reverse against the wind, pivoting off the bow line, which held, until my stern was again snug against the dock for the first time in over half an hour. When I was able to have a look aft prior to hopping out again to secure my stern, I didn't have to. Andrew had docked his boat, the *Andrea*, and come out onto the dock. Then he secured my stern and when I looked up at his cheerful visage as the adrenaline began to ebb from mine, he handed me the bitter end of the line he had cut cleanly through, in exactly the right place. I still have that line on my mantle. Herw was a mariner who said little, knew a lot, and did just the right thing, no more.

In sum, I have learned that is not how fast a boat, nor how modern or electronically equipped. I stake the likely outcome of a voyage on who you trust, how they behave, what skills they have, and whether they will they protect me and my crew. That man, Captain Andrew, did so. I would go to sea with him any day or night, and am honored to have been his shipmate.

There must be a reason the expression "swears like a sailor" is accepted as normal. Here are one-line vignettes set in the IYAC sailor's bar:

Manager Jen framed a cover of my book; that night a pool cue shattered it.
A French single-hander won a non-stop round-world race, too late to get in.
Arriving from Trinidad, Jane tells me "you're not supposed to sink the boats."
In late for showing of film on *Queen's Birthday Storm*, bearded faces all teary.
Visiting sailors ask me "Ever sailed a 12-meter?" "No, but I *sank* one," I said!

It's a funny industry, the yachting racket. I hope that reading some of this memoir, you agree. I, for one, am amazed to be alive and solvent enough to share it with you!

              E. T. W.
              Boston
              May, 2021

When my job on *Rumor* was (mostly) done, I drove from Newport to Los Angeles in 56 hours with a shipmate, and took a bus to San Francisco, staying with boarding school friends who are sailors. One of them took this photo on the St. Francis Yacht Club race committee's inflatable speedboat! They called us alongside a larger boat to accept a delicious boxed lunch and a beverage.

World Map, Islands, Continents & Countries Hailed

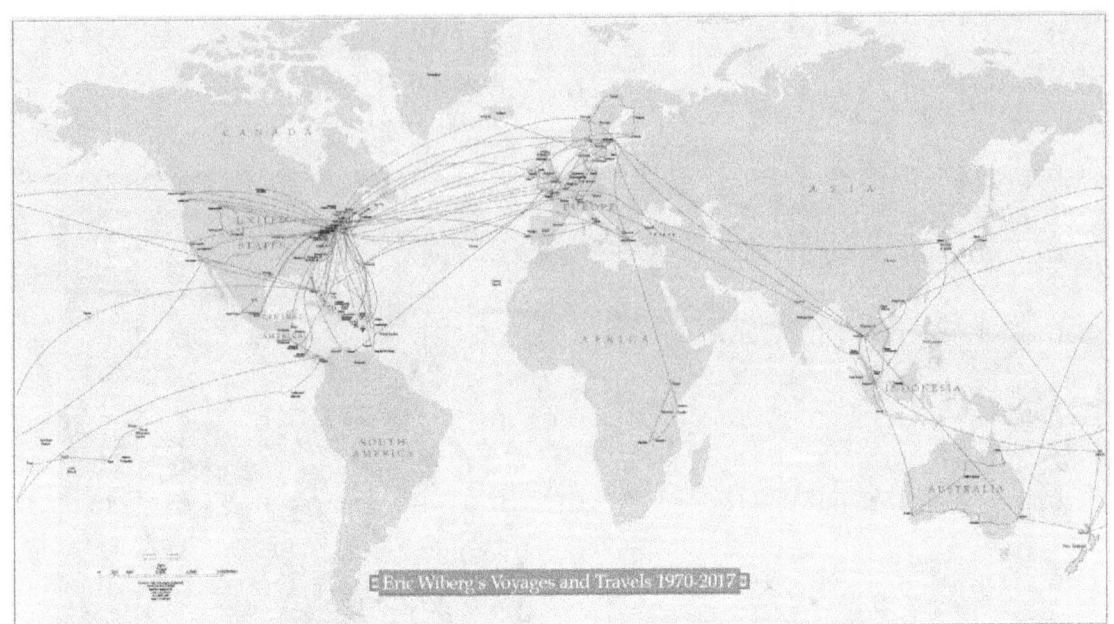

Map by Robert Eller Pratt for the author 2017

Islands Visited, 1970 – 2020

Bahamas (59):
North Bimini, Cat Island, North Eleuthera, South Eleuthera, Spanish Wells, Harbour Island Jacob's Island, Man Island, Current Island, Grand Bahama, Big Harbour Cay, Mayaguana, Schooner Cays, Great Inagua, Ragged Island, Rum Cay, San Salvador, New Providence, Rose Island, Balmoral Island (North Cay), Long Cay, Crystal Cay, Arawak Cay, Hog (Paradise) Island, Athol Island, Salt Cay, Green Cay (Rose Island), Potter's Cay, Great Abaco, Little Abaco, Elbow Cay, Green Turtle Cay, Moore's Island, Acklins Island, Hogsty Reef, Crooked Island, Castle Island, Fortune Island (Long Cay), Fish Cay, North Cay, Great Harbour Cay, Chub Cay, Whale Cay, Bird Cay, Bonds Cay, Ship Channel Cay, Highborne Cay, Staniel Cay, Norman's Cay, Shroud Cay, Halls Pond Cay, Sampson Cay, Great Exuma, Little Sampson Cay, Overyonder Cay, Little Exuma, Great Guana Cay, Mangrove Cay, Man-O-War Cay

Turks & Caicos Islands (4):
Salt Cay, Big Sand Cay, Grand Turk, Providenciales

Canada (3):
Cape Breton, Vancouver Island, St. Helen's Island

Australia & New Zealand (6):
Stewart Island, North Island, South Island, Pohuenui (New Zealand), Rottnest Island (Western Australia), Dunk Island (Queensland)

USA (20):
Long Island, Ellis Island, Liberty Island, Governor's Island, Staten Island, Manhattan, Roosevelt Island, Randall's Island, Ward's Island, City Island, Jones Beach Island, Fire Island, Shelter Island, Long Beach Island, North Haven (NY), Alcatraz Island, Miami Beach, Dodge Island, Palm Beach, Amelia Island

New England (28):
Spectacle Island, Long Island, George's Island (Boston), Uncatena Island, Naushon Island, Cuttyhunk Island, Martha's Vineyard, Nantucket, Penikese Islands, Chappaquiddick Island, West Island (Sakonnet), (Massachusetts), Planting Island, Mount Desert Island, Islesboro, Swans Island (Maine), Beals Island, Vincent Island, Sheffield Island, Grassy Island (Norwalk), Fishers Island, Block Island, Aquidneck Island, Goat Island, Rose Island, Conanicut, Dyer Island, Coasters Harbor Island, Gooseberry Island (Rhode Island)

Caribbean & Bermuda (21):
Antigua, St. Martin, Anguilla, Hispaniola, Bermuda, *Turk*, Guadeloupe, Martinique, Trinidad, Tobago Island, Grenada, Barbados, Dominica, St. Lucia, St. Thomas, Jost Van

Dyke, Frenchman's Cay, Beef Island, Marina Cay, Tortola, Puerto Rico

Pacific (17):
Taboga Island (Panama), Isla Floreana, Islote Caamano, Isla Santa Cruz, Isla de San Cristobal, Isla Lobos, (Galapagos, Ecuador), Tonga'Tapu, Pangaimotu Island (Kingdom of Tonga), Nuku Hiva (Marquesas Islands), Mataiva Atoll, Tahiti, Tahiti-Iti, Moorea, Tetiaroa (French Polynesia), Rarotonga (Cook Islands), O'ahu, Fiji

Asia (27):
Singapore Island, Sentosa, St. John Island, Sister's Islands, Lazarus Island, Kusu Island, Seringat Island, Jurong Island, Pulau Ubin (Republic of Singapore), Borneo (Sarawak), Tioman Island, Pulau Rawa (Malaysia), Batam Island, Bintan Island (Riau Archipelago), Java (Indonesia), Hon Vung Chua (Halong Bay Vietnam) Andaman Islands, Nicobar Islands (India), Taiwan, Honshu Island (Japan), Phucket, Ko Samui, Tup Island, Ko Po Da Nock (Krabi), Ko Pha Ngan, Ko Phi Phi (Thailand)

Europe (46):
Heligoland (sandy & stoney, in Germany), Great Britain, Isle of Wight, St. Mary's (Isles of Scilly), *Jersey*, Guernsey, Alderney (Channel Islands) (UK), Sandon, Telegrafholmen, Lokholmen, Gotland, Landsort, Herrhamra, Valon, Dalaro, Lidingo, Sodermalm (Sweden) Aland (Finland), Kotlin Island (USSR), Andros, Aegina, Hydra, Poros, Corfu, Agistri (Greece), Faial, Sao Jorge, Terceira, Pico islands, (Azores, Portugal), Iceland, Ile Ratonneau, Iles du Frioul, Ile de la Cite, Ile St.-Louis, Ouessant (France), Ireland, Rossmore Island, Brackross Island (Ireland), Skye (Scotland), Sjaelland, Falster, Fehmarn, Lolland, Funen Island (Denmark), Monkholmen, Askoy Island (Norway)

East Africa (1): Zanzibar (Tanzania)

Totals: *232 Islands Visited to 2020*

Continents (6): All except Antarctica
North America (1970-2020), Central & South America (7X, 1993-2017), Europe (1978-2018), Asia (1994-2001), Africa (1992), Australia (3X, 1989-1996)

Countries Visited, 1970-2020 (72+)

North America (18)
Including: USA; 45 states, Hawaii, Puerto Rico, & USVI, Canada; 6 provinces

South & Central America (8)
Panama, Ecuador, Venezuela, Mexico, Belize, Nicaragua, Costa Rica, El Salvador

East Africa (4)
Kenya, Tanzania, Malawi, Zambia

Europe (26)
Sweden, Norway, Finland, USSR, Yugoslavia, East Germany, West Germany, England, Scotland, Ireland, Czechoslovakia, Denmark, Netherlands, Belgium, Luxembourg, France, Italy, The Vatican, Greece, Portugal, Spain, Turkey, Switzerland, Iceland, Monaco, Austria

Asia (10)
Singapore, Malaysia, Vietnam, Indonesia, India, Hong Kong, Taiwan, Japan, Thailand, South Korea

South Pacific (6)
Kingdom of Tonga, French Polynesia, Cook Islands, Fiji, New Zealand, Australia (6 provinces)

Chapter 1

Voyage 1: *Qu'elle Aime*, the Baltic, Sweden, July, 1988

Distant cousin Niclas Lenfeldt and I in the Baltic between Gotland Island and Landsort on the Swedish mainland. Though July, it was cold. He was 15, I was 17. This short but offshore voyage was my sailing baptism of fire.

Entries beginning with **bold dates** *are from my personal diary, or log, written during events*

July 18, 1988, Monday, just awoke. Weather. Grey Cloudy Rainy warm calm. aboard *Qu'elle Aime* 36-foot sail boat with Lars, Niclas and Anna Lenfeldt in the Baltic Sea. Our first destination will be Visby on the offshore island of Gotland, off southeastern Sweden. We are now beginning two-weeks of sailing.

July 19, 1988, Tuesday, 7 am. Storm; high wind pressure, grey, rain. Aboard *Qu'elle Aime*, Visby Harbor, Gotland, with Niclas, Lars, and Anna Lenfeldt. Sailing in the Baltic. Fourth day, and it is exciting. We are in Visby now. Last Saturday was our first day together as a crew, and was busy. My day started off from Stockholm by rail, then we got food, then sailed, then swam. From morning to afternoon, I took the four-hour train from our grandmother's (called *Farmor* for my *father's mother*) in Stockholm. The Lenfeldt family are related to her, and live nearby. Lars is a colonel in the Swedish Army Reserves. We shopped in Västervik (*west bay*), on the mainland, and had a dinner there on Saturday.

By that evening, we were supplied with food, and set sail, but with no winds, we ended up using the engine. We slept at anchor off a secluded island, and bathed by swimming. Normally in the Swedish style, that means without clothing, but it's discretionary. And by anchor, often the captain lowers the front anchor and the crew row a line ashore and tie off to a tree on land, or a large metal loop drilled into the rock. It's usually that calm here!

Lars, the easy-going captain and owner, decided on the voyage, of up to 14 hours, from Västervik to Visby, on a huge island east of the Swedish mainland. We four persons cast off our lines and departed at 9 am on Sunday morning. The Baltic seems like a big ocean, yet rather it is a brackish sea, half salt, half fresh water. We sailed until 6.30 pm to Visby, averaging 5.5 knots of speed, with a best speed of up to 7.5 knots. The total distance is about 110 nm.

I learned that knots are simply nautical-miles-per-hour, with a nautical mile equating to circa 1.18 land miles. That means 7.5 knots equals about 9 miles per hour. A knot is simply a US mile plus .2, and is also used by aircraft. Knots are not supposed to have *per hour* after them, as they are already nautical miles *per hour*. Even though Europeans and Americans differ with metric versus miles and different currencies, thankfully sailors all over the world use the same system of nautical miles and knots.

Qu'elle Aime with Niclas and Anna aboard, in the archipelago, by Lars Lenfeldt. Here they are using the bow to tie to land at two points; notice the captain has literally stepped off the bow pulpit onto land to take the photos. Both the mainsail and jib sail covers are on.

Peak winds were five-to-seven meters-per-second (c.13 knots), from the southeast. Our voyage was almost directly east from the round, or *Rund* lighthouse. We saw lots of thin, flaky seaweed floating in the international shipping lanes, but no ships. My shifts as steerer, or helmsman, were 12 noon to 1 pm and 4 pm to 5 pm, then the same in the morning. Anna, Niclas, and Captain Lars all had shifts. Lars is about 50 years old; he is a distant cousin and friend of my Dad's. Lars' Mama is one of my Dad's aunts, on the Holmström side in Malmo. The eye doctor and his wife had daughters. One of them, my Farmor, with whom I have always been close, became an internationally recognized doctor who helped some 100,000 people flee Communism into Austria in the 1950s. Lars is her nephew.

Lars' son and eldest child Niclas is 15 and, Anna about 13, and shy. We arrived in Visby on Sunday afternoon and I went to a café with Niclas for coffee. On Monday Lars rented a car, and we saw church ruins from the 1100s, or 10th century. Danish, German, Russian, Finnish, and Swedish cultures influenced the cosmopolitan Medieval town, which is surrounded by huge walls. It was an important strategic coastal trading city for the

Hanseatic League, which was also in London and Hamburg. We took a drive to the northwest coast of Gotland. Visby is an impressive place, known as a city of roses and ruins. We saw plenty of both; but too many tourists; even though it's a faraway island, there are many daily ferries. They were a culture-shock for me at first, I felt like an extreme misanthrope. Probably this is from having grown up in a country reliant on mass tourism.

Since I had travelled alone and independently, at least with our small crew, I wanted peace and quiet like on our crew's first night. But on Monday we were asleep on the boat downtown, docked with many other boats in the middle of an elliptical quay, and at the mercy of cars. Lars is a great man and good captain; his having a sense of humor is key. He is also a loving, stern father, whose wife divorced him. His kids, my cousins, are great. We all went to caves on the coast and swam.

The *Qu'elle Aime* crew (it means *what she likes* in French) went to Goat Island, a partly military outpost north of Gotland. The jagged rocky coastal moonscape there has a beautiful beach, and I swam with Lars. Limestone rocks there were like Mont-St.-Michel, the island monastery in northwest France. We saw Crimean War graves for cholera victims; 20 of them, from a British Royal Navy sailor's hospital in 1854. I also heard of the Russian ship *Albatross*, which was chased and engaged by English battleships in the 1850s. Then both sides buried their dead on the southeast point of the island; a touching story. However, another version has the *Albatross* intentionally running around on Gotland in neutral Sweden in the 1940s after German U-boat, or submarine, torpedoed it, then shot it. Legend has it that the German sailors kept shooting at Russian sailors, even when they were dead. I read in the church of St. Marie in Visby that a Russian submarine accidentally sank a Swedish ship in winter, during WWII, Altogether eighty were killed, yet two survived, off Gotland. Later just one lived. There is an old prison is on Gotland in Visby, and I waved to a lonely prisoner gazing out at midnight. He signaled with a lighter. Sad, like the Aids hospital in New York City.

The fictional *Hunt for Red October* ship came towards this island in 1983, when a Russian navy crew mutinied and headed for free Sweden, but the sub was intercepted by the Russian. Swedes knew all along of the escape. There are many fascinating stories about submarine adventures of all nations in the Swedish archipelago, which has some 25,000 islands! Lars has cleared up many pedantic theories and confusions for me. He provided depth, texture, substantiation and long-term significance to pictures of which I once only saw the surface.

Tonight, at 1 am this morning, I am somewhat drunk. Lars and I shared a liter of red wine with fine Italian dishes at the Red Rose Café in Visby, and several coffees over Italian foods. Later Niclas, who has a bad ear infection, and I shared Lowenbrau German beer, and I enjoyed the chance of drinking on the pier. I discussed the long-term powerlessness of man over nature, especially the latter's inevitable victory with time over our self-destructive mankind. Prisons, town halls, churches, sky-scrapers, all will crumble and become overgrown with weeds. All harbors will gradually succumb to waves and hurricanes; bones become dust, crowns melt, and cocaine will blow in the wind. Trees will grow where once were fields, earthquakes crack where once were omnipotent and ever-powerful, mountains. Heroes will live no longer than the lives of select memories.

The next morning, we went to the Harbor Master (*Hamn Vacht*) and they have a Bahamian flag, but will not put it up. I need to be on a bigger ship. Sent a letter home today, the postage of which cost 8:- Swedish Kronor, including a Russian kopek; and a ten-page letter. Tomorrow we begin at 6 am; and will sail 14 to 18 hours. Maybe 20 hours, today, as a big storm left northward at 6 am for Stockholm, three-meter, or 10-foot-high, meaning swells will be very rough and turbulent. We were *a glove in the ocean* to use a Swedish phrase; not a condom! We tossed and turned for two hours; I wanted to continue, Captain Lars said no. We turned back, which was smart, as it was rough going.

Two old Visby fishermen meanwhile caught a lot of flounder, sole and *tjorkt* cod: great catch; brave men. Will that be Frank Baensch and I at Great Exuma in 60 years? I hope so. Returned to berth in Visby by 7:30 am for 8 am weather report. A drastic, unpredicted weather shift; low pressures comes in, which leave pressures also shifting. Huge waves and 11-to-12-meter-per-second [over 25 knot] winds! We listened to radio frequencies with sailors; busy day for lifeboats, Coast Guard. One boat with mechanical difficulty, another sent Maydays (which is simply *m'aidez, aid me*, or *help me* in French), and vague position coordinators off of Oland, southwest of here, still lost and unfound by search parties this evening; possibly dead.

Niclas, Anna and I on a rock with my beloved Fernandez Bay Cat Island t-shirt (from *Geronimo*) on.

I heard Lars and Niclas tell of past unpredicted storms and gales in this ocean. A nine-boat team split up and as my hosts listened, a man, the crew's father, fell overboard and was drowned while his hysterical daughter shrieked alone, deserted in gale in Baltic, with huge waves. Horrible. Survivors who they (Lars and Niclas) met said they slept 36 hours, then said they were nothing in a storm; they could not even see the masts of their friends' boats! Waves were that huge. And to think, my Swiss friend Mecky and I want to sail the world! A lot of ships came to and from Visby today; private vessels from Florida and

Minnesota, USA, England, Denmark, Finland (of course!), Germany, *Holland*, far away and Sweden. Large huge ships filled with interesting tourists like sheep dropped off. I ended up only having a sort of one-night stand in the afternoon with Visby, no relationship; just postcards and photos.

I finished reading Lawrence Durrell's Cyprus memoir *Bitter Lemons* today; my 5th book finished this summer, and then began *Song of Solomon* by Toni Morrison. It's good so far. No names, underlining or pen at all this summer, so reading goes much faster. Went out last night with Niclas, who was convinced into going, by successful, religious, attractive Anders Gustavsson. He has a Christian restaurant, religious *Heaven Up*, in Visby. Encouraging; I was given a Swedish-English bible, good. I've watched the large ships come and go today, the ship *Leonid Brezhnev* from Odessa, on the Crimean Peninsula, USSR, on the Black Sea, came from Tallin, *en route* Visby to Oslo, Norway. They were tourists receiving their political rewards from the Soviet government, like my past ship MV *Ilyich*, which last summer I took on a solo voyage to and from Leningrad [St. Petersburg], to cure me of leftist leanings. Also saw the *Istra* of communist Yugoslavia, whose captain was old, and the bow smashed. Then we saw a ship named *Forest Link* of Sweden, freight cars, trucks, a ship interestingly named *Gotlandslinjen Albatross* (*Gotland's Island* Albatross, like the historic ship and bird), of Mariehamn Island, Finland, and Visby, *en route* Visby from Stockholm.

July 20, 1988, Wednesday, 10 pm. Herrhamra Harbor, the nearest settlement to Landsort Lighthouse, Swedish coast. This place is near the tough, cold rocky island of Öja, on which sits Landsort, past which almost all ocean freight traffic to and from the Baltic, Stockholm, and Lake Malaren passes. The ship's pilots live in the village and the pilots can remain at sea for days! On the open ocean, while steering, I saw an unopened inflatable life boat which may have been lost in yesterday's shipwreck near this place; it was worth $3,000! We left it. We called it the *Jesus H. Christ*!

Thirteen hours of ocean-sailing today, from Visby Gotland Sweden into this quiet coastal harbor on the Swedish mainland, just outside of Stockholm. Yesterday's gale force storms off Gotland moved up here by this morning, and the going was rough from 7 pm tonight. I had about four plates-full of food for dinner. Basically, Lars and I were in control of the vessel. Niclas was ill with flu, earache, and infection all day, and Anna is a thirteen-year-old. Neither took the helm for more than a few minutes, we have no expensive Loran or Decca navigational systems which do all the plotting, and depth. In other words, we have none of the real spoils, and not much time -none that I saw! - was spent on reading charts. Lars, our captain, admitted over dinner that he set our course (north-northwest 350°) from memory. We were leading four boats, yet never made contact with the rest of them, and met no traffic from Stockholm.

That was a disappointment, but the gale was here this morning! Regarding illness, Niclas and Anna were both seasick; Lars a little. I suppose I felt it, but I was certainly never sick, and forced myself out of any ill-feeling. I had to helm our little ship for five hours at one time. Lars for more than seven. Winds were from south-southwest 5-to-10 meters per second, or an average of 6 knots. PS: Coming from Visby, we don't use the toilet, and the seas were too rough. So, all urine and vomit went into a bucket in the cockpit or below, which we then emptied over.

Overall, I was very proud of myself and keen to show my mettle again.

Qu'elle Aime sailing in the Baltic, where Russian *MiG* jets often zoomed by in international waters between Gotland and the mainland, frightening us. It was the height of the Cold War and Sweden was neutral, and so considered a threat by all sides.

July 21, 1988, Thursday, 11 pm. Natural harbor in Ornö, Sweden at mouth of Stockholm's entrances. Red twilight, late, cloudy; it was a sunny day, warm. I swam in water which is 19º C. Six hours' sailing today from the pier at Herrhamra to this peaceful day at Ornö. Many other boats were there, and all of them were Swedish, except one from Tyskland, or Germany. Our neighbor gave us all a haunting revile on his bugle from the wooded hill and everyone took down their flags. It is otherwise silent and wonderfully calm here. We took the little inflatable dinghy over to other rocks, to take in the view with Niclas, and we talked about my brother John. Someone played the flute, several fished, some smoked, a few younger kids swam and argued loudly, but later fell quiet.

I took two wonderful swims today. Here I swam for 15 minutes or so, lost all body warmth through the 18.8º C. (66º F) water! Reading *Song of Solomon* with speed, so that I can get on to Dante's *La Vita Nuova* in English and may be more of Friedrich Nietzsche's *Ecce Homo*, perhaps dig up some of *Thus Spoke Zarathustra* or other excitements. I'd like to read up on music and modern theory, but it's difficult to get a hold of. Reading *Tom and Jerry* cartoons in Swedish, catching on to spelling and pronunciation, it helps my linguistics greatly; such simple pictures. I wish we had spoken more Swedish when younger! I shall look into the Swedish-English bible to better my skills; just think, it's an even more universal book than *Tom and Jerry* (for better or for worse). I spoke with Lars over a glass of red wine as the sun set. We talked about teenage and adult suicides; he said that Finland and Sweden have high rates. As a colonel in the army reserves, Lars has several thousand men under him. Sometimes, I almost think my parents asked him to offer theories and outlooks; philosophies and advice, since he has many. This has filled in a lot of gaps; he will help me get into the Swedish navy.

On Sandhamn Island I met an older man named Wiberg; they are rare! One lives on this island; another one in Rockport, Massachusetts. I heard about him at a poetry fest. Tomorrow will be a busy day; we sail into the Stockholm city harbor, between the Grand Hotel, Kungstradgården, Gröna Lund on Djurgården and Strandvägen. Not a bad or boring place to berth, I must say. Then, in the evening, all of my hosts leave via train down south to a funeral near Norrköping. It's for their neighbor, and for Niclas' friend's father. Then only Niclas and Lars return, as Anna goes off to work, even at age 13. My sister could have used some work at that age!

This means that from Friday to Saturday evenings I have the boat in my possession in the center of Sweden's capital. Not bad. I will probably just do ordinary chores and look around in this city where, I have lived in Sweden for bits of five summers now, but who knows what could happen? Maybe I can be like Wolf Larson, the historical captain in Jack London's book *Sea Wolf*. I'm here watching all along, writing about it. It took Stephen King from September 9, 1981 to December 28, 1985 to write his circa 1,090-page book. Meanwhile, rain is failing onto my little roof. On Sunday, perhaps after a visit to the National Cathedral in Stockholm, they return and we begin the week-long sail south back to Västervik. Either with Niclas and Lars, or only the captain and I. Anna is being a real pain at times, yet I like her, and she has had it tough, sailing and living with we three guys, but really: *hats off* to her!

To spend time in Sweden's islands is to fall under their spell. Someone was playing taps at sunset when this photos was taken, with a row boat in the distance.

July 22, 1988, Friday, 11.40 am. Grey, calm, no wind or rain; nothing. Under auxiliary engine power, *Qu'elle Aime* between Ornö and Stockholm. Today I write what I should have written last night, but didn't! Phone call: last night on the boat radio an unusual thing occurred on radio frequency *OS*; Stockholm Radio. Transmitting from USA to somewhere on the Swedish coast; probably to a yacht, an American speaking to a man named Gerard, who may be Swedish. The American was a young male. He sounded official, technical, talking about leases, rents, and a maid.

His voice and accent were neither New England nor the SE coast, though almost definitely he was rich and from Virginia, Maryland or most likely, Washington DC. He mentioned partner Joe Marelli [possibly mid-western oil investor Nardelli?], spoke respectfully about rents of $66,000 [!] per month, $8,700 another sum; big bucks. A deal closing at $120,000, amazing purchase of yacht, home were among items mentioned. That deal was drawn out because "she" was difficult. Gerard's companion was Maria, probably European, with an American attorney or accountant. The call lasted 52 minutes! Shit! My new mystery American could not have known meanwhile, that any boat in the Baltic Sea or ashore was free to listen. I could have interrupted him to point it that stark fact out, but preferred to think on other speculations.... [Perhaps 30+ years later, this will solve the riddle?].

July 28, 1988, Thursday 12.20 pm. Aboard *Qu'elle Aime*. We are headed for Verkebäck, Sweden, with Lars and Niclas Lenfeldt. Cloudy, grey but warm and calm. In the six days since I have written in this diary, quite a lot has happened but *nothing to write home about*, so to speak. I have focused my mental attention elsewhere; fishing, and *Men who March Away: Poems of World War I*, edited by I. M. Parsons. I have also in that time, written Bahamian artist Uncle Bill Johnson a carefully researched, 16-page letter, with several pages of my own writing which I copied today; some ten pages worth of recent scribbles; the cream of that feeble crop, so, to speak. I also wrote home in ten pages, to Farmor in Stockholm.

I've been kept quite busy yesterday, Wednesday, July 27, we sailed and motor-boated for ten hours, the day before, between Dalarö and Oxelösund, Sweden, heading south-southwest. We were on the ocean for 12 hours. Most of this was in high seas (two-to-four meters) on the ocean stretch from Landsort, and under engine power which makes it much less comfortable. We were practically against the wind the whole time. We covered 62 nm that day. I have learned a real respect for the ocean that day, like others in Visby. It was cold, grey, raining, and all of my things in the bow were wet or damped. And these minor hardships don't compare to trans-Atlantic or other serious voyages! That's where the respect comes from.

We went to Sandhamn for the night of Sunday to Monday, and I saw Katarina (sweet, smiling Katis) Bergstedt again, as well as the American named Calle and Andreas Eriksson (Ade; I met his father, who was the first to circle the globe aboard a motorcycle, and made it to the *Guinness Book of World Records*!), and his little brother. I may see the guys in Stockholm this weekend. Today we end our voyage, tonight and tomorrow.

I return to Misturhult farm estate, near Västervik, built in the traditional style with a hint of Crimea (from the first owner serving with Charles the Twelfth in the Great Northern War in the early 1700s) in large yellow gate. Then Saturday I will be in Stockholm again until Thursday, August 4, which is when I fly home. Since I left home in mid-June, my travels have been wide and varied. I often map my adventures. That will come later. Let me give you a basic outline of our 13 days under sail and at anchor, covering 421 nm.

Actual Itinerary of *Qu'elle Aime's* Baltic Cruise, 1988, by Captain & Owner Lars Lenfeldt

Date	Destination	Nautical miles
Saturday, July 16	Verkebäck to Tangsholm	8
Sunday, July 17	Tangsholm to Visby, Gotland	62
Monday, July 18	car tour of Gotland	0
Tuesday, July 19	gale, failed attempt for Landsort, Stockholm	8
Wednesday, July 20	Visby to Landsort and Herrhamra (13 hours)	72
Thursday, July 21	Herrhamra to Dalarö Castle	27
Friday, July 22	Dalarö to Stockholm (Vasa museum)	34
Saturday, July 23	Lenfeldts to funeral, me to Farmor's	0
Sunday, July 24	Stockholm to Sandhamn	34
Monday, July 25	Sandhamn to Dalarö again	30
Tuesday, July 26	Dalarö to Oxelösund (12 hours)	62
Wednesday, July 27	Oxelösund to Gryhamn (10 hours)	44
Thursday, July 28	Gryhamn to Verkebäck (today)	36

Total: *421 nautical miles over 13 days, at an average of 30 nm per day, incl. rest*

Summary: During this trip I've learned a lot about navigation, tough ship life (especially after Anna left, on Saturday, July 22) knot-tying, army life and the Holmström family! It's been an exciting, adventure-some summer, one of action, watching, reading listening, hearing, rather than, writing so much, as I did last summer. This summer it seems that I have been collecting the scenes, experiences, sights, sounds, and smells. These will surface later, taken up in my writing; always stored in my memory. I have not written or completed a disciplined, edited, pertinent poem for months, it seems: my writing is perhaps deteriorating. A sad thought at age 17, going on 18. I consider a future in law [Note; in 2005 I did actually pass the bar!], psychology, or journalism, with writing as a hobby. My hair is longer now; a ponytail (tiny), as it's been five months since cut!

July 30, 1988, Saturday, 6.30 pm. Aboard an orange-motif SJ train [state-owned since 1856; 284 train stations, 1,200 daily departures], from Västervik to Linköping, then Stockholm. Shifts dramatically from warm, sunny and clear to grey, with heavy rain. Sailing ended on Thursday, when we landed at *Qu'elle Aime*'s home port of Västervik, and Anna met us. After tidying up the boat, it was rainy and cool. The Lenfeldts kindly offered me to stay at their home not far away. My relatives, including my godmother with home I am close and cousin, were at their family summer home named Misterhult, and were expecting me, and I wanted the Lenfeldts to have a reunion without me as well. So I accepted their offer to drive me to the family home instead and was warmly received there.

Then Niclas, Lars and I had *pytt i panna* (*pieces of meat in a pan*) at a restaurant in Västervik. There the cook stared betrayed at the *Ebbe Carlsson Affair* televised hearings (in which a government unable to solve the street murder of its prime minister was aghast to learn the Minister of Justice opened an independent investigation. Of course, they then shut the new investigation down before the Minister, whose job it was to solve crimes, could solve it, leaving Olaf Palme's assassination still unsolved to 2021, and a national embarrassment). The following afternoon, after inviting me to stay with them, the Lenfeldt family dropped me off at Misturhult, a Wiberg, Von Essen family estate circa 50 kilometers south of Västervik, after Blankaholm. When Lars and the kids saw that it was more of a manor house or estate he whistled under his breath and exclaimed before they left how now he understood which I was keen to stay there and not their little home, which stung a little, but we parted very amicably, and I think very highly of Lars as a captain, relative, person and good conversationalist.

Epilogue: The following year Niclas came and stayed with us in Bahamas for a bit and I think he enjoyed it. I haven't seen Anna since, but Lars visited my Farmor, his aunt, several times, and I saw photos and sent them several postcards and letters over the year. Ironically, just as Lars found it so remarkable about the friend whose funeral he attended, Lars also unfortunately died quite young, in his 50s, and in good health with no vices to speak of.

July 4, 1990, (at sea, two years later) ....my favorite meal is still ....the hot large portion of ham stew with buttered potatoes prepared by skipper Lars Lenfeldt after our crossing from Visby to Landsort, Sweden aboard *Qu'elle Aime,* three summers ago.....

Voyage 2: Family power boats *Viking* and *Ma'Wessel* 1 & 2, Nassau, 1978 – 1994

Viking, the family's first sizeable boat, a Silverton 28 with a gasoline engine, which is not what my Dad would have preferred. This is in 1980, in the Lyford Cay Marina, hosting guests for our American grandparent's 50th Wedding Anniversary. Taken by my mother. The constant air traffic over the boat meant that the four children and our guests spent a great deal of time scrubbing the white decks and tops. It's not too unusual perhaps, but we probably spent as much time cleaning it as going out on it.

Overview of family boats in Nassau, Bahamas, 1970's to 2020

1 *Runabout 1*, 1967-1974: Dad, also a licensed airplane pilot, bought a simple outboard power boat to get from marina to beach for the family of six (four children born 1966 to 1972) in Nassau. Old Fort Bay, western New Providence was preferred, as we lived and he worked in Cable Beach and at that time there was no other marina to the west except Lyford Cay. We know this small car-like boat from family photos of the time. This was sold before it entered the children's conscious.

Before owning a motor boat, we had a dozen inflatable boats, including an old Gray Avon dinghy with a Seagull single-stroke engine built for the British military that was always being tested in a barrel full of water, very noisily at home. When our ministrations failed, one of us would take it to be repaired by an eccentric British mechanic who lived in a colonial loft in an old square with his Malay wife downtown. I once knocked on his door in a torrential rain just as the lightning struck. When his wife swung the large wooden door open atop wide cement steps in a piazza which resembled the execution courtyard at Devil's Island with a hanging tree as its centerpiece, we were all terrified. After our young Swedish houseguest and I discerned his frail figure in the inner distance, he begged me to tell no one what I saw. And for 40 years I haven't.

2 *Viking*, 1978-1982. Our parents purchased a Silverton 28' gasoline inboard single-screw fiberglass boat with raised wheelhouse. On our maiden voyage with her we actually ran hard aground just off the western tip of Long Cay, which is also known as Silver Cay, and owned by record guru Chris Blackwell. I was nominated to go ashore for help in the small sailing boat of an English family with a lovely daughter, who was a year or so older than me. I accomplished nothing of course, and never saw her again. It was a maintenance nightmare, no one was hired to look after it, yet we had lots of mostly fun trips. We actually made it all the way to Staniel Cay and back on the *Viking*, a distance of some 200 nm round trip! She was sold after the big 50th Anniversary party of my grandparents, since the kids started heading off to boarding school.

3 *Ma'Wessel* the first, 1986-1989: this shaky, high-sided fiberglass single-engine outboard was neither fast, sexy, or particularly safe, but it was easy to handle and maintain, great fun, and it could fit many young people and take them skiing. Her high sides with *faux*-Colin-Archer ridges that made it look wooden, prevented (or retarded, or at least slowed) drunken passengers from falling overboard. This was important, as by that point our friend's mother had been killed by falling off the front of a speedboat into propellers (with her family onboard), teenagers were running folks over, brother John had badly cut the palm of his hand in a propeller after falling off, and I had fallen off my friend Frank's fast dinghy; intentionally as a prank, which is not reassuring either. So *Ma'Wessel*'s attributes of slow and stable were actually good in our world. We were only going from marina to beach, roughly half a mile away. Eventually I believe the boat simply developed too many cracks in the flimsy fiberglass – no one has a clue what model she was, probably for inland lakes, and it's unlikely it was designed for ocean swells, waves, reefs. Sold.

Note: Contrary to all logic, we learned that if you are steering a boat and a person falls off either side (they rarely fall off the centerline unless dangling from that ridiculous location), your job is to *turn sharply towards the side they fall off*. The reason is that this will kick the propeller, rudder; generally the deadly stuff - out to the opposite side. Since they have already fallen, you will not hit them with the bow by turning towards them. Counterintuitive yet correct, like this trivia: Going west through the Panama Canal a vessel emerges into the Caribbean Sea, or Atlantic Ocean. The first capital city directly south of Miami is Panama City. Ecuador is not the only country named for a line of longitude or latitude – Equatorial Guinea is as well. And toilets do flush a different direction depending on whether north of the equator (clockwise) or counterclockwise south of it. Even storms currents, winds, rotate differently depending on which half of the planet they occur…

4 - *Ma'Wessel* the second, 1989-1993: This was the only Boston Whaler we owned. My parents bought it to be indestructible and a good spearfishing and recreational watercraft-towing and trolling boat, easy to clean and maintain. For many friends in our age bracket in the US and Bahamas it was the family starter boat. This 15-foot center-console, single-Evinrude 85-hp-outboard model, named *Ma'Wessel* like its predecessor, gave us good working years, but by the end it was literally held together with cables. For its size I believe it ventured offshore and into deep water waves too often: if we spearfished on a shallow reef, it was not uncommon to have to escape rolling waves by getting airborne at full speed to avoid being swamped. And hitting reef was not unknown either; finding the propeller and cotter pin was not easy. Ultimately the engine of this boat was so completely burnt out that the boat and motor had to be sold as a floating wreck on a trailer. This was purchased my last year in high school and destroyed the autumn after graduation from college. Sold for scrap at a yard sale.

5 – *Shoal Shaker*, the only, 1994-2021: This is my brother John's boat, which is nominally owned and fueled by my father, yet completely maintained, refurbished, captained and benevolently run by John, without whom no doubt it would have been lost its first week or in the over 25 years since. Keeping the tradition of maiden voyage wrecks, it ran aground and sank in storm swells on the west side of Bimini on the voyage from auction in Florida, hence its name. John, Dad and brother James left Florida in calm conditions, but 50 miles later the wind sprang up against the Gulf Stream, which created horrific, short, steep boxy seas. The captain headed for the nearest shore, Bimini, and anchored. However soon the water overwhelmed the boat from the bows, and flooded the batteries aft. Small boaters will recognize the sting of battery acid in the water on one's feet and legs; it's not a pleasant feeling. Without batteries, no engine ignition and no bilge pumps. If the inflow of water continued, there could be only one outcome. Our younger brother James, a teenager, became alarmed and asked:

"Dad, are we going to sink?" to which our father calmly – and correctly – replied:

"Yes, James, we are going to sink. Now put on your life vest and jump in the water to swim to shore." They did swim, the boat did break free of the anchor after losing all power, and the hull did wash up on the beach upside down. There, my brother hungry, cold, and stressed older brother John stayed by it. With local help it was towed into Alice Town, righted, shipped to Nassau, repowered, repaired, and lives! Mariners are very sensitive to the attitudes of their fellows: had John behaved like some new boat owners do, with a shrug and "oh well, the insurance will take care of it," there would not have been much left of the boat by dawn. But the locals recognized John's dedication and seriousness, and went out of their way to help him, mariner to mariner. The boat is not a big part of this story, since I was in the Galapagos at the time and never returned to live at home in Nassau after that. Still in family. I believe over 40 years.

On the busy stretch of West Bay Street, on which Sir Sean Connery (aka James Bond, 007), famously drove without lights in a sportscar, a 50-foot wooden motor fishing boat wrecked, and we saw it every day going to and from school past the airport. The owner of that boat literally never left that boat's side until it was pulled off weeks later. He made a small camp with a fire and clung to the side of his craft, notwithstanding that 10 feet away was the major traffic artery of a young nation's capital, including the majority of incoming and outgoing tourists. He literally brought the toughness of island culture to the big island.

July 16, 1987, we own our family motorboat now, in Lyford Cay Marina, western New Providence Island. At 20 feet long, with a single outboard engine of 50 horsepower, cable steering, and a mono hull which wobbles a lot in waves, we named it *Ma'Wessel*, for *My Vessel*. The letters are painted with the Rastafarian motif; red, yellow, green. My fondest memories were of the end of the manager's eggnog Christmas party at the main club of

Lyford Cay, on the lawn, which was on the beach. When it wound down we would head out for *Ma'Wessel*, docked nearby beside the school we went to. Less than sober, because we celebrated Christmas the Swedish way, on Christmas Eve, we would change behind the fences out of a coat and tie and into swim shorts, then hop into the boat and head out to Old Fort Bay for a prolonged afternoon of drinking, frisbee, camp fire roasts of hot dogs or fresh-caught crawfish. Back then the beach had no homes or clubs on it and was just lovely.

March 14, 1988, Sunday, 12:21 am. On a St. George's School Choir tour, Peterborough, northeast of London, UK. English, a little chill, slight rain, foggy, grey. I just returned from two-and-a-half weeks of drinking, flirting and family loving over Christmas at home in the Bahamas. We rode our newly christened boat *Ma'Wessel* on the high seas to Old Fort Beach, and hit Lyford Cay, Junkanoo, Club Waterloo, Confetti's waterfront nightclub, and our own Punk Party, enjoying being happy hosts and getting drunk as a family. Truly fun. Perhaps most importantly, I met when our mothers agreed that I would take her out on *Ma'Wessel*, our Bahamian fun boat. We ended up dating over a period of years in at least three countries, so it was a good match.

Sister Ann and I with a Swede painting the first *Ma'Wessel* in Rasta colors; we had met Bob, Rita, and Ziggy Marley, who kept a hotel near ours, over the years. The Swede was visiting staying at my parent's business, nicknamed Cable Beach Kibbutz, as often young people stayed and worked there. From our pale faces it is clear I've just returned from New England and school.

September 5, 1988, Sunday was a family day aboard *Ma'Wessel* at Old Fort Beach; my childhood friend Frank joined us. As far as family travels go, John, my older brother age 19, returned from Maui, Hawaii where he stayed for two weeks after Martha's Vineyard, and James returned from his roommate's place on the Charleston seashore. On return to Nassau I went to Club Waterloo. During the day I took *Ma'Wessel* to Malcolm's house in downtown Nassau Harbor, which was dangerous. After Club Waterloo we drove to Paradise Island and Club Pastiche. On the drive back down the bridge from Paradise Island we recklessly overtook another car. Then we went to the Green Shutters……

Note the ridiculous wiring to keep *Ma'Wessel*'s Evinrude 85-hp engine and stern from falling in the water! And the very 1980's waist-pack! I am sharpening a spear for crawfish.

July 22, 1992, I am to memorize lock combinations for the lock on *Ma'Wessel*'s boat box at dock.

September 30, 1993, so, I sit here, under-fed since dinner at the 15th St. Fishery last night, hungover, sleep-deprived, depressed, and craving numerous and sundry dinks. I'm on my fourth carton of Marlboro red hard-packs in as many weeks, and all does not look well. Well, I should appreciate my stay here; take the small family power boat named *Ma'Wessel* out for spins, and document my time for a captain's license.....

Recollection: Back when I still drank, I drank heavily. One of my secret activities was to drive the family kid's car with a backpack full of gin and tonic, lime, a cup and knife, fire up *Ma'Wessel*, and just take it on a voyage to nowhere. Primarily I would go to the center of Old Fort Bay, far enough from the telescope voyeurs on shore or the traffic in the Lyford Cay Marina channel, cut the engine, drink several gin and tonics, smoke many cigarettes, strip naked, swim, get back in the boat, and repeat, for hours.

Then I would motor *Ma'Wessel* back to the dock and drive home in the rainy steam of late afternoon in time for semi-coherent dinner. I can still recall those trips vividly, and when later conveying the experiences into poetry, I described the wake the boat made across the oil sunset surface of the summer sea as a slick, semen-sticky trail. The elderly lady proof-reading my poetry projects found that language to be evocative.

The magic moment of transformation from country club bounder swilling weapons-grade eggnog to boaters! My brothers John and James and shedding ties for shorts to take *Ma'Wessel* out on Christmas Day. Being Swedes, we celebrated and opened our gifts on Christmas Eve.

Voyage 3: *Geronimo*, Cat Island, Bahamas, Spring, 1987

This boat was run by Captain Stephen Connett, my mentor. I sailed or worked on the St. George's School student shark and turtle-tagging research vessel *Geronimo*, the older aluminum ketch, between March of 1987 in the Bahamas and June of 1993, in Newport, including going aboard in Bermuda in 1989. My relationship with the boat began in 1985 or so when I saw her in Nassau Harbor, my home port, and I decided to apply to the parent, or owning school, St. George's in Newport. Though I never sailed aboard the new boat with a new captain, I went to law school with one of her captains, and have maintained steady contact with the original captain and his family for the intervening decades. I have always sought out his advice, and he has always willingly shared it, and it has invariably helped me.

My first year at St. George's, I took the mailboat *North Cat Island Special* to the Bahamian island named Cat and was taught how to sail at night, steer by the compass and stars, and sleep on deck. The captain's technique was to pretend to ignore me until I put his ship "in irons" or locked out of the wind, then calmly but sternly tell me what to do to get out of the mess I had created. He did not grab the wheel from me, which most captains would have done. Rather Captain Connett forced me to acknowledge my mistakes and fix them myself.

Captain Connett, or Steve as my son and I now know him, hired me to day work or short alumni trips aboard *Geronimo* in several ports over several decades. He has lived aboard a power boat in the Bahamas for years and was one of the first private vessels to reach the devastated Abaco islands from Eleuthera after Hurricane Dorian. His monthly newsletter on the conservation of sea life, particularly sea turtles, is admired by many. Many turtles owe their lives to him, scientist owe their tag-tracking data to him, and fishermen have learned alternatives to turtling from him.

Probably more than any person, Steve and his crews over nearly half a century have gradually changed perceptions of turtle conservation and winding down the fisheries in according with United Nations CITES Convention on International Trade in Endangered Species of Wild Fauna and Flora and other treaties to which the Bahamas is signatory. As a fellow chelonian, my first book with my brother was *Turtle Report* at age 10, and my first published journalistic article, at age 17, was about the loggerhead turtle washed up at St. George's School, titled *Big, Dead, Headless*. As kids, my brothers, friends, and I captured and bred fresh-water turtles, and I have released them from polluted ponds to cleaner ones in the Bahamas as well as Singapore.

Steve now lives in the same nodes that I have most of my life, Newport and the Bahamas. I thank him for all he has imparted to me over the years, whether in Charlie's Good Egg and Gary's Handy Lunch in Newport, in St. George's Bermuda, or the Nassau Harbour Club at home. I will return the compliment he has shown others: *he has shaken more water out of his boots than I have sailed across*. I also recognize the guidance his wife Barbara (Babs) provided me, and won't forget the day a siren wailed, her head popped out of *Geronimo* on hard land, and she simply flew down the ladder then set off running to their home on Washington Street, knowing it was on fire (it was.)

Truck with teachers, friends and family, Fernandez Bay, Cat Island, Bahamas, 1987.

April 1, 1987, between March 17 and March 19, I visited Chrissie Connett and family aboard *Geronimo*, the school boat, and Fernandez Bay Resort on Cat Island, southeastern Bahamas, before the final two months of my sophomore year at St. George's School. Looking back: A tremendous amount of uncertainty went into my spending three days on the school boat in Cat Island, Bahamas, but it was worth every moment. An older St. George's student, nicknamed Digger, was to have joined me to fly to Cat Island. His family was staying on Paradise Island. The weather was very lousy, and on a bike ride to meet the other boy I saw a yacht which had wrecked the night before in Goodman's Bay. It was the *Sea Wolf* from Boston and her skipper entered the wrong channel, I believe mistaking a new lit tower on Coral Cay for the Paradise Island light. I parked my bike and swam to it, it was mostly out of water in the sandy bay. While I was on the mostly sunken boat, a small powerboat came over and, once the people in it realized I was not the owner, they started stripping items from it, like swim fins and masks. It was sickening.

Anyway, Digger ended up backing out of the trip, and my parents said they would only send me on such a fun trip if I brought my younger brother. With two teen girls on the other end, I didn't want him to spoil any of my chances, so I said "no." Poor kid. He was probably pretty excited about the trip. Trying to beat the system (they said they would only pay for flight if I took James), I instead took the much cheaper mailboat, named the *North Cat Island Special*, down to Cat Island. It went slowly, since it was new, and I met some neat passengers. *Geronimo* was in the same port when I arrived, then we drove to the airport and met some teachers there.

The school had rented a lovely full villa at Fernandez Bay Resort, and I guess because of the bad weather the Connetts decided the teachers would stay on the boat and we would go ashore. We did an overnight passage the first night, and it was absolutely magical to me. The phosphorescence, the birds, lapping of waves, talking with turtle fishermen, every single thing about it. I was allowed to steer, even though I had very little experience – none on big boats, really. I learned a lot from my mistakes.

Then we anchored near shore, and I was able to sleep on deck. I felt so infused with the Bahamian island experience and all of it, the youth, the knowledge I had yet to learn ahead, that freedom of mobility and interaction with nature which I had never, or barely, experienced that way before. I was enthused by the danger of fucking up, the ownership of fucking up, the self-reliance and inter-reliance upon each other, the breaking down of formal teacher barriers; all of it. But most of all, I loved the power of being able to just up and go anywhere in the world; after all *Geronimo* went to Europe pretty much every summer. I truly was not just mesmerized, but hooked.

Chrissy and Natasha at Fernandez Bay, taken by an enchanted schoolmate.

Swimming in the moonlight with two girls, while all of us were staying in a bungalow eating leg of lamb and drinking cold beer! I flew back to Nassau after a few magical days, in a haze of happiness. The photos of us all digging holes in the lovely crescent Fernandez Bay beach with local kids and beers propped in the sand are still with me, as is my friendship with the family. Better yet, when I returned to school, to have the captain's daughter acknowledge me and later even give me a haircut boosted my infinitesimal standing on campus just enough to bolster me for a tough year ahead. Also, this trip enabled the suburban son of diplomats to catch a glimpse of the beauty and allure of a corner of the country far away from the capital, and to do it via mailboat, which was not considered the *de rigueur* way to travel once air routes were commonplace, and still isn't. Other encounters with *Geronimo* included:

July 1, 1989, Saturday, 7 am. Commercial Wharf, St. George's Harbour, Bermuda. Wind from south-southwest at circa 15 knots, cloudy, choppy, wet. So began a typical day. Last night I was given shore leave …to visit the Connetts aboard *Geronimo* nearby. I met with Chrissy, Chris, Cindy E., Sara G., Michele M. (last two were on the swim team with me), and John, from Texas. I walked with Terence, also of St. George's.

August 18, 1989, 10.23 am. Port Augusta, Australia. I recently heard a horrifying story of my friends on *Geronimo*, to the effect that the crew, six student friends of mine, two of them Bahamian, found the corpse of a woman floating in the Atlantic in July! Leah K. from home, told me Captain Connett was shocked. [Yacht *Anaulis* of New York, delivery captain Nicholas Abbott, 14 days adrift, Abbott swam away and drowned, she was rescued and taken to Bermuda – no corpses after all! Extraordinary that I found out in Australia, but the story did make the cover of *People* magazine].

June 19, 1990, Tuesday, 9.30 am. JFK Airport, NYC …I worked three weeks on a dry-docked St. George's School *Geronimo*, on which my schoolmates discovered a shipwrecked woman off Bermuda last year.

August 19, 1991, sailing in tandem with us are the classic yawl *Stormy Weather* and a large *Swan* yacht named *Loophole* with owner and skipper Chris R; the dinghy was called *Deduction*, and it was kept in the tax haven of Channel Islands! This name is the same as Danish-German yacht-builder Abeking and Rasmussen, which built the St. George's School ketch *Geronimo*, on which I have sailed and worked.

June 4, 1993, Friday, 5.15 pm. *Geronimo*, docked along the pier at Goat Island Marina, Newport. Cool, cloudy; it rained this morning scattered sunshine, high tide at 5:32 pm, full moon, temperature 65°F. I have finally and very fortunately secured myself a home here in Newport, where I have to date already spent four years or so of my life between three full years at St. George's, half a summer prepping for and doing the Marion-to-Bermuda Race in 1989 aboard yacht *Rumor*. Then the following summer I was working my ass off at the Candy Store (Clarke Cooke House), and also aboard *Geronimo* as I am now, for the Connetts. I enjoy it a lot, though at times I have four jobs, including delivering fancy food for Gourmet Express, in a bow tie; I quit the first night when the customer thought it was funny to shut the door on me without paying.

June 6, 1993, Sunday, 10.15 pm. Charlie's Good Egg diner at 12 Broadway, between Spring Street and the YMCA and police station in Newport. Rainy, grey, dreary; a late-spring cool. I began work on *Geronimo*, living aboard her in the starboard berth with my blue backpack, with an internal aluminum frame by L. L. Bean. I am inordinately proud to still have and use a green sailor's sack, which is really my Eaglebrook School laundry bag from 1983, a decade ago; it still has my name on a yellow tag on it! I came down here last Friday in order to earn some money and make a life for myself after months of unemployment, or certainly underemployment, since arriving in Camden Maine from Bermuda.

June 9, 1993, Wednesday 12.54 am. Newport. Living aboard *Geronimo* at Pier C, Goat Island Marina. Drizzly, raining lightly, spry, clear, wet. Captain Connett, a former navy man, and I worked well together, my verbosity, or talkativeness aside, until I stepped into clear blue paint on the deck, which I had just painted together with him, including our having added sanded epoxy for grip. Yes, I am hyper, but I am also drunk, and pleased that my bicycle works. My new bicycle is one that I salvaged from the harbor behind a shed at the marina on Lee Wharf downtown. The kindly dockmaster there told me that a young crew from Rye New York had abandoned it when the boat sailed to the Caribbean. Orphaned, it was then discretely propped against a back shed out of sight to the well-heeled yacht owners.

Ultimately the hapless bike found no takers, and it ended up in the shallow tidal basin, half submerged, whether from malice, neglect, or both. I pulled the rusted bicycle out of the harbor a year or two later, found the chain intact, and oiled it up and over a week or so. Over a short period I managed to get it back to riding condition. Taped to the main frame, like a police badge, it had a town sticker from City of Rye, New York. Since the initials are CORNY, I added a couple letters to elevate it from merely *corny,* and renamed the bike *Cornelius*! I felt that *Aloysius*, the Teddy bear from Evelyn Waugh's *Brideshead Revisited* and the pig my friend had to kill after crossing the Atlantic to Barbados, was too much of a stretch. Besides, the oligarch Cornelius Vanderbilt began his career rowing passengers from Staten Island to Brooklyn New York as a boy, and ended up with a huge mansion in Newport, nearby! I may have to re-do the varnish. And certainly the paint with footsteps in it! It looks like a parody of a crime scene; elephant prints in the butter and all that. PS: *Time-Life Books* named the author of *Brideshead Revisited*, Evelyn Waugh, one of my favorite writers, and a veteran of World War II battles in the Baltic, Med and West Africa, one of the best *women* writers from the UK!

June 12, 1993, Saturday, 9.48 pm. Newport Creamery, America's Cup Avenue, Newport. Regrettably in the smoking section. Chilly with a breeze. Today the Connetts and I took the 50-year St. George's reunion (class of 1943) out for a sail. However the happy old codgers took too long to finish lunch and then wait for a launch that could carry them out to us. So, as a compromise Captain Connett opted, in agreement with the New York Yacht Club's, not to approach the pier at Harbor Court with a 9-foot draft [funny, really, given that the boat navigated shallow Bahamas for decades!] So we waited on a mooring nearby, and it was not until after 3:30 pm to 3:45 pm, that they were aboard, with a return time of 4:30 pm to 5 pm, in order to let them prepare for a reunion dinner. This short time precluded our setting sail, which I think was a shame after eight days of work was put into *Geronimo* for this specific event. That evening, I splurged on *Escape*, a cologne for men, by Calvin Klein.

June 16, 1993, Wednesday. Expenditures: Was paid cash on Tuesday in Newport for work on *Geronimo*. ….drinking debt, …..went to the St. George's School store, where I proudly bought an *Geronimo* navy blue polo crew shirt.

June 26, 1993, Worked on *Geronimo* 63 hours of work June 5 to June 14. For boat work and Bermuda race I need to buy jeans, a new marlinspike, helming gloves, warm hat, and sunglasses. I already have a bicycle, backpack, sleeping bag, foul weather jacket, pants and boots. Never leave the boat, as they said in *Electric Kool-Aid Acid Test* and *Apocalypse Now*. I should not have left Newport this afternoon on a bus ride, after living in Newport and working aboard *Geronimo* for almost three weeks. Tomorrow I will be bound for Marion then Bermuda; my plans are indefinite from there. Now I am zonked after two consecutive nights of full raging and heavy drinking and expenditure. Hungover. Got my *Geronimo* pay slip and am basically set to go, only need to edit, or weed out, my belongings and bring them down to a reasonable size in preparation for what might prove half-a-year or more of voyaging ahead. Bermuda, and then where? [My subsequent voyages turned out to be almost 1.5 years].

September 11, 1993, called the Connetts, clean and wash the *Geronimo*, Captain Steve and Mrs. Barbara Connett, a dignified woman. On Tuesday at 9 am, meet them. Painted side of *Geronimo* in the shipyard in Newport on the Point, then known as Newport

Shipyard, near their family home on Washington Street, on the water. Next week, more work, on Goat Island, which I need.

September 17, 1993, I am in Newport. On Tuesday, September 14, I worked on *Geronimo* on Goat Island 9 am to 5 pm, with an advance. Next day, Wednesday, September 15 more on *Geronimo*, rowing to work, between 8 am to 4 pm. A job in New England rowing across the harbor from the mooring where I live on a sailboat, to an island where I work on a sailboat, is a really cool, almost mythically old-school thing to do! Did banking through Seamen's Church and the large downtown Post Office opposite the Red Parrot. Settled accounts, bought supplies for imminently shipping out.

April 9, 2003, In order to help me with graduate studies, I called Steve Connett, once captain of *Geronimo*. Hawksbill CITES paper, protected turtles species [the Convention on International Trade in Endangered Species of Wild Fauna and Flora]. He gave me some good advice and taught me the distinctions between commercial and artisanal fishing which tends to be more low-tech, sustenance and on a local or island-wide level for survival, like farming, rather than for profitable inter-island or international trade.

Epilogue: From 1998 on, I returned to Newport to run yachts and study maritime law. I worked for Oldport Marine Services on Sayers Wharf in Newport for about seven years. Briefly my tenure overlapped with Mrs. Babs Connett. She succumbed to a form of cancer and is sorely missed by many, many people. I remember that she told me she was on the jury judging Claus von Bulow, accused of poisoning his wife Sunny on their Newport Mansion. Captain Connett is a legend in the Bahamas, tagging turtles, saving many generations of them from the pot by educating young and old in Bahamas about their plight. The family returns to Fernandez Bay beach, which my brothers and I returned to in 2019. My son, then 12, and I were waiting in immigration line in Bahamas to return to the US when I spotted Steve and one of his granddaughter, Chrissy's daughter. We had a short meal in the airport and it was great to catch up.

When I ran Echo Yacht Deliveries, Steve was a captain on the roster and was always ready with sound advice. His son was been very active on the boat RIB side as well. When I saw Steve in the airport I blurted out to my son; "there is the man who taught Daddy to sail." That might sound like a country club statement to some, but I learned sailing late in my teens and parlayed it into a profession. He taught me to take it seriously, not as a lark, or just about winning, though all forms have merit.

Voyage 4: *Black Sheep*, Narragansett Bay, 1987-1989

Owner, mentor, captain, friend Brian standing, me steering, nephew in forefront, aboard *Black Sheep* in the spring of 1987, East Passage, Narragansett Bay.

April 17, 1987, Hi! Today is Good Friday, I hosted Lucas the other day, my dormmate from Eaglebrook who is applying to St. George's. I am in my room # 110 in Auchincloss dorm, waiting for Geometry class [given by the same young teacher, Mr. B., who dis-embarked from the plane for *Geronimo* in Cat Island about a month ago!]. My Geometry and Spanish are doing terribly. I am reading *The Great Gatsby* and some Hemingway. Everything is doing great with my girlfriend W., who I met in Nassau's Lyford Cay Club at the end of March break. She came up again from Connecticut last Saturday. Fortunately the weather was good and the school thinks, from a misconstrued letter from my parents, that W. is "family," and so I have blanket permission to spend time with her and visit out of state on the weekends. Since she has her own car, this set-up works well.

That afternoon we all went sailing on the 32-foot sailing sloop *Black Sheep*. It is owned by Newporter Brian Blank. He is wonderfully engaging, charming, hard-working and organized. He's a friend of my older sister, who is at an all-women's college in Boston. Her roommate, Christine, has been dating Brian's best friend Ed for years. There were some lighthearted photos taken, heeling the boat over, hair in faces, various beverages in hand, and sweatshirts emblazoned with St. George's, Pine Manor and so on. It was fun, particularly as I've been struggling a lot academically at school. So much fun in fact that I penned a little poem about it:

Chapel Breezes, 1988

The sail as an escape, to drift away, forget;
to leave behind the times, and schedules unmet.
To sail across the water, pulled across the sea;
to go against the winter gusts, and glide wherever you please.
The worries of the pressure world, are forgot when rope is cast.
But though, believe me, it is loved, our sailing could not last.
As strong as we hold liberty, we know that sails must cease.
Our sailing days are like breaths held; as such they need release.

Chapter 2

Voyage 5: *Rumor*, Marion-Bermuda Race, Bermuda-Newport, June-July, 1989

The foredeck team on *Rumor* waiting for the start gun of the 1989 Marion Bermuda Race. Within 36 hours, one of the contestants was struck in the head by the boom and killed. Andrew, to left, Arnaud, to the right. Both very seasoned mariners. There is so little wind that boats haven't even bothered to raise sails yet. We are also on the course before most others, you can see the boat over Andrew's left shoulder heading to towards the mark. Slowest boats start first, by divisions or classes, and each boat has its own pennant indicating which class. For the curious, each boat carries sheath of papers with the names, ages, role and home town of each person racing. Handy for the single person to read during five days at sea! This was my first-ever big-boat race.

Preface: Senior Spring at St. George's and I was both burnt out and angry; I'd run many clubs, founded the Poetry Club, been captain of a couple teams, set a few swim records, published a collection of art and writing two springs in a row, and had my special project essay on *Alexander the Great East of in the Indus in 325 BC* published nationally. In exchange for which I had been molested for two years and had to turn the perpetrators in to the school psychologist in order to get Frankie fired. I had been offered a job on a sailboat in Deer Island Maine by a school administrator who had colluded in the molest, however the offer was rescinded at the last minute. I had nowhere in the US to go after graduation; my family lived in Bahamas and Sweden; we were to reunite in August for a trip to Australia.

So when I spotted a small, neat job posting on the school announcement board my heart raced: I had "discovered" Bermuda on a map as a child and it was a magical place I always wanted to get to. This family offered me that chance. I called, submitted my limited sailing experience; small boats in Bahamas, a summer in the Baltic, a stint on *Geronimo*, and an unimpressive stint on the St. George's JV sailing team. I was interviewed in person, in particular by Andrew, the right-hand-man to the owner and skipper, who is a kindly, calm, gentle and detail-oriented skipper, which is precisely what a young sailor wants in a leader.

To everyone's surprise, I was offered the job, notwithstanding my mis-communicating when I would arrive for the interview, and my learning later that their relative on campus gave me the thumbs down for being a skate-rat; he needn't have worried: I wasn't good on a skateboard or surfboard either. I began the job the day after I obtained a driver's license, and although the instructor threw me out of the car at the end of the parking lot on my first try, and I was nearly arrested the following midnight test-driving a stick shift on the way to a friend's, I finally borrowed an automatic-gear car which I figured out how to drive. Thurs, I passed the test, and the examiner was not killed by my driving. I lasted at the job until a day or so after we returned from Bermuda. During those six weeks or so I lived about half the time on the boat and half on shore in Newport. I used the boat's dinghy so extensively that I could be seen in bars with a sail tie keeping my shorts up and the black plastic gas line from the dinghy around my waist. This was ostensibly so no one would steal the dink; in fact it was a conversation – not a fire - starter.

In social encounters with the owner's sons I would be introduced as a kind of boat boy, only utilizing a particularly upsetting term which was on the original job posting. One reason this was upsetting was that we were all about the same age and had gone to the same schools. A very nice middle-aged sailor lived on a small cat-boat without a dinghy, so some days I gave him a lift from *Rumor* to shore, as he was literally on my way and the launches were often very busy. Quite quickly I found myself being chided as though he and I had spent the night together. On another occasion I noted an alarm going off on the kids' speedboat, but was conflicted, since it had been made pretty clear to me that the boat was off-limits to me. I mentioned the alarm as soon as I got to the house, a couple of minutes away, and that I thought it was a bilge-level alarm, and was roundly criticized for letting their boat sink, which of course, it didn't.

I mention this not just to kvetch, or for self-pity, but rather simply to demonstrate that I was an underqualified and rather angry young man of 18, about to be plonked into a boat surrounded by experts with very definitive process. For me this was an adventure, focused on the destination. For my shipmates, the focus was on the boat, crew performance, and making different pieces and people work harmoniously. Well, they say if you can't spot the village idiot, then guess who it is? You can judge what happened next. I only want to say that any person, boat, crew, that hired me at that juncture in time, no matter how hard they worked with me, how much I was paid, how many toys – trucks, dinghies, scooters – I was given, I was going to a sulky, self-pitying, mopey teenager. I had an attitude issue, and the environment I stepped into was one controlled by experienced sailors who correctly and sensibly insisted on retaining the control necessary not only to sail to Bermuda offshore, but excel in a great race, have fun with family and friends, eat well, and remain healthy and safe.

So far as I was concerned, I was a recently minted adult who had just signed up for the draft, gotten a driver's license, and after six years of having every half-hour regulated at boarding schools since I was 13, I was now set free! And going on the high seas to a faraway exotic island in the North Atlantic was the ultimate expression of that, even if I hadn't come close to mastering the details of how to get there. So far as my employers were concerned, I was the lowest person on board, the only paid one, and the guy expected to say the least and do as much of the menial stuff as possible; they were fair to assume that, since it was literally in my job description. The thin black lines I was to focus on were not the Rhumb line courses on charts, but rather the pubes in the boat's only head, or toilet; it was my task to keep the boat clean.

June 8, 1989, Thursday, midnight. Mr. Jones' home, Newport, in the room of Stan, upstairs in their home. It was beautiful when I began work Monday afternoon, but foggy since. Thick fog now around this house. I had a cigarette alone while drifting in the harbor tonight aboard the sailboat *Rumor*'s tender. A tourist danced aboard a ship, and the pilot boat came through the fog into the harbor. It was lovely, *film noir*, surreal, romantic, Jazzy, all at once.....

June 11, 1989, Sunday, 6:50 am. Newport Harbor. I like Susan, who works on the long pier at Ida Lewis, where I keep *Rumor*'s dinghy, but she has a boyfriend, and Sandra, a US Air Force or US Navy pilot, next door, but she has an army protecting her. Brenda is around; she is an acoustic and vocalist musician works at Blue Pelican, Pelham's and Perini's, and later Franklin Spa. I miss school friends Han, Matt, and Jane, as well as home. I went sailing in *Rumor* with Stan and Arnaud, a great sailmaker, who lived in the Caribbean as well.

Yesterday I went sailing with the St. George's School class of '39 reunion, which lost nine classmates in the war. I saw famous yacht-racing captain Dennis Connor sailing the *Emeraude* of France. Saw Maxi-yachts racing about two miles off shore: *Sovereign* of Australia (red hull), *Kialoa* of Delaware, and *NCB* which is on its way to Cork, Ireland. My school friends C. & C. of California are over at the New York Yacht Club at Harbour Court.

June 21, 1989, Wednesday, 11:27 pm. Caritas, the waterfront estate of the founding partner in an important yacht brokerage, at Converse Point near Marion, Massachusetts. I was excited, as we tied up alongside *Chasseur*, New York Yacht Club Commodore Frank Snyder's sloop run by Captain Tim Laughbridge [I was to run into Tim in Auckland New Zealand, and Newport years later]. Foggy, grey, windless, cool. First day-sail (motor) on *Rumor* from Newport today. On way to the start of the Marion-Bermuda-race, which starts this Friday morning. The whole crew are here: Fred of Texas (originally of New York, he went to graduate school with Mr. Jones), Arnaud, sail and tall ship connoisseur Andrew, and Mr. Jones, a soft-spoken, thoughtful and gentle man who is both captain and owner], Stan, who once skippered *Rumor* from Bermuda to Newport. He and I share the forecastle. It is a great start. We had dinner together tonight on shore at a lovely French restaurant.

June 23, 1989 Friday, 1.33 pm. Marion Harbor, Buzzards Bay, at the base of Cape Cod, Massachusetts. In 67 seconds the first gun will go off the Beverly Yacht Club and Royal Hamilton Amateur Dinghy Club's Marion-to-Bermuda race. We are third (ranked) in 25-

member E division, or boat class. Stan, Andrew, Fred, Arnaud, Mr. Jones, and I are aboard, our stay at Caritas was wonderful: kegs and chicken dinner, breakfast and the company of various sailors, among them Brits, Aussie, the New York Yacht Club's Commodore and US Navy offshore racing boats, *Fearless, Dauntless, Constellation,* and *Avenger*.

I caught up with Shawn of Toronto, and we figured out that the last time we had met was at the Roger's place in Lyford Cay, Nassau, years ago! PS: Speaking of clubs, I came to understand purely through word of mouth that the Beverly Yacht Club is not in Beverly, near Salem and Gloucester, but in Marion on Buzzard's Bay nearly 100 miles south. Rumor has it this is because sailors of one faith were not feeling entirely welcome in the north-shore sailing community, and felt compelled to strike out on their own to the south – I've only heard this reinforced anecdotally, but if true it's a sad reflection on our society.

June 29, 1989, Sunday, 9.05 am. About 250 nm due south of Marion, in the Gulf Stream. Aboard *Rumor* racing for Bermuda. Seas are 5 to 7 feet, winds 10 to 15 knots. It's relatively mild for the river of hot water known as the Gulf Stream. Our third day of sailing; my first voyage to Bermuda, or even away from US shores. The six of us are tired, but still cheerful. Mr. Jones and Fred were both were sick. Though close, I have not been [I was just about to puke over the side of the cockpit when Mr. Jones ran up and did so ahead of me. Then Stan and I caught each other's eye, and I was unsure what to do. Then he smiled, and I smiled back in a conspiratorial way, and didn't throw up. PS: Fortuitously, I've never been seasick over thousands of sea days since!].

Andrew, Stan, and Arnaud have been excellent, helpful ship-mates. Last night I cooked dinner. As a result, I got no sleep 4 pm to 12 am. I stood the 4 am to 6 am watch, then 8 pm to 12 am, and 4 am to 8 am. Now I sleep till noon. We've got a heavy staysail and mainsail up, doing 7 to 8 knots on course 150 degrees, 5 knots on the speedometer. Last night a pursuer was hot on our tail, but over tense hours, they veered off and were swallowed by the night. Now we are overtaking a different. boat.

Southbound in the Gulf Stream racing on *Rumor*. It took a long time for me to stop talking and let the watch-standing team, who were actively racing the boat, focus. The Gulf Stream gives off a great energy when not angered by counter-currents and boxy waves from wind-over-seas effect. You can breathe the salty heat, see the Sargasso Weed and sea life, and confirm you are in it by just popping a thermometer in the seawater in the toilet! When heeled over, you can see the gorgeous turquoise colors through the hatch, or portal near your bunk, as the yacht digs its shoulders into the seas and shakes itself free of them.

July 1, 1989, Saturday, 7 am. Commercial Wharf, St. George's Harbour, Bermuda. Wind from SSW (south-southwest) at circa 15 knots, cloudy, choppy, wet. So began a typical day. Last night I was given 15 minutes shore leave (11 pm to 11:15 pm) on condition I did not drink, to visit *Geronimo*. I returned, walking with Terence about 11:30 pm, Mr. Jones told me to be up by 6 am the following morning to cast off by 7 am for Newport with Darnell, Andrew, Terence, myself and Mr. Jones aboard. I got up at 2:30 am to check rigging and docking lines; it was windy and the rigging makes a lot of humming and slapping noises, which we call *marina-it is*, or fear. Then I got up at 6 am. Perhaps because of unsettled sleep, our shipmates were not quite ready yet.

Since I was fidgety, it was suggested I have a healthy walk. So, I took time to write in this diary. I take much of it for granted, but it is so new to me (work) and I do try to please. That morning I had insufficient money on me to buy a pack of cigarettes, and had literally smoked all of my last pack so I would not be tempted to smoke on the passage north. So, after crossing the peninsula past the limestone armory in the cliffs and between the golf courses towards Fort St. Catherine, I hid what money I had in the crevices in the limestone cliffs above Tobacco Bay. My teen logic was that next time I came to Bermuda I would always have funds! [That tradition continued to at least 2018; I call it the Wiberg Bank of Bermuda].

July 2, 1989, Sunday, 7.36 am. Circa 100 miles NNW of Bermuda, heading for Newport aboard *Rumor* with Darnell, Terence, et al. I just finished a graveyard watch with Mr. Jones, which lasted from midnight until 7:30 am. A real slog. At midnight we were caught in a heavy rain and squall with gusts to 34 knots. We lowered heavy-weather jib, and hove-to, with a storm trysail and a staysail until dawn. This meant nearly tacking, but allowing wind, rudder to maintain equilibrium and stop our forward motion. We saw only one other boat. Now I sleep. Heading WNW 5 to 6 knots. Winds from NE at 10 to 20 knots. Very (somewhat) exciting watch from 10 to midnight. After dinner of pasta and carrots by Andrew and cooked on shore ahead of time by Patricia, Darnell's wife, I was allowed to sleep from 8 pm till 10 pm. Then at circa 10:45 pm, I was at helm, on course 355° NNW, when I saw a huge ship dead ahead. I took it to be a cruise ship heading very slowly east. After about 15 minutes, I told Mr. Jones about the ship, however, when he saw the ship he was understandably fuming, as we were on a collision course with a steamer! And I had been so calm! We also saw porpoises and two other ships.

July 3, 1989, Monday, 12.49 pm. In the cockpit while airplanes embark from St. David's, in a country that circumstances have not let me truly enjoy: no mopeds, drinking (as I am only 18), getting up late, smoking. Aboard: no pissing overboard, asking superfluous questions, talking to watchman, whistling (superstition), obviously no drinking or smoking. I do all cooking, dishes, cleaning of toilets. Overall, despite my whining, my job is ideal, and Mr. Jones treats me fairly; sometimes lavishly, as in our staying at the house named *Coriolanus* on the water in Somerset Parish, and at others like it.

Our only real confrontation came the morning after we arrived in Bermuda. We came across the finish line, which is just east of St. David's Light, after 4 days, 7 hours, 40 minutes, 48 seconds. We were the 1st in our class across start line, and though we were ranked circa 120th, we placed 18th in unofficial corrected time. I am ecstatic to say that we placed 4th in our class , which shall earn us a trophy in tonight's prize ceremonies, which we shall miss. Our boat has been mentioned in the *Boston Globe* and *Royal Bermuda Gazette*. Plus, there are many articles, T-shirts, mugs, neckties, scarves, celebrate event.

I was very pleased with our standing, though *Circe* beat us across the line. *Fearless* which Shawn is on, beat us. *Aurora*, which Ed, Mike, Patrick W.; a Middlesex sophomore, Wendy, Emmet D., are all affiliated with, did well. They came to *Coriolanus*, our cottage lent to Mr. Jones by the Wilsons. Commodore Snyder on *Chasseur* came 2nd, and *War Baby* (60 feet in 60-foot limit cruise race, owned by Warren Brown) won, with new course record, and earned Bermudians their first Marion-Bermuda victory. An O'Day, or factory-made, fiberglass mold 34-foot boat named *Yukon Jack* won with corrected time. This is a light boat, with a crew of four with experienced navigator and skipper who coaches wrestling. Everyone recognizes the win is of David & Goliath proportions. I embarrassingly recall my pouring salt into coffee in the house in Somerset.

While sailing, I've thought of how I've let myself become isolated from friends, old and new. I've always been a bit of a worrier; a bit sensitive. Hangovers don't help. In Bermuda I didn't get in touch with *one* of at least 10 acquaintances or school-mates who live there. It's easy to make excuses like "I was working," or "too busy." I dreamt of being under blocks, crushing me, of freight ship sending me adrift, of poems. I feel oddly like Joseph Conrad. Terence, who is studying marine biology at the University of Rhode Island, saw a whale last night. This is the offshore sailing I've dreamt about for years! No more school *Coastline* poem yearnings! The real thing. Altogether, I will have sailed circa 1,500 nm; almost enough from Newfoundland to Ireland (trans-Atlantic). Now I can wear red shorts, or even pants, to signify an Atlantic crossing under sail.

I'm learning that it's much more casual sailing back than racing down to Bermuda. Fine people. On the cruising voyage home we are using two things outlawed in the race: the motor in gear (rather than just using the generator or motor to charge batteries and fridges), and Loran: Long Range Navigation system, land-tower-based. This is less sophisticated than the satellite-based Global Positioning System or GPS, which is vastly more accurate. Loran, by contrast, allows fishermen and coastal vessels to determine position from inputs like towers on mainland, like a better version of RDF, or Radio Direction Finding. But it doesn't work far from land and the towers; that is the blind spot or folks like us 400 miles from the nearest dry soil (there's wet land a mile below us).

Watch-standing is now more lenient, which is good and bad. More sleep, despite 8-hour watch. The others tell sailing stories about big racing boats, like the Maxi's or ones I've seen, like *Stars and Stripes* in 1983, *Grey Goose,* and *Shamrock*. One joke is that there are two helms! One for owner, one for skipper, but the owner's one is disconnected! Andrew tells of a tall ship's officer ordering a cadet up rigging then stepping away from spot "x." A minute later, the *swabby*'s (meaning sailor who swabs or mops a lot) knife plummeted to that spot! I should keep the ship's log! No more *Playboy* magazines for me; just sail manuals. I'm dying for a cigarette butt! Past analysis says I am good with abstract thought, but not with precise, calculated, mathematical logic. And I may be slightly dyslexic; Stan calls me stupid. But Andrew encourages me in my diary-keeping and reading, which means a lot. I am unused to working directly for other people; indeed I grew up in a family-run apartment business and hotel. Unfortunately, Mr. Jones suffers for my stubbornness.

I badly missed Bermuda on the 1st day out at sea. That's often how it works; first half of a long voyage you miss those you left behind, the 2nd half you look forward to seeing those on the other end! Mr. Jones is sleeping on starboard bunk. Stan and I shared the loft in the Somerset house, *Coriolanus*, which was visited by a crew from Nahant, Massachusetts, which I didn't even know existed. I am developing poems entitled *Japan* and *This Sea* in my head [see below]. Thought of going out with Larissa, a swimmer, whose parents are professors, who I met in the Bahamas and who loaned me a Turkish anklet, Anne P., a friendly waitress I met at the Ark, lives on Pope Street Newport, and others; I call her Anne P. since she lives on Pope Street; in truth I don't know her surname. I liked the cool musicians, painters I met at Pelham's pool bar. I met an Oregon-American on small sailboat in Stockholm. And in Newport I like catching up over coffee and talking about the Beat poets with a kind woman named Deborah who believes she is Jack Kerouac's illegitimate daughter.

This Sea

This sea, the ocean, waves.
Wrecks here, too; bones, and coral,
built on layers of dead polyps.
This surf, these gales, wind;
death to many, yet life abounding within.
How I wish to become an ocean.

What I've learned:
- The captain's words are always an order, however casually given.
- Skipper is captain, is master.
- Eat what you get.
- Watch-captain runs just a watch, still reports to the only real captain, who would be off duty at the time.
- Silence while others sleep; they need rest as much as you do, or will.
- Navigator figures out course and speed based on previous courses and speeds, plus drift, wind, current, and other mysteries. So keep good records.
- Always offer; remember, a good skipper is always the first one to do the dishes. [French skipper later told me along the *quai* in Pape'ete]
- The ship's cook not only prepares food, but anticipates portions, quantities, duration of supplies, how best to keep provisions fresh, and budgets funds and food and storage and keeps track of what is where and when and how to replenish it, not just in stores, which are few, but by fishing, by making new fresh water, and by turning the eggs and basting them in Vaseline so they last

months, even baking bread and hanging the fruit in little hammocks to keep it aerated and fresh, and weeding out rotten fruit, bread, rusted cans, preventing icebox items from getting freezer-burned or soaked if ice melts.

- Don't introduce new systems when sufficient ones are already in use by everyone else. The danger of them not understanding what you have done could be fatal.
- Equipment: a traveler is a bar on deck almost across the width of the boat, usually in front of the cockpit. A pulley on wheels allows the line connecting the boom and thus the sail to the main hull of the boat to slide to right and left sides of the boats as needed for convenience, safety and speed. The traveler is usually under such tremendous pressure that it can only be moved using winches on drums and winch handles. In racing, it is in constant use, yet while cruising it is moved less often, as the boat can remain on a given point of sail for hours, days or weeks in the trade winds.
- Assholes overboard are not picked up either. While, actually, effort will be made to save anyone, if you are alone and wander out of the cockpit, chances are no one will hear you go over if you take a leak or take unnecessary risks. And only admirals and assholes block the only companionway steps below.
- Piss in the cockpit. Stay in the cockpit. One way to reinforce this is to explain how everyone will try to find a man-overboard, and to not give up. The other way to teach this scary concept is preventative. Skipper throws a cardboard box in the vast ocean and has everyone watch as it immediately sinks. *That's you: you're dead; don't fall overboard.* Think outside the box; what if the skipper goes over? Who will be in charge? What if several people go, or you capsize? Where are the bolt cutters and saws to clear sharp rigging away?
- Stay on the boat at all costs. Clip in all the time. If you don't leave the cockpit, you won't go over.
- If you have to leave the cockpit, use the horn or call out for reinforcements so that someone is up there with you, watching you, listening to you, ready to turn back for you and raise an all-hands-on-deck alarm. Pecking order: BN is boat-boy; then comes crew, deckhand, engineer, mate, watch-captain, captain. Much of the rigidity of larger ships, the extra roles, don't occur on small less formal yachts, but there is still a clear chain-of-command.
- Rigging consists, among others, of a running backstay, halyards, winches, rod or fixed backstay, baby stay, forestay. More for double-mast ketch or yawl, schooner and sailing ships like barks or barques, gaffers, brigantines or brigs, windjammers. Schooner has at least two masts, the front can be lower than back. Bermuda-rig and wishbone rigs are the most common. A cat-boat in Cape Cod is wide, shallow, and has a single mast set way forward that is unstayed, with no standing rigging, and a wishbone rig. It is different, wide and shallow to allow shell fishermen and others to maneuver in sandy bays.

- Other items worth knowing and using are the dodger or canvas spray-guard protecting the cockpit, cabin, cockpit, compass.
- Winches for sailing, size 23 and size 28 Barient-brand winches, three-speed, each with 50 parts. When lubricating and maintaining them, and routine cleaning the springs easily pop out and are lost overboard when you open up a winch to grease it.
- Antennae, wind-ex, or wind direction indicator, tri-color lights at top of main-mast, clear sail-ties, winch self-deck topsides, winch-handle, teak decks, varnish are all other parts and equipment that need stowing, labeling, venting, access. In the cockpit are lazarettes which are airy for paints, varnishes, and wet stuff like running rigging lines, outboard, drop boards, and fenders.
- Boom preventer is a kicker, or restraining line to prevent main boom from accidentally jibing to the other side, and literally clearing the decks of people.
- Sails include spinnaker, gennaker, staysail, 95% jib, storm trysail, heavy jib, mainsail, light jib, storm jib. As boats grow in length and add masts, sailing configurations vary exponentially. The simplest boat is a single-masted sloop with a main sail extending to the back, perhaps a jib sail extending forward.
- Boat makes and models: O'Day, Maxi, J-boats, Hinckley, Concordia yawl.
- Sail types, makes materials: Hood [later met Ted Hood], North [later met Lowell North in UK], Kevlar, Doyle, Lapthorn & Ratsey, Shore, Jasper & Bailey.

Me on Watch: Eyes red; little sleep, intense watching of compass, galley boiling water, sails, ships, bandana, thin goatee, coffee-breath waterproof digital watch; no necklace or bracelets allowed, since snagging them could cause you serious injury, like loss of skin on a ring finger. Bare feet can cause loss of a toe in a deck fitting. Smelly, tan, skin cancer urgh! Lirakis sailor's knife, L. L. Bean shorts (khaki, which means *dust* in Persian) tan lines smoker's cough. Rolled-up torn boxer shorts. Cockpit helm, Sperry topsider shoes.

[Same day]: Monday, 8.51 pm. Things getting worse for me aboard *Rumor*. The team can be very intense and criticizing at times. Accused me of wasting fuel, stove gas, food and water. I'm used to working for and living with myself, not other people; grew up in a family business with island stubbornness. In the 1970s and early 1980s during *Star Wars*, folks cared about future, yet now, in the late 1980s they care about salaries. Now, with a week-long voyage expected to end soon, food, patience, energy, and water are all now running low. As a coping mechanism perhaps, I made a sentimental drawing of my childhood friend Frank and I conch diving off Shark's Bay, Rose Island, Bahamas, after spearfishing, in the summer of 1986, three years earlier. [Clearly I was homesick – we all were]. We were also anxious about the impact of the recent spill of 300,000 of fuel oil on Brenton Reef from the tanker *World Prodigy* while we were in Bermuda.

July 4, 1989, Tuesday, 12.22 pm. Entry: The longest watch yet just ended: 8 am to 12 pm. *Nothing* happened. Darnell woke me up with a shake, saying "dude," at 7.30 am, half hour (not the usual 10 to 15 minutes) before watch! The little shit. I almost pitied him the first night of squalls and 35-to-40-knot winds. Now, *urgh*.... His watch always beeps, he hangs in the shade, he tells me what to do..... Today he told me my watch was 13 seconds too slow! I simply don't say anything... [Darnell told me smoking was just for low-class people nowadays; this hurts all the more since he may have a point, but am jones-ing for a cigarette!]. It is scorching hot and still out here. In response to watch captain's question:

"What's that orange thing floating over there?" I made this satirical drawing entitled *Orange Reefer-fish Skeleton Floating with Life-saving Gear On, Atlantic Ocean, Sargasso Sea, Doldrums, Horse Latitudes*, which I kept. Here it is:

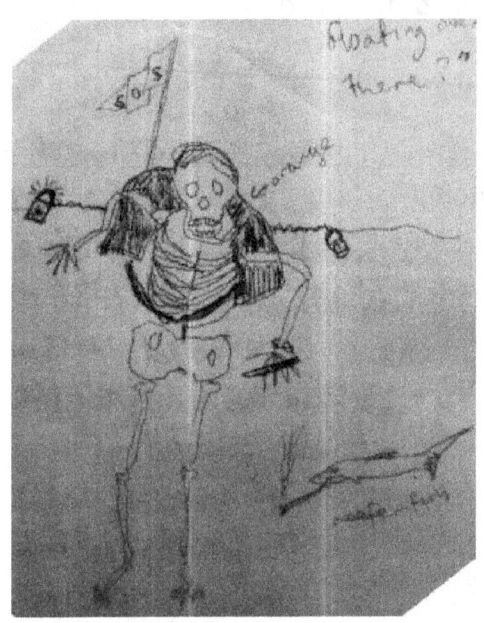

July 5, 1989, Entry: I'm going fucking crazy. Four-plus days, and we're only halfway there. Newport, with its women, cigarettes, relative freedom, and old and new friends, seems very inviting. I'm reading Graham Greene's *A Burnt-out Case*, about a madman in a Congolese leper colony, like Joseph Conrad's *Heart of Darkness*, V. S. Naipaul's *Bend in the River*, and three other Graham Greene books I've read: *Power and the Glory, Our Man on Havana,* and *The Quiet American*. They are vaguely like Durrell's memoir with a political angle called *Bitter Lemons. Heart of Darkness* by Joseph Conrad opens with crew and Captain Marlowe boating up the Thames while smoking and drinking. Their ship is named *Erebus*; a name shared with a Franklin Expedition ship which has come to foreshadow doom. Here we are, seemingly adrift, windless in the Sargasso Sea [not actually]. This drives me mad. Darnell clambers about, asks me to clean my feet. Neither of us want to be at the bottom rung of the social order and struggle to put each other down.

July 8, 1989, Saturday. We sailed into Newport at 1 am, very close to revelers, perhaps even skinny-dippers, in the water at the base of Castle Hill Light. When we entered Newport Harbor, we were met by everyone's wives and the Swiss chef and family, including Darnell's wife, who did such a great job cooking for us for three weeks. I rode my bicycle the half-mile into town, where I saw the One Pelham Street bar literally being closed. I was just able to grab a drink, then buy a pack of cigarettes in the venting machine. As I nervously puffed in the dispersing crowd in the street, I muttered that it was my first cigarette in a week. I woman in her 30's (to me that made her old at the time) muttered back:

"Well, you must be really drunk then." We were worlds apart, but I didn't have the opportunity to bridge the gap before she – and everyone – headed off into the summer mist. I walked the bike home, enjoying the sounds of other people jollifying, and then slept soundly. The next day Darnell and spouse took off. Would I settle back into Newport?

July 11, 1989 Tuesday, 1 pm. Left Newport in a van, bound for Los Angeles. [We arrived 56 hours later. If I was totally honest, I was let go, but this arrangement suited everyone and was characteristically tactful and considerate of Mr. Jones].

Postscript: After the 2000 Newport Bermuda Race Mr. Jones kindly moved *Rumor* out of the way for my crew and I to squeeze out of a tight docking situation in Bermuda following a race. That was *Seeadler*, with Joy, Rory, Linda, and the owner David. It was a bit funny, as I went out of my way to be gracious and humble with the *Rumor* team, and Darnell was there, and they cooperated fully, on the expectation I would skipper "my" boat through the needle-tight gap. So they were a bit surprised and dismayed when I asked the owner, who had thousands of operating hours on the boat, and since this was at his club, to con the boat out, instead of me without a moment of wheel time on it! The expression on Darnell's face, having moved the boat for us, was "all that for this"? I had to chuckle, feeling as I was finally not the lowest of the low.....

Many years later, while applying to pass the bar exam, I wrote to Mr. Jones asking if I had been dismissed, from *Rumor*. He wrote that no, he would *not characterize it as such*, which I thought was a very gentlemanly way to put it, given he was within his rights to skewer me. I started working for him the day after six straight years of boarding school, and I was outright angry and bitter, particularly against authority. So I openly admit I was a difficult employee to manage, shy of actual mutiny. My ignorance made me even more dangerous. I've been in touch with the gang, bumping into them in Singapore, Providence, New York, and of course Newport. I've seen Fred as well. Without them, I believe I would not have a sailing career. Thank you, captain, and family. I learned a lot and am eternally grateful for the opportunity. You were all kinder to me than I deserved. Sadly, Andrew the sage, who made the quite accurate observation that he saw me always writing and reading, and thought I would be better at writing than sailing, passed.

Epilogue: On the third day of this race Dr. Don Hill, a crewmember aboard the 44-foot sloop *Bellatrix*, with teens on board and a neurosurgeon in command, was hit by a rogue wave which caused the boom to dislodge and sweep across the deck, hitting him in the head and killing him instantly. Despite harsh conditions, a Russian spy ship, the *Akademican Vernadsky* of Sevastopol, part of the Russian Academy of Sciences, working on an emergency basis in conjunction with the National Oceanic and Atmospheric Administration (NOAA) in Woods Hole, near Marion, responded to the Mayday and took his body to the US Coast Guard off the Port of New York, and the boat withdrew from the race. We only heard about this in snippets on the radio, and of course on arrival in Bermuda.

In 2020 I was approached by the daughter of the owner of *Bellatrix*, who was eyewitness to events, and is working on a book, or report about it. She is in Vancouver and I sent her to some resources, particularly a book by someone on the same Library Committee with me, Mark Gabrielson, who authored the book *Corinthian Resolve: The Story of the Marion-Bermuda Race*. I am considering writing a script or book about the unlikely O'Day winner *Yukon Jack*; very much like the story of the horse *Secretariat* coming from behind in horse racing.

About 20 years later, Andrew, who encouraged me to pursue my writing, passed after a full life. Not only did I live in the town he lived in – Norwalk Connecticut – for nearly a decade, but one day while rummaging bric-a-brac at Stamford House Wreckers, I found a sailor's knife inscribed with "Newport-Bermuda Race, 1960" or similar, and the sailor's name as well! I tracked down a man of the same name, but he said it was not his. With no other leads I have kept the marlinspike knife, in good condition and high quality. I think of Andrew when I use it. And also about traditions, and sea sense. I am very honored to have been accepted to join the club he and Mr. Jones are members of. And humbled. I have volunteered on the library committee for over a decade and contribute stories, books, research and lectures. The club has become an important part of my family and my lives.

As a sweet footnote, the family had hired another foreign student at St. George's, JC, the summer before. I knew JC, he was a kindly Englishman with the Hugh Grant aura to him. By an extraordinary coincidence, after sailing to Europe to attend Oxford, he and I bumped into each other outside Brasenose College, on the High Street not far from the Carfax Fish & Chips, my favorite. He had a short polite chat, then he hopped on one of the many shuttle busses to London that leave from that spot. It turns out he had studied at Oxford, but I never learned more, and haven't seen him since. I see the Jones family in NYC and Newport every few years and wrote to Mr. Jones to explain my role in the St. George's School fallout (there were an estimated 100 victims like me) and he was highly commiserative and compassionate, and asked what he and they could do. A good person.

Voyage 6: *Rising Star*, Bermuda to Newport, June, 1991

Prepping a 420 two-person racing boat at the MIT Sailing Pavilion on the Charles River, Cambridge, while substituting on the Boston College (BC) big-boat sailing team.

June 19, 1990, Tuesday, 9.30 am. JFK International Airport, New York City. Muggy outside, temperature-controlled within. Flying from New York to Bermuda now. Started in Newport this morning. Will arrive in St. David's, Bermuda by 1:15 pm, local time, which is an hour toward Europe from Eastern Standard Time. I'm being paid to fly down and deliver a sailboat up from Bermuda to Newport, as I did last summer. The sailboat is designed by Argentinian German-Frers; an aluminum 55-foot sloop named *Rising Star*. The skipper is Mike, from Stamford, who recently left the University of Arizona, and his girlfriend Linda, also of Connecticut, who graduated from Boston College; she is a bit older than us.

I called Bermudian photographer Ian MacDonald-Smith, who I met at the Head of the Charles Regatta in Boston casually a few years ago. I shall leave soon; the job was unexpectedly quick. Because of Sunday's awards ceremonies on June 22, the delivery voyage does not begin until Monday, June 23. So, happily, we can all kill a few days down there first. Maybe I will be able to call on Mom's acquaintance Shorty Trimingham, the DesLandes family, Adrian J., James R., and Gregory B. of Eaglebrook, the *Apprentice Reprobates* at the Ram's Head Pub, Jeremy, or Bishi, also of Eaglebrook, or Beverly S. of BC. Staying on the beach perhaps tonight, though security and police on Bermuda are tough as hell!

At 2.40 pm; I have five minutes before our descent to Bermuda. I have just picked out some six to 10 yachts, out of a fleet of 137 contestants in the biennial Newport to Bermuda Race. I worked three weeks on a dry-docked *Geronimo* (whose crew discovered shipwrecked woman off Bermuda last year) and wet- sanded the Hinckley sloop *Night Train*, waxed the yellow-hulled *Troika*. Also for 15 agonizing, tantalizing, nearly life-changing minutes, from 11:45 to 12 pm on *Flyfly*, I was signed aboard for the race itself. I was at the boat with passport, ready to sail for Bermuda, when the guy I was replacing showed up clumsily hungover flailing and yelling his way across the dock with a ponytail. Some employers would have shit-canned him then and there and kept me. Mine didn't.

My papers were torn up and tossed into the harbor, my dream of setting for Bermuda in moments dashed, I untied the boat with a massive lump in my throat, went to the Ark bar (later the Red Parrot), burned a large hole in the outside top of my right hand with a cigarette over shots of Bermudian Black Seal Rum by Gosling's, and went to work that night as a busboy at the Clarke Cooke House. Through no fault of theirs, I summarily quit the following day to join *Rising Star* and gave my bowtie to Tom P., my BU-student roommate at 92 Spring Street; he had worked there before.

Photo of me sailing on Boston's Charles River, by Mom, who was visiting from Nassau with my Dad and brother James from Tabor Academy in Marion. James helped me rig the boat. I would later break one of the masts and T-bone a boat from Harvard, and be gently nudged off the team. Thankfully I retained the camaraderie and varsity privileges like access to football games; I think because each fall I had interesting sea stories to tell.

June 26, 1990, Tuesday, 10.42 am, Bermuda time. Gulf Stream, c.350 nm due NW of St. George's, Bermuda. about 7 knots of wind, seas 3-5 feet, sunny, cloudless seas 89°F. Finally! OFFSHORE! Great voyage between Bermuda and Newport so far; am aboard *Rising Star*, a metal racing sloop. I am making a delivery with four professional sailors: skipper Severin [later captain of a mega-yacht sailing racer owned by a family who own sports teams], his girlfriend and cook Linda. Hank is also from Connecticut, and Chris M. is from Marblehead, north of Boston.

None of us are over the age of 25. We play good rock, folk (Tanita Tikaram from Fiji) or reggae music in the cockpit, have a cooler filled with juices, sodas and seldom–drunk beer, and unlimited access to various munchies. We have been at sea since fueling at St. George, 3 pm on Sunday, June 24. That was about 48 hours ago, and so far we have had only one hot meal, but that was delicious seafood. We can cook whatever, whenever we want. This is all in striking contrast to my crewing experiences aboard *Rumor* between the same locations exactly a year ago!

Our sailing conditions have generally been superb. We had an excellent first day, covering roughly 190 nm of a Rhumb line [direct course point-to-point] out of a total distance to cover of 635 nm, with winds from the SW, or 185° to 210°, SSW at 15 to 20 knots. We've been on one tack, the port tack, or point of sail [wind on port, or left, side], since leaving Kitchen Shoals astern. We've averaged about 6 knots, with a squall and rain hitting me on the graveyard watch (midnight to 3 am), the weather vacuum following which left us with dead winds for an hour or so.

We are adhering to the 6-knot rule, which informally dictates that we maintain that speed via sail or engine power, no matter what! We flew the light-material spinnaker, which requires more man-power and skill to set, maintain, and strike, for the first 15 or so hours, nearly blowing the halyard, which was dangerously frayed yesterday morning. On deliveries, rather than races, a spinnaker is rarely flown at night except in extremely light conditions, as they require dangerous deck-work in the dark. Likewise, we don't fish at night lest a crew get over-excited and go overboard….

This dismasted boat, center above the ensign, with white banner up, has my high school science teacher and sailing coach, Mr. B. on it. The stump of the mast is what is holding up the white triangular pennant, with what looks like a small sail.

The only notable problem came this morning, after midnight, when we realized that the self-furling mechanism on the foresail (genoa in this case) was jammed as a result of a halyard (a line or wire in or outside the mast used to raise and lower sails), snared at the top of the mast or masthead. Experienced Mike was sent up in the Lirakis Chair this morning at about 7 am to rectify that. PS: The bosun's chair; it looks like a Sumo wrestler's outfit, or jockstrap: you wedge into it and are hoisted up the mast using various wires; it can really crunch men's balls and cause rashes on legs and bruises as the sea's motion bangs one's body off and onto the mast. In port going up the mast makes you look like a stud unless you drop tools on your crew mates 80 feet below, in which case you will look like Genghis Khan. At sea, going up the mast makes you look like the metal loop on a string drunk people try to hook to a pole 7 feet away in a bar, or like a fly on flypaper, a mad rock climber on a cliff face, or Erroll Flynn. It's dangerous. The few times I've done foredeck for big-boat racing I've had to work up into an aggressive trance, there are just so many things and strings under high pressure that can, have, and will kill the unsuspecting. Or make you eligible for the Harlem Boys' Choir in an instant.

We just saw what we believe was a Pilot Whale, which are dark like Killer Whales but smaller and highly agile; they even leap out of the water. We also just took a celebratory mid-passage swim, which entails everyone (in groups; not all at once) jumping overboard in the middle of the Gulf Stream and swimming around the ship! (It is said in the Med boats have been found empty with bleeding fingernail scratches all over the full: a swim where everyone accretively hoped into the water and no one lowered a ladder... Watches entail being topsides 1.5 hours, then taking the helm 1.5 hours after that. We intend, at this rate, to achieve Newport in about two days; hopefully by Thursday, June 28! Assuming a strong November westerly wind doesn't spring up, my plans following our arrival in Newport are quite complex and new, as of about five days ago.

Mike, vigilant off the bow of *Rising Star* in Gulf Stream. A good captain instills confidence in the crew. I needed self-confidence, and Mike inspired it in me. He was soft spoken, unflappable, knows his shit, and always seems to be on the verge of a smile.

Rising Star placed 12th in the best class of the 1990 Newport-Bermuda Race. We are delivering her without the stress of racing. I learned that four acquaintances of Mike's delivered *Rising Star* up from Antigua in May. I know about them from asking around and seeing some gear marked with the name Bear left behind. Bear, the previous skipper, is from England, Polly, an American, Lucy, once a classmate of my sister Ann's at St. Andrew's, in Nassau, and Brent, a South African sailor who was denied shore permits by most Caribbean immigration officers. Now is my chance! I will buy a new airplane ticket when I return, renew my Rhode Island driver's license, and move all of my gear from the tiny room I share by sleeping on the floor at Spring Street in Newport back to my home base on Crosby Road, Newton, at the gate to BC. That is my on-and-off girlfriend Celina's place, or my Jesuit teacher's home across the road from her; I've kept stuff in his basement before.

Then I will return to Bermuda on Saturday, June 31, 1990 (three nights after we arrive), in order hopefully to sail for the Azores, starting on Sunday, July 1. The voyage should take 14 days, and from Azores to Lisbon, another seven days at sea; total under a month. Probably the wisest thing for me to have done would have been to drop *Rising Star* and sail straight for Lisbon, but I am dying to get the most offshore experience under my belt. I'm sure Dr. Vassily would have preferred that I cancel *Rising Star*, but I don't like to break my word.

June 28, 1993, Thursday, Newport: We pulled into a marina right downtown Newport. After clearing into the US via the Customs agent who simply walked across from the US Post Office. I can't recall if the boat looked a smidgen lighter on the water level when the officials disembarked; who am I to argue with tradition? I took part in the traditional crew photo, then walked across America's Cup Avenue and across Queen Ann Square. A few steps along Spring Street and up a narrow alley to the back steps of my place and I strode up to the large airy apartment which I shared with fishermen, restaurant workers and other college-age freelance workers.

Pushing the door in, I left my sea bag on the landing and sat down with half-a-dozen other young people, a couple of whom were new to me. Some were pattering upturned water jugs as though they were bongos (this is an oblique hint), others nursing cold Rolling Rock beers, occasionally passing around a bottle of frozen *Jägermeifter* forest liqueur. Tom from the Cooke House asked how my trip was, I said it went well, and the murmur of mellow and eye-watering conversation resumed. About an hour later, another roommate returned home and greeted me more effusively, asking how the voyage from Bermuda went. When the new guys figured out that I my "trip" wasn't simply to Fall River, New Bedford, or Boston, but on a boat overseas from Bermuda, they took a much greater interest and it was good fun to field questions, like

"You literally just stepped off a boat from Bermuda and sat with us?" To me that was a "I have arrived!" moment... Then I left.

September 11, 1993, ...Years later: Captain Mike, from *Rising Star*, might be able to offer me more work, this time on large well-known racing yacht *Congere*. [He later did find me work in Bermuda, and I later found him work on the delivery circuit].

February 2, 1994, Recalling something I learned from Mike on *Rising Star* three years earlier, as a means of celebrating, each of us (except the owner) took a deep and humbling plunge into 12,000-feet depths of the Pacific Ocean. We baked cakes, and I recovered a bit from exhaustion with the distraction and swim. It was fun.

Racing yacht *Rising Star* captain and crew on arrival in Newport, July, 1990; Chris, Hank M., Capt. Mike, Linda. Note the super-sharp knife strapped to the boom vang in upper right corner above the ready bag. That's for urgently cutting stuff free in a tangle.

Postscript: This seems tangential, but please bear with:

1960s: My American grandparents took their only trip to Europe, from New York, where grand-dad was a lawyer. On the bus from Versailles to Paris late one evening, my tall grand-dad saw a drunken Japanese businessman harassing a single young American lady. With gravitas, he intervened, telling the pest that the young lady (a stranger) was in fact their daughter. She then got to know my grandparents, and they stayed in touch.

1999: Annapolis, Maryland. That woman, who has been exchanging annual Christmas photos with my Mom in the Bahamas, visits a yacht, *Sarafina*, I was delivering from Newport to Florida. Her daughter was not there, so she took a photo to show the family.

2000: The daughter, who is a sailor, moves to Newport, and we agree to meet at my place; not the first time I've had "Christmas card reunions." This was the day after a voyage from the Caribbean to Newport. I was a bit nervous, and I think both mothers were more so! I lived in a loft on the harbor, and was cranking music by the Lighthouse Family, which the crew and I listened on the voyage. The whole day I was looking out for the young lady, and actually ran outside twice to speak to the wrong woman. That, of course, was embarrassing. Finally, just as my crew were leaving after getting their payouts, she arrived.

"This music is dumb!" I heard, before she made it to the top of the stairs. The crew looked at me as they descended the steps and shook their heads. They knew it was my favorite music at the time. They were right; the moment was lost before we even met.

Late 2000s: Mike and she married! We all remain friendly, and Mike & I sailed together later.

Chapter 3

Voyage 7: *Circuit* Bermuda to Nassau and Fort Lauderdale, July, 1991

This grainy photo is taken just prior to my boarding *Circuit* for the trans-Atlantic attempt. I am standing in St. George's, the town and island. To the right is the Her Majesty's (HM) Customs and Immigration dock on tiny Quarantine Island, near where I had laid my clothing under a tree and swum out to the boat to get a job. The friendly folks at Ocean Sails; Steve and Suzanne Hollis, is immediately to the left. Also, this photo is taken just a few feet to the left of where the damsel in distress Rachel and her moped were pulled from the water using *Xebec*'s equipment in 1990. Then on the same post in 2018, while on a maritime history conference, I boarded a ferry here to clear brush off the cannons of Fort Cunningham (1815) with the Governor and his bodyguard on Paget Island nearby.

June 25, 1990, Bermuda. In response to ads posted at the Royal Hamilton Amateur Dinghy Club and the Royal Bermuda Yacht Club in Hamilton (my home from last Tuesday to Saturday) I took the bus from Hamilton to St. George, and applied for crew positions on a couple of boats heading for Europe. Through the sailor's grapevine I quickly learned that *Sylvee*, a 45-foot custom-built wooden sailing ketch had just accepted Spike, an American sailor and trans-Atlantic veteran who has raced the second-across-the-line Newport to Bermuda Race entrant *Starlight Express* (about 80 feet) for $1,100 plus a return ticket from Palma, Mallorca, off Spain to a port of his choosing in the US. I got in touch with another yacht, named *Circuit*. She was hooked (anchored) about 200 yards off the St. George's Customs Wharf. Since I had neither radio nor dinghy, and had spent my last dollars and much time getting there, I folded my shorts, with wallet and cigarettes in them, shoes and shirt on the steps of a boat ramp, and swam to her at dusk.

A man on deck stopped work when I proposed employment on *Circuit*, and soon two older gents were summoned, and as I tread water, they explained that they needed crew for a voyage from Bermuda to Portugal, the boat was seaworthy, and they wanted me aboard. They asked me how much I wanted to be paid for the roughly 3,000-nautical-mile passage. I was fighting a current at the time, in the dark and shark-infested waters into which yachts were still pumping untreated sewage, and did not reply. However we agreed on $100 per week as crew, and I only then was I invited onboard, and I explained to them that I needed to make a delivery voyage to Newport, and then I could return immediately to help them sail to Lisbon via the Azores. The skipper Dr. Roger Vassily of Indiana, and the other four or so crew aboard the Henri Wauquiez-designed, fiberglass-hulled, two-mast, 43-foot sailing ketch, accepted this. He also vowed to at least reimburse my ticket back following the delivery from Newport to Bermuda. Later Dr. Vassily is a retired gynecologist who has sailed trans-Atlantic twice, and he generously also promised to help pay for my Eurail expenses once in Portugal. This seemed great to me! Trans-Atlantic at age 19! After we had come to terms and I had signed the articles (a figure of speech – a handshake was always sufficient), they returned me to shore via dinghy. Nothing had been touched.

June 26, 1990, Now is my chance! The voyage should take two weeks to the Azores and a week to Lisbon, for less than a month overall. That would allow me a month of unlimited travel in Europe to meet up with my brother John at our grandmother's or schoolmate Han's place in Rotterdam. My only lament is that I shall not be able to go home, see Gillian, use my free Eastern Airlines round-trip flight from New York to Nassau, and join up with brother John before Eurail, host college roomie Rich in Nassau....

June 28-31, 1990, Arrived in Newport, packed all my things, took them with me in a bus to Boston, stowed all my things in a girlfriend's basement, flew to Bermuda.

June 31, 1990, Saturday, PM: I accomplished the mission I promised Dr. Vassily I would. As agreed, I called his wife, who gave the airline their credit card for the plane ticked (you have to buy a round-trip for immigration purposes, then mail the return leg back for a refund once you arrive – quite silly), packed all my stuff up, and flew one-way to Bermuda. I then went straight to St. George's, mailed a the return air ticket and some quick postcards, pointedly did not buy cigarettes, and made my way straight to HM Customs on Ordnance Island. There they kindly called *Circuit* on my behalf. The rest is the nightmare recounted the following day. Suffice to say, I expected a convivial greeting, to be cleared out of Customs & Immigration, perhaps fed, joined by four other crew (same as when I left), and perhaps sail out the following day together.

July 1, 1990, Sunday, 1.30 pm Bermuda time. 20 hours and 130 miles east of Bermuda. Winds from the SW at 10 to 15 knots, breezy, clear. *Holy Jesus*! Since we set sail yesterday evening, I have been in one of the most hopeless depressions and in a state of suppressed panic. I stepped off the plane in Bermuda, my Dad tells me over the phone that I'll never be able to get a rail pass in Europe, I go down to the docks from the bus station, Captain Roger Vassily meets me by speeding up to the dock in the dinghy. He doesn't shake my hand, drills me about how little experience he suddenly thinks I have (bearing in mind I just stepped off one of the best non-maxi boats in the world, for 650 miles), then lays in with subtle guilt trips about his having to wait. His behavior is erratic; if I didn't know better, I would think he'd been drinking. Or if I knew better....

To top it all off, he blows off clearing out of Bermuda Customs & Immigration, saying he couldn't afford the $30, the cost for me, plus customs clearance. These procedures are sacrosanct to any international sailor; a commodore of a British yacht club in Cornwall was stripped of his duties in the early 1990s for not raising the Quarantine flag and clearing immigration on an overnight voyage from France. Furthermore, the friendly Bermudian officers personally know me, and that I a sailed that evening, on *Circuit*; after all, I used their VHF radio to call the boat. Once we were motoring out of Town Cut and away from the island, I heard them call my name on the radio:

"Eric, you there? Come back!" This is alarming for a rookie to be called out so publicly, so I begged the captain to come down and respond. At that point he simply shut the radio off and went back into the cockpit. This boded very poorly for me. In the meantime, these two older guys, both named Roger, are slightly on the naïve side; one of them is steering naked with his foot.

Compared to my most recent delivery, on *Rising Star*, I am in living hell. *Rising Star* was four days, no tossing around, a dozen feet longer, with five crew, all young, unlimited, ever-available fresh food, sodas, a friendly woman, a great, young skipper, and two affable and knowledgeable crew. I swear to god that we had more problems on *Circuit* in the first hour than we did on *Rising Star* the whole voyage! Rocking and rolling like a fucker, the mainsail (which is tiny in comparison) got caught (batten in a spreader), the jib sail (in this case a genoa) flapped like a bitch, and the mizzen sail is hoisted from the rearmost, smaller mast using the most miniscule winches and winch handles.

By comparison, *Rising Star* had a massive coffee-grinder winch 3 feet high operated by two strapping men standing up. Emotionally, I hear people telling me I'm crazy; stupid. Even my father had serious second thoughts. I mean, this isn't right, and I'm stuck here for three weeks with no contact with anyone, stuck eating moldy bagels, stale bread, beans, beans, beans. I learned that *three* of the previous crew who were supposed to sail to Azores and Portugal; count them *three*, all friends of Vassily, all bailed. Apparently the voyage from Fort Lauderdale to Bermuda was a leaderless living hell of storms and discomfort, and the men hunkered in the bar on arrival all day, forced Roger to place the patheric ad for crew, and as soon as I walked into the snare, they all bolted without anyone telling me!

It's like the title of a Gauguin painting, or the guts of Camus or Sartre novel: *What am I doing here*? How did I get into this situation? Existentialist or dystopian, or who really gives a shit anyway, as I have no choice! I shall *never* let this happen again. I will *plan* from now on. I *miss* Mike and Linda and *Rising Star*. I miss Hank and Chris, and their professional efficiency. I envy the fellow from Maine who is sailing *Sesame* over to Portugal via Azores with a skipper, Andrew, who he's worked with for years.

Phil, the BN (what I was called on *Rumor*) on *Longuest* is sailing to Ireland with *my* former skipper from *Rumor* and a well-known yachtsman. Emmet D., whose father was our landlord on Spring Street, will sail small boats in Newport, *Guia IV*, an Italian-built 45-footer, has a crew of about six. Spike aboard *Sylvee* is getting paid well plus a return flight, and has a professional, easy going young skipper, Neil, and his wife to work with. They'll haul ass over to Europe. In the meanwhile, I remember, the chilling advice of Barbara, BN on *Attitude*, which I happen to help tie up on arrival at the Royal Bermuda Yacht Club and who became my companion in Bermuda and Newport. She told me to hold onto the EPIRB emergency beacon and to know where the life raft is. *So sad, so sad....* These two Rogers sat in the pub watching World Cup while I sailed back, and when they finally bothered to top up on food for a month, provisioned with just celery and water.

I'm crying.

The comfortable, if hot deck of *Circuit* during another quiet day. The bottle of "water" is under the seat cushion to the left to protect it from the sun.

July 2, 1990, Monday, 4 pm. Winds from the SW at 20 to 25 knots, seas 5 to 10 feet. *Letter home:* Dear Mom: I miss you. These guys don't really know anything about me, or even their own boat, with certainty. They look for food without knowing where it is, they did not provision enough because it was too expensive. What the hell? No chocolate or such luxuries. I cannot think of a situation more divorced from the sailing to which I have been accustomed. From now on I stick strictly to racing boats, preferably 50 feet or longer. I'm going crazy. I feel like a helpless ass. We are battered by SW winds and seas 5 to 10 feet which come precisely from the direction which we want to go, which is now home to Nassau, south-west of here. Winds up to 25 knots.

Roger (the nudist) can be consoling to talk to, but it is very difficult for me to keep faith. I was so reckless, for me to have put to sea with these two older strangers whose Indiana lives, 60 or so years longer than mine, have so little in common with mine. Now I am at their disposal, with no land for 200 nm, and a course, headed south with Antigua 700 to 800 nm or less off our bow. I will never let, this happen again. At any minute, they could change their minds and head for Annapolis or some other god-forsaken place where I might be unable to rendezvous with my dear brother John. god help me. What am I doing? How can I rectify this tragically incongruous situation except by mentally preserving, trying to keep optimistic and dreaming of a warm and loving home, even though it's not visible? Dolphins just swam by, I hardly notice any more, I'm in such state of numb fear for my future. It is cloudy, sunless, grey, and rainy. I whistled, as Mike had on *Rising Star*. It made me miss them all, so I cried.

The professor at sea dreaming of the Med, a remote cay in the western Bahamas prior to entering the Gulf Stream, and me and the men! That's an *Island Expedition* T-shirt, and a sail tie from an earlier job around my waist.

July 3, 1990, Tuesday, 10 am. Winds now from west NW at 5 to 10 knots. About 100 miles SSE of Bermuda. The hell voyage continues. Roger is moping. Since both of my shipmates are Roger, I call the one who I speak more comfortably easier with professor Roger. He's single, intelligent, a professor formerly in the CIA and fluent in German. In case I haven't told you, captain Roger called off the voyage to the Azores before our first full day was over, which is fine by me, as I was dreading it with fathomless fear anyway. Now we are trying to head south, SW to Fort Lauderdale, Florida hopefully, via the Bahamas and my homeport Nassau. That would be great! However, we are making about 1 to 3 knots (almost not moving), which is laughably absurd, and at which rate it may take us two weeks to get 7,800 miles. That would suck.

We had Spam (spiced, condensed ham from a tin) for dinner last night. Still can't find milk or rice. I just want to get home as soon as possible, and from now on I shall avoid cruising boats offshore like the plague. Even the Marion to Bermuda Race is off, I think. Maybe the Transpacific Yacht Race to Hawaii from California on Dave G's father's yacht, or maybe I can sail on *Rising Star* up to Newport, or *Vagrant* trans-Atlantic? Who knows? *Never* am I to get in this fucking predicament again. Next time, I familiarize myself with the crew, the provisions, the boat, the pay, the voyage, the skipper, and my own reaction before signing on.

There is hardly a silver lining around this cloud. I've thought about mutiny, abandoning ship, and radioing for an airlift, but they would only worsen a shithole that I put myself into. The nightmare continues with no end in sight. I noticed this afternoon that provisions aren't the only thing lacking or stale; so is humor. Aboard *Rising Star*, Hank and Chris were always guffawing, and Mike had a sly grin turning beneath the surface of his face; obviously and constantly pleased with the companionship; then there was warm and sisterly Linda. At home, in Nassau, some 700 to 600 miles away, is my family. I am terribly homesick, and I cannot wait for this voyage to end. The winds have sprung up again from the SW, which is exactly where we want to go. So, for the meanwhile, several squalls having passed over this morning, we are heading SSE again, towards Antigua, on the easternmost end of the Windward Islands, the Lesser Antilles; the West Indies.

I hope to sail to the Caribbean with Captain Neil Batt from Annapolis aboard *Colt International* which he and Francis run, in November. Right now, I can expect to be at sea at least another week, after four days, and less than three full days at sea. About another full day south, beating, then 600 miles and hopefully no more than 5 to 6 days heading WSW to the NE Providence Channel, south of Abaco, North of Eleuthera, and towards Nassau. We just ate week-old linguini, chili, cucumber soup, and cold beans with stale bread for lunch. I refused to eat anything but the stale bread and leftover cold beans.

There are also some Diet Pepsi sodas with NutraSweet, which has no caffeine and one calorie; in other words, no fucking energy! The good news is that I found some jam, even though the skipper was sure we had none. He is pretty clueless in terms of provisions. He is still looking for some boiled eggs last seen somewhere; I don't want to be the one to find them!, and various cuts of meat, rice, milk. Both Rogers were happy to have made 1 to 2 knots last night! We are doing 2 to 3 knots now! Jesus! In *Rising Star*, we never went below 6 knots boat speed; we weren't allowed to! I am still trying to remain sane, hoping to see land on every horizon, dreaming of cigarettes, the Green Shutters pub at home, my brothers, family, and friends.

July 4, 1990, Wednesday, 3.40 pm. Winds: From the SW at 10 to 15 knots. About 860 nm along a Rhumb line NE of Nassau and circa 300 nm east and, 180 nm south of Bermuda. Resignation, Acceptance. An attempt at realism, then optimism. That is my general shift in attitude, which has been at a low which feels so profound. Undoubtedly my present, prolonged sour spirits have been heightened by an often-subconscious craving for cigarettes, nicotine, tobacco, chocolate, sugar. Yesterday we had a very good meal; our first of this voyage. It was a thick slab of meat, slightly overcooked, with boiled carrots, potatoes, and onions.

During this voyage I have often deliberated on past feasts, and realize how fortunate I was to have had ice cream at Boston College's *Meeting of the Minds*, and my favorite meals are still the family meal at Gibby's Restaurant in Montreal, family feasts on special occasions, and a hot large portion of ham stew with buttered potatoes as prepared by Lars Lenfeldt aboard *Qu'elle Aime,* three summers ago. Last night's meal was good. Spam sandwich and bagel for lunch or breakfast. In terms of what we are accomplishing, this voyage has been, and continues to be, a basic disaster. We have been blown east of Bermuda more than 300 nm since our departure some five days ago. We want to go SW. Since giving up on the Azores on our second day, we have accomplished only about 180 nautical miles southward, which has not brought us expected southeasterly and easterly trade winds. This is especially frustrating for me, because I have generally sailed, and intend to continue sailing, racing yachts, aboard one of which we would have been nearing Nassau by now.

As it stands, we are some 860 nm from Nassau. That will mean at least a week's fucking sail, at this rate more! I can't believe it. This is such a giant fuck-up on my behalf, to have put myself and my plans so entirely at the hands of these pedantic old men and their 16-ton cruising boat. Today, I was forced to learn the state birds and flowers of the United States! They talk about shitting for kicks! Last night we had some 20 knots favorable wind, with the mainsail reefed twice and mizzen up. No genoa. Jesus. Professionals like Stan Jones, Mike, or Captain Bear would have had us hauling!

July 5, 1990, Thursday, 9 am Bermuda time. Winds: From the SSE at 10 to 15 knots. We are at roughly 28°N and about 59°W, in the western Atlantic Ocean. The voyage from hell continues, though I am slightly more tolerant. The truth of the matter is that we are in the middle of nowhere. There's no way in hell we're returning to Bermuda, which is at least 300 nm NW, and which we left illegally, without clearing out and shutting off the VHF radio when Bermuda Harbour Radio, customs and immigration called us specifically as well left at dusk. That leaves us with Nassau as a destination which is 900 nm away. I am appealing to Vassily's frugality in telling him the only port he doesn't have to fly me home to is Nassau. Otherwise there is Newport (not an option) which is about the same distance away; Antigua, which is slightly less of a haul, but then another week or so's sail to or from Nassau, and then the Azores or the American seaboard, but the Azores are too far, and the US mainland is entirely unenticing!

It is the 5th of July today. We began on the June 30. That's four-and-a-half days on our new course, or six actual weekdays at sea. We've travelled about 500 nm so far; last night we went farther east (which is to say: *away* from our destination), than we did south, closer towards it. This is mostly due to our being undermanned with three persons. With one person on watch at night you cannot change sails, and individual limitations; I'm not very experienced, Roger cannot read the compass at night between bottle-cap glasses and the dark, and the captain appears to be drinking. What do we have to look forward to? Nine hundred miles. At a very good 150 miles a day (averaging 6 knots which we haven't done since our first day) we could reach Nassau by next Wednesday or Thursday, which means 6 days more, at least, to July 11. Vassily thinks we will be in that soon. And to think that I was hoping to beat my parents from Europe before the 9th! This means roughly two weeks and up to 1,200 or 1,500 nm at sea. That would mean the equivalent of sailing from Bermuda to the Azores!

At 3 pm, I bid winds more with our SW heading at 5 knots. Also, I just had a talk with the skipper, going over our plans and location. Basically, I could not have worked myself into less professional, less discipline and efficient sailing situation, over the course of several days. While he desperately sailed south looking for trade winds which have never appeared, we managed to be blown some 300 miles east of Bermuda. Hell, we are, or were only about a third more distant from the Azores than the Bahamas, from which we are presently about 1,020 miles 18°, or degrees of longitude, as Nassau is latitude 25°W, longitude 77°N, and we are presently at latitude 28°W and 59°N. Considering that each degree of longitude is about 60 nm (possibly more or less, depending on proximity to the equator), that is a long haul.

We are presently even east of Antigua and the Lesser Antilles! Shit; we're in the middle of fucking nowhere, and I am certain that under Warren Brown on *War Baby,* the skipper or Stan on *Rumor*, Neil on *Colt International,* Mike or Bear on *Rising Star*, or the folks on *Conquest,* I would not be in this ridiculous predicament. Basically, these men's lack of assertiveness, speed and oceanic experience leaves me condemned to another week at sea which really could and should have been avoided.

It is this pervasive air of apologetic indifference which asphyxiates me so. These Rogers have no drive! For example, I woke up this morning for my watch at 2 am and I found the boat floundering, making virtually no headway. Professor Roger had entered the cabin before I even got to the cockpit, leaving the helm. I assumed that he had locked it into place. No. He had left it loose so that before I even laid hands on the helm, we had gone too far into the wind and back-winded! This is a shit position, and I tried to bring her about without the engine. Then Roger, the skipper, who is a light sleeper, came up, started the engine, and set us back on course. I hadn't started the engine for fear of waking him up. At any rate, I took the helm for a few hours, bringing her up to 4-5 knots' boatspeed and keeping her at an angle of 30° to 60° off the wind on a starboard tack. However, the wind was from the south such that we were heading almost due east, towards Africa, and in the opposite direction desired.

I woke Roger, the captain, and together we brought her about, using foredeck lights and harnesses, and bringing the sheets from port to starboard through the intermediate forestay, which allows for a sail change without having to douse the lead, or forward-most sail first. This having been completed, Roger and I enjoyed winds of 5-10 knots from the SSE, which sent us at 4-6 knots to the SW, towards Nassau. The sun rose at 6:10 am, and were doing pretty damn well for the first time in a few days. At around 7 am I proposed that I make breakfast – my first attempt at cooking a meal aboard, and our first hot breakfast. I not only wanted to make breakfast out of hunger, but I felt a certain obligation to make, as I will most likely be paid at landfall. Between 8 and 8:30 am I had procured a pancakes, three each, and 12 sausage links, four each; all hot and ready to be eaten. We summoned professor Roger, who had been fast asleep since I relieved him (or he simply left the cockpit) at around 2 am.

Roger asked him if he wanted pancakes, Roger said yes; I anticipated that we eat together, so I held out Roger's breakfast, of which I was quite proud, for him to see and eat. We knew he was awake, but he wouldn't budge; not even open an eye. He was like a little kid! I left the food on the table, had a good brunch with professor Roger, cleaned the dishes and retired to the forepeak for a rest. Capt Roger had tried to explain Roger's absence, saying that he didn't like being woken and pouted. Roger also noted that Roger had slept through most of his watch, which explains why Roger did not wake me up till an hour or more into my watch, and also why the boat was floundering. At any rate, I awoke again at noon, to find that to my disgust and dismay, not only had Roger not moved or woken, but he had ignored my fine breakfast!

When he finally woke an hour or so later, he complained that the pancakes were too cold for him to eat, and that he would cook his own. The bastard! No thanks, no appreciation. Just whining. He said that he hated being woken up and would only get up for his watch *and if the boat is sinking, and even then, I don't like it*... (I quote). Well tough shit! As far as I'm concerned, when you sign onto a boat, you surrender your sleep to the well-being of that boat, adhering to watches, and remaining at the ready. I am so disgusted hearing a skipper always apologizing for and justifying his friend's and our crew-mate's fuck-ups and his mate whining and not doing his duty!

July 6, 1990, Friday, 9 am. Winds: From the SSW at 7 to 12 knots, seas 1 to 3 feet. I haven't even gotten up to cook breakfast yet; I've been told to wait till Roger gets up. So, I will. Last night should have been a very good shift, making about ten hours of headway to the SW at 4 to 6 knots. However, we lost our SatNav, or satellite navigation system, which calculates through satellite our position to within 15 feet. Now we are sailing and navigating with the Loran, which stands for Long Range Navigation System which is less accurate, but which you can plot by programming a destination, like Abaco Light, and have that registered. Anyway, during my shift from 2 to 5 am, I fell asleep for about 45 minutes (in the military that's punishable by death!) and found us being pushed north. The Loran now reads 28°N, not 26°N; hope that wasn't just me! [Same day] 11 am: The hell voyage continues. GPS is down for good now; we're resorting to sextant soon. Can you believe that on our seventh weekday at sea, we are still 180 nm *east* of Bermuda? And we are *east* of Antigua! Fuck, we're nearly halfway across the Atlantic!

On any other boat I would probably be either in the Bahamas or the States (where I really *don't* want to go) by now. But no: I'm stuck out here. The last thing I heard the skipper say was *we should make it*, and *Oh, it'll be at least a week*. He also says things like *We'll have these winds till December*. Well fuck, I didn't come out here to spend my *life* with these dorks. I still haven't used the head of *Circuit*. I pulled a muscle in my upper left leg. Pain. Makes me clumsy and noisy on deck, and leads the skipper to mumble that I'm a no-good sailor. I came out here to sail, and to get somewhere.

We're sailing slowly west now, but we're hardly getting anywhere! I won't make it to Nassau till halfway through July at this rate; my parents will begin to worry why I haven't called. For the amount of time we've spent out here, we've accomplished next to nothing but slip across the surface of the planet in the wrong direction. Roger still falls asleep (as I have been guilty of doing, but which is an executable offense in most militaries) on his watch, bringing the boat almost to a dead stand-still. Then when he wakes up at about 10 am, he gets excited about "greasing the hatch" and taking a shit! *Jesus! Jesus, Jesus*... I'm just taking it day by day, sitting through Russian violin music, and getting back into Robert Hughes *Fatal Shore*, having finished Thor Heyerdahl's *Ra Expeditions* last night. *Patience*.

July 8, 1990, Sunday, 9 pm. Bermuda time. Latitude 27°30'N, longitude 64°55'W. Winds light at 2 to 6 knots, seas calm, one-foot swell. Things are definitely tenfold better. I really wonder how much my nicotine fit and the fact that I had been very spoiled on *Rising Star* had to do with my depression at first. I still get flashes of despair, especially at our minimal progress, but they are rare, and I am generally contentedly resigned, settled into this somewhat strange but relaxing and un-rigorous daily routine. The food and companionship have gotten progressively better as has sleep, and general cruising conditions, which are flat seas and gentle wind, so very little stress. I hope wind picks up, and we make progress more as we haul west. We've done about 800 nm, and are presently (finally!) west of Bermuda. Our latitude of 27°N, which is about 300 miles south of Bermuda and 100 miles north of Nassau, is quite good, though it has yet to bring us trade winds. Longitude is up from a lousy 54°W to present 65°W, leaving only 12 more longitudinal degrees, each worth about 52 nm, for a total of 625 nm west. We've sailed roughly 100 nm in a curve and have about 700 to 800 more to go.

We have the Vassily family's green *Wild Scottish* spinnaker up now. Still, educating and patient skipper Roger is funny but gross; he talks of farting, penis, pussy, general bigotry. He also drinks Vodka from about 7 am. Though apparently he is secure of his sailing ability, and generally a good guy. Have been meticulously following the saga of Tania Abei, the Swiss-New York teenager in her small sailing sloop *Varuna*, circumnavigating our planet between ages 18 and 21. I'm thinking of subscribing to *Cruising World*, and *Sail Magazine*, and possibly circumnavigating too.

July 10, 1990, 500 nm to go. I've been reading about adventurers Thor Heyerdahl, Voss, Gerbault, Pidgeon, Robinson, Hitchcock, Roth, and Joshua Slocum.

July 11, 1990, 9.30 am. This fucker professor Roger won't get up. Lazy fucking... I pulled 8 hours at helm yesterday, yet he pulled four. With spinnaker giving us 9 to 10 knots downwind, someone has to be at the helm. Roger fills in for him. Roger cooked dinner yesterday, but then I cooked us pancakes, taking an hour and a half. My shift last night was 1 to 4 am, I waited till 5 am, so that Roger could take a shit (really) then was waken about 7 am to strike the complex spinnaker sail. Professor Roger gave up and drifted so I flung on the engine and took the helm for two hours, and Roger hasn't even gotten up. The captain is to wake up professor Roger, which is lame. Now we got him up by yelling. Winds up. Helmed today. Then told me to do 'em tonight, *grrr*. Excuse the blood on opposite page, but I cut my hand while releasing the preventer on jibe (while jibing).

July 12, 1990, Thursday, 8.40 pm. 27°30'N, 73°W, Atlantic. Gusty; a squall just past, with seas 4 to 8 feet. Hello. Excuse foul language and base anger of yesterday's entry. Though things are generally good and we are presently only 230 nm on the Rhumb line from Eleuthera, I am still perturbed by the ravings of our extremely lame captain. We finally struck the spinnaker this morning. We'd had it up three days or so in a row, which was quite a strain on the one-man-a-watch crew, which professor Roger had turned back from being strained for 14 days and 1,900 nm.

Well, we've ended up sailing 1,400 nm so far, with at least 300 nm to go, probably four! Hope that Grandmommy hasn't died. And John hasn't gone to Europe. In Roger's favor, I must say that he is easy to talk to, and makes his nav station, or navigation desk (the corner office of any boat) approachable. This is basically because he has no pretention to hide behind; and little competence, it seems. Of course, he drinks beer or Bloody Mary's (or whatever) from about 7 am on, but I don't think that is the problem. While admittedly I'm a relative sailing neophyte who is clumsy and still an initiate, with zero transatlantic crossings to captain Roger attempting his third, I feel he thinks, he knows everything about sailing. He may a lot when it comes to lake racing, but from what I've gathered of his offshore leadership; naught. He is a nightmare! For example, in 1983 it took them a month *and a half* to get from Gibraltar to Antigua. That's with the wind, 25 days from Canaries to Antigua, and (surprise!) Roger did not provision enough (and he knows diddley shit about provisions on this boat), so that the crew nearly starved: the rations of the last week were a single can of beans for five persons, daily. On a lot of boats you expect to eat large cans of Dinty More or unmarked vegetables form the bilges, but this boat doesn't even seem to have that! Voyage two: for 5 days they set off from Lauderdale, yet their voyage took 7 days. They lost their steering, fell back to using the manual emergency tiller, and limped back to Bermuda, where three of the crew jumped ship (that of course was this voyage, with the three defectors taking off as soon as I showed up!).

Now both the GPS and autopilot have gone down, and we only have a three-man crew. On a better note, the freighter or tanker *Oceanways Harriet* of New York yesterday came up astern of us to *check us out*, startling Roger and I while we discussed provisioning for my planned spring 1993 to 1996 circumnavigation. The American sailors *en route* to Puerto Rico actually diverted and slowed to inspect our spinnaker, which stood out for being green. They tagged behind us a while until professor Roger popped his head up, he eyes went wide in amazement, I turned around to see the bow of this huge ship almost looming over us! We immediately jumped to turn on the radio and they enjoyed telling us they had a pool, ping-pong, ice cream and videos for entertainment. After that we saw many dolphins also. Now our spinnaker sail is down, the genoa is out, and our mainsail is reefed, as is the mizzen sail. Our boat speed is up to 6 to 8 knots, with wind 8 to 18 knots apparent. Our ETA, or estimated time of arrival, is now in two days, or Saturday July 14, in the afternoon. PS: I think Roger and Roger are reading my log, or diary! *Pas bien*!

July 14, 1990, Saturday, 4:30 pm Bahamian time. We are heading into Nassau, with roughly 20 nm to go. We are keeping north of Eleuthera, Current, Rose Island, Atoll and Paradise islands to enter busy Nassau Harbour. *Letter of Reference, for USCG Sea Time Documentation:* Eric Wiberg sailed with Prof. Roger and I between Bermuda and Fort Lauderdale, Florida on a trans-Atlantic attempt taking three weeks and 2,000 nm. Dr. Roger Vassily, *Circuit*, Wauquiez 43-foot ketch, Indianapolis (Signature).

Arrival, July 14 nighttime: Arrival is still a blur. After more than two weeks at sea with no music, women, cigarettes, alcohol, we literally pulled up right in front of one of the happiest busiest bars in Nassau at the time, Nassau Harbour Club, run by a Greek marine construction guru. The pool was often filled with fellow students on *Geronimo*, and boats there included a wooden Concordia 50-foot yacht named *Mya*, owned by Ted Kennedy.

Another yacht there had a name with something about an Iguana. This one was rumored to have been shared between a well-known New England shipping family who had owned the Royal Victoria Hotel and a southern musician known for transposing his non-indigenous foods (cheeseburgers) and drinks which Bahamians never drink (tequila) on the islands for the benefit of his American audiences. I have to admit, my pointing out this misappropriation of culture is deeply unpopular, provoking folks to fall over

themselves to prove they sold him the first cheeseburger or margarita in paradise.....
Legend has it that one of the captains ran off with one of the owner's ladies, so a eunuch was hired in his place, however I have not tested this theory for obvious reasons, nor am I on the market for choristers....

At any rate, I disembarked alone at the Nassau Harbour Club, unwittingly about to start drama and gossip of my own. Groggy but excited, dressed in loose, salt-crusted shorts, and armed with $20, I wobbled on unsteady sea legs to the bar, known as Captain Nemo's. Then I had a beer and bought a pack of Marlboros, which tasted horrible and weak after two weeks without smoking. It is way too much sensory overload for me, and I was damn hungry, my last meal having been meat sauce and anchovies strewn with pubic hair and engine (not vegetable) oil from the bilge.

I bought a hot dog from the rack, and was retreating away from the crowded bar with it, while trying to avoid people, when my head collided with a speaker hung from the wall. I am squished into a corner to avoid attention and eating madly when I wondered to myself how Ketchup got on my hot dog. It was actually blood from a fresh head wound, incurred by walking into the sharp corner of the speaker. My tasseled blonde hair was now pink from blood, which smudged down my cheek, and my white t-shirt was stained with hit. In short, rather than blend in, I stood out like a bloody thumb.

People then start staring at me like I'm crazed, which became a self-fulfilling prophecy. A close friend of my older brother John's, Andrew B., spotted me, knowing I was on the way to Portugal from Bermuda, and triumphantly paraded me around the bar to family friends, which of course terrified me further. I want to find John, knowing he would take care of me. I walked across the street to the *disco-du-jour*, named Club Waterloo, fully expecting to be let in and find my brother. However the big amiable bouncer, named Tiger, who wears a large leather vest giving an impression he is packing a pistol, and who let my sister and brothers and I into the club for decades (often for free), did not let me near the door. I look that bad. He did not recognize me at all.

Then I found myself lost, shoeless, unshaven, sunburnt, and bleeding. To Tiger I was just a poor hobo in a blood-covered T-shirt, nothing more – a menace, to he and his guests. He probably sees half a dozen like me each night of the thousands that were then going to the multi-bar lakefront estate. I gave up trying to get into the club before anyone else I know found me in that state, and stumbled towards the other bar. During the walk I saw a gas station and went in to buy something; anything; sugary. I found a glazed bun, locally made, probably on nearby Fowler Street or Shirley Street. It was wrapped in cellophane, and to eat it in peace I literally crouched, huddling and hiding, behind the wall of some office building near Brown's Marine on East Bast Street, just as during the Great Depression homeless would cook fires under the boats there. This was all in my own home city. I was then discovered by childhood friend Richard K. and his future wife Vanessa M., whose Mum managed our family business. They gently coaxed me, like a wild animal, from behind a low wall, and into Richard's vehicle.

The couple kindly drove me directly home, very near Richard's, and dropped me off. Despite our dogs putting up a barking ruckus, my parents didn't wake, and they allowed me to the back of the boy's wing. Using tricks honed over many years and the obscene skinniness of youth, I push the screen of the small shower window, tippy-toed up and up, and then pushed myself to eye height and into the narrow eight-inch-or-so slat between wall and lower pane. Finally I fell into the bath tub; however only attempt this when drunk, or a desperate sailor.

I knocked from the interior Dutch door separating the boy's room and my parent's room of 50 years, and then and gently called them:

"Mom, Dad." To which my mother responded:

"Who is that? Its 2 am, for god's sake!" Inhaling deeply, I then told my parents the wonderful news, that I was their long-lost son Eric, having made it home after weeks at sea. My parents have four children who have gotten into their fair share of scrapes globally; expulsions, driving off a cliff in Peru, boat accidents, four divorces, numerous car accidents, and plenty of other great stuff; we should have a wing of the rehab clinic named in our honor!

My mother's measured reply was:

"John, you're drunk. Eric is in Portugal. Now go to bed!" I didn't argue, I went to bed. The next morning they found me in John's bed, bloodstains on the pillow case, and famished. We hosted the two Rogers for dinner at our house. CIA Russian and German-speaking Professor Roger studied them and then declared to me that my grandfather's hard-won collection of 12th century Russian icons were fakes. The other Roger regaled us with stories of dogs shitting all over boats. Shit was Roger's favorite topic, after pussy and piss. He is a grown man; I was 19. John and I did make it to Europe, but not till Lisbon till many years later.

August 15, 1990, Corfu, Greece. ...My stay in Nassau was both typical and atypical at the same time. After nearly running aground coming into Nassau, Captain Roger threatened many times to drop anchor, knowing it would have broken my heart not to go ashore in my hometown. I missed Malcolm's birthday party at *Sun And...* restaurant. During the next week, I met up with family and friends, got drunk many times in Nassau and at Nesbitt's, and eventually (I think after 5 to 6 days) I sailed with Vassily to Fort Lauderdale, during which voyage we got lost again, getting blown some 40 nm off course.

Highlights of the layover in Nassau were me literally dodging Bahamas Customs and Immigration officers who boarded while I was "trapped" on board. Since the Captain had not cleared me out of Bermuda I did not, legally, exist. So I had to keep hiding to avoid them seeing me on a small boat. That afternoon, with a viscous hangover, I was hoisted up the mast and left there for hours, mostly by Roger, as a punishment for smoking and drinking after I said I would not. Professor Roger also said "Nassau has made quite an impression on me; a very negative impression," because of the trash and crime and run-down buildings.

Finally, I had a very *laissez faire* attitude to picking Roger's son up at the airport so arrived after they had waited for me and left, meaning I was late and they very nearly left without me. Then at home I worked installing hurricane shutters for Dad. I did a race one weekday afternoon on Peter Christie's sailing sloop, which John arranged. On July 20 I left Nassau aboard *Circuit* to complete the boat's passage to Fort Lauderdale, and on July 23 we arrived in Florida. Professor Roger was irate that the barmen and women would not serve me alcohol as by the estimation of the drinking laws, I was not yet a man, but by his standards I was. Then on July 26 I was back in Nassau again in time to pack for John and my back-packing adventure then back to college in Boston!

August 13, 2002, Paris; Café Noir on the corner of Rue Montmartre and Rue d'Argout. Having a coffee *au lait en une petit Stella Artois (biere!)* at 11 am; on the right bank. ... I also stayed in Paris with brother John in 1990 after my failed attempt to sail across the Atlantic on *Circuit*.... We actually slept beneath the Eifel Tower, on the grass of the Champs d'Mars, and were literally hosed off the lawn at dawn by the Parisian Gendarmes the next day!

Writing in my journal and log at the Café Noir in Paris, where I retreated to after *War Baby* On this occasion I was visiting friends from my years in Singapore. Another memorable visit ended at dawn after a bar crawl by car with a Parisian cop went till sunrise..... The little pouch made of sail cloth on lower right is from a Marion-Bermuda Race.

Voyage 8: *Xebec*, Antigua, St. Maarten, Anguilla, Bermuda, Belgium, May-July, 1991

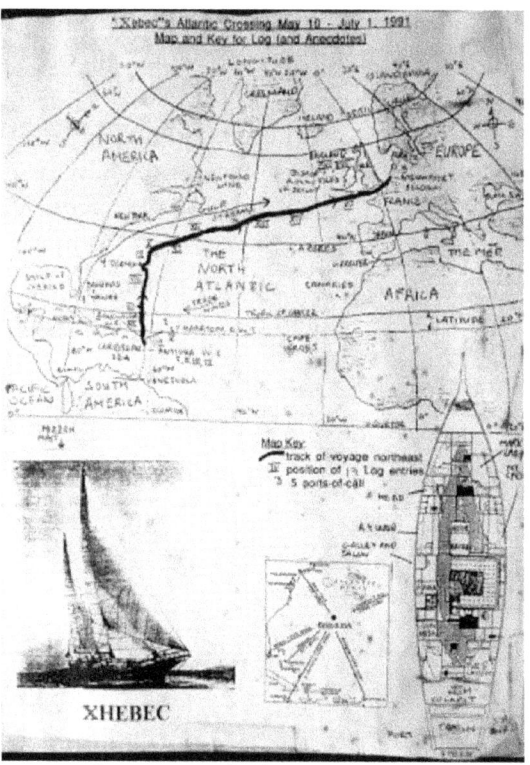

Xebec's route in 1991, excerpts from a yacht brochure which Martin had made for charter guests, and a small map showing distances to and from Bermuda in statute miles.

"We must sail and not drift, nor lie at anchor." Oliver Wendell Holmes, from *The Autocrat at the Breakfast Table, 1858.* At St. George's I was well known to booksellers in Newport (three, at least), and one of them was clearing out old titles from the school library. Though many consider that he was over-zealous, I was the recipient of over 400 books, which, to the bane of those in whose basements I stored them during the summers ahead, I dragged with me wherever I went (it cost more to fly my books than me from Oxford). This obscure book was one of those de-assessed by the Nathaniel P. Hill Library in 1988-1989.

I just finished sophomore year as an undergraduate English major at BC, then flew directly to Antigua, West Indies, on May 10, 1991, after waking up with girlfriend on Lake Street, alongside the Seminary where Cardinal Law lived, in Newton and Chestnut Hill, outside Boston. On arrival in Antigua, I slept aboard 62-foot *Swan Sloop Colt International*. I did this by following the crewing agent's advice to go up to someone on the plane who looked like a sailor and introduce myself. In my case it was Newport yacht navigator Bill Biewenga. After scrubbing *Colt*'s hull, then scrounging around for information all day I got a job as first mate aboard *Xebec* with Belgian Martin Misiree (age 35) was owner and skipper.

Sunday, 12th May 1991, 3:45 pm, Aboard *Xebec*, tied Nelson's Dockyard, English Harbour, Antigua, Winds 10-15 knots SSW. My first night in Antigua I walked to a large sailboat named *Xebec* and. asked for Martin, the Belgian skipper. "Come aboard!" Off with the shoes, hat, and beer, and up the gangplank I went. His back was to me, his face in the shadows, like Brando playing Kurtz in *Apocalypse Now*. The conversation went like this: Martin: "Yes?" Me: "Do you want help going across?" Pause. "Yes. Welcome." Disbelief. Pause. To Martin: "I have five thousand miles." "I've known fools with a hundred thousand miles. Welcome. Where is your beer? Have a Polar." I drank the cheap Venezuelan beer, dizzy with excitement. "Where to?" "Belgium." "How?" "Direct." "When?" "Two days. When I get money." "Who with?" "Me, you. Loco, and Captain Splash." Fear: "Aren't you the skipper?" "This is *Kapitan Splatz*." My new skipper held up a kitten and smiled. "You're welcome. Move your gear aboard tomorrow." I did.

Lovely English Harbour Antigua – having fun! Martin had us dive down and scrub the hull, only the dive tanks he gave us had no oxygen to breathe from in them, so they just weighed us down. Mark took this through the portal in the head, or toilet at anchor. Clearly it was shallow, in order for me to have pushed off the sea floor and get most of my body out of the water! If I spent a year I probably could not recreate this image.

Tuesday, 14th May, 8 am. *Xebec*, English Harbour. Calm, warm, humid, pace slow and languid. Now it is only Martin and I crossing the Atlantic. Loco, a poor Venezuelan, left for a wage on another boat. *Xebec* is a 19.5-metre (65 foot) ketch (2 masts). Her teak deck was laid in Taiwan (strikingly beautiful when clean). She is wide, deep, and heavy, strong and seaworthy, as is Martin. *Xebec* has survived some 16 Atlantic crossings, and Martin almost as many. On Mother's Day I called home and told my mother that I would cross the Atlantic virtually single-handed. The last time I tried that, I ended up on her doorstep after three weeks in the middle of the night – malnourished, bleeding, and barefoot. We sail for St. Maarten tomorrow.

Friday, 17th May, 1 pm. *Xebec*, moored off Philipsburg, St. Maarten, Dutch West Indies. I am now First Mate of *Xebec* – the 2nd in command. There were nine of us, including Splash the cat, on our first voyage. All but four sailors and one passenger have left us here.

Leaving Antigua: Dragging anchor towards coast. Midnight. No skipper. With moments to spare, Martin returns to *Xebec* with an entourage of well-wishers in dinghies. Songs are sung, farewells said, the anchor and sails hoisted, and off we set. Martin has convinced two Antiguan employees of the Galley Bar, Paula and A., to join us (Martin, I, Splash, and Mark, a New Zealand backpacker who'd shown up earlier) all the way across. We bid Antigua farewell under the midnight moon. Martin sets a course and recedes below, not to be seen again until before we make St. Maarten. I pull night watch, trim sail for a dawn squall, and plot course to St. Maarten.

    I was to learn that our skipper was a playboy for whom his mother bought the yacht, the SCUBA tanks we were told to use to scrub the boat's bottom had no air; he picked up different women for the same voyages, one of them threw our only radio in the sea, our crew didn't all have passports and were not always cleared in… Then we set sail from English Harbor, Antigua on Thursday May 16 at midnight. Crew of Mark Aitken of Auckland (former Sea Scout), New Zealand, Alfred aka *Cannon* (drug-smuggler, user and dealer, whose sister married a cop who confiscated his profits to buy a car and Alfred shot his own brother in a duel on a sports pitch) of Antigua, Paula Charles (beautiful waitress at Gallery Bar) of England and Antigua, and *Captain Splash* (alias *Splatz*) the cat rescued from the water of Antigua.

    With an auxiliary crew of Petra Van der Zee (circa 30) of Amsterdam, Netherlands, Grazie (young photographer, of Italy, about 20) Loco, (aka Alexi) of Cumaná, Venezuela. Together we all made Philipsburg, St. Maarten, Dutch West Indies, by 6 pm Thursday while Martin was passed out and Loco, Mark and I sailed the boat. May 16, after an eight-hour voyage. We rested in that large port, and rendezvoused with the *Swan* 49-foot sailing sloop *Loophole* of Guernsey, Channel Islands between the UK and France.

Road Bay, Anguilla, and sailing to Phillipsburg, St. Maarten. Bottom left clockwise: barrel-chested Martin, Mark & Paula I the sunset, and Alfred and Paula on the aft deck later shattered by weather and the preferred place for *Kapitan Splatz* to poop.

Xebec, only some 45 feet at the waterline with long bows and stern for show, is registered to St. John's, Antigua. The crew on *Loophole* are skipper Chris Rasmussen; yes, same as Danish-German yacht-builder Abeking and Rasmussen which built *Geronimo*. Chris is from Finland, and is age about 45, then an older crew nicknamed Padre. Other crew include David of Cowes, Isle of Wight, England, who is age 62 and sometimes called Santa Claus because of his white beard, then Julia, from the UK, in her 30's, and Peter, also in his 30's, from Rhode Island, who was on *Endeavour*, the huge J-boat owned by Elizabeth Meyer who has restored it and others, and co-founded the International Yacht Restoration School, or IYRS, in Newport. Tom is a healthy, spirited young Antiguan, and finally Guy, a good-looking, blonde man, slightly portly, slightly thinning hair; a somewhat affected Britisher who is the paid mate.

A good cook and teller of tall tales; a self-professed Cambridge man; I was later told that he was there all of fourteen weeks before being sent down in mysterious circumstances. His family are said to be owners of numerous boat yards, yacht havens and docks, in the UK, or to have sold them? Anyway, Philipsburg, Dutch St. Maarten was good and cheap. To raise funds, I tried to sell surplus anchor chain which I found unattached on the seafloor when free diving to set *Xebec*'s anchor in the sand. I offered to sell it to a South African on his live-aboard named *Geronimo*, however rather than fair pay, I got paid $4 for about 100 feet, which took me over an hour to pull into the dinghy and then knell in a partially flooded inflatable while feeding rusted jagged chain to him!

As a consolation; knowing he'd screwed me, he fed me some scrambled eggs, and a piece of white toast, which did not replace the calories I expended. The Dutch are sympathetic to *Afrikaners*, or whites of Dutch descent, who are fleeing South Africa as the nation gains racial equality and racists are punished and non-whites given preferential treatment. The Dutch West Indies are about the only Caribbean islands which offer them refuge to anchor and live; the Bahamas welcomed Sol Kerzner and Atlantis when he fled South Africa fearful that Sun City would collapse.

Tuesday, 21st May, 10:40 am. Road Bay, Anguilla; it means "serpent," but the flag is of dolphins. Winds 10-15 knots, gusts to 25, seas choppy outside bay, rain. Arrived 6 pm Sunday 19 May. Took on water, air for diving tanks, cleared customs. I have my own spacious cabin, forward of the salon (where Paula sleeps). Intended for charter guests, it has lockers, bookshelf, two bunks, access to the head (toilet), and hatch leading to the foredeck. Martin is in the aft cabin, A. in port, and Mark in forepeak. The large transom at the stem end of *Xebec* holds our gangplank, the cat's litter box, our fishing gear, and the inflatable dinghy. The four sailors hold six hours of watch alone per day. We are forever on call – dishes to be done, boat cleaned, sails set and altered. Even at anchor we spent the windy night fending off an abandoned ship.

Change of plans. Shall set sail for Bermuda later today.

On *Xebec* north of the Antilles. By this point we were so poorly fed I was losing a lot of body mass. Overall out of about 175 pounds I lost over 35 pounds in seven weeks.

      We left St. Maarten by Sunday, May 19, and made Road Bay, Anguilla a few hours later. There we were treated with what is called a jump-up reggae band (impromptu) at a bar near the government dock called, I believe the Pump House, as it housed numerous large plumbing and pumping devices. We left Anguilla for Bermuda with crew of five total, or six with *Kapitan Splatz* the cat, who over time moved to my cabin in the forward starboard, or right side. We left Anguilla in the afternoon of Tuesday May 21, after a nearly disastrous attempt to anchor off Sandy Cay saw us hit ground several times and abort.

      We then arrived St. George's Bermuda on Monday, May 27. That was a disaster too, as we missed Bermuda entirely, passed to the NE of the island, and Martin had us come to a stop. We spent hours following tracks of planes, calling them fruitlessly on VHF radios, and watching birds and cats and clouds for signs of the direction to the island. Finally, a small transistor radio gave a signal in only one quadrant, our port quarter, so we started the motor and headed there towards the voices in the radio. A few miles east of St. George's a large splash on the starboard bow sent me running forward, only for a massive, possibly fourteen-foot spotted Tiger Shark to slap its tail against *Xebec*'s starboard side amidships just as I scurried along the narrow deck rail there, clinging to the dodger or sun tarp, and only just avoiding being startled into the water.

Xebec on the way in the Trades from Anguilla to Bermuda, from the bowsprit.

Friday, 24th May, 9:35 am. 62°W, 23°N. Kicking up a good 20-35 knot winds SSW, following seas. On starboard tack heading 15-20° NNE. Brisk sail. Offshore at last!.

Monday, 27th May, 10 am. Placid, windless, calm, humid. We missed Bermuda! We finally have St. David's Light within sight. Were due to have sighted land by dawn, after nearly a week at sea. SatNav is down. Stayed up all night – A. and Paula alert as their first real passage nears its end. Seas flat calm. Under power. Failed to hail an aeroplane overhead. Bermuda Radio telling us to be at work on time. At 8 am Martin altered course to WSW – a wise decision. An eerie arc in our wake for only distant whales to observe. A. is devastated when we told him we were missing Bermuda and heading straight for England. Bad joke. Cat prancing with smell of land. Startled by tiger shark, which hit us twice. I was sitting on rail and almost toppled. Bermuda long tail dove circled our mast, and then led us directly to land. I help Martin guide us ashore, having transited Bermuda six times under sail. We're all nervously excited, and toothbrushes and combs surface after days of misuse.

A little background and 2021 perspective: In the spring of 1991, GPS was in such infancy for commercial use that the main system was Loran, where you had dominant towers on land which only reached so far into the ocean. Popular with fishermen for marking favourite locations by triangulations, it was useless far offshore, kind of like an "air gap." Even though Martin had crossed the Atlantic, he said, over dozen times, he never used the sextant. Basically he dead-reckoned, and had the common sense to stop the boat when he recognized we had overshot Bermuda. Since we certainly needed fresh water, provisions, fuel and some festive drinks on shore to continue to Europe, and had gone out of our way to reach Bermuda with *Loophole, Stormy Weather* and others, it made sense that we try to find it, however he never asked for input from any of the crew. What is fascinating is the very low-tech solutions: watch for airplanes and follow them (but are the leaving or landing? We never found out).

Finally we swung a cheap transistor radio around until you hear Bermuda, *voila!* It worked. And watch cats – *Kapitan Splatz* was very attuned to the smell of land and pranced all over when it reached is nostrils. Finally, the Bermuda Long-Tail Doves actually did circle the mast and lead us to land, as dolphins or porpoises where later to guide me on a different boat away from a Polynesian reef. Then, once on Bermuda, the crew improvised to get cheaper provisions from the US Navy base, since Martin refused $500 to sail in circles for a camera as the price was beneath him, while I was making a tiny bit per hour under the table for beer and cigarettes.

Taken by the lovely Rachel who we helped rescue on arrival in Bermuda. *Xebec* in a very prime spot indeed in front of the Wharf Tavern in St. George's. When Martin moved our large boat with a small English one still tied alongside us, the owner was not amused…. You can barely see him leaning over but I believe that is the world-renown wooden yawl classic *Stormy Weather* owned by Captain Paul – that may be him!

Though beleaguered, we were charged exorbitantly for the next ten days in Bermuda till June 6, forcing me to find work. Fortunately, on arrival a young lady with stunning frizzy blonde hair named Rachel, at the Bermuda Biological Station, scooted around tourist on a moped in St. George's Harbour and ended up in the drink, scooter and all. She swam to the dock, was pulled up and then me and other men put my little anchor and line around the moped and pulled it to land. My ultimate act was to dive in and immediately find her moped keys while the guys cleared her bike's carburetor of salt water. That made me a bit of a hero, there was chemistry, and we became lovers for a week or so!

When I went to the Bio Station with other scientists like Bjorn to see the Glow Worms mating, and for a picnic, all the men wanted to know what my secret was to have landed their biggest catch! Thankfully, Alfred and Paula finding distant relatives on the US Navy base who took our cash and bought food at the PX store for significant discounts. Mark and I were waiting outside the impressive base gates and brought the bags of shopping back to the boat. Extremely generous and risky on many people's part!

Sunday, 9th June, 11 pm; on the radio we learned that a man was lost overboard to the south; drowned. 37°N, 62°W, c.300 nm north of Bermuda. Just narrowly avoided a collision with a Bulgarian merchant ship. It passed less than a mile from our port side. We lingered in St. George's, Bermuda, for ten days. Ships and crews rot in port. Someone asked me if *Xebec* was my 'yacht'. No, not mine, and not a 'yacht.' *Xebec* is a sailboat. I help to sail her. *Loophole* and *Stormy Weather* (1936 yawl) alongside us. Paul, captain of *Stormy Weather*, sailed north into the ice packs on the way to France just to chip an iceberg for iced gin and tonics!

Departure at 8 pm on Thursday, 6th June. On stormy departure, *Loophole*'s First Mate caught his jacket on *Xebec* while pushing off from quarantine dock and was stuck with us. We gave him back, which is just as well. He spent 14 weeks at Cambridge. Mark performed the Kiwi All Black Maori war dance in full volume on the foredeck. We blew our horns. *Loophole*'s crew mooned us. Put on our running lights, and headed through the channel. Few times in my life have I been so profoundly moved. Scared might be the word. I'd left that harbour for Portugal the previous summer and never made it. Sombrely I tied up our ensign, dug up the safety harnesses, and prepared for at least three weeks of very trying, very true, sailing. It has proved a gruelling voyage. Separated by *Loophole* within hours. Never saw her again.

Alfred (Cannon), Mark, lovely lady in photo, me, Martin with condom on hand, in salon of *Xebec* in Bermuda.

Monday, 10th June, 9:06 pm. 38°N, 61°W. Today is the glorious celebration of Martin' 35th birthday. We put on the autopilot and engine. The sun shone, and sea spread before us as flat as our pancakes at breakfast. By which time we'd drunk a bottle of Gosling's Black

Seal rum, and were savouring Mark's infamous Gin and Tangs. Sumptuous. Mark and I brought Martin drinks in hammock, tidied up, read.

At the birthday boy's beck and call as we nearly finished our northward leg from Bermuda of 400 miles and prepared for the fiercest and most terrifying two weeks of weather in this sailor's existence. It is literally the calm before the storm and Martin while being served Gin and Tang suggested we hand-wash the railings with fresh water, which we ultimately ran out of.

We finally set off for Belgium, Europe on Thursday, June 6, arriving in Nieuwpoort, Belgium on Thursday, June 27, exactly three weeks (21 days) later, having in the interim run out of refrigeration , and all preserved meats and vegetables, satellite navigation, sugar, milk, eggs, butter, coffee, jam. Even the drinking water was contaminated with rust particles and salty water. We never had more than a final dribble of booze, shavings of tobacco, anything, and the water was cold; usually you can heat water while running the engine, but Martin did not have enough money to fill up with fuel, so we were forced to find harsh extremely windy belts of weather in order to make it to Europe in time for a charter of his and before we starved!

No veggies or fruit, and the crew were upset with me when I traded Goslings Black Seal rum for two packs of cigarettes from Dutch sailors off England; and that I had smoked some residual tobacco I found that provided about two puffs but sent them wild. And Dick Murphie, owner *Maja*, a small sailboat I worked on in St. George's, caringly wrapped four bags of Bourbon Crème chocolate biscuits for me to eat along the way, twice daily after each watch!

Saturday, 15th June, 5 am. 42°N, 46°W. Entry explains itself: 1,120 nm NNE. of Bermuda, 1,900 miles from Bishop's Rock, Scilly Islands, England. North Atlantic. Waters cold and grey. Paula understandably queasy. Captain Splash doesn't know what to make of it. Her litter box washed overboard. *Xebec* running downwind under bare poles, with only the Yankee and Mizzen sails up. We are making 8-12 knots; at times all 35 tons surf down the waves at 15-17 knots! The wind is blowing a steady 40 knots, with gusts as high as 60. The seas are blown in sheets of spray against us. On the Beaufort Scale, we are experiencing the worst Force 10-11. Martin reports that they were blowing 67+ earlier this morning. This is hurricane force wind.

Xebec in a gale mid-Atlantic, all halyards broken and sails lashed, still doing 14 knots down the fronts of 40-foot swells. Our anemometer broke at 67 knots, it was hurricane force.

Sunday, 16th June, 7 pm. 44:15°N, 39:50°W, on *Xebec* headed for Bishop's Rock. Today has to have been one of the shit days of the voyage. I'm afraid, after 1.5 months and 2,500 miles. During my shift from 6 am to 8 am. Martin and I discovered that we had: 1) blown the Main halyard, the sail was whipping on deck, not lashed; 2) blown (torn) the Stays'l; 3) blown the Mizzen and Main preventers; and 4) flayed the awnings and the covers for the varnished rails. I wore safety harness once, changing sails on the bowsprit, clinging half-submerged to doused sails. (Took them 45 minutes to find Jim. He was comatose. He lived. Lucky.) Many a time do I rest with a knot in my stomach. Many a time must I lay down for ten minutes in full gear, thinking about the coming hours on watch? All I can do is put full body weight on the helm, hoping she doesn't turn towards the waves (fatal). Shoulders ache. Hands swollen. We didn't expect the cold. A. wears paper bags on head, hands, and feet. Have an infection festering on my left foot from a scratch in Anguilla. Have not braved a look at it. Too c-c-c-cold to take off boots and socks.

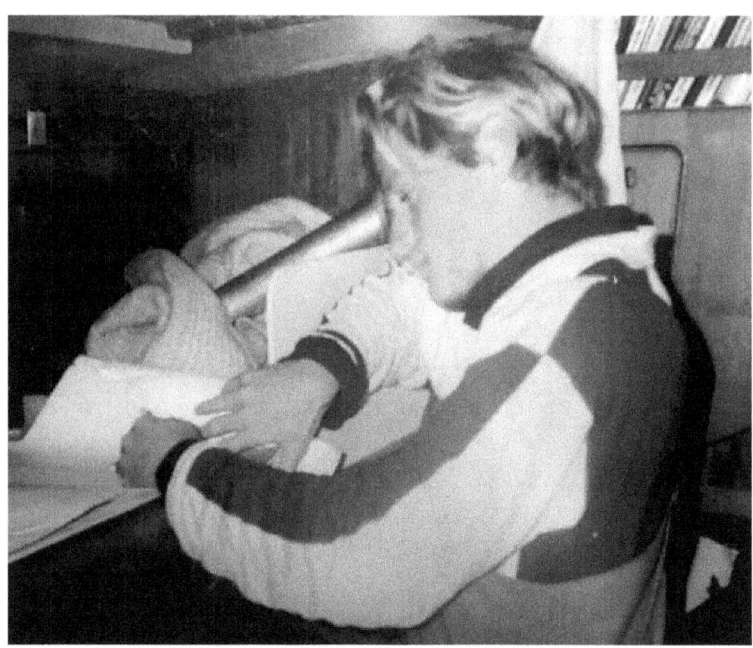

Navigating and trying to keep up with Martin, who missed Bermuda and slept though shorter passages, was difficult. I had to use the back of my other chart – note the silver tube to the right, that is the base of the mast of the sailboat I broke in Boston at MIT. I kept the charts safe in there. The clothing you see never came off, it was too cold. We were all losing a lot of weight by this time – not the right hand.

To his credit, the skipper, Martin made bread every morning, which the crew would fight over to get 1, maybe 2 slices to last the whole day in 40 foot seas and winds recorded at 67 knots before the anemometer was blown away. Parts of our deck were literally splintered and all our sails damaged or destroyed (we still made 14 knots surfing down the waves). Ships offered to save us, and on arrival in Europe our water was rusty and salty, our only daily hot meals were a handful of rice or pasta, we all lost about 30 pounds.

He said he was going to dock our pay for damage done to the toilets, but none of us used the plumbing for 2+ weeks, a female passenger living in the main cabin and galley was constantly pelted by the sharp movements with cutlery, and we were asked on arrival in Belgium how we survived the storm. Since we had lived in the same weather system for over 2 weeks, we naturally asked "what storm" because it had become our norm - it didn't come and go over us, it literally carried us, and we rode in it. The gastronomic problems when we gorged on "real" food in Belgium, including lots of ice cream, chocolate and beer. Oh well...

Sunday, 23rd June, 4:50 GMT, 48°N, 12°W, c.300 nm SW of Bishop's Rock, 65 nm from final destination: Nieuwpoort, Belgium. ETA 27th June. Entry: Am reading Kundera, Marquez, Hesse, Conrad. We listen to tapes of Bee Gees, Gypsy Kings, Santana, Jacques Brel, Paul Anka, and Peruvian music. Stereo lashed down. Couldn't afford to "top up" on provisions or fuel in Bermuda. Only second week and completely out of: eggs, milk, butter, sugar, coffee, oil, crackers, meat, veggies – of course no smokes or booze. For 23 hours after dinner at 9 am we are rationed to two slices of Martin' homemade bread with whatever we find. Rarely anything. Dinner normally pasta or rice.

My trick at the wheel. The noise from shredded awnings and the creaking of broken shattered wooden railings was terrifying and distracting. Even our harness tether, shown here vibrating so rapidly it's mostly invisible in the lower right corner, made a hell of a racket vibrating in the wind as you see.

Accosted Cannon when he came off morning watch and took huge bites from our daily loaf of bread. I called him a thief. Shouldn't have. He drew kitchen knife from the rack and held it to my throat saying he was going to cut me, kill me, poison me, cut my eyes out. I looked up from my book, which had become a blur, and told him to put the knife down. Began to 'read' again. Highly agitated, he pressed throat harder. I looked up at him and told him with surprising honesty that if he drew my blood, I would kill him. On the spot. With my own hands. Paula intervened, shrieking. Grabbed his arm. Stephanie's parting reminder: vessels alter course for Bermuda to drop off bodies of murdered crew and imprison killer. Never have my hands shaken so much at the helm of a boat as when, moments after A's attack, I climbed the companion way and relieved Mark for two hours.

Tuesday, 25th June, 8 pm. Day 19; 7°W., 50°N. *LAND HO!* Just after my 2 pm watch began, deciphered through the fog and drizzle faint trace of an outline of land (Bishop's Rock, England). Strained as they were, my eyes did not deceive me. For a few moments laughed to myself. My smile would have made a Cheshire cat envious. Slid hatch to Martin' cabin open: "Martin?" "Yes?" He was sleeping. "I think I've sighted land." Pause. "What makes you think so?" Pause. I think to myself. Unable to resist: "Because I am looking at it, Martin." Still three days of sailing. Today has truly been one of the happiest days of my life. When we unfurled our mouldy Antiguan flag, its golden sun seemed to bring out the real sun from behind the clouds. After two weeks of grey, we welcomed the warm sunshine as a long-lost friend. Tonight, we whisk past the dark silhouettes of merchant ships, peacefully gliding along the Cornish coast, savouring the womb-like presence of land around us.

Editorial: Most kindergartners know that if you leave North America, as Leif Erikson and Christopher Columbus did ages ago, and sail east for enough weeks or months, the land you end up hitting isn't China or South America, but Europe. Pretty elemental. So to be surprised that we found land after 21 days is just, simply, staggering. Perhaps surrounding himself with all our food addled his mind. Or the deprivation of life without Paula, smokes, drinks, or drugs. At least we had the Bee Gees and Abba though!

Paula, Mark and Mark passing Eddystone Lighthouse, which was featured in *Moby Dick*!

Wednesday, 3rd July, 1991, 12 noon. Train from London to Oxford. We arrived aboard *Xebec* in Nieuwpoort, Belgium, at c.6 pm GMT+2 on Thursday, 27th June, after almost exactly three weeks at sea (21 days virtually to the hour). Captain Splash had a run-about on *terra firma*, and we made our way to warmth, Duivel beer, and Belga cigarettes in the KNYC: Royal Yacht Club at Nieuwpoort. Though can't honestly say that in my state its 'Royalty' meant a damned thing to me, we were treated hospitably. Martin fed us well. The Stats: 4,000 nm sailed. South to North we crossed 35 lines of Latitude; 2,000 nm West to East, some 30 lines of Longitude, for 3,000 nm: 6 time zones, 3 layovers, 7 weeks, 30+ days at sea, 100+ watches each. Innumerable tears, pain, and longings.

Postscript: Anyway, we arrived safely in Belgium, and a few days later, when Martin began to worry I might be a liability and get him in trouble with immigration, and Alfred and Paula had, I met Mrs. Misiree, Martin' mother, who owned most of the boat. Martin made it to the start of a charter for the One-Ton World Cup, in which we saw renown sailing rock-star Laurie Mains and crew.; they liked to be sponsored by cigarette companies like Merit so the could smoke for free! However the proceeds of this windfall which we helped me make, never trickled down to us; rather we were assigned to clean up the mess in the lockers, mostly rotting rags and a rusty soup of old fishing hooks, nails, screws, paint cans, and unusable equipment like his diving gear. It was all ruined by weeks of inundation in salt water.

The noise of storms was such that we would not even have noticed water sloshing at our side. We memorably dined at Nieuwpoort Yacht Club, the highlight of which was eating meat and even a chocolate covered ice cream! But man, was the downside painful, as we grappled with reactivating bowel movements for the first time in nearly three weeks; that process was so excruciating that gastroenterologists informed me that my body manufactured nearly seven feet of redundant intestine for such contingencies, something usually only seen in older sedate men. Also, the surgeries for this condition began in Fall of 1995 in Newport and have spanned half a dozen in Connecticut after 2006 up to 2016, then New York City 2018, and Boston in 2019, and are likely to continue, at one point leading to critical sustained anemia.

Martin' letter of reference read "I give you my favorite souvenir from the Caribbean," as though I were an exotic stripper, not someone whose experience and calm helped him cross oceans while he dithered. He did, however introduce me to a colleague in Nieuwpoort as a reliable mate who helped him accomplish the voyage. By that point the local Belgian customs and immigration were tracking Martin down for people smuggling and not clearing us in, and Alfred and Paula were reported to authorities for attempting to find work in Belgium illegally, as obviously Martin had no intention of paying for them. I personally witnessed an irate government official stride down to the boat and ask who the fuck I was (in French) and where was the goddamn skipper to bring all these foreigners in under his nose? He was clearly about to lose his job because of Martin.

During the fancy race charter, which I was forced to endure, but refused to either leave the boat or work anymore before I was paid, I broke down in tears when a matronly charter guest asked why I was sulking alone hour after hour on the foredeck with my bags packed. Martin was realizing that a pissed off, broke crew could be bad for business, and whatever reputation he had left. When Martin failed to clear me through immigration or to pay me, I finally took the $60 he offered for seven weeks work, a pathetic letter of reference, and his mother hosted me for a sherry-rich debriefing. I thought this would lead to dinner and a good night's sleep, but rather I was ejected, drunk and hungry at 10 pm into a rainy night in a foreign country and forced to hitchhike with my sea-bag from Nieuwpoort to Oostende, where the ferries leave. I arrived soaked and broke and could finally understand Jacques Brel's angry tirade of a song, named *Amsterdam*.

I arrived about 1 am in the terminal, bought a one-way ticket for about $40, and used $10 on more ice cream in a drab but warm café overlooking the harbour. I left about 3 am and arrived by ferry in the UK around dawn. In the queue I was asked how I planned to support myself in the UK for the summer before attending Oxford, on just $15 and no credit card or right to work? I just told him I had a sister in a posh area of London and that my Dad usually took care of us from Bahamas, and amazingly I was admitted!

Then off to London, with no money, arriving in the UK about 2 am on Sunday June 30. After scraping through British immigration and boarding the train to London, I was amazed not to be thrown off, as the conductor did boot another young passenger without enough cash to buy a ticket. I arrived in London's Victoria Station and from there, laden with backpack, foul-smelling laundry bag, and book bag, I boarded the metro or tube, as it is known. It was then sunrise by the time I arrived back to Earl's Court tube (metro) station in London (SW 5), where I'd been during the St. George's School choir tour of March, 1988; to stay with Ann, on Old Brompton Road three years earlier.

I called sister and her boyfriend. After they had slept in and negotiated out of an expensive champagne brunch at a hotel, I walked to their gorgeous and spacious apartment on Harcourt Terrace, in SW 10. They live a mere block or so from the Troubadour Café, between Finbrough Road, Old Brompton and Coleherne roads, where I spent several hours killing time and writing in my diary at the storied venue which launched the careers of many budding musicians in the 1960s London. Off Fulham Road, Harcourt Terrace is notable for its pillared stairways and was used as a setting in scene the dog-crushing scene from Monty Python's film *A Fish Called Wanda*; the offspring of a prime minister lived across the way, and a veteran female journalist shared the same hall.

Fax from London: "Dear Mom & Dad; We reach! I made it safely "across," I'm pleased to say, arriving in Nieuwpoort, Belgium at 8 pm. Thurs 27 June after exactly 3 weeks from leaving Bermuda. All in all a good voyage, though three gales, one with seas up to 30 feet, and winds recorded at 67 knots, gusting to 70 knots (a hurricane starts at 63). Managed to tear all sails but one, rip off awnings, snap planking, etc. Boat very safe, however skipper, very good excellent dinners, though during days only bread and water. Only problem came when the Antiguan crew member threatened me with a knife when I confronted him stealing food. This was never a serious threat. OK I'm now in London…. Came by ferry Sunday June 30. By July 7 I should be aboard War Baby in Lymington, setting off for Scotland. Will visit Oxford. More important: I have absolutely No Money. One change of clothes. I would hate spending five months sponging off people. Can you help? Eric"

To illustrate the money issues I faced: from Bermuda, I had asked Ann to send me some cash which I knew Dad had sent her, on to Belgium for when I arrived flat broke in July. Instead of finding any funds in Belgium, I arrived in London to find my letter begging for funds in Belgium, and a reply being written on the desk – unsent – asking "where are you?" This total miscommunication was compounded by none of the funds which were sent to my sister ever reaching me, and even the clothing my mother sent from L.L. Bean was returned, rather than funds being spent to pay the customs duties.

Finally, many weeks later, the situation wax fixed somewhat by going around her, with funds being sent directly to a rickety supply chain of family friends in the UK, Dublin, and France. The result of course was that for the balance of the summer I was chronically broke, poorly dressed, would not think of spending on a haircut, and was made fun of by fellow crew for my inability to buy rounds of drinks after they had bought me rounds. I felt like shit, and they were right. But that entire summer I was never paid beyond $9 for sailing, and had no other sources of income except day work and sometimes skimming on funds given me to buy the daily paper, to buy a sweet, for which I was caught.

I stayed with them for six days, from June 30 to today, July 6, or Sunday to Saturday. Sunday night I relaxed with a beer at local Hollywood Arms pub nearby on Hollywood Terrace, and had a good dinner; I heard young British Army officers regaling their friends about stints in India and Belize. On day I had afternoon drinks with Sam of Finborough Road days; he lost toes on a failed ascent of Mount Everest so his paramour (and my friend) Ed, Cricket's "other" friend in the US, sent him a pair of flip-flops! The Euro-tunnel (*Chunnel*) from Folkstone, England to near Calais, France is due to open in 1993). We had a great dinner on Monday of Swedish *pytt i panna* (pieces in a pan) with *Punch* sweet and potent Swedish spirits in a chilled bottle, and banana bread. I was starved, after being aboard low-budget *Xebec* for two months! Tuesday night was casual, with fellow *Xebec* survivor Mark coming over in the evening at around 8 pm and staying for dinner. The next morning it was off to Oxford by train, where I registered for courses on Shakespeare and Oxford History past to present at Manchester College where I shall *read*, or study, for three terms.

Later, I saw Mark in Auckland and Cannon, who had shot his own brother and had his earnings stolen by and locked up by his brother-in-law, as well as held a knife to my throat twice on the voyage, and threatened to poison my food and cut my eyes out while I slept) in Antigua. Paula (who saved me from the knife attacks my saying that all my blood would mess up her cabin and that Alfred would go to jail again), and Martin, her unlucky suitor, I never saw again. The voyage may have put hair on my young chest, but it also sure played a destructive number on my innards, from which I'll never fully recover.....

July 17th, 1991, ...My dream goal is to put boating, skippers, family, and school behind me for at least a week or two and run off to Prague, where I would use a cache of US dollars to rent a bed and breakfast and be by myself. There, in privacy, I could make bread, drink, and write in privacy and in a beautiful culture and setting, un-heckled by the hindrances which I ran to sea to escape, and which I find haunting me again. I feel my vulnerability to others changing their plans, as Martin, skipper of *Xebec* did, changing his itinerary and crew several times from Antigua to Belgium via St. Martin, Anguilla, Bermuda and having our destinations changed from Guernsey to Falmouth, Brittany, and Newport.

The cities are too close to me again, the problems of the world to intricately ensuring me again, after my physical and spiritual purge aboard *Xebec*. I've become slothful and fattened by this fine cuisine and nights in harbor. I need to get back out there, on my own. No one has tried to inhibit me, restrain me, betrayed, me even though Martin came close. I've allowed myself to enter into more acts of communion, and surrendered my privacy again. On my next boat the trauma of the *Xebec* voyage became known to all my crewmates, as I would leap out of my bunk in underwear screaming and sweating.

PS: Afterwards *Stormy Weather*'s skipper owner Paul Adamthwaite told me that they had to tie a violent crew member to the mast and deprive him of food until he settled down. On the same passage he claimed to have chipped ice from an iceberg for their gin and tonics, *en route* to a wooden boat festival in Brittany. Perhaps that diversion had driven the errant crew around the bend? [Capt. Paul and I remain in contact].

Saturday, November 16th, 1991, 6:33 pm. Crouched in front of the computer, Manchester College, Oxford. Exceedingly grey and foggy – dangerous weather to bicycle in. Epilogue: Hurricane Grace ravaged Bermuda earlier this month. Several boats were dismasted. *Anna Christina* (95 foot) lost. *Xebec* with Martin, Paula, A. and Captain Splash crossing Atlantic back to Antigua presently. *Kapitan Splatz* – I'm sure sorely missed by fellow-feline in English Harbour. Neither spoken to or heard of any crew of *Xebec* or

Loophole. They now live in a sphere distinct from my own. It is a sphere into which anyone is welcome, but which one only attains by being there. By living in it.

November 22ⁿᵈ, 2001 During law school in my early 30s, I was treated for heavy internal bleeding by Dr. Sanford, gastroenterologist on President's Avenue, north side of Fall River, Massachusetts. Still, I have very bad bleeding from Trans-Atlantic voyage on *Xebec* in 1991. Took two surgeries, four per stay in critically anemic, last surgery 2016.

Chapter 4

Voyage 9: *War Baby*, Lymington, England - Ireland - Brittany, France, 1991
Voyage 30: *War Baby*, Marion - Bermuda Race, Newport, then Pilot's Point, CT, 1999
Voyage 44: *War Baby*, Newport - Bermuda Race, 2000

Postcard of *War Baby* taken by Beken of Cowes, Isle of Wight, given to crewmembers.

July 1, 1991, Monday, *War Baby* Fax: sent from London to Hamilton, Bermuda, care of, Archie Brown & Son, Ltd. "Dear Captain Brown, Hullo again, thank you kindly for your letter of June 18. I look forward very much to familiarizing myself with *War Baby* and more so to meeting you upon your return to England. I was terribly sorry to have missed you in Bermuda during *Xebec*'s trans-Atlantic crossing. As it was, we made a hasty departure in the afternoon of June 6, the very day you were to return to Bermuda. The day was spent in feverous preparations, and I was unable even to call. Regardless, we shall meet within a week here in the UK. The voyage trans-Atlantic aboard *Xebec* was very successful, lasting 21 days, straight to Nieuwpoort, Belgium, This is the soonest that I could fax you. With our missed connections in recent weeks, it seems appropriated that we should meet at *War Baby* on the very eve of what should be wonderful sailing! Until then, sincerely yours, Eric PS My sister enjoyed speaking with you."

July 11, 1991, Thursday, 12.15 pm. Aboard *War Baby* for Captain Jim Leonard's interior tour, Queen Ann's Battery, Plymouth, Devon, SW England. Work list: generator switch, switch off in bosun's locker, engine alternator to right of panel, water heater begins automatically, run time is 1.5 hours. Morning and evening watch should shift engine generator strain. Heater draws 22 amperes; refrigeration needs 3 hours a day, bilge, engine and trays beneath water tanks should remain dry. Fresh water filter, watch for air, pulls Brooks and Gatehouse impellers to clear Perkins engine, which is 4 cc. All dispatch, dip once a week, check in order to top it up, change oil filter with pump engine at top. Fan belts have spaces there for enabling the top-up of oil. Watch not once, but twice daily on main engine. There are three water tanks, of 60 gallons each. Clean bosun's locker, keep screws, change fuel, two huge diesel tanks under main salon seats. When refueling, open the air-release valves, so as to let air out. Check level-measuring dipstick in bosun's locker; 2 inches from bottom is 20 gallons. Don't ever let it get too low, as muck in the bottom of the tank gets sucked into the system and clogs filters, which can shut down the engine. Fuel table of levels is on the door to the bosun's locker at transom, or stern area.

Seals are on top of tanks to enable us to check for leaks. Check water in engine generator on chart, most important are the black dots. Important that we check sea-cocks in toilet, bilge pumps, raw, or salt-water intake valve for refrigerator, aft head discharge. Aft shower sink discharge for galley, Bristol Mafia (mis-spelt a name brand?). Both toilets (or *heads*) have holding tanks. Jim called secretary David Jones at work. Ring road between Brixham and Plymouth. Electrician picked him up at the marina; his name is Richard.

The new crew members are now all aboard Captain Warren Brown's Sparkman and Stevens 60-foot sloop, built in Palmer and Johnson's yard in Wisconsin, and winner of famous 1979 Fastnet Race as *Tenacious* under owner and skipper Ted Turner, who came up with the idea for CNN while sailing on her. What a yacht we are on! And what a comprehensive history, and kaleidoscope-wedge of the sailing world comes with familiarizing ourselves with her. When I say *we* I am referring to myself and the two other new crew-members, Mathew Ratsey (yes, of Ratsey and Lapthorn sail makers in Cowes, England, which *Xebec* used) and Steven Davis, whose father works for British Steel, a major yacht race sponsor, and whose grand-mum lives in Lymington (Matt is from London).

Fortunately, we have joined *War Baby* together on July 6, virtually within minutes of each other. This is very good, as we are all ages 19 to 21, and not overwhelmed by veteran *War Baby* sailors, of which there are hundreds, from Skip Novak and so forth. The other crew already number nearly ten, with Geoff Pack a co-editor for *Yachting Monthly* magazine, for which he is writing an article entitled *One Man and his Boat, Warren Brown and* War Baby, January 1992 edition on pages 94 to 95.

Having "ground," or wound a crew up *War Baby* mast using the winch, I am then photographed by them as I look out for their safety. The round white item on the 2nd spreader up to the left of me is a radar unit. The lines on the spreaders hold canvas sheathing to protect them and the sails from each other. This is the UK, we are at dock, Matthew or Steve took the photo. A smart grinder will select the lightest crewmate to go up, and therefore spare a lot of heavy lifting!

Very importantly, there is Captain Jim Leonard, a wonderful chap, who has logged hearing 100,000 miles on various *War Baby's;* Jim was knocked overboard in the middle of the Gulf Stream on a race to Bermuda and could not swim! He stayed afloat using air pockets created in his clothes for 42 minutes before they found and rescued him. Since then he and his wife (understandably) bought a farm to restore in Wales, far from the ocean! There have been ten yachts owned by Warren Brown and his long-standing Bermudian family who built up Browns of Bermuda; a storied retail firm on Front Street in Hamilton. They are all named *War Baby*, since their inception as a dinghy by Warren's grandfather in Bermuda before or during World War I, and hence the name: a *baby of the war*.

Jim and Geoff left us today, in Plymouth. Jim and his wife Dolly live in a restored farm near Wales, and Geoff and wife both have children, each are about 40 years old. Jim has been skipper on and off for 14 years. The various other skippers of *War Baby* have included the renown American extreme latitudes navigator, Skip Novak of Russian boat *Fazizi* fame, as well as Whitbread 1989 to 1990. Also joining us in Lymington was Charles (Charlie) Berry, a humorous British eccentric of 84 years with a colonel's mustache, a veteran of the Royal Air Force, who has sailed with *War Baby* for thousands of miles including Bermuda races (Marion and Newport) and a cruise north from England along the west coast of Norway to the Lofoten Islands, Spitzbergen, and numerous rarely visited, extremely cold and treacherous corners of the Arctic.

War Baby has been down in the Antarctica and up to the North Pole, along the Greenland coasts, across the Atlantic numerous times, and around the whole of South America, not to mention Admirals Cups, Fastnet races, Antigua Race Week; I could go on forever about the history and cache of *War Baby* and tremendously well-known Warren Brown, and I doubtlessly I will. Films, documentaries, and numerous articles, have been based on her exploits. Warren brought her from US media tycoon Ted Turner in 1980, after she established herself as indestructible and fast in the Fastnet Race which sank and drowned many. She was built on the Great Lakes, designed by Sparkman and Stephens, outfitted by Brooks and Gatehouse of the UK.

In terms of crew, Michael of Bermuda and England, age 60, will join us to the Isles of Scilly off the English west coast, then we'll pick up a couple and hopefully a cook in Dublin. We've sailed 100 miles so far, departing beginning 10 am Tuesday, July 9, and arriving Weymouth that evening. Then we departed Weymouth at 9 am July 8, rounding Portland Bill, during which we were swamped, or pooped (when a wave from behind fills the cockpit), by a rogue wave in the cockpit. This surprise left us all up to our chests in water with cigarettes floating! The boat is well equipped and none of the water got below.

We then arrived in Plymouth circa 7 pm. We leave for Salcombe [which we passed] and Dartmouth tomorrow. In Plymouth, on my first day, a gentleman who personally sailed with world-renowned sailors Miles and Beryl Smeeton, authors of *The Sea was Our Village, Once is Enough, Because the Horn is There*, and *High Endeavours*, paid *War Baby* a visit and socialized with Warren in the main saloon. Listening to them talk brought mythic figures to life [and I was learning that by the third bottle of rum sailor's stories can transport fiction to fact if the listener is not careful!].

One of our fellow crew kindly took and mailed this photo after I had had a chance to fatten up. Capt. Warren is fond of dipping our ensign, seen here to the right, forcing naval vessels to return the courtesy, only it takes much more effort for them to usually!

July 17, 1991, Wednesday 11.35 am, GMT plus 2. Aboard *War Baby* between Dartmouth and Lymington. No wind, or very little, with seas flat. Partly sunny, hazy, and humid. Major change of plans. Last night *War Baby* suffered the worst damage that she has sustained in the decade-plus that Warren has owned her. Dartmouth is a beautiful historic town nestled along the River Dart, at its mouth; the setting of various films, including *Treasure Island* and *Kidnapped*. The current in the river, however, during the shift of tides, is up to five knots, maybe even more. The tides are very strong.

For the second time we attempted to depart for Falmouth, on the SW tip of England, on the ebbing tide between 1 and 2 am. The night before, the engine had failed to work, and we stayed yesterday to repair drained solenoids and poor connections between the starter motor solenoids, and the gear box of the Perkins cylinder engine. This morning at 2.15 am, mere minutes after falling in from our bunks, we young crew pulled up the sacrificial anodes; aluminum or neutralizing nodes, to attract electrical current from other metals ships in harbors and protect the rudder, shafts, motor of the aluminum hull.

Then, as instructed by the after-guard, we cast off the bow and spring and stern lines from a moored trawler in the middle of the River Dart. We then tried to shove off our starboard side from the abandoned hulk, with the bow pointing directly down-river, towards the mouth. Before we even had the engine in gear, the yacht was veering precariously to starboard, pushed against the trawler by a cross-current, against which three young crew and older (as in their sixties and seventies) Charlie and Michael shoved.

Sadly, we didn't shove hard enough to clear the 60-foot boat clear of the Admiralty Buoy, a huge, floating steel drum which serves as a mooring for the trawler. The entire starboard side, meanwhile, sustained a grabbing crash with the moored trawler, at the bow and trailing past midships to the stern. The worst has yet to come. The stern swirled off to starboard, dragged harshly against the trawler and our high-tech, ultra-modern (and costly) equipment. The forwardmost part, or bowsprit, of the trawler's port side loomed a good six feet or more over our toe-rail, or deck.

With a loud tearing noise, soon accompanied by sparks and popping sounds, the steel mast which holds our Furuno radar module, antennas, and radio equipment, was torn from its base and dragged by the force of the moving boat behind us, resting askew across and transom. Finally, we cleared the mooring, but only after the man-overboard module (MOM) had also been torn free, floating downstream, leaving us with no gaff, or hooked pole, on hand in to rescue it. We struggled in the current and silent darkness to regain the floating bag holding the device until finally, within half an hour, the current pushed us dangerously close to moored sailboats and shallower water.

Then we limped back to the trawler, this time port side to it, with our starboard side, scarred badly, facing outward for all and sundry to see when the sun rose. After launching the dinghy we found that there were three nasty gauges at the bow, which dug right through about four millimeters of enamel coating and paint, to the sensitive base of aluminum. We detached some of the beacons and lashed the broken support mast generally upright before assessing the situation. We opted for orange juices, as we had been feeling pretty groggy from beers, rum and wine from 6 pm to 10 pm, two bottles of wine over dinner and, for the others, stiffer drinks. Warren and the crew tried to determine a good plan.

Five of us (Matthew, Steven and I) have been together aboard *War Baby* for nearly a fortnight (since July 6): we've lost the skipper, Jim, the reporter (Geoff) and Charles' old friend Michael. We lost Michael today, who, with a heavy heart, conceded that to voyage onward to Lymington, as opposed to Falmouth would be more of a problem than a joy. He has to retrieve his car in Plymouth. So, here we are. The time of reckoning again. Underway, making 7 knots and back to where we started.

The plan had been to proceed west to Falmouth, the Isles of Scilly, Dublin, then east to the Scottish Isles, cruising there for almost two weeks before, returning to Lymington by mid-August. There Charlie and Warren were to return to Bermuda, Warren only while *War Baby* had her underside done (cleaned) and basic repairs made before setting off on the third week of August for the Mediterranean Sea. From the Med, *War Baby* is to cruise for up to two or three months before embarking on an Atlantic crossing in November, post-hurricanes. Then, eventually she is to sail on to New Zealand and all the way around the planet.

Now we are scampering to Lymington to lick our wounds, spend up to a week there, repairing this damage, and possibly call off a cruise north to Scotland and Dublin altogether. The change of plans is as of yet completely undecided, though in the meanwhile we have turned east, away from our itinerary. This entails missing the northern islands altogether, which I find disappointing. As the other sailors have all cruised the Scottish Isles before, they don't mind writing it off, but as I saw it, we had the chance to do both, and northern islands, with their isolated settlements and foggy harbors and quiet pubs, has a definite appeal.

Warren is considering heading straight for the Mediterranean ASAP, which can be exciting and rewarding. Mallorca, Corsica, south of France, and Sardinia are in the works. Overall, all I find disappointing is that we've spent 10 good days just *mucking about* along a crowded stretch of coast 100 miles in width. Let's get moving! I get impatient with cruising, yet I have no say. I have several priorities before I resume my studies this year at Oxford. If *War Baby* ends up not progressing as much as hoped, and dawdles, drowning which high hopes, yet with only a few miles under the heel, I have to consider finding a job which pays.

As it stands, I am aiming to spend five months earning $80 in Bermuda, make that $84, including anchor chain I sold to the South African in Philipsburg, St. Martin, West Indies. This is not good. I should have had $1,000 in my pocket when I skipped ashore in Europe after a crossing. Yet I didn't. I had nothing, not even an airfare home; the legal minimum for international crew. It cost my parents up to $500 (already at $300) in expenses from London; where I stay with Ann and Gustaf. The cash they sent to my sister to be mailed to me in Belgium was spent by her shamelessly. The clothing my mom mailed to the UK was sent back to the US without my ever seeing it, notwithstanding that my sister's rent at SW1 is worth my entire annual school allowance. I'm in a bit of a jam, really.

So, my goal is to earn some money in the 2.5 months between now and October 9, which is when I enroll at Manchester College, Oxford. Though I have kept expenses to a minimum by hopping from boat to boat, with room and board covered, I remember earning $2,000 cash in Newport in one month last summer, holding down several jobs at once, to help me realize my other goals of going to see. I ought to find part-time work. My dream goal is to put boating, skippers, family, and school behind me for at least a week or two and run off to Prague, where I would use a cache of US dollars to rent a bed and breakfast and be by myself. There, in privacy, I could make bread, drink, and write and in a beautiful culture and setting, un-heckled by the hindrances which I ran to sea to escape, and which I find haunting me again.

I feel my vulnerability to others changing their plans, as Martin, skipper of *Xebec* did, changing his itinerary and crew several times from Antigua to Belgium via St. Martin, Anguilla, Bermuda and having our destinations changed from Guernsey to Falmouth, Brittany, and Newport. St. George's teacher Coleman also did this to us, essentially hijacking a car load of students in the age bracket he liked and not telling us where he was taking us for the weekend till we could tell which bridge he used; Jamestown Bridge meant New York or New *Jersey*, Tiverton Bridge meant Boston, or at least suggested it.... I want to be free. I want to feel that I'm ready. That I'm earning my independence and enabling myself to escape and step away; to reject what everyone else is struggling to enclose themselves with; consistency, and security. I feel like a courtesan, a boat boy, or worse BN (the *actual* job description in writing on my first summer boat job in New England, a horrific racial epithet). To avoid this is the best of my aspirations and desires.

If I don't step out while I can, it will be too late. I feel heckled. I have to write certain letters, make certain phone calls. The cities are too close to me again, the problems of the world to intricately ensuring me again, after my physical and spiritual purge aboard *Xebec*. I've become slothful and fattened by this fine cuisine and nights in harbor. I need to get back out there, on my own. No one has tried to inhibit me, restrain me, betrayed, me even though Martin came close. I've allowed myself to enter into more acts of communion, and surrendered my privacy again. Living aboard brings with it restraint and reserve and lack of privacy. I've been deliberate in my speech and accent, and am beginning to disguise my sweaty and peed-in bed clothes. I get nightmares, a kind of PTSD awaking shouting and sweating from sleep, sometimes leaping out of the top bunk! But it's receding. Trauma of the *Xebec* voyage. Can't hide any of that from my crew mates; it's a tiny space to live and work everyone hears everything.

Matt, Steve, me, & Howard S., funny cool guy and Vietnam veteran.

July 18, 1991, Thursday. Aboard *War Baby*. Food inventory: This is poignant, since *Xebec*'s food ran out! Freezer: 1 packet with 2 sirloin steaks, 1 packet with 2 rump steaks, 1 sirloin steak, 1 packet with 2 filet steaks, 1 packet with 2 beef burgers, 1 packet of mince beef, 1 packet New Zealand lamb (about 12 chops), 2 liters vanilla ice cream, 1 packet with 2 beef burgers, 2 packet streaky bacon (12 rashers each), 1 packet with 2 beef burgers, 1 packet of 8 rings of pork sausages, 2 1-pound packets of corn, half a packet of peas, 1 loaf of white bread.

A dinghy gives us a greater sense of freedom than the largest yacht because it is the largest. Death is the greatest fear, because it becomes greater. Smaller vessels have less to lose, ambition parallel. Boring. Danger, feelings mute quiet gut silky hair it's getting dark, cold, damp, cliffs scale a boat and crew are dinner to return to. I could have chosen more creative stone designs, but a full concept footstep growth rings of artistic potential. The truth of the bloody matter is that I feel old. Old. Tired. Bored. Lazy, Pathetic. We're not moving any-where now.

He we are aboard *War Baby*, which I worked so hard to be in invited to sail on when sending 50 or more letters during sophomore year, and my life is grinding to a mundane subservience under the overwhelmingly generous patronage of Warren Brown. I feel socially dull, and borderline inept, only I feel disinterested. I haven't lived as much as I did between Boston, the last heroic thrust of work consuming two to three weeks prior to departure, Antigua, and ultimately Nieuwpoort, Belgium. Arriving in Antigua, I was free as a bird, able to choose whether I wanted to stay or sail on a moment's notice, and better yet *where* to sail: Europe, Gibraltar, the Mediterranean, Newport, Brazil, Maine; anywhere!

Another night tonight. Going nowhere. Been here for too long; Lymington, on the Solent. It's Wednesday, and I've been here laid up with the boat almost a week? I crossed the fucking ocean for this; sitting on the best sailing machine I've ever boarded, with, very unlike *Xebec* or most boats, almost no expense limitations, and fitted out with the maximum, thorough degree of preparation. And we're not actually *going* anywhere yet (even though I could have done more to prevent the accident that landed us here, by pushing boats of many tons off each other in a thick current; not feasible at all!)

Thinking of having lived in Bahamas, the US eight years, Sweden six summers, and visits to and travel through Canada, Antigua, Norway, Finland, USSR, Ireland, Great Britain, Netherlands, Belgium, Luxembourg, France, Italy, Greece, Turkey, Yugoslavia, Czechoslovakia, Denmark, West & East Germany, Australia, and Anguilla. Forty bloody states, yet now I'm sitting in Lymington, England, holed up by the rain. Oxford is seeming quite foreboding now.

The people in England are almost too distant, even for me. Oxford seems to curtail its students' activities. Keeping tabs, so to speak. A list in each airport has every visiting student and which college in the UK. Very traditional, very stifling. Very proper. Basically, that's everything I sought to avoid after prep school, everything I succeeded at avoiding after arriving my first year at BC. Yet convention began to encroach the last year, living with seven others, dressing, acting, dating more conventionally, without the crazy drunken travels and job in a liquor store with ex-convicts.

At Walsh Hall in Boston during my sophomore year I started giving myself out to others; girlfriends like Veronica, Nicola and Megan; roommates, social contacts. Then I actually got along quite well with Martin for the last month. The wandering. The rest seems a litany of odd company; jobless bar-hand, the aspiring beautiful waitress and me; the generous student running away from school, social standing, relationships, responsibility; now across the pond the slow way to Europe. I think I strongly desire and need southern Europe. I want to rediscover peaceful Greek Isles. I want to hole myself up in a cheap room in Prague, surrounded by books and people who don't know me, and not necessarily people who don't know me.

Sam S. and I while getting water out of the dinghy. I am looking for Florence Arthaud, a crush, to sail past (she invited us all for a sail!). Clearly Sam has taken a swim.

July 30, 1991, Howth, Ireland, on peninsula about 12 miles NE of Dublin. How sad. I just learned in the *Irish Times* that Casandra Clunie-Ross, Cocos Islands clan environmental campaigner, aged just 25 is presumed dead on Vanuatu, in the Pacific islands. Princess of life, embarking on campaigns to save forestry, having just graduated from Cambridge and Oxford, full of hope and ambition! A fellow traveler, been to forests the world over to defend our planet's natural resources. Her plane piloted by a 34-year-old English pilot crashed in jungle. Whose parents are coming to grips with his death. Casandra praised by her older sister for being able to survive in jungle conditions, like other botanists, who had been living in camps. Seven bodies confirmed found. How sad. *Merd*! Another stingingly hot day.

August 4, 1991, Sunday. Royal Cork Yacht Club, founded in 1720. Oldest yacht club in world, though Neva Yacht Club might be two years older. In the port of Crosshaven, County Cork, southwest Ireland; I was last here in 1984. My debts, or IOU's: Warren: £10 Irish pounds. Steve Davis: £5.70 British pounds. The time is 7:53 pm. I am sitting in a tiny, den-like cave on the southern coast of Ireland, outside Crosshaven, overlooking the Irish sea. Enjoying the equivalent of an *après-smoke*, quietly snug in a natural dens, safe from the wind and the sea, on this barren, rugged coast. This beautiful stretch of coastline is reminiscent of Newport. I've been wandering through crags and over points of rock alone during the spring and winter of my final year at St. George's.

Especially once, I remember rehearsing my chapel talk; a self-composed address on individuality. Wonderful, lonely recollections of my sauntering around on my mountain-bike, reading, writing in my diary composing poems, such as *Boots*, and having those thick cigarettes. Perhaps enhancing my feeling of prep-school-hood is the new addition aboard *War Baby* of Howard and his wife Suzanne, and their daughter Tabor, who know Warren from Bermuda. *War Baby* will move from Crosshaven along Ireland's west coast before returning to England.

August 11, 1991, Sunday. Is Captain Jim to come down? *How to Anchor* book? Alan Boyd, yard manager at Berthon's who taught us to say "very unforgiving, those Genoa sheets!" with a Scottish brogue, returns to *War Baby* on September 1. She lies out of the water, *on the hard*, or propped up on land at Berthon's Marina, in Lymington. We've received sail repairs from Peter at Sanders Sails Limited sailmakers, on Bath Road here. Schedule: boat moving in a week: Alan says the boat will be out Tuesday to Wednesday, and back before next weekend.

After she was lifted a new coat of antifouling, and a new coat of paint will be applied, then testing of the auto-helm. Overlap: everyone has tasks. My punch-list of duties on *War Baby* in Lymington at drydock: re-inflate fender at air hose in yard, prepare dinghy engine, go over dinghy, go up mast to look at and cross out wind-vane shearing, pull out stove for Jill, help with laundry, fender socks, paint bottom, wash down heads (toilets) with hose and sponge, then dry, and wash out wet lockers without hatch on rear.

Oops! Our boat was too tall for the depth which the dockmaster mistakenly tucked us into, and worse, only the skipper noticed as the condiments rolled off the table! St. Malo, France.

August 17, 1991, Saturday morning. Stockholm, at Farmor's apartment. Sunny, partly cloudy, yet breezy and cool. Finally, away from boats. Last night I was treated with my siter and her fiancé, who are in Sweden for a sort of *engagement tour*, to dinner, compliments of Fredrik Posse at Paul and Norbert's *nouveau cuisine* restaurant on posh Strandvägen, which means *beach avenue*, on the harbor. Fredrik arrived on a very powerful black motorbike. After this final dinner we proceeded to a popular large night club for drinks and dancing. Called the Stork Club or something near Club Melody and Birger Jarlsgatan, a major nightlife thoroughfare downtown. We all had a very good time. We struggled home to our Farmor's on Karlavägen at 4 am after, for me alone, nearly three packs, and at least a dozen Scotch on the rocks.

I feel somewhat tired. Been at sea virtually non-stop for three months, nearly 6,000 miles. In that time, I've always been on call, at times it was dangerous, often tiring, and no real independence or pay. Taking orders and so on, which is the mode abroad any vessel. I want to go home. Being here is very good for my health. Mental health. I imagine that setting for Oxford will be a bit of a strain. They do keep close tabs on you, so I believe, though I have general advantages, such as extensive travel, having lived and worked in different environs, months spent in England, and having visited Oxford twice. It should still be a question of adapting. It shall be good to go home, photos from there are comforting and warm-seeming. Good to get there within a month (young). My birthday is coming up soon. I will probably call Andreas Ade this afternoon, in order to see him again.

August 20, 1991, *War Baby* notes from studying inventory as part of crew training by Captain Jim Leonard: Two outboard motors, cruising, a number two genoa, a 2.2-ounce spinnaker, diving tank, eleven-volt Hoover, two wire halyards, two rope halyards, deck cleats, life jackets, two LPG gas tanks, six 5-gallon water tanks, one cooler box, one Bombardier dinghy with rigid floor-boards. We are to leave September 2nd. Fifty British pounds. Warren Brown's assistant; Mrs. Pennyweather, at Marylebone, London W1. I am to be there Tuesday, September 3rd, at 1.55 pm. International call. We are to sail to the European continent: Channel Islands. Matthew Ratsey, family home in Kensington. Proposal! Last Wednesday's call home. Friday morning, Stockholm. Call Ann, photocopy letters, September 28. Assemble emergency lamp, with battery. Fix forward running light lenses; lock. Drain bilge in aft head. Attach lamps to harnesses, sail bags for genoa. Mrs. Hutchins (Steve Davis's grandmother), 14 Daniel's Walk Lymington, (she protested being asked to clean crew laundry!).

August 23, 1991, Friday 1 pm. West Cowes Marina, Cowes, Isle of Wight, southern extreme of England.

August 24, 1991, Saturday, 5.30 pm (GMT-1). No longer in Cowes. Rather, we are underway halfway to Channel Islands (Alderney) on our way to *Bretagne* (Brittany) or Cherbourg, France arriving Monday, August 26. It is three days till my 21st birthday. I'll call home collect then, yay! Go home soon. Lines *Hee, hee he*. Thinking of Clara M. of Karlaplan, Stockholm, whose father went to school with our father.

August 25, 1991, Sunday, 5.15 pm. Alderney, Channel Islands, UK. Foggy, cool, breezy, struggling sunshine. Sent letter and fax correspondence.

Oops! With friends like this... the crew have draped the mast and rigging with a poster naming me and wishing me Happy 21st Birthday, as well as Warren, the same day. However it was on the back of a white sheet and they wrote the large messages with black magic marker on white deck. Next day I worked my hangover off by scrubbing the ink out of the hallowed deck! That's Sam, Teddy, Jill and Warren. Channel Islands.

August 27, 1991, Tuesday, *War Baby* Fax: "Good morning all! I miss *Ma'Wessel*, our home, Chippy & Paunch, everyone! I've given my word to help sail War Baby till sept. 19. Then I will fly either Nantes or Paris France to Miami to Nassau. All well here, though I am tired, I shall come home ASAP. Am in Guernsey, Channel Islands. It is Skipper Warren Brown's birthday too! Cakes, Banners, gifts, etc. for both, thought I miss home and wish I could be with you! Thanks for many letters and faxes. My sailing now is an investment to be paid in future: references, and so on. Though Maybe I work in Nassau. Please send my annual dues to Hassle Free Inc. crew agency for me, the check I mailed bounced. Sorry about the turtle raft in the pond sinking. I went to the British Maritime Museum in Greenwich, Churchill."

August 30, 1991, Friday, *War Baby* letter: To Paul & Norbert restaurant, Stockholm. "I am writing in order to return your silverware, which I accidentally carried from your restaurant after dinner on Friday, August 16. I dined there to celebrate the engagement of my sister to a Swedish friend. I had the steak entrecote. However, as desert was served, I found a dental problem increasingly annoying. After an unsuccessful attempt to clear the problem in the wash closet, I carried the enclosed fork with me back there, and cleared my teeth. Unfortunately, the fork remained forgotten in the pocket of my jacket. Having only arrived in Stockholm the day before, I had only two days left in the city. During this time I never managed to bring the silverware back to Paul and Norbert. When passing the restaurant I hadn't the fork, and visa-versa. I apologize for any inconvenience that this has caused. Yours, Eric. PS It is only through a pack of Paul and Norbert matches that I was able to have your address – they have been most practical!

They wrote me back on restaurant letterhead to the Bahamas thanking me for my letter and declaring that the fork was very happily reunited with the other silverware at their waterfront restaurant! (Background; located at historic Strandvägen 9, on Östermalm in Stockholm, it was opened in 1982 by Paul Beck and chef Norbert Lang. It closed in 2010 after Beck died in 1998 and renovations loomed).

September 1, 1991, In St. Malo, France aboard *War Baby*.

Leave our Boats in the Water

There's something sacrilegious about pulling a boat out of the water (pulling teeth),
something unnatural, something rude, about pulling a boat out of the water.
Something powerless about standing beneath a dry-docked boat,
something scary about the underbelly of a fish
intent on remaining belly down, shiny and silvery,
like the sun's glow through prism slivers of gold, dazzling blind fish predators beneath.

There's something rude about investigating the through-hull anii of a boat out of the water,
while a mosquito without wings, jackals without voices, women without wombs. Whoa....
Boats settle so easily so luxuriously into the water; they belong there; they fit.
Something volatile about a hull exposed to the air;
too H2O low, too vulnerable, yet poised of Damocles, waiting to crush
waiting to crumble down upon you. Rib. By. Rib. Vertebrae by vertebrae, voice by voice
The slow cocking death of boats sinking into the air,
of birds floating featherless *Icarus* and *Daedalus*, wax-undoing,
larger exposed, farther away; greater the fall.

Keep them in the water, keep your heart in your chest, keep your homes on land,
keep your cars, keep your jobs....
only let our boats remain in the water.

September 2, 1991, Monday, 11.30 pm GMT (France summer time). *Le Café Di Dauphin* (Dolphin, Talbot Photos) St. Malo, Bretagne, France. Finally! The bottom of the barrel, in letter-writing! Here it goes: I've responded to every fucking letter, whether business or pleasure, by hand, May 10 to September 2: four months, over 25 packets. Wrote Hassle Free agents in Florida, and Professor Roger from *Circuit*. The other morning, quite early, we were docked port-side-to on the inner harbor quai, behind the large Polish state tall ship, training ship named *Dar Młodzieży*, whose sailmaker repaired our damaged mainsail for free. Several things happened in quick succession which feel surreal:

I hear chatter in the cockpit and climb up the companionway from getting coffee to find Steve, Sam and Ted sitting there contentedly as the sun made its way through the lovely buildings of the city and across the wide and open cobble dock space; acres wide and empty. I was sitting to one side of the companionway taking it all in when another crew, the friendly Cathy, also came up, and also was awed by the stillness and beauty of the scene. She then just gave a friendly rub to my shoulders – purely spontaneous and kind.

At that moment, to my right, into my line of vision walked an elderly woman in dignified dress out of a morning summer stroll with her son and daughter, or son and daughter-in-law. They too, seemed to be walking on air, and when they saw us on this lovely large sailing yacht giving each other backrubs in the French morning sunlight, they paused and took our scene in, and smiled. We, who were far from home and families for many months, also watched them admiringly as they continued down the large quay haltingly, on foot.

Then, suddenly, the older woman simply dropped to the ground less than 100 feet from us. None of us had the slightest clue how to perform CPR or do anything useful, and I guess the doctor on the Polish ship did not know about it, and none of us spoke French well. Ted had been playing football on the beach in Bermuda when an American college kid he never med threw a dirty tackle across the back of his legs, disabling him for life, so that he had to be raised to the dock using the winches and lines, so he could not spring to action. So we did, well, nothing. An ambulance was called, I will never forget the look of panicked helplessness of the son kneeling over his dying mother, and soon they were gone away, rather silently, in the ambulance. I've never seen, before or since, such an affirmation of life and joy so suddenly squelched by sudden death, with absolutely no forewarning. I take it as an admonition; enjoy, enjoy, enjoy every last second as though it is your last. It really may be. Because I am prone to bi-polar behavior anyway, this experience heightens my sense for danger and the need to be vigilant when things seem to be going too well…. Watch out! There may by some asshole in the clouds with a lightning bolt that has your name on it!

September 6, 1991, Friday; *War Baby* Fax: From the Swedish Consulate in Brest, Brittany, France. "Dear Mom and Dad; Hullo, hope all is well! I am in Brest now, and War Baby's voyages are basically over for now. I will probably spend the weekend in Brest, then travel to Paris. I may drive to Paris in a car rented by Skipper brown. The Swedish Consul here Mr. Maurice is very helpful. Love you, can't wait to get home!"

September 8, 1991, Sunday. Brest France. Calls to Paris. Sent from *Port du Plaisance*, the yacht marina in Brest *War Baby,* letters and chores for tomorrow. France include *Rumor*'s skipper, Florence Arthaud, Mike aboard *Sayonara*, Captain Charles, Edward M. (Ted) Gosling, Paget Bermuda. Fellow crew Cathy, San Francisco, Steve, Worcester and Portsmouth Polytechnic.

September 12, 1991, Thursday, 2.55 am. Staying at Hotel St. Andre-des-Artes, St.-Germane-des-Pres, Sur Seine, Paris, in room 25. Balcony, cool, humid rain this afternoon. *Je* *suis en Paris, Les voyages et fin par le moment, et je returné a mon familie sur les Bahamas dernierre.* I am going home.

March 5, 1992, Thursday. Wrote to Frederique, young lady at Café Catamaran in Brest, when aboard *War Baby*.

May 13, 1992, Wednesday. Matt Ratsey of *War Baby*, dinner Friday, May 29.

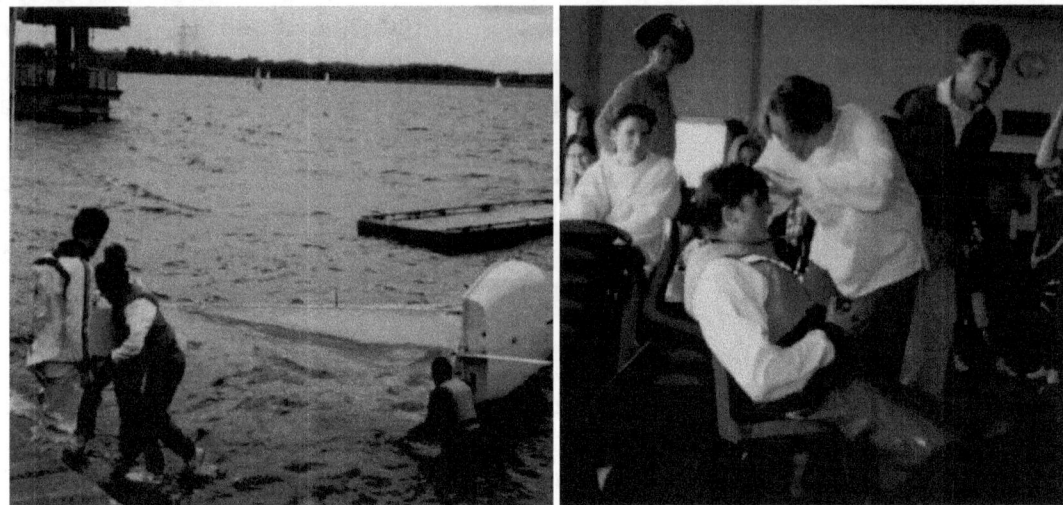

For just an afternoon fellow sailors for Boston College and I were able to sail with Oxford's senior sailing team on a reservoir. It was blustery, and capsizes were common. This fellow was bleeding from a boom blow to the head, and everyone was as merry as you can be, as you see. No wonder the British have won so many wars!

Carting one of the eight-person boats into the Merton College boat house in Oxford where the Thames becomes the Cherwell River. I was privileged to row in the Merton 2nd VIII for two terms. We didn't run over or "bump" enough competitor's boats to earn a blade. I dated one of the coaches from Lady Margaret Hall (*hush hush!*)

September 6, 1994, Tuesday, 2 pm. Staying at Hereford Avenue, Christchurch, Canterbury, New Zealand: Thompson couple, care of *War Baby*....

September 11, 1994, In New Zealand I wrote to Jill B. in Alameda, California; postcard of Mirror Lake; thanked her for introduction to the Thompsons vai Warren Brown, and thanked the Thompsons for their hospitality.

March 20, 1995, Tuesday. Calling Howard, *War Baby* shipmate, at Bluebell Shipping, New York. [He and I remain in contact in 2020]

April 10, 1995, Monday. Mailing: Cover letter typed and sent to Warren Brow, who is a Yalie like Bill Buckley, Jr. who reviewed my African story. Appointment in Lyford Cay with Mr. Buckley at Seaside, to discuss my writing.

December 29, 1995, 9:15 am. Am aboard the tanker *Edmo* in India. I woke up terrified in the early morning, due to the sound made by the door between me and my clothes closet, on way to the head (bathroom) banging. This happened before; in fact, it has been happening since at least *War Baby*, in the summer of 1991. This episode at 8:30 am local, Singapore minus 2.5 at 1.5 days one day out of Visakhapatnam, East coast India.

June 1, 2000, Thursday. Newport. German date Carolina from Mallorca, grew up on a yacht petite very sweet cooked me dinner. Comes home to her yacht tomorrow, and my loft on Lee Wharf, which is very near where they dock. We bring each other meals. Years later, I welcomed a racer-cruiser into Newport from the Bermuda Race only to learn that they had been jolted awake that morning by a whale-strike while doing 6+ knots. They reported seeing the whale limping off in a cloud of blood. The whale carcass that washed ashore on a tourist-trodden beach in Newport that 4th of July weekend was attributed by the local papers to a "tanker strike." My usually loquacious tongue was uncharacteristically silent, and to this day I cannot recall who told me what when.

War Baby crew photo at RBYC by Lady Halifax, 2000. That necktie belonged to my grandfather, an attorney in NYC who didn't sail much but loved to wear Madras coats. It was lost in 2000 when *Stiarna* caught fire and sank off Trinidad, but a burnt remnant popped up, and I have it still.

August 20, 2002, Tuesday. Newport. I sailed off to Bermuda on *War Baby*, and in doing so pointedly ignored a petite sailor Carolina. She was born German and raised in Mallorca with a tiller in her hand. We dated briefly, but I was away often, and she naturally dated another sailor. I'm embarrassed to say we split a bit dramatically, she storming out of IYAC [International Yacht and Athletic Club] when he, younger than I, walked in on she and my conversation, then the two of them stormed out. Yet then, as we left Newport on *War Baby*, she was waiting on the back of her sailboat at the mooring field for when we sailed past. We recognized each other, but I did not acknowledge her. This was insensitive and cruel and I regret it. [In 2020 we reestablished slight contact on social media].

January 8, 2003, Through *War Baby* I was introduced to Bill Whitlock, Sparkman & Stephens broker, and he was very supportive of me and we remained in touch.

October 6, 2005, as part of Echo Yacht Delivery, Warren asked me for yacht crew, and I matched them with retired executive Marvin R., who did a 7-year circum-navigation. He captains yachts and does offshore coaching, passages. Got him what he asked for: a Trans-Atlantic voyage on *War Baby*. Visited them in their home in Charlestown, part of Boston, on the water. He was a canal-boat captain in Lowell Massachusetts, while that was still on offer. All parties seemed satisfied with how it turned out. Jill, however, when she learned I earned a small finder's fee, tried to intervene and prevent it.

Voyage 10: *Young Endeavour* **Port Canaveral, Florida - Nassau, August, 1992**

August 10, 1992, Monday, *Young Endeavour* FAX: From the Australian Commission, Kingston, Jamaica. To my parents: "Sorry for the delay in getting back to you regarding Eric. I did in fact telex the ship directly, but apparently they are experiencing problems, with signals being lost somewhere in the atmosphere... The Commanding Officer, Frank Alica, says they are all looking forward to meeting Eric in Port Canaveral. The ship's assigned berth is South Cargo Pier 48 (the port is reasonably small, so he shouldn't have too many problems finding the ship). ....I trust Eric will have an enjoyable trip. Cheers!.... PS The ship has a cellular phone until departure from Port Canaveral, but apparently provides an unreliable service."

Australian Tall Ship **Young Endeavour, The Nassau Tribune, 20 August, 1992**

Resembling a large bird with its wings tucked at its sides, the Australian training tall ship, The *Young Endeavour* welcomed a young Nassuvian aboard at Port Canaveral in Florida last week in preparation for its voyage to the Bahamas. A gift from the United Kingdom to the people of Australia in 1988 in honor of their bicentennial celebration, the 44 meter (145 foot) brigantine has just begun the third and final leg of its first voyage around the world in commemoration of the voyages of discovery made by Christopher Columbus and James Cook.

The *Young Endeavour* is a traditional tall ship equipped with modem safety and comfort features. The actual sailing is still done manually. The crew consists of 24 select young men and women from around Australia led by a competent staff of eight Royal Australian navy crewmen and Commander Frank Alica. Due to arrive in Sydney, Australia, by Christmas, they have already sailed across the Indian and Atlantic oceans; often accompanied by other tall ships.

Thanks to an invitation from the Australian High Commission in Kingston, Jamaica, and Captain Alica, I was able to join the crew in Florida on Thursday, August 13. I was "hands-on" of their tallest mast, with its traditional "square-rig" yards. The hull is blue and white, with all its flags aflutter, the *Young Endeavour* is a beautiful and sturdy ship. Its decks are rich teak and its ten sails are a complex "web of power" hand hoisted by the crew. The crew's smiles and genuine reception belies the strenuous job that they must perform onboard. On Friday morning, the crew gathered for breakfast at 7am. After cleaning their bunks, all 33 hands and staff met for a briefing at 8am. The white Australian naval ensign was hoisted and the national anthem sung, followed by talks by the captain, navigator and executive officer.

We then spent an hour or more scrubbing, polishing and dusting the brass, wood, gallery and all. At 10am, with uniforms on and inspection complete we pushed off from Port Canaveral, Florida, for the Bahamas. On Friday the vessel cruised south along Florida's East Coast, against the crew set sail and steered eastward across the Gulf Stream for Grand Bahama. All Friday night we sailed and by dawn were rearing Grand Bahama's West End light, making the North West Providence Channel.

Young Endeavour's crew spent Saturday setting and striking her massive main gaff topsail, and foresails according to the winds. We paused in the afternoon between the Berry Islands and Abaco's Hole to celebrate two birthdays; the captain and crew dined on ice cream and cake in the warm Bahamian sun. By Saturday night we were passing massive cruise liners and heading south for Nassau. Sunday morning was brilliant and clear. Under full sail we plied the clear blue waters, hailing western New Providence on the horizon late in the morning. After a peaceful religious service led by Commander Alica, complete with guitars and songs, we began to "tack" along the Nassau Coast towards. All hands were on the deck to heave the sails and keep us off the reefs.

By 2:45 pm all the sails were "doused" and tied up, and the brass was all shining. With the crew lining the tall yards of the square sails, we entered Nassau Harbour docking at the Prince George Wharf at 3 pm, in Navy style. There to greet us were the Australian High Commissioner and staff and the Dean of the Consular Corps and family members, one of whom (yours truly) was granted the highest mast perch! *Young Endeavour*'s crew have since performed a sea chanty pantomime for children at the Ranfurly Home and received dignitaries aboard. The ship welcomed visitors between one and 5pm daily, on Thursday, August 20, it left Nassau and sailed home to Australia via the Caribbean and the Pacific. From their Bahamian hosts, "*bon voyage!*"

September 6, 1992, Sunday, Boston. Hurricane Andrew made first landfall on Harbour Island on the afternoon and night of August 23. My employer, Freddie Wanklyn had given the family a free week in Whale Villa, which despite the *Young Endeavour* racing out of Bahamas to Jamaica to avoid Hurricane Andrew, we accepted the offer. John, James and I were trapped there after parents, sister and her new fiancé Gustaf secured the last seats on the last plane to safety in Nassau. That fall I was training for the varsity big boat team for BC in Boston Harbor. We were off Logan Airport when a large gust took my Young Endeavour cap off my head and into the choppy seas. Obviously we could not interrupt a race to go back and get it; it was an amateur mistake for me to have made. What my fellow crew delighted in learning though, was that it had come from an Australian tall ship which I had helped escape from Bahamas and the clutches of a hurricane a few weeks before! I hope whoever found the cap made use of it.

July 1, 1993, Lincolnville Maine: August 11, before Hurricane Andrew, we had to rush to gather all the crew off islands and bars to emergency evacuate Bahamas to Kingston Jamaica long before Bahamians were making serious preparations. The Australian tall-ship officers were Royal Australian Navy, and got their information from weather bureaus and naval intelligence globally. Pretty impressive.

October 9, 1994, Sunday, 3.50 pm. Sydney, Australia. We walk with Gert to see *Young Endeavour*. ...going back to Thursday October 6, on arrival in Sydney I reached out to former shipmates, including mutual crush Veronica from the tall ship, in Sydney. Then the fun crew named Tucker from Melbourne. Both proved to be a no-go, I could not reach them. Tucker's family was surprised, saying he had gone; left on August 28.

May 30, 2002, Calls: Dave S. of Australian tall ship *Young Endeavor*.

Young Endeavour crew, in Port Canaveral, Florida, mid-August, 1992

Chapter 5

Voyage 11: *Whisper of Maine,* Newport, Vineyard, Nantucket training, 1992-1993
Voyage 12: *Whisper of Maine*, Marion - Bermuda Race, June, 1993
Voyage 13: *Whisper of Maine*, Bermuda-Camden-Newport, July-September, 1993

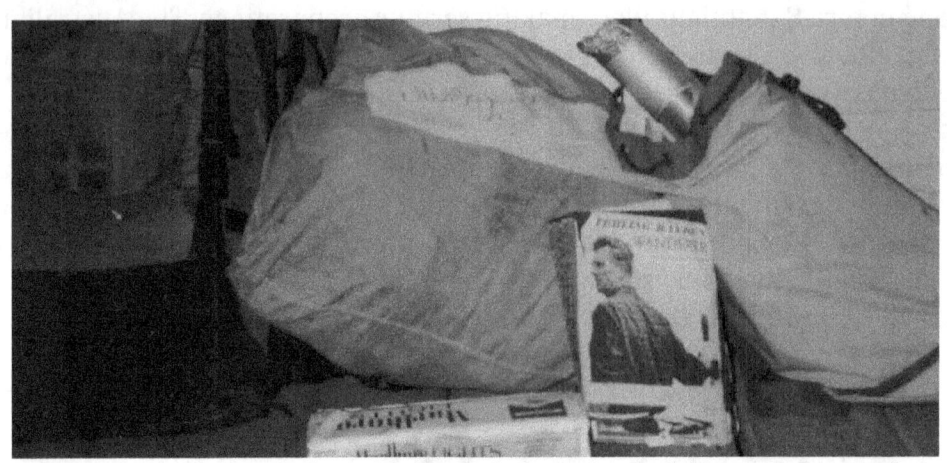

My gear after college: backpack from LL Bean (taken through Europe, burned and sank on *Stiarna*), Eaglebrook laundry bag, inspirational book by Sterling Hayden, prep-school kid, tall ship skipper, movie star, author, the actual mast base from the MIT boat I wrecked in Boston, and a Swedish-themed tote back with a secret pouch in the bottom. And smokes. They are often cheaper by the carton in Duty Free, not packing enough smokes on a long voyage leads to crew friction.

"Don't bleed on my deck." An ex-Navy man coined this classic reprimand, and for an aluminum test hull which didn't get bloodstained anyway! One of us had cut ourselves struggling to get the mate back on board during a botched winter-time tack. He also considered the rusted tins of Dinty Moore meat stew in the bilges top-rate cuisine. There were character-building trips, in one case with just the two of us for days.

October 21, 1992, Wednesday, 5 pm. Crunched comfortably under my bed in a soft lounge chair in Greycliff Honors House, Boston College (BC), Room 104, Honor's House, 2051 Commonwealth Avenue, Chestnut Hill, MA. Overcast and generally cloudy, gray but crispened by bright oranges of nocturnal twilight refracted from foliage of trees across Greycliff Road in St. John's Seminary and apple orchard, which are visible from my window. Various sailing ventures including aboard sailing coach Norm Reid's 41-foot sloop, *Face Off* from Marblehead to Boston. *Face Off* was formerly *Flirt of Paget*, and had belonged to Shorty Trimingham of Bermuda, who Mom and Dad met outside a major musical on Broadway, and they somehow exchanged tickets! I also joined other BC sailors on at least four sailing ventures from Norm's marina berth in Boston to the city harbor, including around Logan Airport, to practice for the MacMillan Cup in Annapolis twice, plus cruises with his father, wife, son, and daughter, and boss, BC's grounds and buildings czar, Tom.

Other good voyages have taken me back home to Newport with Dr. Sheldon Brotman on his boat *Whisper of Maine*, call sign WTG-9346, from Newport to Martha's Vineyard, then Newport and Block Island with my brother John, his friend Cliff, and my Greycliff girlfriend Carla, my friend and dorm neighbor Rich W., and BC sailor Alex J. of Long Island New York, whose father is British and in the pharmaceutical industry, and who also went to Oxford, at Mansfield College. Rich, also went to Oxford with me, same college.

June 4, 1993, Friday, 5.15 pm. Aboard *Geronimo*, Goat Island Marina, Newport. Cool, cloudy; it rained this morning scattered sunshine, high tide at 5:32 pm, full moon, temperature 65°F. I am working and living aboard this beautiful sturdy craft for the following 10 or so days before shipping off on the 1993 Marion-to-Bermuda Race aboard Dr. Sheldon Brotman's *Whisper of Maine*; since his daughter Liz is at BC, he found me on the big-boat sailing program there. I anticipate a good race, especially as we have a good crew, an excellent boat of light aluminum designed by famous Argentinian German Frers, and hopefully sufficient food and provisions. In training, we eat from large rusty cans of Dinty Moore stored wet in the salty bilge. Tomorrow morning, for the first time in many a month, I shall resume actual work for money, which I have not done since last summer, when I worked for my parents in the Bahamas.

June 15, 1993, I have a bicycle (fellow crew Bill Steady's), in Newport, backpack, sleeping bag, foul weather jacket, pants and boots. Tomorrow I ship aboard SY *Whisper of Maine* bound for Marion then Bermuda. I am very bummed out that my girlfriend Clarissa has gone off to work, and I was unable to get a bus out of Newport any sooner than 2 pm, and am now here at 4:45 pm without a real host, or hostess, and feel left high-and-dry in an ugly town where I really no longer belong. I need rest. *Blah*. I leave Boston tomorrow. Quote of the day: Landlords are not good skippers. BC Health Center: tetanus immunization and insurance, last tetanus was in 1988. I needed a new one to cover having cut my legs salvaging old bike *Cornelius* from Newport Harbor at Lee Wharf, I was sent by the Connetts to the former St. George's School physician on Red Cross Lane.

Bonanza Bus leaves Boston at 2 pm and 4 pm. My Newport roommate and BU student Tom told me that Ogunquit and Camden, Maine are yuppie, Bar Harbor is a summer area, with schooners, and that Acadia National Park is lovely by Bar Harbor. Look into 42-foot Hinkley *Silver Lining*. Wayfarer Marine boatyard in central Camden Harbor. Look up Jack Gordon at Portland Yacht Club or basin; call then. Farnsworth has eight to 10 days of work from June 22 to June 24, in *Condé Nast Traveler* magazine. Boston; a good place to write in peace is the old Copley Plaza Hotel bar [Fairmont, Copley Square].

June 16, 1993, Wednesday. Am wanted on *Whisper of Maine*. Am generally out of my element or parity with my peers, dollar for dollar.

June 17, 1993, Thursday. Alone aboard *Whisper of Maine*, contentedly winding up chores and work. I will need: four small batteries, four packs of smokes, a marlinspike. Find and call Rachel's number in Bermuda [*Xebec* companion, 1991 *en route* Antigua to Belgium, Bermuda Biological Station. She and her boyfriend, a sailor met us later on *Whisper of Maine* in Bermuda]. On eve of Marion-to-Bermuda Race mailed mostly postcards.

June 18, 1993, start of Marion-Bermuda Race, Friday: What follows are log book entries. The following are entries transcribed from the *Whisper* official logbook verbatim, unless otherwise indicated. Most were written by your 12 pm to 4 pm watch captain (yours truly), with a few significant others included to give sense of the Marion-to-Bermuda Race and return aboard *Whisper*. Start: 3:40 pm, fog and precipitation. Race committee calls, but no answer, so we beat down Buzzard's Bay. All standing #1 (headsail up) speeds 6 knots and visibility poor. Sow and Pigs Light passed at 8 pm. Eased sheets, course 166°. Captain, Dr. Sheldon Brotman. Abbreviations. 4.10 EST (eastern standard time), position 40°28'.5 N. Latitude (north or south), 70°22'.6W, longitude (east or west). Water temperature 60°F., apparent boat speed 7.8 knots. Course 175° SSE, 557 nm to finish line at St. David's Light, Bermuda.

Notes: Headsail change from heavy #1 to #3, all hands on deck; most were harnessed, changed tack briefly, checked boat speed, all well, fog clearing 12 yachts visible, passed at least one. Dawn breaking two-man 4 pm to 8 pm watch, of Mr. Z. and Adam, are on. Liz, Turner, Eric, 3.10 am June, 7.22 pm, out of Marion Boat speed 8 knots, wind 20 knots. Water temperature 71°F.; we are nearing the Gulf Stream. Gulf weeds visible, one yacht astern, three are ahead. Sail change from #2 to #3 headsails. At 12 pm, reefed main once at 11.45 am to 12 pm, using all hands. Loran has been turned off. 12–to-4 pm watch, Liz. Speed 8 knots, small squall, course 170° SSE. No sail changes. Saw three boats, wind shifted from SW-W. Battery, mechanical problem, appeared to be small fire in starboard forward locker, at 10 pm.

June 20, 1993, Sunday, 1:10 pm. Aboard *Whisper of Maine* racing to Bermuda. I'm standing the 12 to 4 pm watch. 36°25'N, 67°30'W. According to race rules that has been skillfully determined by owner skipper Dr. Sheldon Brotman and his team using the old-school, non-electronic sextant. Shooting the sun and the horizon began at 12:30 pm. Several shots were taken at the meridian passage. Noon sights were observed at 12:34 pm and the corrected latitude was 36°29'N. Dr. Brotman and I calculated or plotted this on the chart. The position puts us roughly 270 nm from Bermuda, showing that we have already covered some 350-400 nm from Marion. Our first noon sight was successful.

Whisper's boat speed is 7.9 to 8 knots, the apparent wind angle is 65°, wind speed is 18 to 19 knots, and our course is 165° to 170°, or SSE, with Captain Brotman's daughter Liz at helm. We are presently flying the mainsail with a single reef in it, and the #3 genoa foresail, also reefed. At about 5 am, after a strong run from midnight to 4 am (the dog watch), all is well! We have overtaken yachts. [At 5.30 pm same day] On the noon to 4 pm watch. Course altered from 175° SSE to 160° SE. I did a spell of two hours on the helm. We are averaging 7–to-8 knots, sometimes achieving 9 knots.

Ocean water temperature, measured by leaving a thermometer in a toilet bowl filled with seawater, is 76°F., and we see both Sargasso-type seaweed and Portuguese Man-o-War jellyfish; all are strong indicators that we have reached and are in the hot river of water known as the Gulf Stream. We've seen two Beluga whales astern, bearing roughly 150°. Weather is sunny, breezy, and warm, so the crew are airing out. Liz and her younger brother Watson are on cabin duty. Clothes and crew are all sunning and airing out. We ran the motor in neutral and generator this morning to charge the batteries which run navigation lights, pumps, and other systems. Dr. Brotman is honored on Father's Day with cards and gifts from Liz, his other son Turner, and Watson. We are now flying the un-reefed main and un-reefed the #3 Genoa as well, given that it's daylight and more settled conditions. We took out a flattening reef from the mainsail at 5 pm. Mr. Z., Dr. Brotman's age), at helm steers us downwind.

Blow-pop candies for all boosted morale. Three vessels were sighted; two off to port, one amidships about 7 miles away. All is well. We intend to rejoin the fleet this evening as we all converge on the race finish line off the eastern tip of Bermuda. Bearing down on North Rock and Northeast Beacon off Bermuda. Our ETA is now late Monday, June 21 (tomorrow), or early Tuesday, June 22. Eric, Liz, and Turner are on the noon to 4 pm watch. It's now 4.30 am so the 4 am to 6 am watch are on duty. Boat speed is 7 to 8 knots, pushing 9 knots, wind speed is 10 to 15 knots.

We are now flying the full mainsail and what is called a reacher, or drifter sail, which is a handy, light, versatile sail for reaching upwind; note that spinnakers and gennaker sails are prohibited in this family-style race. Prizes and incentives are given to those with the most and youngest family members. Our course is still 165° SSE. Off the starboard beam are two boats, with another to the port, or left side, angle 50° from our bow. Sunrise will be around 4.30 am local time. We sighted a lovely bird, the white Bermuda Longtail Dove. Roughly 100 nm remain. Presently, and predictably, five yachts are converging. This is like a vortex; the closing of a triangle, as we have one yacht to starboard and two others to port. Additionally, there is a yacht ahead and to port, leading to intensity on board as we approach the finish line and end to our outward voyage.

June 22, 1993, Aboard *Whisper* after the 12 am to 4 am watch. We finished at 5.45 am. At 5 am the yacht *Galileo* on the finish line. The committee boat spoke with us via radio. Five nm from St. David's Light, at Kitchen Shoals. We crossed the invisible line bearing 45° magnetic with the other yachts *Insurgente, Katama* and *Akka* behind us. Crossed finish at 5:45 am on boat time, which was 6:45 am local, or Bermudian time. I radioed in to the race committee within two minutes. After some 84 hours elapsed time, *Whisper* was 9th across the finish line with at least six other boats. The course is over 650 nm in a straight, or Rhumb line. No yachts were visible to us far behind, but it was still dawn. We took a waterborne tour past St. George's at sunrise, then motored along Bermuda's north shore to the capital, Hamilton. This route took us via The Narrows. Given that I'd been there several times and know the dock master, Tom Hayden, I helped to negotiate a berth for *Whisper* at the RHADC, or Royal Hamilton Amateur Dinghy Club. Tom, the dockmaster, found us a good spot between *Sea Strange* and *Attractor*, on the front dock which affords access to everything and an easy escape when ready in several days. We immediately drank two Dark and Stormy rum drinks in the early but daylit morning! Losing one's lands legs for sure, yet, *gotta do it*!

June 28, 1993, Monday, 10:45 am. Aboard *Whisper of Maine* at roughly 36°N, 64°W, roughly 300 nm NNE of Bermuda and about 500 nm south of Mohegan Island, Penobscot Bay, Maine; which we are aiming for, outside Cape Cod; this will be my first time in those waters. Entry: All well. The return, or delivery crew post-race is riding strong seas in winds gusting beyond 20 knots, but no serious threat. Bill is watch captain of Watson now, and I shall take over from him watch captain duties for Turner and Isaac of Maine, starting in roughly an hour for the noon to four watch. Dr. Brotman is being temperamental; he is very competitive, does not like not to collect silver, but this is understandable I suppose. We are no expert helmsmen, are young and fairly easily distracted, but overall, I feel we're doing a more-than-satisfactory job, especially considering that I think Turner may not want to be here; he is, after all, a teenager!

Bill, a navy man from Newport, is good, and Mr. Z., has a great sense of humor. Isaac is now cleaning the bilge with detergent. It *reeks! Urghh. Celestial navigation exercises:* LAN stands for local apparent noon, meridian sailing without a clock, phenomenon within time zone earlier, east to west; you add. East you subtract, one time zone is one hour, one hour is 15 degrees, one degree is four minutes.

Bermuda to Camden after the 1993 Marion-to-Bermuda Race, Sheldon Brotman, MD, USN (Ret.) and I in the Gulf Stream on *Whisper of Maine*. I liked sailing with him; he was tough, but also I never broke. The boat was like *Rising Star*, except stripped. Like *War Baby*, my participation was voluntary, so it was always a delicate balance of taking and giving. Dr. Brotman was the biggest, quietest, bad-ass in the smallest body of any skipper I sailed under. Before saying anything, he carefully thought it through like the war-vet trauma surgeon that he was. He simplified sailing for me, bringing the emphasis away from fancy equipment, yacht clubs and protocols, and placing the sailors, their hearts and hands at the center, manipulating basic equipment to achieve their ends. This was a really important lesson as yachts quickly became very reliant on increasingly complex electronics for toilets, navigation, lights, raising and lowering sails, drawing more from generators and fuel tanks. Yachts can now feature retractable keels as well as TVs that go in and out of panels, with hot and cold air, their own water-makers, and military-grade communications and navigation far beyond the sextant which Brotman was a master of. For Sheldon and his young acolytes, it was just you and him and a metal hull with hand-hauled sails and an anchor. The most valued asset on his boat was seamanship, and if you had that, you were quickly promoted.

June 29, 1993, Tuesday, 1.50 pm. At 12:40 pm I determined the local meridian passing at the meridian 12:03 pm, per *Reid's Nautical Almanac*, a mariner's bible; about four books are typical need to calculate a star sight. Local apparent noon is your local time. 39°02'N, at our date in *Reid's Nautical Almanac* was 12:03 pm, per page 128.66°57'W from 75°W to 67°W is 8°. 8° at 12:03 pm is one hour multiplied by four minutes, minus 32 minutes is 11:31 am, and so factoring daylight savings time is 32 minutes, so becomes 12:31 pm.

June 30, 1993, Wednesday, 10 am. Aboard *Whisper of Maine*, at roughly 40°40'N, 67°30'N. Between St. George's Bermuda, and Camden Maine, on our 5th day (4th full day) with Dr. Brotman our captain, Mr. Z. a watch captain on the 4-8 pm watch, Bill Steady, watch captain on 8-12 pm watch, myself, with the noon-4 pm turn was watch captain. Sons Watson and Turner and their friend Isaac are reliable crew. Adam M. and Liz Brotman, who was my co-watch captain during the race, have returned to New England by air. *Whisper of Maine* was the 9th boat across the line out of a fleet of 120 yachts racing. Overall, however we were knocked down to about 60th place, or 7th in Class A, which consisted of 24 yachts.

July 1, 1993, Brotmans, Lincolnville Maine: I can see a freighter barge making its way up Penobscot Bay, SE-central Maine coast, now; it is pushed by a tug. Beautiful here. I'll need to make some money of my own. We'll see. Looks as though Cannell, Payne & Page, a waterfront yacht brokerage firm co-owned by friendly Bill Cannell in Camden, are my best bet for a reliable delivery contract. Talked to my girlfriend Clarissa last night. She asked if I was capable of bringing a yacht from Sweden to here. I said yes, because I feel I am. Especially from Göteborg, avoiding the Helsingfors passage at sea.

July 3, 1993, Saturday, 1.40 am. At the Brotman family homestead, Saturday Cove, Lincolnville. Home from the bars of Camden. What a trip it's been with John Bintan and his acquaintance David, co-owner of the sailboat *Halo*. We ambled from the Salty Dog to Cappy's (actually the Crow's Nest, which is upstairs), then to Gilbert's. Spoke to Mom and Dad this evening. All well there, though my conversation was mono-syllabic. *Rhetorically:* Home? Where for art thou home? At sea, my boy, at sea! Go east! Go west! Who the fuck cares where I go? Drinking beer and *Jägermeister*, a German bitters or liqueur drink; it was a full night. We drank up the Wayfarer Marine Friday afternoon Happy Hour on the dock, too [it's owned by Tom Watson, founding family of IBM, and his former yacht skipper, an older German, still has employ there). Happy.

Apprehension. Saturday, evening, in Lincolnville. Sitting upon a rock which is the crux of a large granite boulder along this evergreen pine coastline of forest on Penobscot Bay in Maine, thinking. Today's thoughts, in the wake-up late, groggy hangover state of a dozen beers the night before in three or more places between 3:30 pm to 1:30 am leaves me now tired, worn, with smoke-filled lungs (again). It is overcast, grey, foggy. I chainsawed and hammered my way through late morning, early afternoon, working on the Brotman's large impressive dock in the tidal bay, and am now tired. I'm thinking that, having gone into Camden this pm for an hour with Dr. Brotman, drank Mochaccino at the Blue Café, and read local and national news, walked with my foul-weather gear through town.

We saw and talked to Ricardo, a yacht skipper, and Brian the mate whose yacht suffered a broken shroud cap at the top of the mast, when it was stepped or put in place with cranes today by Scott of Wayfarer. This is sad; not good. In the morning while in town I called about a job offer as first mate (ha!) and followed up regarding work aboard the slower sloop *Dovetail*. Mr. William, Bill, Sampson, her owner, met with me at 1.30 pm at The Camden Yacht Club, and offered me ten hours of work a week worth at an hourly rate. Work would start in three days, on now, on Wednesday, possibly Tuesday. Hans is the skipper of another boat; we'll see? We finally finished rebuilding the dock at the Brotman house. Had a conversation with Mom and Dad last night about risk and security. Signed the register at the Blue Café.

From Camden a couple silly stories; on arrival from Bermuda in a very still dusk in July we did a victory lap of the inner harbor, and there was a young man sitting on a floating dock when we entered and when we left. He had a ponytail and was, it seems, just chilling. Never had it happen before or since, but as we motored slowly passed where he sat, he actually "shushed" us; a family of happy people on a 50-foot yacht into their home port from overseas, with no music, just excited voices. The next day I read a blurb in the local paper with a photo of the same guy, saying that he was about to set off on a great adventure to many countries. Here was this prick who hadn't even left on his adventures, telling those who were returning from actually doing it, to shut up. I cannot imagine he got far, or that if he did, on his return a 15-year-old told him to pipe down. The schism between folks who do something and those that sit on the sidelines and complain was never clearer to me, and hardened my resolve to stay my course, and keep going farther. It's true, I often published about adventures – but always after I had lived them. That's what Admiral Morison told me to do; *dream, write but live your dreams out first.*

I was introduced by friends of my grandparents, the Jacksons, to a young lady recently graduated from Harvard who was single-handedly sailing New England while living aboard her own lovely wooden boat. She met me at the Camden Yacht Club, and rowed me to her 35-footer. We were relaxing in the main cabin over small talk as she prepared some coffee. Mid-way through the kettle boiling she interrupted to check for a gas line leak. This meant her listening to a hiss, then using detergent soap on the copper line. She showed me where it bubbled, and then repaired it. While greatly impressed and on one hand attracted to her self-sufficiency, on the other I do admit that at a fellow, and fellow boater, I was also a bit intimidated by her self-sufficiency. She had a greater skill set than I possessed, an eye for detail I lacked, and I recognized – perhaps she did as well – that I felt at least a smidgen threatened by this [decades later ,women friends on the dating circuit told me how they have to tamper down talk of their own careers lest the man they just met felt threatened; in fact some women say that to get rid of men in bars they say they are physicists!]

Then, a young man on another single-hander set off on a long voyage on his own wooden boat. He told me that for years, everyone in the family ignored him and the plan and told him to *get over it, give it up, move on*, until they realized he really was going to do it! Then, on the day of departure, his family and friends were all there on the dock with baskets of supplies and gifts of things for him to eat and read and use. His resolve convinced them to be resolved as well. He seemed to say – do it and they will follow, eventually. The same fellow described how had a love letter from a past girlfriend that he wanted to keep, and of course did not want his present live-aboard to read. So, he hid it very carefully in the one document least likely to be read: reduction table almanac for celestial navigation, which is just dates and data. That evening, he came back from work in the shipyard to an angry and hurt shipmate, and had to explain the letter...... [Later, a mate that supplanted off a boat in Panama was boat-sitting for a couple and would stay up all night on drugs reading their love-letters to each other, jealous of someone he barely knew! And on a trans-Atlantic passage an absent owner left his laptop for us to use for navigation, however he left a lot more than that for the crew to see over a month becalmed.]

July 7, 1993, Wednesday, 7.17 am. The Brotman's pier, Saturday Cove,. Quiet in the early morning, but for a small lobster boat navigating between ports having set out from a pier down the bay. There comes the lobster boat now; an open aluminum skiff, with a small outboard made by Seagull or Johnson. From the high dock I am sitting on, the little boat is just below my feet. The father and son team pulled up their trap, with the father navigating and pulling, the son sorting, the father smoking. He passes forward one decent-sized lobster in the first trap; I don't know about the second. A good day so far for them, I hope, though maybe not for the lobster. I need to confirm a time for me to pick up my copy of *The Bermudian* magazine from charismatic Brian Mullaney, of Ireland on *Zaberdast*, who were in the same Bermuda race as us and also came to Camden – he's a generous host at the bar to a broke sailor like me. He and crew, under Captain Clive sail for England today. At low tide lobster claws are visible in shallows.... seal visible parsing through the water looking both feline, and canine. Working in the dock on Wednesday.

July 9, 1993, Today, or tonight, I go down to town again to seek out evening life. It be Friday, the ninth of July, *anno Domini* 1993**,** *Anno* Eric 22. Sitting on the end of the pier in the evening placidity of the bay, with a couple getting off from Saturday Cove in their 20-odd-foot-boat for an overnight sleep aboard, with Jeff Shecher nearing me in his lobster boat, and an airplane skirting overhead from Islesboro, and me on our freshly updated pier with new railings and all, looking prim and safe. How quiet, and what ancient pursuits, as we each reflect on a day and a week generally well-spent. Tuesday was spent early working aboard the Dutch, Jongert-built 98-foot sailing sloop *Flying Magic* for Michael and Hans (*in absentia*), a tour of Camden Tuesday afternoon and then on Wednesday.

Calling Mr. Sampson to set up a Thursday work day. Quietude, placidity, tranquility; these characterize my story, here on the Maine coast above Saturday Cove in the convivial home and hearth, the welcoming easygoing family of Susan and Dr. Sheldon Brotman. I'm happy again, and after a tedious and exasperating year (or two, or three) at college. Now, I breathe clear air, see stars setting brilliantly above me overhead from the pier; all there tonight. I called the home of Mrs. Jackson, our grandparent's friends from Winter Park, Florida, and I suspect that after I'd left my message, they had rushed to the phone to pick it up, who knows? I can't tell. Difficult to know. We'll see. *Happy.*

July 21, 1993, Wednesday, 2.30 am. I sit atop the car; my favorite perch, lid closed, in my long-john underwear. Tonight, I could not sleep after reading Sterling Hayden's *Voyage: A Novel of 1896*, which demonstrates his masterful insight into characters, by fireside, with smokes and coffee but too many interruptions. For me, the bachelor, I am seeking freedom, seeking employment, seeking a future. I've got to move; I've got to get out and earn. Get moving, and get working. What am I doing? I'm broke. I flat out need something, and can't wait forever. I must leave. I am studying a way, trying to finish the varnish and then cash in my check from work on *Dovetail*. Then I would like to take the funds owed me and hitch to Boston on Monday or Sunday, should I be able to earn enough funds by then. I feel a pressing need to get out of here. I've got to do something independent; travel, see my girlfriend again, find peace.

Need to get my money for work done. Move on. Move, move, move. Settle up, go to new post, take a vacation from hell. Can't wait. Move. So ideal. Now it Wednesday morning. To Boston Sunday, in traffic in the afternoon. Sunday to Wednesday with Susan, Mrs. B. *Things to be resolved now:* Assert to Mom and Dad that I'm not going home right now; independence (said). Settle up business affairs, and see friends in Boston. Work in sailboats in Newport. Leave Camden by Tuesday. You don't want to be here when Dr. Brotman returns; he wants you to sail for free throughout the Maine islands, but you simply can't afford it. Tomorrow Newport.

August 9, 1993, Thursday, 4 pm. I'm on a Bonanza Bus from Newport to Boston; my 100th such trip? I give up on sorting this sailing affair out entirely on my own. From now on, I must mediate and balance between the fallacy of complete independence, and the reality that others' decisions and actions are significantly determining factors in my own progress. I called all my sail agents and contacts, even in Maine (giving them the Brotman's address and phone) to discover the not-entirely-surprising truth that others are not holding nuggets promising me a prosperous future for me but rather that I must assess my own venues and opportunities, a cliché, and act up on my own impulses, on my own volition, as Clarissa would say, and work with my own brawn before greater to me.

Just spoke with my mother, covering several of these issues with her; the importance of foresight, integrity and commitment, good faith. From her perspective, the willingness to let an obsession such as I have with sailing passages go in order to pursue a career, which I am not too eager to cede (sail) and pursue (journalism); certainly not in the immediate future. I intend to use the leeway time which I allowed myself, and which I feel I deserve, is my right after ten years in preparation and for finishing school. Thus, I persist, and continue to pursue my own mirror career in the endeavor of my heart; travel through sailing. I consider myself fortunate in my early maturity, on which I trust and rely, and with which I shall also follow my heart for one year. *Amazing Grace, how sweet the sound. That saved a wretch like me! I once was lost, but now I'm found, I once was slave, now free.*

August 25, 1993, Wednesday, 6.30 pm. Aboard a Peter Pan bus depot, Portland Maine. In transit to Belfast, and the Brotmans. Am returning to Maine, having left as early as mid-July. I think about exactly one month ago, actually to July 25 or so. Since leaving in the Brotman van, I stopped at Boston to see Clarissa with Watson to go to airport, Susan driving, with young Daniel being left at home. Then, the following morning Clarissa and I made Swedish pancakes before zipping into Newport. I spent a few hours in public relations, pushing my sailing career. Clarissa is bound cross-country with her friend.

What I earned lasted only a half-week, including sharing a drink with Bill P. of Palm Beach Florida at Goat Island Pub (we got drunk) [Bill, from Woods Hole originally, and I would become on-off-again roommates 1998 to 1999 in Newport]. A bus ticket to Boston soon followed thereafter. I stayed at BC roommate Jay's friend Greg's roomies a Belmead Manor on Bellevue Avenue, which was free, so fair enough. Trouble with Clarissa and me over my reluctance to return to Camden, where I felt I had failed to secure full-time work. Shame, but I couldn't bring myself to pay for the bus to a cocktail party around August 8. I went to Newport on the day of Jazz Festival to buy Sterling Hayden's autobiography *The Wanderer*. Then, in Coral Gables at the Books and Books café and bookstore, I saw Julie C. again, after three years at St. George's together. It has been four years since we knew each other quite well. I now return to a welcome reception and work at Brotman's. Nothing for Captain Sampson on *Dovetail*. Saw *Mutiny on the Bounty*, by Nordhoff and Hall, two Americans living in Tahiti or Polynesia.

August 31, 1993, Tuesday. In Newport. From Dr. Brotman. Instructions for living aboard *Whisper of Maine* this fall. Under port after bunk electrical grounding switch. Multiple-use battery switch, batteries and propane tanks are under starboard after-bunk. Third battery activated. Rule; *my* battery has red tape. I must be sure to turn off everything before I get off, scrub off decks, rags applied to the blue freeboard. Apply Murphy's Oil, dust the interior, pump bilge once and week, and keep food from spoiling in ice box. Free accommodating, reliant on a dinghy or boat launch to get ashore for work or play; did that in 1989 summer with *Rumor*.

September 11, 1993, Saturday, 1.20 am. Stamford railway station, Connecticut. Just parted with Clarissa. Calls: Mom and Dad, Bill Steady, Brotmans, Captain Nils Christensen, Danish-American, taciturn. I met with Nils and his spouse at their boat. I offered to help him with yacht delivery. 2:23 pm, depart Amtrak train, Stamford for Newport.

September 12, 1993, Sunday. Aboard *Whisper of Maine*. Where will be next? My own place! Next came *Breathless*, Newport Marina, off New York, Cape Hatteras, Sargasso Sea, Gulf Stream to Bimini, at anchor, off Bahamas, then Fort Lauderdale, 17th Street Marina, Florida. *Zarathustra Lives!* That's my rallying cry since hitchhiking alone in Africa.

September 27, 1993, Summer overview: Lived on *Whisper of Maine* afloat in Newport Harbor, various day jobs, then *Breathless* southbound back to Bahamas.

April 4, 1994, After Easter and April Fool's. I've had to come this far to realize that what I've escaped, I seek. Listening to the cassette mix of meaningful and sentimental songs made by Clarissa last summer, as I left her home in Greenwich and moved alone aboard *Whisper of Maine* in Newport Harbor. It was crisp and cold and I knew I had to settle in and survive or split, and I split.

January 31, 1999, Newport. Dr. Sheldon Brotman, Danville, Pennsylvania. I reached out to see whether *Whisper of Maine* will do the 1999 Marion-to-Bermuda Race.

May 27, 2005, Today I honor the passing of my skipper. Dr. Brotman. Taught at US Navy base in Great Lakes, Michigan. New *Jersey*, Pennsylvania Mattapoisett MA, Lincolnville, Maine. My mentor, the owner *Whisper of Maine*. Emergency Room trauma surgeon and doctor. Died. US Navy, retired, he and his wife served in Vietnam.

Epilogue: Dr. Brotman, ever competitive, participated in many more Bermuda Races, re-married another woman of Swedish descent, and settled in Mattapoisett, on the Cape Cod Canal and near *Whisper of Maine*. I went back to their cottage in rural Maine, it looked as lovely as ever however I knew I was being watched going there and back in a black city car with New York plates! There is a communal dock in Saturday Cove, yet it all looks comfortingly familiar.

Dr. Brotman and I spoke on various docks in Marion and Bermuda over the years and he cheerful tracked my boat's progress, but the big victory in a Bermuda race eluded he and his *Whisper* crews to the end, probably due to the penalty on it being built to eat the kind of cruising boats the Marion Bermuda Race was designed for, for breakfast. The aluminum hull still had original metal-cutting chalk marks on it! It was not designed for long-range comfortable cruising, rather that would be like taking the shell of mobile home, before the interior has been fitted out, around a continent. That might explain the electrical fire up forward, starboard.

I've not kept in contact with his children, Susan, or even my Camden buddies, except for Brian Mullaney, the affable older Irishman with a great sense of humor who hosted me for drinks at the RBYC in Bermuda after racing *Zaberdast*, the wooden hulled British boat down and then staying in Camden for the summer, where we met again at the Friday afternoon BBQ's at the Wayfarer Shipyard, along with the captain of the Tom Watson family's yacht *Palawan*. In about 2015 I was in London on business and caught up with Brian in the bar of the Royal Thames Yacht Club, where I was staying. We had a jolly gam with a younger Finnish sailor, talking about the Bermuda races and so on. Brian's career as a developer was clearly not suffering, as he was in white tie and tails, having just returned from a dinner hosted by royals at Buckingham Palace; I believe by Her Majesty herself!

Voyage 14: *Dovetail* Camden-Penobscot Bay, July-September, 1993

July 3, 1993, In the morning while in town I called about a job offer as first mate (ha!) and followed up regarding work aboard the slower sloop *Dovetail*. Mr. William (Bill) Sampson, her owner, met with me at 1.30 pm at The Camden Yacht Club, and offered me ten hours of work a week worth. Work would start in three days; we'll see?

July 6, 1993, Coffee and smoke for me before beginning the day. Should call Mr. Sampson, about 80, right now about work on *Dovetail*. I need steady employ, income.

July 7, 1993, Thursday at 9 am have meeting Bill Sampson at Camden Yacht Club then spent a good day preparing his 32-foot white sailing sloop *Dovetail*, then sailing her from 1 pm to 4 pm out of the bay with his wife Ruth and friend Constance. All are Harvard or Radcliffe graduates. Now, having spent today doing odd chores here in the morning on the pier more, I rest after a nap (and a physically vicious *sesh*, or drinking session, and its effects on the head) with my Pepsi and a Marlboro and a sunset while Brotman boy Watson reorganizes his cottage, and his brother reads his novels and their Mom Susan catches up on the phone.

July 21, 1993 Lincolnville. I put in 20 hours with *Dovetail*.

August 25, 1993, Wednesday, 6.30 pm. No work for Bill Sampson, *Dovetail*.

Planner	*Date*	*Place*	*Obligation, work, people*
Wednesday	July 21	Camden	Brotman House and *Dovetail*
Thursday	July 22	Camden	*Dovetail*, 8 hours
Friday	July 23	Camden	*Dovetail*, 8 hours
Saturday	July 24	Camden	*Dovetail*, 8 hours
Sunday	July 25	Camden	settle up, *Dovetail* pay, then Boston
Monday	July 26	Camden	work on, finish varnish, *Dovetail* pay
Tuesday	July 27	Boston	drive early am, Susan, Clarissa
Wednesday	July 28	Newport	business there settle up. Then Free!

September 12, 1993, Sunday. Aboard small sloop *Dovetail*, waiting for varnish to dry to re-paint, on a mooring near the Sampson's home in Camden Harbor.

July 5, 1994, I learned on a later visit from one of his friendly neighbors that Bill died and bequeathed *Dovetail* to a charity locally.

Epilogue: In the fall of 2005 my new bride and I were curious about Islesboro, the island the Sampsons were fond of sailing to and around. Since she and I were staying in Camden, and her good friend's husband grew up on the island, we took a ferry to Dark Harbor, with the car. We had a picnic on a pebbly beach and dinner at one of the few restaurants open. That evening we went to the local church to hear a former CIA agent talk about a book he published. As folks strolled out in sunset, I introduced myself to a gentleman wearing garb from the same club at I. Turns out that was a life-altering meeting, since half a year later he employed me in Stamford, we moved to Norwalk, and I remained in the tri-state area until 2019….

Voyage 15: *Wave of Peace*, Daywork, Camden, Newport, August, September 1993

August 5, 1993, Thursday, 10:30 am. At Balmead Manor, astride Ruggles Avenue and Bellevue Avenue, Newport. Sitting here in the kitchen on this bright sunny day after three days of solid work aboard *Wave of Peace,* the yellow-hulled Dutch 72-foot Jongert-built Dutch sailing yacht with a 105-foot mast! It is presently berthed at Bannister's Wharf, right downtown and down-dock from the Clarke Cooke House, where I once worked. The skipper is Andrew of Perth, Australia, and his companion Fiona.

It's good work with Bongo of Antigua, a jovial fellow in his 30s who is sending money to his Mum, in assistance. I spent 29 hours working aboard, which I spent in just a few hours following payoff. Shame on me. Will be fortunate to deposit any. Return to Boston this afternoon at 2 pm, unless an offer to be flown to Greece and sail aboard a 192-foot schooner named *Mistress* for six months, comes through Worldwide Yachting Company, run by Norma Trease in Florida.

Further Reading: For more on Andrew of *Wave of Peace*, see account of delivery of *Swan* yacht *Pericles*, from Lockeport Nova Scotia to Newport; same captain, Australian Andrew, hired me again on the cusp; the shortest activation of my career, thanks to Captain Andrew Burton in Newport, about August, 1999. He had broken up with his mate by then.

Chapter 6

Voyage 16: *Breathless*, Newport-Lauderdale via Bahamas, Sept.-October, 1993

September 14, 1993, Tuesday. I worked on *Geronimo*, rowing to work, then on Thursday September 16, I moved off *Whisper* first thing, onto *Breathless*. Did banking through Seamen's Church and the large downtown Post Office opposite the Red Parrot. Settled accounts, bought supplies. Woke aboard the *Whisper of Maine,* moored on heavy mooring ball number 865 off Ida Lewis Yacht Club on the way to Brenton Cove in Newport Harbor. This morning from 8 am to 10:30 am I cleared off her, playing Pearl Jam's *Alive*, and *Black*, and Enya's Clannad while packing, washing, rinsing, and taking inventory for Dr. Brotman, the generous skipper, owner patron. Then at 10:30 am the Oldport Launch under Matt Galvin came serving Brenton Cove and having been summoned via VHF radio, took me and my gear across the inner harbor to SY *Breathless*. This is my new home, having been recruited at Zelda's one evening recently by Manfred, Samantha and their friend Kimberly.

September 16, 1993, Thursday, 5pm. Newport Marina, Lee Wharf and Brown & Howard wharves. Aboard the Mason-designed, 64-foot sailing sloop *Breathless*, Manfred Advent of Jamestown, skipper, in Newport. His British girlfriend Samantha is mate. Wet, cool to cold, overcast. Winds 15-20 knots, ESE. Temperature 60°F. It is the very busy annual Newport Boat Show. Business day: First money in my possession (which hasn't been overdrafted) in over two months. Now I'm preparing to ship out on a paid passage to home port at Lyford Cay Marina Nassau, Bahamas. I cashed Delta's check reimbursement for my damaged computer at the Seamen's Institute (they ask no questions of sailors or fishermen, as does Mrs. Mary Salas at the eponymous restaurant), got settled, and mailed all debts and credit, and bought supplies to seal it.

September 17, 1993, Friday, Newport. Work schedule aboard SY *Breathless*. Arrived in Newport from Greenwich by train and then a generous ride offered by Angela's brother, who happened to have a St. George's sticker on the back of Dad's Volvo (Angela was with her Spanish boyfriend on the same train). Stayed and slept on *Whisper*, Sunday, September 12. Was offered hot showers. The next day I hit the docks looked for an apartment from about 5 pm. Then I met Manfred and Samantha, with Kimberly at O'Brian's on Lower Thames Street, near Scales and Shells. Kimberly did all she could to get me the job, but everyone was stumped by the "trans-Atlantic attempt" on my CV! Work on *Breathless* began, so I slept aboard. On first full day I mailed her dock package, cleaned aft cabin, ran errands, applied grease gun to propeller shaft, and doused the # 3 jib sail.

September 18, 1993, Saturday, my second day of work. Went for charts at Armchair Sailor Bookstore nearby [I later worked there 1998-1999], inspected # 3 jib, laundry, taped window, cleaned lazarettes, vacuumed and cleaned interior, bought oil filter clamp. Sunday September 19, third day of work; clear, sunny. Cushions, returned tracker, called Lyford Cay, set cooler, provisions.

September 20, 1993, Monday; we are estimated to depart at noon. Mast checked, dinghy hoisted up onto deck, diesel and water tanks topped up at nearby fuel dock, and we pushed off. Log by crew of *Breathless* Newport to Nassau: 64-foot sloop, delivery south.

September 21, 1993, Tuesday, 2.30 pm. Wet, rainy, seas are three to five feet on the beam (amidships). Barometric pressure 1018.5 millibars, wind two to five knots, Force 3 apparent, from the SSW. Course 225º, SW. Bound from Newport to Nassau, Bahamas via Cape Hatteras, North Carolina. Position 39ºN, 70ºW. So, this is what is meant by *delivery*: we've been flying our Detroit sail since leaning Newport, meaning we've been only motoring with our strong Detroit Diesel engine against a reasonably calm but dead-on-the-nose swell. We have sighted many, many vessels all through yesterday evening and last night through this morning when I stood watch alone from 6-9 am. We stand three-hour day watches, with nine hours off, then two hours at night with six hours off. I cooked Beef Stroganov with noodles last night; it was basically Hamburger Helper out of the box, so I just read the directions, with rice and salad followed by coffee and smokes. Today someone else cooks. We'll see. Delivery is constant; we are speeding to get there; Samantha must leave the US in order to renew her via in Fort Lauderdale, or at least that's the plan. What happens now? My atlas. *Escapism*; geography is not visible.

What we will know or believe of one another is limited. What we will not know about one another is infinite. To know and to believe are two very different perceptions, but what is knowledge without the connection of belief to support it and what is belief without the desire, believe or the resignation to acknowledge I pose these questions to all. [Drawings: *The Horror, the Horror*, Marlowe in *The Heart of Darkness,* and Kurtz in *Apocalypse Now*, *Regnar Mycket* (it rains a lot), *Café in the Grass in the Weeds, Upside Down*, and *The Inquisitor*].

September 22, 1993, Wednesday, 5 pm. Aboard *Breathless*, on the forwardmost point or bowsprit, heading SSE in the Gulf Stream, 35ºN, 74ºW, about 150 nm off Cape Hatteras, bound for Nassau. Clear, cool, warm, sunny, partly cloudy. I'm sitting here on the bowsprit in a slatted wooden seat at the pointing end of *Breathless,* after our crew beer and smokes and ratings of the day and jokes [a tradition Manfred and Samantha believe in and I see the merits of, as we mostly stand watches alone and silently]. I am very content and joyfully relieved by them; not racing or bound somewhere north, but cruising south with the sails (mainsail and jib #3, both full) swung out to starboard on a beam reach, bound home!

Today two firsts; after accidently stepping on the cover on the engine switches in cockpit, I inadvertently shut off the engine in full stride last night, I today dropped our only winch handle over the starboard side while hydraulically setting the jib and mainsails, but then accidentally pushed the buttons which activated the winches against my manual efforts, forcing the metal handle out of the grooves at the top of the winch and into the air, bouncing on the deck and over the side, for some marine archaeologist to find. Fortunately, I soon thereafter managed to pull in an edible dolphin fish, or dorado, so it's okay. My hands were pulsating after the effort of reeling in the heavy fish.

At 5:26 pm we were all just interrupted in what we were doing (mostly personal things, like listening, and reading) to appreciate a mammoth grey whale, which was broaching both near and far. The cycle of life seems to come to life after we threaded a regurgitated fry (small fish), from the dorado's belly onto our hook, ha! Sitting here, it has been hard to rekindle those original nostalgic urges which have plagued me so often. Going back to sea on both the smallest and greatest of days and voyages, this is in a sense an urge, an intangible feeling, or yearning.

For years in the musty cloisters of Oxford and asphyxiating rot of suburban USA, it has remained dormant, yet I am as determined as ever. I knew that I had to return to sea, and that I have indefinitely. I understand more tangibly why this offshore breeze, clear and cool, all the visual blues, and the scent of Vince Johnson's dinner wafting up from below spurs thoughts of over-inherited relationships ashore; the promise of hard cash on arrival, which is a new sensation. All of these stimulants merely remind me and reinforce my desire to be back at sea and my gratitude for being here now, not languishing in port alone and largely unpaid, which is how I seem to have spent much of the summer.

September 24, 1993, Friday, 4.45 pm. 31°15'.44N, 75°52'.96W. At 3:40 pm *Breathless* altered course from 225° SW to 270° W and reduced speed. Within minutes, we had retrieved a battered orange life-ring. This was the culmination of days of my scouring the horizon with eyes. I in particular had developed an obsession with finding a life raft filled with a crew of sailing survivors, or at least seeing them and coming to their assistance. I had become convinced, over the course of days in increasing calm waters, that we were in an ideal situation to retrieve flotsam and survivors of shipwreck. We were coasting along on a belly-flat sea under motor power in relatively remote waters of the confluence of the western fringe of the wide Sargasso Sea and the eastern fringe of the Gulf Stream. This orange life-ring floated daintily with its emergency strobe-light dangling from a coarse yellow line. It also had a dozen or more fish of several varieties seeking shelter beneath it. It was labelled on large black stencil print: *Philadelphia, New York, NY*. The discovery and subsequent retrieval by Vince and I in the bow, with our long telescoping boat hook, was at the same time enervating and unnerving.

On bringing it aboard and make it part of our small community, a sort of eerie peace settled over us. That was most of yesterday, and after I had cooked and served a dinner of spaghetti with pesto sauce, Italian sausage, and corn kernels, complemented with a salad of carrot shavings, cucumber, tomato and green peppers with honey-mustard sauce and our daily beer, we cut off the engine and simply drifted in a most magnificent and splendid manner to the sounds of Enya and her band Clannad. With that soothing instrumental and vocal music, whales in the distance and the sunset surrounding us, I really understood why I love the sea.

September 25, 1993, Saturday, 9.45 am. We are roughly 280 miles north of Grand Bahama, and Freeport. That's 200 nm east of St. Augustine, Florida. We are heading SSW, and 225° to Bimini; not our original destination of Nassau and Lyford Cay. It is clear, sunny, and warm, with my 6 am to 9 am watch duty in sunrise behind me, alone with more fishing line out. We have diverted from Lyford Cay Nassau, Bahamas to Miami, due to the owner's accountant; these individuals are known to swing from open floodgates of expenditure to counting toothbrushes bought, depending on the owner's moods. At 5.40 pm, same day: 29°20'N, 74°7'W, opposite Cape Canaveral. Heading SW at 6.9 knots. The mainsail is up, and I'm with Captain Mark, Mate, Samantha and Vince Johnson. 8.10 pm. Alone on watch; rain clouds, and thunder. Ship seen dead ahead on radar, four miles to the SW. We are just coasting along, all well. Going south, finally hoping to call in at Bimini for a Birthday beer and bash for Samantha there. Only about 24 hours out from Bimini, not accounting for the strong three to four knot Gulf Stream current against us.

September 26, 1993, Sunday, 9 pm. The current is against us in the Gulf Stream, NNW at about four knots. Bimini is visible, despite being low and flat. It is clear, calm, humid, hot. Entry: We decided over our evening beer together that we would bypass rushing for Bimini tonight in favor of delaying all night, arriving early morning one week after departure from Newport. Manfred and Samantha's plan is to anchor outside in deeper water in order to do work like refitting the boat and general cleanup as needed. Reasons include waiting till after the passage, and because by week's end the owner shall inspect *Breathless* after months and any funds spent. Then it will be decision time as to whether Manfred and Samantha remain aboard as Captain-Mate-Chef couple combination. This will also determine whether I stay on for the trip down-island to the US Virgin Islands and Antigua or not; it is something I could easily do by flying from Nassau to Fort Lauderdale, and I could use the money.

Meanwhile I think that after 6-7 days of confinement, calm, torpor, languishing and its corrosive toll, I'll feel a bit the butt of ill-humor, but it's all well. We'll see, right? What awaits me in Florida? Other deliveries south? The fabled ultimate role: ascending to the industry throne of captaincy? This voyage is in stark contrast to those of Dr. Brotman and family. I'm the youngest aboard, and perhaps the least friendly and least responsible. [Same day, half an hour later]: 9:30 pm. Bimini is only 30 nm, or eight hours away. We are still bucking the Gulf Stream, that hot river of water which is about three feet higher and several degrees hotter than the water either side of it.

Joseph Conrad wrote *A Personal Record*, a wonderful work about being a merchant marine officer. This is a personal record of mine. Simultaneously, I am keeping intermittently a voyage log of *Breathless*' passage south from Newport to Miami initially bound for my home port of Lyford cay, Nassau, and now via Bimini, Berry Islands, Bahamas, and Fort Lauderdale, Florida, from whence to uber-wealthy Fisher's Island, Miami, from whence the owner owns and controls a large shoe brand. I say personal record because, from this afternoon, I'll play closer attention to the personal aspects of this voyage, and the crew who initiate and carry it out. I have learned that as our character roles settle down into an established pattern of sorts, I find the evidence of alchemy unsettling.

The results of this are sure to be evidenced soon: my prediction is that over his own general wishes, the owner will cease the contract of Manfred and Samantha to run the boat, and, or, I will find sufficient reason to leave the ship in Miami, with a flight to Nassau having been paid out on a *per diem* basis over up to the 14 days of my service. This is beyond satisfactory, and will enable me to open an account with Barclay's Bank PLC, in Nassau, and wait there, possibly in Cable Beach Manor's Apartment 1, until I find and ship out on another vessel. Otherwise, the situation with the owner may well be ripe for the confirmation of the voyage from Florida south, and the eventual chartering of *Breathless* down–island, which I believe is Manfred and Samantha's preferred outcome.

Several factors, however, work against this scenario; the most obvious is the immediate threat of us all being axed from the boat, by a dissatisfied or disgruntled owner fed stories of financial irregularities or worth graft by Manfred and Samantha. This is basically beyond all of our control, except insomuch as we can best prepare the vessel for review by the owner next week. More unsettling for me is recent evidence that I have become seen as, or worse, have proven myself to be, a less contributive, even to the same number of a limited crew. Manfred is an apt Captain, very deft at engine maintenance and alterations, and is doing well at getting us there happily. Though we are not yet cleared in at Bimini, we are also just a short voyage west to Fort Lauderdale. All well.

September 27, 1993, 5.30 pm. *Some humorous moments from this voyage:* I received shit from fellow crew for chop-stick straddling a fence (one leg at the time) in Newport when trying to leave a party drunk, with rum in hand, but took a wrong turn and was seen by folks arriving for the same party! Owning and actually riding *Cornelius*, my rusty old bicycle dredged from Lee's Wharf. Dropping a winch handle overboard. Melting a plastic bread wrapper onto the surface of Samantha's *Breathless* microwave. Getting so very excited over discovery and retrieval of the life ring for the tug *Philadelphia*, which I plan to check in as hand-carried luggage for the flight to Nassau. I've gotten credit for donating three adventure team flashlights to boat, cleaning the interior, making Swedish pancakes.

Some of my jokes were well received, as in when, in O'Brien's Pub, local and Salve Regina watering hole near the IYAC bar and IYRS yacht restoration school, a female photographer assembled some guys for a group photo, but made an off-hand question about the size and depth of the group, to which I made a quick-tongued retort. Timing: comedy is tragedy plus time. Vince on deck, describing catching rays to us at happy hour in the cockpit: *I found myself lying in a pool of sweat*, he says. *Well, whose was it*? I asked! I got laughs from Captain Manfred especially for that one.

Vince has gotten guffaws for his (feigned) anxiety to greet and bash *homos* in port, as in our homeport, Newport. He's an ex-navy safety officer from New Bedford. My imitation of Camden and Maine accents draw laughs. Manfred secretly radioed me on a yacht as I made my entry into navigation station, or cockpit for strategy. He used a portable VHF hand-held radio from the cockpit, to say *You are lost*. I came up to the cockpit where he was and acted confused, saying that a lonely merchant mariner called me, (playing along with it). Then I said; *Well, I am not lost; I can find my way to and from my bunk, and I know my way to and from cockpit and galley*! This drew laughs from our captain and navi-guesser (ribbing for navigator). It also led to a great reenactment that evening by Manfred at happy hour.

I earned great brownie points by volunteering to hold anchor watch on our one projected night in Bimini; in other words, to remain aboard while they galivanted ashore in my home country. A striking thing happened on arrival in the morning; we anchored in about 100 feet of clear turquoise water, unable to see the limestone bottom. Because of all the Sargasso weed getting tangled up in the delicate instruments like odometer, which could only be cleared by pulling the plug (thus letting water into the boat for a few seconds), inserting a dud plug in the hole while you clear off the weed and so on, Manfred sent Vince over the side to do what he could to inspect the through-hull instruments for other weeds or impediments, as we still had problems with the reading, which effected our log and predictions for the voyage (GPS was not fully accessible yet, or at least we didn't just rely on it).

Well, Vince gamely hopped over, but we had not yet remembered to lower a swimming ladder or platform for him at the stern or the side of the boat. He made about two dives on the starboard side, which was facing south, full emblazoned by the sun, and all three of his crewmates were watching him to learn what he found and could fix. Suddenly I noticed two brown dots either side of him, growing in size quickly. They were sharks. Aggressive sharks, making full speed from very deep right for Vince, one on either side. He surfaced and innocently looked up at us for input on the through-hull fittings. I grabbed the nearest jib sheet, or sailing line, about an inch thick, and quickly threw it over the side of the boat at him, knowing it was secured to the boat.

Very calmly, evenly, but clearly intently, I said to him: Vince, I've lowered the line to you. You have to grab it and climb up the side of the boat – immediately! Don't ask questions and don't look around. Being a navy veteran who had put out fires under attack in the Middle East, Vince did exactly as he was told and only learned of the dreaded sharks after he was safely on board *Breathless*' hot, dry decks. Work on the through-hulls could wait till Florida. But alas, this service was not needed, because after frenzied work and shuttle diplomacy from 9 am to 4 pm we were still unable to clear the yacht into Bahamas. At about 4 pm we pulled up anchor from offshore Bimini, outside and west or the Florida side of Alice Town, and left.

Some first experiences for me of this voyage: the eastern seaboard, Newport to Miami; absolutely glass-calm ocean, Sargasso Sea. Retrieving a genuine life ring from the Saragossa Sea. Eerie, damn-near collision (near-miss, they are called), by a mere two boat lengths last night; I was nearly crushed to death in my cabin. The next day (today!) we were hailed and closely inspected by US Coast Guard island class patrol boat *Maui* [WPB-1304, in the Persian Gulf in 2019]! This led to several odd exchanges. They call us, Manfred replies. They ask where we are going, are told Fort Lauderdale from Newport. They ask why we deviated to Bimini Bahamas for a few hours and sent a boat ashore and had a boat come back with us. Manfred has trouble explaining that one, since we never cleared in or out, and remember we are all in our twenties!

As they approach closer, Vince and I are in the cockpit with a partially empty case of Budweiser beer and empty and full cans, so we start frantically calling out *Hide the Bud, hide the Bud*! and handing it down below and out of sight of the coasties. The coast guard officer asks what we are doing on *Breathless*, and because Manfred does not want his girlfriend busted for immigration infringement, which was our entire purpose of going to

Bahamas for a US visa and immigration renewal, and he doesn't want to declare earnings, either, he nonchalantly says we are friends of the owners, just moving his boat for him.

The USCGC *Maui* intercepts us. I had to crop out faces, but you can see the right shoulder of the helmsman to the right and the Bimini top wrapped up in between them.

But when the USCG ask us for the name and address of the owner, Manfred panics and asks, where is the fucking owner's name? And there is a scramble while they rifle through papers to find it! Some friends, huh? Didn't know his name! Finally, when we get clearance to proceed, the starboard side of cutter *Maui*, which is the only side we've been permitted to see, is turned away from us and suddenly we see for the first time that on the opposite side are half a dozen fully armed assault troops in black gear ready to fire on us!

And, to top it off, they are equipped with huge domes for listening to voices far away, and could almost certainly hear, or so we believed, us desperately yelling *Hide the Bud*! And *Who is the owner*? And still they let us through, perhaps assuming we were dumber than dangerous. Samantha's birthday is tomorrow. Manfred and Samantha below watching *Star Trek*. Vince, after many beers, is at rest. Enough for now. I have a boat to sail, and to hold

September 30, 1993, Thursday, 4.45 pm. I'm sitting and writing on sister Ann's porch, which is our Farmor's favorite perch, at Mom and Dad's home *Palmeiras*, Nassau, Bahamas. Thoroughly depressed. Today I left the ship. And though it may be mere days, perhaps two weeks until I ship back out; utilizing, say, the ticket purchased by *Breathless* for today's flight, which I didn't use, as Dad bought me one, and is good for a return to Fort Lauderdale by October 18. It is disheartening and lonely to pack up so quickly this morning, then part with Vince and crew at 10 am, and return to *Breathless* for only a few minutes to say farewell. What is most saddening is to think of the dreary prospects awaiting Manfred and Samantha, the young couple who have been together for three years. Now they must now return to the sobering reunion with the owner in Fisher's Island, off Miami then discuss and contemplate their future aboard her.

Breathless immediate future is far from certain; ideally, they continue along their way south, rendezvousing with Dan off *Reverie* in Miami, for a passage south to the US Virgin Islands, and onward to Antigua. The owner wants to put the brakes on spending, Manfred and Samantha prefer to remove the governor, or breaks, and let loose south! I'm learning about an under-the-table industry which thrives meanwhile, in the form of T-shirts, with costs for maintenance and upkeep, remaining high. The Detroit Diesel representative who drove from Massachusetts to overhaul and service the engines in Newport cost a ton, starting the moment they left their home to the boat. Then we left the good oil on the dock. I dread the outcome of this imminent, yet only their second, encounter with the owner, who seems a sincere and positive enough character. A clothing industry CEO or owner, he hopes to buy a new boat.

Whether or not Samantha and Manfred remain aboard the first boat (*Breathless*), or even the prospective new boat, remains to be seen. Mark, I think, would like to see me help sail the boat south from Miami, so might I. Samantha, I think, is lukewarm; after all, I did melt a bread wrapper on the microwave top and drop a winch handle in the sea! We shall see. Manfred and I shall talk within a week, and shall know then whether his plans or mine will reach fruition or fall asunder, leaving possibly all of us, with the exception probably of Vince Johnson, on the beach.

Vince returns to Boston this afternoon, at noon, to stay with his sister and then return to Newport to resume a passage north aboard a summer tourist passenger schooner name *Madeleine* for several weeks before packing up and moving south to South Beach, Miami to paint and renovate the Avalon Hotel there, which is owned by a successful middle-aged Newport hospitality entrepreneur (Don Glassie), who build a luxury passenger ship from an old steel fishing hull to create the *Arabella* [I often saw him alone at the bar of the *Asterix and Obelix*, or A&O in the Fifth Ward, Newport, owned by a Dane named Jan].

I miss them each and all already, and though my own immediate future looks promising, as I am set to fill in for a crew departing the 192-foot schooner *Mistress* in mid-October in Greece, nothing is finite. Manfred and Samantha and the owner's going-ons are beyond my control, so meanwhile, here I sit, exhausted after 16 days constant wear and general lack of sleep. I of course had to be extra alert while watch keeping on *Breathless* or drinking ashore in Newport at O'Brien's, Zelda's Cafe, The Downtown AC, or International Yacht and Athletic Club; aka IYAC, or *I-yack*, and at parties. Then in Fort Lauderdale what sailor's watering holes like Flannigan's, The Quarterdeck, Coconut's, Bahia Bay, where we went last night, briefly, and the infamous Pink Pussy Cat. René was our dancer, conversationally age 20, and Samantha the bouncer, barwoman. The Booby Trap, was constructed of two actual huge pink domes with nipples on top on SE 17th Street, right beside the crew agencies, has seen come down, but was a famous spot for sailors to go for legs and eggs and strippers at the *Snort Liquordale* Center for the Performing Arts.

So, I sit here, under-fed since dinner at the 15th Street Fishery restaurant where Dad took me last night, hungover, sleep-deprived, depressed, and craving numerous and sundry dinks. I'm on my fourth carton of Marlboro red hard-packs in as many weeks, and all does not look well. Well I'm not too spoilt, I should appreciate my stay here; take the small family power boat named *Ma'Wessel* out for spins and document my time for a captain's license. I need to get CPR, or cardiopulmonary resuscitation health certification from the Red Cross. *Wanderer*'s crew under skipper Sterling Hayden's 1950 voyage visit to Nassau must still be in the microfiche reels in the National Archives off Blue Hill Road downtown.

October 1, 1993, Friday. Home in Nassau *Breathless* is still in south Florida.

October 5, 1993 Tuesday, 3.30 am. Not truly happy here, and Clarissa's visit really threatened that. I was at risk of spending all my remaining money from *Breathless* work and remain here, never fully committing to proposed work at Cable Beach Manor, the family business. Otherwise I ship back to Florida or Newport as soon as possible to resume work aboard boats. I could deliver one south from Newport, picking one up through World-wide Yacht Services in Florida, though their business model is to get the first month's wage and deliveries hardly last two weeks most of the time. It may need doing sooner than expected. I may of course, find more work in boats and restorations in Nassau, or even Harbor Island. Who the fuck knows? Meanwhile, I'm *rotting*. If I ain't happy, then get out! And I've got a cold, since I smoke to much! I need to call Newport Yachting Services' (NYS) Nigel Henderson, who helped with *Breathless*. I need to fax my resumé to Worldwide Yachting Services' Norma Trease regarding Greece, Hassle Free, Crew Finders, photocopy.

Aargh! Fuck! I am *on the beach* again. Fucking beached whale! [Same day]: 4.50 am, same (not sane!). I am still in apartment #1. [Same day]: Tuesday, 12:45 pm. Cable Beach Manor, in the manager's apartment, first door on right insight gate, cover the main entrance. Nassau. Synopsis of my recent eight-day voyage on the good ship *Breathless*. Two pairs of nicotine and caffeine-addicted sailors driving a boat south for 1,500 miles and eight days. We all had two cartons of cigarettes, Marlboro reds or lights, and consumed about two gallons of coffee grounds: about one quart-sized packet of grounds each! Great! We had supplies. On my return to Nassau after a decade of school in New England, I experienced a tannic, or acidic reminder of my lot.

Today when port-controller Leon Flowers rejected my application for captain', or master's license; also, the Bahamian car registry denied my application for a driver's license as I don't live her, or cannot legally live here! Where I have rights, the US, I have no home, and where I have a home, Bahamas, I have no rights. Possible homes for me to pursue…. South America; who the fuck knows! Sweden? Solution: an island somewhere!

October 10, 1993, Sunday, 3.20 pm. Apartment #1, Cable Beach Manor., family business. My life and conduct here has been pitiful, disgraceful. Need to work towards my master's license. From recent discussions *ashore* (with Vince Johnson) I am an armchair proletariat. The truth is, I'd like to be living, the truly physical, pragmatic, and inspirational, life aboard and offshore. Or to be holed up and hibernating in a secluded peace, fully frenetically writing on my own ashore. Either-or; I hate this middle-ground, interim; being a fish out of water. Large yacht *Mistress* left Greece and is in Spain or Barcelona taking on fuel to bunker for trans-Atlantic voyage, possible via or to Bahamas. *Breathless* is in Florida, possibly to Antigua later. *Black Knight* at Lyford, thence to USA, probably Long Island Sound, New York, where the owner lives.

Note: For the details of my efforts over the next decades to both preserve the life ring against hurricanes and neglect, and reunite it with the ship it was lost from, see the Appendices, "2018 Outline of details of the Life Ring *Breathless* and ITB *Philadelphia* story," with photos.

Voyage 17: *Power Play* **Palm Beach, November, 1993**

Motor yacht *Power Play* under way; a condition I was never able to observe, as the gear box broke a few hundred yards from Brazilian Avenue Dock, Palm Beach. Note the Cadillac on the upper deck. There was an oxygen machine near the master cabin bunk. This was the second and last yacht with it's own postcard that I worked on.

August 5, 1993, Newport. ....unless an offer to be flown to Greece and sail aboard a 192-foot schooner named *Mistress* for six months, comes through Worldwide Yachting Company in Fort Lauderdale, run by Norma Trease.

November 11, 1993, Thursday, 7.30 pm. Aboard the motor yacht *Power Play* on Brazilian Dock Marina, at the sheltered, or western side of the island of Palm Beach, Florida. I'm already a bit homesick, and as my mister says, feeling sorry for myself. I have found no girls here, at least not ones who would date a hired sailing hand. And even the fancy New York City bank here would not open an account for me on such a pittance of a salary; and because all the other employees of he and *Mistress* have disappointed them and not lasted long. A bit beleaguering. I do have access to a car, though. And I just shopped around for other motor yacht positions. We'll see. I'm ready to grow to love the single rewards, or fail and be again on the beach and marooned. *Destiny*. I had lovely farewell wishes from Celine and Brent are good friends of John's from their summers on Nantucket, and she's John's girlfriend. Both are from Wellington, New Zealand. *Mistress* seems ready to daily drop out of the sky any day as she struggles to cross the North Atlantic from Gibraltar with harsh weather, contaminated fuel, and an inability to properly sail.

November 12, 1993, Friday, 11.44 am. Aboard the motor yacht MV *Power Play*, Palm Beach, Florida. god, I feel lonely and homesick. I just want to go home again, and work on my correspondence and my US Coast Guard license. If only I could establish some friendly intimate contact. How appealing work tomorrow now sounds; how much I want to be happy again! No security, and left off, now calling in earnest. *The future belongs to those who believe in the beauty of their dreams*, said Eleanor Roosevelt, cousin and wife of FDR, who named many of the Liberty ships launched in World War II.

November 14, 1993, Sunday, 4 am. At Brazilian Dock, aboard *Power Play*, Palm Beach, Florida at slip 118, under Captain Banjo of a quarry town in Maine. Hello. All well. Much better than the oppressive self-pity and self- disgust a much has characterized my outlook recently or threatened to derail and sink me during the past few months. Meanwhile, things are going pretty well, and they certainly could be a lot worse. I have a job with a decent income and this is good. I will undoubtedly learn much in the coming months, and this is my first season in the south, and Palm Beach in particular. I've done several seasons in New England, at Newport, in Maine, even toured Nantucket and the Vineyard. Now it's a time to see how it's done down south; not even the Swedish-English season, but the American one, where the snow-birds come to escape the cold. I have a lot to learn, and the attentive ear and eye shall be rewarded. A few months of stability, commitment and income can only do me well, anyway.

PS: This is the third full day that I have had this elegant 118-foot motor yacht to myself, and it has been relaxing and wonderful, overlooking the intracoastal waterway, the Royal Park Bridge, which leads to Royal Palm Way, which dissects the island south of its midriff. I revel in seeing the boats, the cars, the yachts, the people. Though I could, I haven't left the boat at all, but have concerned myself with reading and writing and absorbing all the stimuli, and learning more information about this new realm; the mega-yachts, the power yachts, the yachts that go to the Pacific, the Mediterranean, the Indian Ocean, the Caribbean, the eastern seaboard and west coast of North America; what range!

Oh, the adventures I should have, to paraphrase Dr. Seuss! And the responsibilities I have been given and already entrusted to. True to my word, I have showed up for work, and was treated in kind here. When ship's power was lost, it meant my having to find and switch on the main circuit breaker, and without lights or training in it. I succeeded nevertheless. Tuesday evening at 5:45 pm, while watching the film *Midnight Express* on video player in the aft salon, starboard or shoreward side, all shore power in the area cut out. Unable to see the film, I rested 6 pm until midnight, then reactivated the power since *Power Play* had lost all power, and it would not have been good for all the frozen and refrigerated items to melt, especially before Thanksgiving, with the Owners bringing friends and family aboard for a feast laid on by Mr. Owner's Canadian wife *dieux*.

November 16, 1993, Tuesday, midnight. All well abroad *Power Play*. I am happy and content, the weather is clear, and good-to-great news and confidence booster begs to be told. I feel lazier by being stateside. All is well here after this weekend work resumed without Captain Banjo and Zebulon the mate and engineer. I have swum twice, on Sunday evenings. I have watched French and other films: *Midnight Express, Blues Brothers, Le Gran Blue, or Big Blue, and Das Boot, or The Boat (U-93)*.

Tonight, a riddle: she is the wife of my love, of course, but the humor is that she married my true love- myself, ha! The boat *Mistress* was built in the shipyard in Australia as their first of a kind, yet Owner created a lot of modifications, left without paying, and sued them out of business! On the voyage east to the Americas they are said to have caught a couple sailfish or similar near Panama, but nothing else. I'm in Palm Beach! Warm, and I love it! Broken neck, teeth insurance travel, work shop, no sinks. For Banjo and his wife, business versus friendship are always at play. Banjo tells me the owner has 15 known ongoing lawsuits; one against family, as in his own daughter, others against adopted children, one against or by Captain Banjo for injuries from falling into the engine room not once but more. But what really pisses Banjo off is that in all that time the Owner never learned or remembered Mrs. Banjo's name.

November 18, 1993, Thursday noon. Aboard *Power Play* on Brazilian Dock in Palm Beach. Here I am, waiting for an unfamiliar and dreaded scenario to unfold around me; to envelope the little cocoon of an existence that I have woven around myself during my first week here aboard *Power Play* in recent weeks. Within the hour the owner Mr. Owner is coming aboard until at least December 12. As the good Captain Banjo says, *Hurry up, Jim!* British sea captain James is still making their way from Spain. Captain James will bring *Mistress* in soon! Then the owners will welcome her back and prepare for a cruising season in the Bahamas.

November 21, 1993, Sunday. The Heart of Palm Beach Hotel and Restaurant, 180 Royal Palm Way, on the corner of South County Road. I am still happy, and progressing well at my favorite hobby of letter-writing, which continues untraced perhaps, or even inspired by three bunkbeds to sleep in, my first one in and weeks and plenty, plenty, of coffee: about a dozen per day. I sat in the Cape Cod Café on South County Road. Then, after a swim near a wharf I was hit in the face by a surf board on the beach. Then and now the restaurant has three brands and four types of coffee at this bar when I'm just clinching backup mail! Things to do: mail thirty postcards and letters, gifts, and cards from the US.

November 25, 1993, Thursday. Palm Beach. Thanksgiving. [Critical editorial input: I abruptly quit my job on *Power Play* after about two weeks, the first and only time I did so. Dad received a once-in-a-lifetime fax job offer from Chris Orient and Tina Lark aboard *Stornoway* in Panama offering me a mate position to sail from Panama to Galápagos, Marquesas, Rarotonga, Tahiti, Cook Islands, Fiji, Tonga, and New Zealand. It would be paid per week. They would fly me to Panama right away and after repairs from a lightning strike set off, and pay my return airfare from New Zealand to the Bahamas. I had met Matt the crew in Nassau in September. They had sailed via Jamaica but had crew problems and Skip the captain and Vietnam veteran, had quit, leaving them stranded. Tony the mate had been fired. With a bit of encouragement from Dad, perhaps living vicariously, I accepted. I told Captain Banjo that I quit right after Thanksgiving. He told Mr. Owner who swore angrily and called Norma Trease the agent who also was upset. I was just glad to have gotten the hell out of there before *Mistress* even showed up. Guess the bank in Palm Beach was right: I wasn't going to stick around long anyway.

Narrative of the *Power Play* Experience from *Round the World* memoir: I needed work, which I eventually found in Palm Beach. I signed on to the 118-foot, 20-year old motor yacht, *Power Play,* as a training session to become a deck hand. I was training to join a monstrosity of a mega-yacht, all two hundred feet, and a fleet of vessels and vehicles called *Mistress*, a massive power yacht with sails for decoration, an elevator, art collection, and an oxygen machine beside the bed. She was due to cross the Atlantic to Florida any week. I expected it to be the beginning of a career in yachting. By joining what sailors call a 'stinkpot' I had gone to the dark side.

My time aboard *Power Play* was peaceful, private, and otherwise terrible.

A call from my father a week before Thanksgiving interrupted my comfortable, albeit dull, routine. My employer, a New *Jersey* real estate magnate named Eddie Owner answered it, transferring Dad to an ostensibly more private line aboard. I imagine he could hear just fine, because Banjo told me it was his habit to pick up another phone. *Stornoway* had contacted me, my father said. They wanted me to go sailing across the Pacific.

I felt insulted; and disrupted. I had already dealt with the disappointment of *Stornoway*; they hadn't called, and I moved on. I got over it and found work, convinced myself that scrubbing toilets was what yachting was all about. They put me off for nearly two months, and then expect me to come running back? Was I that easy? My father seemed to think so. I will never forget the boyish excitement in his voice:

"Eric! Guess what arrived? You have a chance to sail across the Pacific! Listen to this!" He narrated the fax for me. I could sense his thinly concealed disappointment when I retorted "I have a job, Dad; a good one. The big yacht comes next week. I can't move now. I have commitments. I won't take it." I felt as though he was trying to live through me vicariously – Dad had always given the four of us freedom to choose. His father had insisted on Dad giving up engineering to study law and work for the family business back in Sweden, and demonstrated his natural skill as an engineer at home and the business.

"Look, I'll send this fax through to you. Don't make the decision right now. Wait until you at least see it." As I returned from the phone call, Mr. Owner came up to me in the corridor. It's not that I had to regain my composure; I didn't think I'd ever lost it. And yet he asked me if everything was alright.

"Of course!" I snapped, resentfully. It was for him, I felt, however indirectly, that I had turned down *Stornoway*. Of course I was alright. "That was my father. He wants me to be sure to be home for Christmas," I explained. He seemed to understand. "And maybe a few days at Thanksgiving," I continued. That would be during the following week. I kept going, "And I wanted to know if I'd be able to live ashore while *Mistress* is berthed in Nassau this January." I was being unfair, but I just couldn't help myself.

Later, sitting in my berth, I was annoyed. Now I had a decision to make - an adult decision - whereas before it was made for me. Before I got the offer, if things hadn't turned out the way I wanted, I could console myself that I had done everything I could. But now... Thanksgiving was coming soon, and with it my employer's family. After that, the larger boat would be pulling in from a trans-Atlantic voyage and I would be needed. The agents had recommended me for this job, and it could take me places; the Caribbean, the Mediterranean. The pay was decent, but the larger boat hardly ever seemed to sail. Then there was the postal kiosk in Palm Beach, where the proprietor had snickered at my current job, "That boat," he had scoffed, "we open and close more boxes for crew that quit than for any other boat that comes through here." I didn't like him laughing at me, but I had to admit, being turned down at a Palm Beach bank for trying to open an account on a deckhand's salary of $1,000 a month wasn't pleasant either.

Tina's fax reached me a couple days later. I knew, before even opening the envelope, that soon I would have to talk to my employer. Very candidly. Or carry the weight of my silence in the form of a deep regret, possibly for the rest of my life. The offer marked the last days of my youth. I half wanted to just put it away, shelve it, and not make a decision. But, with trembling fingers and increasing excitement, I opened the envelope. Galapagos, Marquesas, Bora Bora, Tahiti? Excitement started to take hold. It wouldn't be easy, but nothing worth doing ever was, right? A follow-up fax added that I would be mate, with one crew reporting to me. I would get my own room and head (bathroom), and my airfare out and back would be covered. I was sold.

Accepting the offer was easy. Quitting the job I'd committed to, less so. Two agonizing mornings after I had received and accepted the offer, I waited outside the swinging door of the salon until my employer had finished his breakfast.

"Good morning, Sir," it had gone... "I have something to tell you that I feel is important..." [gulp] ... "...And that you should be the first to know." He looked up from his coffee and the paper.

"Sit down, Eric. What is it? What's on your mind?"

"Thank you. I'll be as candid as possible. As you know, I really wanted this job. Badly. I think *Mistress* is a unique boat, and I'll miss not having the chance to see her. As you probably don't know, this year is meant to be my year off for traveling. I plan to return to school after a year or so..." This wasn't easy, but so far so good.

"It's been a dream of mine since childhood," I continued, "to sail around the world. I know it sounds foolish, but ever since my parents gave me [well, they gave my brother] a signed copy of Robin Graham's book *Dove*, about a 16-year-old boy sailing around the world alone in a twenty-four-foot sloop ... Well, I'd honestly hoped that working on *Mistress* would be the beginning: Greece, the Med., crossing the Atlantic again. Only now it's already late in the fall, and I haven't even seen her yet." That wasn't his fault — there was an angry captain somewhere mid-Atlantic as we spoke, stuck with thousands of gallons of contaminated fuel and forced to use the sails, or "rags" as he apparently called them - on his retirement voyage, no less. I was beating around the bush and finally came out with it.

"I've received another offer. From a sailboat..."

"Which one? Who is she? How big?" his competitive streak piqued, probably thinking it was a mega-yacht like his, something he could understand and compete with.

"Her name is *Stornoway*; she's a vintage sailing ketch; probably a rust-bucket, but that's what I really love. She's going across the Pacific, and is waiting for me in Panama now. They want me to be mate. The pay is less than half of what you pay (*but I planned to be at least twice as happy*, I thought to myself). As you probably know, I've never worked on powerboats before. It's different. I feel that I'm not really cut out for it (*it's too bloody sterile: I just clean and wipe, clean and wipe – one of his crew told me that British tycoon Robert Maxwell literally wiped his ass with the yacht's towels before jumping off his yacht*). Really, I'm just a dirty sailor. I like the wind in my hair, the salt on my skin..." I was getting into my lines, already viewing myself as this romantic character pursuing a dream.

I wrapped it up by saying that my bags were fully packed and I was prepared [hoping] to leave *Power Play*, waiving the two weeks' wages due me, if my employer had heard enough and wanted me off his boat. I could understand that. But if he felt he needed me, I would be willing to work on for as long as he felt I was obliged.

There it was in a nutshell. Over to you, Mr. Employer.

"Oh, Hell! Have you told the captain? Banjo! Get in here!" Now it was Banjo's turn to pretend he hadn't been listening; he scurried around the corner from the wheel. "Eric here has decided he's leaving. Find out what you can about his wages and have them sent down. We'll need him through Thanksgiving, which is two weeks even. Five hundred bucks, right?" Captain Banjo didn't seem too surprised. I could still hear the ring of his sage witticisms in my ear, and perhaps he could sense the echo of his own youthful ambitions in mine. Prophetically, the day before I took my stand with our employer, he had offered me a parting volley. Facing down Brazilian Docks and the avenue beyond, he'd looked me hard in the eyes, and said resolutely:

"You could leave this boat now. Just up and go down that dock, and it wouldn't hurt you a bit. You got an education, kid. A real fuckin' education. You got a chance. I don't know what you're doing here. Do something with it." And so I did. I knew that Captain Banjo had a *Stornoway* in his past, too. His wife had told me; it was Alaska. He'd always wanted to go, to do something there, live, and work. And he hadn't. Even turned an offer down once. And that regret rang every time he heard the word Alaska mentioned.

The owner's wife was convinced I was leaving in pursuit of higher wages, and told me so. That's what a string of other absconders had said. It was a simple enough motive, neat and tidy, so I didn't object.

Quitting was invigorating, freeing. But by far the best part of that morning was overhearing my employer's banter with my Victorian-seeming agent, Norma Trease, down in Lauderdale, the one who 'knew the ropes,' and had 'been there' herself. *Been where?* I thought - *Where I was leaving!* The same one who told me, when I walked into her Newport office after a month as watch captain racing to Bermuda and back to Maine, to get rid of the goatee and scrap the earring (that Clarissa had given me) before she'd even talk to me. She had also told me that only engineers become captains.

"Eric's leaving," my employer had begun. Captain and mate were in the wheelhouse too, listening.

"Oh shit!" That was the only time I heard that from her. She had known that I didn't know my ass from my elbow about engines, yet had posted me on a motor-sailor. A "two hundred-foot Australian schooner," she had described it. She knew how to place, and economize, her words. She needn't have said more. I was hooked with that. Too bad for her that Tina was just as good at putting words together. And economizing – the lightning was Tina's only hint. At least I'd seen *Stornoway*, if not actually boarded her. The clincher hurt, but not too much:

"Looks like Eric's not the reliable guy you said he was."

"Looks like it," we heard the agent over the cackle, before she busied herself trying to replace the month's wages she'd just lost. She probably dropped my file in the bin as she reached for some new sucker's CV. The exchange would have hurt the boy who had gone into his salon that morning, but it slid right off me when I emerged. It hadn't been that bad after all, even for a middle child mortified by confrontation, convinced I could always make concessions, mollify, and build a consensus.

After moving my backpack and sailing gear onto the dock I helped untie *Power Play* for its rendezvous with *Mistress* in Miami. The current carried her into midstream, where the main bridge on Okeechobee Boulevard opened for her transit out, stopping traffic both ways. But she just sat there, looking so regal, facing the open bridge. Minutes ticked by. Car horns started blaring. I could hear urgent VHF chatter from nearby boats. *Power Play* would not slip into forward gear – could not move ahead. Resignedly, Banjo and Zebulon were forced to quit and maneuver her back to the berth using only reverse gear, a challenging operation. Hopefully the local newsmen didn't pick up on it.

Not one to bolt or gloat (!), I dutifully tied her back up and, embarrassed by such public face losing, scurried down the docks without looking back. This rat had jumped ship – just in time, it seemed. I left *Power Play* in Palm Beach the morning after Thanksgiving, bound first home to Nassau, then up to New York to see Clarissa, and back to Nassau, before finally pushing off for Panama a week later. It's funny, but in the over 25 years since then, I never used a crew agent again, except as the captain and employer of crew (as in, their payer of bill and client), or as an equal, with my own delivery agency where we would convivially share candidates as it suited everyone to do so. My days as an agency commodity, of paying an enrollment fee to be told not to bother stopping by the office, and told how to look, were over. I've never worn a captain's hat.

Chapter 7

Voyage 18: *Stornoway*, Panama-Galapagos, November 1993 to May, 1994

This is a very worn image of a poster I made representing *Stornoway* at anchor in Nuku Hiva, Marquesas, with Panama to the upper right, New Zealand to the lower left, and different panels depicting key events. I hand-made about 50 of these and mailed them around the world. Perhaps inspired by the primitive art style of Paul Gauguin, Peruvian French primitivist sculptor and painter who I greatly admire.

December 4, 1993, Saturday. Panama City, Republic of Panama. Shopping spree. Then, another boat-focused shopping spree in Panama City with Tina and Chris in a rented cab with my first pay and remnants of my bank account. I bought a nautical ashtray with a sandbag to pervert it sliding off tables which in Spanish is *cenicero con arena*, or *ashtray with sand*.

December 7, 1993, Outer mooring, just south of the massive trans–continental Bridge of the Americas, aboard *Stornoway*, Balboa Yacht Club in Amador. Chris and Tina orchestrated the crew changes, fortunately sparing me that onerous task (I'm not well suited to be the heavy, or bad guy). Now, with the cyclone and monsoon seasons settling in, we are faced with the prospect of riding out the stormy season in nearby Costa Rica's Pacific coast. It would be an un-planned, extended six-month layover, living aboard in heavy rains, month after month; yet I did not sign up for boat-sitting, rather sailing, voyaging, and moving, which is what I've always done in my yacht delivery career so far, and why I left *Breathless*.

Stornoway's roster will soon be added to by a new captain, Roger , former engineer in the Royal Navy, owns a yacht and condo in Fort Lauderdale, always dreamed of crossing the South Pacific. With Skip saying farewell after the handover, the bloodletting was finally over, with three of the five sailors I met in Nassau culled, and two added, leaving us one person short from the original, with four: Chris, Tina, Roger, and me. A lot of tact and diplomacy, communication, secrets, money and logistics were required to achieve this successfully, which is a credit to Chris and Tina. Roger is now, having done an inventory and audit of the boat, in Panama City working on negotiating the purchase of a new or refurbished life raft, possibly with his own credit card.

December 10, 1993, Friday. I will be crossing the Pacific all of this winter of 1993 and into spring of 1994, returning during or after the cyclone season. This is the question; Ecuador. Balboa Yacht Club, Panama, on the narrow peninsular of Amador, where General Manuel Noriega holed up during the US invasion of the country begun December 20, 1989; just four years earlier. *Errands in Panama City and Balboa*: fill propane tank, taxi to Panama City with Chris, refill five 15-gallon drums with diesel oil, pay with Chris, send fax from the yacht club officer to Dad, permission to buy gifts at Armchair Sailor. We will only remain here until tomorrow, Saturday.

December 11, 1993, Saturday, 11.23 pm. Aboard *Stornoway,* Balboa. Cool and clear, though riddled or sprinkled, or dappled, with overhead clouds and a rainy spray. This is Panamanian winter; mild. Thus far, mostly shopping, spending my weekly stipend. We have bought many more provisions, given that Panama is comparatively cheap and practical and we have up to half a year ahead of us, with the only other city being Tahiti. Also one is supposed to add 30% to whatever duration of voyage you expect, as a safety precaution for if and when things go wrong and you find yourselves adrift with no mast or engine, or sinking, or shorthanded; all manner of scenarios. I bought six (6!) cartons of Marlboro red hard-pack cigarettes, one dozen rolls of 35-milimeter film, several pornographic magazines, and a wide-base sailor's coffee mug. I also bought a lovely white Balboa Yacht Club polo shirt with a light blue and gold crest from the friendly team in the front office [who allowed thousands of club dues receipts from rich people's yachts to be burned at the low water mark, but when the ocean came it doused the fire and all the personal details were sent drifting in and out of the canal, leading to a scramble in boats and on foot to recapture them! Worse still, a couple years later, on February 18, 1999, friends' parents watched the club burn but not until the managers and security had ensured homeless drifters and drunks had been paid to vacate the area; insurance lightning I think it's called].

I also bought a unique Guatemalan hand-woven vest in red, yellow and green Rasta colors, called a *ping-ping* vest. Nowadays I am increasingly working on the boat, inspired by Roger's work ethic after being dispirited by the lack of one shown by Mathew or Chris. I am checking cotter pins at the base of the standing, or metal and wire rigging for the large aluminum main mast. Also, the sheaths or metal tubing around the fixed, metal and wire rigging (as opposed to running rigging called lines or sheets and made of many materials, including polypropylene, nylon, polyester, or in the old days, rope, hemp, or manila), and toe-rail caps are all aluminum.

This was per Chris' practical express desire not to have high-maintenance varnish to work on all the time, and I could not agree more with his philosophy; he also build an engine room you can sleep in which has a Mercedes diesel which you can walk around in strong light and stay warm next to! This is all Roger's marlinspike seamanship, which I find refreshing and hands-on. We also tuned the aft, or mizzen mast, which has been my favorite since *Xebec,* since it's small and you can rig and douse it single-handedly while steering, as the mast is above or just behind the steering wheel. Other tasks involved clearing decks cluttered by our being stationary for weeks, re-fueling, provisioning, buying parts and detergents.

Around this time an extraordinary thing happened; we were at anchor when a major microburst heeled us over nearly sideways right before sunrise and I ran into the cockpit alone. When the storm settled, I heard and saw a black large RIB inflatable motor boat with many electronic items on its; highly unusual looking, and it had not flag that I could see, which is illegal and makes it, technically, a pirate. I ran below to grab my old 35-mm camera and was fumbling with the case and to get it open when the first of several boats past my transom. I saw large machine guns mounted, a tiny American flag painted, and a man with face painted black, a black bandana, gloves, and camouflage. He saw me fumbling with his camera and without saying anything he simply raised his right hand and an index finger, and waved it from right to left to say 'no, no, no, bad idea!'

Seeing this, I slowly lowered my camera and all the boats passed. They had obviously planned to make it back to the nearby base (Fort Kobbe or several others) across the canal when weather or other factors caused them to be seen by a few minutes of sunlight. I learned only later that a few days before, on 2 December, 1993, Columbian drug kingpin Pablo Escobar was assassinated on a roof while speaking to his son at boarding school in the US. Columbian authorities who killed him had the help of US special forces and officials in the DEA. It would have taken a few days for boats and ships return from the Colombian coast to Panama…. And they would not have wanted to be photographed….

Tomorrow on Sunday December 12 in the early morning, we plan under leaderships of Roger to set sail for the Taboga Islands, which are just eight miles out, to the SSW, below the Pacific entrance to the canal. We then plan to return Monday to confirm insurance coverage, pick up the final spares for radar and navigation and SSB [radio equipment which were damaged by the lightning strike in Panama at anchorage before either of us arrived. Then we're off!

December 15, 1993, Wednesday, 10 am. I saw a French captain named Pasqual Patrice and his American and French crew leaving on the large blue Californian sloop *Perseverance*. Also, at the yacht club, I see an 80-foot red catamaran.

December 18, 1993, Saturday 6:30 am. Aboard *Stornoway*, Panama. Clear and cool, orange-tinged sky. Just hailed the *Swan* 53-foot sloop *Ms. Blu* aft of us verbally to say that Darren, crew from California, will be resting ashore this morning through noon, rather than return aboard a busy boat. [He was with my recent date and her brother, Zonies, after a long night of live music and drinking in parked cars at basketball courts in the Canal Zone, American-inhabited if no longer controlled. The crew of their boat still replay my reply of *they tend not to be*, when asked if the moorings are occupied on weekends]. It is sunrise over the Pacific entrance of the Panama Canal. And *Ms. Blu*'s sister ship *Perseverance* just pulled out with the 60-foot ketch *Felicity*, also from California. She arrived first of the two for Antiqua from Tahiti via Panama. The latter will turn right outside the Caribbean canal entrance, for Cartagena Columbia, on her passage from California. One captain, Frenchman Pasqual Patrice, jovial, is with his nephew, and Dolan, the other skipper just had triple-bypass heart surgery. All well. We've been here too long, and my social performance shows it.

December 19, 1993, Sunday, 11.10 pm. Aboard *Stornoway*, bound for Galápagos. We are offshore, outward bound, on a shakedown cruise, or leg one, that is roughly 1,000 nm. Making good speed on a southwesterly course under the #1 jib, and a roller-furling headsail and full main, all of which I just set and hoisted on my own between 9 pm and 10.30 pm. When Chris and I ground Roger up the mast using a winch and windlass, I was breathless and sweating in the heat, despite the breeze. Admittedly, I've been smoking heavily as of late.

Also, I was able to kiss a young woman, age 20 (I'm now 23) named Marci, daughter of a US State Department official who was found by embassy staff at 15 in Mexico City. I was fortunate enough to meet, chat with her then intimately converse with the other everything. Though I thought we were staying a few days to settle up, that night *Stornoway* was motoring in Balboa from the yacht club, listening to a band of American locals and residents played an angry tune about signs fucking up the view [*Signs*, by the Five Man Electrical Band in 1971]. Then we went to a suburb in the Zone. Then we all went to an upscale Zonian suburb called Alemania, but possibly Paraiso. I was very much attracted to her finest, noble, almost-Korean features; she reminded me of Empress Cleopatra, as depicted by Shakespeare.

Then, unfortunately, though she invited me to the apartment she and her brother shared, and indeed Darren accepted, I felt strongly compelled to return to the boat, something I always adhered to in foreign ports, lest I be left behind or shirk my duties, or be seen as a slacker. So, abandoning the prospect of immediate gratification, unslept and un-sober, I let them take me back to the yacht club and my new employers and companions on *Stornoway* so as not to miss our imminent departure, that only we knew about, not Darren or Marci. We slipped out of port after refueling, without, I don't think, paying the full bill. I never saw or heard from Marci again, sadly; I hope Darren has!

December 20, 1993, Monday 8.54 pm. 5°N, 87°W. Aboard *Stornoway*, pushing WSW for the Galápagos Islands, Ecuador. So far, we have covered some 320 miles in 50 hours since departure. We can expect at least three days to cover 500-plus miles left. All very well here, in my comfortable and recently much-enlarged cabin in the home and transport for four people which we call *Stornoway*. I just cleaned my head (toilet) with the chemical named Mr. Clean, having cleaned bulwarks and commode of cabin. I now have my own spacious crescent seating and entertainment leisure reading area to myself at the very front of the boat, after it was cleared by Chris and I yesterday.

Today was a wonderful and glorious day, with Chris and I helming and setting sail from having no wind and using just the engine to obtaining an impressive 6 knots by the 7-11 am watch. Later he and I stood the 3-7 am watch mostly motoring, until we finally set MPS, or multipurpose sail, which is more flexible than a full spinnaker in that it does not require a cumbersome, heavy and dangerous spinnaker pole to be set like a whisker diagonally from the mast. We had the sail up during our 1-7 pm watch. Chris cooked a succulent dorado fish steak on the grill placed on the stern railing, after diving birds visited and ate with us. The ship's cat Davie basked happily in the sun, the, boat hummed, and we were all happy. [Diagram of boat's interior].

December 22, 1993, Leg One: Panama to Galápagos, day five. Entry! All very well. *Stornoway* at 7 pm on Wednesday, making 7 knots. Chris is cooking tuna fish, which, along with fresh fried rice is to be served in cockpit. Van Morrison is serenading me in my spacious, cozy cabin. Morale was low this morning, with rainy cold wet layers overlaying us. We are all a bit fatigued by Roger's rigorous watch-standing system, which demands fourteens hours per day on watch from each of us. We had heaving, confused seas on the nose, but these have largely have subsided. The sun, birds, flying fish, and bananas peeped out with us. Dreams were permitted only after 10:30 pm when we finished dousing the forwardmost jib sail in heavy rain.

December 23, 1993, Thursday, 3.34 pm. Eve-of-Christmas Eve! Aboard *Stornoway* under full sail, one-degree, or 1°N, 88°W. We are coasting along the eastern Pacific Ocean on our sixth day out from Panama, buffeted north by the confluence of the Peruvian and Humboldt currents. All of us are enjoying a brisk sail, though the inner staysail rather than the full #1 jib, whose roller-furling drum broke two nights ago, and two reefs in the mainsail, with breezes of 15 knots from off our port bow. It is certainly a nice sail, enhanced by motor. As my forepeak bunk is to starboard, with the outer hull inches from my face, and my feet from the bow, and we are on a port-tack beat, I slide out board and comfortably against the bulkhead, or cabin side. All is well aboard; it appears that tensions eased with better weather, namely sun, less rain, and lumpy seas. Also, we are all getting more rest after an adjustment to the watch roster. This allows Tina and Chris to spend some much-needed quality time together. I am sitting at the helm as I write, and Roger is at the navigation station, or nav desk with a sextant reading.

[Same day, at 11.55 pm]: We are now roughly in 0°.18"N and 89°.50W. We are approaching Puerto Ayora, in Academy Bay, which is on the south coast of Santa Cruz Island, in the Galápagos Islands, which are owned by the mainland nation of Ecuador, which is named after the equator. More importantly *Stornoway* is on the very threshold of crossing the equator, that dividing line dissecting our planet Earth, as a geographic constraint, at the shore of Santa Cruz, going from north to south. Though I have crossed the equator four times in the past (to and from Australia in 1989 and to and from London and Mombasa in 1992), I have yet to take the infamous nautical passage and to see it from the shipboard perspective! To make the thrill more satisfactory, I am preparing to do so not as a passenger on a cruise liner, or a swabbie on a navy ship, but aboard a 70-foot ocean cruiser. Maybe this will lead to my being given my first beer of the passage. And on Christmas Eve, at age 23! Due to Galápagos or Islas De Colon, fabled isles, sometimes tomorrow noon is a mere 150 or so miles distant after 7:20 am we have just taken a sight for Roger's celestial navigation.

December 26, 1993, Sunday, 11 pm. Puerto Ayora, Santa Cruz, Galápagos. Noteworthy scenes and settings of Christmas, 1993. It is my first away-from-home. At midnight on Christmas Eve we cross the equator north to southern hemisphere. At around noon, December 24, King Neptune and Queen Nefertiti held court, directing the jailor to bind and gag the measly mollusk, or pollywog crew, *Enrique* (Eric) who is accused, and tried from the throng aft. There he was found guilty of tiptoeing across the equator without King Neptune's permission. He may be keel-hauled, which is painful, being dragged under and across the entire hull by hand.

As punishment he is bound and forced to kneel and kiss the feet of Queen Nefertiti, who only wears pasties on her nipples. Then he, the pollywog or mollusk suffers to be photographed as he is punished by having a pie made of rotten bananas and baking soda in and across his face. Two dorados were fortuitously then caught and summarily eaten, all but raw. *Rocas Gordon* (Gordon's Rock, a dive site), is sighted and we weave towards it. By 2 pm on Friday, Christmas Eve!, *Stornoway* rounds the Plaza Islands, passes inside Isla Santa Fe, and enters wide, turquoise Academy Bay, on Santa Cruz, which hosts are large airport on an island named Baltra to the north. We then tuck our worthy ship away, with two anchors. We go ashore and chat with (and donate rum to) the naval port captain in charge of the base, mostly talking about soccer. Then Roger and go to the bar on the waterfront of bustline hamlet Puerto Ayora.

There we met Washington and Antonio. That Friday night [still Christmas Eve], after dinner I clambered ashore with Roger, to rendezvous with Antonio and his partner, Alejandra, for a drink at *Cinco Dedos*, or Five Fingers Bar and Disco. Then the four of us set off to *Tiro Fito*, or Bull's Eye Bar, which is one of three owned by Washington and Abraham. There is clearly chemistry between Captain Roger and Alejandra, Washington's friend from

Quito. They later trundled off to Five Fingers to go dancing. At the clubs and dance halls with several Germans and Ecuadorians, I met and Israeli scientist named Tila. I hope for nookie (action), yet am denied. None. I did however manage to sleep at her place, and early Christmas morning I coffee in café between her pension and the port. It was only about 20 cents, as I contemplated my family opening gifts back home in Nassau. Then I went back to boat with Chris: Roger went off to a Christmas lunch. That evening, we all shared profuse gifts, wine with Chris and Tina aboard in the spacious cockpit, which was decked with colorful lights. I received a metal money clip from Roger, and a T-shirt from Stockholm Café from my sister and her husband.

That afternoon at 2 pm Roger pulled up in a smallish blue chartered speedboat, and so off he and I go with Alejandra, Captain Ramiro and a Swiss couple who are completing a year's jaunt through South America. We went to Isla Commando, a seal rookery in the middle of Academy Bay, to swim with seals and marine guanos. It was fantastic! Then it was off to Lover's Canyon after a walk for a naked cliff dive. Then a boat-ride to a long gulley filled with white-tip sharks. Roger and the Swiss girl swam with sharks. Then we went to Tortuga Bay to the Simon George Beach Observatory for flamingos, but there were none there. [Then Monday, December 27 at 2 am]. Along the way we came across a pair of turtles mating afloat. A bull seal was aggressive towards us. Then we met an eccentric hermit, German émigré who moved to the islands in 1931, possibly named Gustav Engelmier. Then it was back to *Stornoway*, after which Roger went ashore to Alejandra. Chris and Tina then met with Ramiro at Five Fingers, but were interrupted by the pushy Tila, and I ended up talking with her for hours again. No progress. She didn't pass out till 3:30 am, and I went home to *Stornoway* via dingy aboard. She is very aggressive, and has white hair. *Arrrgh!*

December 27, 1993, Monday 1.30 am. Aboard *Stornoway* at anchor in Puerto Ayora, Isla Santa Cruz, the Galápagos. *Things to do*: Process the *zarpe*, or ship's immigration and customs clearance papers with Roger to get stamps on passports and inward and outward clearance stamped for the port captain in the next destination. From the local bus station find a minibus to take us to the mountains to see farms and giant tortoises. As the newest on board, Roger incautiously placed a number of boat-related expenses and charges for fuel and flights, on his personal credit card, not that of the owner, Chris. Rookie mistake.

January 1, 1994, New Year's Day, Saturday, 10.40 am. I came back aboard after swimming the dinghy behind me, as it ran out of fuel at 6:30 am. It was a big night aboard *Stornoway* aboard, with dinner, champagne and even family at a British expat party, an open house by the British High Commissioner, David Balfour. I did some shopping prior to our very long passage to the Marquesas. Bought two more cartons of Marlboro red cigarettes, and tons of Ecuadorian soft suck-able candy to help when I run out of cigarettes. I bought about 3,500 total candies, thinking I could barter them too later in the trip; I hope the South Pacific has a sweet tooth, or good dentists for me!

January 2, 1994, We are anchored in the former German settlement of Black Beach Bay, Floreana, on Santa Maria Island, Galápagos, Ecuador. There is a clear sky, and it is cool, especially for the equator. There is a gentle breeze, and flat calm. As we anchored here in this tranquil, glassy smooth and quiet bay, a tiny seal pup surfaced around us breathing and flopping excited in welcome, coming alongside mere inches from our bodies, which are all leaned over *Stornoway*'s toe-rail. Now we are securely and peaceably rooted to the seafloor for the morning of the second day of the New Year. My nicotine cigarette addiction is being substituted by a candy, fruit, and mint fetish not by six cartons of Marlboros, as before, but now six sacks of sweets! All well to me. I must put postcards in the mail tomorrow, then we set sail for the Marquesas!

January 4, 1994, Tuesday, 5.30 pm. Shipwreck Bay (*Bahía Naufragio*), at Puerto Baquerizo Moreno, the administrative and naval capital of the Galápagos, on San Cristóbal, Ecuador. Breezy, clear, sunny, cool, beautiful. Entry: Aboard *Stornoway* anchored. New and rather uproarious changes today. Captain Roger decided as we departed Academy Bay, Santa Cruz Island last Sunday bound for the Marquesas, that he would no longer sail the good ship *Stornoway* west across the Pacific Ocean to New Zealand, as planned. As I and owners Chris and Tina anticipated, his reasons are manifold. Some are personal, as stated in an (overly) quasi-legal format affidavit, which he read to us in the salon while anchored in Black Beach Bay, Floreana. Roger cited, in person and confidentially to Tina, who asked him to affirm his commitment to our voyage today, many reasons. Among them is his lack of faith in the yacht, the owners, and the crew; meaning me! He told us that he plans to leave us here in Galápagos rather than take us to Quito, on the Ecuadorian mainland, as he may have planned, and where he may see Alejandra. So, for now that is that. As Kant would say, *Das Ding an sich*; the thing as it is, or as itself. *Onward*?

Chris, Tina and I crossing Wreck Bay from *Stornoway* to our French neighbor's boat.

January 5, 1994, Wednesday, 4 am. We've gone from passage-making to puddle-jumping. That is the derisive comment I just made to our ex-captain, lame duck in the cockpit when he found me smoking and made a snide remark about not having the resolve to quit, *à-propos* to my very visible purchase of thousands of sweets, over coffee. Clearly my, and our, respect for him has diminished significantly, particularly after he pulled the boat over on the wrong bay in Floreana; tiny lighthouse at Black Beach Bay rather than the popular Post Office Bay. He didn't even know where we were, and could have wrecked us any manner of ways. It's like landing on the wrong airport.

January 6, 1994, Thursday, 6.30 am. Wreck Bay, Galápagos. This is not mutiny, it's voluntary. This afternoon, in my favorite café in the village; the one which looks like a Wild West saloon with faded chipped green wooden walls and a wide verandah, Chris and Tina heard my ruminations and considered propositions and solutions which I laid before them concerning Roger's proposed abandonment of *Stornoway* for Ecuador. In short, I offered my services as captain, stating my faith in my own navigation abilities and the confidence we all share in the boat under control of five, or at least four, persons. They accepted my proposal, and appointed me captain. Obviously, there are many considerations and responsibilities consummate in my becoming captain of a 68-foot vessel for at least a 4,000-nautical-mile voyage, just to start with, from the Galápagos to Marquesas. Then we won't even be halfway there, so onwards to Tahiti and possibly New Zealand.

The conditions, proposals, ultimatums, and considerations as I laid out were, first: that Roger, the abdicated captain, leaves *Stornoway* immediately. That he hands over ship's papers, or *zarpe*, that we sign on a fourth crew; Delfin of France, that we clear out, with passports, and depart, and that their insurance company in Montreal receives my papers and agrees to insure me on as captain on the basis of my credentials, and finally that we then get underway. Then, that we consider crew with captain change only in Tahiti. That GPS is reliable (it is) and that I inspect vessel, systems and certify my trust in them. That the voyage continues west as soon as safely possibly. Contrary to his intent, we are all agreed that a neutered Roger must go. These are all invigorating and rewarding prospects! The voyage must continue under my experienced tutelage if necessary. It is a strange and startling, not to mention surprising and hurtful circumstance, that Roger has acted in such an evasive and elusive manner, shirking his responsibilities to the boat and its people as captain, in such an indirect and apparently selfish way.

We are all still reeling from the realization that he has diverted us here for his own ends, especially Tina, who brought or enticed him on board, and for whom he apparently had a crush, notwithstanding his romance with Alejandra and hers with Chris, the boss. And apparently Roger was acting not for the betterment of *Stornoway*, the vessel in which all of us have invested our home and hopes, and her progress westward. We are left with few options but to continue on our voyage without him. Indeed, we have no choice without either stopping, sailing back east to the mainland, or flying in some other expensive professional captain at great expense of time and money. But by making do with the three of us, two owners, a new mate, and captain, and a new crew, we three triumvirate have no doubts as to the ability of *Stornoway* to complete the voyages ahead safely.

The long and the short of the situation is that, within reason, or as soon as we can replace Roger, with an adequate crew, and I can rehearse the responsibility of full captain, then we shall settle accounts ashore, muster aboard, ignite the engine, weigh anchor, and push out the harbor bound WSW for the Marquesas Islands. This will be much as the Captain and crew of this morning's Beneteau 50-foot sloop, British sailors Stephen, Raz, Richard, and Guy, did this morning after a romp with the seals and run ashore at the rookery. This will undoubtedly prove the boldest, assertive, move decisive move of my life thus far. What a different world of decisions I inhabit, now than if I was the lowest crew on a power yacht in Palm Beach! [Same day, afternoon]: We serve the boat; as captain, one is merely a physician or nurse to the boat, determining the best and safest cures and balms to coax the boat along and keep it trim and fit to carry we and our lives onwards for as long as possible.

Some reflections of the day, at the prospect of assuming command of *Stornoway* within the week. On navigation, sailing offshore, and blue water. As I see it, land serves three purposes; as a point of departure, as a point of arrival, and as a point of destruction. Put simply, a sailboat either hails land, leaves it astern, or wrecks on it. Conclusion; that the safest place for the boat is the sea. There is no system of propulsion which I would trust at sea more than sailing on wind, versus motoring on fuel or drifting in the current. Anachronism; that the experience and sense of overwhelming, yet exhilarating responsibility, inherent in a young man's assuming command of a sea-going vessel could only possibly be compared to that felt by a young woman at the prospect of giving birth. There is no bolder move than the severance of your anchor rode, or chain. Enough witticisms for the day.

Tomorrow centers on these prospects; an all-crew encounter with Roger quite early in the morning; we need to know his departure time, we need an electrician, an introduction to the senior naval officer, Port Captain Francisco Ramiro, to receive his closing remarks and instructions. We *don't* need hassles. Also, I hope to receive a fax from the family in response to their learning I will be captain. It certainly is an exciting day; one of the most crucial in my life.

January 7, 1994, Friday, 10.45 pm. We have just held a meeting, *ad hoc*, in the cockpit, with canvas overhead which the cat Davie punctured with his claws on Christmas Day. During the brief discussion Chris rather authoritatively told Roger that we would prefer he leave the boat. Quick on the uptake, Roger agreed to catch the next, and only, daily flight out, first to the Ecuadorian mainland. He added (as if we cared), that he would fly to Quito via Guayaquil (for all we knew, to see Alejandra, the one-armed divorcee he met in Academy Bay) and then on to Fort Lauderdale, his home. This is, obviously, good, since, when confronted by Tina, he conceded and agreed to leave *Stornoway* right away.

This has been an unpleasant shock to all of us, and I might feel like Lyndon B. Johnson taking command after President John F. Kennedy's assassination, except that Roger has really and publicly self-immolated himself. Much like our grandfather, Åke, who was so dismayed by politics that he ultimately took his own life while hunting. So, it is with mixed but enthusiastic feelings that I anticipate becoming, if only by default, the captain, aboard, and of, this lovely vessel and those within it.

I guess you can say I've risen from downstairs to upstairs, with authority on matters of safety and seamanship over my own boss and paymistress! Quite a shake-up at age 23 and four months. This should take effect this afternoon. So, therefore, we have it. Delfin is a young French sailor crewing on a French catamaran at anchor in the same bay and being crewed by two brothers named Karl and Marco from LeHavre, who we call *Karl Marx* for short. We need to invite Delfin aboard and possibly charm her into making the long passage ahead with us. She has expressed a real desire to get to Tahiti the fastest way possible and Karl Marx and their captain are delaying, for example they have a local man who has been helping them here, believing that he will be paid a lot, yet they have almost no intention to pay him. I believe that the appeal of *Stornoway*'s luxurious interior, combined with Tina's charming approach, should win Delfin over. But at the same time, I have found (from Paula on *Xebec* and Jill on *War Baby* just two years ago) that sailing boats on long voyages are only big enough for a single woman and matriarchal figure. The tension and competition becomes too much for both the women and men aboard if not. So, if Delfin does not work out, we need to be receptive to any other crew who shall pass through, or if necessary that we can dig up.

All is rather well, I suppose. Herein I assume control. Safely west. This *is* the moment I have been waiting for. So be it. Let's go. *Onward*! Here are some slogans I find inspirational at this critical juncture in my sailing careers. The national motto of the Commonwealth of the Bahamas is *Forward upward onward together*. Regarding anything on board from tools to mugs: Don't put it down; put it away! About blocking a passageway, particularly the critical safety one between the interior and cockpit; only admirals and assholes stand in a companionway. The mushroom theory of crew management is; keep them in the dark and feed them shit. Fair enough. We begin. *Je suis capitaine dans l'océan pacifique. Au sud! Aux îles Marquise; aux îles polynésiennes.* The mega-yacht *Timoneer*, which I was considered by Kitty at Hassle Free to crew aboard, arrives in the Galápagos in three days. *Tamure, Leap Frog* on their way south. I learned that Queen Sylvia of Sweden was vacationing in the Galápagos on a SCUBA diving trip to the northern islands when we arrived.

We need crew, no more sub-service and second-hand sycophants. I take control. Waiting. Delfin is the question, possibly the solution. Roger is a jam in the spokes of the wheel. Chris's pessimism could likely endanger progress. I am reading the label of a food packet: *Arnott's farm baked cookies. The taste of home. Win a trip on the Kingston Flyer and a family holiday for four in Queenstown, New Zealand: see inside for details*. We were spoken to by the Capitán de Puerto, or port captain, yesterday; on Friday. We went to him since we needed papers, or *zarpe*, minus Roger plus, possibly another, like French-woman Delfin, who wants to join her boyfriend in Raiatea. Also, we need electronic parts, and 30 gallons of diesel. *Vamos a las Marquesas*, I say, we all say; let's go to the Marquesas!

January 11, 1994, Tuesday. The port captain now knows that we have no new crew confirmed yet. We are to pay for 60 gallons of diesel, shared by the Ecuadorian Navy, for $120. Also, he processed our ship's *zarpe*, passports, papers for any new crew, electrician, electronics, garbage, or *basura*, and battery parts, which were flown in from their naval base in Guayaquil. The yacht *Timoneer* is here, under the command of Captain Philip. It is 118 or so feet long, and they don't say anything, but remain aloof. It's the first time we have been outdone by a larger sailing yacht in the same port at the same time.

By Friday, January 17, 1994 at latest *Stornoway* must leave. The trash truck provided by the Navy takes our garbage at 9 am. They are strict here regarding hygiene; each of us had to carry taped-over jars with fecal samples to the port captain on arrival. After all there is no holding tank in use: the crap, piss, and food waste goes right into the pristine waters. We went to town to fax people from the government post office and sent inquiries, mostly to Fort Lauderdale, but all over, looking for crew. Chris and Tina are working on the insurance. The Spanish word for crew is *tripulación*, and for owners *propietario*. There is no rush, we may not need to sail now until January 20.

January 12, 1994, Wednesday. Depart the Galápagos five days from now. Ship's registration, request to extend to nine days. *Notes*: $6, a day is $50 total, 30 gallons of diesel to buy on Monday, January 17, our deadline to sail. Boat meeting on January 10, between Tina, Chris, and Eric. Our itinerary; we must rush to avoid cyclones in Polynesia along our route, particularly in Marquesas, our first stop. Other reasons to wait include two to three days for battery parts to be flown in from mainland Ecuador by their navy, three to six days to fly in replacement autohelm parts [it never worked, we hand-steered for nearly a year total from Florida]. Another three to eight days' delay for a 4th crew. I got scissors, rid of the garbage. The port captain is kosher. From January 3, our fees due for remaining in the Galápagos are only $6 per-day, and $56 for nine days. That includes filling tanks with Ecuadorian Navy fresh potable water. There are some 85 SSB radio frequencies gives the crew options.

One very happy evening the three of us took our dinghy over to the smallish yacht of a single-handing Frenchman named Jean-Luc. It is named *Dance of the Cow over the Moon*, *Moondance* yacht; *Guinche a Lune*. It is black with a red stripe; Pascal had lots of photos and good French music. Told us about Autona, Hiva Oa, and another yacht named *Quaucaren*. He is from Marseilles; made a Jacques Brel tape for me, of music has collected through voyages in the Amazon River, Brazil, Martinique, Venezuela and beyond. The photos had plenty of relaxed French cruising sailors without clothing; for me that was a fun break from norm! They say a Frenchman will build or buy a yacht half the size of an American's one yet sail it more than twice the distance!

Señor, or Don, Francisco Ricardo, the Capitán de Puerto at Baquerizo Moreno. We will need ship's registration. Richard and Melissa, of Boroko, Papua New Guinea; he told me in her presence that he wanted to join us, she, his fiancé Melissa said no; they recommended Trevor in his place! Good choice for all. Our mail can be forwarded to yacht *Stornoway*, care-of the port captain, Pape'ete, Tahiti, French Polynesia.

January 14, 1994, Friday. Hassle Free; thanks, we are okay now. Jennifer Borchardt; thank you for applying, we found Trevor locally. Trevor White's parents in BC.

January 16, 1994, Sunday, 1.30 pm. Sitting here surrounded by owners of the Merida Maz, the restaurant of a talkative family! Rosita's Café and restaurant in the capital of Puerto Baquerizo Moreno, on San Cristóbal, Galápagos. Living aboard *Stornoway*. Well, Roger left the boat on the evening of January 7. It is now January 16. In the week since he flew out after debate, I have been acting captain, and so I set out on a quest for a fourth, or even a fifth, crew member and to familiarize myself with and know the system of water pump-age, water maker, battery charging, I have cleared at least a few days remaining time here since our expected Wednesday departure, and now have grafted the services and commitment of Senior Angel, electronics officer in the Navy to recharge batteries.

The primary charge of the nine hours has been to master the SSB radio. GPS and other navigation tools, like training with sextant sights, reductions, and reading of the many astrological tables, weather, plotting, and charts. Of primary concern in *Stornoway*'s progress westward. Firstly, to Tahiti via Marquesas is to confirm insurance backing with our present crew of four: Chris, myself, Tina and Trevor a new crew from Canada (ex-tourists) or with an additional fifth; Jennifer Borchardt.

This is pending by tomorrow afternoon we should have rigged a satisfactory battery charging system, confirmed at least a fourth (Trevor) and possibly the pending arrival of a fifth crew; possibly Jen Borchardt [see obit. below]. Crew and should begin processing our *zarpe* for a departure from here by late Tuesday or mid-day Wednesday in league with at least two of seven yachts being delivered from St.-Gilles, France and Spain to Polynesia. [*Horribly Sad Note: Peter Pavlis, the 76-year-old founder of The Muesli Company, has pleaded guilty to murdering co-director Jennifer Borchardt, 49, at her Richmond home on July 25, 2017.* From *Daily Mail* story July 30, 2018].

January 18, 1994, Tuesday. Roger is gone, I have been appointed captain Cleared with port captain, bought 400 gallons of diesel fuel. Paid for diesel; struck deal to anchor $6, repair water-maker, fill water tanks from naval ship too. They put a floating dock alongside their ship at anchor to accommodate *Stornoway*, which was exceptionally helpful; I can't see them doing that for yachts in Bahamas! Rationed electrical power, re-charge batteries, found fourth crew-member, Trevor.

Now must pass insurance coverage in Montreal (where it is called *Assurance*), provision tomorrow, on Wednesday morning, clear out, pay 17 days' worth of stay, or $102, clear Trevor's passports to match boat, fit through-hull valves to prevent water ingress and ensure hull integrity, and non-return valves for engine exhaust so the engine is not somehow swamped and choked off by a rogue wave, as Roger formally requested. We should depart this Wednesday afternoon. Deck preparations: lash drums, stow lines, clean dinghy and hoist, clean anchor chain, re-run running backstays, clean boot top, prop, wheel, douse tarpaulin; poison gas for the roaches.

They say that once you've gone *cap* you never go back. This, I'd have to say, for better or worse, must be true, because there's no role aboard quite like it. This is an odd instance where not being and yet being appointed captain allows some glory, with responsibility shared between Chris and I. Chris spoke very clearly to me today saying *take it easy, go slow, and let's try to have a few days of rest and recreation (R-and-R) before pushing off on a long passage.* All the better. We are still in Wreck Bay. Now sitting peacefully admiring the sunset wafting in sweet jazz music in the Green Café with Trevor to my right, and the rosy glow of orange lamps above. This voyage is a determining factor in my present life after school; crossing the Pacific. Makes me also think of Samuel Beckett, *Waiting for Godot*.

January 20, 1994, Thursday. *Errands*: Pick up faxes, mail letters and postcards, buy ten more cartons of ciggies, meet with port captain, introduce Trevor, with his passport, in order to obtain fresh *zarpe*. Thank him for the services of Señor Angel [who coincidentally I had to physically lift and throw him off the dinghy onto the dock he and his companions were so drunk and incoherent]. Problems solved, Christian split with $50. We must fill center tank, empty the drums like stainless steel wine canisters stowed up forward, that we will need to buy 35 gallons of combustible fuel. We must check and perhaps change oil and filters for the generator, main engine, and water-making equipment. It will cost $6 to buy generator lubricating oil for the water-maker generator oil. Anchor fees from January 3 to January 22, accrued to $170 over 19 days. Medical advice based on results of tests of all our fecal samples: we are each to take anti-bacterial antibiotic medicine called Fasygin.

The tablets at $2.20, take one tab each, every eight hours for four days. [Other words incorrectly scribbled down were Rubella, for German Measles, and Zantac, which is just over-the-counter antacid medication and not relevant, and I assume both words are just red herrings and may be mis-spelling of the doctor or clinic]. Hoped-for ports-of-call from December, 1993 in Nassau, to Miami, Panama, to January, 1994 in the Galápagos, was three ports. In February of 1994 we should be in the Marquesas. Then Tahiti, for two Polynesian ports and Cook Islands, a protectorate of New Zealand, and Tonga, which is a sovereign kingdom. Pasqual Patrice was the skipper of *Perseverance* in Panama, which was going on charter to Trump in St. Martin, French West Indies, but got soaked along the way and left two American women ashore in the Marquesas *en route*. The marooned women wrote very long letters to the owner complaining about him, and his response was "do you want me to write a 20-page letter as well? What would that achieve?"

January 25, 1994, Tuesday, 10 pm. 1°15'S, 91°22'W. We are 70 nm WSW of Post Office Bay, Floreana, Galápagos. My first command has proceeded with mixed sentiments, but generally positive results. We weighed anchor from San Cristóbal, Wreck Bay at 1 pm, Sunday, January 23 [two days ago], bound for Hiva Oa, Marquesas, where Gauguin and Brel are buried. Within several hours, passing along the Southern shore of Santa Fe, the owner, Chris Orient, breached his concerned over the integrity of the hull, which has now endured and withstood some 30 years' worth of heat bolted through keelson and garboard strake to a lead keel of some seven tons, plus there was a concern over saltwater intake into the bilges while underway.

And so, Chris, who knows the boat probably better than any man alive, suggested that because of alarmingly high and fast water ingress, we call in at Post Office Bay and anchor off one of the Galápagos Islands. This will allow us to take stack of the problem and effect possible repairs, mainly by an underwater inspection and tacking lead plates. Through at first reluctant, I agreed with him that we should do so, and so we altered course WSW for Post Office Bay, Floreana, arriving at 10:30 pm in the somewhat tight anchorage in the inlet to the ENE extreme corner.

The bay is large but shallow reefs make it smaller We have been anchored here for two nights. Were joined by the 30-foot Chilean-flagged sailing sloop *Tamure* the following morning rendezvoused late morning to chat, and share some loose rigging lines with them. Hector and Cathy had muffins, and he resumed his instruction to me of celestial navigation with the sextant, which he had begun in San Cristóbal. He is a former naval officer in the Chilean Navy, so training was thorough and extensive. After extensive systems monitoring, we had run through bolting heels on tighter, released leakage, pressurized the water tanks, cleared bilges, ran energy-sealant, checked the sails, and set off this early afternoon at 12 noon for the Marquesas, which are, at 3,325 nm away, one of the most remote in the world from any large land mass. All is well, though admittedly for the one in the hot seat it's been exhausting, yet exhilarating. I've had ten hours navigation in the last 24, to have Chris spring system-maintenance on us after supper? *Argh*! And when he first broached his idea (order really) that we turn back and repair.

After we had done nothing but turn back and repair since Roger and we left Academy Bay, retreated to the wrong bay at Black Beach Bay, then Post Office Bay, then Wreck Bay, then Post Office Bay, I was fit to be tied, however, fortuitously at that moment the fishing line suddenly made the *whiiizzzzz!* sound, meaning we had caught a tasty dorado fish about three feet long. I sprang at the reel, raced it in quickly, and rather than gaff and kill it with alcohol, as we usually would, I pummeled its head into a bleeding spray of blood. Grinning ear to hear with blood all over me, an acquiesced to Chris and we turned *Stornoway* round and made for Post Office Bay. Who likes sending postcards more than me anyway, right?

January 27, 1994, Thursday, 1.50 pm. 4°30'S, 95°40'W: Some 380 miles along our course in about 48 hours! First two days really sorting themselves out: First happier hour and after dinner chat because a confrontational debate on how to handle, share bilge, systems responsibilities, second (last night) was a brief debate on our course, navigational tactics instigated by Chris (with 50° course damage from reach upwind on port track SSW to run off to 290° west. It ended decisively with my confirming course to more north than WSW regardless of wind patterns sail configuration and shared interest in keeping current and SE trade winds while something to cut across WSW maybe west to Hiva Oa Marquesas along 8th degree of latitude south and from 6° WSW, 2,500 more miles. All well. Your navigator, captain held the field and wants his (mates).

February 2, 1994, Wednesday, 7.30 pm [GMT -8]. 5°45'S, 116°20'W. Aboard *Stornoway*, in the skipper's berth over-looking now deck station. At 4:15 am this morning on our eight day at sea since leaving Post Office Bay, Floreana, Galápagos, astern, we hit our midway point roughly halfway along the 3,000-mile route Galápagos to the Marquesas. As a means of celebrating, and also to use up or kill (without assigning a helmsman) the dead-hour cost to GMT when passing 115°W, I proposed we wind down all sails; this was quickly done to the genoa, mainsail and mizzen sail, which were easily lashed down. Then we turned the motor on in neutral at 10 am, and at noon we hove-to without propulsion and Tina, Trevor and I each and all took a deep and humbling plunge into 12,000-feet depths of the Pacific Ocean; the world's largest at some 20 million square nm. We baked cakes, and I recovered a bit from exhaustion with the distraction and swim. It was fun; something I learned from Mike on *Rising Star* three years earlier.

February 7, 1994, Monday, 12.20 pm (GMT -9 hours, as of today). Position 7°S, 130°W. Heading 290° WNW, on course 260°W to Hiva Oa, Marquesas, expected to arrive in about four days, 600 nm remaining; due in on Friday, February 11. All well. This morning after my 8-10 pm watch, which was spent motoring, reading *Cosmopolitan Magazine* back-issues stashed by Tina again, drinking coffee and smoking, I handed the helm to *Monsieur Blanc* (Trevor White, interpreter, radioman, and *tripulación*, or crew), and went about getting the boat moving properly again. This meant cutting the engine, pulling out the hydraulic genoa headsail, setting the mizzen sail to port, or on starboard tack, and locking it into place with the kicker, or preventer, and finally having Trevor steer *Stornoway* upwind for me, so that I could then jump and grind the mainsail all 85 feet up off of the deck to the top of the mast, where it belongs. I then used the sheet, brought the boom down with a preventer (the vang drum leaked hydraulics and so is no good), and we were golden with an extra knot of boat-speed bringing us to WNW at 7.5 knots. My morning began while I was sleeping off-duty below and was broken by a very loud cracking bang sound, made by the spinnaker blowing out in a squall. Then we spent an hour running generator in order to make fresh water, cleaning the limber holes in order to keep the bilges flowing from front to back of the boat, wiping up and oil in the bilge with Joy detergent, checking the fuel system. Also, last night Trevor spent hours monitoring SSB frequency and getting new on weather.

February 11, 1994, Friday 9 pm. In Baie Taioae, Nuku Hiva, *Les îles Marquises*, South Pacific Ocean, French Polynesia! Aboard yacht *Stornoway* anchored in the bay. Some thoughts and considerations, good and bad; I've been working aboard *Stornoway* for ten weeks now. I flew from Nassau to Miami, Panama, on December 1 on a reimbursed ticket I have been paid upfront, in cash, on written agreement for seven of these ten weeks. I am owed three weeks wages, flight reimbursement bounced: Dad is furthermore owed to reimburse the flight he paid from Nassau to Panama.

Since being promoted and declared, for insurance reasons, captain of *Stornoway* on January 7, I've neither asked for, nor received a raise from our originally agreed mate's wages per week. Indications are that my basic legal right to a return flight (in this case, from point of disembarkation somewhere in the Marquesas to New Zealand, at latest destination) is now jeopardized for me, and a new crew threatened that he must receive a flight from New Zealand to Los Angeles California on completion of the voyage, or bust. Thus, I have been reneged on for a promised initial flight from Nassau, during which I went shopping one evening for and on behalf of our shared home, this boat). And I now stand at risk of losing my return flight New Zealand to Nassau, which was my point of departure. Not a comfortable position to be in; vulnerable but I am used to it.

February 14, 1994, Resolution, since the following day, Chris and Tina agreed; actually they volunteered, that payment would better and only realistically be made in major port as Tahiti or actually New Zealand, and that both Trevor and I can rest and be assured of return flight tickets home and coverage for the flight from Nassau. On top of this, I was given a cash advance. Meanwhile I photocopied and mailed home any documents needed for my defense. Log documenting my appointment to captain on January 17 in the Galápagos, confirming insurance acceptance of me as captain. Log books maintained, initialized by me, specifics of voyage, log charts, log captain log, all about 100 pages, copy of *zarpe* clearing me and crew out of Galápagos as captain others crew, copy of *zarpe* clearing us into French Polynesia, on my Swedish passport. Crew, me copy of team listing crew specifics, Swedish passport. Ask Rose Courser, matriarch of a resort on the hill who has sailed these waters for decades. Where did the prep school drop-out desert? On Nuku

Hiva, a hermit with a name like Givada and a village in the north named Hatihe'u, and nearby and Ha'atuatua Bay; all intentionally vague, I reckon, and they locals including her were sheltering the boy and I was the last person he wanted to see.

There are dozens of stone platforms. According to guide book author David Stanley (*South Pacific Handbook*, our bible): the Marquesas has a total population in the 1990s of 7,500. Atuona on Hiva Oa are where Jacques Brel and Paul Gauguin are buried near one another. Nuku Hiva he talks about living for three months using just cash but one must get a visa, and those require an expensive cash down-payment of thousands per person with the *gendarmerie*. [Same day]. Monday, 12.15 pm (GMT minus 9.30) Marquesas time, French Polynesia. Sitting here on the stem of a wooden pontoon paddling canoe at the mouth of remote Comptroller Bay, a kilometer's walk beyond Ho'oumi Village at the base of Cape Tikapō in the Taipivai, or what Herman Melville entitled his book, *Typee Valley*. Trevor and I are enjoying baking afternoon, sunshine with fresh streams seaward on either side, horses and goats grazing, chickens cawing, and papayas, lemons, guavas, bananas, all drooping ripe and heavy on their limbs. We were up at 6 am this morning after multiple rums at Rose Courser's He'e Tai Inn, and dinner at Chez Rose, Happy Hour with Lyle Walsh last night, and a Japanese dinner with wine and film with Katheryn Hepburn autobiography film last night into the morning.

February 18, 1994, Friday 10.45 pm. Aboard *Stornoway*, weather is mild, balmy, humid, after a blow of 30-to-50 knots for 2-3 days from the ESE. Nuku Hiva, Marquesas, from Polynesia. Still board after almost three months, becoming a test of endurance more than anything. I knew during the fortnight of preparations in Wreck Bay, Galápagos as Captain, and the outset of the last 3,000-mile leg that our landfall at Marquesas, if achieved, safely, would be a major water- shed in the voyage, and particularly for me personally. I said as much to Trevor. This has proven very true.

Frankly, no other excuses brought to bear, I'm burnt out. Graham Green's novel *A Burnt-Out Case*, Congo River, Africa, man. Reached a major passé. I've never had to endure a single yacht, a single job, a single voyage, or even a single girlfriend! for this long. Three months and half of my life liberated, and it's not half bad. All that I dreamed of doing, only doing it now and it's hard to transfer over Melville's running away to pull together the strength and will and excitement and suppress the doubts and lethargy, even the fears (of seas, of cyclones, of getting gipped for all that I've worked for and actually earning (deserving, seeing) less of. No one's fault but my own.

I never realized that a single voyage could be so immense. That a captain's position of that is so harmless and often so lonely, secluded in the realm of his own concerns, hopes, doubts, and constantly being cross-checked and cross-referenced, questioned, and confronted, who it for a puppet position whose greatest asset is actually learning a lot of more than the systems about navigation and seamanship and quiet firm leadership by example, about remaining calm and self-reserved. And making the proper safe decisions, often unpopular. Who knows? Three-week passage completed successfully in Marquesas, west for Tahiti, as early as tomorrow. We'll see.

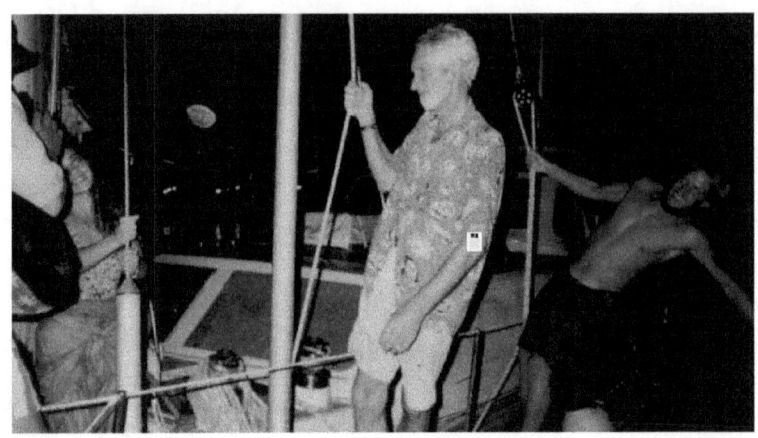

February 20, 1994, Sunday, 00.30 am. Half a day's voyage out of Pape'ete. Thought: There are a thousand and one ways to undertake a project (any project) on a sailboat: the right way, and a thousand other ways, at least getting paid. [Same day, Sunday, 4.30 am, GMT -10]: 100 miles and about 18 hours 55 nm west of Nuku Hiva, capital of the Marquesas. It's been said that many lose themselves in their work, or take their work home with them. In the case of giving your life every waking and sleeping hour all consumption, all expulsion (as you eat, and as you shit) all you dream, think, and especially invest in the drawing table of the sailboat, you have a travel aboard. This is by far the most expensive, broad and ambitious voyage independent undertaking of my life. Trevor stepped aboard a month and a half ago. I had lost myself and the ability to identify and relate to myself independently of *Stornoway*, being so totally immersed in two other people's virtually life-long dream. [Sunday, same date, 1 pm]. Continuing SSW aboard *Stornoway* content though in sweltering (scorching?) heat. Will gladly contact M. Michel Solari in Pape'ete, and push my mail belongings there, indulge in them and savor some time to myself in the city and hopefully become romantically involved with one of the many young'uns doubtlessly abounding there. We'll see, as a booster and my silent thoughts alone on a sleepless night spent working on the foredeck. Last night thought of family and friends strikes me with a range of emotions from affection to love to remorse to lukewarm confused regret.

February 21, 1994, Monday, 11.40 am. *Advice*: For a young man seeking adventure, ship aboard in sailing vessel; go west, young man; but don't escalate beyond mate. Though you may aspire if you will, in this gain adventure, experience and tutoring from a good captain while being able to enjoy the voyage from the perspective of one removed from the immediacy of responsibility: safety navigation, speed, soothing owners and crew. Crew is best for this as they are above all physical bodies (gorillas or cooks) needed for any or all physical tasks, deck thrills but not in dispensable and removed from decision-making. If a young man wants STRESS and overwhelming responsibility, try SKIPPERING; Especially of a large vessel ship (70 foot) across vast oceans with the owner and mates! *Arghh!*

March 5, 1994, Saturday 4.30 pm. Somewhere in the hills of Presque Isle, or Tahiti-Iti (*Presque Isle* means almost island). A mountainous island connected to Tahiti by a narrow isthmus. I am sitting beneath a corrugated iron roof of an open verandah-like concrete platform amidst a large cemetery having just hiked from Port Phaeton. Began at 7.30 am to hitchhike around while island. Calling in of Swedish anthropologist, author Bengt Danielsen's enclosure along way but I passed. Had a beer in one truck, big lunch exhausted, slept in rain. I am as far as I can possibly be from *Stornoway*. That an old Irish ability to laugh at oneself! Trevor interpolated my humor around blood, sweat, tears, isolation and if it's blood you want, try a strange vegetarian high fiber beet, rice diet and or irritate the old anus and like heads from iron cross of fresh working on my first independent. I love it! Noon starts now? Good luck, Wiberg. *Presque Isle* continued. Which pleases me after not having slept ashore since Nassau nearly four months ago.

Looking back to November 1993, when Chris gave quite a straight forward disclaimer the other day offering the option to fly onward or homeward and to be paid off for it in on *Stornoway* must sensibly wait and the deluge of hurricane and rainy season in safe Pape'ete until as late as April; at least two weeks more than the one we've waited and possibly more before limping along to Tonga and eventually New Zealand via the Cook Islands, possibly. By now Trevor is probably ripe for revolt or ascension; skipper? *Ha!* And Chris and Tina probably needy of some privacy, attention, tending loving
care to their sadly aligned decrepit boat. We'll see free?

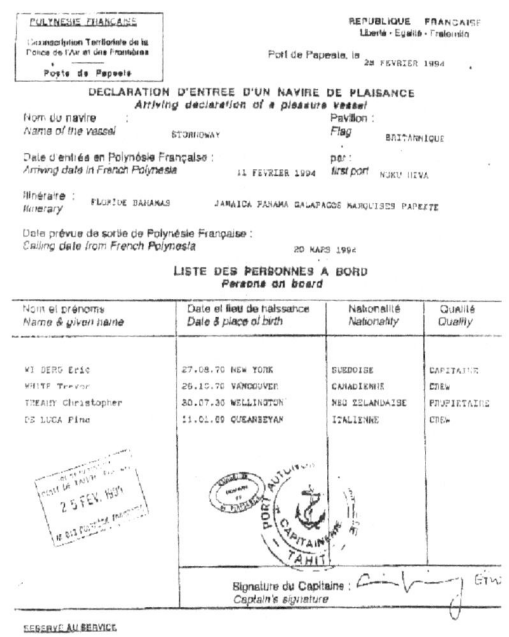

March 13, 1994, Sunday, 11.30 am. In a Chinese, Polynesian café in Cook's Bay, Mo'orea, Society Islands, *Polynésie Française*. I'm hanging out with Trev. We hiked from the ferry dock from Tahiti at Vai'are, facing Pape'ete over steep mountains, along precipitous ridges and then down around [and very nearly straight down] a 300-foot-high waterfall hidden from us by dense jungle. We descended down the other side, passing through a grove of marijuana under cultivation. [Trevor had mountain climbing experience planting saplings in western Canada, but we just eyeballed it]. We made it, thankfully without falling off the cliff or being shot, to Cook's Bay on the north coast by yesterday afternoon, which was Saturday. On the pleasant hike over we drank from a fresh stream, then walked to Club Bali Hai Mo'orea Hotel. This is Cook's Bay famous yachting and marine South Sea hangout, bar and club. There we drank with Robert and Margaret, two Seattle sailors, living aboard a *Swan*. We had heard via the SSB, or single-side-band community, which Trevor managed for the boat, about the captain of the yacht *Taurus*, out of Wilmington, Delaware.

On their suggestion we were able to leave our stuff aboard and crash on the deck and benches aboard an old passenger catamaran of aluminum nick-named the *Liki Tiki*, which was very kind of the staff as well, since we could not afford our own accommodation. At about 9 pm were met an American industrialist who owned a large power yacht named *Bondo*, after the anti-rust paste which he invented in Atlanta, Georgia. The adhesive works on boats, too. On his encouragement, and after he knew we were broke, he, Trevor and I went out frolicking and roaming with him till the hours; as in after 3 am. I met Jean, an American visitor, and we danced and partied at a low-key wooden shack called a club populated largely by plenty of young transvestite beauties who caught the eye of Mr. Bondo. From there, after midnight, we had our chartered taxi driver drive us to the large Club Med, however our benefactor, on being charged at the gate to watch the shows in the club, refused, became belligerent, and was soon heard screaming horrible racial epithets (this troglodyte actually used the *n* word), at these poor, then infuriated Polynesians.

Even our cab driver refused to have anything to do with him after that, and it was clearly a very near thing that he avoided being soundly thrashed by them. On return he went back to his mega-yacht, which was shipped out but dumped in Tahiti, and was not seaworthy enough to get back to the US on its own, since it was basically a gin palace for show. The yacht's mate told us he blamed the whole late night on Trevor and I, framing us as racists who liked cross-dressers! I set the record straight when I saw them in Tahiti). Exhausted, Trevor and I slept on the *Liki Tiki*, mostly in the open, however it did not rain. Our hiking boots were rather smelly, to the extent that when I asked a tattoo artist to ink a band around my toe, he refused. In order to catch the ferry from Vai'are, roughly four miles along the coast, we split up, and I was able to hope on the back of a friendly scooter rider most of the way, seeing many sacred totems called *tabu*s set into the grass along the way. I waited in a large waiting area for the high-speed aluminum-hulled catamaran, smoking and reading. Feeling very lonely, I went to the public pool and the library in Pape'ete, then waited nervously outside when they closed, hoping to meet a lovely blonde I'd seen there several times, but I lost my nerve as she walked past then when hitchhiking put my hand down when she drove past.

March 14, 1994, Pape'ete: We are moored Tahiti-style, stern-to, eating onions, potatoes. For weather service go to Fa'a'ā International Airport on foot, up the hill, road curves to left after bridge, electricity general, call failed. Mr. Solari, Swedish Consul. Find crew on yacht *Destiny*, Captain Ericson of Seattle, or Café Morison in Pape'ete.

March 17, 1994, Thursday. I received some cash wages from Chris on *Stornoway* to afford sending mail and faxes. Other times I would tell other broke sailors like Trevor that

I got paid and would bluff our way into a club with newfound confidence to steal unfinished drinks from well-heeled younger patrons. We neither got caught nor got Herpes.

March 19, 1994, Saturday, noon. Pape'ete. The nebulous gaseous aura surrounding the head and body of one who has consumed copious amounts of alcohol recently: the smell of a drunk. As lingers, wafting, around me and oh so depresses one after another bout of heavy prolonged drinking and smoking. Yesterday (this morning's beginning at noon yesterday with Patrice of Michel's, sailor then dinner ice cream with. Petro Café boozing at Morrison. The Club 5 Bar. Or Boulevard Queen Pômaré whisky flask of Rob chef of *Destiny*, which is *en route* from Florida to Malaysia.

Blonde stewardess, whom I met and have since managed to miss successively several on the frustration, expiration endless absence of intimate female company. *Argh*! Thoughts while strolling back to the capital; I am a bastard without identity or country. Sailing west under MPS and mainsail aboard the good ship *Stornoway*. Bound towards, but possibly past, Rotorua. Real position, I'm either calm in this light air, consistent gentle what I'd originally expected. I suppose in the final conclusion this Pacific is really just an exceptionally large ocean. Calm cheer, peaceful. We left on Friday afternoon, March 18. My watch duties have been spent on the wheel alone as follows; from 2-6 am on watch (with Peers Prospect), then Monday 6-12 pm, and 2-4 am. Now from 10:30 am to 1:40 pm. Not much speed in three days, but happy with it. After all, it was my turn to prepare lunch!

March 21, 1994, Monday. The shiniest conditions since our first day of out of Pape'ete. Today has been just as I would envision Pacific voyaging under sail; smooth seas from behind, with gentle but noticeable following ocean swell, winds light, but generally steady from 5 to 10 knots. Calm, clear, hot, relaxing, jogging along under full light sail.

March 24, 1994 Thursday, 12.15 pm. about 20°S, 154°W; three days out of Pape'ete. Bound WSW for Rarotonga, Southern Cooks, Mauke Island looms in the distance. On the radio we hailed the Russian cruise ship *Azerbadezhyaya* bound from Auckland, New Zealand to Pape'ete, the other night. No word since our first evening from MV *Destiny*; the large power yacht from Fort Lauderdale with Swedish Captain, Arne Saxon, and Chief Engineer Andreas, who are bound for Fiji. By reports of this morning Arnold (weatherman out of Rarotonga) Cyclone Thomas is now circling around Fiji in a clockwise direction from WSW to SE this morning.

It is vicious and dangerous, especially for *Destiny*, which should be approaching there about now. I'm sure captain and ship are safe (all 17 of them) but it could be a dangerous encounter. We are fortunately some 1,000 to 1,500 nm east of it now, it moves away, and we will be okay in relation to it. But should be here southward toward Tonga Islands. We'll see. Of course, I am concerned, but we are safe so far and we have a good information feed. We will layover in Rarotonga after an expected arrival in two days, or the afternoon of Saturday, March 26, then see about the final leg of this trip, from Tonga to New Zealand, across the world's largest ocean on my first command.

March 28, 1994 Monday, 9 am. Aboard *Stornoway* anchored Avatiu Harbor inlet on the island of Rarotonga, Southern Cook Isles. Good morning, faithful friend. Now, southward of our present location we are nearing the Tropic of Capricorn. There are many islands to the south, and the closest we've gotten to them was San Cristóbal, Galápagos, and it begins again. I'd better begin gathering my little nuts like a squirrel, and finding a place to bring them back to a den or cave, in order to wait it out this winter and possibly write.

April 1, 1994 Friday, 12.45 pm. Between Rarotonga and Tongatapu, on passage from the Cook Islands to Tonga Islands. *Stornoway*'s second day out; having covered 130 nm. Position 21°S, 162°W. As autumn came to Newport in September last fall, so winter and fall caught up with me aboard *Whisper of Maine,* blowing across our cheeks now, we on *Stornoway* can feel cold air from Antarctica to our left, or south. We heaved anchor out of Avatiu, Rarotonga, and make our way soon westwards towards Tonga and our first 1,000-nm run down SW to New Zealand. The voyage is in its throes. Thoughts include reflection of sobering effect of colder weather, survived, difficult adjustment to a new nation and a way of going about through being paid out and severed from my half-year tenure aboard *Stornoway* and the daunting prospect of having to fend for myself in foreign, even urban settings. The cold chill to the air saber: seems reality check, time is money, buy time.

Travel in the relationship commitment with no one or another. We'll see? Cold? One bid. Hauling ass westward 150 nm in eighteen hours! April 7. *FEAR*. With understanding and experience of dangers inherent in this passage, naïveté and ignorance are nullified and yet not having traversed these waters (like I have the North Atlantic) each wave, each mile, is new and potentially intimidating. Fear. The sheer power of this vessel under full sail. Fear. The strength and endurance called upon each of us to conduct it safety onward and into a notoriously rough and cold, windy sea (New Zealand). Fear. The responsibility of leadership, of keeping cool and collected, of ensuring personal safety for each and all: and I personally have dodged death twice in this voyage (off the sea): these start with assault, tumultuous and the vast precipice of Mo'orea.

I must deal for the first time in my life with the grind of merrowing fear in this endeavor. Metaphors: Sea captain is to sailor as Jesuit Priest is to clergyman. University professor is to teacher. Field commander is to soldier. Puccini soloist is to chorister. Winter is to drinker. Conductor is to symphony. Ringmaster is to circus. Ingredients: Inception, unitive, responsibility, loss. Fear, anxiety, self-assurance, leaders, nurturing, protection, surety, precision, confidence, prime mover, decisive action. Great decisions.

April 4, 1994, Monday 12.45 pm, Cooks to Tonga with no engine; Captain's log, day four. We are 640 miles west of 850 nm to Cooks to Tonga, with no engine, no means to charge the batteries, no generator or alternators. For the first time in this half year I found myself able to weep openly, it began with , many months of suppressed anxiety upon arrival in Nuka Hiva, Marquesas, safely through exhausted, from Galápagos, and even then, try as I might, with insomnia and reminisce, I could hardly manage and the release I sought in hem. Then with an agonizingly slow passage and angst upon angst, frustration, lethargy, apathy, resentment, pent up in the Pape'ete, Tahiti.

About the only releasees was drinking, getting slowly, coarsely and flirting danger and desperation with highest, the pulp, or film of suppressed emotion finally burst with our calm and safe, even happy arrival after four peaceful days in Southern Cook Islands, finally surrounded by photos reminiscent of happiness, burst in here was relieved. After Easter and April Fool's. I've had to come this far to realize that what I've escaped I seek. I find myself lying on my back listening, and in the privacy of my warm, dark and secluded cabin to Van Morrison, old friend and it seems singing again of *it feels like a brand-new day, I was lost, double crossed, by down at the railroad tracks, and it feels like, yes, it seems like, a brand-new day, yes it does*. Does my new day about really a new life for myself in New Zealand? Or perhaps more realistically and consoling in a life which I now appreciate more back friends and family, and Newport?

April 7, 1994, Thursday. *Stornoway* Nuku'alofa Harbor, Tonga Tapu, Tonga. Wages paid by Chris Orient. November to April; originally planned to get Christmas gift in Nuku'alofa, Tonga, now over four months ago. There is no gift here. I wasn't was wildly optimistic (unrealistic) as Skip, another of *Stornoway*'s failed captains, who filled the boat to the gills with barrels of diesel to make it to Auckland by Christmas like General Patton in a tank! Like the rest of them he was armed, in his case with a loaded pistol.

April 25, 1994, Monday, 10.30 am. After a generally miserable and angst-ridden week or two following our arrival here April 6 to April 7, finally outlook and general feeling back to humane and more congenial levels. Extremely frustrating start here with no real money coming in. All of us are broke, the main engine start motor busted without repair here (it was damaged more than Dane Bjorn Neilson) and sent off to Wellington, New Zealand for repairs. Water-maker, battery charger, even video machine has been damaged or broken while here. was extremely bummed out which rubbed off on all of us. The MAF (Agriculture; high German, Conrad Engberg's) hired to kidnap kill our cat, the weather furious, 25 to 35 knots virtually constantly from arrival. Wind east, then NE for 35 to 45 knots, riding out on an anchor, not from south. Snorkeling shell on quiet yesterday with Trevor, haircuts in my office at the Cable and Wireless, faxes, Hula Bar at The Island and a modest waterfront bar. Lobster and sea-view. Late drinks with English musician Richard at yacht and International Dateline Hotel. Fairly Scot-free-loving now too, the same is possible and the personal card.

Tonga can be a funny place, fraught with pitfalls. After a night of drinking in Nuku'alofa, one of our group told me he would disregard my advice (and that of local cops) and try to find some pot to smoke with the locals. I took the dinghy back and passed out in my cabin with the hatch open. For two hours I heard (and ignored) his plaintive cries from the breakwater. I was too drunk and apathetic to pick him up. He ultimately swam, putting himself at risk.

A week or so later the same mate dropped me from the dinghy over an anchor which we had let go in a storm. I was holding the heavy end of anchor chain and treading water when he decided to go into the port to have a chat with someone calling from shore. He left, leaving me for about 15 minutes unwilling to release and possibly lose our anchor, but very tired and peeved. He was fairly inexperienced, and I had to make the point that when faced with the option of attending to complete strangers or standing by to help a member of the crew in distress, it's best to help them first particularly if they are your captain and employer.

May 16, 1994, Monday. Auckland. Pick up Wednesday at 2 pm. Develop film, haircut, return books. Jason's Bond High Street. Get wages, drop of pillows on land to dry. Get letter of reference typeset, with *Stornoway* stationary, sign sea miles: 8,000, 5.5 months, two days. Go to Delta, check on Travel for Less, get flight home to Nassau. Remuera, cement contact March and, or family Living. Four hours behind, 9:40 pm, Tonga 2:30 am, Monday, May 2, Connecticut, is 9.30 Sunday. Station-to-station left yesterday morning, movie in Greenwich. Queen Street Backpackers [our crew Stefan Kahlsson was robbed of is invaluable and irreplaceable foul-weather jacket there].

May 19, 1994, Thursday. Auckland. Swedish consulate, Australian High Commission. India in May. Met with Mark Aitken of *Xebec*; by coincidence he hailed me on the street, making Auckland feel a lot smaller and friendlier. Richard of Tonga is in the UK.

Epilogue: Seven of the yachts fleeing New Zealand for Tonga that fall were lost in fierce gales. Three persons; a couple and their son, were lost. These words are for those who never make it.

Trevor and Stefan (Canada and Sweden) on *Stornoway* (Scotland) heading between Tonga and New Zealand right before the Queen's Birthday Storm.

Chapter 8

Voyage 19: *Goldenhome* Turks & Caicos-Hogsty-Exumas-Nassau, Spring, 1995
Voyage 20: *Simpatico*, Crooked, Acklins Islands, Bahamas, Island Expedition, 1995

January 11, 1995, Friday, 6 pm. I'm a volunteer and fundraiser for Island Expeditions, created over a decade ago by brothers Niclas & Dragan Popov of Nassau. At our family business, Cable Beach Manor focusing on the layout for the annual Island Expedition picnic hosted by my parents for my colleagues. Bar-b-que at our family beachfront property side, by shuffle-board. Storage space, electricity, slides. How many persons? We were told by the Popov Brothers to plan for as many as 150 to 200 students, families, patrons. Fridges to store food. Parking, ice $25 tickets. Danish-owned yacht SY *Goldenhome* will be at Captain Nemo's restaurant on Saturday January until Sunday January 15. One of the greatest partners in setting up this party is Fijian Prince Felix Colatanavanua, who has become an expert boat handler, managing the crew to and from the small red Expedition sailboat named *Simpatico*, as well as hard worker to facilitate the many details of setting up the part. [Drawing of layout of bar-b-que event]. I'm working at the family apartment business now, but between January and April, 1995 I will meet and network to gain work in the shipping industry.

January 15, 1995, Sunday, 12:30 pm. Notes regarding Island Expedition fund-raising ticket sales. My notes for a presentation on Common Sense at Sea: Vaccinations, health and diet foresights, not going overboard, faint, always wear shoes, go minimal on jewelry, strong on hygiene for the sake of the other crew. Underscore what a nightmare experiencing a man overboard is for person watching as well as the one drowning. Crew selection, a new angle, sign-language, a good skipper should not shout or drink, but always remain calm. This will have a calming and reassuring effect on all those around them

Simpatico under sail in a building gale off Hogsty Reef, remote southern Bahamas. Years later my son and brothers and cousins and I were in the bridge of a mailboat going to Inagua, direct from Nassau. It being a two-day trip, we had time to dream of other islands. I asked my son to pull up a picture of Hogsty Reef, which I had enjoyed so much fishing and camping on in the Island Expedition. He showed me a photo of the small lighthouse tower there and then exclaimed when he read the photo credit – his Dad submitted it to a database of lighthouses which has lacking a decent recent phot of the light, which featured in the RAF, drug-smuggling, Nazi-gold novel *Bahama Passage* by a local pilot.

January 26, 1995, February 19 and March 3, my diary entry shows an arrow to Nicolas Popov of Bahamas Out Island Expeditions in Puerto Plata, Dominican Republic. An anticipated voyage with ten photos. On Tuesday I met with Brooke, Tony and Tim, Australian teachers and volunteers, at the West Ridge Pub, then Rock-n-Roll Café, and the Zoo nightclub, dancing. They stay in cheap accommodation, almost like barracks, behind Malcolm's Garage on West Bay Street. Soon thereafter I met with Brooke for lunch at the Cabana bar, followed by a quiet night. I'm excited to join the expedition in Puerto Plata in a week to ten days. I have generously been given an open invitation between March 16 to March 17 to the Turks and Caicos aboard the Bahamas Out Island Expedition small sailboat named *Simpatico* and also their large Inflatable to the Turks and Caicos. Great. Expedition: To make 15-minute movies. They are going to the Silver Bank or Mouchoir Bank, north of the Dominican Republic, around March 5. I am to rendezvous in Puerto Plata, north coast of DR or the Dominican Republic; look for a hard-hull dinghy. Witty, sardonic comment.

February 22, 1995, Tuesday, 9.30 am. On Friday March 3 depart Miami at 5 pm. Where will I rendezvous with Bahamas Out Island Expedition, which port or country? Call Paul, Jane Popov, Buffy and expedition volunteers from Europe and Australia, including Rhonda, Rolf, Mauro, Marie Solomon, or in Punta Grand, Dominican Republic, Duarte

Montinos, or Sonora and tell them I'm coming. Also contacted Gretel Costellano in the Turks and Caicos Islands (TCI).

March 20, 1995, Tuesday. Return to Out Island Expedition, confirm who I met at the Clay Hostel on Washington Street and Española Way in Miami Beach. Contact Minard Johnson at Shipping International Freight, and Clarence Smith.

March 29, 1995, First phase of a major skipping mailing: copies of *Bahamas Out Island Expedition* books (care of student Dante)... means a lot of papers. And no sleep.

June 14, 1995, Wednesday. Home, in Nassau. [I returned here ill on June 10, four days ago]. Photos: four Philippe Heurlin, Paris, expedition, photos five Kristian and Marianne *Goldenhome*, photos.

September 3, 1995, Wednesday. Mail to Dragan Popov, Island Expedition,

June 6, 1996, Afternoon, aboard tanker *Edmo*; 1995 is over, and for my part, I'm glad. It was not a happy year for me, except for the Island Expedition, and time at home.

April 29, 2003, Sought the input of Nicolas Popov of the Bahamas Island expedition for my paper in turtle's expedition, on CITES Treaty for my graduate degree, Masters in Marine Affairs from URI in 2005.

March 15, 2005, I am to send mail to Island Expedition, Nicolas Popov, on Cowes.

Aboard the smaller Island Expedition vessel, *Simpatico*, taken by the skipper, Niclas Popov, on arrival at Salt Cay, Turks & Caicos in March 1995. There is a story behind the hard-to-find New Zealand-made foul-weather jacket I'm wearing, by Line 7 in Auckland. It belonged to a British yacht captain named Bear, and he left it behind on *Rising Star* to move up the ladder to a bigger boat. I inherited it as I needed it badly to start my career and could not afford a new one. I then left it aboard David Ray's 90-foot wooden classic Hinckley sailboat *Nirvana* in Newport, where no doubt someone else made use of it. It had the name Bear in black ink on the upper right shoulder. That fall, I commissioned a Line7 vest at Team One Newport in Wellington Square (where I later worked for Armchair Sailor Books), and it had the Stornoway voyage monogrammed on the upper left breast – that almost got me in a fight on Rottnest Island, Western Australia, early in 1996 when was living in Singapore and visiting my Perth girlfriend, but that's another story...

Voyage 21: *The Dollar*, Newport-Block Island, August, 1995

Simply put, the boat named *The Dollar* was a large high-performance racing sailboat owned by someone in high finance at that stock exchange in NYC. The captain was a friend of my girlfriend Kimberly and mine. It being my last birthday in the US before I head to Asia for several years, she coordinated that we join the captain and his fiancé on a shake-down cruise over to nearby Block Island from Newport. Sounds harmless, yes? On the approach to the northeast side of the island we saw a small plane doing maneuvers, more like stunts, along the coast. Then on approach or doing other antics, or in distress (we will never know), the plane struck some power lines along the coastal road as it headed inland with one pilot. As (horrible) luck would have it, he happened to crash land in the ONLY gas station on the entire island! It blew up, of course on impact, sending a large plume of dark gray smoke into the air visible for many miles. Immediately the airwaves of VHF etc. were abuzz with witness and the US Coast Guard in nearby Block Island and Point Judith, RI.

Tragically, when the Block Island fire department arrived to douse their worst fire in years, the fire chief thought he recognized one of the cars incinerated by the inferno – he did, it was his mother's, and she as well as an attendant (so I believe) were also killed. Just horrible. We stayed a couple nights and my girlfriend and I flew back to Newport rather than wait for the boat, and at the airport it was very sad and subdued with such a tragedy effecting the small community and of course the small aviation world there too, as the pilot had taken off from that strip.

Voyage 22: *Luna*, Newport-Bra d'Or, Canada, June-July, 1995

June 29, 1995, Depart for Canada. Work for Captain Dyson Roberts on *Luna*, Severin's Little Harbor sailing yacht, about 65 feet. It was very foggy outbound from Newport Bridge and I was blowing the horn like hell on the bow to warn a little fishing boat at anchor. Later on: ...Signed off *Luna* in Bras d'Or, Nova Scotia, Canada. Advanced cash and air tickets by Severin Arrived Boston. Geoff at Seven's. US Government Printing Office, Causeway, Federal Building. Bookstore.

August 7, 1995, Reimbursed by Severin, for air tickets receipts for *Luna* crewing job... Nice to have an upfront honest owner who pays and reimburses!

October 2, 1995, Monday. Severin loaned *Luna* to an uncle of his wife, to go to Nantucket; her father was a US Navy veteran who managed significant properties in Nassau, which is part of how I got the job; the nexus with the Bahamas.

November 30, 1995, Severin was in the market in Nantucket, the A&P, which stands for Atlantic & Pacific? Perhaps I should introduce him to Denis & Wendy Metcalfe of Nantucket Moorings, for whom brother John worked.

Chapter 9

Voyage 23: *Endless Summer*, Bermuda-Newport, July, 1996

Voyage 27: *Endless Summer* Newport-Bermuda Race, June, 1998

Endless Summer at Cuttyhunk Island, Elizabeth Islands, between Padanaram, New Bedford and Menemsha, Martha's Vineyard, with just Brian and me, 1995.

Background: A friend of my older sisters through our mutual friend Ed, Brian has un-hesitatingly taken me under his wing and helped me from age 17 to today. from Bermuda to Nantucket to the Vineyard, introducing me to Cuttyhunk and Padanaram, always ready with a helping hand, the chance to earn my keep or room, and most of all welcoming me into his family with Peter & Lisa. Thank you, Brian. You have literally shown me the ropes. He was the skipper and owner of *Black Sheep*, then *Endless Summer*, and now a fleet of charter sailboats for Bareboat Sailing in Newport. I might have dedicated this book to he and his wife Lisa and son Peter, yet I have done so in the past....

When I was broke or between bunks, he always found a paintbrush for me to use, some hull to sand, or a yacht to charter to deliver to keep me on track, and having grown up as part of a large family in Newport, he knew exactly who would cash a check, or have a room needing a tenant, or a handyman. I stepped of my first voyage from Bermuda to Newport and into his wedding, without him I could not have held onto my high school sweetheart, and had he not insisted I return from Singapore to Newport at least every year, I might not have stepped off his boat *Endless Summer* and into a date which led to my quitting my job in Asia and returning to Newport in order to work at the Armchair Sailor and write. Like almost every captain and owner in this book, Brian also immediately filled, signed, notarized and returned the Sea Service forms for my US Coast Guard license, required every five years.

December 10, 1995, In Singapore, dreaming of summer: spoke to owner of *Endless Summer,* my longtime friend Brian's. She is at Oldport Marine in Newport repairing a backstay.

December 11, 1995, Monday. Day 83 in Singapore: Monastery of the Royal Palace at Huế in Vietnam. Brian Blank: Blank, *Endless Summer*. I'd like to crew on way down, skipper back Bermuda to Newport.

February 12, 1996, 8:55 am. Singapore; voyage planning; Hamilton, Bermuda to Nassau is 822 nm. Nassau to Newport is 1,028 nm. Newport to Bermuda 652 nm, or 100 hours at six knots. Nassau to Bermuda is six days. Nassau to Newport is seven days. Newport to Bermuda is five days or a bit less. I am to depart Monday arrive Saturday. My Norwegian tanker chartering boss, Trønd called off his Truk Lagoon SCUBA diving trip which makes the prospect of my taking command delivery of *Endless Summer* seems suddenly less likely.

April 22, 1996, Monday, 10 am. Midnight. 1996 Race. Fax Brian my sailing résumé, with, date of birth. *Endless Summer*, Bermuda. Plan. Todd Middagh. It is very strict in Singapore. Regimented.

June 10, 1996, Arrive Bermuda. Rachel, New York. Riverside Drive, delivery crew assembles. *Endless Summer*. Sailed from Hamilton, St. George's, Newport.

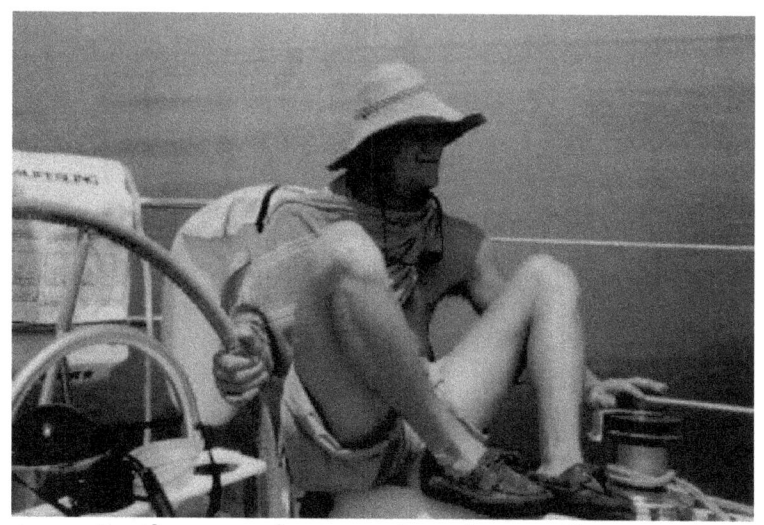
Deliveries do not require the same dress as aboard some Newport-Bermuda Race boats.

June 23, 1998, Tuesday. Location: 39°N, 70°W, 300 nm from Bermuda. Aboard *Endless Summer*, a lovely sloop by Beneteau; she is 42-foot designed by German Frers and his brother. Dear diary, I am at sea again, this time *en route* between Newport and Bermuda direct, as opposed to via Marion, for the Newport-to-Bermuda Race in 1998. Am thinking very much about Lara recently. We met years ago, on the train from to move aboard *Whisper of Maine* in the fall of 1993. Then, in about 1997 in Singapore, I came across her photo and address in the St. Paul's student booklet which my friend brought with him to Asia. On a whim, I wrote her, urgently, prior to coming back to Newport from this trip.

What undoubtedly hooked me the eve of this voyage after a series of fruitless and formal flirts was communiques from me. Was a lovely and lovely, refreshing and reassuring telephone conversation which I think we both enjoyed on Tuesday night, the day before I sailed out of and she drove long to Newport. I think that even in a lengthy and probing conversation at Newport with she in her apartment on Beacon Hill in Boston, was the harbinger of our being the soulmates. Good families, high expectations, a caring nature, an independent will, a disinclination towards wealth in itself except as a mean of sustenance; happiness, fulfilment Newport. I will try to visit her in Boston, this Friday, with any luck; I'll keep you posted! Happy, hopeful.

Dinty More, or canned beef stew from the bilge heated with a hand torch on *Endless Summer*.

June 26, 1998, I arrived on land to find this very thoughtful and out-of-character (given our family's stoicism) fax to the Royal Bermuda Yacht Club in Hamilton:

For and regarding Eric Wiberg crewing on Endless Summer *in the 1998 Newport-to-Bermuda Race. Please, let us know when* Endless Summer *arrives, or arrived. We assume they are caught in the off-shore doldrums unless and until we hear from you. Thanks. Signed Anders Wiberg, father.*

Voyage 24: Power boats; Singapore-Sentosa Island, numerous day trips, 1995-1998

October 2, 1995, Monday. Singapore social life: At 3 am saw River Towers, 5 pm, dinner, rest, joined Atle at 9 pm for cards party, at midnight at Fabrice's night club off Orchard Road. At 3 am home. Then at 2 pm Sunday, set off to joined Atle, Trønd K. to go boating passed Sentosa and out to anchor off Kusu, or Turtle Island, or St. John Island, Lazarus Island, or the Sisters Islands. At 4 pm to 6 pm ski at 6 pm anchor *Silus* on the beach, off Sentosa Island. It is a yacht owned by one of Atle's bosses, a New Zealander high up in Stolt-Nielsen who would later flee back to New Zealand;

At ease off the Singapore islands, 1995-1997; our host is checking out a bottle of perfume we found.

December 1, 1995, Second floor to right. First level of Cruise Terminal Lounge. Clock anchor off Sentosa. World Trade Centre. Speed boat, ministering Christmas Service, 5 pm to 6 pm back. How to find Cruise Ship. *Sunward II*, Captain Kjell Smitterberg, of Visby Gotland; very memorable, with Filipino crew singing hymns and the Norwegians and Swedes throwing back Schnapps! She is a Norwegian Caribbean Lines ship which my father had the family invited on board for a voyage to Miami in the late 1970s. The good captain was kind enough to extend his warm welcome and generosity 20 years later!

December 23, 1995, Christmas holiday, monitoring incoming calls log: Hung-up, Peder Møller, Mark, Burma, Myanmar, Mandalay Hotel at noon. Trond Kyrkjebø means *church hill* in Norwegian. A ship owner who I barely know owned a small power boat and took it to Sentosa, it was great fun and generous of him.

February 18, 1996, Singapore. 9:21 pm. Later, my new Dutch girlfriend visited me in Singapore. She is living as a student at Lorong Beluntas, Hedan Damansara, Kuala Lumpur. Landscape architecture student in Kuala Lumpur. She is lovely, as well as driving my teammates to distraction at rugby practice, she stayed with me at the dive Mitre Hotel. Later we went boating with Peder to the islands south of Sentosa, with the Norwegian artist Einstein Christiansen, who is now on kids' programs on Norwegian airlines, Greg B., Sten K. and Marius H. She said she'd never spent time with *pretty boys* before!

May 6, 1996, ...I didn't call Mr. Chew, didn't call Seawell Agencies in time, didn't liaise with Arif, (rush job on position list today), did take shit from agencies, did go boating to Sentosa, didn't mail Sally's photo. Ian W.: refineries out for overseas bunker supply to our 20 ships at moment. Cape Town, maintenance, available low-storage not great.....

Voyage 25: *Cheoy Lee sloop*, Jurong-Changi ship yards, Singapore, 1997-1998

Peder and volunteers from the US & Scandinavia, and the prize purchase, Singapore, 1997.

    This story is simple and a bit funny. Danish friend who lives life very intensely seeks an aquatic release. He has money, I have some expertise with old sailboats. About the time we start looking for a bargain starter boat in places like Pulau Ubin and Changi anchorages, the Singapore government decides to clean out abandoned commercial and recreational yachts and issues a firm and fast edict for all yacht owners to get rid of abandoned derelict boats or pay for their removal. Well, well; a Taiwan-build fiberglass Cheoy Lee with charming and solid lines in poor shape but strong bones comes on the market. Seven sails, a working Volvo Penta engine, looks horrible, but is afloat and moves. Peder and I offer $10,000 and it's agreed. but then I do what is inexcusable in shipping; I back trade. I get cold feet after realizing I don't have $5,000 and would lose what little else I had on an old boat. Peder tells the seller this who thinks it's a ploy but is under the gun and sells it at half price.

    To make up to Peder I spend many hours ripping junk out of it then moving the boat sail and power from the river anchorage near Johore to a Tanjong Pagar yacht yard near the opposite of Sentosa, quite charming actually. Well I remove a plug in the fuel tank which means after boat is launched for more in repairs than it cost. Then on being slowly lowered into the water, it sinks due to water ingress from the keel, and Peder gets a further discount due to me! We spend many happy hours there and a Danish girlfriend breaks up with me on the phone as I won't leave the boat to go on a date with her and we all joke about it until my friends go home and get laid and I don't... Peder ended up buying a larger power yacht and moving to Sentosa.

Voyage 26: *Artemis*, **Jurong to Changi Sailing Club, Singapore, 1995-1998**

July 15, 1996, Monday. Return to work, Singapore 9:15, Wednesday. For being up at 6 am; too late to be coming in (personal grooming). Where? Brit, Arabic? Boat Quay, 7 pm to 8 pm. Par-la-Ville Place, in Bermuda. Swim. Brian's car. Tanjong Pagar, August 25. Brian Miller, owner and captain of *Artemis* called; the Miller family graciously joined me for a house warming in my shophouse room at Spottiswoode Park; some of the only to do so. I think only Sten, from across the street, did. Very sweet.

September 18, 1996, Contact Bill Lindse, owner of a small sailboat, Changi Sailing Club. Miller's sailboat named *Artemis*, a Wauquiez 45 or so, my first bid. Delivery there, back? Louise, Olivia, Morten. Sten, Norwegian. Glen. Joneser (my personal nickname). Diane. I was once so terribly hung over that I arrived over an hour early for Sunday morning racing and in that time could not for the life of me figure out how I had made it home the night before! I also looked at a couple of beat up small sailing boats as live-aboards but even alone could not see it making sense financially or just in terms of having clothing clean and pressed.

August 29, 2000, Tuesday, 9:10 am;. Brian Miller called from Newport – their son Michael and spouse (who he met in Church in Singapore) and their children live in New *Jersey*; he's in banking.

September 18, 2000, Monday. Brian and Caroline Miller called from Newport. I was shipping out on a charter yacht *Ascent* when they called to say they were in Newport, and if I went back ashore in the launch I probably would have missed the last boat and been fired; I was studying for law school entry exams and was kind of on probation for drinking as it was, so chose not to and got a good night sleep instead – missed them though; good family. This was nicer than some other pranksters from Singapore who broke into my apartment and went upstairs, where my landlady caught them taking photos of each other on my toilet! Awkward for all concerned....

October 1, 2000, I emailed thanks for help with USCG license to: Severin and family, John Hirshler of Sightsailing, Peder Møller, Carol and Brian Miller......

Yes, I actually kept a written record of those I sent email thank-you letters to!

Chapter 10

Voyage 28: *Youth*, Stratford CT-Portsmouth RI, Spring, 1999

Voyage 33: *Youth*, Jamestown-Block-Cuttyhunk, MV-Nantucket, Padanaram, 1999

Voyage 59: *Youth*, Newport-Portsmouth RI, Summer 2000

Since yacht delivery skippers are a bit like firemen, showing up with little notice most of the time. That's not because we are the first choice or best choice ,but rather since we are one of the only choices. There are no trucks or ships making it convenient on most of our routes. I did, however once get a call in winter from Coast Guard asking if our client's yacht was sailing at 65 miles an hour across Dakota when Jack was trucking *Williwaw* to Seattle and the EPIRP shook loose and went off), it is rare to have two or three stints on the same boat, all of them without meeting the owner.

Such was my experience with *Youth*; a nice but groggy single-handed skipper showed me her ropes (and ripped some teak off when he stubbed his toe on it!), then I had to learn all the systems on a crash course basis or lose my tips (I didn't learn fast enough and lost my tips), and then just got to take her for a spin up the coast, knowing that if I went between Goat Island and Rose Island I would hit hard stuff a few feet below, and a very hard thing – Senator Claiborne Pell's namesake bridge – if I went too low beneath it (I graduated from the same Newport school as he, and had spent a voyage from Bermuda to Newport dreaming of taking his granddaughter to dinner….). So here are just short vignettes of *Youth*…. The hungover skipper just threw a piece of teak in the water on my first trip with her. Then we found a nice fender in a blue sock, and the fender was still there.

Just a simple trip of a few miles, couple hours at most, up the Long Island Sound, but no one wanted a skipper alone on a paid delivery. Post-race repairs or charter positioning probably. We all need that extra person who will at least to stop and us up if we go overboard. The yacht broker's assistant took me early one spring morning across bridge Newport to Stratford. Having studied all of, and seen many of William Shakespeare's plays and comedies at Oxford, I was fascinated to see a town of that name in Connecticut, and to try to see their theater. When we arrived the captain is washing up had a big night.

May 17, 2000, Saturday. *Calls: Seeadler*: David, Bermuda, yacht owner, J-160, Dr. CC, owner of *Swan Youth*, which I delivered several times for brokers….

July 9, 2001, (from *Breathless* and *The Dollar* days, 8 years before) called, I am to move *Youth* from Newport to NEB, New England Boat Works, up the coast in Portsmouth.

June 28, 2002, Return call to Brian, Manfred, re: *Youth*; to manage boat. This was one of my first charters. The owner could not have been nicer, and was trying really hard to understand keel-boat management. I got very little shore support so some things like wiring, panels and batteries were not solved right away, and nor were the full usages of a whisker pole and even unfortunately a head, or marine toilet which kicked and refused to work the first night in Block Island. While they dined on shore I had to pull it apart, and the Mrs. was not pleased at all about the invasion of privacy, understandably!

From Block Island we hustled into the anchorage outside of Cuttyhunk, Massachusetts just before the sun set. All beds in the Inn were booked; meaning all moorings were taken, so we had to rush anchor outside the breakwater. In my rush, I dropped the anchor with the sail still up and never reversed to sufficiently dig the anchor in. The guidebook said the anchorage was eel grass over tightly packed sand but "safe in all but a northwesterly, which is rare." The seafloor was such as hard as concrete, and usually I would throw on a mask and look myself, but being the only crew, with a dinghy to launch and food to prepare, I wasn't able to in the dark. So, predictably, we dragged anchor. By about 3 in the morning a strong northwesterly had dragged us into the mouth of a very narrow channel and aground on a gently shelving beach.

I was woken by the metal channel buoy hitting our hull, leapt on deck and managed to lasso it before we dragged much further ashore. When I fired up the engine the charterer joined me and asked if all was alright.

"Absolutely not" I said, "I need your help, you gun the engine, I'll take up slack on the buoy, and we'll kedge off this beach." After we had stabilized the situation, his bleary-eyed wife popped up and asked if everything was OK. Not missing a beat, he sang out

"Just fine, dear. You can go back to sleep." My punishment was a night on deck fending off other boats as they dragged anchor. By dawn I was sheepishly (and sleeplessly) on display to curious fishermen using the channel.

We later motored to Edgartown and anchored in Kitamet but I was out of cigarettes and miserable. On Nantucket I saw the Buena Vista Social Club. To make up for being turned away from most nice spot in southern New England we felt better by going to Padanaram for cozy family fun and were as always very welcomed by the New Bedford Yacht Club who opened their dining showers and laundry to us like long lost friends even though we were not members. Thank goodness for them.

The *denouement* was that I was paid out and they disembarked at Goat Island Marina and my other employers who managed the yacht for a charter pool from a base off Lower Thames near Zelda's (Susan and Caroline), told me to dock it at Jamestown Marina. I saw a great spot but fishermen had strung some cables across the slip, which is *verbotten*, but I had no time to complain, and commercial fishermen are not a recommended target for screaming at from a yacht. I had to change plans and reverse into a narrow spot between yachts post-haste, before anyone could even help me! The surprise on the professional French and other skippers was palpable as they had not met me before and assumed I was a charterer with little experience who was mad to even attempt the maneuver! That was gratifying, and what my frail ego and empty tips-jar needed at that moment. They took me back to Newport across the bay in a dinghy. The fishermen of course didn't even notice.

Epilogue: *Youth* has always been a popular boat and done well in Bermuda races and the *Swan* Regattas in Newport and elsewhere. The owner seems astute and actually able to cover costs with chartering the boat out – good for him. I had a few friendly bit a bit odd run-ins with the first skipper. For some unknown reason, during the big 2001 celebration at Cowes Week for the America's Cup, which I had to miss it to enroll in law school, I met a lovely young lady from the UK who is an exceptionally gifted marine artist. She was staying at the same flat as the delivery skipper, not far from my place, and I stayed up late chatting, probably to the chagrin of the leaseholder!

Early the same morning I rushed to get to a boat I was running (I think *Föhn Wind*) near Bowen's Wharf, it was one of those nights; I left my cell at their place, and had some trouble explaining to my girlfriend at the time, who was getting ready to race from Boston to France, how I lost my phone…. But at some point he cornered me about collecting a sales brokerage commission on the *Stiarna*, or the *Columbia*, which the owner bought after *Stiarna* sank under our feet. Well, I didn't obtain any commission – I showed the buyer my client *War Baby* and he demurred. So I really could not help the captain collect from anyone else, but it was awkward and uncomfortable. That's the world of yachting, folks! Very interwoven, and you haven't been paid what you were promised till you *have* been paid.

Voyage 29: *Flambé*, Antigua - Newport via Bermuda, May-June, 1999

Everything was almost too easy with this boat; here the breeze keeps her off the fuel dock while I tie a forward spring line, Ed holds the stern and Kent takes a photo. Antigua in May.

This was my happiest voyage ever, yet almost all the diary and log keeping was in the boat: Freddy was Swiss but US via marriage and got overseas pay in Switzerland for US banking! Bob was the broker, nicest guy around his wife Polly helped at Oyster Goat Island. Best friends Kent and Ed were by my side, and Wayne. Great food as Ed is a chef – ham basted in brown sugar, sprite, and cloves. Fishing was good too. The main engine was a Yanmar, water-maker worked.

Kent's story about "I could change course, or you could?" is about a motor ship on horizon, and was a funny one. Being in the commercial tanker and bulker business, I cold often tell from the color and type and course of a ship – before the technology shared such things, where they were going and what they were carrying. For example, I would on a calm boring day call on the VHF: "Would the 30,000 deadweight Odfjell parcel tanker bound from Gibraltar to Houston in ballast please come back to *Flambé* on Channel 16."

Since it came out of the blue, with them rarely being able to see us and with a USA accent, this practice often scared the shit out of the Filipino or Indian deck officer sitting on the bridge, and they assumed we must be in some military drone or aircraft. After a couple minutes of back and forth about things like weather ("there is much wind where we came from," one captain told me), they were usually willing to alter their course – bearing in mind they were 30 to 50 times or 100 times bigger than us – to accommodate us! The tail wagging the dog; great fun.

Flambé's crew minutes after arrival in Bermuda, at the Starlight bar, or the late-night one down the steps from the bus stop and liquor store, west of Silk Alley. Me, Ed, Kent, Wayne. I appreciate the many global clocks. It is a chill place for reasonably priced drinks, local company, and a quiet beer and game of pool, being dark around the clock. It was to this place which my would-be grafters took me at 3 am when I was younger, and set me up with a paid tab and introductions, four of them having asked me for money just minutes before…..

In Bermuda we raised hell; the classic call of "is my daughter on board? And she was! Ed's sister joined us, while the captain and a guest were indisposed. That sailor both took a wrong turn on the dock at night onto lovely golf-course grass on the water, and later misjudged US and Bermuda time and the mate had to literally grab her from my arms to get her on the boat before it sailed; a tall ship full of students, with horns blaring and flags fluttering to find her, as we had been on the Young Endeavor to find crew before Hurricane Andrew in Nassau in 1992.

This trip is also how Kent met another sailor, which lead to his meeting said sailor's friends, which let to Kent meeting his future and present spouse! When we arrived in perfect weather on a quiet Friday morning at Goat Island fuel dock, we simply cranked up Frank Sinatra's *Fly Me to the Moon*, and scrubbed the boat down right in front of our employer's office, and I recall the steam coming off the dark hull from the cold New England water. Great pay, particularly after what I was earning as a part-time book cataloguer in Newport store! And then I was convinced me to quit my job in the book store, got job thanks to chart-monger and racing guru Tony Bessinger.

May 30, 1999, Voyage, Antigua. Messages, on my return from Antigua. Eric's Sailboat arrived safely in Newport. Message to my parents. Refused all full-time work to deliver instead. Bermuda. Thursday Delta flight #210. Departs Bermuda 5 pm, and arrives Boston 6:18 pm. *Geymen.* Robin, Kent's good friend, land in New York. ....June 27 Warren, Hamilton. Dinghy. Fueled. Ed of Block Island. Today 6:41 am, Kent, in New York City.

October 5, 2000, Ian, call, jobs? Looking for work. Freddy, Swiss-American banker and owner of lovely Hinckley 52-foot sloop *Flambé*.

September 2, 2003, *Flambé*. Captain Woody, who bailed me and Ennalls B. out of the *Congo* fiasco in the Carolinas, might be able to cover me on *Flambé* this time?

Anecdotes of *Flambé*: After saying goodbye with his best friend Hienrich in Antigua, the owner set off for the airport. To my subdued panic I heard him on the VHF radio saying he was coming back to the boat to get his daughter's graduation speech which was on the boat. The crew did not reply to my calls on the VHF. So as Freddy screeched to a halt in the taxi van with limited time to catch a flight, and I whisked him in the dinghy to the boat at anchor, I was dreading what we would find. The load reggae blaring explained why they didn't hear the VHF radio. But to everyone's relief the crew were hard at work prepping the boats, stowing food, airing sheets, packing and inventorying. He grabbed his speech and was off, and I kept the job.....

"Has anyone here seen my daughter?" Not what any skipper – or parent – wants to hear. It was a mother from New York in her 50s that had been partying with us all the night before, no one knowing who to dance with she or her 24-or-so-year-old daughter? Well, the boat on the dock was owned and crewed by half a dozen gentlemen who were not interested I the overnight company of ladies, and everyone was perfectly comfortable with that, so they simply called out "it wasn't us!" in a cheerful voice and the mother looked beyond them understandingly – to our boat! I was hung over and had a visitor myself, so I simply managed to ask:

"Does anyone on board have this ladies' daughter?" A door flung open up forward starboard and one of the guys kissed the young lady good morning. As she scrambled awkwardly for the companionway and escape, I asked to goodbye please slow down. She needed to lace up some eyefuls up front before bringing them up on deck and in public for admiration – she agreed and tucked everything away. She and mother were reunited. What a question!

"Who has my daughter?"

A few months later I ran into Teddy, his entire crew abandoned him and he sailed the boat back to Newport himself, having numerous solo swims in the Gulf Stream to fix broken equipment. Months later I received a long hand-written letter. It was from one of our many jolly and happy playmates in Bermuda that voyage, and she wrote admiringly of how when we all walked to Fort St. Catherine in a group, she would admire my hair, how the moon shone off my checks, my smile, voice, I was quite excited to learn who she was and why she hadn't let me know sooner! I soon found out – the author was one of the crew on the boat between us and the dock. He and I did not keep the correspondence up, though the letter counts as probably the most flattering I have received…

Voyage 31: *Diviner*, Southwest Harbor Maine - Jamestown RI, July, 1999

This is where Echo Yacht Deliveries Worldwide was founded at 3 Lee Wharf, Newport, in July of 1999, following successful voyages on *Flambé, Youth*, and *War Baby*. The blue plastic crate at left was the company filing system. I was determined not to be another "Capt. John Doe Deliveries," meaning a one-man-band. Rather tried to broaden and diversify the number and locations of captains available globally, and to make the sector more accountable, professional and transparent, with a paper trail for every step of the way. I quickly learned that the *Captain Ron* parody and piratical impression of yacht delivery skippers is hard to budge, and that ultimately owners are really just focused on safe, fast results in budget, and not in long reports about their yachts deficiencies, or excuses for over-runs. Owners seem wary of hiring a wing-nut going in, and so the word of mouth referral system is vital, however burn-out rates for delivery crew is high. Also, since delivery skippers and owners often do not meet, the issue of how compatible they are is largely moot. Parties often prefer, as I did, to just do the job and get paid and go home; it is after the anti-charter, the anti-full-time-captain scenario. Regarding the desktop computer in this photo, when I returned to Newport after working my tail off in the tanker space for three years I was basically penniless, and my parents helped me buy this desktop: cell phones were pretty standard in 1998, but the internet and email was for many, or at least me, just taking root. The first thing I did was develop an informative and richly illustrated website, with help from Giuseppe and Marta from *War Baby* and Rich Schlegel of Computer Zen. Then I plastered printed cards in every crew laundry area in the North Atlantic from the Channel Islands to the Azores, Trinidad to Halifax and Little Creek.

Based on a bright idea while I was banished so the cockpit so that crew could sunbathe topless on the bow on a return to Newport from Bermuda in July, I quit my job in the book store. Then I launched Echo Yacht Delivery Worldwide with a vengeance, posting the internet as well as lockers, hallways, post-it boards of all the marinas I could find. Then I waited. Then, well, the sound of crickets. It was middle of summer, when boats tend to already be where the owner needs them to be. The first voyage came from the same gent who shared the *Flambé* opportunity with me; Bob, then of Bartram & Brackenhoff. The boat was based in Jamestown and named *Diviner*. Beloved by its owners, who I never met, to me the older whale-bottomed craft seemed cranky and heavy, yet my salvation! I was told to meet it in Southwest Harbor, Maine, the home of the storied Hinckley Yachts, the next day, and bring it to Jamestown, a mile or so west of Newport.

I could not find crew, went to Zelda's Café on Lower Thames, on I assume a Tuesday night. I tried to find a sailor to help me, and did find a man in his early 50s, thin, slight, who had owned a MacGregor 65 or so; a fast sailing boat. Thankfully, he agreed he would help me, and sure enough I met him at 5 am on the curb outside Zelda's in my car. He was wearing the lapels of a Russian or French sailor, blue and white stripes, which I found endearing. We drove to Boston's Logan Airport then flew to airport near Bar Harbor.

During the flight I remember a British socialite and man-about-town who insisted on dropping several names and that we all recognize his many languages and global graces. I think he believed we would find him to be a superior person, and ourselves inferior. I found him bemusing, yet pitied his silent wife and whatever host they were sponging off. Quite a character; a hero in his own mind; if there had been any that fit his age, I am sure he would have told us how he had managed to win it.

Two, quieter members of the jet-set studied my tide book with Echo Yacht Delivery pasted all over it with the red and blue company logo, clearly recognizing that trickle-down extends to moving yachts! We then took a cab to the boat yard, and that afternoon I asked my mate to wait on the dock while I met Cuyler Morris of Morris Yachts. Cuyler and I went to St. George's and grew up in family businesses; he could not have been nicer. That said, there had been a miscommunication, and it would take a few days for repairs to a panel to be complete before we could sail. That was fine with me.

Since we now had time, I decided to hire another sailor for the trip. Marta was Giuseppe from *War Baby*'s Italian girlfriend. They had been staying at my place, helping with the website, and borrowing my car. The owner of *Diviner*, or at least the person who managed my participation, was a woman, and was fine with paying for Marta to fly up. When Marta, the Zelda's sailor, and I were refueling at the lobster dock in Southwest Harbor, Cuyler and members of his team found time in their busy day to say hello, it was a *Babette's Feast* moment! I believe the local boatbuilder clique was a bit curious to meet the Italian beauty who moves boats. [This is in contrast to a smaller Maine port which banned a certain yacht club from visiting during their annual cruises as they were considered too uppity!]

When I over-engaged with tourists admiring the seals from the adjacent lobster restaurant, the fuel overflowed. My professional and personal worlds collided as I then looked inattentive to the crew, who had never sailed with me. The passage was fine, and even though the wheel was too small for ease of steering, she did not like me messing with or commenting on it. There was no override autohelm option, as it was a cruising boat. Everyone had a good time, and most importantly it was safe. I completed the first voyage of Echo Yacht Delivery without drama, and stayed in touch with Cuyler as well! The money turned out to be hidden in cash in the navigation station. It was one of those goldilocks trips – not too long, not too short, and I'm just grateful that when I asked for additional crew just inside the necessary envelope, my decision was affirmed by a client I never met.

August 30, 2001, *Diviner,* for four days. She just didn't tell us where the payout was until we had picked up the mooring at our final destination at Jamestown Boat Yard; very clever! The couple who owned it had no interest in learning the faults, which was important to me, as I had advertised as a sales gimmick that I would thoroughly details a yacht's failings to the owners and then realized: *perhaps not such a great idea.* [The gent running Jamestown Boat Yard at the time, or recently, was Captain Johnno, who with his wife Susan own and run the Cuttyhunk Island ferry service from New Bedford in 2020!]

August, 27, 2005, My 28th birthday. Hurricane Katrina. Cuyler Morris, owner of Morris Yacht in Maine; graduate of St. George's. Key Bank of Ellsworth, Maine.

Voyage 32: *Pericles*, Lockeport, Nova Scotia-Newport, RI August, 1999

At 6.30 am, my phone rings, it's from the owner of a small yacht delivery network like mine. A captain of his has pulled into a remote fishing village in Nova Scotia on a passage from the Marblehead Halifax Race to Newport and is unhappy with the crew, so he's dumped him ashore (a friend of the owner). Captain is Australian and friendly – turned out he was my captain on the *Wave of Peace*; Andrew, of Perth, then dating Fiona. I agreed to deploy immediately, grabbed my gear and back, drove to Boston took the next flight from Logan Airport to Halifax, but was faced with a long wait for a bus to Yarmouth close to Lockeport where I needed to go, to the southeast. So I hitchhiked, and one lift giver was a former Canadian Army intelligence officer who won a lottery to hear Churchill speak in Parliament. I had time to pick a lot of blueberries.

I was next given a long lift by a kindly middle-aged bearded, heavyset man who was very Christian. It was raining hard and he could not bring himself to drop me with a 3 mile walk in the forest late at night so he drove me to the village and captain Andrew met me. Not much to the trip, now wind, the previous crew was an insecure windbag. Two items *en route*; at daylight we saw lats of swordfish harpooning boats with long bows as well as lots of whale spotting boats. On skirting the coast to Provincetown Harbor low on fuel and eager to make it before the pumps closed, we were so close to the beach that we could see a lesbian couple with one going down on the other, so of course we slowed down and tested the binoculars! Then we pulled into Provincetown for fuel. He put on a loud red cap and posted me as a sentry in the rigging, *in case he was attacked by homosexuals*! I did hear US Coast Guard sailors complaining that they often had to hose amorous couples from their large lawn.

We made it to Newport via the Cape Cod Canal, and were paid out, not a big deal. Andy B., a respected Canadian captain and exemplary organizer was in overall charge, paid us promptly, and went into the ship model business afterwards. One moral of this voyage was then even when flat calm, with no external danger, crew can drive each other to extremes, and boats are more likely to run out of fuel, and still might run into swordfishermen with harpoons, like in the days of *Moby Dick* and In the *Heart of the Sea*!

Voyage 35: *Marblic*, SW Harbor ME-Newport, September, 1999

Me and Tugboat Anthony, a merchant mariner, a bit older, who barely said a thing and when he did it always came out angry. Tug and I did half a dozen voyages (*Lapwing* from the same port being one), mostly as the only crew or only professionals, so we were pretty familiar with each other. Between us, it was strictly business, and he mostly was skipper, but other times I originated the business and he joined me. He considered himself evolved from the school of hard knocks, and me, well, not. We flew up to the little airport off Mount Desert Island, which still called itself Bar Harbor, the main settlement on that island. We arrived by cab at the Hinckley facility too late to get a drink, but did manage a brief meal. Andy liked to chew tobacco and I smoked. We had cold food for the passage, maybe a hotdog or bread to heat in a microwave. This was a picnic boat twin screw diesel, fast, comfortable, dry, which had all the bells and whistles.

We both got up before sunrise for the tide then clicked off four states (Maine, New Hampshire, Massachusetts, using the Cape Cod Canal, and Newport, in Rhode Island) from sunrise to sunset, averaging over 40 knots even with the different winds and speed adjustments, which were basically south for most, west for some, and north for the final little bit. Cool! Manfred Advent (of *Breathless*)'s brother Chris was there to take our lines at sunset at Goat Island Marina. It was really a memorable and enjoyable and trouble-free transit with the wind and seas negligible or behind us. Four states in one day. I like that. The experience positively alters – improves – our sense of time and distance, as on a sailboat it can take three days at 6 knots with all kinds of issues.

Chapter 11

Aaron: A Preamble to *Sarafina, Crested, Triton*, and *Femme*, Fall 1999

AARON DICKSON, CANADA: LIFE SAVER

    As a middle child not prone to admitting his dependence on others, who started five small companies and is fiercely protective, to a fault, of his independence, I have to openly say that without Aaron Dickson of Halifax, Nova Scotia, my small startup Echo Yacht Deliveries would either not have survived for over 20 years, or been just local in reach.

    Aaron and I were able to meet in the company's first fall season, 1999, which was riven by numerous hurricanes, as well has high demand for boats to go from Newport to Fort Lauderdale for boat shows. There was also pressure to get owners to the Caribbean for the once-in-a-lifetime millennial New Year. Here are the boats on which Aaron was my mate. For about four months we were inseparable, living either on four boats, or in my waterfront loft in Newport. This includes the boats along with the weather systems we endured together:

Sarafina (Oyster 53'), Newport-Port Canaveral via Annapolis, Charleston in September.
   Crew: Eric, Aaron, Lisa (later a new Eric for Lisa when she left in Charleston)
   Hurricane Dennis hit North Carolina prior to departure on *Sarafina* mid-September. Hurricane Floyd passed over, just east of Annapolis, where *Sarafina* was berthed with *Wentje* (Cronkite) & *Flying Colors* (lost, all young hands, Gulf Stream, 2003). Hurricane Gert headed for eastern seaboard, veered to Bermuda and Nova Scotia. Hurricane Harvey strengthened in Gulf of Mexico as we rounded Hatteras, forcing a duck into Charleston, where one of our crew (Lisa) left, and a new Eric joined.

Crested (Little Harbor 54') Newport-Lauderdale via Beaufort, Charleston, in October.
   Crew: Eric, Aaron, and Dave
   Gale leaving Newport caused me to be knocked overboard, 100 nm off Block Island. Hurricane Irene wound up the US east Coast of Florida (mostly rain): passed over and just east of Charleston where we had ducked in aboard *Crested* to avoid it.

Triton (Little Harbor 52') Newport-Lauderdale, Norfolk, Charleston, October-November.
   Crew: Eric, Aaron, and Ed.
   Gale, 50-knot, 18-25-foot-seas, hammered Cape Hatteras, forcing *Triton* to Norfolk.
   Femme (Beneteau 43') Newport-Tortola, BVI, via Bermuda, in December.
   Crew: Eric, Aaron, Ed. Bill P. (he left in Bermuda)
   November Gale; this 40-knot, 20-foot-seas system blew through New England, halting retrieval of debris EgyptAir crash off Long Island, before *Femme*'s dash. Bermuda Gale; microburst, 180-degree 60 knot wind. Hit 10 large boats moored stern-to at St. George's Dinghy Club, damaged our port quarter, led to a dry-dock. Hurricane Lenny; *Femme* dashed to Bermuda to avoid Lenny, large seas, east Caribs.

The working relationship which Aaron and I developed was simplified by the boarding school system of keeping ourselves so busy that you don't have time to think. He wanted to further his skills and experience towards his captain's license, and we both wanted the money before the fall became winter and opportunities dried up in the north, where we both lived – he in Halifax, where his dad is a marine artist. We both really wanted to make the foundling Echo Yacht Deliveries work, which was a value-added I sorely needed.

Aaron is an exemplary loyal, honest, hard-working person and a solid reliable mariner; precisely the person I relied upon while I ran around in person and online getting new business, mollifying brokers and customers, paying and collecting money and arranging repairs to all the items from leaking steering quadrants to jammed goosenecks, and making docking reservations, paying bills, finding diesel mechanics, booking hospital visits, and taking calls from brokers at 9 pm ordering us into a 40-knot gale and blinding rain to make it to the boat show on time. For Aaron and I, there were many highlights, like making it to port safely, meeting other young mariners like the team at Charleston's City Marina, exploring West End, Tortola, cutting a mooring line off the propeller at night on approach to another Tortola anchorage, buying a year's supply of cereal and toilet paper near the St. George's Community Center in Bermuda. Often we could be found trying to either get into the St. George's Dinghy & Sport's Club, or just get the tokens for hot showers and get out.

Although Aaron retained the rank of mate, or second-in-command on all vessels we ran together (or perhaps because of it), when I would bring in older and perhaps more experienced sailors for passages, they appeared to have been miffed by that. I needed Aaron badly, and he was available for non-stop full time work throughout the fall, on call in my guest area, while the others were not. They did not make more money than us on boats I ran, but in some cases they had full-time day jobs and "lived it up" on shore more than we could afford to do. That also caused tensions.

On the nearly 1,000-mile passage to the Virgin Islands from Bermuda we lost all electronics – even speed gauges and anemometers – forcing me to navigate on short bursts of a hand-held, battery-powered GPS. That meant that calling for sail changes or sail reductions (cautious reefing or shortening of sails) in the evenings might be met with resistance, since we all became more torpid in the gentle tradewinds. Then, I was aghast to learn that even though we were beyond the 100-fathom line and many miles north of the Virgin Islands, there were blue-water fishing traps with floats and markers on the surface, which posed a threat to our propeller, and safety. So I posted a watch stander on the bow. Since we were all exhausted, as many crew are when the approach shore after a week-long passage, that was not well-received either.

So there was not a total lack of friction, as there naturally would be over nearly half a year in life-threatening voyages, and most of it was between my new and existing crew. I admit that towards Christmas and New Year, I just stopped mediating. The fact is that Aaron and I not only needed but relied on each other not only for our livelihood, but also our lives. He saved my life by organizing my retrieval from the horrific, lonely, cold, and terrifying man overboard near-tragedy off *Crested* in October, 1999.

It says a lot about our working relationship that over two decades passed before Aaron read my account of his rescue as *de-facto* captain of *Crested*, when I was helpless and spoke up with the correct version. I had only heard a sloppy, bar-room version from Dave, and Aaron, who led the charge and saved me, had not once volunteered his version. He let his accomplishment and skill speak for itself. That, and I believe we all found and still find the events traumatizing and raw. This book helps to set the record straight. Aaron did benefit from getting Echo off the ground, he saved the pay, earned the sea time, and obtained a significant merchant marine license in Canada which he has parlayed into a port captain role. I would have expected no less.

Words cannot tell how much of an inflection point, or fundamentally life-altering experience it was, since all experts and anyone who has survived something like it, recognized that in strictly scientific terms, I was minutes at most from death, and largely hypothermic, which blue face and lips, and shivering terribly when retrieved. Aaron did exactly the right thing- they lay me down on a warm bed, covered me in many layers of warm blankets, offered me hot tea, an told me that they would stand my next watch for me.

Then Aaron wisely radioed the safety net and told them we had survived a MOB incident and gave the position of the life ring horseshoe with flashing light which was lost when pulling me in.

Obviously I am eternally and unspeakably humbly and thankfully grateful to Aaron and Dave for that, and on behalf of my son and for every happy event of my life since, for every event. It's pretty heavy stuff for us to digest, still. Without Captain Aaron Dickson, I would not be alive. Thank you, Aaron, and thank you for agreeing to write this *Foreword* as well. When I called Aaron's employer from my fleet-owning employer in Manhattan on a work-related issue some years ago, the woman managing the calls had been there a while so I asked if she know Aaron. She brightened up and said, why of course she did. I started to say

"Well, years ago I was his captain, and he saved me when I fell overboard in a snowstorm." – I got that far alright, but when I got to

"I would like him to meet my son someday…." But of course my voice cracked and I could say no more. She was very understanding. I don't think was used to hearing sea captains break down when talking about each other, though!

Aaron: you never let me down. We both went through more shit that fall than either of us wanted or expected. I didn't always make the best and fastest decision, and I hope that you forgive me for that. I am glad that we remain in touch and look forward to our families having a picnic someday, so we can tell sea stories of making it through.

This is taken by my Mom's friend from and in Annapolis. Her daughter eventually married my captain from *Rising Star*! From *Newport Sailor, Caribbean Sailor*, editor Jim Long, 2000

Voyage 36: *Sarafina* **Newport-Port Canaveral via Annapolis & Charleston**

A chicken farmer from Indiana found a Bentley-style sailing yacht which had caught fire and been condemned. He then bought the insurance write-off for pennies on the dollar, and after a total refit, using the loyal broker Bob. I never noticed any fire damage in nearly a month. The new owners calls the Oyster-England-made 53-foot yacht *Sarafina*, and drives like a madman, yelling at people with out-of-state plates, even when he, too, is visiting. But, unlike plenty of fancy owners or brokers I've met, this one supports his crew and always pays. When we got stuck in Hurricane Floyd in Annapolis at Petrini's Boatyard next to Walter Cronkite's yacht *Wentje* and another named *Flying Colors* with Alden Anderson in charge, he told us to buy used carpets to drape on the side, and to wear swimming masks! Wasn't a Laura Ashley or Martha Stewart solution perhaps, but it made a lot of practical sense.

I had single-handedly moved the boat across Newport Harbor earlier in the summer, and come to know the boat a little bit that way, including raising and lowering the dodger, or collapsible window in front of the helmsman. So, in a case of closing the barn door after the horses have fled, we set off from Newport as an untested crew during a busy weekend evening with dozens of boats rounding Fort Adams inbound and out. Even on my tippy-toes on the cockpit combing, or ledge, I could not see over the dodger. Only I knew took a few seconds to release and lower.

Before we entered the hectic channel, I asked the Aaron and Lisa to lower it and they both demurred, saying it would take too long, given the crowded state of the harbor. I could not do it myself, as I could not leave the wheel. At that point in time we were the largest boat in the mix, and were increasingly surrounded by small power boats, which Newport sailors refer to, unfairly I think, as the Cranston Navy. So I let my crew's mini-mutiny slide. As a consequence, I could not see when we entered a blender of anger, and within minutes we were being justifiably berated by angry skippers who we had unintentionally nearly run over. That juvenile taunt

"Get a copy of the *Rules of the Road*!" was hurled at us more than once, and I just took it on the chin. Fortunately for the owner, it was before cell-phones could take videos, and his yacht was going far away for a long time. It would have been better for me, the crew, and all concerned had I laid down the law at the outset, more explicitly ordered the dodger lowered post-haste, and explained why. My failure to do so almost caused a collision during the first minutes of a weeks-long voyage, and undermined my authority in the eyes of the crew. The crew told me later that they would have preferred a stronger hand at the outset which let them know they, and my, position. I was reminded that sometimes it is necessary not to care if you sound like a dick, particularly in the interest of safety.

Crew Lisa and I, southbound to Canaveral. Due to storms we took three times longer than expected and she had to go back to Newport. I've never lost a crew and rather than pay the airfare I wrongly paid just for a bus fare. When I told the owner, he was upset with me and said I should have raided the boat's petty cash (I handn't known where it was till then). I have tried to catch up with Lisa and repay and apologize, but boating creates great distances just as it closes them. I did not do that again. And she had a chuckle when the Charleston currents pinned us for hours. She had been on a yacht which lost a rudder off Bermuda and seen more danger than many of us.
Credit: Capt. Aaron Dickson, First Mate

This voyage had so many weather delays that my crew's time commitments were stretched to breaking point. Sadly, for the first time ever, I had to let a crew, Lisa, go, as she needed to get back to Newport. She is an excellent sailor, Irish, and has survived the loss of a rudder in Bermuda. She was and friendly shipmate and we were sorry to have to see her off in Charleston. It was we, not she, who were two weeks late. She had to take a bus home, as I foolishly did not pay the full flight back to Rhode Island. That is something I regret to this day; I had staked my reputation on being fair to crew, and in this instance I let she and I and Echo down.

Perhaps as poetic justice, I was unused to river and so after Lisa untied us and as we were backing out of City Marina, the strength of the river current caught klutz skipper by surprise. Immediately we were pinned indecorously against the sterns of two vessels and several pilings. I stopped the throttled immediately and stabilized so that we just waited. She was there to lend a hand, and helped us save face and avoid further damage. We sat in that awkward and highly visible position for several hours until the tide freed us. She boarded the bus to her boyfriend. I'm sure that our fellow sailors at IYAC shared a chuckle or two at my expense – again, deservedly!

The thing is that before and during I had been influenced by sailors regarding Lisa's disloyalty, though it was not her fault, she was being honest, and having never made these trips I thought two weeks would be fair. I didn't hear the others side – the owner's perspective until after Lisa had left. He said by all means I should have opened the ship's safe and bought her an air ticket, particularly being a single woman, and I should have done so. For one, I was not willing to take a penny for the boat's kitty, particularly for a crew conundrum of my own making, until I'd pre-approved it.

As a not-quite-on-par replacement, we recruited a waiter and tour guide named Eric. There was a back story which I will try to abbreviate. At a great bar named the Blind Tiger, our friendly waitress, Cindy, said she did know of a sailor we could hire. He then gave me a number to call when we were ready. I then invited Cindy back to the boat for a tour. During said tour, she learned that the number he had given me to call him was in fact her number; although she was a single mother, he had assumed he would be shacking up with her when needed. Quite a few wheels-in-wheels. Instead of having two Erics in her world, she very quickly ensured there would be none! A big, bearded guy, he did come in handy warding off a psychotic fisherman off Mayport, Jacksonville Florida, and the submarine base in Brunswick, Georgia.

We arrive in Canaveral and all was well, except for the delays. Characteristically the owner was hands-on and waiting for us with a rental car, and sped at terrifying speed to Orland Airport, reminding us that the rental car had New York plates, so his driving would be blamed on them. He also enlightened us to the vast money-gobbling conspiracy which is NASA [before SpaceEx]. This trip then backed up my next two trips to the Fort Lauderdale Boat Show.

Voyage 37: *Crested* Newport-Lauderdale via Beaufort, Charleston

Snow before a voyage south, winter in Newport, here we are having a bit of fun and welcoming the crew of the large yacht to the right while clearing decks of the yacht to the left for a passage south, including throwing a snowball or two. British ensign: Oysters.

On 8th October last year, my delivery crew of two and I were 100 miles south of Block Island, Rhode Island, aboard a 53-foot cruising sloop headed southwest into 20- to 30-knot winds and six- to eight-foot seas. It was our first full day on the second of three consecutive deliveries from New England to Fort Lauderdale, Florida. The voyage, with me as captain, Aaron as mate and a youth sailing coach from California named Dave, a young student from University of Rhode Island (URI) as crew.

We left Newport bound for the Fort Lauderdale Boat Show via Morehead City, North Carolina, and Charleston a Little Harbor (aka *Little Horror*, per the graffiti in the stalls of the men who made them), named *Crested*, formerly one of the *Robins*; meaning it sells for more since the found of the company owned it, and it once had a light-blue hull like robin's egg. The boats are perfect for what they are designed for, the saying goes: "to get their owners into the fanciest yacht clubs."

While I was off watch and resting below, a loud crack – followed immediately by the sound of flailing lines and sails – woke me and brought me into the cockpit dressed in only a pair of boxer shorts; clearly a preventably vulnerable state in winter. The mainsheet had parted, and the boom swung wildly across the deck. After heading into the wind, we rolled and furled the main. I reefed the genoa for stability, and then began securing the boom, mainsheet, and tackle. In hindsight, this would have been an ideal time to suit up and clip in with a harness.

I grabbed the errant mainsheet with my left hand and a metal dorade guard with my right. Moments later, the weight of the boom pried my right hand free; I was lifted and swung over the lifelines. My open-air glide didn't last long. When the boom smashed into the starboard shrouds, my body continued its outward trajectory, and I was flicked into the sea. Electrified with adrenaline, I came sputtering to the surface. In an effort to save my wristwatch, the band was loose, I noted the time: 2:24 p.m. From that point on, I maintained a steady, very salty, stream of commands to keep the crew active and to regain control.

"Duck!" I yelled. "Don't let the boom hit you! Throw me the life sling!" Aaron made it aft of the boom and threw out the all-important man-overboard equipment, which if we had more hands would have been soon sooner. Sod's rule of course, he found more of our equipment failed through no fault of his own; the cloth release handle of the white Lifesling disintegrated in his hands, its fibres degraded by sunlight. The portside horseshoe, with 100 feet or more of floating line, was lashed too tightly for him to release quickly. Again, this was entirely my fault as captain. Remaining calm and pragmatic, Aaron then managed quickly to throw the starboard-side horseshoe to me. It had a strobe light was attached to it.

During my short time in the water, the genoa remained full and pulled the boat farther away. In the cockpit, the seriousness of the situation hit the two young men, and minutes were lost in the confusion and life-and-death pressure. For my part, once I had the life-ling, all I could do was wait. After ten minutes, cold and true fear set in. My teeth began to chatter. In horrible conditions, and with a large, disabled yacht, the short-handed crew managed to jibe the genoa and sail back toward me. With the boat's considerable windage, however, they soon sailed passed me.

"Turn on the engine," I shouted, losing my voice to help save my life. "Come back!" Thankfully, Aaron started the engine, which I could tell from the exhaust and steaming water from the waterline. Instead of risking another jibe, he jammed the engine in reverse; a wise if unorthodox thing to do. Given my fading mental and physical state and low life expectancy at this point, it was a brilliant act on Aaron's part. Working against the flailing genoa, they back-paddled the boat toward me to complete the rescue.

Once *Crested* was near enough to me, I reached one arm up towards Aaron and Dave, some four feet above me, and as soon as our fingers touched, these swarthy and brave men plucked me out of the cold October seas as thought my nearly 200 pounds were a feather. Smiles broke across our tear-streaked faces, and quick, warm embraces were shared in one big jumble. It was 2:40 pm. Orthodox or not, Aaron had successfully led my rescue, and Dave had immediately alerted him to the danger, despite numerous equipment failures which only I, as captain, can bear responsibility for.

The entire rescue took 16 minutes in rough, daylight conditions, with water temperatures of 56°F., or 13°C. I was extremely fortunate, and I owe my life to the actions and dedication of my crew. At 4 pm that day, we informed Herb Hilgenberg, via his *Southbound II* SSB net, that our strobe and horseshoe had been lost when I was retrieved. Aaron and Dave then thoughtfully wisely lay me horizontal under many layers of warm bedding and kindly told me they would cover the next watch. It was extremely stressful to them as it was for me; in fact to this day Aaron still wrestles with the "what if" aspects. Based on Aaron and my observations, Dave did not recover throughout the entire weeks-long ordeal.

Since I did not – could not – witness or appreciate all the effort that went into rescuing me, I had until recently a tainted perspective of events, as filtered through Dave. Because of the need for Aaron and I to maintain a degree of discipline, even formality as we continued to move four yachts back-to-back for many thousands of miles in three countries, we never went over all the details. So, just as other captains and crew – he is an accomplished merchant marine officer, captain and official in Halifax, here is his perspective of events, as mate of *Crested* during that absolutely terrifying quarter-hour:

> "I too was off-watch and completely asleep, when the panic ensued. It was a young, inexperienced deckhand who was on-watch when you went up to check the loud crack, got flung over, and ended up in the ocean. What I remember clearly after all these years, was him then coming down below, yelling and waking me up saying that you fell overboard. I remember coming up on deck half awake, and seeing you far behind the boat at that point, much to my horror. I quickly noticed that no one had thrown you a life ring at which point that was my first reaction. I distinctly remember coming to terms with the situation, and realizing I had a crewmember with me who was in shock (as was I), dealing with what turned out to be an unreliable with unmaintained lifesaving equipment. I realized at this moment I had only one mission; I had to make sure that you were saved. This meant that I had to do whatever it took to make that happen. So, with the grace of God, I managed to remain steadfast and calm enough to hold it together to the point where my mind became clear in all the panic. With sheer determination, I was able to manoeuver the boat to reach you and provide a lee from the winds and waves, to a point where Dave and I could finally haul you back onboard.
>
> In hindsight, I can only imagine how this must have been a nightmare for you, as it would have been for me too if it had turned out the other way. Although it has been over 21 years, I still often think of how my life would have turned out if things had gone the other way and I'm grateful God was on our side that day. One thing for certain is that not all sailors who fall overboard, in only their shorts, in the middle of the ocean in 30 plus knots of wind and 6-8 foot seas, live to tell their story. Looking back after all these years, I suppose it wasn't the perfect rescue as far as rescues go; and I can totally understand that from your perspective. However, the most important thing is that you survived, which is something I am extremely proud of and count my blessings for every day."

Post-mortem: Studying all that happened, we found the sheet intact. The entire ordeal had begun when a tooth-sized stainless-steel pin that held the mainsheet block to the deck broke. This was my fault; I had pulled the mainsheet too taught using just electronic winches, and also tightened the topping lift and boom vang, to minimalize the tremendous racket and noise of the boat in a gale while Aaron and I tried to rest off watch. That made it inevitable that at least some piece of equipment "had to give" under all that pressure compounded by over 30 knot winds and 5-8-foot, jarring seas from dead ahead. Had we briefly inspected our equipment before leaving, we might have noticed the worn metal at the base of the block and the frayed lines of our man-overboard module.

This was a life-changing event for all of us. I had been extremely stressed and insomniac since some stressful years in boarding school (yes, *that*). The unlikely emergence from death and back aboard *Crested* thanks to Aaron and the crew cured me forever of insomnia. I decided not to live the dangerous life of sea when less than a year later *Stiarna* burned and sank beneath me between Trinidad and Venezuela, and went to graduate school for maritime law and a masters in marine affairs instead. Out over nearly 150 offshore voyages, this counts as my worst. Subdued terror most of the time, wondering what part of boat, crew, or command (me) was going to break next. I told my family a week later in the Bahamas, and a cheerful group of several tables fell deathly silent and aghast when I was done, including tables near ours; they felt they were seeing a dead man walking, and we all were.....

Aaron soon proved his mettle again and on the same voyage, when he did an extraordinarily skilled job at plotting us into Moorhead City with a "dead ship" except for the main engine. When I realized just how much of our equipment was toast I actually, for the only time in my life had a "why me?" moment and lost bladder control, but Aaron remained focused and professional. We sailed under staysail alone at 6 knots into headwinds up a narrow channel, and despite my not issuing a *Sécurité* as I should have, all local traffic avoided our unlit boat at night until we managed to secure to the nearest dock under the principle of *force majeure*. The condo owners protested our continued presence, but without a starter motor they hadn't much choice but to wait for our repairs and forbear a daily traffic of mechanics through their complex.

On the same passage the broker lost his cool on the phone, yelling "get that 3#$%&@ boat back on the water now." As a result we left Charleston at midnight in 40 knots and got pinned in the fairway between two huge ships, which is something I would never do again unless in a rescue capacity. When he realized that we were going out in the drenching rain and high winds, the City Marina manager for that night refused to take our money for the use of the front slip while fueling; that should tell you something! (We all later exchanged holiday cards). Herb Hilgenberg, our SSB router, commented wryly "this can only be a delivery."

Like Lisa on *Sarafina*, Dave found himself trapped for many weeks on a voyage slated to take two, because of the busy hurricane season. His ex-girlfriend had calculated he would return after a week and accused him of assaulting her in Rhode Island on a day that he was, in fact, still part of our drawn-out voyage. On return to college, he was assaulted by her other boyfriends, but presented his travel receipts to prove he was away, and she admitted the fabrication. Unfortunately his car had been towed and retrieving it and paying for storage cost him about as much as he had been paid — after all, he couldn't exactly rely on his girlfriend to get it out of the pen!

I took these of me re-living the horror years later in Rhode Island. Some text copyright *Cruising World Magazine*; *A Delivery Skipper Sees His Life in Minutes*, November 2001.

Voyage 38: *Triton*, Newport-Lauderdale via Norfolk, Charleston

This was an Aaron-and-Ed quick voyage that went well as I have almost no recollection of it. The broker as I recall was very soft spoken, considerate, kind and thus highly unusual in my experience! We had light winds from Newport towards Hatteras. That made us motor a lot. Then the owner, who I was never in contact with, asked via the broker, why we were not sailing more? Because there was insufficient wind, I explained. I decided to pull into Chesapeake Bay to refuel before Hatteras. Little Creek, which I had never been to, was closest and easiest. On the approach there was a significant shortcut which we might have taken, but I told Aaron I was done with being second-guessed, and we would play it safe. After a night out, we set out again, but learned of a dreadful system waiting for us on the other side of Hatteras. I felt too high-masted and inexperienced with the Intracoastal Waterway (ICW) to try that route. We were overtaken in close proximity by a USCG cutter and called for weather advice, but they would not answer, I still don't know why. So, rather than face 20-foot seas and strong headwinds on the tip of Hatteras on a lee shore, it was back to Little Creek for us.

In that sordid US Marines amphibious training base we were disappointed by strip joints which did not permit stripping, but found equal color in the local water-top drinking shacks. The entertainment varied from a taxi ride to faraway Virginia Beach where I dated the mother of a skateboarder and a bar on the dock which looked like the Blue Oyster Bar from the farce *Police Academy*, in which a heavy set merchant marine captain was showing off his nipple rings. We skipped town before anyone got hitched, and headed for our other favorite, Charlestown. From there the Lauderdale Boat Show with no damage or injuries. The best kind of delivery voyage is one where nothing went wrong and you can concentrate on the good food and companionship, and the warmth of your bunk; *boring is good!* As I told an interviewer for *Offshore Magazine*, from Newport, Annie Sherman, at the Sail Loft in Boston, "I like a steady delivery when I can simply *chain-smoke and chit-chat!*"

Aaron and Ed watching as *Triton* returned for the second time to Little Creek after another failed attempt to round Hatteras without getting hammered by gales. Eerily calm, 1999. Little Creek is best known as a proving grown for amphibious troop carriers for the US Marines and others. The beaches on the right have been used by many a large hovercraft.

Voyage 39: *Femme*, Newport-Tortola, BVI, via Bermuda, November-December, 1999

Landfall on *Femme* British Virgin Islands last week of the last century. We had not instruments except handheld GPS for a week. Credit: Capt. Aaron Dickson, First Mate

The owner of *Femme* and his business partner owned a lighting industrial strength business in Providence area, very nice. The actual namesake was his sister who was sick. They didn't tell us until too late that the boat had been trashed and thrown ashore in a hurricane on the streets of Newport. First impression it was late fall cold and rough. Small dock in Jamestown. We take the boat for a spin with his young impressionable son. Owner says son thinks I'm Australian or something and exotic like a pirate. We go to dock, I've never handled this boat, he asks me to helm her alongside in the strong wind, then the poor guy falls into the open water while trying to help. Luckily he was rescued, but leather jacket and phone got wet. He was a very good sport. His buddy joined us to Bermuda, where I swore in a bar – blasphemy – he was shocked, and I was fortunate not to have been thrown out.

Many of the small crew were mutinous as completely hated each other, the happy-go-lucky Ed and stolid Aaron. I just threw hands in air at the end. In the middle of the Gulf Stream we were getting tossed around a bit and ankle-deep in water which flowed in from the split seams at the stern as well as ruptured fresh water bladders amidship. I tasted brackish water, which didn't help solve the issue at all! During this shitshow, all members of the crew broke out their personal handheld battery-fired GPS devices, which makes Einsteins out of elves, and told the right course to take. I explained calmly how:

"Gentlemen, there are 360 options to take when devising a course, and while I appreciate your professional input, fortunately there is only one person relegated to make that decision, and that person is me, and here is the number that I have chosen for us to steer to Bermuda!" I've often felt that skippers need to be psychologists as well; I've seen a few mutinies put down, but none that needed a fist or a gun. In the midst of an uprising in the windless Bermuda High without enough water or fuel or food, I stood my friend the captain at the mast dreading what would come next.

"Eric," he whispered, "go down and find the case of beer in the bilges, and grab some of your porn too, and bring it all up." He blasted Hootie and the Blowfish for hours and by sunset the loyalists were back in charge while the insubordinates slept it off happily.

I had to throw off Bill when he kept complaining the convection (or microwave) oven wasn't working to his satisfaction. Without the Gulf Stream we just didn't need an extra mouth to feed, even though the leg to the Caribbean is 30% longer. In Bermuda, Ed was so set on spending his time my sister's (other) former roommate that he would be gone for days. As a prank, Aaron and I would move the boat around to try to confuse him into thinking we ditched him and left, but then invariably along would come Ed, nonchalantly wandering on up to the boat before we left port! He had a Rhode Islander's instinct for not being left behind, what with being from Block Island and all. I guess finding crew who are lifelong friends pays off both ways, since Ed knew I would never leave him.

In Bermuda I met Dermot, a fellow captain who became a life-long friend and spoke at our wedding. He is a vastly more experienced sailor than me, after all, he survived the Fastnet race, which was fatal to many. He could be curmudgeonly and opinionated, but below that crusty shell and beard and behind the thick glasses is a warm heart, quick wit, and loyal friend. He knows a ton about sailboats and can dock one without engine, as we can see, and no crew over 25, or male, while holding a Guinness and expounding on whether to take the Straits of Magellan or round the Horn!

Damage to *Femme* in the 60-knot microburst at St. George's Amateur Dinghy and Sailing Club. Tom Wayland, same gent who had been welcoming us as dockmaster since *Rumor* in 1989, was there to adjudicate and prevent more damage, even before dawn!

The microburst from the perspective of another captain, Irish skipper Dermot, a veteran of the 1979 Fastnet Race which *War Baby* had won as *Tenacious*. He and his all-female crew on the battered, recently salvaged fiberglass sloop *Rogue*, was in harbor at the same time and befriended up:

> Sometime in this period (not recorded though) a major squall line passed over Bermuda and at about 0700 in the morning it struck with winds up to 60 knots, we in the lee of the land registered 55 knots, the whole anchorage was a mass of blinding rain and spume, several boats seriously dragged their anchors and one small 35 footer was a total write off on the rocks across the harbour. The boats on the Dinghy Club dock suffered damage in particular Eric's boat *Femme*, her transom had to have some serious work undertaken. This meant that Eric and Aaron ended up at the boatyard hauled out to have the work done. They spent Thanksgiving on *Rogue*, also not recorded in my original writing. The girls put on a feast for about 10 crew and guests, showing how large *Rogue*'s saloon was.

Regarding the damage, at least one yacht was destroyed; we saw its owner with a beer and a chainsaw at dawn after the remnants was dumped on the dock, cutting off the winches of his dream boat that was going to carry him from the Bermuda Biological Station to the Caribbean for his new life after a divorce and retirement.

Riding *Femme* up the Travel-Lift in St. George's Boatyard, Bermuda.
Not the safest thing to do. Note two fifty-gallon drum barrels of diesel on transom
Credit: Capt. Aaron Dickson, First Mate

We on *Femme* had automatically set two anchors and held fine with no motor, and none of us were warned of the weather burst. But when it hit about 4 am, we learned that most other yachts adjacent to us did not do so and fell on top of us, sometimes with engines fully engaged, pushing us onto the sea wall and doing this damage which took a week to repair. I tried to stave off panic among nearby sailors by calmly brewing coffee and disembarking and slowly going up and down the lines and crew on the docks, wishing them a cheerful good morning. They looked at me like I had two heads or ignored me, and my tactic did not really work. Panic spreads faster than caffeine, and the skippers who took it calmly had that "cold as ice in crisis gene" already, and didn't need me.

As an indicator of culpability I did get the owner of the other yacht to pay a good sum towards the repair. When the repairs were over the yard owner and manager (where I had worked for cash on *Xebec*) stopped lowering the boat right as the keel dipped in the translucent Bermudian waters.

"No cash, no splash!" he chuckled with a smile, and we went in to call the owner for payment. Sensible policy. We were pretty miserable and the boat was damaged in a massive microburst at the St. George's Amateur Dinghy Club and had to go to the yard in St. George's. We made it to Tortola, but lost most instruments so I was almost blind. The bladders leaked in the Gulf Stream making us think we were sinking (it was leaking in the stern seam) but then it was fresh water from our dinking supply.

Dermot keeps an extraordinary detailed log, and since we were to work together on *Femme, Rogue*, he ran *Verite* for Echo Yacht Delivery (first time I trusted anyone to that), and *Sinai, Farr Away, Alcyone*, and probably one or two more. Here is his perspective of Aaron, me and *Femme* from *Rogue*, his crew being Rowena and Fran, later Kristy as well, all Australian and young. He missed Bill and Ed wasn't around to mingle with us at that time…. Logbook and notes by Capt. Dermot, S/Y *Rogue*, Bermuda same time as we on *Femme*.

>Saturday 25th November 1999: I could write a book about the last 10 days but I will fill you in on a few preliminaries…… Eric and Aron; "Professional" Delivery skipper of SY *Femme* a 43 Beneteau damaged at The St. George's Dinghy Yacht Club spent a week in St. George's Boatyard, Eric was a classic public school, Swedish parentage, knew even less about engines than I do, excellent radio procedure. Stole the heart of Rowena, and disappeared into the sunset. I am not allowed to comment on his actions. Aron, his crew had a quite relationship with Fran. His expertise was with radios, he did manage to tune *Rogue*'s SSB.

Regarding the Canadian sailboat *Windrift*: Dermot writes that

>After finding her on the dock near our boat at dawn looking very lonely, I went over and signed Kristy aboard the Customs guys were relieved to see her go to a boat with women aboard, Kirsty is from Australia, where else, and knows friends of Fran. The position she was in on this Canadian Yacht from Chester NS was horrendous. I had been asked by the girls earlier on if I would take Kirsty if she wanted to jump ship from *Windrift*, over the next few days I observed the yacht and owner and advised her through Fran that she should leave. Later that stay….. Rowena is moping around like a gull with a broken wing upset with Eric from *Femme*. Scott, Frank and Greg: Crew of *Windrift,* captain and owner madman Scott, well in with local street traders in St. George's, scared the shit out of Kirsty, on the route to Bermuda, total control freak, wouldn't even let the crew know where they were, they almost sailed past Bermuda.

During this period occurred an episode which shames me as a captain. Of the six young sailors from the Canadian *Windrift* described by Dermot above, landed an earnest young 'Hippy' girl with Rasta locks and lots of piercings and tattoos. She made an impression on boat crew and townsfolk in the small town, and the boat's charismatic, good-looking young owner about 25 years old, did as well. Then there was an odd assortment of rather gruff, hard-working landsmen with trades like electrician and plumber and farmer, each loaded with tools they planned to start new lives with in the Virgin Islands.

What was pretty strange is that even though the boat was not on charter, almost no one asides from the captain knew anything about sailing. The girl was begging Aaron to take her off the boat and he wanted her to go on *Femme*, which I really could not do, in part since the owner's best friend was on board. Bermuda is a "small place" where secrets don't last long, and St. Joe's as it is known, is even tinier. It was therefore very quickly common knowledge that the young Canadians had spent the summer growing marijuana in rural Canada, and were sailing that cargo on their boat to the Caribbean where they planned to made a windfall! Talk about bringing coal to Newcastle and ice to Eskimos.

There were two major problems: if the government took the official route, the boat and entire cargo and all crew would be arrested and the boat would never leave, the crew might be there for years dragging through the judicial system, probably resulting in a long stay in the women's penitentiary overlooking the Bio Station nearby (I've seen prisons with waterfront views in Tauranga, New Zealand, Boston, Sunset Heights, Brooklyn, Vancouver, BC, Alcatraz, and Visby). Second, pot is, or was, illegal in Bermuda. Third, there was some strain of a contagious disease said to have broken out on board – it wasn't dysentery (symptoms mainly diarrhea) it was, as I recall, diphtheria, which is quite serious and bred in very unhygienic conditions. It is described as "an acute, highly contagious bacterial disease causing inflammation of the mucous membranes, formation of a false membrane in the throat that hinders breathing and swallowing...." Well; we all had a problem on our hands if that boat came to the dock! It was, at all times, out at the anchorage, not ashore.

So the government made a very pragmatic decision: all crew were to be sent out of Bermuda on whatever boat would take them, and the boat would find a crew asap to sail out of Bermuda. As a result, I was "offered" a competent, sensible-looking 35-year-old electrician with this tools to go on *Femme*. But, while like every other captain in the harbor, I was trying to be helpful, I was also not going to infect my crew. So several other captains and I took this poor fellow, tan, weathered, very short hair, clean shaven, earnest look, winter jacket, to the doctor's clinic, which was conveniently above the bank right in the public square in St. George's.

In the small clinic the doctor asked this guy lots of personal medical questions, did a swab sample test, then got the results quite quickly. I recall the sheer inhumanity of it, like he was cattle, and him just submitting to it. Whatever the result – I can't remember to be honest – I turned him down because he could become symptomatic during the trip, even if he failed the test. And sadly, since I have felt like a taken-for-granted crew in the same port, I didn't pay the $35 or so fee; the crew who we rejected even *after* he passed the test, did. Looking back, I really regret not passing a hat around with the captains and doctors and paying his fee. I never did see him again, I believe we took off soon thereafter. Perhaps there is a strain of ganja in Bermuda with the name of that boat?

Rogue set out before us, and we did see a sailboat ghosting in the early morning sea mist far away. However, they must not have seen us, or did see us and didn't hail us, so we sailed on. Later, when they called, it was *Rogue*, and they needed us to come over, stand by and help. This was a little peeving, as we had passed them hours before but clearly not been seen, and resumed course away from them. One must, of course go to the aid of any fellow mariner, friend, lover all of the above. Dermot relates what was going on aboard *Rogue*:

> I left last Tuesday and on Wednesday morning the engine died we were motoring in 5 knots of breeze. So, we started to change the Racor filter, bleed the system but the lift-pump on the engine didn't seem to work. We had a radio schedule with the boys off *Femme,* and they were only 15 miles away, so they sailed over to us. Launching the dinghy, Fran got in then I did and was immediately struck by the fact that there was a layer of 4mm of Hypalon rubber between me and the bottom of the ocean two miles down! Weird, we rowed over and borrowed their hand pump which they had to get diesel from barrels to their tank.
>
> So, we went back to *Rogue* with the lift pump so I could expel the last of the water out of my tank which was sitting under 100 gallons of fuel. It didn't work, so I removed the hatch cover on the tank and low and behold there was no fuel in the tank at all just some watery sludge at the bottom of the well. I knew at once what had happened, Mark the engineer who had helped us the other day when we had to sail on to the dock, had thrown a valve believing it to be in the system. But this had decanted the contents

down into a well tank on the keel. I had no method of getting this fuel up nor did I want to cos I wasn't sure what was in the tank. The mystery is that over 80 gallons went into a tank that we thought was a 22-gallon capacity tank. So, we were 160 miles off Bermuda and 750 from the Islands, what choice did I have. At this stage the wind picked up decanting the tool box right into the bilge! I asked if Rowena wanted to go across to return the pump as she was out of sorts with Eric for ending their relationship so abruptly. We said our goodbyes to the lads and set off, two days on the nose back to St. George's. We arrived at 11:00 pm at night and sailed in down the town cut across the harbour to our friendly boat yard, and assessed if we could pick up a mooring can, but opted to drop the anchor. 11:30 pm on Thursday night we were back in Bermuda.

Capt. Dermot Bremner shuttles fuel and filters between his command, *Rogue*, and mine, *Femme*, hundreds of miles south of Bermuda, December 1999, as we all rush to get the boats to their owners for the Millennium.
Credit: Capt. Aaron Dickson, First Mate

Tree Frogs in the Boatyard
A Poem by Capt. Dermot

The incessant howl of wind in rigging not at sea.
Dark and stormy skies scud over St. George's Hill.
Azure blue water, palm trees indicate the warmth,
but not in his heart.
She wants to stay, but deep down knows she can't
Why did she let him take her that way?
Years of avoiding that pit fall.
Now all that's left is the call of the tree frogs
in an empty boatyard.

by the captain of *Rogue* 400 nm south of Bermuda, December, 1999

This poem, by a fellow captain at sea after I had both broken the heart of his crew and then gone to their rescue and not been warm and sentimental enough to her when she rowed over to see me (I was "on deck" helping a colleague at sea and aware of being watched by my all-male crew), makes me quite sad. It was a pairing of two lonely young persons, afraid for the future and eager to share last days of warmth together before more storms, cold, damage, and hardship.

One irony about this, which only I amongst the sailors knew, is that about three nights before our last night in Bermuda, when we had our only tryst under the tree frogs in wintry blasts of wind, I had been meant to take out an American recent college graduate. Days earlier we had met and she told me at the Wharf Tavern that she had to host several people, and could we wait to court until three days later? Well, as agreed, on the final night, she joined our group of a dozen male or female sailors. Predictably, she, being a landswoman, was quickly ignored; this is something which folks in the bulk shipping and ship-broking industry are prone to do as well.

As the poem relates, though she and I took chances to be with one another and left the safety of our emotional harbors (she was a commercial fisherwoman off the northwest coast of Australia; Broome, Port Hedland, or Geraldton, I believe the latter), we were also unrequited, inasmuch as we met on the high seas for an hour, just missed seeing each other at Foxy's on Jost van Dyke, and then briefly at Bomba Shack, but by then we had a guest rescued from there, which did not make the small-at-best one-room hotel for three of us any easier.

It is an empathetic, sonorous, melodious, poem in the minor cay for a reason: the events it shares and sheds light into were as well. We never saw each other again, and Dermot had to do a lot of the emotional sorting in an all-woman crew, which was not much to his liking, though we have remained friends. Here is his candid yet restrained perspective on the same events:

Sunday 19th December ....At 2:10 pm, we dropped anchor in Great Harbour, Jost Van Dyke, I dinghied ashore with the papers whilst the others cleaned up. [The *Femme* crew witnessed this, but did not know it was our friends on *Rogue*. A day or two later, less than 10 days to the new millennium, which was much-hyped and a big reason many of us were paid to said to the Caribbean in rough conditions before 2000.] Dermot continues:

In the evening we met up with crew of *Something Else*, and *Femme*. Earlier we had met the remains of *Windrift*, not that we had wanted to. But it was good to see the others, even if I did have to remind Eric about basic etiquette in dealing with other people's crew, it is amazing how people forget there are some primary rules in relationships at sea that don't hold on land, as I have always maintained sex and sailing do not mix.

It might be appropriate, since captains are discussing poor Rowena, without her having the benefit of input, for me to chime in. I agree with Dermot – lovemaking within the fraternity of the seas is literally fucking too close to water and at the least unprofessional, on one's own command, if you don't own it, and the are no rings. I've been told not only is there no privacy, but crew tend to feel the captain is being "controlled" and "not the real boss" and their authority is eroded by intimacy with another on board, whatever the gender of captain and mate.

Either way, I've passed on at least a dozen opportunities to make the most of being on the same boat for that reason, and at times regretted it. With Rowena and I, and I speak for myself at least, I was terribly lonely and a bit scared, and appreciated her companionship very much. Still, we held back. Then, not knowing *Rogue*'s itinerary, and assuming she and I would never see one another again, I thought the right thing to do was not lead each other on, but make a clean break. I was wrong, we did see each other, at sea and on shore – which neither of us would have predicted – and it was rather emotionally dicey for both.

Ironically, when me and the boys, and they had ribbed me a bit for having a relationship talk with Rowena on the high seas, saw the *Rogue* team in the Virgin Islands, we had the audacity to think that we might be greeted favorably. Having gone out of our way if not both times, then once, and rendered aid which enabled them to make Bermuda, which enabled them in turn to make it to the USVI before New Year's without calling for government help, we were prepping for a hero's welcome and accolades, rather than the talking-to about the Birds and the Bees which we actually were dealt. Fortunately, all of being adults (OK, less than 30, but still....), we made the post of the bottled fermentation process and bygones were bygones and with claps on the shoulders we made nice! Dermot's postscript written in 2008:

This delivery was my first on the North Atlantic to Caribbean circuit and it has become one of the legends of my sailing stories because so much happened in such a short time. The resulting period spent in the Virgin

Islands at the end of the trip ended up in my staying in St. Croix and meeting Page, and falling in love with her, it took three years to fall out of love. I met Eric Wiberg on this trip and he became a substantial friend to this day, He put me in touch with Jon of *Alcyone* who became my daughter's God Father. I am reminded of this trip in that I am sailing *Alcyone* which is also a ketch down from Newport RI to Virgin Gorda via Bermuda.

We paid crew out and I waited a week at Bomba Shack area in West End to fly back on the owner's private plane, which he did, and left me in Nassau; home! In time for the millennial. We did rescue an Idaho Hippy from a son of a prominent bar owner on an adjacent island, by smuggling her out on the bottom of a boat... she then set out to sleep in my bunk but I was wary of taking advantage of her and demurred.

Ed of course was self-sufficient, but Aaron and I were to part ways for the final time, and he needed to be paid. So we moved the boat to from Soper's Hole far west of Tortola to the far east, into East End Bay to Penn's Landing Marina, near Parham Town and not far from the airport and Beef Island. Well, for whatever reason we made the move at sunset, and of course the Tradewinds blow from the east, and they were pretty strong that night. It piped up, the seas built, there was poor radar, and lots of local obstructions, from moorings to traps and just my general unease about my first time in the Virgin Islands and all the rest.

Because we were expecting to go stern-to and had been told the bay is a mite shallow, I took out some heavy mooring lines for docking using all four points of the boat. I was nervous. Well, laying out the thick lines on the bow at night not only showed me to not have much faith in the crew, but I was micro-managing, and not well, as we shall see. Suddenly, a shuddering *KLUNK*!, and *Femme*'s propeller stopped. The line from the bow had fallen in the water in the rough seas and seized the propeller.

Quick damage control assessment revealed no leaking, no prop shaft ripped out of the boat, but as pain in the ass, all my fault of course, but still I was resentful. We threw out the anchor, cut off the engine, threw on deck lights, launched the dinghy, and with one guy in the dink shining a powerful torch, I hopped in with a line around my waist in case I was attacked by sharks, and freed the line. Big pain in the ass and a bit dangerous but not really that bad. Line was freed, I swore like – well, like a sailor! – we upped the anchor and just took a fucking mooring for the night. We could dinghy in and dock in the daytime.

Ralph and his girlfriend, who were very nice, arrived and paid us out and then took off on a romantic week's cruise. I wanted to fly back private and enjoy the freedom of Tortola for a week, which Aaron, me and for a while Ed did. West coast by Soper's Hole. Did a bit of hiking to different bays and hitchhiking between them.

My memory of the flight home was that we all had headphones and were listening to *My Love is Your Love*, by Whitney Houston, which of course is a bit ironic since I'd just been such a dick towards Rowena. We could see the Turks & Caicos as we flew over it and spoke with a German pilot, and over Mayaguana I asked if there was a means to piss. Over the radio I was told that there was a funnel to my right, and that on using it I simply opened a valve, which went right out into the air! Pretty basic but cool. I was deposited at the

Millionaire private air base, my Mom drove the two of them to one of the nice hotels at Cable Beach, and we parted ways.

    I wonder what has happened to Ralph's son and if he remembers the yacht captain with the funny accent who flubbed docking his Dad's yacht and sent Pops in to the cold New England waters? My siblings and I all remember Lindsay, the Australian yacht captain staying on a similar sailboat at the Elbow Cay Inn in Bahamas in the early 1980s when we met him, and naturally looked up to him.

Chapter 12

Voyage 40: *Valentine* Newport, Jamestown, Hundreds of Short Trips, 1999-2001

  About 300 trips over three years, with between one and six passengers, so on average I would have carried over 1,000 persons. These were single-handed voyages with no electronics or charts, or plumbing or privacy, sometimes 3-5 miles round trip, with just a little putt-putt outboard and hand-raised sails. The boat is a durable 19-foot Pearson Ensign. The route was not just around Newport Harbor and Narragansett Bay, from the base dock at Bowen's Wharf to Brenton Cove to Jamestown to Castle Island Light and Rose Island, Goat Island, and even inside Clingstone on high tide days, if you dared (I did).

  Many high points included a middle-aged mother who stripped off to skinny-dip (that was actually a logistical nightmare, since her mum and daughter were on board; I believe she was 'touched,' as we say in the Bahamas), college kids on a sunset cruise who drank too much and all had to take turns I a tiny cuddy to pee, as darkness fell and I would not allow them to go over the side. The worst was a family who did not understand English with a tiny toddler child for whom I did not have a lifebelt, and to whom my safety instructions were just gibberish. So when the child started to walk on the bench and over the side, I was in a panic: how to rescue the child *and* run the boat?

  A boat used to follow very close behind, dangerously so, for sport. So one day I did a massive and dangerous sharp U-turn, missing grazing his hull with my bow by perhaps 2 inches at best. Man, was he irate! Jumping up and down red in the face screaming about calling the harbor master (Tim, who we all knew). I was a bit scared, not realizing how close I came to a collision. The guy never called Tim, and at the same time, he never did that again to me either.... Fun notes were seeing lovely fun Camilla in her boat dashing back and forth solo under sail, waving cheerfully to me....

Valentine under sail, not by me. The small engine for docking or getting home at sunset when the wind is completely dead is lowered here. We skippers were responsible for doing all maintenance – no pay – in the spring to get the boat ready. I remember wishing I had a VHF, and other items that worked. The biggest scares were babies in the water or drunks swimming. Overall it was very intense, solo work but fun with interesting clientele. It was neat exploring the coasts in very close detail – here is the New York Yacht Club's Harbour Court and nearby Ida Lewis Yacht Club. There was camaraderie between other boats most of the time too. The simplicity and speed of this design explains why it is both popular and profitable.

Worst low point was a massive Nor'easter you could taste, in October, the sky all grey-black and snorting cold wind blasting from over the island, highly unusual compared to summer south-westerlies. So I tacked back and forth wet of Goat Island, in the lee, not having fun at all, on a two-hour cruise with half a dozen mid-western farm wives. Well, finally we drifted or were blown too close to Rose Island, looking to spot some Harbor Seals, and wouldn't you know it, we ran aground, and in 30 knots steady (not good). I hit once and bounced, it was a keel boat of six feet or so depth, I was usually at that area on *Quick Step*, a motor boat, or the Patriot, drawing about three feet. They all look at me, and Bam! We hit again. The second time I wait till we bounce off again, look calmly at my watch, and say aloud, kind of stage-whisper like:

"Just where I thought we should be at this time – time to head back." They all looked relieved, and were when we docked. I gave the owner the keys and went home for the day. I think it was Confucius or Cicero who said that surfing the web is safer than taking a bunch of flat-landers out in a Nor'east gale in New England in October in the equivalent of a soda-can. The owner is an affable young man just a bit older than I who lived with his mother a short walk from the dock and had a small fleet of fun, accessible sailboats of unpretentious manufacture, like O'Day or the highly popular and flexible, durable Ensign. Starting in 1962, there were a total of 1776 (the year of independence) Ensigns built by both Pearson Yachts of Bristol, nearby in RI, and a firm in Dunedin, Florida named Ensign Spars.

Voyage 41: *Stiarna*, Chaguaramas, Trinidad-Grenada, February, 2000

Yacht *Stiarna* in the Solent, UK, during her former glory, in an original print which I bought from Beken of Cowes, world-renown British yacht photographers.

It was cold in Newport in January 2000; all the buildup to the New Millennium, and visions of meeting Mrs. Right, single at age 30 had crashed. As we pulled up to the big party at a beach front manse in my hometown in the Bahamas, my host passed out, and his wife insisted I dance with her all night, leaving him in sand. There had been no mistletoe for me.

So when my best friend, who like me was recently returned from the Far East, he as a helicopter salesman, me as a tankship operator, told me his boss in the IT sector in Cambridge Massachusetts was buying a boat in Trinidad and needed an experienced, trustworthy captain, I jumped at it. I packed for three months, watered a couple Ficus' in my garage loft on the commercial waterfront in Newport, took a Peter Pan bus to Logan Airport, and after explaining I needed to go to Trinidad five times to the local travel agent (yes, they used to have those), and watching five flights leave for Trinidad, I boarded a plane about 9 pm from San Juan, Puerto Rico, aka the airport equivalent of an ashtray of the Caribbean. It may be a step up from Guantanamo, but I hope to never find out.

A few hours later we landed in the small plane, and I was welcomed to Tobago Island – not Trinidad. I groggily asked the flight attendant when we were taking off for Port of Spain, Trinidad. She told me that Tobago was the final stop, and to disembark. It was nearly midnight. Scarborough is the main settlement on the island of about 20,000 persons, and it is made famous for Prince Charles having landed there. Having him sleep with you seems hardly something worth celebrating, but after my night there I give him a lot more credit, because the hundreds of European women I met wanted nothing to do with me. Their eyes were set on a handsome and happy cluster of local men. They had to have felt like cattle being corralled.

Being a newly re-minted yacht captain in town for just one night before assuming command of a classic yacht, I was determined not to walk back to my humid little cabin off the main drag a short walk from the airport. There was a huge stage in an amphitheater - like concert space and back areas for drinks, bathrooms, and flirting. I entered a drinking contest, won a yellow Carib beer umbrella and cap, and most importantly was able to speak on the mic to the audience about who I was and where I was from.

Nothing. I walked home alone about 2 am.

About 8 am I flew to Trinidad for only about $50.

Then I went to Chaguaramas where I moved aboard the shittiest boat I've ever seen.

It was full of slopping oil water. The mosquitoes were bred by US fighter planes and pumped to B-24 Mitchell bomber proportions by my blood; Chaguaramas had been a US Naval base to fight U-Boats in World War II. The inhospitable boat was matched only by the we-don't-give-a-fuck-about-you insouciance shown by the project lead, who was half the time lost in pot and the other half, well, lost in pot. Having gradually been pushed out of various ports in the Caribbean, starting, as so many do, in the US Virgin Islands, this fellow Tom had skills as a shipwright, but I was never able to observe them in action.

The new owner was a decent if pliable client. Tom opted to treat a client who ordered a new Sitka Spruce mast (tree) from the Pacific Northwest by basically ignoring him, and his boat. The mast was rotten, the survey Jim had made was neither dated nor signed – in fact though everyone knew it was Tom's; he didn't even put his name on it – and actually won an insurance case over that issue in Boston. Tom's money and crew and efforts and skill went into his personal yacht, the scene of a grisly murder of its couple of owners by a young German hitchhiker in the 1980s, who after soaking their blood into the floorboards, threw them overboard and had the gall to cruise the Caribbean saying he had never heard of them when suspicious friends inquired. Well, Tom and his crew ground that blood out while I begged for help starting the motors and rewinding starters, and changing the oil and waiting till dark to empty the oily bilges, and swimming below to fill through-hull openings with pegs.

Thank goodness the owner and his son were delayed several days by a Boston blizzard. I worked my ass off in a ratty pair of shorts covered in oil (made some teen girls giggle), and showering several times a day in pouring rain and suffocating humidity. Another British, young, shipwright named Ash looked over the boat long enough to refuse to go up the mast so he loaned us some small sails so as not to strain the mast under way to Grenada, 75 miles north. Owners arrived. I picked them up, in the car they asked me what I thought of their new, 1936-built, pedigreed wooden yacht built by Camper & Nicholson. A thoroughbred – once. Now it had a side-mounted blue Perkins in it, aft, near the large cockpit.

"Your boat is a piece of shit," I told them while navigating oxen crossing the road to populous Port of Spain.

"What do you expect me to do about that?" asked the unflummoxed owner, who grew up in France.

"I expect you to hire a tug to help us get to Tom's new greenfield yard in Grenada, or fix it here."

"Why wouldn't I hire a tug?" he asked – He and I had never met, only the son and I had, in a café in Cambridge.

"Because you hired me to do the passage," I said, "and it will cost quite a bit – over $5,000 for the tug, and you are already paying me."

"Hire the tug," he said.

I said "Sir, I've been doing this for over a dozen years, and you are the first person to follow my advice. Why?"

"I'm not in the yachting business, I'm in the *business* business, and when you hire an expert outside you field of expertise, and they give you hard advice, you don't pretend, as a CEO, to be smarter than everyone, you listen to it, and you follow it. And if you don't you're an arrogant fool putting yourself and others at risk."

That decision most likely saved his life, that of his son, and possibly all of us, because less than an hour out of port a couple days later, with five of us on board – the owner, his son, me, the young shipwright (not Tom) and a Trinidadian shipwright of indeterminate age named Coelho, the boat caught fire viscously and quickly – again in less than an hour – sank.

"Save our luggage," they begged, and I said I would. "It has our computers in it!"

I ran forward though the fire and smoke and grabbed the passports and cash – except for Ash's, as he insisted on keeping his passport, and it was lost (I never force anyone to let me keep their passport when captain). Paul Coelho went first, to the tug named *Carthage II*, and made it, then we threw off the gasoline tanks for the dinghy, and they were quickly swept in the current. Then the father went with Ash, and the son with a bag of computers. After they all leapt into the water to the gangway of the tug, which was also a bit like a freighter with a burly American captain, I stuffed the cash in my pocket, stuck the passports in my mouth, kicked off my shoes to swim better without, ignored the bags of computers on the transom and jumped in.

Everyone was out except me, and the current was running hard, but I was a good swimmer. As I swam up current to the ladder, the tug captain started pointing and yelling, at first I thought it was a shark:

"Fifty Dollars!," he yelled – "There's a 20 dollar bill! – Cash! Get the cash!" he was frantic. Realizing that the ship's cash was spilling out of my pocket, I submerged and followed the green bills, just like the baby boy in the swimming pool of the Nirvana album *Nevermind*, swimming for a dollar bill in the bright blue water. Of course it only took grabbing a bill and stuffing my pocket full before I surfaced and blurted out to him:

"Fuck the money – if you want it so much come in and get it – please get me out of here!" They got it. Once I was taken to the bridge, kind of a courtesy thing – I lay my matches and cigarettes on the lip of the windows to dry. It was going to take a while, so I turned to the crew and captain, patted my empty pockets and said:

"Gee, I'm all out of matches and smokes, and it's been a hell of a morning: does anyone have a light for me?" And behind me, framed in the window was my yacht completely consumed my flames and smoke! We asked for a camera via VHF radio to document the drama for insurance, since no life or limb was in peril we did not think it a Mayday situation. We had effectively rescued ourselves. But the Trinidad & Tobago Coast Guard sent out a RIB to rescue us, they braved the flames to get the luggage, and interviewed us and gave us tea till the large cutter arrived, a gift from the USA.

Then they took us to base where we were kept in a cold old warehouse with air conditioning but no cigarettes, we were interviewed, released, taken to customs an immigration where they drew great mirth from our misfortune after decades of being mistreated by yachtsmen and we stood soaking wet in pools of water, no shoes, just the life ring and some debris popped when the boat sank. It made the immigration officer's day to process a band of humbled, near naked and wet shipwrecked sailors with nothing but passports and a burnt life-ring to show for themselves. He was so tickled that he took photos of us through plexiglass that so many rich entitled foreign yachties had hurled insults and abuse at him through for decades. While we were standing there, even the other yachties ignored us as our teeth chattered and puddled formed around our feet, and we emitted *eau-de-burnt-yacht*. The mirthful officer was texting photos to his friends and called his wife to make sure no one missed this crowning glory in his career in officialdom, guarding the gates of Trinidad and Tobago against invasion of wet, cold shipwreck survivors.

I feel that this team from all over were the best-behaved crew I ever had only worked under me for less than an hour. They all evacuated the fire-enshrouded spaces quickly and cooperatively and jumped overboard when told to. Despite a huge disparity in ages (70+ to early 20s), using the buddy system all five of us were rescued by a nearby tug. The yacht we were trying to overtake at the time ignored our sinking, as did a nearby tanker.

Tom was aghast it sank, but really he had no one to blame but himself. In Viking times my crew might have strung him up and trussed him. His plan of opening a new yard in Grenada was shelved – he was upset with me that I planned to enter Grenada in the main port anyway. I flew via Grenada, since the owner bought me some shoes and gave cash – and my passport was all wet. In Grenada I was supposed to stay three months but three days sufficed. I told the barmaid of my story and she was not impressed but suggested I meet a red haired German nurse who often sat alone and was studying at the Grenada medical college. Anna was from Munich, where my uncle lived, and we got along rather well. Aside from the complaint that locals were hard to photograph due to being so dark skinned, it was fine, we swam, took the bus, stayed in a local guest house and she went to Germany, I went to Boston.

Back in Newport, friend keeping bar at the IYAC dryly commented that part of being a sailing professional entailed keeping the boats afloat. She was gently suggesting I had fundamentally missed the mark and should perhaps go back to more terrestrial pursuits. To the observation that I am not supposed to sink them, I could only reply that if a truck driver moves more than 100 rigs, it's reasonable to think he or she will wreck one of them. But her husband Billy moves yachts by truck and she seemed pretty unconvinced!

I visited Anna in Munich a week later, after I was reimbursed. She was the masseuse to my uncle's wife, a former Lufthansa executive, in Munich. There is a story about a Moroccan belly dancer, 19, who I met in the New York airport for the flight via Frankfort, however that did not – *not* – end with a mile-high encounter, and is better left for another story. Suffice to say, some older female members of a Danish motor biker group (I mustn't use the term gang, as we did not make each other's acquaintance) who saw me canoodling a Moroccan in the Copenhagen airport, and then saw me being welcomed and kissed by Anna, who does not look Moroccan, caused me a little anxiety. To get to Anna, who had borrowed her boss' car to show me around, I had to formally enter Germany first.

Junior German immigration officer:

"*Vy is your passport wet?*" Me:

"You see, darndest thing, I was on a yacht that sank, the passport was in my mouth and it was like the Nirvana album *Nevermind*, you see, in Trinidad last week, and salt does not dry...."

Senior German immigration officer, who now joined in:

"*So, you not only bring a wet passport to Deutschland, yet on top of dis, you insult my colleague and I with this ridiculous story about shipwreck? Now go! Raus!*" And so I entered Germany and escaped the Danish biker gang, German immigration, and Moroccan belly dancer from Lyon as well.... All in one day. And after all that, when my uncle's girlfriend, the countess, met my German hostess Anna, she reported back to my mother in Nassau, who is, that my date was not a *real* redhead, but dyed...

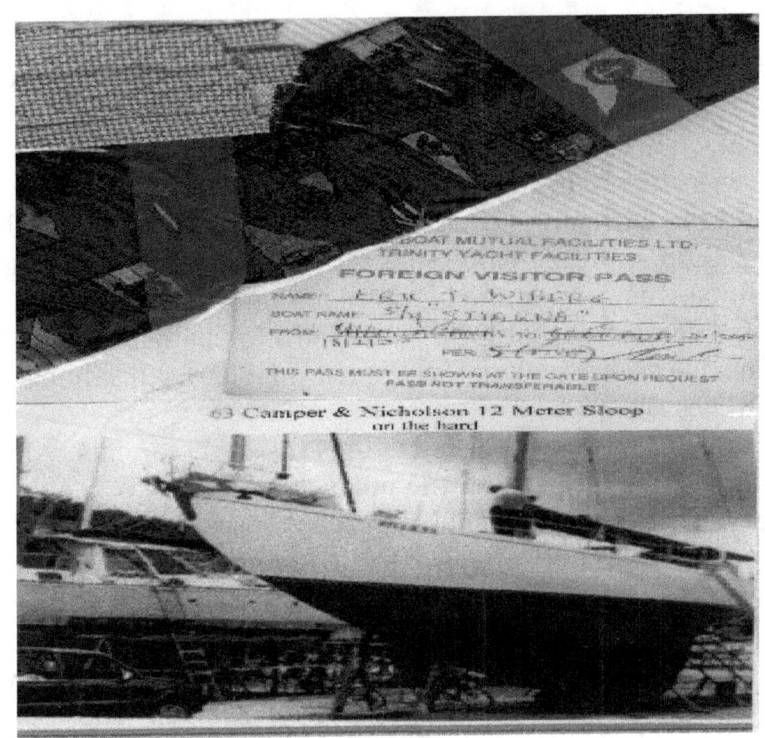

My grandfather's tie, my shipyard ID card or pass, and other relics of *Stiarna*, RIP. Granddad had a great sense of humor and liked to win "most clashed outfit" competitions in the retirement town in Florida they settled in. He was not a nautical man, so this tie, whose flags have no discernible meaning, were for fun and I inherited it. He probably would never have guessed it would burn, sink, and be salvaged off Trinidad!
PS You may recognize the necktie from Lady Halifax's photo during *War Baby* at RBYC, 2000.

Voyage 34: *Sabbatical,* **Newport cross-harbor, Mooring to Marina, Winter, 2000**

Voyage 42 *Sabbatical*, **Newport-Tortola, BVI, via Bermuda, Winter-Spring, 2000**

Just what it was – me and Captain Ian Strump, an engineer, bringing the large 55-footer Mercedes of yachts from a mooring into the haul-out slip at Newport Shipyard, which itself was recently purchased by a family friend in the Bahamas. Mostly I remember close inspections of the batteries with Bob, the amiable affable broker, whose office, once he moved from Bartram & Brackenhoff to Oyster USA with his wife Molly and friend Will at Goat Island nearby.

My highest-skilled and happiest crew: four captains, an engineer, former skipper of a chartered America's Cup boat, a medic and a cook, at the IYAC in Newport, winter 2000. Me, Ian, Mike, and Chad. The team gave me a handcrafted wooden cigarette case with this photo on it, which I still cherish.

One broken lightbulb, 2,000 miles in March and April. This was teamwork more than just a voyage. I was blessed with an extraordinary crew and highly supportive owner. He just bought the boat and would do anything to get it down to the Caribbean so he and his mates could fly from California and have a go with it. We obliged and literally delivered. We developed wonderful friends in two sisters who we had all known in Newport. All of us hung out together, including their cousin, who was out of college. It was a cold winter so we all appreciated the diversion.

We learned the hard way, before Zoom, that the metal of ships and docks in Newport Harbor was so bad at interfering with SSB radio that several times we sailed into Narragansett Bay and had to cut off our own motor to get best reception, which was scary as winds were rough, temperatures cold and SSB was distracting and East Passage from Fort Wetherill, near Clinging Rock, in Jamestown to Fort Adams. We heeled over so much with motor sailing on a flat see the last 100 miles to Bermuda that we had to shut the water intakes on the airborne side, it was so much out of the water it sucked air! Ian engineered that.

Lastly, a kind of hippy wealthy New York City family – father a good sailor, good boat, with very young kids – like three children ages 1, 3 and 5 were cooped up for weeks, and frustrated in Bermuda and wanted to get out of there. So, when they learned we were dashing south trying to beat an occluded front, the skipper begged me to know if he could go too. I told him, look man, we are paid to get our asses kick and no one gives a shit about our comfort, even we don't at times. Your young family are different. Your purpose and voyage are different. Unlike him, I told him that I benefit from having three full time captains with me at all times, you do not. I suggest waiting. They left anyway, his prerogative, they could not keep up with us, and got their asses kicked, and had to listen to their plaintive talks with Herb. Finally after two days of getting our teeth kicked in Herb simply told me to stand up and look in front, out the starboard saloon window. I did. He asked me if I could see the first blue sky and sunshine in days, I said I could He said simply in his German fatherly way

"Well, go there. Enter the sunny spot, turn left, and keep going, and stay on the course till you get to Tortola in about a week." We did, it did, we arrived that way! The owner was waiting for us on the dock in Soper's Hole, Tortola, with his buddies, even called via SSB and VHF before we arrived and sent a little boat out to welcome us in which was nice. The dinner and drinks were only marred aby about six loads of linen laundry, we pumped the boat full of fuel and diesel the next day and they were off on their voyage!

PS: I saw a documentary later about a rich girl right there in Soper's Hole who was taken advantage of by two shady guys and the show heavily implied that they guys killed her there on the rocks, as they had forensic sand in their shoes that matched that coast, but were only lightly, if ever escaped punishment. It was a weird scary story, we never met any participants but that it happened around then was scary. We rescued an 18-year-old Idaho gal named Heidi from someone she old us had tried to sexually assault her on Jost van Dyke, over a period of days. She was convinced that worst was to happen that night, and the individual held quite some say on the island. It seemed dramatic at the time, hiding her under blankets and whisking her to a new acquaintances' power boat down the dock as the assailant ran after us. We then all ducked, leapt aboard with our breathing bundle, rapidly undocked, revved up the engines of an old diesel boat and got the hell out of there! Odd…

March 23, 2000, 2:30 pm. *Southbound II* Herb Hilgenberg radio record, simplex telex, Alpha callsign WCX 5856 logged in at 2:35 pm, EST [eastern standard time, or New York time] then 2:55 pm tango, 7 pm and 6 pm, uniform, interference Ocean 50, *Schooner America*; key, *Sabbatical Nassau, Aquaria Crown, Ocean Joy, Sunrise Euro*, and *Danika Brown*. South of open waters, tug *Defender 10* from Puerto Rico to Bahamas, others dispersed, *Lady Georgina* summer play with Andros, Bahamas to Florida. *Wind Walker*. Titles, coastal area, *Capella, Whistle, Sweet Freedom, Turtle Spotted Goose, Kat, NautiCat, Sunburn, Andros, Aristar, Colony Creek, Breakaway 99*, and on March 24 *Sabbatical* too.

The weather front is laying off Chesapeake Bay with 25 to 30 knots from SW Saturday, Gulf of Maine low front 25 to 30 knots NW cold sun, Chesapeake, Lake Eerie front, low storm into Tuesday. Revised ETD [estimated time of departure] mid-late week, March 29 into April, Thursday to Saturday. That's all, standby Caribbean boats, *Resolute, Esprit, Breakaway 99, Capella,* same one from Bermuda. Difficult copy, static crashing interference, *Geyser* to Iceland, *Sabbatical* Newport, *Titus* to Cape Town, *String of Pearls.* We will try Monday, March 27, *Salt Whistle, Spotted Goose* [winds 15-20 knots, barometer 10.27 millibars, SW, seas three feet to five feet] *Lady Georgina, Sea Shuttle*, one hour, *Ocean Joy*, sunrise, Danika, *Moondancer* the tug *Defender*, Florida to Bahamas, across to Florida.

Pam again, *Agape, Dragon Lady, Sea Cloud, Sweet Freedom Vixen.* Log book for *Sabbatical.* Connections travel agency, lawyer Richard D'Addario, When unsure if destination was Nassau Bahamas or Tortola BVI [British Virgin Islands], tentative flight booking: Delta late morning landing, Providence, March 20 Nassau to Providence, USAir, noon Philadelphia to Providence. Chad leaves on April 12, Nassau to Providence, Ian April 10 Nassau to Boston to Philadelphia, Mike on April 12. Delta 12:15 pm, Atlanta to Savannah. Andy has warehouse in Connecticut for new dinghy. New order of 150 Echo Yacht Delivery T-shirts: 30 extra-large, 70 large, ten extra-extra-large, 20 medium, ten small, ten infant size. Three phone messages: Jane change, Bill, Teresa at work. My work started March 23.

April 21, 2000, At sea, aboard SY *Sabbatical*, with First Mate Mike B. Lithgow, Engineer Ian Strump, and EMT, Cook and Crew Chad Jackson, all US Coast Guard-licensed captains in their own rights. 200 nm north of the BVI.

Voyage 43: *Seeadler*, Bermuda-Newport, May, 2000

Heeled over extremely aboard *Seeadler* on the approach to Rhode Island in sunset as the team tried to cook. Half the entire crew was women, the largest ratio until *Maiden 2* in 2002.

Superstition: With a crew of four, half of them women, I cranked the mate two thirds of the way up the mast to make an inspection when he suddenly requested to be lowered to deck. When I asked him what the problem was, he admitted he simply had a "bad feeling" in his gut about the potentially dangerous chore. Rather than make a fuss, I went with his instinct and we inspected it later when he felt better.

Even though we were at least ostensibly two couples, and I had gone out with one of the women, I make it a rule not to cohabit at sea. I'd heard too many instances where skippers were seen as compromised or controlled by their mates. I'm not sure I was right on that instance, though. Of course we don't drink at sea either, but smoking is permitted where it doesn't go below. One hard and fast rule is that no one leaves the cockpit alone, and remains clipped in. If they have to they can pee in the scuppers. If you are always clipped in to the cockpit, you won't fall overboard. There is a horn or whistle to call for help.

May 17, 2000, Saturday. *Seeadler*: Owned by Henry in Bermuda, J-160. May 16 to June 3, Henry, Mike, Rebecca, Mark, yacht broker at Bartram Brackenhoff. Next Tuesday on Goat Island, Nicole, *Swan*, David Laicz, ex-*Alchemy* 69-footer, Lauderdale, new owner 1985 Hotel St. Martin, Bermudian sloop, huge mainsail but small jib, tack line carbon fiber. Gear: two primary winches, electric, snatch lock regular main, lazy jacks, monofilament lines, four points along, into wind Yanmar 88-horsepower turbo diesel, 100-gallon jerry jugs, two gallons per hour, one gallon per hour, because of house must leave by May 21 before the Monday team. [Mike] arrives. Two refrigeration, air-conditioning, engine. Both feed off Westerbeke, generator. *Seeadler*, Chris Cannon.

October 6, 2000, Morning. Henry, British from Bermuda owns *Seeadler*. Capt. Joy in Newport. Brown & Howard Wharf. 31st birthday [just two weeks before 9-11].

August 30, 2001 David Willems arrived Saturday, St. Thomas. Introduced Henry, *Seeadler*.

Laura and I reading in the cockpit of the strong and fast sloop *Seeadler* with a lovely supportive British owner, Henry. We must have just left Bermuda since I am reading the *Royal Bermuda Gazette* and she is reading a magazine, and neither of those mediums hold up well to rough wet conditions on a boat! Rory, her Canadian partner, took the phot from the main companionway which is only for temporary occupancy except perhaps captains, admirals, those taking sun sights with a sextant, or navigators at the start of a race who have to jolt from the mounted VHF radio and charts. I notice that I am smoking, wearing jeans (something I almost never did at sea), and socks, which means we had to have left St. George's that day, and I got dressed up to walk through town and from the cruise ship terminal, past the Wharf Tavern and Annie's little book shop to Ordinance Island and back. The white and red belt is from excellent sailing outfitters Team One Newport which Severin's wife Hope supported at its inception with *Luna* gear for Alysse, and whose store was beside the Armchair Sailor bookstore when I worked there, and which my parents used to equip me for sailing for St. George's School. Finally, I laugh to note that my Carib Beer cap is atop my head; not only did I win it in a beer drinking competition in Tobago, but the umbrella I also won was burned and sank with *Stiarna* off Trinidad that winter, so that hat is one of the only personal possessions of mine so survive the fire and sinking! I literally just had my shorts, boxers, belt, short, no shoes, socks, or baggage or any kind: the cap must have been stuffed in my pocket or tied to a lanyard tied to the collar of my shirt! I'm amazed it survived that long; it is a relic.

Voyage 45: *Dancer*, Bermuda-Azores-Channel Islands, UK

Nigel, Craig, me, taken by Mick, Wahoo, between Bermuda and Azores on *Dancer*.

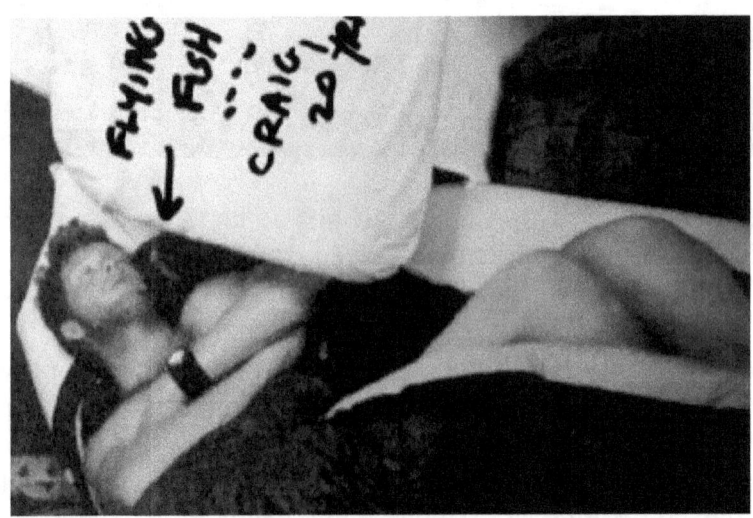

Craig, a divinity student, at rest on *Dancer* trans-Atlantic, calm as a millpond on the Azores High. Note flying fish we gave Craig as a companion to his copious reading of large books which had a tendency to fall through the cockpit hatch onto the head of the Australian chef skipper sleeping below!

Once we arrived in the Channel Islands, we basically killed time waiting to be paid. This did not accrue to the owner's advantage very long, as we were expecting to be paid while waiting, so the bill just went up by doing nothing. We of course were interested in the local ladies, but they were on such short supply that after watching the most popular one the club, Spanish, blonde, young, an excellent dancer and dressed to impress, I bought her precisely her drink (Rum and Cola) when hers ran out. Her response? She looked me in the face for the only time, looked at the drink, identical to her empty one down to the lime, and stubbed her cigarette out in the drink to go back dancing with her admiring coterie. It was then then that I knew we would not too well on that island, even with our trans-Atlantic-on-a-yacht backstory.

Then the forward toilet, or head broke, and we filled it with bleach and taped it up. Eventually Mick decided to take action, so we hopped on a tiny plane and flew to tiny airfield on mainland, which happened to be a former RAF base now civilian commercial virtually made of grass runways and quite charming actually. We ended up in a pub in Piccadilly Circus, waiting for skipper to squeeze all that money from all those ATMs in a sports car. Then payout, Nigerians watching intently, I show them all our cash! Later the Ozzie crew was my gest in NY Yacht Club with mates in Manhattan.

July 11, 2003, got a call from Craig B., care of Mick, our skipper. Crossed Atlantic on *Dancer* with him. Collecting money from ATM's in London from a Ferrari.

Voyage 46: *La Souris Qui Rugit*, **Christmas Cove, Maine - Newport, May, 2001**

Something I find charming about this images is that it shows how small some of our craft are. Here, Ken is taking the boat off the dock himself, in the background to left is a small inflatable dinghy which folks use to catch stripers and bluefish or shuttle to and from boats in the mooring field in all weather. Look at how large the horseshoe life ring looks compared to this boat, and how close to the water the captain is! His feet are basically below the water line, and if he wanted he could probably reach the lifelines on both sides without moving his feet. And two of us took this boat through four states. I joke that I prefer sailing over flying because I have so much less distance to go until I hit the sea surface. That point is amply illustrated here. And Hinckley, like *Swan* yachts, are designed for sailors who like to be close to the elements. I once serviced a yacht in Newport Harbor that had complete mosquito netting around the entire cockpit, and everything was redundant or in triplicate, starting with the anchors. Every sharp edge was padded, blunted, covered. Its name? *Seize the Day*! ....

"What have you done to save the world?" That was the question posed to me by a new skipper as I boarded this small but elegant Hinckley yacht in Newport heading (where else?) to Maine.

May 10, 2001, Books to buy at Armchair Sailor; *Trouble-Shooting Marine Diesels*. Sail, *La Souris Qui Rugit* August 3 to 5. Delivery prospect with Dan Thomason.

July 11, 2002, After *Violin*. Dan Thomason, calling. Ken Hand. Small Hinkley. sloop named *La Souris Qui Rugit* Marion this Saturday....

Chapter 13

Voyage 47: *Lapwing*, Southwest Harbor, Maine-Bristol RI

Really odd, sad story in a way, but at least no one in the making of this voyage was hurt. Grandson of very respected investor in the Bahamas and farm developer in the Bahamas. Ran coin operated laundry business and lived in charming colonial style home near water in downtown Bristol Rhode Island. However must have had diabetes or similar, and very overweight. My buddy Tugboat (Anthony Neighbors) and I were hired to join the owner and take over a newly purchased, large heavy yacht lovingly maintained.

They did not want to sell to anyone who would not love and care for the boat, named after a rare duck, unless they met the standard. They sold this guy anyway and he could hardly get out of a chair much less sail. Off Provincetown I threw a life cushion into the sea at dusk and never found it (*oops*!). it was supposed to be a man overboard drill but was a fail. He asked how I was to pay for the damage and a mount I knocked off clumsily and accidentally with my feet.

Sad thing was that this boat sat off Poppasquash all winter long for years getting totally trashed, the sails flapping off the roller furling drum, what a mess! Exactly what the sellers had dreaded but could not explicitly prevent, of course.

Voyage 48: *Ascent*, Rock Hall, MD-Block-Newport-Cuttyhunk-Vineyard-Newport

I did a lot of law school exam preparation, starting with the LSAT standardized test, on this boat. The owners super nice, flew us on a private plane and all. They very nearly left me on the dock in the Vineyard when I was late one day after an over-drinking session with folks affiliated with the Irish dance troupe *Riverdance*, which is a punishment I surely would have deserved. If it weren't for a kindly cab driver driving back empty who took me back, I might still be asleep or passed out in the dunes! It's ironic since I was trying so hard to behave for the passage out that I moved on board and went to sleep early, which cost me a chance to meet Brian and Caroline Miller, the family who kindly invited me to race on *Artemis* in Singapore!

Ascent in New York Harbor, near Liberty and Ellis Islands, World Trade Center towers in background, roughly a year before they fell.

August 29, 2000 Tuesday, 9:10 am. Missy, Tim, super friendly couple who own the boat, came very highly recommended by Bob. Boat's base in Rock Hall, Maryland, east side of the Chesapeake Bay, so named as it was some kind of quarry. Charts? 48.5 miles to Morristown airport. Private plane. Airport to Caldwell boat. Captain John. Rock Hall, across from Baltimore, in Maryland. Fly into Eastern Shore on a private charter with others from Summit Airport, NJ. Yacht *Ascent*.

Time management. Kimberly checking for us. We ended up going straight offshore, Cape May to the Massachusetts islands on the first leg, in good weather. On the way back, since we sailed often together, we dropped into Hell's Gate, from Long Island Sound to East River, Manhattan, saw and spoke with their daughter, who was expecting us on the jogging esplanade, then into lower New York Bay and out via Sandy Hook.

Voyage 49: *McKinna 57*, Newport-South Norwalk, CT, September, 2000

September 18, 2000 Monday. Fellow agent, John Jenkins. Power, Newport to Norwalk. Bob Millions, Norwalk, Connecticut. McKinna Corporation. Marina in South Norwalk named Total Marine Pat *Hunter*. 56-foot custom, Italian. We are to dock starboard-side-to, in a moving river. No breakwater. Chris Lukas at McGregor's. Broker Bob Millions, to take place right after the annual Newport Boat Show. Oldport Marine's *Quick Step* and *Amazing Grace* captain, Pat *Hunter*, owner of Spatz the dog.

Voyage 50: *Ivory*, Newport-Bermuda-St. Thomas, April, 2000

March 21, 2000, Capt. Michael B. Lithgow of Hilton Head, Cape May to Little Harbor. He and I and Ian are friends, and Mike is a childhood friend of Kent's and veteran of tips like *Sabbatical* in winter. He has skippered charters in American's Cup boat *Stars & Stripes* too.

October 6, 2000, Morning. Yacht *Ivory* US Coast Guard Master, pm. Thursday. Crew from *Ivory*, confidant of Capt. Mike's from Newport [narrowly avoided trouble in Zanzibar, as had I!] Capt. Mike Lithgow. On arrival Bermuda Harbour Radio came down to say hullo – then, as we jokingly interpreted it, tried to convert us to religion and rent us a mooring! We really just wanted to hit the pubs.

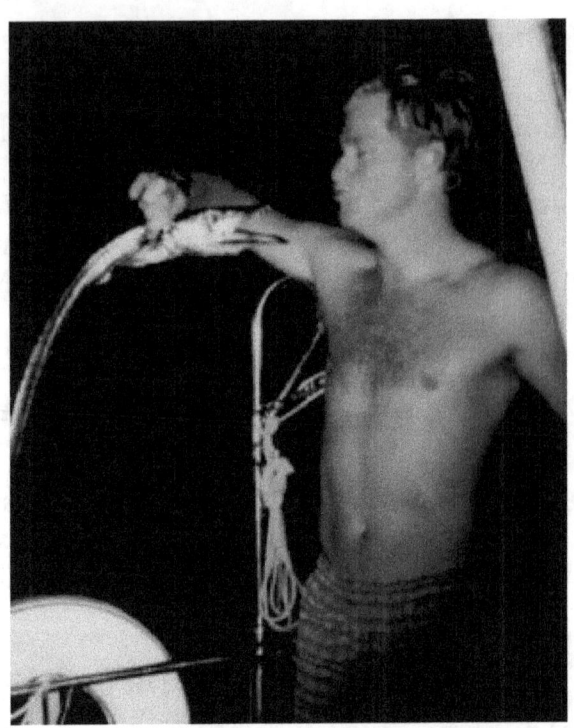

The mysteries of the deep: I sent photos of this fish to marine biologists at Woods Hole Oceanographic Institute and the labs at University of Rhode Island. Nothing really conclusive identifying it came back but no alarm either. We didn't eat it, rather released it.

The first leg was a record to Bermuda for me, out of more than 30 voyages to or from there. We were about 10 miles south of Brenton Reef, Newport, gauging all the weather information and speaking with Herb in Canada around 4 pm. We hailed a smallish Hinckley sailboat and asked the skipper where he was going.

"Bermuda, hell or high water, I've had enough of waiting for the weather," was his reply. At some point you just gotta pull your thumb out. So after waiting ourselves, but not waiting for more input, we discussed it, agreed we were willing to give it a shot, and the captain made the decision. We would just go for it and get down to Bermuda ASAP.

This was notwithstanding 40 knots each day, and we did it! Downwind, wing-and-wing, whisker pole out, nervously, slowly at times swinging side to side, but hauling the mail. With the wind from behind it's harder to gauge just how fierce it is blowing! The distance point to point for the race is 636 nm, and so with meandering and getting to and from docks, plus Gulf Stream offset, let's say we sailed 650 nm in 72 hours- hardly ever using the motor, not in gear at all except to enter Town Cut in St. George's. That an average – average – of 9 knots. Fast! The kind of trip you hear the ocean racing past your ear when you sleep, separated from the sea by just a few millimeters of fiberglass which on a bright day you can see through, and you can see deep into the ocean through the close portholes when you heel over, which is often.

Then Bermuda Harbour Radio did us the unusual courtesy of permitting us entry, I believe it was my 11th voyage there in 15 months and I had submitted a float plan so detailed it had our next of kin!

On shore, we drank. A lot. I darn-near ended up in Tobacco Bay on a scooter about 3 am. I told Mike the next day that I had a bad feeling in my gut about sailing that day. His classic retort was that I had a hangover in my gut and head, and we postponed leaving due to weather, not my and the other crew's drinking. One of the crew had to leave and Mike pulled double-watches, which I always admire him for. He also was the kind of captain never concerned about turning back, if it was the right thing to do, he did it, end of story.

Chapter 14

Voyage 51: *Sinai*, Antigua-Bermuda-Block Island-Black Rock CT

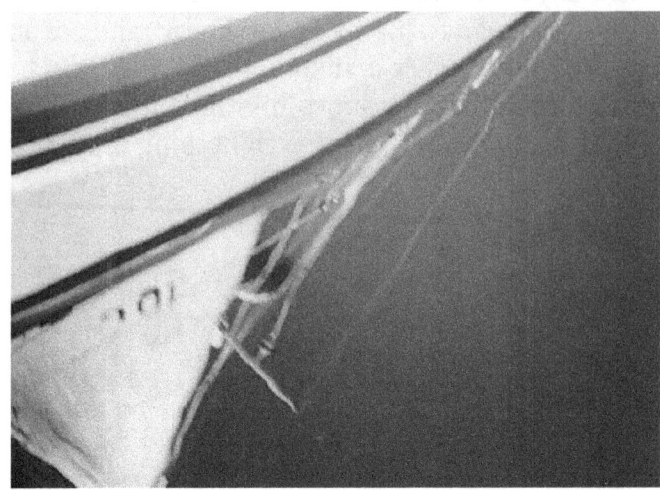

Funny voyage, interesting owner. He was a divorce attorney in the Bridgeport Connecticut area, with family homes in Antigua, where his brother lived part time. We know this since, on the second day of work on the boat, we were visited by a stranger who watched us work without introducing himself. Crew were Dermot and an Antiguan fiberglass expert and cook nicknamed Jobe, as in the patient biblical fellow.

On the way down, Dermot asked for, and of course received, special air routing from the DC area via the USVI so he could see his close friend Page. Jobe made sure to take us to a reputed place of ill repute, which met with no objections. The next morning I insisted on keeping my reputation clean by having the mate (not me!) row the ladies ashore, fully expecting to be shamed out of my job. As soon as they saw the ladies making for the opposite shore at Nelson's Dockyard, English Harbour, the owners of boats nearby, who were almost all bachelors of a certain age and European, inundated me with questions about where they might find some dates of their own; in other words, I didn't get fired, I got promoted!

While the sun shone, we pulled and re-stepped the mast, placing a coin under it. We followed the advice of a veteran carpenter and used green wood named heart of oak, something like that; stronger than steel they say. We enjoyed the experience, and I learned a lot, having not pulled a rig before. We had an issue finding batteries for the hand-held GPS, easily solved by finding a corner grocer in a wooden building. The boat was in pretty rotten shape, having not been used much in recent years. Like many yachts, to all outward appearances it was in all respects ready, and yet down below one finds a loose floorboard or a bucket filled with all (all) the spare nuts and bolts. I found it a bit endearing. There were smokables inside the pages of a book, and some adult literature under cupboards elsewhere; not the only sailor to bring that.....

In calm seas on *Sinai* with Jobe and Dermot: when you have great crew; you don't need more than a small cadre of good sailors, and in calm weather, you can relax and enjoy. Between Antigua and Bermuda, more than a decade after my first such passage. While I've done many coastal voyages with just two on board, unless I own the boat, I won't leave harbor with only one person, except delivery launches to Block or the Vineyard.

Alas! We set sail for New York via Bermuda, and lost the gas cannister valve (but not the gas) about three says out of Bermuda. Jobe had smashed a valve as a kid and knew how to glue them back together, particularly since he really wanted that hot food! Dermot says "the gas regulator was repaired by Jobe ingeniously using just a piece of a match and superglue!" I'm very fortunate, as it's not often that a team member paints and draws the yacht and records dozens of pages of recollections and share them with you *gratis* after the trip! Dermot is another close friend who I try to have on board when possible because he is a vastly more experience and accomplished sailor than me, and so I can sleep, dry or wet, knowing he will get me out of whatever pickle I put us into. And he has no issue – as you will see – with putting me right in my place! I assure that he's more than worth an occasional friendly badgering.

Dermot contributes that we managed to erroneously set the autopilot with a 15 degree course error, and thus it's extraordinary that we found Bermuda or Block Island at all. He also recalls an amusing incident of Herb the weather-routing guru telling me that our wind estimate was wrong, until after five boats reported the same 5-knot northerly. He eventually got the message and apologized to me. My being uncharacteristically taciturn is because not only is Herb a sea-dog who is held in awe by younger mariners like me, but he is almost always right. Herb is a volunteer, very deft at letting participants know their place in the pecking order, and being corrected and reprimanded by him is very public, I found it safter to tread softly in his airspace…. Two extremes are being lumped in with a bunch of other boats in the same area and routes and told to listen to their brief silently, or the one time he went to a NOAA conference and only took care of three boats; one of them a tug going to Greenland, another was our boat!

I made Jobe smoke everything found inside various books, with titles like *Thousand and One Nights*, before we arrived in Bermuda, so he was pretty well stoned the last few days. Dermot made a friend – in a big way – a jovial woman who was, as recall, a policewoman when not towering over him like a pair of headphones. We sailed in due course in light winds for Montauk but could not make it with limited fuel and no way to properly gauge it, so in thick fog about midnight we pulled into New Harbor, Block Island. Dermot then generously adds that "you understate the finding of the R"4" Buoy, flashing red every 6 seconds, with a whistle, between Southwest Ledge light (R"2") and SW Point, Block Island in that pea-soup of a fog at night. That super-impressed Jobe, who being accustomed to Antiguan and Caribbean weather was uncomfortable and unfamiliar around so much fog and so near a landfall.

Our approach was so unorthodox – a springtime landing of a small vessel in thick fog from international waters doing 5 knots and navigating without self-doubt to the tiny entrance of New Harbor, that the US Coast Guard launched a speedboat at night to investigate us. When they saw we were in fact just more crazy yachtsmen, they carried on without event hailing us via VHF. Block Island is not an official port of entry to the US, more like a setting for *The Russians are Coming* in May, so we could not expect officialdom to meet us. It was more a case of *force majeure*; insufficient fuel. The fuel would not open till next day, so we were stuck for the night, so I sheepishly asked the Federal authorities for permission to disembark during our visit. Fortunately and amazingly, the US Customs person in Nashville told us:

"I didn't see you go ashore" when I asked if we could. Then a rollicking time was had by all. We befuddled some locals with how three gents from Europe, the Caribbean and US showed up when there hadn't been a recent ferry arrival, and the airport was socked in by fog. We shared the only taxi back to the dock with a woman who told me her boyfriend was also a yacht sailor, but in Fort Lauderdale. Rather than capitalize on his absence, my efforts to pronounce "snort liquor-dale" at that point failed abysmally, further confirming that the skipper would bunk alone.

After we fueled up in Block Island we headed west to The Race entering Long Island Sound along the shore of Fishers Island. Dermot explains why we suddenly heard five short blasts (imminent collision) and had to do an emergency U-turn when suddenly at dawn Cross-Sound Ferry seemed about to T-bone us….. He explains that "the ferry on the Radar was heading straight at us, and we could barely tell, because the Radar was the old green-screen type, which had to be subjectively interpreted" by the user and was thus prone to a wider margin of error."

This is really no joke, as that choke-point has vicious currents four times a day, plenty of rocks, recreational fishermen, lobstermen, constant ferries, the entire Long Island Sound from the East River and Hell Gate, a US Navy submarine base at New London, and much besides it entering and leaving at a place strewn with rocks. In fact, on the same spot the 600-foot bulk ship *Barkald* ran right over and sank the 92-foot sailing yacht *Essence* on delivery from Newport to Greenwich at 4 am on September 20, 2006. Gina Bortolotti, 30 was killed, while her fiancé, crew Nardus Blue Bothma and Captain Ian Robberts, were taken to New Haven with hypothermia. The boat was later found in 90 feet of water.

We arrived at the small inlet on the north side of Long Island Sound and entered Black Rock Connecticut near Bridgeport the next afternoon. The tight space is at the end of a canal almost touching the I-95 highway connecting Canada to Key West like the Autobahn which inspired Eisenhauer to build it. I had trouble figuring which marina was Captain's, and so naturally just asked someone for help. They slowly pointed to the huge *Captain's Marina* sign painted on the roof of the place we sought. This did not make me feel particularly perceptive, but provided them with a chuckle. It was like the Maine joke by Bert and I, when the New Yorker asks a local how to get to Millinocket, and the reply is

"Don't ya' move a goddamn step!"

Black Rock was a very busy bustling small boat scene lined with ropewalk restaurants, a bit like Florida. A booze cruise from Manhattan ambled up the canal in slow mode; you know the ones, all glass, booming music and cheesy multi-colored lighting with like a totally different event on each floor; on one a Bat Mitzvah, another a college graduation, and a third a 50th wedding anniversary. A lovely and voluptuous blonde woman in her early 30's was rather enjoying the office party and shared images of her ample bosom a-la-Mardi Gras on request. I was about to request a *gratis* showing when the boat pulled right alongside *Sinai*. Even though none of us had not seen anything so lovely since Antigua (and those weren't free), I demurred asking. This was a good thing, since for the rest of the night an angry boyfriend and she loudly argued above our heads....

The following morning I coordinated with the owner for Immigration officers to drive down to meet us and clear the boat and crew in. Jobe scoffed when the immigration authority questioned if he would leave in three months, to which Jobe replied "of course I will, it gets cold after that!" We were paid cash, Dermot got the traditional post-voyage meal. Dermot went back to Annapolis, me to Newport, and Jobe to friends and family in New York City. Another uneventful voyage.

Dermot and my camaraderie also thrives so long as I provide a solid meal at the other end with Guinness suitable to his high demands of provenance, specifications of temperature, volume, alcohol content, and preferable a lovely server: hold the mid-West accent, in favor of a West Indian lilt.... We all get long marvelously. Dermot gave what I think was a most memorable and authentic short talk at our nuptials, and we have both provided work and hospitality to each other in Connecticut, Annapolis, Newport, the UK, Ireland and the Med, where he has been raising a family.

Such friendships, in my experience, are rare when both participants possess alpha personalities, are frugal, and enjoy talking, particularly about themselves; yet in Dermot and my case or fondness for each other has always remained true, to this day. I once dated someone I found work for, and when she returned to Newport from the West Indies, we all naturally went for a drink to celebrate. Since I couldn't charge the usual Echo agency fee and still have a girlfriend, for administrative purposes, I made a ceremony of taking out a dollar, giving it to Dermot to give to her. He then asked her to give it to me in front of people, so I could say it was all work-related. Of course, this befuddled everyone but Dermot, Jerry Harrington my Newport tax guy, and the eight lawyers in my family!

Dermot Bremner's Log of SY *Sinai*

Prologue: I was asked by Eric of Echo Yacht Deliveries if I would go as Mate with him on a fixed price contract delivery of the Mariner 47 *Sinai* from Antigua to Connecticut. There would be a third person, the guy who looked after the boat. He was going to New York to see his woman. This was all agreed in a matter of days and I opted to fly on Monday (the deal closed on Friday) to St. Croix and spend 48 hours with Page, then fly to Antigua. There was a question of the boat failing its survey because of the chain plates. I later tended to agree with the surveyors. So here is the tale or log of *Sinai*.
Signed, Dermot Bremner, Sheldrake International
Yacht Racing Management, June 2001

May 23, Antigua: First night's reunion: After running over a guy's bicycle parked under our rear wheels, we left and made the boat by nightfall. Eric and I then dinghied over to the dockyard for dinner and met between the dinner table and the Mad Mongoose half of English Harbour on the scrounge and as Eric had sailed with them over the years he was obliged to cough up, trouble was this happened every hour or so, so it got a bit wearing, Some British lord's wife was whooping it up in the Mad Mongoose, so it was a bit like *Le Café Douche* by midnight. We retired early in the morning back to the boat and mosquitoes, we were only 30 feet from the mangroves. Welcome back to the Caribbean!

May 25, Antigua: Then on to the Piano Club and heard apple jam being played, of all music! Hands-up those who understand what I mean! Then we went back to the Antigua Yacht Club bar, where Eric was greeted like a long-lost friend. There were a few more people around this time and we stayed out late as usual

June 5, Tuesday: 30.19.3N 64.24.3W, log 832 nm, still no wind, around lunch time the lads caught a second dorado and after 40 minutes in the pot the gas runs out!!!! NO GAS. This had been a side-issue in Antigua but we thought that the tank was full enough for the three of us, considering that 20 lbs. in *Rogue* [see *Femme*] had done me four months of which two months was for four persons. So we have no gas, little wind, and are conserving the last of our diesel. However we are nearing Bermuda. Dinner was half-cooked dorado and thank goodness Eric had picked up a tin of new potatoes something I would never have done in the past.

Wednesday, June 6: 8 am, 33.22.82N 64.40.69W, Log 955 nm: In the early hours we are overtaken by *Antarie* a 100' ketch, the big boat. We are sailing on a beam reach on port tack doing 6-7 knots as Bermuda's south shore comes into view. Eric calls Bermuda Harbour Radio and is answered by name! A cruise ship enters ahead of us through the cut as we approach St David's. Reefed, we fetch up to the Sea Buoy, no tacking, no problem, lowered head sails, sail up to cut transfer fuel from jerry to main tank byway of a siphon, Jobe has the ability to drink diesel with no obvious effect. Then we motored in through

Town Cut. Clear customs by 10.00 and Bernie calls down tells us two weeks ago 130 yachts arrived in one day! We go down to St. George's Boat Yard for diesel and water.

Next day, June 7: Thursday. We went to St. George's Dinghy club and did the washing. Well; Eric did, and we won't let him do that again.

Me again: One great thing about ending a yacht delivery between Sag Harbor, Long Island and New York City, and Mamaroneck, New York and Essex Connecticut; basically the Long Island Sound, is the ease of finding ferries across the sound and also catching many train, bus and car options along the Connecticut coasts, even access to JFK, LaGuardia, Providence are easy. After my cash payout, I took the train to my friend Brian's place in Old Saybrook where I spent the afternoon horse-trading over a dozen used Saab cars. Finally I spent most of my income on a Turbo 900S black sunroof of the stick shift variety which I loved. Then, after just three months the decade-long overhaul of Mount Hope Bridge, which I had to cross daily to get law school in Bristol, RI resulted in my staving in the bow against a large American automobile, totaling it. Sad.

The yacht *Sinai* then began a long ignoble decline, of at least a decades on the props at Calf Pasture Beach in a large marina named as I recall Norwalk Cove Marina, where I lived from 2006-2015. It's transom and name-plate faced the road, so I often saw the boat. I dated a young French lady from Lyford Cay Club; *pied noire*, North African French, who claimed to have sailed aboard her in Martha's Vineyard and knew the owner. The owner's version of buying the boat climaxes when the boat yard went bust and he sent a team of extractors to break the chains on their shed to take the most valuable asset they had, *Sinai*, in the dead of night.

Then I arranged to meet him at the Red Barn, a large family country restaurant in Norwalk to talk about marine business in the Caribbean, about 2009. As I might have expected having found pot in a book and interesting literature (which of course I very much appreciated), he was a bit rambling and eccentric. I have a job doing business development for a captain friend's brother in law on Park Avenue South, and he had a client who was looking to build a breakwater for a cruise terminal in the Virgin Islands. I put together the Norwegian owner of a quarry with a small Oslo bulk ship operator based in Nevis, West Indies, and the *Sinai* owner was going to provide some financing. Well, things did not go so well.

I must be a bit delicate how to relay the next few chaotic hours, but they were very stressful to me. I learned of bad deals with a high-end automobile retailer, then what I am sure was an intentional episode of getting lost at LaGuardia Airport between Norwalk and Manhattan, by someone who knew the area well. Then an almost entire change of clothing on Park Avenue, which was applauded by several young ladies dining nearby. Finally nearly two hours late we met with the older gentleman who, thankfully for me, was as kooky as any of us and no one had any intention of actually getting anything done, but rather preferred to talk about it, and themselves. My Norwegian associates, while spared this time-waste, took it in stride, didn't hold it against me, and hosted me at Gorham Island in Westport and an old fortress in Oslo as well.

My wages from *Sinai* allowed me to purchase my favorite car, a used Saab 900S Turbo the day I arrived back in the US. This photo is taken in Marion, where my brother and Kent schooled. Note the paint-trashed shoes, which were sometimes held together by wire or tape; during my heyday of deliveries I would send the boat shoes, sunglasses and leatherman-type tools to the factories for tune ups or replacements, and they would send me letters of admiration for how quickly I destroyed their stuff, saying the lab learned a lot!

Voyage 52: *Samburu*, Marion Bermuda Race, June, 2001

This was the only time I truly behaved like a "hired hand" and a brat in the non-professional Marion Bermuda Race, which I first did a dozen years before. I was rather a sore loser, and regret it. I was navigator, and we were well ahead of the fleet with a highly aggressive young crew who like the owners were mostly dinghy and endurance, round-Bermuda windsurf racers. We pushed the smallish yacht too far and hard, and in the boxy seas characteristic of the Gulf Stream, doing over 14 knots down waves. Then one of the bolts holding up a spreader in the rig, mast division, sheared off, and fell loudly to the deck, leaving it hanging limply. It was like a bird having a broken wing.

I recommended that we rig another running back-stay in order to take the pressure off while we figured out a more permanent solution, but the feeling was

"Without our being able to aggressively sail, what was the point?" Since further racing seemed pointless, as navigator I was asked to call in our withdrawal from the race. We caught some flak for giving our position which lowered morale among racers (we were so far ahead) and gave intel to others, but I felt it only fair to do, so since we were no longer racing; there was little guidance about this: if you are racing, obviously don't give your location, but if you are no longer racing, what is the protocol?

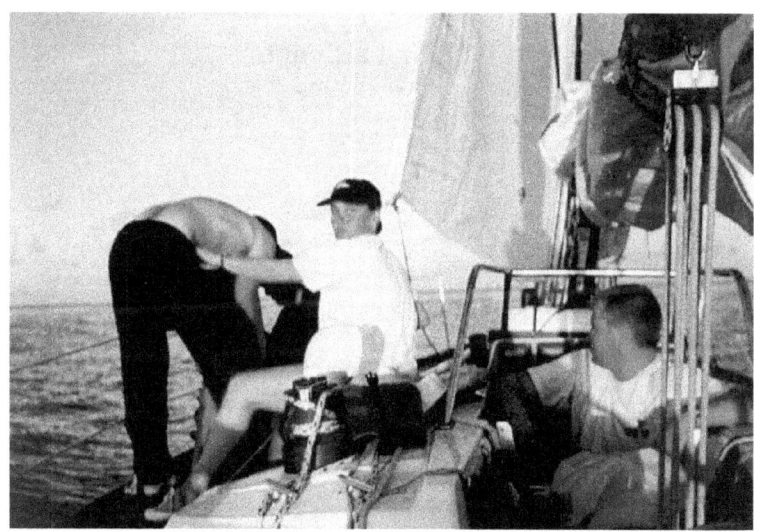

Making sure the skipper, who is repairing broken running rigging, doesn't go overboard on *Samburu* in June 2002, after we were forced by equipment failure to withdraw from the Marion-Bermuda Race.

Then after two days of no wind and so us just motoring to Bermuda, where everyone was from except me, we saw a large yacht motoring as well. Having done my share of yacht-to-yacht transfers, for fuel, cigarettes, rum and just someone to talk to, I wanted to hail them and, with permission go over to them and get extra fuel to enable us to not worry about refueling; remember, we had rationed fuel to sail and race to the island. My idea was shot down, and I fumed a bit. Yachts and their personnel understandably cherish their self-reliance, and it had been difficult enough quitting a race without also begging for fuel.

We arrived in Bermuda, but due to typical Bermuda High conditions of light wind in a belt around the island at the end of June, we were several days ahead of the fleet. I opted to head back to Boston to see my girlfriend before she went off on another round-world adventure. So I abandoned the crew, even turned down an offer to stay for free at Spanish Point. All before a single plate of silver was proffered to our fellow racers.

While it's true some owners leave the island before collecting their silver, I feel badly that I behaved poorly and with poor sportsmanship. At the least I should have stuck around for the sake of my crew. I guess my behavior reflected that of a yacht delivery sailor; a bit mercenary, on to the next voyage before the last one was barely cold, not prone to sticking around to fix and test all the shit he broke, or even feelings we hurt.

One factor is that, although it's true I may have secured a paying berth back to the US by mingling for a few days, it's not uncommon to burn through whatever you earned if you are not careful. I recall one night at a popular club on Front Street I spent the evening and all my funds on charming a young lady who vacationed on the island. As we left the club at closing, I was unable to afford the taxi to her place, and another competitor swooped in and carried her away; according to him, they even fooled around on the front lawn between taxi and home.... I feel it was my loss to have left Bermuda before the race, and it turned out to be quite sad to bid farewell to my girlfriend, even though they successfully broke a round-world-non-stop record on that attempt.

Voyage 53: *Tetiaroa*, Padanaram, Martha's Vineyard, Cuttyhunk, 'Tucket, Padanaram

This was an unexceptional family charter, which is good. The only drama lasted a few seconds, when a fellow at sunset was racing from Vineyard Haven to Falmouth on Cape Cod failed to see that we had a fishing line trailing behind the sailboat, and had in fact recently caught a bluefish. We tried to yell and wave, but he just cut our stern and the fishing line jerked down and the rod and line swung back in a jerking motion, which describes the guy (jerk), but he of course didn't notice a thing, and kept going.

Tetiaroa, in Padanaram, or South Dartmouth, Massachusetts, for a handover. After a week with a mid-size family with only you in charge of every detail (except cooking), there is a tendency for a charter skipper (at least this one) to be emotionally and physically exhausted, but hide it. The inclination is to burrow into a dark quiet place. However often one has a back-to back group to prepare for and adjust to. I still enjoyed having a paid cruise with interesting friendly people to some very neat corners of maritime New England! And have remained in contact with many of my charter guests, upon whom I also depended. This particular charterer and I stayed in touch, we were all brought together by it being the last happy week before 9-11. He later introduced me to a big financial player, who also had been a yacht delivery skipper, and was a subject of the film *The Big Short*, as one of those who beat the system.

Then there were the unpleasant antics at the end of the voyage, which I logged carefully. While I, the only paid sailor on board, was busy cleaning off sheets and the boat, the owner paid a diver to poke around under the hull and pesto! Predictably they found a "nick" in the leading edge of the rudder, either fictional or could have been caused by anything, at any time. As they correctly anticipated, I was too frazzled and busy to don a mask and verify, and it was not my pay at risk, so the charterer had to pay several hundred dollars, right when he should, or could, have been thinking about what to tip me! Pity.

I am convinced that this is a scam which the owner and diver go into with all of the charterers they get, and very few persons push back, as I should have done. For it to make sense, obviously, the diver would have to charge less than the penalty. I could have leapt in there in seconds, but just had way too much stuff to do.

Voyage 54: *Quick Step*, Newport, Portsmouth, Mooring Maintenance, Towing

Captain Pat Hunter and I and his dog Spatz, so named for the fancy shoes black and white, went around the largish Newport Harbor pulling up old mooring mushrooms for service and repair. Once you are good enough you get to create your own signature twist of the wire so folks who go after know who it was who set the mooring. I found a rare Coca Cola bottle made in Newport, behind the 7-11 and Tennis Hall of Fame, and tried to sell it on E-Bay but only lost money, which is pathetic. Ultimately I was not welcomed back as some of the gossip I was told made it to the wrong ears due to my lack of circumspection, which I regret as I like Pat and always learned from and enjoyed working with him. He drove a VW Golf diesel car (similar to my gasoline version) from Warren and was a former fisherman. We together delivered the McKinna 57-footer to Norwalk.

Voyage 55: Sailboat Tow, Fairhaven MA-Newport

     This was with Pat, who I enjoyed and worked with quite a lot, despite his taciturn New England nature, I liked his skills, confidence, and bravado. He's done commercial fishing, large passenger ferries, mooring maintenance and snow plowing to boot! And Mrs. Hunter always made him the best lunches. A typical tow, nothing too special around one of my favorite lighthouses, the sparkplug light called Sakonnet Light and my old school chapel St. George's at Sachuest Point. This was the route from the marinas at Fairhaven, opposite the huge commercial fishing port in New Bedford, and Aquidneck or Conanicut Island.

     As you would expect, there are dozens of ports and Islands in Narragansett Bay, bounded roughly by Point Judith, Sakonnet, Somerset and Fall River and Brayton Point in Mount Hope Bay area, and Providence, and the West Passage, including Quonset. There were several other non-urgent tows we did, I recall to Portsmouth as well as Common Fence Point opposite Fall River and Tiverton. Because nothing went horribly wrong like fouling the prop or crashing the tow, these trips gave me an exaggerated sense of my skill set.

Voyage 56: Launch *Rounder*, Newport–Edgartown Martha's Vineyard

A visiting Irish *au pair* was sitting on the bench reading Joyce when I arrived in Edgartown, Martha's Vineyard, and during the hour before I had to fly out I managed to get her to take this photo. I tried to impress upon her that I'd arrived alone from Newport, however she was unimpressed. The other skipper ran the base on the Vineyard at the time – his predecessor went on to purchase Echo Yacht Delivery from me.

Voyage 57: Launch *Hope* Newport–Block Island, for Oldport

Voyage 64: *Quick Step, Patriot*, Newport-Bristol-Newport; July 4, US Navy Charters

This is the Oldport Marine Services depot in a vacant lot from 28 Young Street in downtown Newport, before about 2002 when a co-founder of Oldport, my friend Ron Ackman (US Navy Vietnam vet) built a large home there. Between September 1998 and 2005 when I left Newport I was a part-time captain, mooring maintainer, boat-tower, and mooring-ball painter. Fortunately my commute from the home I rented from Peter Warwick, a British yacht captain, and Ron's and Oldport's yard was about 3 inches, or the width of the fence! The Volvo I bought from a fellow law student after the Saab Turbo I bought with *Sinai* earnings was wrecked on Mount Hope Bridge.

This is on one of the Oldport Marine Launch boats, probably *Hope* or *Rounder*, an open boat with 26 person capacity, Yanmar Diesel, and built by Oldport in their shed right downtown in Newport. The displaced the clunky whale-bottomed Crosby Launches popular in yacht clubs with a sleeker, more nimble and ergonomic boat. A passenger took this photos. Our hours were not bad; about 8 am to 2 pm and then the next run to 10 pm. The owners often lived on boats (*Aurora* and *Karin*), or someone was manning the office much of the time. Also Tim, the Harbor Master had our backs if we needed it – like the time a drunk knocked a launch driver out, threw him in the boat, drove it to a ship in the deep bay, hopped on his anchored ship, and cast the launch off for the poor boy to fend for himself. When he woke up and sent a Mayday the crew and ship were arrested. These were fun versatile boats, my only regrets being unable to know all 500 mooring locations and capacities, and the time my colleague ran aground on Brenton Reef and I dropped my passengers off to make room for his first, during which time he backed himself off without me… For my wedding in Newport co-owner Ron gave me the use of a launch for a few hours to show out-of-town guests around, and a spin on *Amazing Grace* too!

Mooring ball maintenance, and twisting metal into signatures to show who made a chain fast to a mooring. Ran many launches for Oldport from 1998 to 2004. Lived next to their yard, did repairs and maintenance, tows, passenger runs like this to Brenton Cove, and the Sail Newport dock past Ida Lewis Yacht club and to the Sayer's Wharf dock of Oldport. The biggest pains in the ass were a large family with a dog who lived aboard in the summer. They got a season's pass and abused it, to the extent they expected the launch driver to pull alongside every couple hours, take the dog ashore (out of the route) and on the way back pick them up to the boat! The company should really have given the season's pass back and they should have bought a small tender for the dirty business.

Voyage 58: *Elba*, Barrington-Jamestown

My brother and his sailing wife, who is a daughter of the commodore of the Torquay Yacht Club in UK, were very excited for this trip as their first-born was named *Elba* like the boat. I was about one minute out of the New York Yacht club where we were meeting at 7 am when the phone rang asking where I was! All good, we had a great an uneventful trip from Harbour Court to Portsmouth, even sailed! And the photos taken have been keepsakes of they and their daughter since. For me and Matt G. the skipper, it was another short positioning job for a racing boat.

Voyage 60: *Erebus*, Portsmouth-Newport

About an hour trip, a way to stay honest, make come money, and probably ran the trip myself, as I sometimes did. Straight shot around Rose Island up East Passage to Portsmouth after the navy base and inside an island called Prudence. Sunny summer day, a chance to hum and sing and enjoy! No sense putting up the sails.

Voyage 61: *Katahdin*, Newport-Port Jefferson, NY

It came as a surprise to me when the dock owner where the boats was kept harbored rather sharp enmity towards my mate, or crew. In fact the one, who was my neighbor, so despised the other, who was my erstwhile roommate, that he would not allow my crew to set foot on the dock. Since the dock owner lived on a boat at the dock, and I could not carry my mate onto the boat, he ultimately had to jump onto the yacht from the street! We cut our lines and fled. Then, tornado-like fierce winds heeled us over so very far that I was able to take fuel out of the choked filter and it just poured into a cup I held, the boat was that tilted! Owner was waiting outside the breakwater in Port Jefferson in a dinghy for us. It was cold and he let us stay the night at his horse farm. I later went to the island where *Katahdin* skis are made outside Seattle.

Bill on *Katahdin* before the tornado which we ducked, and right before having to heel over real far to get diesel out of the starboard tank after changing the clogged fuel filter.....

Chapter 15

My sister Ann and nephews visiting friends of mine aboard a round-world racer in Stockholm c.2002.

Voyage 62: *Katabatic*, Hull MA-Jamestown RI

Cold, but an interesting start and the Cape Cod Canal is interesting most days, when the current isn't overall boss. Captain and I got along great, till I was too passed out to meet him for a 4.30 am delivery in Jamestown and I wasn't called again, though I kept a bottle of cheap champagne in my trunk for years after that to apologize to him with.

Voyage 63: *Violin*, South Freeport ME-Nahant MA

Started off with humor when we told the marina crew to bring the yacht around to the dock from the mooring while we nibbled lobster with the friendly owner, she was a nuclear scientist living on a spit of land north of Boston south of Marblehead called Nahant. Then as we dropped into the South Freeport creek and the water with lots of rocks and islands, the weather worsened to a snorting Nor'easter by time we made Nahant, low tide, which neither of us had been to. The launch driver finally came out to get us, I have to return a pin from the anchor that was in a pocket, and on Route 1A south we saw a bad but non-injurious accident where a driver came onto the highway without seeing the car to the left and just kept bashing them into the rail. We didn't stop. We were exhausted and wind-blown.

Voyage 65: *Papaya*, Jamestown RI-Rye NY

Captain was an experienced sailor and toll collector on the bridge. Her former fiancé Mike Plant on a yacht named Coyote, also from Jamestown, let of his EPIRB signal mid-north-Atlantic (not a nice place) in training for a round-the-world solo race. His yacht was found months later, they never found Mike or his body. Local hero around Newport. Figure his keel fell off. Well, it happens that Jamie, from the IYAC and yacht racing circuit, had been killed in a Round Block Island race in which a girl-friend was participating about two weeks before.

When it got sunny the skipper and I got to cranking up the music 1970s-style, and dancing on the cabin top, I took off my shirt and it was fun in the dawn sunshine. My biggest fear was that Jamie's body, which went missing when a spinnaker exploded at head height on the foredeck, would rise as they tend to do. It did, at that spot, but a few days later. Jamie, also had been engaged. Very sad. Lost at least half a dozen fellow sailors to accidents like that including *Flying Colors*, a Little Harbor literally swallowed whole in a hurricane in the Gulf Stream, Bahamas to Carolinas.

Voyage 66: *Maiden 2* (ex-*PlayStation*) Newport-Westport MA

There were two parts to my brief involvement to *Maiden II*'s record-setting arrival in Newport. This was for the former *PlayStation* and a super-fast catamaran. Welcome to Newport, USA. record setting crew of mega sailing catamaran *Maiden II*, ex-*PlayStation*. Ado, Eric, Sid, Sara, Mickey, John, Carl, Regis. The only exposure I had before to this type of vessel was when Isabelle Autissier the famous woman solo racer from a French maritime publishing family, invited other crew, Sam S., and I from *War Baby* out for a cruise on her racing cat at Port d' Plaissance in Brest, France in the later summer of 1992.

The spring in question other boats had not arrived yet, I was driving launch for Oldport Marine, and my on and off girlfriend, an Australian navigatrix, concert pianist, maritime attorney, and meteorologist who set about five world speed records that year along including fastest non-stop round the world with Steve Fossett and fasted 24-hour speed record, told me to arrange a reception for she and the crew in Newport. They skipped

Bermuda, and from Antigua to Castle Hill, where I was out watching the official boat, they set a new record.

Then the chaos started. She didn't name me in her biography and so I won't here. I managed to get some weather routers and other support team members to the boat at a mooring via launch. Beers and cigarettes were had. Then the skipper, Brian, docked the boat at American (aka Newport) Shipyard, and US immigration and customs were called. The sailors were understandably famished and so many pizza pies surfaced in the office of the marina. After lots of hemming and hawing and appreciative crosstalk the female USCG and US Customs & Immigration approved the polyglot crew, and they moved to their crew house in downtown Newport near where I lived as property manager.

Well, I had ordered hundreds of clams and made huge vats of *bouillabaisse* and rice and white wine and ashtrays and with the French that was about all that was required. The next morning early my date got a message accusing her of somehow cheating on a record, and dashed out, and I didn't see her for about three days, during which all the horrific crap her crew and she had left behind – old stew, oysters, clams, cigarette butts, and spilled beer and wine – festered in the head of my old loft. Not much fun at all. It was so bad in fact that a few days later a an attractive, if sturdy older European member of the crew bumped into me on the street near our respective homes and made it quite clear that I was welcome to seek solace in her arms – I should have accepted!

The voyage: two days after arrival I was allowed the one and only chance to sail on *Maiden II*, whose color configuration still had both names on it. My main memories were of how level and flat the boat was under way, being two-hulled with a massive tennis-court-sized net in the middle of either side. Also all the fasteners were not the characteristic metal or twin but rather Velcro! If one ever needed a great advertisement for Velcro, this was it. And last of all speed: my goodness, could that boat go fast!

In what seemed effortless, the crew managed to work the boat up off Brayton Point south of Newport to an astounding 42 knots! Within moments it seemed we were off Cuttyhunk and the Vineyard Sound, with Buzzards Bay to leeward. I honestly felt that a large power yacht aiming for Cape Cod Canal slowed down, wary of us. It was the only time in a sailboat that I felt superior to a power vessel in speed power and agility. Quite a feeling – I recommend it!

Voyage 67: *Alcyone*, Newport-Bristol

This story began on the BQE, or Bronx Queens Expressway, some 20 years ago, and continues to this day in Mallorca, Spain. I got a call while driving, in fact after an accident where I hit a convicted felon in a Cadillac with a poodle and his girlfriend (I never got the insurance from him after discovering him in Georgia on PrisonPenpals site). A client whose business was traffic signals for the State of California asked me to deliver his new boat, named *Alcyone*. I could not, but recommended a dear friend and accomplished skipper, from Ireland. The owner, Jon, moved to Newport and bought a home (he was in his 20s) and the good captain moved from Maryland (he was in his 50s) and they have been symbiotically looking after the boat ever since.

I was given a standard finder's fee which I was told was high – yet considering the years of service and total refits and major ocean passages undertaken, I feel everyone received high valued. On this day we left in a snorting nor'easter, rather cold, rough and unpleasant, and went up the East Passage to Bristol, Rhode Island, closer to the Mount Hope Bridge. I remember wondering if we would have to find anchor on the lee of Aquidneck Island in Portsmouth, and what the purpose of the trip was, yet everyone had a rollicking time. That rough day on *Alcyone*, Dermot recollects that given the fierce wind, Dermot said it was a major feat to get her off the dock and out into the channel with no damage.

Voyage 68: *Föhn Wind*, Padanaram-Vineyard-Tucket-Hadley-Menemsha, Voyage 69: *Föhn Wind* RI-Block I, Cuttyhunk, Vineyard, Tucket

This was a family charter. The charterer is an experienced owner and captain in his own right, the children were good fun and stayed out of the way, and the only drama was when we snagged a lobster pot while approaching Nantucket and I dove in to unsnag it yet when it was free, I wished to remain connected to the boat and not left behind miles from shore. A passing boat asked if they could help, I said sure, and they simply stood by till it was all clear, about 10 minutes. Also the family were interviewed for the local TV program and we took in a movie at the old gas light theater.

Padanaram is South Dartmouth, a charming yacht-building and owning town famous for Rebecca's Ice Cream, the gated Mishaum Point community, and the Concordia Yawls, all of which are allegedly afloat or accounted for. Menemsha is a northwestern village and port on Martha's Vineyard near where JFK Jr.'s plane crashed with his wife Caroline and her sister. The village was used in the set of *Jaws* movies and Carly Simon, James Taylor and other notables like David McCullough the historian have lived in the same Chilmark town.

Having a lovely swim and watching the horses in private Hadley's Harbor. Even for non-Forbes family, one is welcome to anchor and swim – just not to go ashore.

Hadley Harbor is a secluded anchorage away from the maddening and embarrassing currents of Woods Hole where a list of members of the Forbes Family is posted: If you are on it, you may land, if not you may not. The Forbes family owned the entire Elizabeth Islands, see? Cuttyhunk is a very desirable, small village on a small island less than a mile square with no more than 11 full-time inhabitants. Shouldn't have told ya! Neighboring Penikese Island has only one resident.

April 23, 2003, Garden of my home on Young Street in downtown Newport, up from Lee Wharf. *Farr Away*: Mid-May. Charleston to New *Jersey*. Stamford, Sandy Hook.

August 6, 2003, Yacht owner seeks captain. New business cards. Adam, welcome back. Old wagon, van, camper, Volvo. July 7. Captain John C. touch base. *Farr Away*.

Chapter 16

Voyage 70: *Turk*, Nantucket-Sag Harbor NY

The only time as captain I woke up to find we were already moving! My "mate" drank less than me and figured he'd make good on the tides and head out at sunrise, so he did! Kind of a relief actually. We hailed friends of his while rounding Sow and Pigs shoals off Cuttyhunk, they were on a much bigger boat, and looked at us as though from a tank to a rickshaw....

June 9, 2002, Crew finder. SY means sail yacht. Call Manfred Advent, once of *Breathless*, when contract *Turk*, a sail yacht. Tell Oldport Marine so they can schedule around the delivery.

June 18, 2002, Saturday. Sag Harbor. Beneteau 42-footer. *Turk*, within a week of May 24. Onset Massachusetts to New York City, 25-foot Chris-Craft power boat. Quoted per day and expenses. Single engine, at 13 hours. Destination 79th Street Pier, mooring 25, one mile north of aircraft carrier. *Cancelled.*

Note: If it was a different yacht then forgive me, but it was during this busy summer of short voyages that billing piled up and as Echo Yacht Delivery blossomed, it was harder for me to monitor, and with email easier to for crew to avoid pitching in their finder's fee of 10%. In this – or a similar – case the owner had done nothing wrong, but one of my colleagues had a disagreement with me and I was forced to endure a browbeating in front of her crew, who had up till then known and looked up to me to provide work.

I was hurt and humiliated and tried to recoup it from this owner, who I had never met. At one point I called and he was in Turkey on business and clearly did not appreciate the call. I told them that a discretionary tip would be much appreciated, as I had been stiffed by someone else. The check duly arrived in the mail for exactly $00.07 – seven cents! – above the invoice! *Touche*!

In later years, I developed an alarm-tripping network so that if my name was ever posted as delinquent from a club, folks would call or text me and it would be quickly resolved. I would return the favor and when I see friends on delinquent lists at clubs I take a photo and email or text it to them. But the same cheap fellows that stiffed me for $50 or $75 finders' fees, forcing me to chase it for months? When I see their delinquencies for all to stare and snicker at, I do absolutely – nothing.

Voyage 71: *Farr Away*, Bermuda-Port Jefferson, NY

Dermot, Chad, Austin and I on the racing sled *Farr Away* at Penno's Landing, Bermuda in June, 2002, all wearing the Echo Yacht Delivery T-shirt with a big chart on back, and flying the Echo flag. Behind is what was the Naval Operating Base, St. David's Bermuda, where the *Xebec* crew bought subsidized food for the ill-fated voyage to Belgium 11 years earlier.

June 8, 2002, Wednesday. *Farr Away*. Friday, June 21. Booked to fly there via economy. Eric W., Dermot, Chad Jackson, Austin Ian's birthday.

June 22, 2002, Saturday. 3:15 pm. We were clear of St. George's fuel dock, setting Jib. 4:30 pm, 32°23'2N by 64°37'.71W. 400 EST Wednesday. Log: jib up, main up, jib down wind down, anchored, no fuel, united, *Farr Away*, continued of fuel on approach overtaking at 1,800 RPM Main up RPM 800 maximum. Barometer 6 pm jib up. Main engine off up, sail with engine on ran fridge at 1,500 RPM Main up winddown jib down main engine on no wired. Still no Engine RPM up checked 9 am wind up down, RPM up to 1,750, jib up, down jib up down, three dolphins.

Autopilot off, SSB on, port tack, SSB, wind up, wind mon up 20 knots, jib up, hours 2,774, jib up, main up, main engine down #4, reef main Squalls 3,025 to 1,024 millibars (down) down seas down, main engine on for batteries, 193.5, two is 13. Some spray on VHF 16 channel 22, directed then to sea lark. They will tow with give *bottle in* ARC rally. AM Engine hours. Radio log. Saturday 22, 6, 7 on Zulu 12 to 3 on. *Mensae*, which is leaving now. Numbers 34°N. *Tiger Too. Kodiak*. SSW tomorrow with light stronger wind Monday 34°N to 38°N, 18 to 20 knots.

Monday, long-range to New York. Front back to 64°N. Tuesday into Wednesday, winds 15 knots. Wednesday up to 20 knots. *Emily's Moon*, 8:30 am. VHF channels 16 to 72. *Blondies*. Captain Valerie Doan. SY *Mensae Swan* 50-footer. Gulf Stream. Chart entry point. 34°N to 69°W. Waypoint 35°N by 69°W. Bottom of a Gulf Stream meander. Two entries. West end of New York and Rhode Island. 37°N by 70°W. Entry to 37°30'N by 67°W. Eastern

Entry. Out 39°30'N by 68°30'W. 3:30 pm to 4 pm, EST EOT 6:30 pm to 5:15 pm Racing with TV and one plastic fork.

Main engine hours: 257.3 at 8.30 pm, 10 pm and then 6-8 pm. Was 252 hours at start from St. George's, 2 hours, am 247 hours when Echo joined *Farr Away* and three hours. Hamilton, St. George's. Note 4 am turn off lights after sun up including installation lights. June 23 at noon: batteries #2 is 12.25 volts, #1 is 12.75 volts. Noon position plotted: at 95. Dermot: please wake Eric up at 3:30 pm (Zulu, or local time) for SSB radio duty, thanks. Also Dimple; laptop at night. Boats Nobel Tec, GPS integration back up and running. Navigation.

Austin fileting a fish we caught on *Farr Away*. Earlier we had transferred fuel to a needy boat which was trying to make Bermuda before dusk, and nearing the US we obtained cigarettes in exchange for Bermudian rum from the scalloper *Kismet*, under Captain Gordon. Austin required butterfly stitches to his left eyebrow due to a bottle falling on it.

June 24, 2002, 1 pm. Our position plotted on race chart, we are at 75 nm east of Rhumb line to Newport but that's okay for eddies are being headed from with NW by at 2 knot counter current, H_2O temperature up to 76°F., wind up 18 to 22 knots steady NW, seas up lumpy 6 feet to 11 feet NW, autopilot not viable in these seas, otherwise 10 am to 11 am, we passed through dense long line west to east of thick squalls, rain, wind, with that Herb's frontal; trough? Compass course 335° to 345° is Okay, WNW.

Presently 36°34'N, 66°16'.9W, only 65 nm SE of Gulf Stream. Entry SOG [speed over ground], or actual speed up 6 to 7 knots SOW [speed over water] is 7 to 9 knots, NE pushed 10.5 knots in squalls. Total 45 hours. We are at 270 nm as crew flies to Bermuda is an average speed over ground over 6 knots (not bad). At 3:30 pm boat time (6:30 Zulu), we must shut off systems for Herb Hilgenberg's SSB broadcast called *Southbound II*. Barometer

13:20 millibars! 10:22 millibars (down by 6 millibars). Dropped sails. Batteries gone down so. 730 am. H_2O 26°C., 250 nm from Block Island.

June 25, 2002, *Navigation Notes*: Noon, 125 nm covered noon to noon now 340 nm from BDI. 25, 6 *Morning Glory, Vanish, Emily's Moon, Spirit, Mischievous, Farr Away. Vanish, Emily's Moon, Ace*, Thursday 25 to 30 knots, up to gale force, east 45 eddy, favorable current. 37°04'N, gradual backing winds 38°N by 75°W, front to east, back to with speed over ground well. Wind still 15 to 20 knots into Wednesday evening; 20 knots gusts up to 25 to 30 knots offshore near East less front south of New York, 8 pm 39°20'N with *Mistress M.*, group *Kanook*, intuition our barometer reads 1024.

Pre-frontal *Ace*, 37°48'N, 68°34'W. SW 8 to 10 knots wind, slight band 30°N to 34°N, till 20 to 25 knots up winds on Thursday. Break behind with SW 25 knots near coast break 50 to 60 nm offshore a gale out of stream cold eddy 37°10'N, 68°40'W. *Tiger Too, Jared*. 36°58'N, 67°29'W, barometer to 1,021, 5 knots north Gulf Stream wall to 37°40'N by 72°W to 38°N by 70°W to 35°N by 68°80'W to 38°30'N by 68°38'W, SW over the morning 15 knots, 40°N, 68°W by Wednesday in winds SW 20-25 knots, then 30-35 knots into Thursday.

This affects *Windswept, Evictus* missed us and *Emily's Moon*. VHF tried, vessel four times on VHF 16. On the border of the low, it missed us. *Note*: On VHF channel 16 we are hailing vessel at one nautical mile distance, oil tank port bow. 9.08 pm on June 25. Checked oil seventh time, now that engine is off: dipstick fine but cannot remove oil lid while aiming light not working? Spare bulbs. oil checks added. (00.01 am). Water temperature 76°F. Log 430 nm. Ship and clocks engine on at 2 am, motor-sailing, storm jib down, tack 2,000 RPM grid. Main Engine 1,700 RPM. Rolling out jib, pull main up. #3 jib up (delivery sail), main up full main engine RPM 1,800. Jib down. Tried sailing for an hour no radar, for coming, horn in cockpit 2,000 RPM. jib down wind down, main engine up. Pilot Whales in sight. They lift shy fog on bow three miles. A little rain and light fog.

June 26, 2002, *Engine Notes*: Oil checked good June 26, low, unscrewed cap (very tight) added 1 quart. Type: SAE 30, transmission fluid, okay, coolant oil, salt, H_2O intake okay. Engine hours 4 am: 304, at start (St. George's) 252 so 52 hours steamed. Rob now is 30 gallons, is 40 gallons, start and C9 added is 49 to one third; (10) 39 on board (Electrical Reservoir). Circa fifty hours consumed at 20 gallons, so a great two hours per gal at X revs, is 30 gallons. Remaining on board (ROB) at half-gallons per hour is 60 hours steaming so RPM up to 2,000 at 3.30 am to make Block Island if need be, can go up to Block Island or Montauk *en route*, plus we have at 3.6 gallons.

At 180 nm to Fishers Island and The Race, entry to Long Island Sound, is at 30 hours at 6 knots is at 15 gallons. and we have at 35 gallons. Race is Port Jefferson is at 50 nm, at 6 knots is circa eight hours is about 5 gallons is we have on top of whirl, fuel, SW winds 20 to 25, even up to 30 knots expected this morning, sail. Red Aframax bulker westbound, New York approaches 40°N, 69°W. Herb 3:50 pm. 40°17'.7N and 70°09'W.

Morning Glory, Emily's Moon. Stampede, Sukanosh, Intuition II, Ace, Tiger Too, Jared, Sea Hawk, Windswept, Alphida, Farr Away, Intuition II, Champs. Building winds 20-25 knots, closer to 25 knots up. 40°15'N, 70°20W, June 19, barometer 10.28 near *Farr Away*. Same forecast increasing SW flow by morning 25-30 knots. Later stronger in New York after, from Newport Friday, secondary pre-frontal line main front offshore, Saturday will be okay. Rounded SE of Block Island and Narraganset Bay approach at 2.10 am, SW, Block Island clear at 3.15 am. 4.15 am, Main engine on for batteries, fridge, auto.

Passing through The Race into Long Island at 7.19 am. Cleared lots of fishing boats. Going for Amtrak train 842, via the 7 pm ferry to Bridgeport. Donald, Stephen Arruda. New Haven. US Customs and Immigration. Setauket Yacht Club. Cheryl, Ali Zapp Cool. Comments. Wind SW, so jib and main sail up full, main engine off. Past sailing. Shipping channel. Mainsail with one reef. 3 pm mainsail down, storm jib up, engine on, off. Sleighride downhill, spotted Buoy A, ETA at Gull Rock at 8 am. Rounded Block Island's Cerberus Shoal at 6 am. Pam's VK, GI at 7.19 am. Jib down, main fuse, 2,100 RPM. Favorable current. Engine hours 319.6. Fastest day's run. 7.2 knots average boat-speed.

June 27, 2002, Thursday. US Customs New York US-flagged noncommercial, three US, one non-US, fax. Rhode Island DOM [Department of Marine] valid to 2004. Notice of arrival. US customs, Newark. Inspector C., US Immigration, New *Jersey*. 11.15 am, must go to New York maritime unit. Dermot writes that "we left from RBYC in Hamilton then went to St George's. I remember two things about that voyage, firstly that the boat was exceptionally wet, and secondly that it was impossible to sail without having eight guys on the rail once the wind came up." The other was the ferry crossing on the ferry across the Sound after the trip it was archaic. I have never been on such a utilitarian ship before pretending to be a passenger ship.

Dermot took this, overlooking the large white Bermuda Customs and Immigration & Police station on Ordinance Island, Bermuda, clearly in their winter. The boats to left are exactly where *Circuit* was anchored when I swam to them and obtained work to Europe in 1991, having left my clothing and wallet at the station. Bermuda Harbour Radio, with Scott and the team, is right above my shoulder, to the right, with Antennae. It is easy to see how a crew might face a week at half (or no) pay with not much to do, and would need entertaining; scooters, busses, trips in the dinghy to watch turtles, beaches, Hamilton, museums, lighthouses, and inevitably, drinking. In this photo, it's a Blackberry and I have to still report to the owner, brokers, marina in the Caribbean, and still keep new job prospects and clients warm, because by January deliveries in the northeast are almost all done.

Voyage 72: *Oniwa*, Newport Harbor Christmas Lights, December

This was just a fun evening cruise on a lovely restored power yacht named *Oniwa* around Newport Harbor decorated or festooned with lights and music, great fun, skipper Casey is well known and super kind to invite me, I was a line handler and helmsman at times only.

Voyage 73: *Congo* Wilmington NC to Beaufort, NC

Very odd voyage: Call during law exams, my friend the captain had broken ribs from being thrown around off Carolina capes on this smallish yacht, could I receive him ASAP. Yes. I took a train from Rhode Island to a small North Carolina stop called Rocky Mount where a high black pimp on a bicycle who must have been pretty high since he kept circling the station with a stereo playing, he alone and me along. He pissed of the local (white) boys by offering me a Russian – or black – hooker. The train arrived, my friend got off broken ribs and all, and I boarded it southbound.

Instructions from Capt. Ennalls, friend from Newport: 4 am. In Rocky Mount railroad station, North Carolina. Amtrak. Express pick up. *Congo*. Commanders router Richard. Richard, mechanic. Dry cell. Voltage regulator not problem? 42-foot Hinckley in Wilmington, North Carolina. *Congo*; to Southport, or South Harbor, NC. This short trip turned out to be a horrible boat which broke Ennalls' ribs and almost blew my crew and us all up! Tony S., friend of a friend's from Fenwick, Old Saybrook. I tried to squeeze in short voyage US coast before flying Caribbean, failed. Andy G.. Both US mate. 57 gallons. Westerbeke, regulator part by FedEx.

I met the boat and a young demoralized crew. The boat kept trying to kill us, a charge alternator broke so raw battery acid gasses filled the interior, there was not wind but lots of rain so we opened hatched and lit the stove for the kittle for tea and almost blew us all to smithereens! Could barely see or breathe, the plastic covers to CDs and other items melted, we tied the boat up in Beaufort, splashed each other with hose water and no shirts in front of a bunch of middle age women who wine and dine. Then we handed the boat over to a local captain as we considered it unsafe.

May 10, 2003, South Port, North Carolina: Mechanic, working on the pump. Check out whole system either alternative with wired system. Westerbeke, service center in Massachusetts. Service manager. After sales. Bob B. Telephone Captain Woody W. Jamestown token, Amtrak train. $5 meals Amtrak, Richard including use of car. Fuel and 3 days dockage, Southport and ice. Car trip to Jim C., Southport. Fuel; 20 gallons diesel. Dockage in Beaufort. Advance Andy (wages). Groceries in South Port. Dinner for three Beaufort for trip ($15 each). Two days lunches, three persons. Southport Deli. Laundry, rental car. *Note*: credit card machine down at Beaufort. Fuel. Over to Capt. Woody. After the voyage, we drove the younger crew to his mom's in Kingston, the other, Tony back to Newport or Saybrook aka Fenwick.

Voyage 74: *Andromeda*, St. Martin-Bermuda-Sag Harbor, NY

May 16, 2003 Tom (owner). Need letter of introduction from boat for arriving at St. Martin Immigration. Crew options; Roger D., Randy, Mike of *Rising Star*.

May 18, 2003, Sunday. SY *Andromeda*, St. Martin to Bermuda then to New York. Sag Harbor in the Hamptons, eastern Long Island. 57-foot Bristol build in Rhode Island in 1994. Generator power sail. *Sloop Andromeda* and *Fresia*. Tom. James Carley. I did this voyage, and my girlfriend met me Sag Harbor. Cook Cathy V. Brian M.. 5th back up needed on top of owner and me. Educated, well-spoken crew. New Rochelle. Princess Yacht Club in Simpson Lagoon. Adam on *Andromeda*. Stephen M. *Andromeda* marine survey. Derek G. referred me intro. Tom's Captain mid-1970s. loves to be on the boat. Jody LoCasio to 5,000 nm last year in Connecticut. Adam Smith capable captain out of St. Augustine. The resort bay *Anse Marcel* and the owner playing games, going or not. French lady I had dated in Singapore was working there then.

May 20, 2003, Commanders Weather, ably run by Ken Campbell. *Andromeda*. Simpsons Bay. 57-foot Bristol sloop. *Weather Notes*: Light. Today stronger Sunday, SSW to new front. 25°N and 30°N by 60°W. Late Wednesday, Thursday, NE 15 to 25 knots. Geordie; work being done, boat race? Rudder. Diesel tank. Jimmy H. *Twilight*.

Dear Pisshead, if you wake up before we're back, then call us on channel 16. Love Crew. Please call. Thanks, 3 pm on the VHF 16, dinghy! [Another reason I'm glad I quit drinking in 2006; this behavior cannot have helped my reputation!].

In Bermuda I unintentionally pulled an Israeli military Uzi submachine gun out of a satchel in a fully manned police and immigration and customs office in St. George's. Tom had told me it was just a harmless old hunting pistol when I insisted I know about any weapons or drugs on board. He waited weeks then finally when we were docked at Her Majesty's Customs, he told me to unscrew panels to find the old gun. The packet was locked when I slid it to an officer, but he ordered me to open it for inventory purposes before I surrendered it during our stay. Imagine my terror and their surprise when I slowly extracted a bloody Uzi, which far outpowered what was on their hips; yet several of them drew their weapons an pointed them at me, ordering me firmly to lower the (unloaded) submachine gun. I did, of course.

That was one of the least smart things I've done. They took it, demanded to know our departure to the minute. Two minutes before that time I heard scooters stop, the crunch of police boots in the gravel, they walked down the dock with the carefully guarded back in which the Uzi was, handed it to me the precise minute we were to leave, we cast off and set sail, and they sat on the dock until we were out of the Town Cut and out of sight! *Non circum coitus*, as Queens College, Oxford says on their rowing gear: No fucking around!

SY *Andromeda*, sport. 1984. Custom Canada. No cutter. Westerbeke. Draft 7'10". BVI, Tortola British Virgin Islands, May 9. Echo's best Captains: Andy Burton, Mike of *Rising Star*, Patrick Childress, Dermot, Captain Steve Connett, Mickey Spillane, Chad Jackson, in New York City? Bill M., Donald of the *Connecticut Post*. Tom knows the boat absentee owner. Kathy and Brian. South African. *Andromeda* expenses. Ricky, engineer, crew dinner, Diesel, Dockage, immigration clearing, laundry and detergent, cab to airport, cabin, balance on airfare, top up diesel St. Mark, ferry and bridge tolls.

June 17, 2003, Catriona; Sharkey got delivery back? *X–Base* photos? Sails from *Andromeda*, Hamptons. Thomas Bernard said he'll travel back. Photos. Tom, owner of SY *Andromeda*. [I hosted owner Tom and his girlfriend at the NY Yacht Club in Manhattan about 2015].

After we waited over half an hour for this Bahamas-flagged cruise ship to leave St. George's (I admit I'd become accustomed to being first dibs at entry), I permitted the crew – and me – to offer this salute (of sorts) on the hallowed waters where Bermuda races have been finishing for over 100 years.

There was a lovely Swedish girl walking in cave and all way to fuel dock and back. Johanna from Goteborg, but then I choked. On voyage from Norway past Iceland in November how the Arctic fishing boats played the *Titanic* film soundtrack to scare them! Dead corpse towed behind boat then cut free from dinghy. On the storied 1930s yacht *Stormy Weather* before, a man was tied to mast and deprived till he calmed down. I also met Capt. Dale Norley aboard a lovely yellow catamaran which she was taking from South Africa to the US. She is an incredibly impressive mariner, person, and writer. We remained in contact and I ultimately entrusted Echo on to her. She also submitted several articles to *Latitudes and Attitudes*, some of which mentioned Echo Yacht Delivery favorably.

Relaxed in over 50 knots of wind on the strong *Andromeda*, approaching Gulf Stream. About *Xebec* over a decade before, which was poorly run by a terrified and underfed, cold, crew trying to kill each other, this exuberance barely made it to the surface.

Chapter 17

Voyage 75: *Pollux*, Marion-Bermuda Race, 3rd Place

Odd voyage, the only time on a Bermuda Race that I felt things was a bit fake and just felt, well 'off.' Said we hit a whale, it was just stiff rudder stock bearings. Nearly earned us a seamanship award. Owner never left his cabin except to have folks clean the crap and vomit off the head walls and floor. Not nice. Creepy. No crew cohesion. But somehow it worked and we placed 3rd in class, and I was navigator, so you never know, do you? With no rudder, the bearings having shot on *Pollux* we had to hand-steer with John B. to RHADC at night

May 20, 2003, Swede, ex-intelligence officer, union publisher, yacht owner, *Pollux* (work). Marion to Bermuda. Perhaps after the race, from the Carolinas to northern Italy. This October. Milford, CT. New rudder.

June 17, 2003, Bunker Hill, Charlestown, Suffolk County. Boston. Letter of program. St. Gabriel's, mooring. Low across Appalachians. High coming in from WNW, out of Buzzard's Bay. laptop internet. Club. Beneteau 42-foot. *Hiro Maru*. *Cassiopeia*. Marion Bermuda Race preparation. *Firefly, Starry Trail*, six dinner tickets. *Firefly*. Wilmerdings. Two hours crew. *Eclipse*, Zach Cutler, *Starr Trail, Hiro Maru*, Catriona, Sharkey. Skippers meeting. *Fandango* pulled out, due to having broken down in Long Island Sound on the way to the race. James Lurtz, 1936 Bermuda Race. 78 boats this year? [Note: I omitted five pages of weather before race which, as navigator it was my duty to compile and analyze]. This was such a strange trip that I am opting for less is best. We hand-steered to the dock due to a whale strike, or stiff bearings on a new rudder.

This was one of the few times I was relieved to leave Bermuda, at least from a professional point of view. On a personal level my girlfriend flew down and we had a lovely time, notwithstanding a butcher of a haircut, which I should have foreseen as I lowered myself into an old barber chair in a wooden shack to find myself surrounded by large posters of professional boxers looming and leering over the knocked-out bodies of guys who looked like, well they looked kind of like me! Before the haircut. There was also an ill-advised shortcut on an old railway line which would have resulted in one of us losing a calf – or having a cow! – had not a strong metal chain arrested this bulldog's lunge.

Voyage 76: *Aviatrix*, Newport, Narragansett Bay

Just a fun outing on the bay which led to a hot tub ashore.

Voyage 77: *Impulse*, Newport-Hyannis-Nantucket MA

First and only Figawi Race from Hyannis to Nantucket, the crew were so tired from beer and sun by the end of the race we could hardly function, much less coax a 50-foot *Swan* to victory. A funny guy approached my fiancé on the dock and asked "is that sweater wool, or can hit be felt?" A less funny guy asked if he could take photos down the cleavage of my date at the Rope Walk. Then we were asked to sign petitions both for an against Cape Wind turbines in the space of a few minutes!

That evening while having a cigarette alone, I got to hear Senator Ted Kennedy speak on the back of his yacht *Myla*, I think. Wow, it was like hearing a Kennedy speak from the 1960s! The race T-shirts were deemed to have been disrespectful to participants in AA as well as the LGBTQ community, it was pointed out to me in a public place; Providence's T. F. Green Airport.

Voyage 78: *Eclipse*, Bristol-Newport-Bristol RI

Lots of fun short sails and general maintenance work with friend Zach on this yacht, *Eclipse*, the *Swan* 42 he lived on. Zach was a groomsman in our wedding in Newport. Others put a lot more time into maintaining and sailing *Eclipse* than I did, yet he was still very generous in introducing me to join the NY Yacht Club. I salvaged a dinghy from my law school campus on Mount Hope Bay after a hurricane and tied it to the roof of my Saab. I had to drain and drag the thing uphill on a campus filled with healthy young people who did not help me. Then crossing the Mount Hope Bridge in a Nor'easter I was afraid car and all would be sucked off the bridge by a gust! It sank on the tether at Lee Wharf where I lived. Once back home, I christened it *Harbour Courtship* as a way to thank him for getting me into Harbour Court. After we tied it to a pier, afloat, we inadvertently abandoned it where the bike Cornelius has been abandoned in 1993. It is probably a barnacle today.

Where Echo Yacht Deliveries was run, overlooking Lee Wharf, IYRS, the old Armchair Sailor Bookstore, near Gary's Handy Lunch, the new Armchair Sailor, Zelda's, O'Brien's, IYAC, several marinas including Casey's, and Oldport Marine Services where I worked. This was base from 1998 when I returned from Singapore to mid-2001, when I moved just half a dozen buildings up the street, to 28 Young Street, closer to the Newport Public Library, which was my base until early 2005, after we were married, then moved to Boston and Norwalk. It was not unusual for sailors, clients, fishermen and women, to see the banner and pop in – not all of them between 9 to 5; I had the option of finding out who was there by opening the French Doors on the second floor and looking down. Newport is, after all, known as 'a drinking town with a sailing problem.'

June 17, 2003 Bunker Hill, Charlestown, Suffolk County. Boston. Zach Cutler won second sunset drinks at the New York Yacht Club at Harbor Court rather than losing and hosting us at his place. Zach third 7 pm. Two hours crew. *Eclipse,* Zach Cutler.

Voyage 79: *Regimen*, Islip, Long Island, NY-Portsmouth, RI

Fun short voyage, stayed on the boat at the family dock in Islip, south Long Island, New York, Chad did most of the work, frankly, but we took turns. Gentle swell, no traffic, no worries, good company, cold food but hot coffee. And pay. Sunny and clear, stereo on, a great experience. That what preparation, a good owner, and having a fellow captain you know well can bring.

September 10, 2004, Friday. Log: Both crew aboard 9.30 pm. 10 pm engine tested, oil, transmission, coolant filter okay.

September 11, 2004, Log, MV *Regimen*, Legacy 28-foot, Yanmar 300-horsepower, Bayshore, Islip Long Island, New York, to Brewers Sakonnet, Rhode Island. Captain Eric, Chad Jackson mate, from Yawgoo Mountain ski resort, owned by his family, in Rhode Island, and Middletown Connecticut. At 6 am, main engine on. 06:15 am main engine off, all well, shore power off. 6:30 am under way, all fuel tanks full, engine 3,402 hours. 7:19 am cleared Fire Island Inlet. 11:15 am rounded Montauk to port. All well. 2 pm around Brewers Sakonnet Marina. Hailed VHF channels 72, 74, 71 then 9 am to 2:30 pm, berthed outside B, the T-shaped pier, at pump out. 3 pm berthed a 30-foot slip with the help of Joe, stern to starboard side, finished with engines. Called Roe O'Brien told only one fender. Washdown, crew returns to Newport. Save voyage log books.

Voyage 80: *La Mer*, Padanaram MA-Newport

A good friend, captain, engineer, former cop, invited me on this trip for a very friendly full time owner and it was uneventful as they should be. Good weather, some issue with the anchor, great company, paid promptly, no drama, all good. I worked for Jack again and he introduced me to Maiwenn. She is a fellow captain, and provided critical shore support for McKenna 57', has worked on commercial fishing boats, and a Welsh woman, has more licenses and experience than many of the sailors I know. She's worked in the Falklands on a fishing boat. Jack is close with my son and his mother as well. He famously was driving to Seattle with the boat when I got a call from the US Coast Guard:

"Sir are you sailing at 60 miles an hour across the Dakotas?"

I called Jack to say his EPIRB device must have shaken loose and been giving a global signal of distress form a very land locked area! Solved. Switched off.

I've met and caught up with Jack in Newport, Boston, Connecticut, Seattle, NY, FL and beyond, and would go anywhere with him. He's also a very talented engineer and inventor who holds patents in the automotive space. The kind of person you want running your vessel, who also happens to be quiet and unassuming.

Chapter 18

Voyage 81: *Ranger*, Eliot Maine-Portsmouth, RI

October 5, 2004, Log of MV *Ranger* for yacht broker Roe O'Brien. Mate, Tango. Port engine hours, starboard; 1,064, 1,052. Port engine 1,067, 1,061.6. Port generator 1,030, starboard generator 10,523. 1,067. Enquires star 1,066.4 1,064 port. Log trip 63.76 and about 80 part. Log total 843 nm. Total trip is 146 nm. New owner. 1987-built, 43-feet length overall. Delivery log MV *Ranger*, Eliot Maine, Sakonnet Brewers Marina in Portsmouth, just north of Tiverton, Rhode Island. Captain, me, mate, Tango.

October 11, 2004, Voyage log: Monday. 9:30 am, MV *Ranger*, a 43-foot power yacht, engines on. After systems checks, familiarization and engine warm-up, at 10:30 am, clear Great Cove Boat Club, Kittery, Maine. This was a family job, and Tango's sister drove us from North Shore Boston to Maine for this delivery to Portsmouth, Rhode Island early. The weather was blowing a strong gale but 95% of it would be behind us, so we went for it. Total log; 696.8 nm. With a 40-knot tailwind I decided we could power from the Maine-NH border to Newport quickly and without incident in a 40+ foot twin-diesel power boat that was just sold (and stripped of equipment). It was late October, and we were the only boat out there. Abreast Isle of Shoals, New Hampshire. RPM [propeller shaft revolutions per minute] up to 3,100. Boat speed up to 23.5 knots. 2:45 pm, starboard prop snagged by over 50 feet of 6-inch Manila hawser line.

We had almost made the Cape Cod Canal when a 6"-thick polypropylene towing line seized one of our engines. Problem was, there wasn't a tool on board the boat. Starboard engine off. Realizing what tasks lay ahead, and limited crew and tools, and foul weather on a lee shore highly trafficked, I put out a Pan-Pan message (for *Panne*, or breakdown in French), to US Coast Guard, Cape Cod Canal on VHF channel 16. It's between Mayday (*M'aidez*, for help me) and *Sécurité*, for safety. In 6-8' seas and freezing water I calculated the time I could last before hypothermia set in, and jumped in to clear the line. I had just a pair of keys and, later, a small Swiss Army knife. The prop, jerking back and forth on the anchor, hit me in the face, and the hull, bouncing up and down, crowned me on the head repeatedly. The mate sensibly ignored the Coast Guard's replies asking for clarification on the radio. Instead he gave me his totally undivided attention. It's very dangerous to cut the hawser off the propeller, yet necessary to regain reliable propulsion in a gale on a lee shore.

After swimming with a pen-knife for about 7 minutes and sustaining lacerations to hands and blows to the head by hull and propeller as the boat jerked wildly at anchor, I had to get out and find better tools, using my car keys. It's because the boat was sold "stripped" that we had insufficient tools. After 18 minutes I was already turning blue and the mate insisted I get out of the water.

A huge, rusty fishing boat kindly diverted to help. We had to tell the very helpful fishermen which came by to assist that we were fine. I waved them off, and thanked them via VHF later. Finally, at 2:50 pm the 50-foot hawser was on board. The line was cleared from the prop, but then the anchor stuck and the windlass broke - all with the breakwater a few hundred feet alee. We got the anchor at the cost of a lobster pot, while taking turns being immersed on the foredeck. We had nearly lost the skipper and boat yards from shelter. Looking back, we could have limped into shelter on one engine, but I was afraid that then both would seize on the line; sod's law dictates that what can go wrong will go wrong, and we would have placed ourselves in a significant disadvantage in rough seas.

2:55 pm, anchored in position 41°78'.6N, 70°48'.4W. 3 pm, captain in water with knife to clear prop. 3:20 pm, hawser cut free from starboard prop shaft. 3:25 pm, hailed by US Coast Guard, Cape Cod Canal on VHF channel 16, then we stepped up to channel 22. At 3:30 pm, starboard engine all well. Began hoisting anchor. At 3:45 pm the anchor windlass power supply light indicates it is off. 4:15 pm; generator having trouble shifting, so hand-hauled anchor up. At 4:25 pm we entered Cape Cod Canal. Engine running fine. By 5.30 pm we were clear of Cape Cod Canal, Onset Massachusetts, RPM up to 3,200, boat speed up to 23 knots.

At 7.30 pm we rounded Sakonnet Light, Schuyler Ledge and began one of the toughest parts of the voyage, since all the heavy wind and waves that had been behind us all day were now in our face, blinding us with spray. It was cold, very dark, heavy drenching, not great Radar coverage, and neither of us have ever transited up the Sakonnet River, which while deep and wide, has islands and rocks in it. Also, Tango and I were tired, pretty emotionally drained from earlier events, and getting hungry and cold to boot.

At 8.45 pm entered narrow, current-riddled pass between a new and a destroyed bridge, with Tiverton to starboard, and Portsmouth to port. By 8:55 pm were clear of old swing bridge. At 9 pm entered Brewers' North Marina in Cedar Island Pond, aka Safe Harbor Sakonnet, looking for free berths, but finding none. Bumped stern backing in and out. We then called the marina on VHF channel 9, no reply. At 9:20 pm were clear of North Marina. 9:30 pm, docked outside, sewer pump port station, cell called.

Here I will say the electronics were amazing, as they showed every foot of our progress on a bright color screen, in high-definition, preventing my running aground. 9:45 pm, unberth south dock, went around to north dock again. 9:50 pm, we re-entered North Marina. 10 pm berthed in haul-out slip on the advice of Joe, night manager. By 10:10 pm we were finished with engines, all well. We then slept on only warm items we could find; moth-eaten old blankets used as drop-cloths for painting in the boat yard. They had bedbugs or fleas from pets, and were not comfortable, but I wanted to get the extra half-day's pay by staying on board till handover.

October 24, 2004, our wedding, in Newport! During the ring ceremony at St. George's School chapel, my ring finger and hands were still cut up from clearing line from *Ranger*'s prop.

Voyage 82: *Tangerine,* Bermuda–Marion MA, June

This was the cautionary tale against having the crew be all the owner's friends. No one listened to me, the captain who had dropped into Bermuda, they deferred to an alpha executive talking about CEO stuff and human resources benefits. Meanwhile the radio antennae just fell off at the outset, the boom vang dropped to the deck with no pin, and all kinds of other mishaps. I said a gallon of water per person per day, the CEO dufus kept hosing down the head after showering, so we ran out of water. Despite over 30 voyages to or from Bermuda, admittedly this time I was distracted and not navigating in the Stream well, so the owner's kids could see our signal online and second-guess us, he wanted me to go between Nantucket and the Vineyard abut I refueled, we ended up in Marion, the crew didn't help me clean the boat or laundry, only the youngest crew had any sympathy for me.

As for the older fellows, they all figured I'd screwed up, and on the navigation side perhaps I did as a boat which left after us arrived the same time as us. It was a miserable disaster and I got a lift to the bus station to take the Peter Pan to Fall River and Newport, and the owner had to limp along very tilted over on his final voyage as we filled the water tanks but could not open tanks on one side to balance the boat. *Urgh!*

May 27, 2005, Randy of *Tangerine*: we are to go to No-Man's-Island behind Martha's Vineyard. Tuckernuck? Six persons plastic life-raft. Hydraulic autopilot. Triple-reef, roller furling in storm. Marion, where brother James and good friend Kent studied and we played them from St. George's, by Thursday June 16 or June 15. 40-foot *Legacy*. Bermuda. Depart Newport to Bermuda. Hyannis Yacht Club pick double pendant. Mooring of Randy. Visas. Crew: Wiberg, Tommy and Frankie, age 48, Bob, 54, and Jim, 24 years. I boat track dot com. 60 minutes of cell phone, $1.39 per min, $1.59 per minute. Global Marine Travel. Sold Echo Yacht on account briefly prefer to book myself. Newport and North Shore Boston; look for friend Cameron in Bermuda: Bermuda; *Sky High*. Lower house, *Sky Lark*. We met at the RBYC. Voyage logs. Callsign WDB *XXX*. Bermuda to Marion, Massachusetts, after race. Yacht SY *Tangerine*. Eaglebrook friend Forster, Pitts Bay Road, Pembroke. Herb Hilgenberg, *Southbound II* free weather routing.

June 26, 2005, *Day 1: Southbound II*. Some thunderstorms in stream Tuesday. Heavier winds Wednesday. Frontal band along coast 30°N Cape Cod. Build from SW 20 to 25 knots west. An associated low-pressure system is moving south from the Gulf of St. Lawrence. North of 40°N, SW to 25 knots and two mild days. Strong wind pattern starts Wednesday. 35°N by 65°46'W, current. 37°N by 68°W to 36°N and 30°N by 65°W. Easterly set current by Monday morning 36°N not well defended 37°30'N with a NW set.

Gulf Stream meander east, set current to 37°N, then current north to NNW at 39°N and 67°W. So, keep going, north is windy and rain 32°52'N by 69°51'W, current set 7 knots to SSE and then SSW 35°N at 3 knots. Tuesday SW winds, high through US, isolated squalls. End up Wednesday north of 39°N in 20 to 25 knots of wind. Entry: 37°56'N and 69°5'W, in SSW winds and favorable current, to 35°N. *Shearwater*.

June 27, 2005, Monday. *Day 2*: Herb *Tangerine*. East to SE in the Gulf Stream current. Eight knots easterly meander gone 38°N, 65°W and, 36°40'N, Tuesday light southerly southeasterly. In north end of Gulf Stream 15-20 knots by Tuesday pm, June 29 into Wednesday June 30, with large low-pressure system in the Gulf of St. Lawrence. Frontal boundary Wednesday SW 15-20 knots could go 20-25 knots. Buzzard's Bay. This severe gale force conducting 30 knots wind Thursday into Friday. This will affect *God Spell* and *Lindy's Leap*. 34°53'N, 66°45'W. SE light 37°47'N, 69°43'W.

June 28, 2005, *Day 3:* From 4 pm to 7 pm Zulu Herb, *Lindy's Leap* on. Our position is 37°N, 67°25'W, 38°5'N by 68°5'W. Strongest wind. Thursday 20-25 knots in the am. 41°N by 65°W to 33°N, 70°W to 30°N by 74°W. Pre-frontal boundary, variable, west of 36°N gale conditions in Gulf Stream. South to SSW, approached Newport Friday 15-20 to 25 knots increase to 42 knots up 15-20 knots. Stronger wind, Thursday afternoon. *Ariel* to 36°10'N, 69°32'W, 25 miles from Gulf Stream, 36°30'N by 70°W to pleasant crossing up 15 knots slowly building winds Wednesday am to Thursday. 20 knots, wind speed is up, lull, NW to west fill in from south. Front crosses Buzzards Bay. Cold eddy 2.5 to 3.5 knot drift 210° 35°40'N by 69°10'W. *Shearwater*, 36°33'N to 61°30'W, 34°N by 64°W. 7 pm to 4 pm, and 3-5 am. Log. *Tangerine*.

Bermuda to Marion. Commander's Weather, run by founder Ken Campbell in New Hampshire. Boat cell 37°48'.2N, 68°02'.4W. Friend Kent is a member. Buzzard's Bay, 39°05'N by 68°55'W, big wash to NE. Four and one hour. Harden up 39°N, 69°30'W. 70°W separated. Over eddy storm, squalls. East of eddy hauled by SW wind. ETA to 40°N, cold front is mid-day Saturday. SW and southerly, 3-5 knots north, so take care of thick fog. US Customs Inspector in Hyannis cell phone and office. Have deal. Took bus to Newport via Fall River alone. Mattapoisett, at entry to Cape Cod Canal. McQuaid 1-hour heads up. To Bequia Island, Grenadines, southeast Caribbean. Burton's Boatyard, Town Dock, little South Office in New Bedford, leave recall 55-footer Newburyport to Barnegat 46-foot *Hunter*.

Retrospective: I had long dreamed of being given command of a boat and a crew that I had never met or worked with. I imagined laconically telling them in Bermuda "let's get this tub out of here," before nonchalantly pushing off for Newport. When finally I got to live out this fantasy of sorts, the reality proved jarringly disappointing. It was to be my 31st Bermuda voyage, and has proved to be my last since. The owner had lost his job in the post-9/11 downsizing and had contracted to sell the factory-made boat after doing one last Bermuda race. To save costs, he insisted on only hiring one person for the delivery: me. The rest were volunteers. One was a former colleague and his brother-in-law who was the CEO of a mid-size firm and a kind of a proxy for the owner. No one except me had sailed from Bermuda. I had insisted that the owner offer his neighbor's son a berth, as felt needed at least one compliant "yes man" aboard. The other crew had raced down and was modest and helpful but a passive presence aboard.

Introductions: In Bermuda, as pre-arranged, I waited at the airport for the crew to assemble there, in part to consolidate the taxi cost. One by one they slipped passed me and hopped into separate cabs to go to the yacht club, where i finally tracked them down. I rehearsed them ad-nauseam about my undocking procedure, outlining each person's role, only to have the owner spring aboard, grab the wheel, cast off a few lines, and start moving. This sent all of us scrambling.

On the passage to St. George's we did a Man Overboard drill during which I felt compelled to step in and work the traveler. The main sheet was let go in my hands, and it badly burned my fingers. Confidentially, I told the owner that he needed to let go and let me do the job he had hired me to do, I explained that it wouldn't do the crew much good to learn his management style, but rather, on the eve of his departure it would be helpful if they learned mine. But it was an opportunity lost. In the eyes of a mostly older crew I had been publicly upstaged by one of their contemporaries.

Once we were berthed, I tried to interest the crew in the town or the boat. Instead, the CEO immediately held forth on a group-wide discussion of IRA benefits, pensions, and corporate mumbo-jumbo that had no relevance at all to our tasks ahead, but was squarely in his comfort zone. I didn't break in, but instead broke away for a swim. The morning of our departure I encouraged everyone to stretch their legs with me by taking a scenic walk - they thought I was nuts, or worse, and none joined.

The paperwork necessitated my being separated from the crew much of the time. We hardly knew each other until we were underway together. Departure: We raised sail in the protected lagoon in St. George's and cleared out with Harbor Patrol via VHF. We hung out some bunting, reefed the main and headsail, and breezed through the narrow channel with a farewell toot of the horn to the sailors lining the rail at the dinghy club; so far so good.

Things fall apart: There were no incoming cruise ships for us to moon, and soon we had shaken out our reefs and cleared the actual reefs into deep water. Immediately the "race-ready" boat began to literally fall apart. Within the space of five minutes under full sail the SSB and VHF radio antennae, ail 13+ feet of fiberglass Shake Spear (a great name), snapped at the base and fell into the sea. When we went too close the gate in the safety tines, the wire railing literally came off right into my hands. Next the vang, ostensibly holding the boom up, separated and crashed to deck. It was suddenly a triage situation.

The CEO created an ingenious sheathe from PVC piping and clamps for the antennae. I saved face by threading the pin of a shackle the wrong way to hold up the vang. It wasn't pretty, but it worked and restored some of my credibility. An inauspicious start, though.

I explained the watch system to the crew, added how a suggestion from the skipper is the equivalent of an order, and outlined our intended route. I permitted one shower per person for the whole trip.

Though we had no internet updates on board, unbeknownst to me our progress was being tracked, using a beacon on our transom, almost hourly by the owners family. By the third day the kids were screaming self-righteously and saying "don't go that way; *noooo!* You were almost out of the stream!" I was losing street-cred 500 miles away, and didn't know it, as we were beyond cell phone range. After nearly 24 hours in the stream the crew were exhausted, and I was concerned too. To ease the strain on boat and crew, I bore off for a few hours to run with wind and current that made our predicament worse. The low point was when, during my off-watch at about 4 am, the CEO shook me awake to point out his impression that a plot fix of mine from many hours before was inaccurate.

To humor them I had allowed the crew to plot our course on the chart in pencil after making bi-hourly log entries. I entered our actual position in ink, ignoring their sloppy work (l used protractors, they guesstimated with rulers, which shifted with the boat's motion. I knew that, they did not. I didn't tell them. The net result was that they believed their own erroneous data, and I had let them. Accustomed to behaving imperiously, this fellow had woken the skipper on a non-urgent matter during my valuable off-watch rest, to make an academic point in which he was wrong. Disgusted and angry, I explained his error and went back to sleep. I did not dress him down on it. The opportunity came after the stream, in light airs. I had given the 6-knot rule; if we fall below 6 knots, crack on the engine to make up for the deficiency in speed. We had been slating around for an hour making about 2 knots when I pounced into the cockpit from my bunk, fired up the engine, set it at 1,500 RPM, and went below in a silent huff.

This incident reminded me of three crew, each with his own GPS and ideas of how to exit the stream. I put the hammer down, reminding them that at least only one of us had to make the call. I pointed our bow to Bermuda and sped the engines. There is a comfort in the clarity of command and a risk of too much of a democracy. On the other hand, I've had skippers take a vote while underway on whether to proceed, and then respect the crew's input, whether it called for turning back or lunging onwards. On another voyage we were so engulfed by a dense squall and terrifying lightning that none of us, even using radar, know which direction it was coming or going. Finally I just pointed us towards our destination and sent the trusty Yanmar into turbo overdrive to get us out of danger.

Approach: We were all worn out from the stormy stream, and the CEO refreshed with a shower; a very long one. Unbeknownst to me, he was showering daily and then using the fresh water to clean and rinse the whole head area. By day five we were out of fresh water, with no way of replenishing it. He had disobeyed a strict instruction, in fact a generous allowance - and I did not openly reprimand him. He was teamed with his brother-in-law, and all of the crew but me had relationships to keep with the owner. In short, we were a Balkanized crew with conflicting loyalties. Having no common experience threshold bred suspicion and misunderstanding. I decided to just put up with it till the trip was over. Though difficult and frustrating, I still think this was better than a showdown over something we could not change. The crew, all of us deprived of showers, meted out a muted punishment as admonishment to him.

Arrival: It turned out that our very costly easting came to naught. The tidal rips between 'Tucket and the Vineyard combined with nightfall to eliminate that route as an option. Then the owner advised by cell phone that we could not clear immigration in Falmouth anyway, but a special post-race customs service was available in Marion, where the race originated. On arrival we tied up opposite from a yacht filled with some of the more condescending and unfriendly sailors I've met. They derided us for having taken so long and boasted having left Bermuda later than us and arrived sooner. "Why had we gone east?" they openly asked? To use the Muskeget Channel would be madness, they said. They gloated at having outsmarted a professional skipper. The fact that they were right did not assuage my fuming sense of disappointment.

The crew asked me what I expected of them, and I said they were to remove their belongings, shower if they must, then report back to wipe down their individual living spaces aboard with a mix of vinegar and water. With the exception of the youngest crew, they all raced to the showers and didn't return to wipe down the boat. Their consensus was that I was the only paid crew on board and they weren't going to do my job. To me a team wipe-down is a standard, if only a courteous, measure. It is what you do when you leave a boat. They would have none of it, so I did it for them. My lack of discipline had deprived them of showers and they took their sweet time taking them ashore. We just didn't see the same issue from the same perspective. On some boats the crew would clean up while the skipper took care of larger tasks such as clearing in and arranging food, fuel, money, water, checking in with the owner, etc.

In the rush to get the boat ready for the owner, we filled up an empty water tank, but could not get one deck fitting open, it had been sealed tight for some time. The owner didn't care, as he had already sold the boat. So he set off to solo the boat to Falmouth (perhaps to avoid paying me for an extra 12 hours or so) with a very lopsided boat. It was not a sight to be proud of, and not a stable-looking deck. He would be in full view to summer traffic. This reminded me of the owners who insisted we hand their boat to them ASAP after arrival in the BVI, with the result that they spent the first week of their holiday with three weeks' worth of the delivery crew's dirty linen.

Postscript: We said farewells. I could already imagine the CEO boasting that he wouldn't take orders from a kid. guess in his mind he outsmarted me. The crew who raced down gave me a ride to the depot. He told me he thought I did a good job, and was upset at the lack of cooperation I received. I took a bus home. It was a humbling and humiliating last hurrah for me, made worse by my navigational hubris and my failure to instill a proper team spirit and discipline. My own cockiness, an impulse to outsmart the rest of the fleet (on what was, after all, a delivery and not a race), had cost my crew and I more hours at sea in a hostile environment; indeed in the Gulf Stream itself. This is exactly what a good skipper minimizes, instead I had maximized our time in the capricious stream.

Whatever its shortcomings, I had kept a frail boat and an untested crew out longer than I should have to test my navigational mettle, and had failed. I could have foregone a walk ashore in Bermuda in order to get the best and latest Gulf Stream imagery. I consoled myself that, by covering a lot more ground we had actually gone faster than the boat which beat us in, but that defies my rule of "the shorter the voyage, the safer" and was hardly a palliative. My main consolation is that no one was hurt, and the only bruises were to my ego. The rest, the emotional element, the team spirit, the blame game, came secondary to that priority, at least on a short passage. On a longer voyage, my authority might not have recovered, just as the water supply would not have been replenished. As a delivery skipper, I strive always for the most uneventful voyage possible.

Irony: On this trip there had been no refueling missions off Bermuda, no shark attacks or whale strikes, no conversations with rescue aircraft or spotting of derelict boats and no high-seas exchanges of Bermudian rum for American cigarettes with draggers on the continental shelf, as on other voyages. I set out on this swan-song of a voyage hoping that my impressionable crew would learn something. Instead it was I that hit a learning curve, and I'm not particularly proud of what that crew are likely to have taken away from my leadership style, or lack thereof. Hopefully they took more than the empty water cups on offer.

For me this trip is summed up by me sitting in an empty bus stop with my sea bag, alone.

Voyage 83: *Endearment,* Newport-Portsmouth

An afternoon voyage, anchored and swam. Two nightclub owners from Nashville apparently owned it. Great fun, west of Prudence Island off Newport, with the maid of honor, our friend the good captain, fiancé and her mother. Anchor, swims, and chill.

Voyage 84: *Kikynos*, Portsmouth RI-Portland, ME

Who is the captain? The owner sent me aboard this large *Swan* yacht which had a good reputation for aggressive racing in order for me to "observe" his full-time captain. I assumed I was to be the lead, asked for and was paid the captain's wage, and when I went to the boat I acted as a skipper would towards a crew. However, when the real skipper, who I knew from the IYAC, showed up, he quickly fixed my attitude. Assuring me that he was in full command, he introduced me to his Dad, a Pan Am pilot, who had even more gravitas! Turns out that we had a great time, and the owner was none the wiser.

Folks sometimes play mind games which require the participants in the games suspending common sense and volition. As for myself, I was more than happy to work and stress a lot less for the same wage for a few days. I later ran into the real skipper at a food court near Downtown Crossing in Boston, behind the Orpheum Theater, on Washington Street.

Voyage 85: *Bellatrix*, Newport-Wilson's Creek, Norwalk CT

Took the wrong boat. Only found out when the owner told us the slip number. It went like this: we were told to take the boat in the late afternoon from such-and-such marina, and it was a 35-foot sailing sloop. This marina, off West Street in Newport, was pretty shallow, so most of the boats were that size. We were in a bit of a rush to make the tide, and the boats were all docked the easy way – ass-end-out, meaning we could not read the name on the transom, except with great awkwardness and in a flat-calm sea, or from shore... you get the idea.

Almost all keys are kept in the same place (don't tell anyone, but under the binnacle cover or on a hook in the starboard lazarette, or in a dorade vent). Thank goodness this owner didn't put it any of those places, and we called the owner a bit perturbed. He finally explained the right slip number, and boat name, neither of which matched the boat we were on! From acting like we owned it, we hopped off the boat quite quickly. What a mess that would have been, if we delivered the wrong boat!

I was very clear that in the flat boring coast between Point Judith and the start of Fisher's Island, I was going to lay down, to be woken when we passed Westerly, Rhode Island. Trying to be nice, the mate let me sleep an extra hour. Suddenly I was startled awake in The Race when he shook me hard and told me he could see a strange light which he could not interpret. I dashed on deck in the dark to see as a man on his front lawn frantically waving a torch light. He was screaming to get out of his private cove in Fisher's Island; he was trying to help us as well as prevent big drama on his huge lawn! Dashing to the wheel, and knowing nothing about our predicament except that behind us must be safe, for us to have made it that far without running aground, I did a U-turn post-haste and tried to delete the track on the computer once we were clear.

The owner is super nice. On arrival we were met by a kindly uncle and had a lunch at Rowayton Seafood on the charming Five Mile River. Hurricane Katrina was playing out during all this voyage, as was my birthday.

Voyage 86: *Williwaw*, Newport RI-Larchmont NY

Young Polish girl. Never been to New York City but heading back to Warsaw in a few days. Our indefatigable leader is Jack again (same as *La Mer* earlier), and he knows the boat's systems and handling characteristics as well as anyone afloat, since he's both an engineer and captain. We arrive after anxious passage down Long Island's notoriously strong currents, and the owner insists we be given a hot eggs breakfast by the Filipina cook.

Then this thoughtful fellow mariner let us borrow a car of his to see New York City and we go to Rue 57 the patisserie and restaurant near Central Park South and have a great time, then head home. Great! And the owner is an aficionado of maritime memorabilia and self-made shipping man, importer and terminal owner. Cool indeed.

Chapter 19

Voyage 87: *Alpine*, Shelter Island, NY-Block Island-Wickford, RI

Was in a passenger van from LaGuardia airport to the Seafarer's International House in Manhattan when a client called the number for my yacht delivery agency, Echo Yacht Delivery, late one fall. He was going through a divorce, needed his mid-sized sailing yacht moved from New York to Rhode Island's Narragansett Bay, and would only do it with me, the founder. Usually such requests were only made by folks with large yachts on blue-water passages, say to the Caribbean, and that was normally all I would take, but I joined him.

We got along well, he was a tax attorney anxiously discussing the logistics of a large divorce settlement with international assets (hiding funds in Central American real estate only to have it quadruple in value). We partied in Greenport Long Island, then caught the last ferry to Shelter Island, and had the next day after coffee and pastries in cold windy weather, a lousy, spray-filled passage to Block Island. After a rest in spacious, not-quite-lonely New Harbor, then on to Wickford, on the mainland. It was humbling to have to step down a bi to a wide bodied production boat in heavy cold wind right on the nose and not even be able to just power through it. Exasperating and a fairly novel sensation after many years.

He and I were actually pretty close for a few weeks; I stayed at his place in Manhattan, visited his new place in Boston, and even invited him to my in-law's Christmas party to which he did not show. They say sailboat cruising is the art of following the wind-indicating arrow to where you are going; in other words, going straight into opposing winds. Another silly expression is that cruising on a boat is simply "repairing your yacht in interesting countries."

"Nothing goes upwind like a Boeing 747," or the captain's counter to the owner racing to, say, Bermuda, Halifax, Block Island, Fastnet, Fernando de Naronha, Gotland, wherever the offshore destination is that is their first away from land.

"Just look around you sir, or madam," the captain says, sweeping the horizon for miles around, with no land: "Everything you see, you own!"

An awkward pause, then the owner whimpers;

"But, I still can't see land, and I'm feeling seasick and panicky."

To which the heartless skipper replies beguilingly:

"Not to worry! Land is a mere mile away from us right now."

"But where?" blathers the once-mighty owner....

"Right down there," says the captain, pointing a sun-tanned finger at the sea's surface, beneath the boat: "but they say you only feel the first hundred feet."

Admiral Lord Horatio Nelson once famously replied to the question of how to avoid seasickness, from which he suffered his life-long career:

"Sit beneath a tree."

Here are two radically different yachting reactions to not being able to spend time with your spouse. Before AIS, one maritime and divorce law strategy was to use a power boat to pull a rigged sailboat sideways, so it was lower, and slide it under a tall bridge as though in a limbo move in country club. The idea is that opposing counsel will only look in those marinas below bridges too low to allow the boat under. That way the owner can avoid letting the ex-spouse during a divorce seize the asset, preventing them from preventing him or her the use and enjoyment on the yacht.

Here's another version. I was working in corporate recruiting in Cos Cob, Connecticut and eating lunch along the Mianus River, alone. A well-known Norwegian shipowner and skipper named Oddvar Nygaard, but known mostly by his VHF handle Pappa Fish, kept his fleet there. I speak a smattering of Scandinavian and sea-speak, so I asked him about his tugboat, which has a woman's name. He told me simply that it was named for his wife, *Cayah*, and that when she died, he and a friend took the tug for a spin into the Hudson River, about 50 miles away. I ate another bit of his son's Vedar and Jagard's Fjord Fisheries sushi while digesting this small talk.

Then, Oddvar said, he and his buddy continued into the canal, and into the Great Lakes. *Aha*! I thought, my interest now piqued. This was no longer a day trip. Soon they took the 362-mile Erie Canal into the lakes Ontario, Erie, St. Clair, Huron and Michigan, and reached Chicago. Did they turn back? *Hell no!*, down the Mississippi they went, still getting over his beloved Cayah's death. New Orleans, no less, then Key West, and up the entire US East Coast. Eventually, over a year later, the tug returned that exact spot. I got the impression the vessel will remain pristine and rarely move. During Oddvar's lifetime I doubt it will either sell or be renamed. A year or two later a group of charter guests and I waited to board his larger boat to watch 12-Meter races. Since Oddvar was uncharacteristically late, I went down and looked into the main saloon where I was startled to see the good captain holding a boom handle and small anchor, his white captain's uniform completely soaked in fresh blood splatter.

"Raccoon in the galley," he explained with insouciance as he went to wash off before the guests arrived. I don't envy the US Marshalls sent to arrest Oddvar's fleet on behalf of Caterpillar Financial, and I certainly hope they didn't dress as raccoons.

Meanwhile my Boston-bound client on the tub battle fall gales in Narragansett Bay was going through a divorce and moving home and job to a new city. At the same time, I was leaving Newport for a new state to get married and find a career job. It was Christmas as well, so there were some silly drinking stories, less about which later.

Voyage 88: *J-40*, Day-racing, Riverside YC, Connecticut

Just racing around the buoys visible from my office opposite the Cos Cob MetroNorth Railway train station. Highlights were being treated at the Riverside Yacht Club to dark n' stormy Bermuda rum drinks with amiable Shep and Ian Murray, the founders and owners of the Vineyard Vines apparel line (I managed to repay the favor by helping to expose fraudulent knock-offs at a lacrosse tournament I attended out-of-state with family. Since I wouldn't take reimbursement for the samples I bought, Shep sent me a receipt for the books of mine they bought! Old school....).

Low-points were that I was still addicted to both nicotine (smoking cigarettes) as well as alcohol. I noticed disapproving looks from the skipper when I would sidle over fences to take calls on the cell in the garden in violation of club rules, sneak out for cigarettes, and in general drink too much. I have no doubt that this – justifiably – led to my "not being invited back," as the euphemism goes.

Voyage 89: *Kamchatka*, Bermuda-Newport

Tossing a coin at midnight and flying to Bermuda against your spouse's wishes to take a sailing yacht to Newport, leaving her with a newborn child is *not* the best recipe for marital bliss, even if you were unemployed and made some money.

My good friend Dermot called me after the financial Bear Stearns collapse of 2008 and I was unemployed. Said a Canadian client was finishing a multi-year round-world family voyage and needed a hand for the final leg Bermuda to Newport. St. George's Bermuda is one of my favorite places, since I started my bank of coins in the cliffs overlooking Tobacco Bay there at age 18.

I rationalized to myself, I had the offer and skill, wanted to earn a bit of money for the family, and could do with a healthy outdoor activity to take my mind off the rat race in a rat race. So I discussed with my wife at the time, she was confused and against it, by the time she came home I had already booked the tickets, I said I was willing to risk the yes/no on a coin toss. It was 10 am I won and at 5 am was heading to Bermuda via the airports.

Mistake, as most of you reading already know: my mother sure did!

The trip ruined my (now former) spouse's week and her mother's as well, and starting on the bus from the airport to the boat I was barraged and inundated with angry calls, guilt trips, threats, and all manner of unpleasantries. Thanks to the wonders of communication, these continued throughout the voyage, which was the only smooth an uneventful part of the experience.

Leaving St. George's Bermuda for Newport aboard *Kamchatchka* in 2008, for my last offshore sailing passage..

    The owner turned down a chance to stop at my yacht club to cap off his round-world voyage and instead went to an industrial marina where under the watchful eye of several superyacht stewardesses he completely choked the docking, managing after about 15 minutes to get us close enough to get a line ashore without damage. That was about it.
    I remember good cereal for breakfast and lunch, a comfortable cabin and yacht, great sea stories and good company, and considerable trepidation on all of our parts about going home! I took my lumps on the chin on arrival and was told the payment I received was nothing compared to the costs I incurred, and despite over 31 Bermuda voyages, in the 15 years since I have never sailed to or from Bermuda – even as a single man!
    Dermot commented "I didn't realize that you got so much grief for doing that trip! I enjoyed it. Remember the AIS plot with USS *Enterprise*, 700' wide! I think that was your first trip with AIS, or automatic identification system. It was just Dermot, the owner and me, unusual for a Gulf Stream crossing, but then again each crew was an experienced captain.
    I met a Swedish single-handed sailor in Panama about 2010 who recounted living his dream of motoring up the interior of a mysterious river in West Africa, the only sound being that of the jungle and the hum of his hand-made boat's motor. He was entranced, euphoric. He had forgotten to turn off his cell phone in all the rapture, and when it rang for emergencies only from his girlfriend in Stockholm, he picked it up, concerned.
    The washing machine at home had broken.
    PS: In the dozen years since, I have never been offshore in a sailboat.

Voyage 90: *Allure*, Old Saybrook-Norwalk CT

Some buddies and I drove up to the Connecticut River where it meets the Long Island Sound one September afternoon to move the boat from eastern to western Connecticut, where the tides are the biggest player in The Race between Fishers Island and Plum Island. Our first turn out of the Connecticut River took us past a small lighthouse and Fenwick, inhabited by Katherine Hepburn herself, and a place our son was later fond of crabbing. With a lunch packed of fried chicken and lots of soft drinks, we nursed our respective hangovers or celebrated a few hours out of the marital and parental home by taking a lovely voyage down the sound to the boat's home-port.

The vessel, now positioned in Palm Beach with its owner, operates a bit as a cooperative, with team members and crew helping with large maintenance projects like caulking and overhaul as well as cleaning, in exchange for which they get to go deep sea fishing off Montauk, Long Island, Block Island, and right on down to Florida. I was honored to be able to help as a crew this day, and our captain, owner and host was as generous and gracious as ever, in the communal way his fishing boat operated.

When the trip was over and I had hosed down I offered to stick around and help but the tight core of crew dismissed me. By the bye, I had a nightmare that I was sinking on a sailing yacht between New England and Bermuda in the fall (not too far-fetched given over 30 Bermuda voyages, mostly from New England in summer, winter or fall), and I grabbed the radio and spoke to the same skipper of *Allure* – in my dream – and told him I was out, but he should marry my widow and raise our son!

Voyage 91: *Water Taxis*, Boston Harbor Cruises, August, 2019-March, 2000

Between August 30, 2019 when I started, and March 23, 2020, when COVID-19 shut down all operations of Boston Harbor Cruises in this storied Massachusetts harbor, I was trained aboard half a dozen Oldport launches called water taxis, then operated my own vessel throughout the winter. Sent out at about 6.30 am every day of the winter, four similar sized water taxis (some larger *Catalina* Boats to service the anchored fleet on the *Catalina* Islands off Los Angeles) would set out on a shift until about 2 pm. Then a new boat would leave the base in Mystic inlet for Long Wharf at the Boston Marriott for the handover, and take over the boats until 10 pm, at which point they would clean them down and by 4.30 pm the original watch was gearing up to resume.

My boat could carry 25 or so passengers, including bicycles, luggage, and pets, with a bow area as well. There were about 24 stops between Seaport, Logan Airport, Spaulding Hospital in Charlestown, the Toronto Dominion Bank Garden (formerly Boston Garden at North Station), and Reel House restaurant at Whitten Point in East Boston. I enjoyed it and found time to write and publish a photo book named *Boston Harbor*. The boats I operated were often named for members of the owning family (we were sold to the largest passenger vessel operator in the US when I was there). *Gina, Bonnie, Andrea*, and *Lynda* were some examples.

Since I had worked for the manufacturer of many of the boats, Oldport Marine in Newport, on and off for seven years during graduate school, I was familiar with the boats and the faithful grey bullet-proof Japanese Yanmar diesel as well; it can warm the boat with the hatch open or head dinner by placing tins on the engine. Truly magnificent machines! To find out if they are healthy all one has to do is study the exhaust; light grey? Healthy. Dark black? Problems.

There were excitements, like nearly being run over by a tractor tug late at night while emailing an ex-girlfriend (he turned on his searchlights and yelled at me on loudspeaker since my radio was on mute), the stern sinking down so that a large party of Boston College graduates celebrating a bridal shower or hen party of some sort had their lovely shoes soaked in salt water, and very friendly commuters who would remember our names. There was the rescue of another boat with something in the engine intake for which I was criticized for towing him in backwards, and lots of dangerous debris to hit.

Overall I would estimate with four shifts a week, 25 passengers a day, over just under seven months, I would have carried around 750 passengers, bearing in mind that the August and September time frames were still good weather and officially summer much of the time, with many more passengers. I called urgently on the radio when I saw a mid-size passenger ship going in reverse down the harbor on an August day, only to be asked why the hell I didn't mind my own business. That captain was let go that day; he was on a dangerous lark. Wildlife included all kinds of seals, birds (from gulls to egrets to ducks, Canadian Geese, cormorants, Eider Ducks, warblers, and Razorbills; ornithologists rode with us daily) and others reported a whale and harbor dolphins. Here is my brief introduction to the book:

The idea for this project came on a whim as a way to thank my employers for giving me a chance to get back on the water as the captain of a smallish passenger vessel going to 24 different docks around Boston Harbor. My fellow captains and I start out solo before dawn and have two shifts going till ten in the night, in all weather. I started taking photos of birds, seals, old wharves, new and old buildings and so on. I shied away from photos of people out of professional courtesy, and because this book celebrates a workaday way of life which is new to many readers; and yet which employs thousands of men and women on the water, most of them federally licensed, whether ship's pilots, deckhands, cooks or servers, or captains.

The daily commuters are part of that waterborne fabric. Also this is not about a waterfront so much as being on the water itself; seeing the City of Boston and it's people and activities from the water itself; away from it, yet part of it, and helping it's people get to and from work, from the airport, hospitals, sports games and concerts, hotels and marinas. For several passengers it is the first time in a boat, and for many it is a very special time of their day, month, or year. We witness proposals and take people to weddings as well as wakes.

Over a 30-year maritime career I began with racing sailboats for Boston College on the Charles River and around Logan Airport, then racing to Annapolis and Bermuda. Over the years I raced and delivered some 130 vessels, mostly sailboats, as well as power, to many countries, from New Zealand to Sweden. Then I became a fleet operator from shore of tanker ships, with a dabble in dry-bulks ships. I then had various mostly sales roles representing salvage tugs and barges and workboats, and tractor tugs. Working for a leading bulk shipping newspaper that covered every kind of watercraft which could float enabled me to travel widely, mostly between Athens and Vancouver.

Years as a part-time launch driver taking folks between their boats and shore in Newport for Oldport Marine during graduate school sparked an idea when I returned to Boston unexpectedly to be near our son in mid-2019. As I explored Boston Harbor from a base on Eagle Hill in East Boston, I was drawn to the types of equipment which people operate around the clock in Boston Harbor, including bridges, dredges, fire boats and police boats. There are whole teams working round the clock as engineers on the vessels and buildings, as bridge operators and dispatchers, on payroll and balancing the day's revenues, calling from hotels to send passengers aboard, and graciously providing places of shelter and relief to mariners around the harbor. Without them, the boats and their captains could not operate, serving as just one example a region without pipelines for its fuel and gas for all rolling stock, cars, trucks, planes, and gas for building and oil for power generation.

This book aims to be unusual; there is very little text, as the images are meant to be self-explanatory. Themes such as weather, geography, wind, snow, rain, fog and dark all become characters of sorts, as do the vessels themselves. Though the reader cannot hear the VHF radios cackle , and the slap of a ship's wake hitting one's boat, or the wind lifting and dropping awnings like the sigh of bellows, and the churn of a faithful propeller around the debris which is a constant threat to all but the biggest ships, the hope is that the images will provide some kind of tactile experience and exposure.

Inside each water taxi, a captain works alone in a little cocoon, but in tandem with a team of other captains, who then interact with dispatchers, supervisors, and the captains of myriad other craft, from survey boats to whale watchers, tugs, push-boats, oil-supply boats (called bunker barges), others carrying distillates like methanol, some anchored, some public safety boats whizzing by well lit, others rowing, or in fast dinghies, paddle boards, electric-powered boards, and little Sunfish, all being dodged by ferries to Hingham, Hull, Provincetown, Salem, the casino in Everett, commuter boats to Lovejoy and Constitution Wharf; massive cruise ships, LNG tankers, product tankers and articulated tug and barges; all in a day's work, and more.

There is a bit of the wide-eyed-wonder of *Katie and Big Snow* or *Mike Mulligan and His Steam Shovel* in this narrative. In April I moved to East Boston from the West Village in Manhattan where I'd been writing about German submarines besieging New England and leaving five never-found TMC-type mines between Graves Island and Nahant. I left Boston before the Big Dig was completed and was astounded at the difference between seeing the water taxi 'wars' off Logan Airport (which Massport ably suppressed), in the early 2000's and the fall months between August and mid-December in 2019. It is like a city revitalized, and utilizing the water to connect rather than separate its populace and many visitors.

Boston Harbor is an extraordinary and busy and lively and commercial place. It is also a danger-fraught region of the nations' waterways where global mega-ships carrying cargoes that range from cars to Egyptian salt to gypsum intermingle with cross-harbor water- taxis and water workers of all stripes and dialects; the radios convey a myriad of accents from far eastern to colloquial Boston and Charlestown; Braintree and the Bayou and maritime academies all mixed, whether raising a bridge or requesting permission to pass, or inquiring whether a certain boat may have cables out, that might trip up your boat.

The central characters of this book are not buildings, but boats; not people so much as the weather they are constantly adjusting to. There is a cycle at play; on a summer afternoon it seems like a delicate ballet as unspoken rules allow a dozen boats to untangle from a wharf without hitting each other. That cycle can turn brutal as smaller vessels struggle against three-or-four foot waves, four runs of current (tide?) daily, each at least nine feet high, debris, radio messages not received, very cold conditions, challenging lack of visibility, and pure tedium.

But please remember that no one in Boston Harbor knows everything, and if they claim to, they probably shouldn't be out there, operating equipment. And boats need to refuel just as those who operate them, so surprising acquaintances can be made at one of the few fuel docks, between enforcers and those being monitored, and vessel operators and the birds and seals they strive to protect from pollution. Odds and ends are found floating in the harbor and taken to a place they are less like to harm other boats, or are taken home as nautical decorations for the mantle, or toys as playthings for children, as you will see. Boston Harbor is a fascinating place to live and work, as I hope this short slice of images convey.

Voyage 92: *Blue Moon*, **sea trials Narragansett Bay, Portsmouth RI, July, 2020**

On 4th of July weekend a German friend who I had known at Oxford and met up with in Newport and New York since, called to say that due to Covid-19-induced life changes, he was looking at buying a large yacht which was presently lying in Newport. Since I happened to be there that weekend with our son, we gave the lovely boat a look-see and sent photos from my iPhone. Within three weeks he was the proud owner of a 100-foot super yacht built by a highly reputable firm in Finland. I had the honor of serving as owner's representative, since he was unable visit and see her himself due to Covid-19 travel restrictions. I was fortunately in a position to appoint Manfred, who had been my skipper on *Breathless* 27 years before and found me so much work since, work with a tanker captain, a yacht skipper who had also studied in Oxford, and meet some really neat folks in the brokerage, sail making, and yacht repair sectors.

Part of the process was to take the mother-yacht as well as the inboard turbo tender out for a spin, testing half a dozen or more sails, with the best in the business from the region on board. It was a sunny, calm day and the broker's friend took her in circles around us was we put the boat through the tests. I would have to say that I felt there was more talent on that boat than any boat I'd been aboard in terms of specific skills, from sail making to rigging to racing to engineering (racing the Farr 50 *Black Jack* in the Posidonia Cup in Piraeus twice was the most intense racing team I've sailed with, up there with *War Baby* on a Newport Bermuda Race).

The boat was successfully purchased. One of my pleasing assignments after the sale was to drive to Thomaston, Maine and load and return with some boat equipment. I stopped in the boat-building and commercial fishing port of Friendship, Maine, south of Waldeboro, and watched the lobster boats at work. A lovely day. Like Cuttyhunk, Friendship was refreshing to find a place which is made difficult to get to, as the nature of those there tends to be more on the persistent and self-sufficient side; I've always tended towards such island traits, including stubbornness and perhaps a bit of color tainting one's thinking; perhaps you have noticed....

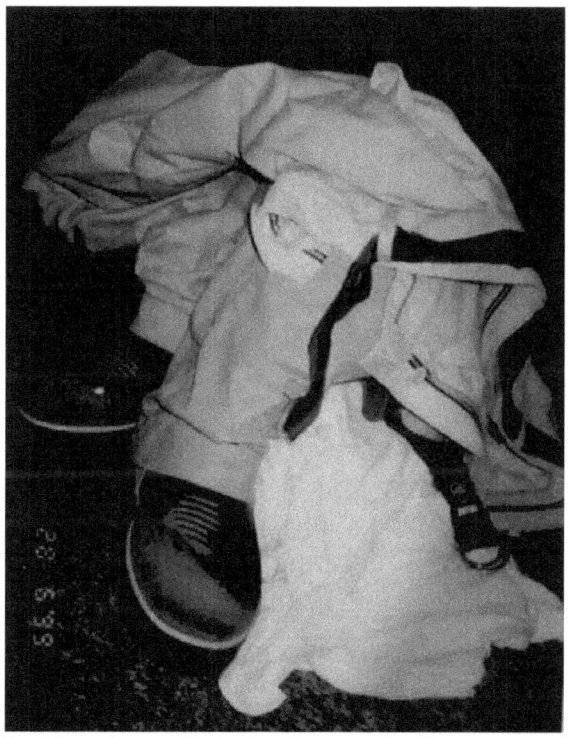

Home at last! Sleep, unplug the phone, lock the door and take responsibility for nothing and no one for a few days, though crew would at times stage and stay with me in Newport, waiting for a break in winter weather. Some neighbors were perplexed since they would rarely see me except when I returned from a voyage, went to the balcony, shut all the French doors, and didn't emerge for days.

Chapter 20

Joseph Conrad's *Initiation*, in *The Mirror of the Sea*

Joseph Conrad's story *Initiation*, from *The Mirror of the Sea* and its impact on my maritime life. A retrospective and book review for the New York Yacht Club.

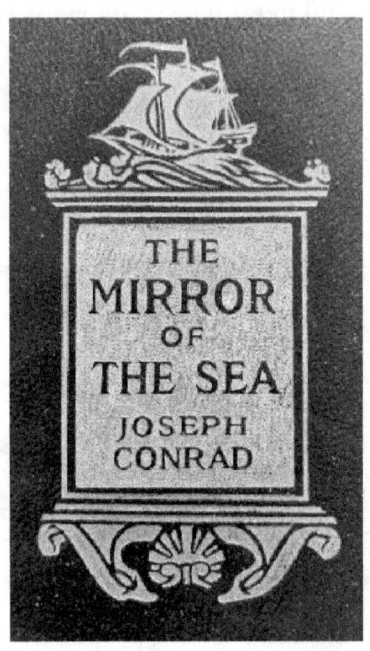

The 1925 edition of Conrad's *The Mirror of the Sea* which my grandfather, a Manhattan attorney, purchased, and which my mother saved to inspire me.

At the last, when you have sailed long and far enough, you come to understand that the sea is everything. It is calm and restless, stormy and laughing, many-hued and one-hued, and one-colored, salty and fresh, warm and cold, an enemy and a friend, a help and a hindrance, a tragedy and a jest. Everything! Sufficient for every mood, for every dream, for every hope, for every sorrow. It will give you health and it will break you. It will teach you strength and turn your courage to water....

And so in your youth, when the bridge-watch comes, you regard that sea which took your boyhood and gave you a certain wisdom and joy, warily, as a fencer regards his foe. And something of the mystery, something of the wonder, something of the clean, innocent and sincere love you gave to deep-water goes slowly away, never to return.

From *Way for a Sailor!*, Albert Richard Wetjen (1900-1948), British-American merchant mariner and author. From *The Oxford Book of the Sea*, Jonathan Raban, editor, Oxford University Press, 1993, pages 396-398

Joseph Conrad was born Józef Teodor Konrad Korzeniowski in what is now the Ukraine in 1857 a Russian subject in what became Poland, and died in Kent, England as a British subject in 1924. Along with Jack Kerouac, whose first language was French, Conrad is notable as an Anglophile author in English whose mother tongue was Polish. He is known as one of the finest modernist novelists of the 19th Century, having published over 20 novels, dozens of short stories, and over a dozen essays.

Conrad is remarkable for the nautical realism, rich description, and technical accuracy blended with a sense for portraying the fantastic in the weather, in maritime mistake, and in human characters such as *Lord Jim*. He portrayed a major colonial and then global expansion and interactions 'twixt traders and sailors in the Atlantic and Indian and Pacific oceans and the South China Sea. If there were a comparison with a character on a tramp steamer in the Far East by William Somerset Maugham, Conrad would have been more than the narrator; he would also have been the captain.

While a success as an officer in the French and British merchant marine, and as a writer, Conrad was also moody, at times lonely and morose. As a consequence, at age 20 he shot himself in the chest with a revolver in Marseilles, France, largely due to worries about finances. But for continued intervention and support by his Polish uncle Tadeusz Bobrowski, the Conrad's already turbulent life of global voyages would have doubtlessly been even more unstable and dangerous.

Many members of the New York Yacht Cub will be familiar with Conrad's writing already, having at a minimum read a book or two of his before college and during university. Being sailors, members will have been imbued with a knowledge of his skill as a mariner and someone who almost sensually portrayed the dank jungles of the Far East in books like *Lord Jim* and the intrigue and mystery of going up river in *The Heart of Darkness*, which morphed into Francis Ford Coppola's 1970s epic *Apocalypse Now*, and his wife's documentary *Hearts of Darkness* about the madness of making the film.

In mid-2020, as COVID-19 cut most of us off from the shelves of Conrad on 44th Street and the Library at Harbour Court, I took as keen an interest as anyone in trying to help members to engage with the club in new and novel ways. I was asked to contribute a book review to the Library Committee, on which I have been honored to serve for some years. The club has given me much to learn from, and a safe haven to shelter in during winters and economic blasts, and I am happy to oblige and do what I can. After all, I launched one of my maritime history books there, and have had the privilege to present on a book or two as well. In fact, several of the books I've published have been researched and written in both club houses. So here we are!

How does this relate, and how is this review organized? A gentleman who frequented the Harvard Club beside the NYYC from the 1940s to the 1970s as a managing partner of Reid & Priest, purchased the 1925 leather bound, gold-embossed Doubleday edition of *The Mirror of the Sea* by Joseph Conrad. His name was Ralph Manewal McDermid and his daughter Jane worked across the street from the club at *The New Yorker* in the early 1960's. She cherished the book, and on his graduation from college she gave this treasure to her son – your author. The cover of this book is on the title page of this essay, and the original sits in front of me as I type. It is propped near a window overlooking the Bunker Hill Monument in Boston from East Boston, across the harbor I spent the winter as captain of passenger boats, often taking fresh arrivals from Logan International Airport downtown.

The parallels between the revered Conrad and my modest efforts to keep up with him are few, but can be briefly brush-stroked. I was mate across the Atlantic at age 21, then watch captain on an aluminum Frers-50 racing sloop on the Marion to Bermuda Race, right after college, and rose to first command from Galapagos to New Zealand of a leaking wooden 68-footer at age 23. I know the loneliness of being separated from ones mates, having survived 16 minutes in the water in an afternoon snowstorm, farm from land and having watched the yacht I had so recently commanded sail out of sight.

By coincidence, the wrecked ship central to the core story is a "Danish brig homeward bound from the West Indies." In 2003, as law school ended for the year, I was hired to fly from Newport to St. Martin and deliver a Bristol 57' sloop to Sag Harbour. On the leg from Bermuda we went through over 50 knots of gales trying to enter the Gulf Stream, and unbeknownst to me our South African crew had a strong bond with an audacious and tenacious young Danish skipper. He was running a slight and fast stripped-down 40-foot-or-so racing sloop named *X-Base* for X-Yachts. And damn if that boat was not always at our side as we emerged from gales, storms, fog, rain, all of it – we were his insurance policy and they never gave in! At one point they came along side and threw some birthday cake onto our deck, everyone doing over 7 knots under sail. I marveled at and admired that Danish captain as the young Third Officer Conrad did the Danish ship master who survived the sinking brig, as they all sculled back to the ship that evening.

In 2000 the 1936 classic Camper & Nicholson *Stiarna* sank under our feet, aflame, north of Trinidad, thankfully east of Venezuela. I was hit by a Thai long-boat off Rai Lay, and was malnourished when the freezer broke on the first week of a 21-day trans-Atlantic passage in severe weather, Bermuda to Belgium. Like many readers had a few other unpleasant experiences due to the ocean, failures of equipment, and people – more often than not me. I've been so scared at times across some 125 boats and 75,000 nm that I'd frankly rather not say – but Conrad more comfortable sharing his misgivings, and lays his out for all of us to appreciate, respect, and relate to, whether we admit it or not.

So let's all enjoy parsing his words and mine with a sprinkling of criticism or critical thinking, pretend we are young again and going to the aid or wrecked wretches. Here is how this is organized: Part I - *Initiation*, in *Mirror of the Sea*, and Part II – Conrad's appearing in my logs & diaries, his writing influencing mine. There is of course a brief *Introduction, Conclusion* and *Further Reading* each. *Enjoy!*

In late August, 23-year old 1880 Joseph Conrad enlisted as third mate on an iron clipper ship, the *Loch Etive*. The next day the ship left London, arriving in Sydney in late November. The return voyage began in January of 1881. In his 1905 retrospective of insights gained from sea experience named *The Mirror of the Sea* Conrad describes for the readers his ship's rescue of a doomed Danish brigantine overtaken by a hurricane between the West Indies and Europe and adrift with nine men for over three weeks (the exact days are left a bit in doubt as the Danish captain is told the actual date and falls silent). The *Loch Etive* arrived in London late in April, roughly four months after leaving Australia.

The vignette known as *Initiation* is one of the coming-of-age stories which Conrad shares. To set the stage, he write how he "felt its dread for the first time in mid-Atlantic one day, many years ago, when we took off the crew of a Danish brig homeward bound from the West Indies." Peter Villiers, in *Joseph Conrad, Master Mariner*, begins by assuming the incident occurred in 1881 aboard *Loch Etive*, but concludes it is an amalgam of several incidents, possibly the wrecked *Able Seaman* in 1879, rescued by the *Duke of Southerland* off Canada (pages 37-43). Conrad himself prefers to leave his novels vague and imprecise in origin, as Villiers notes; "…he heartily disliked too close an attention being paid to the origins of his writings." Conrad wrote directly to an inquisitive fan that "It is a strange fate that everything I have, of set artistic purpose, laboured to leave indefinite, suggestive…. Should have that light turned on it and its insignificance… for any fool to comment upon." (Villiers, pp.42-43, Curle, Richard (ed.) *Conrad to a Friend: 150 Selected Letters to Richard Curle*, Wright, Low, Marston & Co., London, 1928, ibid.)

Conrad speaks of men's working relationship with vessels as being driven by a pride of endurance, which I find is true of offshore voyages, and races. He observes that the anthropomorphism which men and women apply to machines or animals fails in their interactions with the sea, which "has no generosity. No display of manly qualities - courage, hardihood, endurance, faithfulness - has ever been known to touch its irresponsible consciousness of power." Humans "cannot brook the slightest appearance of defiance," without incurring its wrath, since the sea "is always stealthily ready for a drowning. The most amazing wonder of the deep is its unfathomable cruelty."

We readers recognize that this will be no ordinary evening in the doldrums, or after a storm, when the lookout on Conrad's ship is so alarmed at the sight of living bodies on the wreck that they shout on with "a most extraordinary voice - a voice never heard before in our ship; the amazing voice of a stranger." The once-mighty rescue ship – and its crew – become reduced to drifting "silent and white as a ghost, towards her mutilated and wounded sister, come upon at the point of death in the sunlit haze of a calm day at sea." Already the reader and narrator drift into a surreal world of phantasm, with dusk's onset blurring life and death, afloat and sunk….

Conrad is a junior officer at the time – entirely the point of the story, and as he become master of a small row boat, he realizes that "It takes many lessons to make a real seaman." Rescue boats race towards the sinking hulk. "The issue of our enterprise hung on a hair above that abyss of waters which will not give up its dead till the Day of Judgment. It was a race of two ship's boats matched against Death for a prize of nine men's lives, and Death had a long start. …Already, her bulwarks were gone fore and aft, and one saw her bare deck low-lying like a raft and swept clean of boats."

Then, as launch captain to brig's captain, Conrad prepares to receive his counterpart, with he and the reader perhaps expecting a salute, tip of hat, or handing of ceremonial sword. As it was, there was no *Captain Sorensen, I presume* heroic Victorian flourish, rather "....the captain... literally let himself fall into my arms." No bugles and cavalry charge there. In fact, the participants note that "it had been a weirdly silent rescue - a rescue without a hail, without a single uttered word, without a gesture or a sign, without a conscious exchange of glances." Rather, the surviving nine mariners could not take their eyes of the pumps until one final order was given to cease, and then they stood, without caps, with the salt drying gray in the wrinkles and folds of their hairy, haggard faces, blinking stupidly at us their red eyelids, they made a bolt away from the handles, tottering and jostling against each other, and positively flung themselves over upon our very heads. The clatter they made tumbling into the boats had an extraordinarily destructive effect upon the illusion of tragic dignity our self-esteem had thrown over the contests of mankind with the sea.

The narrator relates the devastating effect this had on him, as though an acolyte become swiftly an atheist, or at least an agnostic.

> On that exquisite day of gently breathing peace and veiled sunshine perished my romantic love ....the cynical indifference of the sea to the merits of human suffering and courage, laid bare in this ridiculous, panic-tainted performance extorted from the dire extremity of nine good and honorable seamen, revolted me. I saw the duplicity of the sea's most tender mood. It was so because it could not help itself, but the awed respect of the early days was gone. I felt ready to smile bitterly at its enchanting charm and glare viciously at its furies. In a moment, before we shoved off, I had looked coolly at the life of my choice. Its illusions were gone, but its fascination remained. I had become a seaman at last.

The captain of the sinking brigantine explained to Conrad, in the thwarts of the rescue boat on its way to the new mothership, that "the ships they sighted failed to make them out, the leak gained upon them slowly, and the seas had left them nothing to make a raft of. It was very hard to see ship after ship pass by at a distance, as if everybody had agreed that we must be left to drown." The rescuers have narrower recollection of the rescue, which took an hour or so, than the survivors, who were adrift nearly a month after a hurricane. Conrad describes that even in retirement, "I remember the dark-brown feet, hands, and faces of two of these men whose hearts had been broken by the sea. They were lying very still on their sides on the bottom boards between the thwarts, curled up like dogs."

Suddenly, with no word spoken, the brig's captain emits a groan, and Conrad loses command of his boat to his Scandinavian stranger: "....after a glance over his shoulder, [he] stood up with a low exclamation, my men feathered their oars instinctively, without an order, and the boat lost her way." Then "... he pointed a denunciatory finger at the immense tranquility of the ocean. .....the amazing energy of his immobilized gesture made my heart beat faster with the anticipation of something monstrous... the stillness around us became crushing."

Brilliantly, Conrad makes his men, perhaps even the readers witnessing, complicit in what happens next, as the surge of the swell destined to condemn the Danish brig to the depths passes beneath the mother ship and the launch, lifting them all up, even for just a moment, informing them of it's inevitable intent...

> For a moment the succession of silky undulations ran on innocently. I saw each of them swell up the misty line of the horizon, far, far away beyond the derelict brig, and, the next moment, with a slight friendly toss of our boat, it had passed under us and was gone. The lulling cadence of the rise and fall, the invariable gentleness of this irresistible force, the great charm of the deep waters, warmed my breast deliciously, like the subtle poison of a love-potion. ...As if at a given signal, the run of the smooth undulations seemed checked suddenly around the brig.

This description is extraordinarily accurate, in my experience. As a new captain of a historic yacht which caught fire, I watched I dismay from a Trinidadian Coast Guard cutter as the wooden, oil-soaked vessel, freshly loaded the night before with 72 gallons of diesel in bladders, became engulfed in flames leaping higher than the cotton sails and booms. We men who had swum to the safety of another boat waited for the diesel to explode, but nothing but a "poof" emitted: grey steam and hot air. Then the water tanks when. And finally, when the moment arrived and the fire had eaten like leprosy from one side right through to the other so that we could see gaping, smile-like holes in the 64-year old hull, after the mast had toppled onto itself like a broken matchstick, all of us hats off an in awe, the owner's recent baby imperceptibly rose to the top of a whale-back, silky smooth swell, and every so gently and almost silently was enveloped in the forever embrace of the ocean.

The boat sank 134 feet down into the seas over which German U-boats had ferociously fought the US and UN navies in The Bocas, or Mouth of the Dragon. It was all so oily, silent, anti-climactic, sorrowful or even wan, drained of emotion. It was so actual and matter-of-fact, like the sliding of a corpse off a tray from under a flag, anchor chain on ankles, into the depth. It just happens. The absence of a stunning sensation is in itself a bit stunning. Watch these on the internet, and you will notice – that ships and yachts often do go out with a whimper, a whisper, a puff of air. In my case since I had three months of belongings on board, the coast guard RIB found pieces of my grandfather's nautical tie, of an old Oxford shirt, and the boat's charred life-ring with its name. The owner quickly went on to own *Columbia*.

And then, the *coup-de-grâce*, as the narrator related how

> by a strange optical delusion the whole sea appeared to rise upon her in one overwhelming heave of its silky surface, where in one spot a smother of foam broke out ferociously. And then the effort subsided. It was all over,

and the smooth swell ran on as before from the horizon in uninterrupted cadence of motion, passing under us with a slight friendly toss of our boat. Far away, where the brig had been, an angry white stain, undulating on the surface of steely-gray waters, shot with gleams of green, diminished swiftly, without a hiss, like a patch of pure snow melting in the sun.

Following this stark experience, the young officer forever changed by them relates his new perspective of his host, livelihood, and adversary. The sunken brig, ne notes as he watches the devastated Danish master, "...had lived, he had loved her; she had suffered, and he was glad she was at rest." Conrad ruminates on the future for he and his own men as they fall under the shadow cast by their home'

> Ships are all right." They are. They who live with the sea have got to hold by that creed first and last; and it came to me, as I glanced at him sideways, that some men were not altogether unworthy in honor and conscience to pronounce the funereal eulogium of a ship. This smile of the worthy descendant of the most ancient sea-folk [Danes], whose audacity and hardihood had left no trace of greatness and glory upon the waters, completed the cycle of my initiation [into] the sea, which has betrayed so many ships, so many proud men, so many towering ambitions of fame, power, wealth, greatness!

Being welcomed by cheering shipmates and congratulated, even backhandedly by a wizened captain of his ship, Conrad ensures the survivors make it to the deck of his ship and then the author ruminates.

> It was not for [my Captain] to discern upon me the marks of my recent initiation. And yet I was not exactly the same youngster who had taken the boat away - all impatience for a race against death, with the prize of nine men's lives at the end. Already I looked with other eyes upon the sea. I knew it capable of betraying the generous ardor of youth as implacably as, indifferent to evil and good. ....My conception of its magnanimous greatness was gone. And I looked upon the true sea - the sea that plays with men till their hearts are broken, and wears stout ships to death. Open to all and faithful to none, it exercises its fascination for the undoing of the best.

The somewhat absorbent effect of reading *Initiation* on an aspiring and ambitious young sailor reminds me of a winter day in the southern hemisphere, on the commercial fishing dock in the village of Oban, on Halfmoon Bay, Stewart Island, at 47 degrees south in the Roaring Forties. I was 24 and finishing a memoir of sailing to New Zealand, and while waiting for new typewriter ribbons to arrive on the ferry from Invercargill, I struck up a conversation with an older fisherman. He was chewing something and in a philosophical mood – I'd lived on the island about three months and was considered OK to speak to I guess. He spread his arm across the entire horizon in a sweeping grand gesture on that steel gray cold, still afternoon and said to me:

"My son is in construction. He takes me to Dunedin and Invercargill and Christ Church and shows me all the buildings he's helped to put up. When he comes here to Stewart Island and I want show him what I have to show after more than five decades of fishing these waters, this is all that I have. There's not one damn thing to show him for all that work. The sea hasn't noticed me."

Next we look at the dozen or more times that Conrad's works, thoughts and experiences have bled into my personal diaries and voyage logs over more than 30 years. They are pulled from a 750-page compendium of 55 diaries largely collated and in one of the alcoves of the 44th Street clubhouse last year – the one nearest the new *Tenacious* model, which is fitting as I sailed and raced her as War Baby from 1991 to 2001, and remember RAF veteran Charlie Berry being up to his chest in water in that cockpit when rounding Portland Bill, UK, in the summer of my 21st years. These diary entries are meant to show how reading Conrad interwove with my own coming-of-age as a sailor.....

On August 22, 1987, I was a week from turning 17 when I wrote that on a flight, "a lady who sat next to me for three hours Miami to New York finally asked me, *Can I buy that when it's a novel*? See, I'd been writing in my diary for hour after hour! *Live by the pen, die by the pen. Come home wearing your mainsail or in it*, said Saint George's teacher and sailing coach, Mr. B., who had been my Junior Varsity sailing coach. In 1990 or 1991, I saw Coach B. crushed, broken, sobbing uncontrollably after their sailboat was dismasted racing to Bermuda and moments after days of living hell and a tow, he made it to the payphone booth (where I was also calling my parents), and called his. It was like a Joseph Conrad short story from *The Mirror of the Sea*, the single text which most impresses me with its saltiness, as the film *White Squall*, about the loss of the training ship *Albatross* does as well, with Jeff Bridges and an amazing soundtrack of the ocean under way. The experience helped teach me that can still deal with reality while accepting the romantic."

On the 3rd of July, 1989, I was 18 and in that wild summer between six years of boarding school and four of university. I had the good fortune to sail as boat boy on the Marion-Bermuda Race, then the voyage back to Newport, with some trepidation, since the tanker *World Prodigy* had spilled some 300,000 of fuel oil on Brenton Reef the previous week:

> I dreamt of being under blocks, crushing me, of a freight ship sending me adrift, of poems. I feel like Joseph Conrad. Terence, studying marine biology at URI, saw a whale last night. This is the offshore sailing I've dreamt about for years! No more school poems of and yearning for the sea! This he real thing. Circa 1,500 nm; almost enough from Newfoundland to Ireland (trans-Atlantic). Now I can wear red shorts or even pants..... [Nantucket Reds from Murray's Toggery Shop are considered in some circles a sign that one

crossed the Atlantic under sail; though you won't find many clips of stolen valor confrontations on Youtube].

A month or so later I enrolled in Boston College as an English Major, joined the big boat sailing team (really contributing nothing to it, sadly), and the first day of summer I set off sailing; after Freshman year I bicycled to Newport, caught a boat back from Bermuda Race, then another to Europe. The next summer I blindly caught a one-way ticket to Antigua and found a boat to Belgium where I could join *War Baby* ex-*Tenacious*, then attend Oxford. During this time I was submitting stories of voyages to Bermuda, on the Australian tall ship *Young Endeavour* in Bahamas, and *Xebec* across the North Atlantic to the school paper in Boston, *The Nassau Tribune*, and *What's On Bahamas*, and the St. George's School *Bulletin*. As a result of these forays I became a journalist for a while, covering everything from robberies at the local store to a coup in Haiti, a struggle for LGBTQ tolerance and round-the-world yacht races, allowing me to meet participants in the BOC Challenge and even Florence Arthaud.

During this stint I attended a lecture on Graham Greene given by his most assiduous biographer (Boston College, holds much of Greene's papers). His name is Norman Sherry, and he published *Conrad's Eastern World*, and *Conrad's Western World* in the 1970's, one colorful illustrated edition of which was gifted to me to read during three years helping to operate a commercial fleet of tankers from Singapore. It was ideal, and I still have it. Sherry also completed a monumental three-volume biography entitled *The Life of Graham Greene*; he is funny, and no slouch. So I faced the world empowered by the words of Greene, the humor of Sherry, the adventurism and skill of Conrad, the socially skewering wordsmithing of Somerset Maugham, and a bit of the inaccessibility of Lawrence Durrell and the sardonic humor and sly British wit of Evelyn Waugh, who might have been mistaken for an effete artiste were it not for his having participated as a soldier in numerous World War II campaigns, from Scandinavia to the Med, as well as West Africa. Overall, being able to meet one of Conrad's biographers brought me a step close to him, and to his worldly travels.

Years later, on August 25, 1993, two days before my 23rd birthday, and after graduating from college in Boston, I set off for a career at sea, and wrote: "Books I recently read: *Looking for a Ship*, John McPhee, *Lord Jim*, by Joseph Conrad, *Voyage, a Novel of 1896* and *Wanderer*, by Sterling Hayden, *Alive!*, the story of Chilean air crash victims and survivors; cannibalism, *North by Northeast*, by Ray Ellis and Walter Cronkite, *Islands of Maine*, by Bill Caldwell, *The Sufferings of Young Werther*, by Goethe, and *Mutiny on the Bounty*, by Nordhoff and Hall, two Americans living in Tahiti, in French Polynesia."

A month later, the final Conrad entry of my youth; on September 26, 1993, a Sunday at 9 pm, I was a crew with a young couple in command and a friendly former naval officer from New Bedford, also very nice. We were between Newport and the Bahamas on a 60-foot sloop, emerging from a crappy first half and into a sunny second one:

> The current is against us in the Gulf Stream, NNW at about four knots. Bimini is visible, despite being low and flat. It is clear, calm, humid, hot. We decided over our evening beer together that we would bypass rushing for

Bimini tonight in favor of delaying all night, arriving early morning one week after departure from Newport. The captain's plan is to anchor outside in deeper water in order to do work like refitting the boat and general cleanup as needed.

This may determine whether I stay on board for the trip down-island to the US Virgin Islands and Antigua or not; it is something I could easily do by flying from Nassau to Fort Lauderdale, and I could use the money. Meanwhile I think after six to seven days of confinement, calm, torpor, languishing and its corrosive toll, I'll feel a bit the butt of ill-humor, but it's all well. We'll see, right? What awaits me in Florida? Other deliveries south? The fabled ultimate role: ascending to the industry throne of captaincy?

9:30 pm. Bimini is only 30 nm, or eight hours away. We are still bucking the Gulf Stream, that hot river of water which is about three feet higher and several degrees hotter than the water either side of it. Joseph Conrad wrote *A Personal Record*, a wonderful work about being a professional merchant marine officer. This diary or log is the personal record of mine. Simultaneously, I am keeping a voyage log of *Breathless*' passage south from Newport to Miami initially bound for my home port of Lyford Cay, Nassau, and now via Bimini, Berry Islands, Bahamas, and Fort Lauderdale. I say *personal record* because, from this afternoon, I'll play closer attention to the personal aspects of this voyage, and the crew who initiate and carry it out. I have learned that as our character roles settle down into an established pattern of sorts, I find the evidence of alchemy unsettling.

Another Diary entry for Friday, August 18, 1994, after arriving by sea in New Zealand, reads: "....Ho Chi Minh City, which makes me think of the film *Apocalypse Now*, based on regicide and Conrad's *Heart of Darkness*...." This is due to my final paper for documentary film in college was based on the influence of Conrad in *Apocalypse Now*. I considered much of my assumption of first command and subsequent travels in the light of Conrad-esque perception, coloring it with the wide-eyed gone-more-cynical outlook which this story in particular encapsulates so well. And I don't see it translating to other professions as easily. Had those nine men on the Danish brig lost their fight at the pumps, going up and down like an eternal, infernal pump trolly or railway handcar, they would have been lost forever, with no remains to make it into the local church. Just the vast heaving surface of the sea, over 139 million square miles just of the salty stuff.

From my early teens to the daunting, scary yet emboldening assumption of my first command, trans-ocean, at age 23, I have always felt that Joseph Conrad has been by my side to guide and support me. Like some of my other heroes, including Sterling Hayden, Felix von Luckner, and Samuel Eliot Morison, Conrad went out and *did it* first. It is extraordinary for someone to write such lovely, evocative prose about the ocean we all so deeply cherish. What I admire and respect about these men, and others including Albert Richard Wetjen, is that they often quit reputable schooling and families to experience the hard knocks of an ocean-going global life first-hand, before they share their perspectives as writers.

One thing which is clear to me from all this, and may be to you, the fellow reader, is that references to Conrad, comparisons, thoughts, memories of he and his writing and the high bar of example he set for me, depression and self-doubt and all – are things I've not only literally carried around with me most of my life, but interwoven and used it as well. Conrad is not passive. You breath, fear, see, and sweat or tremble right alongside him.

And now I return to him – to Conrad – as I do when I sit at the feet of the statue of Admiral Samuel Morison on Commonwealth Avenue in Boston. I do so at the start of my second half-century, chastened, hardened to the sea perhaps, as scared of the sea as ever, and as the account in *Initiation* makes clear, wiser, less bedazzled, better prepared and with fewer expectations and almost none of the rose-tinted innocence left. Having known true terror alone at watch at sea, fumbling for the emergency cockpit fog horn before realizing it won't cure me of the terrors, I have some round to Conrad's view that almost anyone can be brave. It takes someone who has been terrified to go back to sea afterwards that constitutes more than just wisdom. I think it constitutes bravery, which is made more by the underlying terror.

Though in this instance Conrad shows us how a shipwreck can end, the truth is that in many instances, no one is left to relate how their shipwreck ended.

Thank you, Captain Conrad.

Conclusion

The statue of Samuel Eliot Morison (1887–1976), professor, admiral, who has inspired me since I discovered this lovely sculpture on the Mall on Commonwealth Avenue, between Exeter and Fairfield streets, in Boston, where he grew up. It is said of him that "Throughout his life, and particularly in his later years, Morison challenged younger generations to take a more immersive approach to their historical work." With me it worked, and he was a live-changing, even life-defining motivator to. Don't just dream and write, he invoked: get out there and *do* it first!

Morison was related T. S. Eliot; I've spent time in the Back Bay neighborhood where he grew up, he sailed to the Bahamas to better understand Columbus, he taught at Oxford, I studied there, he taught at Harvard, they granted me library system access in 2019 when I moved back to Boston. The image of text on this statue is on my writer's home page. I visit the statue often and have had interesting conversations there. This Boston Literary District monument was funded by the George B. Henderson Foundation. Not in over 70 countries and hundreds of cities have I found a statue to a maritime historian.

I've been to his Birthplace in Boston, and his grave in Northeast Harbor, Maine, and like him written several books of World War II history and studied at Oxford and even as a guest of the Harvard Library system and member of the Boston Athenaeum. When my boarding school allowed me to address the entire school right when my angst at being kept on campuses for six years was reaching its boiling point, I exhorted young students to get out and do it, whatever it was they wanted to do, and ended by throwing this quote by the German philosopher Johann Wolfgang von Goethe, who was the literary equivalent of a rock star in his early twenties:

Whatever you think you can do, whatever you dream you can do: BEGIN IT.

Since my teens, I have tried my damnedest to do just that. I hope you enjoy the results, which you have just read.

From Wanderlust to World Weary
1995 story for Armchair Sailor bookstore, Newport

I sailed around the world. Well, not quite. About halfway, really. Stockholm to Auckland. Wanderlust to World Weary. Took me about seven years. On more than a dozen boats. Went from bilge-boy to mate, watch-captain to full captain. The most memorable of these voyages were the first, the worst, and the last. Then I burnt out. The sea gave me strength. Then it stripped me of it and offered in its place subservience - a humble pill, difficult for a young man to swallow, especially when you have a lump in your throat. Trouble was, I got scared. And like a flyer or a diver, when you recognize that fear, you either confront it or you hang up your hat. I opted to hang up my hat.

My sailing idols were Sterling Hayden, Melville, Conrad. Now I am fighting not to end up like Hayden. Thing is, that when, like him, you're first command is of a wooden sailing vessel crossing the vast Pacific to Tahiti and beyond, in your youth, the rest of what life has to offer sometimes seems a tinge disappointing. The first, and the last. My first voyage was a venture across a corner of the Baltic Sea. I was seventeen, and when the skipper rounded the breakwater to find mounting seas that sent ferries scurrying, only I called to press onward. We pressed on later, he and I at the helm. At anchor in the lee of a pilot station that night, we shared a fine meal and the warmth of satisfaction. I'd found something that truly thrilled me - something I could be good at.

I used to skate, cycle - run to the statue of the man on Boston's Commonwealth Avenue. Sam Eliot Morison. He and I whittled away many a chilly Boston night together. I memorized his words, and as much as I could, I lived by them. An hour or so after my final exam Sophomore year in college, I was southbound on a flight to Antigua, hoping to find a yacht for a passage to Europe, where I would study the following year. I found one, and thus began two months of, if not the worst, then the most terrifying seas I had ever beheld, much less sailed across .

The shock of crossing a fierce North Atlantic at age 20 didn't catch up with me until the following fall. The editor of our college rag asked me to write a few words about the voyage. Prodded by my keyboard, a rush of emotions that I had canned at the time broke forth. Twenty five pages later, I was still writing, still regurgitating, still trying to wring the haunting experiences of daunting combers shattering our transom, of daily rations and knife fights over food, the cold loneliness of mid-Atlantic in June, still 2,000 miles from Bishop's Rock - from myself. The recollections left me shuddering and whimpering for hours.

It was all too much for the editor. And it has proved too much for me. Those were some of the hard parts the ones that plague you later. The same voyage also gave me a real sense of adulthood, a surge of self-assurance, power, even, when I needed it. After my first trans-Atlantic voyage, I felt like the single-handed sailor who, peeling himself out of his sloop after a long passage is met on the jetty by a blazer-wearing prig telling him he can't dock there. Without a word, the single-minded one brushes the blurter aside, and into the water, on his way to the bar .

As I strode toward the fountain of knowledge at university that fall, I found it difficult to sit in a room taking instruction from a man who had never been to sea. Still a young man myself, I begun to assess adults, my seniors, differently - by different criteria. In the years ahead it seemed more and more of my fellow sailors succumbed to accidents, to living to excess, and died, several of them "missing" at sea. With them a certain innocence to the sea which I had managed to keep alive, was also lost. These words are for them - that family on its way from New Zealand to Tonga during the end of my first command, who all went missing, and those sailors those fishermen, those merchant-men, who go down to the sea in ships and do not return.

My role models for leadership under stressful voyage conditions range from Count Felix von Luckner of *Seeadler* (*Sea Eagle*), to Bernard Rogge of the successful World War II raider *Atlantis*, Carl von Muller of the *Emden*, and of course Sir Ernest Shackleton on the *Endeavour* and later *James Caird* and other life and rescue boats. Specific mention should be made of U-Boat commander Wolfgang Luth's *Problems of Leadership in a Submarine*; a lecture he gave in 1943, the politics of which I explicitly disavow.

I would like to summarize aspects of the delivery skipper's chosen lot by sharing several well-worn, perhaps pithy observations. To laypeople I describe the job as "taking a boat you have never seen, with a crew you have never worked with into the shoulders of the worst seasons of the year, for an owner you may never meet." I've learned lots of great jokes making fun of bareboat charterers and even owners (about there being two wheels). The reality, though, is that the joke is on us: I've found that the future for a delivery skipper is too easily dead, drunk, or divorced - and not necessarily in that order.

Some of the best skippers I know managed to break up with the bottle. You don't see them in pubs so often as out on the water, quietly doing their jobs. I've heard some wry comments from skippers who have "shaken more water out of their boots than I've sailed over" about "a license does not a sailor make," - and nor does their clothing. I've found that some of the most expensive "name brand" yachts have been the most hellish to handle and live aboard in a sea; their expensive electronics easily scrambled, the whale hulls and retractable keels making them weave in a following sea.

I would like to share insight gained the most painful way, from mistakes and failures. Like our mistakes and failures on shore, I find that a lot of them trace back to poor interaction or communication skills, a lack of "situational awareness" and sometimes poor judgment as a result of fatigue. Not all of the examples have unhappy endings. Most of them deal with crew management and differing reactions to crises as well as successes.

The impetus for this article was a specific voyage which was to have been the crowning of the Bermuda portion of my career. For over a decade I had tried to bring a boat into my home port of Nassau, Bahamas and been stymied thrice. First, we limped into Nassau in darkness after diverting from Lisbon (yes, Portugal). Two other times the owners diverted cur boats away from the Bahamas *en route*; once to Lauderdale and another time to the BVIs, depriving me of a triumphant homecoming command. Without this crowning glory, I had to settle for the second-best feather in my cap.

Good crew: Some of the best crew was significantly older than me, and many of them knew more about sailing than I did, but under the circumstances they behaved admirably well, contributed immensely with their skill and collaboration, and hardly grumbled. (This may be simply because I was paymaster). Others had to be scared to humility by the rest of the crew. One trick was to move the boat surreptitiously around the port while they were in the bar and make them find us. To deal with drunks I would enforce a dry ship policy. It is amazing how much some crew can drink before a mid-morning departure! Waiting at anchorage to clear in, we would sometimes tap into the owner's booze supply, which lead to interesting and expensive expeditions to replace the exotic liqueurs we had drunk.

A colleague of mine had an unfortunate experience, which I realized when the US Coast Guard called my cell the day after Christmas to report them overdue in the USVI. The crew spent December moving a cruising sailboat from Massachusetts south. The owner, a farmer, placed his trusted boat crew, a young lady, on board. But after weeks of chopping ice off the deck and waterline, she opted to fly to the USVI and meet the boat there, tacitly approving of the Echo crew to finish the job. Well, not surprisingly, more delays in Bermuda but finally the fellows managed to arrive in the USVI. Immediately on arrival a high-speed power boat pulled up, the girl hopped aboard, scampered down the companionway with – by the accounts of three separate persons I interviewed – no underwear, dug round in the aft cabin for five minutes, emerged, left the boat on the speed boat, and was never seen again.

Well, wouldn't you know that back on shore she called the owner to report that the captain and crew had stolen the boat's cash entrusted to her by the owner. The owner sent his local buddies down to the boat to detain everyone from leaving and rifle through all their personal belongings for the cash, which of course is exactly how every hardworking crew wants to end a voyage! They had no idea there even was a lockbox of cash, much less where it was and how to get into it, though sailors can find anything on a boat.

The owner, a New England apple grower, called me up right away, and I attested to the high moral and professional caliber of the captain, who I had known for years, worked with me at other companies, and did business with for another decade after Echo. the boat to the islands with the own. They would have probably been jailed had not the stewardess not suddenly quit her job on the boat's arrival and been seen spending lavishly on chartered boats, etcetera, drawing the blame onto herself. Overall this was a massive squander of time, resources, reputations, and effort.

Detaining my crew in the absence of law enforcement after a long and dangerous voyage was also most likely illegal. To me at least, and this is largely conjecture, it appears the young lady arrived in the USVI and started as the weeks of delays increased, to live a champagne lifestyle on a coca cola budget. When the boat returned, she saw her opportunity to grab the cash she now owed for apartment, transport, and god only knows what else, and bolt, blaming that genus of humanity known as yacht delivery crew: they were smelly men in from a month at sea with beards, she was a mere damsel in distress.

It almost worked, since the owner and his family could simply not acknowledge that this pretty little think was ripping us all of. My guys were much more convenient; the last ones on stage. It was a frustrating episode, an illustrates that even when you do the job right and bring the boat and crew in safely, you are still a yacht delivery crew, and can still be blamed for kidnapping the Lindbergh baby.

While crossing the South Pacific, I heard about a cruising boat that had been completely outfitted for a circumnavigation, starting in California. On the first week out they were hit with a difficult storm in which all the crew became sick. In the grips of *mal-de-mer*, someone left the water faucet on and, in the din, the sound of the tap water and pump running went unnoticed. Through the night all the fresh water drained into the bilge. A combination of the water and bilge pumps in continuous operation drained the batteries and left the electronic sails useless. Because of a simple human error, a boat with infinite range had its horizon restricted from global to local, as without power or water or sails they had to turn back. Also, it used up all their fresh water supplies and the batteries they would need to make water using the filtration reverse-osmosis systems.

Off season, living alone in Newport in winter; I was walking along the empty shore at Fort Adams at sunrise. Out of the opaque fog of sunrise emerged the white hull of a modest lobster boat, heading determinedly to Newport's Fish Pier with its catch. As they rounded the point beneath my feet, I felt that making no gesture would be inadequate, so I offered a short and simple salute. The skipper caught the sign of respect, and probably assuming I was US Army, which still control much Fort Adams, from Robert E. Lee of West Point who designed it to General Dwight Eisenhower who lived there, he smiled back.

When I was in my early 20s and ambitious to become a yacht skipper, I interviewed a lot of skippers about what makes a good captain. I thought a captain might be defined by how often and how high he hung the crew from the yardarm. The best reply I heard, from a very experienced French captain as we stood under a palm tree in Pape'ete, was that "a captain is the first one to offer to clean the dishes." In other words he and she was defined not by the discipline they mete out but the humility, spirit of cooperation, and team work which they lead by example.

The surviving members of a delivery crew in Tahiti told me how one of their members had been eliminated. The skipper flew four British crew from a half-way house for adolescent reprobates into Gibraltar for the trip. On arrival, he learned he was given a smaller boat to move, and only needed three crew. As a trial, he invited them all for drinks. The most responsible crew volunteered to stay behind and mind the boat. The next morning he found himself left behind as the voyage of his dreams pulled out without him. His conscientiousness had gotten him eliminated.

Later on the same voyage, the same skipper woke up off the Canaries and asked why they had gotten underway without his consent. He'd forgotten that he'd stormed aboard earlier that morning three sheets to the wind and cast the boat off in dark squalls. They nicked several nearby boats. Two crew had to prop him behind the wheel . Then the neophytes managed to get the boat beyond the breakwater and underway.

Amazing what a young man or woman can still discover out there on the wide, unforgiving sea, isn't it? The only way is to get out there, and see it from deck level yourself. I hope you agree that I tried.

Appendices

Appendix 1 - Echo Yacht Deliveries - Ranks & Roles

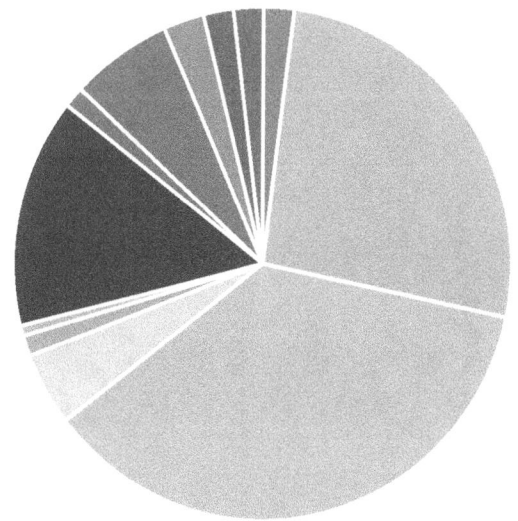

Roles and Ranks:
Orange is Captain, Gray is Crew

- Boat boy
- Captain
- Crew
- Guest
- Labor
- Liaison
- Mate
- Navigator
- Passengers
- Student
- Trainee
- Watch Captain

Mileage By Rank:
Capt. 25,503, Crew 19,497, Mate 7,308

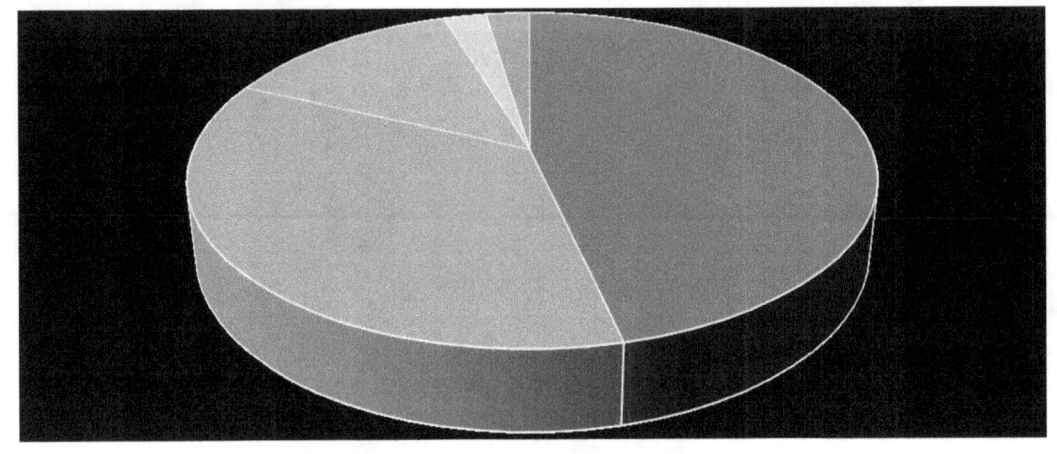

- Captain   - Crew   - Mate   - Navigator   - Watch Captain

Captain by Type: Delivery 21,548 nm, 26 boats Charter 3,230 27 boats

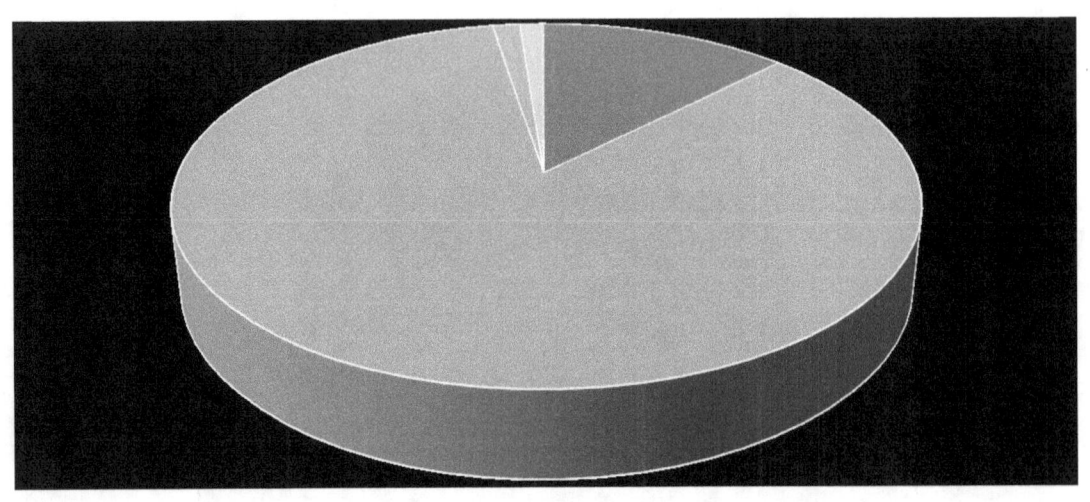

- Charter   - Delivery   - Leisure   - Workboat

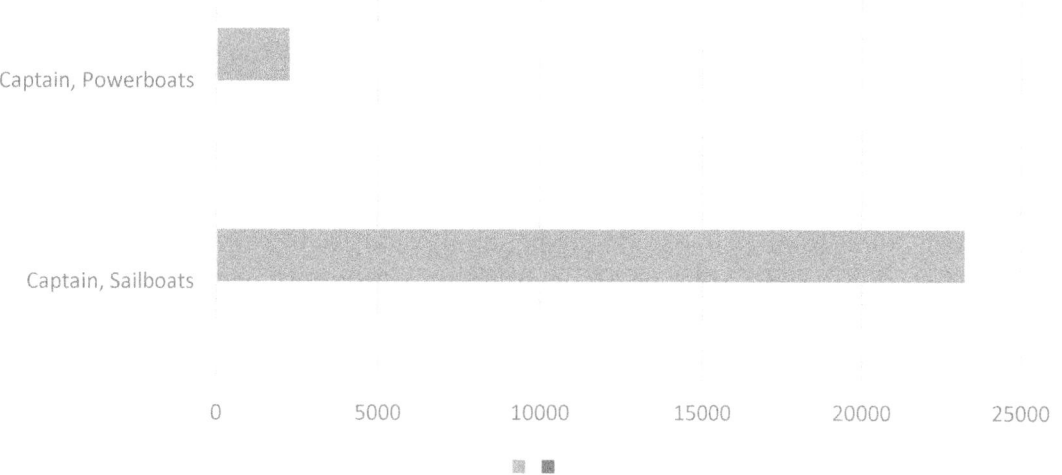

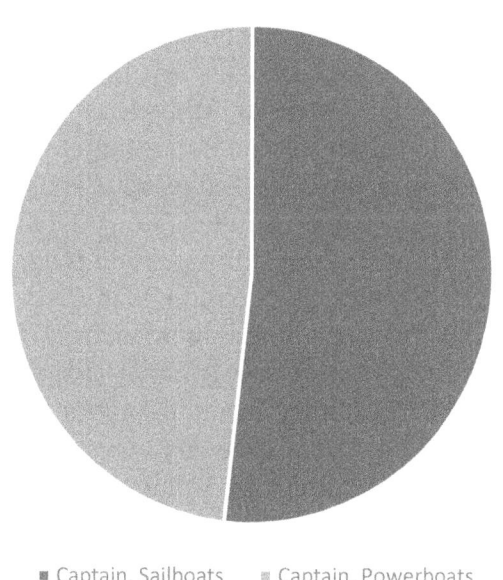

Appendix 2 - Sample Echo Yacht Delivery voyages

Sample Echo Yacht Delivery voyages: circulated, bid on, but not necessarily won.

ECHO VOYAGE 110/2005/27.4: 53' Super Maramu, Turkey-St. Maarten, end Nov. '05
ECHO VOYAGE 136/2005/30.4: 45' *Hunter* sloop, Annapolis-Belize, Nov. '05
ECHO VOYAGE 152/2005/16.5: 45' sail, crew, owner assist, Lauderdale-New Zealand, Oct.
ECHO VOYAGE 187/2005/12.6: 41' sail, owner-assist, US W. Coast-Brisbane OZ, Aug.-Dec.
ECHO VOYAGE 197/2005/17.6: 59' Hinckley, US E. Coast-W. Coast, Hawaii, Japan, '05
ECHO VOYAGE 198/2005/18.6: 36' sail TransAt, Charleston SC to Cadiz, Spain, Nov. '05
ECHO VOYAGE 2003/57/27.10: 61' sailing ketch, USVI to CA, Oct.-Dec. 2003
ECHO VOYAGE 2003/58/3.11: 40' CS *Sloop*, Annapolis-Newport, early June, 2004
ECHO VOYAGE 2003/60/4.11: 50' Gulf Star, Annapolis-Tortola, BVI, Dec. 2003
ECHO VOYAGE 202/2005/21.6: 40' Power, NY-FLA, Nov. '05
ECHO VOYAGE 204/2005/22.6: 41' Beneteau, Croatia-Australia, mid-end 2005
ECHO VOYAGE 206/2005/3.7: 33' catamaran, Fort Myers FL-USVI, Nov./Dec. '05
ECHO VOYAGE 207/2005/3.7: 60' trawler, Gibraltar-Ft. Lauderdale, Oct-Dec. '05
ECHO VOYAGE 208/2005/3.7: 50' Bavaria, sail BVI-Spain, April-May 2006
ECHO VOYAGE 216/2005/7.7: 40' sloop, LA, Calif.-Darwin, OZ, Sept. '05
ECHO VOYAGE 2005/13.7: Crew/cruise Med-Canary-Cape Verde-Argentina, Sum/Fall
ECHO VOYAGE 226/2005/13.7: 43' *Swan*, crew, St. Lucia-USVI, cruising, Summer '05
ECHO VOYAGE 229/2005/15.7: 60' Little Harbour, mate, deck, New England, Summer
ECHO VOYAGE 230/2005/19.7: 40' sail, Hawaii-CAL, non-paid Crew, Aug 1, '05
ECHO VOYAGE 233/2005/24.7: 37' Beneteau, Athens-UK, Fall '05
ECHO VOYAGE 235/2005/26.7: Italian Service Rep sought for builder, US, Europe, full time
ECHO VOYAGE 238/2005/4.8: Charter Boat Deliveries, Caps/Mate/Crew Fall '05-Jan. '06
ECHO VOYAGE 240/2005/4.8: 35' power, Lauderdale-BVI, Fall '05
ECHO VOYAGE 241/2005/5.8: *Catamaran* skipper, Fleet Mngr, New Eng-Caribs, Fall '05
ECHO VOYAGE 242/2005/8.8: 36' sail, San Leandro-San Diego CA, 15 Oct., '05
ECHO VOYAGE 244/2005/8.8: 36' sail, Fla. & Bahamas, training voyage/s, Nov./Dec., '05
ECHO VOYAGE 245/2005/.8.8: 80' motor-sail, Antalya Turkey-La Paz, Mexico, Nov. '05
ECHO VOYAGE 246/2005/11.8: 46' ketch, Grenada-Lauderdale FL, Nov '05
ECHO VOYAGE 249/2005/13.8: 54' Hylas, crew, pay-to-sail, NY-RI-BDA-BVI, Oct.-Nov. '05
ECHO VOYAGE 251/2005/15.8: 41' Beneteau, Annapolis to Lauderdale, Nov. '05
ECHO VOYAGE 252/2005/17.8: 42' sail, Palma de Mallorca-Germany, Oct. '05
ECHO VOYAGE 254/2005/21.8: 35' power, Key West-Roatan, Honduras, end-Sept. '05
ECHO VOYAGE 256/2005/21.8: 114' power, engineer & stewardess, RI-Caribs, ASAP-Fall
ECHO VOYAGE 259/2005/25.8 : 57' Lagoon, full-time Capt., Bahamas & FLA, ASAP
ECHO VOYAGE 260/2005/25.8 : 37' trimaran, sail, New Brunswick, Canada-FLA ,Oct.
ECHO VOYAGE 261/2005/25.8 : 37' sail, Cabo San Lucas, Mexico-San Fran., CAL, Nov. '05
ECHO VOYAGE 262/2005/25.8 : 32' sail, TransAt, Tampa, FL-England, May 2006
ECHO VOYAGE 263/2005/27.8: 25' sail, New Haven CT-Cancun Mexico, Fall '05

ECHO VOYAGE 264/2005/28.8: 80' power, TransAt, Martinique, FWI-Dubrovnik, Fall
ECHO VOYAGE 265/2005/28.8: 42' Chris-Craft power, Seattle-Portland early Oct. 2005
ECHO VOYAGE 267/2005/30.8: 36' sail, Antigua-Northern Ireland, Spring 2006
ECHO VOYAGE 268/2005/30.8: 42' *Hunter*, Houston TX-US Virgin Islands, Nov. 1, 2005
ECHO VOYAGE 269/2005/31.8: 57' trawler, Fort Lauderdale FL-Seattle WA, Fall '05
ECHO VOYAGE 270/2005/31.8: 34' Chris-Craft, Newport-Miami Oct.-Nov., 2005
ECHO VOYAGE 271/2005/6.9: 29' sail, owner-assist, Portland OR-Bremerton Washington
ECHO VOYAGE 272/2005/6.9: 40' power, Barcelona-Stockholm, Oct./Nov. 2005
ECHO VOYAGE 275/2005/11.9: 56' power catamaran, San Diego-Saudi Arabia, Nov. 2005
ECHO VOYAGE 276/2005/12.9: 46' *Swan*, racing crew, Fall 2005–Summer, 2006
ECHO VOYAGE 277/2005/13.9: 45' sail, Balt. MD-Cairns, Australia, winter 2005-2006
ECHO VOYAGE 278/2005/13.9: 26' sail, Barrington RI-Greenport NY, Fall weekend
ECHO VOYAGE 279/2005/13.9: 43' catamaran, FLA-San Fran CA, Oct .20 05
ECHO VOYAGE 280/2005/16.9: 42' sloop, St. Thomas USVI to Miami FLA, Nov. ' 05
ECHO VOYAGE 281/2005/16.9: 54' schooner, Bermuda-Beaufort NC, ASAP
ECHO VOYAGE 282/2005/17.9: 95' paddle wheeler seeks 2 non-paid crew, Great Lakes
ECHO VOYAGE 284/2005/21.9: Full-time mate & cook, Caribbean-New Eng., Sep. '05
ECHO VOYAGE 285/2005/21.9: 32' sloop, Miami to Toronto, Fall '05-Spring '06
ECHO VOYAGE 286/2005/21.9: 41' sloop, Portsmouth RI-Rock Hall Maryland, Sept. '05
ECHO VOYAGE 287/2005/21.9: 50' sail, Tortola BVI-OZ, FLA, or Mexico, Oct. '05
ECHO VOYAGE 288/2005/22.9: 42' catamaran, crew, New England to St. Maartin DWI, Fall
ECHO VOYAGE 289/2005/26.9 : 30' sail, San Fran-Sidney, BC Canada, Oct. '05
ECHO VOYAGE 290/2005/26.9: 37' sail, Charleston SC-Galveston, TX, Oct.-Dec., '05
ECHO VOYAGE 291/2005/26.9: 70' racer-crew, Vancouver-Singapore, non-pay, ASAP
ECHO VOYAGE 51/2005/2.26: 50' wooden ketch, crew share, Grenada-Panama-NZ, 2005
ECHO VOYAGE 58/2005/3.5: 36' Beneteau, Mexico-FLA, Oct., 2005
ECHO VOYAGE 59/2005/4.5: 33' foot sloop, Bermuda to Bahamas or US, next spring.
ECHO VOYAGE 79/2005/24.3: 46' sail, Med-Singapore, Sep. 2005
ECHO VOYAGE 92/2005/6.4: 36' power, NJ-Miami FLA, Nov.-Dec., 2005
ECHO VOYAGE 167/2005/1.6: 40' sail Tahiti-Vancouver Aug.-Oct., 2005

Appendix 3 - Life Ring Story: *Breathless* & ITB *Philadelphia*

2018 Outline of details of the Life Ring *Breathless*
and tanker barge ITB *Philadelphia* story:

October 1993 on S/V *Breathless* in the Sargasso Sea, as a paid crew I found a Life-ring from one of US Shipping Partners' vessels, the ITB *Philadelphia* is presently in Great Bitter Lake, Egypt, per wikipedia.org.

Bullet Points:

Nassau, Bahamas - my home is where I delivered it, to my parents business, Cable Beach Mano Bahamas (since sold)

Diary – I kept a careful record of the details and Lat / Long and time of the find.

Photos – Ten extensive photos, though I cannot 100% guarantee it will still be at my parent's shop 25 years later, after hurricanes.

ABS Report - I pulled it at the Bahamas Maritime Authority about 1995

Book – My maritime memoir *Round the World in the Wrong Season* opens with the sentence "I had a life-ring round my feet....." – this life-ring!

Today the ship is at anchor in Egypt off the Suez Canal, basically unusable.

on Marinetraffic.com and other AIS-tracking websites.

I would like to find out when, how and why and where the life-ring was lost overboard? Was it a casual mistake, a storm, a rescue, was anyone killed? I would love to return the life-ring to the ITB *Philadelphia*, however, though I have photos of the life ring in Nassau, it appears to have been lost, or thrown out with other debris in a hurricane years ago and my parents have sold the property, Cable Beach Manor Apartments.

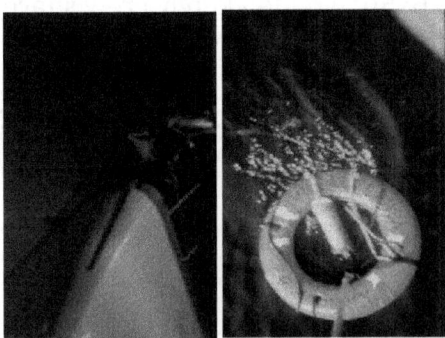

Retrieving the life ring from ITB *Philadelphia* onto *Breathless*, September 24, 1993, Sargasso Sea.

ITB *Philadelphia* in the Great Bitter Lake in the middle of the Suez Canal.

Appendix 4 - Float Plan for *Ivory*

Float Plan for S/Y *Ivory*, Newport-Bermuda-USVI, 24 Oct. 2XXX

Please be advised of the following Float Plan, or voyage itinerary, for the sailing yacht *Ivory*. Vessel: *Ivory* is a 54-foot, single-masted, white-hulled sailing vessel with Westerbeke Diesel 100 hp auxiliary propulsion and a cutter-rig (three sails). Her rig is 72' high. She is fiberglass hulled, built by Little Harbor of Portsmouth RI (USA) in 1991. She is US Flagged, registered to XX, XX. For aircraft, her deck is teak.

Callsign: WX... XY.....

EPIRP: 410 MGHZ Cat2 Litton, Model # 952-00.... The NOAA ID Code is XXXX... for Bermuda Harbor Radio. Inspected 8 Jan XX valid till 8 Feb. XX.

Life raft: Givens 12-persons last inspected Oct. XXXX

Itinerary:

09:00 EDT Weds. 25th Oct. XXXX: Expect Depart Newport RI

mid-day Sun. 29th Oct.: ETA in St. George's Bermuda

The voyage is about 650 nm, and *Ivory* motor-sails at about 7 knots. So voyage time is 95-100 hours, or four full days. Weather is predicted to be less than 20 knots from NNE to E till we are through the Gulf Stream. Thereafter still below 25 till within a day of Bermuda, thereafter possible SE or on the nose at 20-25 knots for the final approach, subject to the movement of a low which we will track daily via SSB Radio.

Captain/Crew:

Captain: Capt. Zebulon. XXX, USCG 100-ton

- Mate: Eric..., USCG 100-ton
- Engineer: Ian...: USCG 100-ton
- Crew: K..., Newport RI
- Owner: Mr. XXXX
- Contacts on shore in US/Canada/Bermuda/Bahamas:
- Bermuda Harbour Radio *[N/A]*
- Herb Hilgengerg, *Southbound II* voluntary WX radio net, (emergencies only)
- [....*Crew's family's contact details*......]

Trust that above clarifies. From Bermuda we will be sailing to St. Thomas, USVI (XXXX Resort and Marina, person in charge Freddie), with an ETA in the USVI of roughly 10-14 November XXXX. This will be advised once we've waited for a weather window from Bermuda. I will personally TRY to update as many parties as possible of our progress in Bermuda, however time online there is costly, and the best way is for me to respond to those who write back (remote email). Otherwise we will be keeping Bermuda Harbor Radio, Herb Hilgenberg in Canada (SSB) and our parents closely advised of the itinerary. I will send a voyage completion memo from Newport sometime mid-November.

Thanks for following this one: we have a 3-day weather window for a four-day voyage, which in October is unusually favorable.

Note: In actual fact we managed an extraordinarily fast passage of 72-hours, all with some 40 knots dead down-wind, no need for the engine, arrived at night, and were permitted to anchor inside before clearing immigration the next day.

Appendix 5 - Timings of the Loss of *Stiarna*

ECHO YACHT DELIVERIES WORLDWIDE
3 LEE'S WHARF, NEWPORT, RI
02840 USA Tel. (401) 845 0052
www.echoyachtdelivery.com

Cruise Inn, Chaguaramas Trinidad
Thurs. 24 Feb. 2000, 12:00 AM LT

AFFADAVIT:

MASTER'S STATEMENT OF EVENTS, S/Y "STIARNA" FIRE & SINKING CASUALTY, TRINIDAD, 24 FEB. 2000

To Whom it May Concern:

I, Capt. Eric T. Wiberg, served as Master of S/Y "Stiarna" between Weds. 16 and Weds. 23 Feb. 2000.

Please find herewith a summary of events of the morning of Weds. 23 Feb., 2000, covering the loss of S/Y "Stiarna", a 1937-built Camper & Nicholson wooden sloop (#642218, US Flag, white hull) to fire and sinking:

04:45 – Oil level checked, main engine (Perkins, 1957-built 6-cylinder diesel) started to warm up
05:00 – crew of five (5) on board: Wiberg, Butler, A. Hanover, D. Hanover, K. Cavalhos
06:00 – S/Y "Stiarna" cleared the fuel dock at Power Boats, Chaguaramas, Trinidad with outward clearance
06:50 – smoke, white in color and only moderately dense, observed emanating from engine space, Revs. reduced
06:55 – Main Engine (M/E) oil pressure dropped from 50 – 20, M/E temp. Temp. abt. 170 degrees F., shut off
06:56 – smoke became thick & dense in pilot house above engine, flames 'crackling' heard, seen in companionway
06:57 – Captain of "Stiarna" called nearby vessel "Calypso II" via VHF requesting standby assistance, reports fire
07:02 – crew use all extinguishers on fire but unable to pinpoint source or extinguish same; I order abandon ship
07:03 – fire aboard "Stiarna" fills pilot house, stopping access from cockpit or main cabin, visibility very poor
07:03 – all five crew members and four bags assemble on aft transom, M/V "Calypso II" manouvers close astern
07:04 – I order abandon ship, Keith C. first, then Hanovers, then Mate Butler, then Wiberg (captain) jump into sea
07:06 – all "Stiarna" crew reach ladder of "Calypso II" safely
07:08 – all "Stiarna" crew safely aboard "Calypso II"
07:09 – fire aboard "Stiarna" has consumed pilot house, has reached boom
07:10 – I consult with Capt. Tom Coulter of "Calypso II" about fire pumps, assistance, we call TTCG for assistance
07:40 – TTCG Rigid Inflatible on-site, a TTCG officer takes info. From me, they assist AH to retreive 2 bags
08:00 – fire aboard "Stiarna" envelopes midriff, moves aft then forward, mast topples to starboard above 1° spreader
08:15 – fire has gutted whole hull of "Stiarna", boom stern midships, topsides burnt through port mid, starboard aft
08:20 – S/Y "Stiarna" sinks in a 3-second heave in one piece, taking with it mast and rigging, ejecting life-sling, ash
08:25 – TTCG "Corozal Point" on site
08:40 – TTCG Rigid Inflatable transfer five "Stiarna" Crew from "Calypso II" to TTCG "Corozal Point"
09:20 – (timings are rough estimates), five "Stiarna" Crew arrive ashore at TTCG base, Trinidad all safe, no burns.

All times in A.M. local time in Trinidad.

Signed: Co-Signed

Capt. Eric T. Wiberg, USCG 100-Ton Master
Email: ericwiberg@lworld
Web site: www.echoyachtdelivery.com

Appendix 6 - Echo Three-Season Summary, to End 1999

A Three-Season Summary of Voyages: Spring, Summer & Fall, 1999

Newport, Thursday 7 February, 2000

By way of background, Echo Yacht Deliveries Worldwide is a small delivery-management company founded in July, 1999. Happily, it turned out to fill quite a niche in the yacht transport market, and the past three seasons were by most standards, a success. Some 15 voyages were undertaken in that time, covering more than twenty ports in four countries and 10 states. We employed almost a dozen sailors, one of whom effectively paid off his college loans with Echo earnings. The only 'downside' was that the weather, especially in the Fall (see list of nine storms below), made it difficult for us to provide our clients with voyages as expeditious and economical as we all would have liked.

Here follows a list of voyages undertaken and performed by the Echo team, with, undersigned as skipper or mate: [*Only boats not named above are included*]

April, 1999 *Pam*, 68' motor launch, hull work, shed, Wickford
June-Sept. S/V *Quintessence*, 53' sloop, day-work, bottom sanding, fall photo-shoot
Oct. 1999 S/V *Carolina*, S/V *Endless Summer*, & S/V *Summer Wind*; shifting & tending

For enabling us to anticipate and avoid serious weather systems (like those listed above) safely, hearty and sincere thanks go to Mr. Herb Hilgenberg, who provides a complimentary Single Sideband (SSB) radio net called *Southbound II*, to mariners who log on for daily weather analysis. His service undoubtedly provided life-saving advice to dozens of sailors in the Atlantic this season. One example: when we aboard S/V *Femme* came to the assistance of S/V *Rogue* (53' Gallion ketch) 100 miles SE of Bermuda, Herb tracked *Rogue*'s return voyage to Bermuda with no engine, a weak SSB, and no VHF – we helped to relay SSB.

The eight voyages May (*Flambé*) to Aug. (*Marblic*) were accomplished in comparatively light and warm summer conditions. The 'most loyal crew': Aaron Dickson (mate, 5 boats *Sabbatical-Sarafina, Triton, Crested, & Femme*, & Ed (chef/crew *Flambé, Triton, & Femme*). Most voyages were happy affairs: crew well fed, warm, dry, and well-rested. Auto-pilots & GPS invaluable labor-saving devices.

Appendix 7 - Echo Sample Yacht Delivery Contract

S/Y *Sample*, 48' *Sloop*, Bermuda to Anywhere Port (USA), end May, 20XX

This agreement is made and entered into in Tucson, Arizona, on Thursday April 16th between Mrs., owner of the vessel S/Y *Sample*, a 48-foot sloop by...., built 19..., draft 0'0" sailing sloop, registered to......Official Documentation Number 1..., Call-sign WD..., and Capt. Eric T. Wiberg (USCG 100-ton sail-endorsed license #8..... valid to 2.. Aug. 20XX), d/b/a Echo Yacht Deliveries Worldwide, XX, Newport, RI, USA [*Echo moved RI-MA-PA-CT-FL-MA*].

1.) Agreement:
Owner agrees to retain the services of the Captain to command delivery of and operate aforesaid vessel from Hamilton and/or St. George's, Bermuda to the dock or mooring at *Anywhere Port* by whichever route the Captain finds expedient and safe according to established navigational practice for a vessel of *Sample*'s size and fuel capacity. Intended route: St. George's-Anywhere Bay-Anywhere Port, USA.

2.) Definitions:
Delivery: Assuming command of the vessel, without passengers, only for the purpose of moving her on her hull, from one port to another, within the US or between foreign ports or vice-versa, excepting locations off limits to US citizens.

Expenses: Expenses are defined as food, fuel, oil, supplies, customs and immigration fees, berth and port fees, emergencies and transportation, local and international, to and from the point of departure and destination for Captain and all Crew.

3.) Rate and Terms:
Owner agrees to pay the Captain, on behalf of Echo Yacht Deliveries, $XX... lumpsum, plus vessel expenses. Captain is to purchase his own airfare tickets. If, due to no fault of captain, the $1XX change penalty applies, owner is to cover this cost. The voyage is estimated to take 5-7 days including vessel/voyage preparation, actual voyage and repatriation. A very rough itinerary would be: Capt/Crew arrival Bermuda *Any Date*, depart Hamilton Any Date, refuel and clear out of St. George's, depart Bermuda Any Date, (weather permitting), 4-5 days or so at sea, ETA ...port.. about Any Date, followed by boat clean-up and Captain's repatriation (likely bus or car to Newport).

It is mutually agreed that if the voyage takes longer than one (1) week, Captain to be paid $100 *per diem* for extra time. It is agreed that this length of time is very unlikely.

The delivery fee shall be paid as follows: A $XX... will be paid to Captain on completion of the voyage in Any Port USA. Payment shall be made in US dollars by cash, check, bank draft or money order to Echo Yacht Deliveries in person on completion of delivery. The owner agrees to pay reimbursement of reasonable vessel expenses on receipt of final invoice with receipts, preferably within a week of the voyage's completion.

4.) Crew:
It is understood that Capt. Eric T. Wiberg will be Master of the vessel, and Crew required in addition to the Captain will be nominated by the Owner and retained by the

Captain to assist in the delivery voyage. If, for any reason, Capt. Wiberg is unable to personally perform the voyage, he will notify the Owner right away, and offer a qualified, available captain as substitute, subject to the Owner's approval. Failing this, the Owner has the right to terminate this contract before Crew have left to join the vessel.

There will a total of five persons onboard, subject to Captain's approval and approval of Owner's nominees. The Captain reserves the right to 'hire and fire' crew, whether selected by the owner or captain, and to place additional crew aboard, say, in Bermuda, if deemed necessary for safety.

If the owner wishes to add remove Crew in agreement with the Captain, then additional Crew's travel expenses, wages, etc. are to be borne by the Owner or Crew, not by the Captain or Echo Yacht Delivery.

Of course the Captain and Crew will be courteous and hospitable to Owner and his guests in Bermuda. On *Any Date*, the Crew list is Wiberg, Crew 1, 2, 3, & 4. Each Crew will be responsible for arriving Bermuda by Any Date.

5.) Inspection and Equipment Failure:

The Owner and a Surveyor of his nomination represent the vessel to be seaworthy. However, if upon inspection and preparation or *en route* (underway), mechanical, electronic, electrical failure, loss or damage occurs or has occurred to said vessel or its equipment which, in the Captain's judgment, hinders her ability to make or continue a safe voyage, the Owner must correct it, or authorize corrective action, at the Owner's expense.

The voyage may be terminated by the Captain if, in the Captain's judgment, the vessel is considered unsafe, then he will be paid a daily fee of US$500 for the Echo team, plus expenses incurred including return air/ground fare to their home base. All remaining monies advanced in excess of what be due to him will be returned to the Owner or his agent by the Captain.

6.) Expense Money:

Adequate expense money (to be mutually agreed) will be made available in cash and or cashier's checks in advance of the proposed departure of said vessel. The Captain will submit an itemized book with receipts, petty cash slips and invoices, where procurable, as basis for final accounting to the Owner. If the expenses exceed the amount of the advance, then the Owner will provide funds to cover the deficiency. To cover provisioning and fuel an amount of roughly US or Bermuda $XX... should be made available to the Captain on the boat's behalf before departure, depending on needs. Since Owner and family plan to sail with crew from Hamilton-St. George's Bermuda, and fuel and provisions will be aboard, there may be no need for a cash advance.

7.) Marine Insurance:

A valid marine insurance policy will be provided by the Owner, with the Captain, Mate, and Crew included as additionally insured parties to cover possible liabilities including, but not limited to, damages to the vessel and all expenses related to injuries and/or sickness to the Captain and/or Mate and Crew. Coverage shall also include public liability and property damage. A copy of the policy will be faxed, mailed or emailed to the Captain for review.

Resumes showing experience and qualifications (i.e.: licenses and resumes) of the Captain, Mate and Crew will be made available by the Captain to both the Owner and the Insurers. Captain will provide full sailing CV plus copies of his USCG-issued Master's license, front and back, for insurer's perusal (emailed *Any Date* to Owner). Note Any Insurers have accepted Captains' USCG license and a rider for voyage with delivery crew is in place as per discussion between Owner and Captain.

8.) Hold Harmless:
The Captain is not responsible for normal wear and tear, nor for equipment failure under prudent operation consistent with established practices, nor for loss resulting from acts of God (i.e.: lightning, hurricanes, etc.). The Captain is not responsible for losses due to acts of war, piracy, government's actions, or insurgencies, nor for damage to the vessel or injuries to the Crew sustained there from, nor for the termination of the voyage caused as a practical consequence thereof.

9.) Illegal Activities:
All obligations of the Captain under this agreement will become null and void if the said vessel is engaged in any illegal activity or violation of the Zero Tolerance government regulations regarding transportation or use of illegal drugs or smuggling on board. The Captain and Crew will uphold the law, report such activities and support the authorities conducting any investigation whether on land or on the high seas. It is understood that when arriving in the United States from overseas (i.e. Bermuda) international requires that the vessel hoist the Quarantine ('Q') flag and advise US Customs and Immigration of the vessel's arrival, and the vessel be cleared into the states with INS (Immigration and Naturalization Services) and US Customs.

10.) Rules of Responsibility:
The Owner, his guests and supplied Crew will adhere to Rules of Responsibility as outlined by the Captain. These will include, but not be limited to: 1.) No consumption of alcoholic beverages while underway, 2.) No smoking in the interior spaces, 3.) Carry no contraband onboard vessel, 4.) Present all firearms, including the flare gun, for inspection, in Bermuda, the US and any other jurisdiction, and 5.) Follow all reasonable instructions issued by the Captain.

11.) Addendum:
A.) That adequate berthing quarters will be available to the Captain for full voyage.

B.) That currently certified and dated lifesaving devices be onboard vessel prior to departure (i.e.: SOLAS 6 Plastimo, person life raft, flares, working EPIRB, SSB, VHF and Satellite telephone). If out of date, items will be acquired or inspected at Owner's expense. It is understood that there is Radar on board. It is understood that the vessel qualified for the Bermuda Race 20XX and is fitted out for offshore racing and cruising.

C.) Wire instructions: "Credit to the account of XXX, Acct. No. Any Bank, etc."

D.) Owner agrees to compose and forward letters of introduction to enable the Captain, Mate, and Crew (to be named) addressed to Bermuda Department of Immigration, setting out that they are in Bermuda in order to join and depart aboard S/Y *Sample*. Copies of this letter should be mailed by the owner to Bermuda Immigration, with Mate and Crew copies given in person or sent to Eric Wiberg, …. prior to the start of the XX-Bermuda Race, preferably on letterhead or assertion showing ownership.

Note *Any Owner* has already filled out and sent five letters to the complete Crew to facilitate their arrival in Bermuda.

Signed:

_____	_____	<u>Any Date</u>
Owner/Agent	**Captain**	**Date**

Post Delivery Statement *(to be completed at end of delivery):*

The vessel has been delivered to its final destination in good condition. The Captain has been paid in full and holds no claim to the above-named vessel or its Owner.

_____	_____	<u>Any Date</u>
Captain	**Owner/Agent**	**Date**

Appendix 8 - 2005 Echo Yacht Delivery's Second-Quarterly Summary

Transat Toulon France-Baltimore, 56' *Sundeer*, Capt. D. N. Sept.
Jamestown RI-Cold Spring Hbr. NY, 30' *Sabre*, Capt. D. A., Aug.
Tortola BVI-Newport, 47' *Tayana*, Capt. B. & Jay S., July/Aug.
Tortola BVI-Turks & Caicos, 29' *Bayliner*, Capt. R. D. & T. O., July/Aug.
Ixtapa Zihutanejo Mexico-Golfita Costa Rica 34' *Irwin*, Capt. Ken S., July
Fort Lauderdale FL-Newport RI 113' *Destiny*, Mate Vin S., July
Newburyport MA-Bernegat NJ, 46' *Hunter* sloop, Capt. Everett H., July
TransAt, SW Hbr. ME-Azores-Spain, 52' Hinckley *Flambé*, Capt. Andrew B.,
July Lowell, NY-New England Cruise, 50' Jeneau *Farr Away*, Capt. Kevin L., Jun-Aug.
Portsmouth RI-Little Creek VA, 38' *Hunter*, Capt. Dave H., June
St. Martin, DWI-Newport RI, 72' *Holland Sloop*, Ignacio B., May
West Palm Beach FL-Manlius NY, 47' *Catalina*, Capt.s P. & H., May
Fall River MA-Laurence NJ, 36' *Jersey*, Capt. Kevin L., Apr.
St. Thomas USVI-Caribs, 46' *Gran Soliel*, Capt. Mike C., Mar.
Annapolis MD-Beaufort NC, 40' sail, Capt. Jeremy H., Jan.
    Total: *17 Voyages, 20,000+ nm (2 x 4,000-mile Trans-Ats), 19 captains & mates*

Newport to St. Martin, Oyster 55', Nov. Capt. Andy B.
Georgia to NJ, 42' *Sloop*, Capt. V., Oct.
Onsett MA to Huntington NY, S/Y O'Dea 32', Sept., Capt. Kevin L.
New England Charter, 42' S/Y, Aug., Capt. John C.
Bermuda-Newport, 42' *Swan* S/Y, Catriona L-C., Crew
Marion-Bermuda Race, 42' *Swan* S/Y, Jun., Catriona L-C., Crew
Daimler-Benz Trans-At Race, RI-Germany 80' S/Y, Greg H., Crew
Florida-NY, 40' *Legacy*, Capt. Kevin L., May
USG-Panama-Galapagos-Easter-Chile, Cape Horn-Falklands-arg-Caribs-Key West, Kevin L.
Newport-Wickford RI, Winter, 42' power, Casey F., Todd C.
New England Charter, Beneteau 44' S/Y, Jun., Capt. John C.
Transatlantic MA-Azores-Ireland, Dehler 40', May-Jun, Adam S.
Trans-Atlantic, Bermuda-Azores-UK, S/Y, Jul, Adam S.
North Carolina – New Jersey, 35' *Catamaran* S/Y, Jun., Stephen D.
NY-Maine, 45' *Sloop* S/Y, Capt. Mike, July
Cape Cod-USVI, *Swan* 60' S/Y, Oct, two Echo Crew
Bermuda-City Island NY, Jenneau 37', June, unnamed skipper
Trans-Pac San Diego-Cairns, Australia, 43' Saga, Apr-Jun, Amy, Crew

Bermuda-Newport, *Swan* 46', May, Chad J.

Lauderdale-Beaufort-Annapolis-Newport, Capt. Dermot, Aug.

E. Greenwhich RI - Camden ME, 46 Jefferson, Capt. John C., Aug.

Marion MA-Boothbay, ME, S/Y Pearson 36', Capt. John C., July

Essex CT-Bristol RI, 41' Bristol S/Y, Capt. Dan T., Nov.

Jamestown RI-Southwest Harbor, ME, 52' Hinckley *Flambé*, Kevin L., Oct.

Lauderdale-New York, 50' Baltic *Sloop Verite*, Capt. Dermot, June

Appendix 9 - Echo Yacht Delivery Wall of Fame

Brokers:
Bob; *Flambé, Diviner, Sabbatical, Sarafina, Femme, Sabbatical, Ascent, Ascent, Flambé* – 9 from 1999-2000, supported by Polly, Will. Also Susan C. & Carolyn C., Swan Yacht Charters Newport, Lisa, Bill, Eric, Hank, Georges, Annie and many others.

Captains:
Capt. Dan: S/Y *Down Home*, Essex CT – Bristol RI, Nov. 2000
Capt. Mike C.: S/Y *Ivory*, Newport – St. Thomas, via Bermuda, Oct.-Nov. 2000
Capt. Kevin L.: S/Y *Flambé*, Jamestown RI–SW Harbor, Oct. 2000
Capt. Pat H.: McKinna 57, Newport – Norwalk Ct, Sept. 2000
Capt. Ken H.: S/Y *La Souris Qui Rugit*, Christmas Cove, Maine-Newport, Aug. 2000
Capt. Dermot: S/Y *Verite*, Fort Lauderdale – New York, 2000
Capt. Mick M.: S/Y *Dancer*, Bermuda–Azores–Channel Islands Jun. 2000
Capt. Anthony 'Tugboat' N.: *Marblic*, SW Harbor Maine – Newport, Sept. 1999

Mentors:
Brian Blank, Bareboat Sailing Charters, *Endless Summer, Summer Magic, Summer Wind,*
Capt. Warren Brown, *War Baby*
Capt. Stephen Connett, *Geronimo*.

Mates:
Aaron Dickson: S/Ys *Femme, Triton, Crested, Sarafina, Sabbatical*.
Capt. Mike: S/Y *Sabbatical*, RI – USVI Nov. 2000
Capt. Joy: S/Y *Seeadler*, Bermuda – Newport, May 2000
Ed: S/Y *Flambé* Plus Chef/Mate on *Ascent, Femme, Triton*.
Anthony "Tugboat" Neighbors: S/Y *Lapwing*, & *Marblic*, Maine – RI

Crew:
Ian Strump, Engineer & Chad Jackson, *Sabbatical*. Rory & Laura, *Seeadler*, Dave C., *Crested*, Marta and Hugh, *Diviner*, Lisa, *Sarafina*, Kent & Wayne, *Flambé*.

On Shore:
Susan at Armchair Sailor, Bill Harnett at PostAll, Capt. Ted P. of F/V *Gertrude H.*, John Hirshler of Sightsailer & Tony Bessinger at Armchair for encouragement

Canadians Laura and Rory on *Seeadler*, espying an oceanic sunfish and raising the Echo Yacht Deliveries banner in St. George's Bermuda. It was the only voyage I made with parity of genders, and also one of the most relaxed, healthy, and enjoyable.

Appendix 10 - Working Voyages: 56 vessels, 1,510 miles

Trip	Name/s	Year	From	To	Miles	Role	Notes
1	lobster boat	1993	Lincolnville, Maine	Penobscot Bay, Maine	18	Crew	1 day
1	Jongert 65' *Serenity Of Sea*	1993	Camden Maine, Newport RI	Newport RI	0	Labor	
1	water tanker *Titas*, 5,000	1995	Nassau	Morgan's Bluff, Andros	86	Guest	consultant
1	lobster boat *Gertrude H.*	2000	to c.100 nm offshore	Newport	215	Crew	4am-10pm
1	workboat	2009	Freeport, GB	Freeport, GB	65	Capt.	backup
1	shuttle boat	2009	Freeport, GB	Freeport, GB	300	Capt.	oil platform
1	tug *Victoria*	2009	Freeport, GB	Freeport, GB	75	Crew	lived 2 mos.
2	BC Ferries	2010	Vancouver, Tsawwassen	Victoria, Swartz Bay	58	Pax.	work
8	NYC ferries many	1975-2019	Sandy Hook, Staten I.	North Manhattan	150	Pax.	
5	Hudson River, NYC	1977-2018	Statue of Liberty	Ellis Island, tours	75	Pax.	
4	Bridgeport-Port Jefferson ferries	1985-2019	Bridgeport CT	Port Jefferson NY	75	Pax.	
7	Block Island ferries	1987-2015	Newport, Pt. Judith	Block Island	75	Pax.	
2	Greenport, LI ferry	1988-2018	New London, CT	Greenport LI	50	Pax.	
4	Bermuda ferries	1989-2018	St. George's	Hamilton, Somerset	50	Pax.	
1	*Quick Step*	1999-2004	Newport, RI	Fairhaven, MA	120	Mate	moor, tows
6	Puget Sound islands	2005-2015	Seattle, Bainbridge	Vashon, Bremerton	48	Pax.	work, fam.
12	12 McAllister Tugs	2013-2018	Puerto Rico	Portland	50	Guest	12+ ports
56					1510		

Appendix 11 - Passenger Voyages: 178 vessels, 12,240 miles

Trips	Name/s	Year	From	To	NM	Notes
2	Turkey	1991	Dardanelles	Istanbul	1	
1	Corfu to Athens (Piraeus), Greece	1991	Brindisi Italy-Corfu	to Piraeus	250	backpacking
1	canoe Kilifi Kenya Salim	1992	south bank	north Kilifi, Kenya	0.5	adventure
1	Modern ferry	1992	Zanzibar	Dar Es Salaam	55	
1	fishing boat *Sea Star*	1992	Sandy Point, Abaco	Nassau, Bahamas	60	mail trip
3	Ecuador	1993	Academy Bay, local	Wreck Bay, local	30	
2	Tonga ferries	1994	Tonga'tapu	Paingaimoto	6	very close by
1	French Polynesia	1994	Moorea	Pap'ete	23	
3	New Zealand inter-island	1994	Wellington, Invercargill	Picton, Stewart Isl.	97	N-S Stewart
1	Finnish lake ferry	2000	Keuru	Lake central Finland	5	
1	Napier New Zealand fishing charter	2000	Napier, NZ	fishing charter Napier NZ	10	wedding trip
1	France	2007	Marseilles	offlying islet	15	
1	Charles River, Boston	2019	tours	tours	8	
1	Maine ferries	2020	Mt. Desert	*Swans* Island	25	
1	Cuttyhunk, Penikese charter	2020	Cuttyhunk, MA to Naushon Island	Penikese Islands, back	10	
3	Dutch various	1977-2007	Rotterdam port	Amsterdam cruises	50	
1	Mailboat, various	1977-2019	Nassau (hub)	Little Abaco	50	research
1	Mailboat, various	1977-2019	Nassau (hub)	Berry Islands	100	research
1	Mailboat, various	1977-2019	Nassau (hub)	Rum Cay	300	research
1	Mailboat, various	1977-2019	Nassau (hub)	San Salvador	300	research
3	Mailboat, various	1977-2019	Nassau (hub)	Andros Island	300	research
1	Mailboat, various	1977-2019	Nassau (hub)	Crooked Island	500	research
2	Mailboat, various	1977-2019	Nassau (hub)	Acklins Island	500	research

Trips	Name/s	Year	From	To	NM	Notes
1	Mailboat, various	1977-2019	Nassau (hub)	Mayaguana	600	research
1	Mailboat, various	1977-2019	Nassau (hub)	Inagua	600	research
2	Mailboat, various	1977-2019	Nassau (hub)	Cat Island	700	research
3	Mailboat, various	1977-2019	Nassau (hub)	Exuma, various	750	research
4	Mailboat, various	1977-2019	Nassau (hub)	Abaco, various	1,500	research
4	Mailboat, various	1977-2019	Nassau (hub)	Eleuthera	3,050	research
2	Waterway cruises, Florida	1980-2018	Winter Park, South Beach	Fort Lauderdale, Miami	20	
3	England various	1984-2018	Lymington, Southhampton	Cowes, Isle of Wight	40	
3	Narragansett Bay	1986-2019	Warren, RI	Newport, various	30	school
6	Jamestown & Rose Island	1986-2019	Narragansett Bay	Newport	75	dinghies, ferries
7	Sandhamn ferries	1987-2007	Stockholm area	Sandhamn Island	200	
10	Martha's Vineyard ferries	1987-2012	Woods Hole	Martha's Vineyard	110	
2	Connecticut River ferry	1987-2014	Gilette Castle	Hadlyme CT	3	
3	Norway	1987-2017	Bergen local	Trondheim, Oslo	72	
4	San Francisco Bay	1989-1994	St Francis Yacht Club	Alcatraz, race work	13	
4	Sydney Ferries	1989-1994	Sydney	Outer bays	15	
2	Rottnest ferry	1989-1997	Kwinana, Freemantle	Rottnest Island	48	
12	Eleuthera water taxis, to Harbour Island	1989-2018	Three Islands, Bahamas	Harbour Island, Eleuthera	50	
8	Nantucket ferries	1990-2014	Hyannisport, MA	Nantucket	170	
2	Chappaquidick	1993-2013	Edgardtown	Martha's Vineyard	2	voyages
2	Panama	1993-2013	Balboa	Islas Tabogas	30	spearfish
3	Cuttyhunk Ferries	1993-2021	New Bedford	Cuttyhunk, Vineyard	48	

Trips	Name/s	Year	From	To	NM	Notes
15	Longboats, ferries	1994-2000	Ao Nang, Railay	Phi Railway, Chicken, Phucket	150	
6	Thai ferries	1994-2000	Surathani, Samui	Ko Pha Ngan	250	
1	Charter junk	1995-1998	Ha Long Bay	northern Vietnam	25	
4	Tioman Ferries	1995-1998	Tioman, Rawa	mainland Malaysia	450	
2	Vermont Lake Champlain ferry	1995-2015	Vergennes, VT	Champlain to New York State	30	
2	Providence Ferries	2000-2001	Providence RI	Newport RI	15	
2	Fishers Island ferries	2002-2006	New London	Fishers Island	7	
5	Shelter Island Sag Harbor ferry	2003-2018	Sag Harbor	Greenport LI	4	
5	Long Island Sound, CT	2003-2018	tours, cruises	tours	25	
3	Maine ferries	2003-2020	Lincolnville	Islesboro	12	
6	Greece various	2013-2018	Angkistri, Aegina	Poros, Hydra, Andros	200	
5	Boston Island ferries	2019-2020	Boston, Hull Hingham	Harbour Isls, Provincetown	250	
178					12,240	

Appendix 12 – "A Summer Under Sail for Eric Aboard *Rumor*"
The Nassau Tribune, Bahamas, August, 1989

This June, *Rumor* crossed the starting line off Marion, Massachusetts, with a Bahamian crew-member aboard, and set a course for Bermuda. Around midday on June 23, the seventh biennial Marion-Bermuda race began, and though the following four days brought thrill and victory to our boat, they also brought wreckage and death to others. A record 163 boats, some as long as 60 feet in length started the Marion-to-Bermuda Race that was begun by David Kingery in 1977. Kingery was frustrated that the Newport-Bermuda race, begun in 1906, had become too competitive. So, the cruising yachts that compete from Marion with all-amateur crews and are not permitted to raise spinnaker racing sails or use satellite navigation.

Cruisers, instead must use, sextants and star-sightings to navigate more than 625 nm from Buzzards Bay, New England, to St. David's Light, Bermuda. Then they thread their way through the reefs to a rendezvous at the Royal Hamilton Amateur Dinghy, which, along with Marion's Beverly Yacht Club and the Royal Bermuda Yacht Club, sponsors the race. As newsmen from *Cruising World* and Bermuda's *Royal Gazette* observed, the yachts made their way offshore by nightfall of the first day.

Rumor found herself drifting at midnight in light winds; the boat is two ton, with a sloop-rig, and it flounders without wind. However, by the race's first dawn, the crew of six had *Rumor* moving at six knots in conditions which would last us the race: winds 15-to-25 knots and seas 4-to-7 feet. Among the 800 individual participants, I was the only Bahamian. Although the race was my first real introduction to offshore or blue-water sailing, *Rumor*'s crew had sailed 30 Bermuda races among them. Our skipper, Mr. Jones, and his son, Stan, had long since mastered their ship. Andrew, my watch-captain, had raced to Bermuda more than 20 times; and a fifth crewmember had made *Rumor*'s sails, so I felt in safe hands. My position of boat-boy this summer entailed preparing *Rumor* in Newport, and crewing aboard her to and from Bermuda. I held watch between midnight and 4 a.m. (graveyard watch), 8 a.m. till noon, 4 p.m. to 6 p.m. (dog watch), then a switch. I was also responsible for cooking and general cleaning and up-keep.

The work was often exciting and always varied. Though our ages ranged from my teens into the sixties, our crew amicably gathered over pre-cooked dinner, salad and sandwich lunches, porridge, and snacks. As *Rumor* sailed through her second day, all attention focused on achieving maximum speed: I either steadied the helm, used my weight to steady the ship, or busied myself setting and striking as many as three sails. With the wind behind us, we sped along at up to nine knots with the mainsail to starboard, and two huge light headsails. By the third day we had overtaken several boats, and a few had come very close upon our stern before veering off. Even at night vessels were never far off, sometimes trailing our lights at intimidating distances.

Our only mishaps included a snapped boom vang (an adjustable metal strut which supports the boom from the base of the mast, near the deck), and a loss of lights and speed-gauging equipment. However the nearby Canadian yacht *Bellatrix* was not so fortunate: the

44-foot Canadian yacht broke its rudder on the night of the 25th. Shortly thereafter, the preventer, a temporary black and tackle system to prevent the boom sweeping suddenly across deck and cockpit, snapped, and the swinging boom killed crewmember Dr. Donald Hill, a 52-year-old Vancouver doctor. The Russian research vessel *Akademik Vernadskry* then came out of cover and towed the damaged *Bellatrix* to a waiting US Coast Guard ship outside of New York.

Meanwhile, aboard *Rumor*, where participants had very limited radio communications to prevent changing strategies based on what others are doing, we knew nothing of the tragic mishap. By the third day were crossing I the Gulf Stream, where we sighted whales, porpoises, Sargasso weed and sharks. The weather warmed and the water temperature shot to 80 degrees as we neared Bermuda on the evening of the third day.

Although plastic debris hinted land, we didn't sight St. George's, Bermuda, until dawn of the fourth day. Bermuda long-tail doves welcomed us as we cruised across the finish line past the yacht *Pirate* off St David's Light in North East Bermuda. When *Rumor* and her crew pulled along the "winners' wharf" of the Royal Hamilton Amateur Dinghy Club, even though we started the race ranked 123rd overall in D Class, we had crossed the line 53rd, and had placed with a corrected time (with handicaps) of 18th!

The crew received a trophy and various souvenirs for placing. Bermudian Warren Brown's ship *War Baby* won line, honors and Commodore Frank Snyder's *Chasseur* won A Class. The smaller yacht *Yukon Jack*, an O'Day 34-footer won on corrected, time; which was a David & Goliath story, in a more accessible type of yacht run by a wrestling coach. About 20 boats withdrew in the finishes' light winds, or earlier on in the 30-knot gusts. As for me, I enjoyed my first visit to Bermuda, which was wonderfully similar to the Bahamas, before the week long return to Newport. I only hope that I am not the last Marion-Bermuda-Bahamian.

Appendix 13 – "23 Year Old Nassuvian Skippers 70 Foot Sailing Yacht Across Pacific"

What's On Bahamas, January & February, 1995

S/Y *Stornoway*'s voyage westwards, essentially from one boatyard in the US, to another, in New Zealand, was an often impeded and at times almost abandoned voyage. The Christmas and New Year's season of 1994 found *Stornoway* laying disconsolately in the Galapagos Islands, off South America, with only the owners and me aboard. The options facing them were few and stark. They had no captain. The hull was showing signs of leakage, and the dreaded cyclone season bore down on them daily. A lightning bolt had scrambled valuable electrical gear, including automatic steering. They would need hands, and more than three pairs of them. Their insurance was revoked. And they had a South American navy breathing down their backs.

In a desperate bid to wrest his prized yacht from seizure by the local port captain, the owner appointed me as acting captain, responsible for recruiting and training needed crew, navigating, sailing, and delegating watch-system and emergency duties. With 7,000 more miles of open ocean between they and the repairs awaiting *Stornoway* to New Zealand, I assumed his first command. What follows is my account of how *Stornoway* and her meager crew ended up in their Galapagos predicament, and, more importantly, how they sailed their way out of it.

Smoke and soul wafted around my older brother and I as we sat in Mr. Nesbitt's bar in Delaport, on the fringe of Cable Beach, outside Nassau. The ice in our drinks was melting fast, but we weren't bothered. It was the last night of November 1993, and I was about to ship out to sea once more, for the longest in my 23 years. We were in earnest conversation. I lay my concerns out on the table like pieces of tangled driftwood:

"I mean, it's a big ocean out there. A long time. A lot can happen, They may *ask me to become Captain*." The solace of Otis and Aretha from the jukebox, the comfort of familiar faces, the buzz of conversation, all seemed to recede before that word: Captain. Virtually unutterable among young sailing crew except as a term of address — or of conspired mutiny. John and I talked about *Stornoway*, that stately sheer of dark blue and stained wood, the majestic outline of her masts, forming the yacht which we had both gone to admire in Nassau harbor. We'd both been sailing awhile, but the very size of *Stornoway*, and the scope of her voyage, was beyond what either of us had faced.

"Don't do it, Eric," he said, "...it's too much, *too soon. Don't let 'em even ask you...*" Though I had to agree, I also felt a restless excitement: it would be a fine way to cap off a steady progression: six summers' worth of working my way from bilge-boy to watch-captain. I had the sailing bug that fall. I'd had it bad since graduating from college in May, and even another Bermuda Race and a yacht delivery (through the Sargasso Sea from New England to the Bahamas) that summer hadn't satiated me.

I first spotted *Stornoway* on my flight home from a decade of schooling in New England and England. As our plane swooped down Nassau harbor towards Paradise Island, her proud figure briefly filled my portal. I would fulfill my burning again. The following day

I was by the yacht's side at the Nassau Harbor Club for a closer look and to learn as much as I could of her. *Stornoway* was hand-crafted out of Burma teak in her port of registry, Greenock, Scotland, more than thirty years ago. Her owner of fifteen years, Chris, is near twice as old as *Stornoway*. He and the ship's chef, an Italian-Australian woman named Tina, had just spent four years, in Florida preparing for the voyage.

They were bound for Chris' birthplace of New Zealand; two large islands, which lie, nudged between Antarctica and Australia. Theirs promised to be a rare undertaking: sometimes tip-toeing, at others barreling, across an expanse of ocean twenty million square miles in breadth: the Pacific, the largest and among the least populated, watery regions of the world. In October my brother and I saw *Stornoway* off as she made for; Panama via Jamaica. Already her crew, selected at the last minute, was causing concern aboard. I gave Chris arid Tina my sailing resume, and my brother and I walked away. Late that November, a fax machine on Cable Beach hummed with a tantalizing offer. The letterhead read S/Y *Stornoway*, Greenock. the sending station was Balboa, Panama.

The message, marked URGENT, was brief:

Eric - We've studied your sailing file again, and would like you to join us as First Mate of Stornoway, *effective on acceptance. Weekly wage, flight down to Panama, return airfare from New Zealand. Yon will have your own cabin, 'head' (toilet area), and crew to administer. Original mate to be sent home. Plan to push off within the week,.*

Ports-of-call: Panama, the Galapagos Islands, the Marquesas, Bora-Bora, and Papeete, Tahiti, in French Polynesia. Then the Southern Cook Islands, Kingdom of Tonga, Fiji, and the Bay of Islands, finishing in Auckland, New Zealand, hopefully before the cyclones!

For the "voyage of a lifetime", please respond ASAP. Yours, Chris, Panama.

Tahiti? Galapagos? Marquesas? Islands to an island boy, they sounded so exotic – the offer almost too good to be true. As a student and a dreaming sailor, I had long conspired to hit the highways and sea-ways of the world... I packed my gear, backed out of a power-yacht job in Palm Beach, Fla., and trundled off to Central America. On the first of December, I landed in the rainy season in Panama City, a capital of coups, and signed aboard.

Right away, as we lay moored under (the Bridge of the Americas, at the Pacific entrance of the Panama Canal, the power structure aboard was thoroughly shaken. I clung on tenaciously as first the mate, then the crew, and finally *Stornoway*'s second skipper packed it in and flew home. They were told that the voyage was off, that the yacht would be mothballed. But no sooner had they left, in the first of December, than a new captain— veteran sailor Roger—whisked aboard in a flurry and readied us to get underway.

After an overnight 'shakedown' sail to the Taboga Cays, and several weeks spent tinkering with the gear and partying with Canal 'Zonies', yachties, and Panamanians, the four of us slipped out of the Balboa yacht under cover of bound 800 miles westwards, for the Galapagos Islands, astride the Equator. The morning of Christmas Eve broke full and clear over us six days later, as *Stornoway* made her approach to our first Pacific landfall. Tradition called for Equator-crossing celebrations, and, as the youngest, I was selected to be the 'Equatorial Virgin', crossing the seams of the earth by sea for the first time. Dressed as 'the Jailor' in stuffed stockings, Chris roused me from my off watch slumber in the forward most cabin, handcuffed me, and led me aft, to the transom, where I was tried and condemned as the 'virgin' by a costumed 'King Neptune' (Roger), and forced to pay homage to an all-but topless Queen Nefertiti: Tina!

After dousings of food and a feast of fresh-caught fish, we sluiced our way around the island of Santa Cruz and sailed up into Academy Bay, home of the Charles Darwin Research Station. Nestled among passenger ships and yachts, we dropped two 'hooks', or anchors, folded our wings, and settled down for a week of Yuletide festivities. We spent the followings days languishing aboard, among nearby islands, or along Tortuga Beach. We swam with playful sea-lions, dared a dip among the sharks, plodded with the tortoises, mimicked the penguins, and dove from the ravines. We celebrated Christmas, Tina's Birthday, and New Year's aboard a decked-out and Christmas lit *Stornoway*, harnessing Tina's cat and letting him roam the decks.

The drums of Junkanoo were replaced by the palpitations of Latin music in the sultry heat, and I ushered in the dawn of the New Year not on Bay Street or Harbour Island, but in a sun-baked Galapagos cafe after partying the morning away at the British Consul's home and the local discos. Despite all the excitement, though, all did not bode well aboard Our 'magic carpet' ride and the security of yacht and team would soon be whisked from beneath us. The first days of the New Year found us aground in Wreck Bay, our trusty captain stuffing his bags and jumping ship in a flurry of angry recriminations and sexual jealousies, leaving Chris, Tina, and I, in the hands of a militant South American Navy, stranded on the equator, without a certified captain or the means to fly one in.

Because of the unhappy skipper's shenanigans, the Ecuadorian Navy were I threatening to have us to wed to Guayaquil, 1,000 miles to the East Beneath us reefs, around us insidious water seeped in. To the West lay some 4,000 miles of open-ocean to the Marquesas—the most remote islands in the world. Chris needed someone who could, and was willing to, navigate across that blue eternity, the mysterious, barren eastern Pacific about which we knew so little. Though not licensed, I had the most sailing experience. I offered my services as navigator and, if needed, as captain. Chris accepted, and on that first week of January, when cleared in (by the insurers) and called forward from the consolation of the back bench to the trials of the 'hot seat Clarissa responded duly. Bucking eager outwardly, somberly scared within, I stepped up to assume my first command.

"*I wanted a mission,*" muses Captain Willard in the opening scenes of Coppola's film *Apocalypse Now*, "*and for my sins, they gave me one. And when it was over,*" he continues, "*I knew I never wanted another.*"

The first week of my command found me frazzled and exasperated in Wreck Bay, on San Cristobal, capital of the Galapagos Islands. New Year's 1994 and a skipper had come and gone. The Ecuadorian Navy was threatening to impound and confiscate *Stornoway* if we lingered, but we needed crew to continue. While sitting in my favorite cafe, studying a file of crew resumes faxed to me from the Caribbean, I grew frustrated by the paperwork. Looking up, I finally just called over to a nearby table, which was filled with travelers:

"Anyone want to sail to New Zealand?" A young man blurted back:
"Sure. I'll go!" but the girl sitting beside him grabbed his arm with a firm
"You will not!"

He couldn't, but he introduced me to another traveler who might. In khaki and a beard, Trevor made a fine impression. He is my age, and also a recent college graduate. We sped out to *Stornoway* in the dingy. He came aboard with me and met Tina, topless on deck, and, Chris, who he also liked. I exercised my full authority to recruit him aboard as our needed fourth crewman, to man the wheel and satisfy the insurers. Though slated to return to his travels and family in Vancouver, Trevor joined us. On the spot. A brave man. We'd found our fourth: Chris is an amiable gentleman who with Tina and their cat, Davie, made a triumvirate. Now I had a comrade too.

We spent two more weeks tinkering in the Galapagos. I taught Trevor as much as he'd need to know while I 'crammed' studying *Stornoway*'s complex systems and navigational gear. Then we fumigated the hold of roaches and readied to set off on our longest passage - to the Marquesas, in French Polynesia. On the 23rd of January we pulled *Stornoway*'s anchors and headed out to sea. Right away there was trouble down below. We were taking on alarming levels of water through the seams of *Stornoway*'s 30-year-old teakwood hull. For weeks, even months, there would be no land.

On Chris' suggestion I agreed to sail us to the nearest anchorage, on Santa Maria Island. It was hairy. After a nighttime approach on an unfamiliar, barely charted shore, we anchored in the historic whaling depot of Post Office Bay, where sailors can still leave letters in an old barrel to be carried on for free. In the morning we saw just how close we'd come to foundering in the reef-strewn bay. I alone discovered, a smudge of our paint on one of them. So close to disaster. I kept quiet. We bribed a local official with cigarettes and hunkered down to repairs. Two nights at anchor, with flamingos, turtles, fish and lobster everywhere. I practiced the mysterious, ancient art of celestial navigation, tutored by a Chilean Navy officer. We had a universe of constellations to 'shoot' sights of with a sextant. Having tightened the bolts attaching keel to our hull, we were ready.

Our first offshore passage together, and Trevor's first ever, was massive. After eight days and a few flare-ups between Chris and I (shifting the power-structure: his boat, my command, and thus my 'ass on the line'...), we hove-to, coming to an eerie halt. I called for a mid-passage swim, a skipper's and crews' tradition meant to boost morale. It would prove a dangerous exercise. We were clocking a smart 200 miles daily and crossed our third time zone since Panama. 1500 miles from the Galapagos, we stopped in about the most remote spot in the world. The fabled Marquesas Islands are farther from a continent than any others. Halfway to the ends of the earth can be a lonely place.

To keep your cool when you know you're in the middle of friggin' nowhere and that you're accountable for the lives of four people and your employer's property, insured in the seven-digit range, takes effort. That passage in particular is known for its dangers - freight containers floating just beneath the surface, whales striking the hull in unexplained aggression... silent killers for which there is no warning, little recourse for help, very little time, and a long way to drift if you are sunk. I was one scared puppy, but I kept it to myself.

We all did.

We made the Marquesas Islands in an almost record 17 days, swinging into glorious Taiohae Bay, Nuku Hiva to proudly drop our hooks in French Polynesia. In that very bay the young sailor Herman Melville had jumped ship and fled to the Valley of the Cannibals, known on charts and on his book as *Typee*. Artist Paul Gauguin, writers Jack London, R L Stevenson, and others have sailed, lived, even died there. I brought our ship's papers (called 'Zarpe') from the Galapagos to the French Gendarmerie and cleared in yacht and crew. The officials administer a colonial society, sending out police or welfare cheques from behind barbed wire enclosures. The cyclone season, which we were openly defying, bore on us daily, but we were permitted only a brief stay.

I returned to *Stornoway* and collapsed, exhausted. Though relieved, the navigation and stress were wearing me down. We hiked ashore, rested, and enjoyed a few 'happy hours' and a Valentine's Day' feast before pushing off for Tahiti, where we hoped mail and new faces awaited us. We were fraught with anxiety over threading the Tuamotu, or 'Dangerous' Archipelago of coral lagoons in the passage ahead. Though fringed in palms trees, these atolls, are razored in reefs on which, the *Kon Tiki* balsa-log raft expedition and others have met grief.

We consumed most of our costly diesel to burst through the Tuamotus ('motu' means atoll) and into a glass-calm, unrippled sea, with 400 miles to go to Tahiti. Drifting for days with neither fuel nor wind, we went slowly mad. Our reflections shone "clearly"; on the unrippled "mirror of the sea" of which Conrad wrote. Trevor and deck in the eerie silence, lapsing into fits of giggling and mad conversations. During night watches the depth-meter sometimes went from an infinite reading (the seafloor a mile or more beneath us) to flashing a depth of 4-5 feet. This meant, something was passing beneath us at that depth. But what? As always, we continued to flush food, waste, even blood overboard. Our cabins heavy with sweat and heat, the lure of the pond-like sea around us proved too tempting.

Late on the second morning, we swam. Chris had seen a dark shadow beneath us at dawn. All we saw were fish - plenty of them. I swam deep. The others tired and went aboard. The waters were so clear that at 30 feet I could mimic the gestures - smiles and fingers - of the crew from deck. Then horror. First on the face of Tina. Then Trevor. Then Chris ran to the railing too, and I knew I was in trouble. They pointed behind me. I looked. And there it was. A triangle of teeth framed by a black jaw and two eyes, mounted by one tall fin. Its tail switched from side to side, propelling the shark towards me from directly below.

No time to think. I turned and swam for our ladder, an eon away. It moved in for the kill. Thank god I had no flippers on. only one toehold on our ladder I catapulted onto *Stornoway*'s scorching deck. The shark struck. Its teeth closed around our ladder and wrenched half of it away. Silence and panting. Shock and disbelief. The shark had been trailing us - stalking the mother ship - for days, waiting for food. It had come seconds from having me. *Never leave the ship.*

The wind finally picked up. We approached Tahiti, making Venus Point, of Captain Cook fame, in a howling squall. The wind also picked up Chris' "Bahama Papa" hat, and took it. We did pirouettes in the sea to retrieve it. The storm brewed over Papeete, capital city, but we barreled into the harbor jubilantly chanting, "*It's a long way to Pap -ay- ete*" - our own rendition of the song *"Tipperary,"* also sung by Germans in *Das Boot*. The French thought we were mad, which should say something for us! (...pot calling the kettle black...)

We were one month in Papeete, the capital city of Tahiti, waiting for the cyclones to break. Ships and crew rot in port. In the colorful tapestry which is Tahiti, in the rainy season, in a town of wash-ups, escapists, and even criminals, we languished. Tahiti was what we had come to the Pacific for, I think. In the overall picture, when we conspire our escapes to sea, when we think of the South Seas, perhaps, it is Tahiti that we think of.

On the rock of that expectation our dreams perhaps run aground. In truth, Papeete can be a sad town. A town where dreams are hung up. The 'women' of the night are as likely to be local men dressed in drag. On the waterfront, where the sailors curl up on abandoned wrecks, where wine, bread, and pot are the diets of many, everyone talks of somewhere else. Dolphins of Papeete, returning from Tetiaroa, Patrick *Tropical Souidade*, late, mutinous passengers, they steered us off reefs to harbour and port safely by making noises.

We had covered more than 4,000 miles in less than a month; like sailing trans-Atlantic, from Nassau to London. Yet we found ourselves not 'across' any ocean, but stuck in the middle of one. It takes days just to *fly* to Tahiti! Chris and I had crossed the Atlantic, but the Pacific seemed just too vast to fathom. We all felt the desperate isolation and struggled with it. Tahiti was the peak of our outward-bound voyage. Though our morale and stamina were sapped, we each chose to continue. We wouldn't quit, wouldn't fly. At the end of March we packed up to head out. The weeklong passage to Rarotonga, in the Cook Islands, was mild but steady, with a swell from Antarctica nudging us. It really was 'pacific', or calm - a 'milk run', despite the threats.

We dodged Cyclone Ursula to nip into Avatiu Harbour, Rarotonga for a few days' rest. The only other sailboat there was bound from New Zealand to Nassau - the opposite of our route. On April Fool's Day we motored out of the basin, watched by the 'happy hour' crowd at Trader Jack's. Just as we passed the wreck of the brig *Yankee* our engine caught fire, spumed smoke, and cut out.

We had a reef on either side, 100 yards to go back, and 1,000 nm to the next port I said nothing as we slid to a silent halt Just started pulling those trusty sails out, one by one. I am a sailor, specializing in simply moving boats from one port, or one island, to another - not in winning races or repairing engines, perhaps, but in getting there. And if to get to there we would have to sail, then sail we would. And sail we did. Chris understood.

We were all becoming a bit testy. We had been abandoned by our skipper, had fended off attempts to seize *Stornoway*, had sprung leaks, nearly run aground, been attacked by a shark, harassed by a cyclone, and finally lost our engine. We were pissed off, and I proposed we sail directly to New Zealand - that we end the voyage after nearly half a year. With winter brewing over New Zealand, though, we weren't prepared for the final passage. We needed our engines and provisions. We set sail for the Kingdom of Tonga, weaving our way westwards around coral lagoons and volcanic seamounts (marked 'position doubtful') in our path. A week later, we threaded past a graveyard of wrecks and into the yacht basin on Nuku'Alofa on Tongatapu with only a foot beneath our keel.

We settled in among Tongans, expats, and ' yachties' for a tedious month of repairs, all but broke. I had deep misgivings about that final passage - a 1,200-lunge mile to the south, out of islands like the Bahamas and into cold and rough seas. The days of my unfettered bravado had passed. Chris asked my conditions to continue. "We need more crew", and we found one - Swedish sailor Stefan. On May 4 we set off.

The seas tore off shreds of *Stornoway*'s paint. We shared watches, manned and pumped the bilges. Yachts flew by. On May 11 the reassuring beacon of Burgess Island Light pierced the dawn; New Zealand at last! Radios all around the gulf flashed warnings of gale conditions due to set in that night. 'Authoritarian' rule gave way to magical teamwork. At midnight we wove around a disabled tanker and punched through to the mouth of Auckland's sprawling harbor. The wind whipped spray on us in sheets as we ducked behind Queen's Wharf, Auckland, and hoisted the yellow 'Q' (for quarantine) flag victoriously. We had made it.

We lashed *Stornoway* to the pilings, which were her final berth and cracked a bottle of Jamaican rum in a warm toast. We - *Stornoway*, her patron Chris, Tina, Eric, Trevor, Stefan, and a boat-ridden cat - had made it. Made it across the South Pacific in all but the wrong season. We knew on arrival that we were each free to keep going - around New Zealand - around the *world* in the wrong season if we liked. Only we would have to go it alone. And that, no doubt caused not just obvious relief, but sadness. A soft, painful, unspoken sadness. We huddled around one another for a week or so, and then we each split off, going our own separate ways - homewards.

Appendix 14 - Employer Letterheads

Miscellaneous images including two short articles, stationary from yachts and yacht owners, the *Young Endeavour* cover to their *World Voyage 1992* brochure, and a copy of one of the US Coast Guard licenses for 100-ton near coastal, sail endorsement I've maintained every five years since 1995:

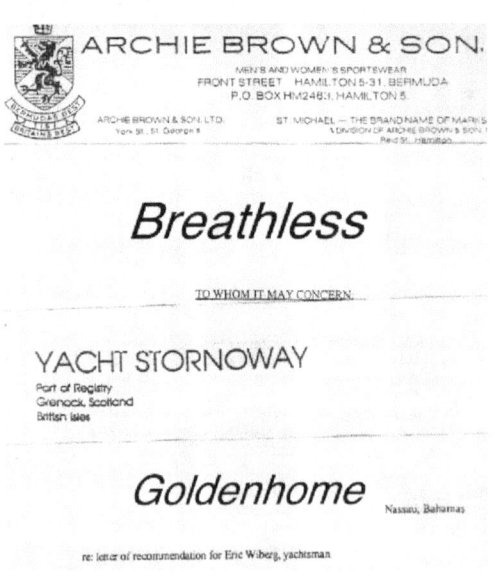

A conversation with a delivery captain
Calls "competence, sense of humor" keys to success

Soon after Eric Wiberg graduated from St. George's School in Newport he set off to sea. Thirteen years and 26 voyages later, CBNS caught up to him on a Saturday morning in October at Gary's Handy Lunch in Newport, a popular spot among sailors and locals which as usual was so packed that there was hardly enough elbow room for Eric to unfold his well-used charts on which he had plotted courses during deliveries to Bermuda, the Caribbean and Europe.

Although Eric, 31 is now living ashore in Newport while

Eric Wiberg spent six months navigating and nursing the 70-foot vintage sailing ketch *STORNOWAY* across the Pacific Ocean, and on a stormy night last May, a battered *STORNOWAY* sailed into New Zealand's Auckland Harbour. It was an epic voyage of some 10,000 miles, taking 72 sea days in the Pacific alone. Eric has written a detailed account of how *STORNOWAY* and her meager crew ended up in their Galapagos predicament, and, more importantly, how they sailed their way out of it. Parties interested in reading this account should contact the Alumni Office.

YACHT SALES • CHARTERS • DONATIONS • NEW CONSTRUCTION
"Professional and Personalized Service Since 1967"

Wm. F. Buckley Jr. * 150 E. 35th St. * New York 10016

Apr 16 95

M. J-C de Revenel
Nassau

Dear Jean-Charles:

You ask my opinion of the writing talent of Eric Wiberg. I have read his essay, "You Can't Get to Mpulungu

Eric Wiberg, Oxford, February, 1992

Looking for **paid crew/Mate** position (pref. offshore) April or June/July '92
Have c.12,000 nautical miles experience as crew/Mate

Appendix 15 - Law Student Sinks Yacht

Part 1: Law Student Sinks Yacht: The law catches up to us in mysterious ways. So I learned this fall when I walked into a 2nd Year Law, Day Division class to find many of my colleagues snickering at me. It turns out that, in the course of research into *Apprendi v. New Jersey* (530 US 466, 2000), my colleague Larry White came across a case, which featured yours truly as the skipper of a yacht, which sank following a fire.

The case is *Reliance National Insurance Company (Europe) Ltd. v. Alain Hanover and Daniel Hanover*, which was heard in the US District Court for Massachusetts on July 22, 2002. Larry handed me a copy of the case in class. I would like to comment on the case in *The Docket* and provide further insight to our colleagues at RWU Law. The case stems from events, which happened in late 1999 and resulted in the sinking of a classic, historic yacht off of the island of Trinidad, in the Lesser Antilles (Caribbean), on 23 February 2000. The issue is whether the yacht's owners are entitled to a jury trial against the insurers, and whether the insurers are entitled to cancel the policy because the owners allegedly misrepresented the purchase price. Both parties allege bad faith, with owners Hanover alleging 'unjust enrichment' by the insurers as well. Judge Richard G. Stearns denied both party's cross-motions for summary judgment, and the case is meant to go to trial within a year (in fact, I understand that I am expected to testify as a witness and give depositions).

For the purpose of this comment, I would like to limit my discussion to the facts of my involvement, and to my perspective, legal or otherwise, on the story of the case. I recommend the reader finds and prints the case - I am mentioned by name six times on page 3). I first heard of the yacht and it's owners in late fall, 1999. A good friend of mine referred me to the Hanovers, with whom he had worked in Boston in the then-booming Internet technology sector. In July of 1999 I had started a small yacht-delivery company (www.echoyachtdelivery.com), and, despite a busy fall seasons (during which I was lost overboard in a snowstorm 100 miles south of Block Island for 16 minutes, and had my index finger stripped almost to the bone by an engine alternator), Christmas holidays had seen me spend my meager savings. By January 2000 I needed work, and Messrs. Hanover offered it.

On February 20, 2000, the Hanovers closed on a deal to buy *Stiarna*, a classic wooden sailing yacht measuring roughly 70 feet on deck, which was built in England (designed by Camper & Nicholson) in 1937. Described as a Twelve Meter, *Stiarna* represents some of the finest in sailing yachts built this century. In 1957 she was fitted with a side-mounted diesel engine. She has one mast. A single owner had owned *Stiarna* for over a decade, and by all accounts her condition had deteriorated during this time. As I understand it, the insurers did not commission their own survey of the vessel, but rather were waiting for the Hanovers and a shipwright, Tom Fredriksen, to overhaul and improve the boat in Tom's new shipyard on the island of Grenada, roughly 80 nm north of Trinidad.

My participation called on me to 1) fly from Boston to Trinidad to assume command of the yacht, 2) organize and implement the delivery voyage from Trinidad to Grenada, in coordination with her caretaker, Tom, 3) oversee the refit in Grenada for up to a year, and

4) skipper her, in restored condition, from Grenada to the Hanover's base in New England, where she would be proudly sailed in Newport. The projected cost of refit exceeded $500,000. My wages were to be comfortable, and included accommodation and transportation in Grenada, which is a beautiful island.

I arrived in Trinidad by air roughly one week before the Hanovers, and immediately set about getting the boat ready for an offshore voyage. This included rewinding the starter motor, changing the oil, bleeding the engine of air locks to make it easier to start, and tightening the fan belts. It also included a check of mast and rigging, available sail inventory, and the seaworthiness (integrity) of the hull. I lived on board, and paid careful attention to the level of bilge water, which led me to seal off several valves, which were fitted 'through the hull'.

I liked Trinidad and found a young man, Ash, who had refit and sailed his own boat, alone, from England to Trinidad, to help me. The island was gearing up for the Carnival, and after long workdays we would unwind in one of two local pubs. The work was hard, the yacht was not too comfortably fitted out, and nights were spent fending off mosquitoes. Work during the day was often filthy, with heavy rains making it more challenging. A snowstorm in Boston delayed the owners for a few precious days, giving me more time to get the boat ready.

On about 21 February I met the owners, Mr. Alain Hanover, and his son Daniel, at Trinidad's international airport. During the drive to the marina at Chaguaramas, they asked me my opinion of the boat. I told them that found the boat to be seaworthy, but recommended that they accept the offer of a local tug boat captain to accompany us for the voyage, with the option of taking *Stiarna* under tow, should the need arise. Mr. Hanover approved this measure, despite a charter cost of several thousand dollars. His attitude was 'if you hire an expert, don't then go and ignore his advice', which I found encouragingly pragmatic.

The owners put us up in a local hotel; we took the yacht for a spin on the engine only, pulled up to the fuel jetty, refueled, and remained there for the night of Feb 22 - 23. The tug *Calypso II* stood by on an adjacent berth, and we agreed to wake at about 4:30 am for a departure before sunrise, which would enable us to accomplish the voyage mostly in daylight. At about 6 am *Stiarna* and *Calypso II* left Chaguaramas, Trinidad, bound in convoy to Grenada. Aboard *Stiarna*, of which I was in command, were five men: myself, Ash, the mate, Mr. Hanover and his son Daniel, and a gentleman named Coelho, of indeterminate age (I estimate around 70 years), who, like Ash, was a shipwright employed by Tom Fredriksen. Aside from white exhaust smoke emanating from the engine space (a pre-existing condition) the voyage proceeded uneventfully as far as the Bocas - a series of islands and channels called, in English, the Mouth of the Dragon - through which all shipping into NW Trinidad must pass.

At roughly 7 am we cleared the Bocas and made a course pretty much due north. The sun rose on a glass-calm sea with very little wind, and just an ocean swell and an easterly-setting current. During several crucial minutes, however, our situation deteriorated rapidly, leading ultimately to all of us abandoning *Stiarna* to her fate. I was pushing the engine to accomplish two things; catch up with *Calypso II* and stay clear of a sailboat to windward of us, when we started to lose power in the engines. By this time the white smoke had turned black, making it very difficult for me to see ahead, except by standing on the deck behind the wheel. I asked Coelho to advise on the oil pressure of the engine, and was told that the pressure had dropped to nil. I immediately shut off the engine, which both stopped the boat and also made it easier to hear.

Ash and Daniel were at the mast, where they had raised one small sail (Ash's orange storm trysail), and were preparing to connect a warp around the base of the mast to a tow line from *Calypso II*, which was returning to assist. Shortly after shutting down the engine I investigated the engine space and heard a distinct 'cackling', which indicated a possible fire on board. Needless to say, fire is an extreme hazard on a yacht, partly because you normally have nowhere to escape to except the sea.

Because the engine is covered by two large doors, which open up on the floor of the yacht's navigation station, it would have been dangerous to open them and ventilate the fire. So I opted to check under a small footstep leading from the cockpit. What I saw dismayed me. Orange flames were already at work in the engine space. We had a fire on board, and visibility was extremely poor in the resulting smoke. I had to act quickly. I tried one small fire extinguisher on the fire, but this did not extinguish it. I reached for the VHF short-range radio and informed *Calypso II* that we had a fire on board, asking her captain to stand by alongside to either fight the fire with pumps or rescue us. *Calypso II* stood by.

Next I ordered Ash and Daniel to gather other extinguishers and fight the fire from within the yacht. They went down below using an entrance amidships and I could hear them using extinguishers there. Meanwhile I threw our gasoline container (for the dinghy engine), into the sea and placed several life vests where they could be easily grabbed. I went forward to investigate the fire and found that all extinguishers had been used, but that the fire persisted. At that point I went to the forward most cabin and collected the passports and the boat's petty cash. Daniel and I also hoisted some of the Hanover's personal baggage onto the deck. The situation looked pretty grim, and we were only about three minutes into the emergency. I knew that not only did we have about 50 gallons of diesel on board, but that virtually the entire boat was made of wood, and that the wood in the bilge was oil-soaked.

I turned off the fuel valve leading to the engine and ordered all crew to assemble on the after (rear) end of the boat. My experience running a fleet of tanker ships (30,000-ton cargo capacity) in Singapore for three years had taught me not to let firefighters become injured at their task, since often other crew will risk their lives to save the injured. This could create a domino effect, whereby, say, Mr. Hanover hears the cries of his injured son, races to the rescue, becomes injured, causing more crew to race to the rescue, and so on until a number of men are incapacitated. I did not want this to happen.

On assembling (with the Hanover's gear) on the aft deck, I called *Calypso II* and informed them that we were sending Coelho into the water to swim to *Calypso II* to set up a fire-fighting pump if possible. Another reason was to save the life of our oldest crew. He assured me he could swim, and did successfully make it to *Calypso II*. By this time we were in danger of losing our VHF communication, as the fire was by now spreading up through the navigation station, only feet from where we stood. I informed the *Calypso II* of my intention to abandon ship, and requested that he stand by to receive us, including placing a ladder over the side. When they complied with my request by stopping their engines a mere 40 feet or so upwind of us, I ordered my remaining crew to don their life vests and abandon ship. They responded with calm efficiency.

Mr. Hanover went first, asking me to bring one of his bags with me. I assigned Ash to go next and look after Mr. Hanover. Third to go was Daniel, with one of his bags, and I, as captain, was the last to leave the ship. I did not bring either the bags or my shoes. In my mouth I held the crew's passports, and the cash was stuffed in my pocket, from which several bills floated out (this created a funny scenario, where the *Calypso II*'s captain directed me to swim and save a number of bills, and I finally gave up on the cash in order to save myself!). Within a few minutes, and by around 10 minutes after 7 am, all five of us and about two bags were safely aboard the *Calypso II*, a sizeable ocean-going commercial vessel. The captain and I contacted the Trinidadian Coast Guard, and they immediately dispatched a RIB boat to the scene - we were roughly four miles north of the coast guard station. They also sent out a larger (former US Coast Guard) cutter to our assistance.

At that point I felt that my primary duty - to save my crew from injury or death - had been accomplished, but we called for any vessels with sufficient fire-fighting capability to come to the scene and a photographer to document the vessel's demise. Neither items were available in such short notice, and for an hour we watched as *Stiarna* burned to the water line in the clear dawn sunlight. The Trinidadian RIB was extremely helpful, took statements from me, the *Calypso II* captain, and Mr. Hanover, and even shuttled Mr. and Daniel Hanover to *Stiarna*, enabling them to retrieve their belongings from the after deck. At about 8 am, her mast fallen, the fire having eaten its way through both sides of the deck around the engine, exploded the diesel and water tanks, and run the length of the boat, *Stiarna* succumbed to the sea and sank in a single, anti-climactic sigh. She left only a few burnt items of clothing and a charred life ring on the surface of the sea, 134 feet above where she finally came to rest.

Shortly after the sinking, the cutter arrived and all five *Stiarna* crew were transferred by RIB to the cutter and taken in to the Coast Guard base in Chaguaramas. We were given a kind of hero's welcome, treated to blankets and coffee, and offered medical attention, which fortunately was not required. After a cold hour in a warehouse room on the base, we were permitted to take a taxi back to the marina, where we discussed the yacht's sad demise with fellow sailors and with a devastated, shocked Tom Fredriksen, who was to have overseen a complete refit of the boat in Grenada.

The owners were extremely understanding of the crew's position. Since only the Hanovers had been able to retrieve personal gear, and they reimbursed each of us for our lost items and provided for us in the form of new clothes, accommodation, etc. This was very generous of them. After giving a number of statements to authorities at the Port of Spain, I flew back to Boston via Grenada the next day, and am now awaiting the opportunity to testify in trial.

In conclusion, I would like to say that I have no regrets regarding the sinking of *Stiarna* - she was a beautiful boat, but could have been the deathbed of my crew and 1.1 acted decisively, and unlike the captain in the case of *M/S Topdalsfjord*, where the captain repeatedly forced a crew into the engine room of a sinking ship, where they died. I did not hesitate to order my crew to abandon ship. Once I issued that order, crew was released from their duties to *Stiarna*, and responsibility for abandoning ship lay exclusively with me, as master. It was the right decision. Flames were already consuming the boom by the time we left. My attitude then was that human life and safety was more important than property, and that claims could be settled for the value of the vessel in a safer forum at a later date. Unfortunately this claim is not yet settled.

Although the Hanovers applied for, and Reliance issued, an insurance policy covering the yacht and crew for that specific voyage, payment of the claim has not been made by end October 2002, nearly three years after the accident. Mr. Hanover has gone to considerable expense to follow up on the claim and settle up with the crew and other parties. I am glad that the parties will soon 'their day in court' and can update you if and when that day comes and I am a participant. Meanwhile, I am proud of my own actions, and of the professional reaction of my crew to a highly difficult and dangerous situation. I am grateful that everyone is safe, and that the litigation involves only loss of property, and not loss of life or limb, as it easily might have been. I will be pleased to discuss this case with fellow students and faculty; after all, *Stiarna*'s loss and the subsequent litigation have played a part in inspiring me to pursue the study of maritime law.

Part II: The Trial (District Court, Boston): In this installment I would like simply to make several brief observations from my experiences as an expert witness in a bench trial in US District Court. The trial took place between Monday 3rd to Wednesday, 5th of February, 2003. Goldman represented plaintiff Reliance with two witnesses and Defendants Hanover were represented by Wolfe, with three witnesses, only two of whom were called. The District Judge presiding was Richard G. Stearns, and the hearings were held in the 21st courtroom, 7th floor of the new and impressive Moakley Federal Court Building in downtown Boston, which boasts splendid views of Boston's skyline, harbor, and working waterways. I learned and observed several things from my first participation in a real trial, much of which will seem obvious to those with experience. First of all, Evidence is actually very, very important. Professor Ritchie had a point! Second, a lawyer who is too aggressive might hurt his or her client's case more than help it. Third, the night before giving testimony can be terrifying, but after a lot of coaching and a good night's sleep the truisms proved true: "relax, answer the question, and above all, be honest".

To recite briefly, Plaintiffs called the yacht's owner, Mr. Hanover, first, and the attorney was very aggressive towards my former employer. So much so that Judge Stearns had to interject several times with "not so argumentative", and "tone it down". After 2 hours or so, Mr. Hanover's attorney spent an hour or so on damage control — Mr. Hanover had also given sworn depositions, and then we were all released for the day, with four witnesses yet to be called. The next day the Plaintiff s witnesses - the man who placed the insurance on the yacht before it sank (he had flown from England) and the man whose job it was to assess/adjust/investigate the claim (he flew from Florida) gave their testimony. I found it interesting (and intimidating) that Defendant's attorney (our party's man) opened his questioning by establishing that neither man had gained formal education beyond high school - a rough way to begin testimony, I thought!

On Wednesday it was my turn to speak, and since Daniel Hanover was not called, I had the floor to myself. Both opposing witnesses had left after the previous day's testimony. Only the Judge, the court Reporter, the stenographer, two attorneys, two Hanovers and I were left in the room. Only one person 'sat in' uninvited on the proceedings, though anyone was welcome to have. I was very fortunate that Mr. Wolfe was a friendly interrogator, while I stood on the threshold of the witness box, he and Mr. Goldman argued over whether I was an expert witness, and thus could give my opinion, and also whether Mr. Goldman could have me first. So I was pleased that Mr. Wolfe won and allowed me to spend five minutes after swearing in introducing myself, education, and maritime career (watch out for letting sailors talk about die sea!)

The first half hour or so went along smoothly, but with events three years in the past, and conflicting testimony having been given by Mr. Hanover, I had to step carefully in recalling the condition of the boat, on which I had spent a week. Much hinged on my testimony, since I was the only 'professional' at court who had gone over the boat before it sank. By clarifying on the side of the court (a few *I-don't-knows*), I was able to proceed without too many hitches, though I suspect that Mr. Wolfe wanted more favorable details from me.

Mr. Goldman wasn't as intimidating as I'd feared he would be, but still he managed to get me against the wall over one issue; intense questioning with only the option of 'yes' or 'no' before you have time to digest the question. Overall, however, I came out alright and stood up to him, asking for clarification when necessary. I was told not to weave tales, just understand and answer the question. Because there were a number of evidentiary objections (fewer than if it had been a jury trial, counsel conceded), there were pauses of several minutes between fines of questions, and clarifications for the stenographer. Both attorney's used my last round of cross-examination and I was released, the judge calling me 'Captain, soon-to-be-attorney' as I left the stand, which was nice.

Readers hopefully had a chance to learn the details of *Stiarna*'s sinking in the last *Docket*, which is still available on fine at *The Docket* homepage. I was a bit disappointed that as a witness I could not 'control the content' of what I said, but was rather limited to answering what was asked of me, often no more. I was never able to describe in court the yacht's actual sinking, because those facts were stipulated, and to say how proud I was of my crew's performance, or how rotten I think it is that insurance still hasn't paid my employer three years afterwards...

My final thoughts on the experience are that evidence is extremely, extremely important whether by deposition, testimony, photographs, old survey reports, insurance documents, correspondence between insurance personnel and also dozens of emails between Messrs. Hanover and myself, some of which was written, by us, with no thought given to whether it would appear in trial years later. Objections were made not as often as

I thought they could be, but most of them were overruled. One objection that was granted spared me an uncomfortable bit of interrogation.

In his closing argument, Mr. Wolfe harkened to the USS *Constitution*, which like *Stiarna* was, is a seaworthy old wooden boat which has an escort vessel standing by it when they take it out for a sail. Given that the *Constitution* was within sight of die courthouse, his closing argument was very poignancy. The judge was helpful to counsel and all of us. Pointing out each day what he found informative and what he wished to learn the following day. Indeed, Justice Stearns is someone that I would gladly clerk for if given the opportunity. He ran a good court. He gave counsel three weeks to draft final legal arguments, and will rule either in the spring or summer of this year. I look forward to his opinion or decision. None of us could really tell which way he was leaning certainly couldn't, but Mr. Wolfe did say that I helped the Hanover's case, and we shall have to see. I will keep you updated in the next *Docket*!

Law Student Sinks Yacht, Loses District Court Case: I wish to add some insight into the judge's ruling in *Reliance v. Hanover.* On March 3rd 2003 Judge Richard G. Stearns of the District Court in Boston published his opinion, in which he essentially found the 60-foot wooden yacht *Stiarna,* of which I was in command when she sank off Trinidad on 23 Feb. 2000, to have been unseaworthy both at the time of inception of the relevant insurance policy and also at the inception of the voyage, which, to use the legal term of art, the time that she "broke ground." Needless to say, my employers, Messrs. Hanover of Boston (who owned *Stiarna* for all of about two weeks), and I are disappointed with the judge's ruling, which followed roughly two years of legal sparring between the parties, two court appearances (July 22 and August 14, 2002), depositions and three days of a bench trial (3-5 February, 2003), in which I testified as an expert witness.

Certainly this holding does not help my reputation. It is bad enough that a vessel under my command sank. Although I continue to be proud of how my crew and I responded to the fire, and that no one was injured or killed in the efforts to extinguish it, abandon *Stiarna*, and reach the rescue vessel *Calypso II* on that fateful dawn more than 3 years ago; to have a judge find that, in the law's view, I left the dock in command of a vessel deemed unseaworthy adds insult to injury. As a law student I am learning to be more circumspect in my analysis and judgment; to follow Justice Holmes' admonition not to think too often with my heart as an aspiring member of the legal profession. So I am willing to say that Judge Stearns' decision on whether *Stiarna* was seaworthy or not must have been about as difficult to make as mine was at the time, at 5 am, with a new employer chomping at the bit for me to take her off across blue water to another country, while goaded on by the captain and a crew of an escort vessel standing by to assist us, and blinded by the white phosphorous smoke of a faulty exhaust system.

Judge Stearns, somewhat poetically, depicts the moment of our breaking ground thus: "There is no question but the loss of the *Stiarna* was an accident. ...Wiberg, who recognized the seriousness of *Stiarna*'s shortcomings, was nonetheless hesitant to disappoint prospective long time employer. Each of the actors, despite his better instincts, had a personal motive for putting caution aside. This perfect storm of bad judgment precipitated the sinking of the *Stiarna*". Fortunately, the judge, (who, from his demeanor, insightful questions, and post-hearing summaries I respect greatly), was not all damning about the owners and I, in his 22 or so references to me he notes, "Despite his relative youth, Wiberg was an experienced captain..." (Id. at 6). He adds that "Wiberg's overall impression was that the *Stiarna* was a *tired* vessel" (Id.), and in this observation of a wooden boat built 63 years before she sank, patchily maintained for a decade, and powered with a diesel engine 48 years old and by a mast which was rendered partly unusable by spots of rot, neither of us were entirely wrong.

Like me, Judge Stearns had to make a decision on the seaworthiness of the boat that morning based on all the information available to him, and knowing that either way he decided, he would be subjecting himself to possible criticism from his peers. What for me were restless employers are to him the Appeals court looming over his shoulder. He knew that he was making a decision that could be challenged and over ruled, just as my analysis of the vessel's seaworthiness has been by him.

In doing the matter of law whether *Stiarna* was fit for its intended purpose at the inception of the voyage, the judge relied in part on compromising testimony given by my employer and the yacht's owner in which he claimed that the yacht was rotten from stem to stem, and that the mast was also rotten (Id. at 3, 4). While I take issue with the treatment of the engine as being in the same condition at the outset as when the owners first inspected it (I and others had put considerable time, effort, and money into improving the engine, though not perfectly), I can understand the court's thought process much better from this conclusion (Id. at 9):

"While the aging engine was the immediate cause of the destructive fire, had the *Stiarna* been able to make the passage under sail as was originally intended, it would not have been necessary to place the stress on the engine that in all likelihood caused it to fail". Despite my assertions that sailing yacht deliveries are often undertaken and executed with reliance on the engines more than sails, sometimes to the tune of 90-100% (many boats make it to Bermuda, for example, after 600-1,000 miles with mere drops of diesel remaining), I do see and appreciate the judge's logic here.

He drives the stake in the heart of our, their defendants arguments with the following missive: "A yacht that cannot safely raise its sails or rely on its engine is by definition unfit for its intended purpose" (Id. at 9). Here the judge is on safe ground - indeed virtually unassailable in maritime- think. The defendants, our task would be to assert and prove that the facts (i.e. actual condition of engine on departing) warrant a finding of seaworthiness.

At the end of the day, my testimony, that after close inspection that I only found limited, specific patch of rot, about 6 inches by 3 inches by 1 inch deep, in the mast, and that we thus decided not to use full sails, failed to dissuade Judge Stearns. While this is the safer holding, I believe that an element of syllogistic argument was in play, i.e.: "The vessel sank after less than an hour of operation. If the vessel had been seaworthy when it left the dock, it would not have caught fire and sank. Ergo, the yacht was not seaworthy when it left the dock". I think that this reasoning, while perfectly human and understandable, clouded and prejudiced our claim.

What is frustrating is that had the yacht *not* sunk, as I envisioned it wouldn't, then there would be no issue; no insurance company revoking their coverage, refunding the premium, and suing my employers in court. That was exactly why the Hanovers sought, applied for, paid for and put in place an insurance policy - in case things went wrong. Well, they did. Five men could quite easily have burned, drowned, or been badly maimed. *Stiarna*, an authentic part of yachting history remains 134 deep north of The Bocas, and we have no judgment money to raise her. When the owners went for compensation from Reliance Insurance (whose American subsidiary went out of business that week), they came up with naught. And now the District Court Judge sitting 100 miles or so north of us agrees with the insurers.

The Hanovers are considering appealing to the Court of Appeals in Boston, and I may be asked to testify again to try and assert the seaworthiness of, say, *Stiarna*'s engine if not the mast. On the advice of friends and mentors, and believing that it is unlikely that First Circuit will overrule the District Court's opinion, I am inclined to decline the offer and sit this one out. I'm not keen to further hold out my reputation as a master. However, if there are changes in this status and the case proceeds further, I will be sure to let you loyal readers of *The Docket* know!

Thanks for bearing with us. The sinking of *Stiarna* still weighs heavily with me, but now that I have an opinion from a legal expert I feel some sense of closure. I am pleased to have at least had our 'day in court', even after three years. It has been an exciting, interesting and stimulating process, from the deck of a stout, 70-year-old sailing craft in the Caribbean to the docket of an esteemed judge in an old New England sailing port. Thank you for coming along for the ride.

Appendix 16 - Poem "*War Baby,* Irish cave"

Thoughts from an Ocean Cave in Ireland, During *War Baby*, 1991

I:
Too public, too many shares in too many people, in too many ventures,
feeling nothingness (not nothing, which could be anything).
Too formal, until freedom (sad word).

II:
Lying backwards, head over heels (heels overhead), kneeling forward, toward the abyss
feeling trembles, tremors of silliness. Passion. Seagulls. Feeling void.

III:
Sometime upon that empirical cliff, drowned in the thoughts of others,
which cascade against, sideways thrust against, the side of a thought,
of a sensation, of jealousy to the point of exasperation,
this is followed up quickly, rapidly, by despair.

IV:
Smelling like firs on an August stroll through the copse of treeless trees,
and unsmiling fences, groping for the communal face of the void.
The void: something which lingers from your tongue, feelingless, numb.
Sugar on raspberries, cream (scream), feel the rush of mellowed smoke,
insipid into your very fibers (fibrosis). Means the moistest to begotten advertisers,
gazing through sheets of neon at their innermost fear (and ally): ignorance.
Creeping upon each of us with the ease of death, until awoken sadly
from the slumber of *I didn't knows* into the filling light
of length and time: measurement standards by which we amount to nothing.
In the very heart of this issue, and the next; this phobia, and that.

V:
And when, on that grumbling premonition, a knock
on the storage bin of our inner selves, we confront boyishness
and the last desire to possess, or at least to conquer (to vanquish), it. Then, a cessation.
With the tools of our labors laid plainly for us to see behind the glass enclosure
of a socialist museum (as though we hadn't ever hands of accomplishment),
as though we hadn't ever, we hadn't ever had too much of the same person –
ourselves, of the same place – here, of the same fears – life.

VI:
Shoes: For trodding, forbidding, for fucking, for disposing of inspiration.

VII:
Through only heroes do people attain some semblance of normality.
(Ebb my portrait, full to brim). Though with defiance, we remain sane.
Feeling? Hey! Eye, beard, nose, tear, house, neck; Ack! Back-breaking.

Photo Credits, Contributions

All original photographs were taken by, or for, the author or gifted to me, including those on the cover. Images which deserve credit are listed here. If I have missed giving credit to anyone – and about a third of them were taken of groups by kind souls using my camera – then I apologize.

- Cover - Blue yacht hitting large wave, top cover, is of *Andromeda*, which Danish Capt. Jasper and his German crew from *X-Base* shared with the author on arrival in Newport, June, 2002.

- Page III – While the black felt lines are mine, I purchased this chart from Armchair Sailor Bookstore when they were on Lee Wharf, Newport in about 1987. It is entitled "North Atlantic Ocean, SE Coast of North America," and is Omega International #108, DMA

- Page XVII – Swedish tall *Svanen* under sail in Sydney, Australia is by Peter Andrews on May 24, 2001, "*Svanen* to Slip at Wollongong," members.ozemail.com.au/~outimage/news/news05.htm

- Page XX – Sailor Aaron Dickson

- Page 30 – World Map of my travels was custom made by cartographer Robert Eller Pratt

- Page 35 – photo of the Swedish sloop *Qu'elle Aime* is courtesy of her owner, Lars Lenfeldt

- Page 44 - The family boat *Viking*, Silverton 28 in 1980, in Lyford Cay Marina, by Jane Wiberg (Mom)

- Page 89, lower images are from a brochure *Xebec*'s owner, Martin Misiree, produced

- Page 95 with me holding a helmet on *Xebec*, was taken by the nice lady I rescued

- Page 106 – The postcard of *War Baby* was taken by Beken of Cowes and was given to me, along with my crew shirt, as a crew. It is courtesy of Warren and Anne Brown of Bermuda

- Page 109 was taken by Lady North (?), widow of a senior British Admiral, at the RBYC, or Royal Bermuda Yacht Club, during a private reception to welcome the *War Baby* sailors home to Bermuda. She generously later mailed it to me.

- Page 148 – The postcard of *Power Play* was given to me as a crew of the vessel.

- Page 206 – Author in cockpit, *Sarafina*, Annapolis, September, 1999 by my mother's friend, and later used by Jim Long, Editor of *Newport Sailor / Caribbean Sailor* in 2000.

- Pages 214 - Account of *Crested* and the MOB appeared in *Cruising World Magazine*, Middletown, RI, November 2000, under the heading "Delivery skipper sees his life in 16 minutes."

- Page 223 – Poem *Tree Frogs In The Boatyard*, by & courtesy of Capt. Dermot Bremner, *Rogue*, 1999

- Page 227 – A passenger on the *Valentine* kindly took and mailed this; she is unknown to me now.

- Page 229 – Beken of Cowes took the *Stiarna* photograph, and I purchase an original print from them

- Pages 229 - 234 – literature and images of *Stiarna* from various yacht brokerage websites

- Page 263 – of my sister, Ann Wiberg Wachtmeister, and her three boys, Oscar, Wilhelm, and Axel, in Stockholm, where they went to see my then girlfriend aboard the racing yacht

- Page 267 – Hadley's Harbor on a dock, swimming, *Tetiaroa*, from Jay, we have remained in touch

- Page 270 – Crew in Echo T-Shirts on *Farr Away*, Bermuda, courtesy of Capt. Dermot Bremner

- Page 273 – Dermot Bremner took this in 2005 during *Kamchatka* passage, possibly *Farr Away*, 2002

- Page 294 - Leaving St. George's Bermuda for Newport aboard *Kamchatchka* in 2008, for my last offshore sailing passage.

- Pages 349-357 were published in the Roger Williams University School of Law student publication *The Docket*, of which Neville Bedford was editor and publisher at the time. It is no longer in print.

- Page 369 – Author photo with son is copyright *The Nassau Tribune*, whose photographer took it on a mailboat series of articles published by them in 2013-2014.

Acknowledgements

I would like to thank Capt. Stephen Connett for writing the *Foreword*. Before I attended St. George's School, I was enamored of it by reason of seeing this sturdy lovely Danish-built sailing ketch with the school name emblazoned on the sail cover, crewed by healthy and happy student crew, sailing into my homeport of Nassau. Then the acceptance telegram arrived in the Bahamas in the spring of 1986. The story of my admiration for and working relationship with Steve Connett is told in the chapter on *Geronimo* early in this book.

For his Foreword I also thank Capt. Aaron Dickson of Halifax who helped me to establish Echo Yacht Delivery as a long-haul blue water and international sailing yacht delivery firm, year-round, in four long months of 1999, and it has lasted over 20 years. During the time we moved *Sarafina, Crested, Triton*, and *Femme* across over 5,000 nm, we were hit each time by hurricanes or major storm systems, had to avoid them, and incur the enmity (and even short-payment) of clients. Those were rough, cold dark months of physical danger and financial stress – one of our crew was paying more in parking fines each day than he was earning.

I also want to thank a friend so close that I consider him a brother, Brian Blank, who was with me, growing his own bareboat sailing yachting business as I also grew, encouraging me, offering me the best opportunities. More about Brian in the chapter on his boat *Endless Summer*. Here are names of other crew and captains, where appropriate. On shore I was inspired by many, particularly Bill Cannell, of Cannell, Payne & Page Yacht Brokers and Peter Specter of *Wooden Boat Magazine* and the *Mariner's Book of Days*, in Camden, Maine. Some folks like Bill helped me more than they know simply by taking me seriously and taking my calls.

I thank George Day, founding editor *of Bluewater Sailing Magazine* in Middletown, for so consistently and often promoting Echo in print and online. Herb McCormick of *Cruising World* encouraged me with his writing to be published as well – so did fellow *Cruising World* editor Bernadette Bernon, who had a look at my *Stornoway* voyage memoir around 2000. Rich du Moulin has always made time for me, even when I was just back from the Pacific and had never held a day job. His generosity still holds true today; his father was in the US Coast Guard in Bahamas in WWII, I thank him for his mentoring and introductions.

Web designer and general IT guru Richard Schlegel stood by me to get Echo Yacht Delivery from 1999 when he made the website to after he left FedEx Kinko's right up to the company's sale in 2006. I thank three captains for keeping Echo going for years when I was not able to: Dale N. from 2005 to 2007, Kevin Ledwell from 2007 to 2015 or so, and Richard Moore from 2015 to 2020, when I bought the company from him. Thank you.

Since 1989 I have been wandering in and out of the 1870-founded L. J. Peretti & Co. tobacconist enigmatically at 2 ½ Park Square, Boston, near where Edgar Alan Poe was born and between the Boston Common, the Public Garden, and the Theater District (not far from Chinatown and what was the Combat Zone in the 1980s). The owner, Stephen Willett, turned out to be a fellow member at the same clubs as my late father-in-law, and Steve,

Tom, and his colleagues have always been exceptionally patient and kind with me, even though I rarely bought more than Mount Vernon Ovals or filter-less Lucky Strikes. When I was sweating over my license books at the Seaman's House on the corner of Winchester and Church Streets in Bay Village, the Nigerian Vicar would wait at the door as I arrived with my sea bag as men from the nearby drag bar Josephine's would take an interest in chatting with me! I always cherish my over 30 years of gams or social calls with Steve and his team, which continue to this day. I was the Where's Waldo to their 150 years of stability, like my anchor.

Farnum Bailey was always there with good conversation as was Wayne, who ran a B&B on Washington Street, and Bill Steady of *Whisper of Maine*, who helped run one just down the street. I am grateful to Ben Brayton, Kevin Doyle, naval architect and loyal friend, Rob Moore, Tom Richardson and Brian Billings, who helped make me feel at home in Bermuda as has my good friend Cameron Clarke and many schoolmates from Eaglebrook over the years: Jamie, Stephen, Gunther, Bishi, Jeremy, the list is lengthy. I appreciate Dave Kennedy reaching out to my brother in Nassau recently, and Philip hosting me in Charlestown after his trans-Atlantic, and Danika hosting me at the Pier 6 there later as well.

I was very fortunate to have met in person with Tania Aebi, William F. Buckley, Jr., received a letter of support from Farley Mowat, and invited to sail by Florence Arthaud in Brest. On a flight to the UK from New York the person in front of me also checking a cumbersome desktop computer through carry-on was yacht designer Bob Humphreys! Through Warren Brown I was able to meet Lowell North of North Sails, and later I met Captain Bill Pinkney of the *Amistad* who circumnavigated solo. I even met a journalist who stayed up all night with Jacques Brel in Paris! I believe from riding a bus with him that Chay Blythe is the most direct-speaking person I've met.

Since I seem to be on a shameless name-dropping quest, I should add that I entered a ship chandlery in Auckland at the same time as America's Cup skipper Russell Coutts, met or saw most of the 1991 BOC Challenge participants before and after the race, and once managed to say hullo to Dennis Connor. Perhaps most memorably, during some of Hall of Fame induction the skipper of *Suhaili*, Sir Robin Knox-Johnston, winner of many awards primarily since winning the first non-stop round-the-world sailing race in 1969, walked into our sailor's bar, the IYAC in Newport. It was late in a summer night and persons were literally three deep to get to the bar. I had heard Sir Robin speak at St. George's before, and immediately recognized him. He was with a fellow his age and a younger English lady.

I was just trying to find a way to help him make it to the bar when, to my continual joy, one by one and entirely silently the entire crowd parted ways, each person looking up, recognizing him, and giving up whatever space he – and they – needed, until they were all comfortably seated at the bar. I feel immense pride at that moment; a venerable, gnarly sailor given an unspoken hero's welcome in a club of brethren; there seems no higher honor in a sailing circles than to give up your barstool and drink for a stranger....

Sir Chay Blyth received an honor when at I was at an event in Marblehead, and we all shared the bus back to Newport afterwards, during one of the round-world races about 2001. My kudos in Newport to fellow sailors Neily Williamson, Glen Neylon, Leonard

Whelan, Tracy Neylon, Alison & Melissa Caldwell, Teresa, and Matt Gurl. I thank half-model maker, captain, and entrepreneur Andy Burton, who backed me up by saying "the license does not the sailor make," just as apparel does not a sailor make, motivated, and hired me. One of the highlights was to commandeer a friend's SUV, with (admittedly) a bribe of a half-empty keg from my sister's college nearby, to arrive in Newport at midnight to see the winner of the round-the-world nonstop yacht race BOC Challenge in 1991. I was able to shake the hand of winner Christophe Auguin of *Groupe Sceta*! I also followed Capt. Bill Pinkney on his solo round the world at the same time; he now runs the *Amistad* at Mystic Seaport. Interviewing Tania Aebi, who set the record for youngest round the world was a major thill as well, particularly in a boat shed on the Charles River in Boston, which I reached by bike in the snow!

In St. George's Bermuda my crew and I have received to many kindnesses to list, from groceries brought to the boat to supplies and repairs at the last minute, bars kept open, an errant ice cube sent via fan to a face being mollified, Scott and the team at Bermuda Harbour Radio, local historians, the Bermuda Biological Station, Bjorn, Rachel, and others, thank you all. But most of all thanks to Steve and Stephanie Hollis of Doyle Sailmakers there, for always making time for a friendly family style chat. Thank you - and your parrot.

On a more personal level, Tony Bessinger from the Armchair Sailor Bookstore inspired me to grab the *Flambé* opportunity and run with it, rationalizing: you have a license: use it. Jenifer N. Lader, Esq., Catriona Lohan-Conway, Catherine Gingras all inspired me with their sailing, as did Capt. Joy Baum and Adrienne C., and Constanze B., Liz and Jen, Jane and Billy, Rivka, Lisa, Mick and Pat of IYAC. Then the team at JT's Ship Chandlery, and the folks who supplied our boats with everything from propane tanks to laundry to fuel, canvas, even old carpets and face masks to protect the hull and ride out a hurricane with! In the interest of discretion I do not always provide last names and rarely include the prefix "Captain," as so many listed are.

Niclas and Anna Lenfeldt, parents Jane & Anders and siblings Ann, John, and James, Christina and Natasha, Brian, Ed, Christian, the Serpa's, Severin, Linda, Hank, Chris M., Dr. Roger V., Prof. Roger D., Leonard Whalen, Commander Frank Alica, RAN and the crew of *Young Endeavour*, Jill, Matt, Sam, Steve, the Story family, the Brotman family, Bill and Ruth Wright, Andrew, Mark and Samantha, Jody, Bruce Varisco, his wife (yup, like Mr. Owner, I forgot her name too!), and AJ. Trevor White, Stefan Kahlsson and Tina of *Stornoway* are forever shipmates, as is Chris Treahy, memorialized above. Captain Kristian and Marianne of *Casadore*, Nicolas and Dragan Popov and team of *Simpatico* and Island Expedition for including me.

My appreciation to Mike, Chas, Hope, Rip and Bay on and following the Bras D'or voyage, as well as Rob and Alyssa. There were too many crewmates on *Endless Summer* to list them all, but Eric Findeisen, Tom & Dave Serpa, Tara Smith of Canada, and many others who took short voyages or prepped Brian's many boats together deserve mention. In Singapore I thank Peder Møller, Simon Wingfield, Chris Jones, Tejan Fadlu-Deen, Atle Sebjornsen, Sten Kittelsen, Thomas Andreasson, Marius Hagen, Esben Ringen, Trond Kyrkjebø, and many others for sharing their boats with me and being beside Peder and I was we all worked on the *Cheoy Lee*. I thank Brian and Caroline Miller, Michael and Mrs. Miller on *Artemis*, along with fellow crew.

At Oldport Marine Services in Newport, Matt Gineo, Matt Galvin, Meredith, Mike and Bev Muessell, Teak, Diesel Mike, Capt. Phil Holmes, and many other fellow drivers made my years there enjoyable. At the adjacent Cooke House I thank Reginald, Stefan, Mike Jenkins, Rosie, Rick, Henry, Eddie Cushing, and David Ray, who was kind enough to take me out on *Nirvana*. For the unforgettable voyages of the Bermuda Hinckley 52' *Flambé* I recognize Wayne, Ed, Kent, and Ed's sister. I appreciate Capt. Anthony Neighbors for hiring me to traverse four states in a day aboard the 42' Little Harbor picnic boat, *Marblic*, and his later help with *Lapwing*. Ed helped me again with *Triton* as well as *Femme,* meaning that with numerous *Black Sheep, Endless Summer*, and other trips covering Block Island to the Vineyard and beyond, he and I have covered a lot of territory: I specifically brought Ed along after falling overboard, as I needed a friend to keep looking for me the extra hour….

John Hirshler and his able team of many others made the *Valentine* voyages possible – thank you. For helping us all survive the *Stiarna* episode, I thank Fred, Raymond, Alain, Daniel, Ash, Roger, and our rescue captain, Tom Coulter of *Calypso II* – thank you, Tom for saving all of our lives; the current was ripping way faster than I could swim that day. *Sabbatical* saw the stellar team of stalwart sailors; Captain Michael Bowie Cassidy, Ian M. Leslie, and Chad Johnson. What a group! *Seeadler* was Joy, Rory and Laura, the latter two a Canadian couple. Thank you, David. Aboard *La Souris Qui Rugit* it was good to accompany Ken Hand, with whom I shared strong thoughts about our boarding school. And on the *Ascent* I am forever indebted to the owners for being informal, fun, and not leaving me behind in Vineyard Haven! I stay in touch with Jobe and Dermot, and it is a testament to my utter confidence in them both that it is the only passage I made over the Gulf Stream with fewer than four persons.

The Bermudian windsurfing team under Martin, with Rick and co., I wish I had the opportunity to have gotten to know each other better, but the rig failure expedited our arrival in Bermuda. Matt on *Elba*, Mark for giving me great work on *Youth*, *Erebus*, and Bill the friendly owner of *Katahdin*, who braved a shitshow of horrible weather in a dinghy to go outside the breakwater of Port Jefferson and welcome us in, then put us up in his farm – thank you. Dan Thomason, photographer extraordinaire, yacht owner with Nancy, captain and great crewmate, I thank you for the chances to share trips with you on *Violin*, *Quintessence* and *Katabatic*, *Down Home*, and others. Once again I apologize for oversleeping on the Jamestown 4.30 am departure, something I have never forgiven myself for.

Captain Patty, moving the *Mango* with you and the conversations engendered therein have stuck with me since. Thank you, Ado, Christian, Brian, and many others for the chance to try a spell on *Maiden II* off Newport that day. Jon and crew on *Alcyone* - fair winds! Mike, thanks, your help both with *Turk* and *Rising Star* – I feel you really ran them both! On *Farr Away*, Austin I only hope the butterfly stitch over your eyebrow didn't heal all the way and that you have a battle wound to show…. Thanks Casey, Todd (fellow Eleutherans), and Earl McMillen, for a brief spin on *Oniwa* and later *Aviatrix*. Mats and Tom, appreciate the opportunity to have participated aboard *Pollux* – saw a newer iteration in Cuttyhunk this fall!

I am grateful to world-class maritime photographer Onne Van Der Wal for his faith and trust in me as a chase-boat skipper for 12-meters. And Charlotte Johnson of Rose Island Lighthouse. And whoever he was, at the Club Wyndham Inn on Long Wharf near the Fish Piers, who looked out the main windows and saw me, freshly arrived by the last bus from Boston, trying to shelter from a winter blizzard, and let me stay somewhere warm till dawn.

Captain Jack Kiragu, kudos to you for the opportunity to sail with you on *La Mer,* and later *Williwaw* as well, and thank you for introducing me to Maiwenn and others. Without naming him, I appreciate Mr. R. B., fellow sailor, serving us hot breakfast on dawn arrival at his home. Clute, thanks for the chance to move *Bellatrix* back to Rowayton, and for other gigs you provided me as well. Chris, enjoyed the short trips on *Alpine* – you were the only owner to insist on sailing with the Eric of Echo. Thank you, Tom Richardson for introducing me to day-racing at the Riverside Yacht Club. Dermot, I appreciate the opportunity to fly down to Bermuda a few hours after getting your call to move *Kamchatka* across the finish line of the round-world trip.

In Newport Andre and Peter Warwick, were very helpful and supportive, as was Casey, whose Marina we stayed at on *Sabbatical*, the team including Gary, Joe and the friendliest team it the world Gary's Handy Lunch (they tell my son what was my favorite meal in the 90s, as well as what day I liked to eat it and in which booth!), Charlies' Good Egg, Mary Salas at Salas', the teams as IYRS, Museum of Yachting, Ida Lewis Yacht Club, the NYYC at Harbour Court, Fort Adams, the Fish Pier (*Gertrude H.*), Newport Shipyard, Goat Island Marina, Bend's Boat Basin, and many others including the Brewer's franchise. The Seamen's Church Institute were immeasurably helpful in letting me cash checks over the years, as was Mrs. Mary Salas. May not sound like much, but it made a huge difference.

And where would I have gone to share stories, find crew, get to know them better and look for Mrs. Right if it were not for the IYAC, Café Zelda, the Red Parrott, the Cooke House and other wonderful spots including West Street Grille, Fajitas n' Ritas and the Sail Loft in Boston? Thank you Pat & Mick at the IYAC, Cal and Co. And to Susan Dye and Ron Barr for always keeping me up to speed and accepting my mail, putting on a story-writing contest, and hosting me to a book signing. And to John Dye and Oakley Jones, other colleagues there, as well as Bill at Postall for hiring an Oxford guy and telling me about Myles Standish State Forest.

At Boston Harbor Cruises there are too many to thank, but Lindsay & Challis, boat driver and team leader Andrew, Chuck, Taylor, Shawn, Jerry, Bonnie, Matthew, and of course David Coffin, I thank you all. Aboard *Blue Moon* I appreciate working with Harry and Freya, Arnulf and Nico, Annie and Georges, Andrew, the team at Hinckley Shipyard in Portsmouth, Rhode Island. As with Mike Toppa, Jon Barrett, Mark Ashton, Will at Oyster, and other pre-eminent leaders in the yachting sector. A note on yacht brokers: in the delivery racket a strong relationship with just a few of these lifelong yachting professionals, many of them captains of impeccable reputation, can make or break a yacht delivery skipper's career. I regret that early on, during the hurricane-bestraddled season of 1999, I squandered much goodwill by taking too much time and costing too much money.

Since warm climates and blue-water passages from New England to the Caribbean on racing-ready boats was my milk run, I was admittedly un prepared for some of the older vessels which hadn't been owned or loved recently that came out of mothballs into the less-than-fully prepared hands of my crew and I. As the boats – and the weather – broke, we were forced into port, whereas on the Caribbean run you had no choice. I took my share of blame and pressure and most of it was well deserved. There were even some awkward evenings with winter approaching where my crew and I found ourselves at the same pubs as folks I had had financial disagreements with, but Newport's a small town and we always manage to figure out a middle way. I own my mistakes, and I did pay for them too, and the captain must always, no matter what, take the blame.

On a brighter note, I did manage to find fantastic support among folks at many levels in the yachting cornucopia, from charter brokers (thank you, Susan Chamier), to brokers who just did nice things, like offer a ride from Logan to Newport (thanks Hank Halsted). Among many I thank Eric Leslie, Bill Titus, Carolyn Cox, and David Laicz; though I have looked on several websites to find everyone's names, I could not - so if you sent work my way, please consider yourself thanked. By far the team that made me feel the most welcome and appreciated, and sent me and my crew the steadiest flow of work, was Bob & Molly Marston, then at Oyster Yachts USA, along with Will, Dermot and others. They were responsible for work big and small from *Sarafina* to several *Sabbatical* and *Ascent* voyages and much more. It was always a pleasure to head to their offices on Goat Island and catch up to the cheerful sounds of their dog or children.

I cannot remember every broker who helped, from those at Jamestown Boatyard to the Bob Tiedemann group and the Earl McMillen team, to Missy Johnson, whose office was across the lot from my loft and who hosted wonderful holiday parties, I am grateful to each and all. Thank you. You put food in my crew and my mouths and gave us opportunities to make extraordinary voyages. I have had fellow sailors in the same small sector with whom I've amiably competed and also almost always ended up sharing work; thank you to John Jenkins of Captains For Hire in Maine, Nick Irving of Reliance Yachts UK, Hank Schmidt of Offshore Passage Opportunities in New York, Andy Burton, Jean-Marie Cabral, Phil Cusumano. Only once was I "trashed" by a competitor, and I realize it we because they had a newborn, living aboard in New England, and it was the middle of winter, so I get it, and forgave it.

Also Nick Tellam, who I met in Pap'ete, Tim Laughbridge, Gino and the team at Lyford Cay Marina, the gang at City Marina Charleston and Goat Island Marina Newport, Andrew Short of New Zealand and Singapore (former paratrooper), the owner of Zelda's, Tom Callahan, for taking me sailing with Kip, Mrs. Jean Smith, neighbor of Lee Wharf, Ruiz of Firehouse Pizza. Captain Justin Zizes. Lawyers; Richard D'Addario in Newport, Seth Holbrook in Boston, John Bohannan in New London, Neil Quartaro at Cozen O'Connor and WFW, the team at Healey & Baillie, Peter and Jim Drakos, Nick Sofos. Norm Reid of BC Sailing is an institution, thank you teammates as well.

And always Lorraine Parsons, Jim Lawrence and colleagues, Lee Denslow and Erin Moore, Carleen Lyden Walker of Morgan Marketing, and Peter Kosseff, and Neil Batt, Bill Biewenga, Lee Bruce, J. P. English, Finally, my gratitude to those have blazed paths before me, Paul Aranha, Craig Symonette, Peter Vlasov, Jerry Kirby, Brad and family at Sail Newport, Eli and family at Newport Shipyard, Johno and Chuck on the Cuttyhunk Ferry, Olympic sailor Mark Holowesko, and Bruce Stewart, who literally showed me the ropes in a man-made lake in the Black Mountains in the mid-1970s. And Craig & Bobby Symonette and Paul Aranha and the folks at BASRA who bravely go out in the thick of it to save people, not least of all Bermuda Harbour Radio.

Shipmates are too numerous to individually thank put I want to recognize longtime sailing comrades Ed Galla, Bill Posgay, my brother John, captain of the family boat. Zachary Cutler, Steve & Lisa, Geoff M., his mate Tim, Dave, the *Dancer* team (Skip, Craig, Nigel), Mark Aitkin, Alfred Byron (Cannon), Paula, Loco, and the *Xebec* squad. As I prepared this book New York City maritime journalists Barry Parker and Justin Zizes, and *TradeWinds* Shipping News features editor Paul Burrell kindly helped me find the back-story to the tanker *Philadelphia* life ring. In the Stamford maritime community I thank Lee Denslow, Erin Moore, Eric Martin and Aaron Kelly as well as career guides Lorraine Parsons and Jim Lawrence, Brad Berman, Johny Kulukundis, Jeff Parry, Harry Kerames, Georgios Stamoulas, Nick Hadjipateras, Chris, Sam, Patsy, Banc, and Peps Jones, Charles Mallory, Clay Maitland, and more than I could possibly name. My sincere gratitude to anyone named in this list and apologies to anyone omitted. Without you, there would have been no sailing experiences for me to share here today.

We all offer our eternal gratitude to fellow blue-water yachtsman and weather volunteer guru Mr. Herb Hilgenberg, who provides a complimentary Single Sideband (SSB) radio net called *Southbound II*, to mariners who log on for daily weather analysis. Herb and his family lived aboard *Southbound II* in my favorite harbor, St. George's in Bermuda, where he worked for the very respected Bermuda Harbour Radio. Nowadays he transmits from his house in Canada. Bermuda Harbour Radio which for years has been led by Scott Simmons and an extraordinary team of professionals has been there at all times in all weather for countless times, and I for one am especially grateful them; we try to walk up the hill to give a token of our appreciation when we arrive in port. I thank generous Captain Makis Kourtesis, his lovely wife Mrs. Ellie Kourtesis, and their son Mike and family, for hosting me in Andros, Greece and aboard the super-fast *Black Watch* in Piraeus for two iterations of the Posidonia Cup.

Without Abdul Rehman Qureshi I could never produce nearly a book a month for over a year; so thank you Abdul and all who help you. That includes Aditi Rae and Sanchit Goel who designed the cover. I also thank Erin Niumata of Folio Literary Management and all the persons and organizations who have published my stories and research over the years, including the *Providence Journal, Offshore, Cruising World, New York Post, Journal of the Bahamas Historical Society,* Eileen Carron, Editor of *The Nassau Tribune* which honored me by publishing two sailing articles in my teens, *BerNews, The Astrolabe* of Turks & Caicos, the *Abaconian, PowerShips*, Neil, Andrew and colleague Nicola at *What's On Bahamas* for publishing me, and many others to whom I am eternally grateful. It was also a treat to sail with Geoff Pack, journalist and co-editor for *Yachting Monthly* magazine, in the UK.

Obviously I cannot name anyone but myself, but I've found plenty of solidarity, support, and sobriety at sea, and it continues to be a complex, decades-long recovery process. Thank you for everyone who has listened and shared over the decades. It may sound strange, but the USCG and the employers who insist on random testing actually help.

I thank Caitlin D. F., fellow writer, for her unwavering support and inspiring company, and her parents for Geoff and Diane for their hospitality. I thank my parents and brothers in Nassau, our sister in Sweden and their/our families, and cousins, nieces and nephews in the US, UK and Sweden, who have paused to hear tell of these voyages over the years, particularly my godsons Wilhelm, Henrik and Oliver. Above all I thank my favorite fellow in the whole wide world; Felix.

About the Author

Eric Wiberg grew up in the Bahamas and has studied in the US and EU. Though a career in shipping, salvage, tug, media, and yacht firms took him to various places, New England has been his base since boarding school in 1983. The author of over 30 books and nearly 1,000 articles and blog posts, Eric's strategy was to live the first 40 years as though they would be his last, and those after 40 documenting the first. His more than five million words of writing occupy over 7,000 pages so far, and have been translated into half a dozen languages. Eric has appeared in French, Norwegian, US and Spanish film documentaries, including CapaTV, the BBC, and Norway's NRK1 show *Tore på Sporet*.

His work has been used by writers for *Rolling Stone*, *Vanity Fair*, and the *Boston Globe*, and the *New York Post* called *U-Boats in New England*, a *Book of the Week* in 2019. His research led to the discovery of US, Italian, German, and Norwegian KIA in World War II, and resulted in the US Navy correcting the records for the sinking of U-84 northeast of the Bahamas, with awards made in the US Senate. In 2020 his writing was runner-up in the Tulip Tree story contest and his book appeared on Cuban TV. His latest of seven books covering World War II and or the Bahamas is 900 pages in length and took 11 years. Other books like this one are *Travel Diaries* and *Sea Stories*, as well as *Round the World in the Wrong Season*. The young man shown in the photo on a mailboat in the Bahamas, which they voyage upon annually, is Eric's favorite fellow; son Felix.